CRITICAL SURVEY
OF
SHORT FICTION

CRITICAL SURVEY
OF
SHORT FICTION

Authors
Pas–Z

6

Edited by
FRANK N. MAGILL

Academic Director
WALTON BEACHAM

SALEM PRESS
Englewood Cliffs, N. J.

LIBRARY OF CONGRESS CATALOG CARD NUMBER: 81-51697

Complete Set: ISBN 0-89356-210-7
Volume 6:   ISBN 0-89356-216-5

PRINTED IN THE UNITED STATES OF AMERICA

LIST OF AUTHORS IN VOLUME 6

BORIS PASTERNAK

Born: Moscow, Russia; February 10, 1890
Died: Peredelkino, near Moscow, U.S.S.R.; May 30, 1960

Principal short fiction

Sochineniya, 1961 (*The Collected Works of Boris Pasternak*).

Other literary forms

Primarily a lyric poet, Boris Pasternak also wrote epic poems upon revolutionary themes and translated English and German classics into Russian. Besides several pieces of short fiction, he wrote two prose autobiographies and an unfinished play, *The Blind Beauty*, intended as a nineteenth century prologue to his single novel, *Doctor Zhivago* (1957), the first major Russian work to be published only outside the Soviet Union. Pasternak won the Nobel Prize for Literature in 1958, but Soviet governmental pressure forced him to refuse it. His lyric "The Nobel Prize" describes him "caught like a beast at bay" in his homeland.

Influence

Most Westerners appreciate only with difficulty the profound impact of literature, and especially poetry, on Russian life. Despite their actions during Pasternak's lifetime, Soviet authorities had by 1972 published 170,000 copies of his collected poetry. Verse recitals before and after the 1917 revolution significantly contributed to the peculiarly Russian combination of art, politics, and morality; and Pasternak's public reading of his works in 1948, for example, evoked outpourings of genuine love for poetry mixed with a fervent desire to watch a poet challenge the restrictions laid down by Soviet authority. Pasternak believed that poetry was in fact prose, "pure prose in its pristine intensity," and by wedding the creative essence of his personality, seen in the poems of Yuri Zhivago, to the objectified prose autobiography of Zhivago's life story, he sought to express the reality of the Soviet revolution's aftermath. Pasternak's short stories as independent literary creations as well as early studies for his novel demonstrate his intense moral concern and his singular defense of Christian values in the context of a newly forged instrument of literary integrity.

Story characteristics

Pasternak's fourteen short stories, all written prior to World War II, mark successive stages in the broad movement of his art from the lyric to the epic mode. His short fiction illustrates his acute poetic observation and his kaleidoscopic disruptions and recombinations of thematic fragments, plot, and time with startlingly impressionistic and synaesthetic effect. Pasternak's earliest stories restate a neoromantic concern with the artist's relation to society, while his later short fiction, principally intended as portions of a projected larger work possibly modeled after Rainer Maria Rilke's *The Notebooks of Malte Laurids Brigge* (1910), which Pasternak felt profoundly influenced his own *Doctor Zhivago*, demonstrates Pasternak's increasingly Christian ethical orientation.

Biography

The eldest son of the celebrated Russian Jewish painter Leonid Pasternak and his wife, the musician Rosa Kaufman, Boris Leonidovich Pasternak abandoned an early interest in music for the study of philosophy at the Universities of Moscow and later Marburg, where he remained until returning to Russia at the outbreak of World War I, at which time he began to write seriously. From his literary debut in 1913 to 1914 with "The Story of a Contraoctave" and a collection of lyrics, "A Twin in the Clouds," Pasternak devoted the whole of his creative life to literature. Most of his short fiction and both long epic poetry and shorter lyrics, headed by the 1922 collection *My Sister Life*, occupied him for the next fifteen years. His first autobiography, *Safe Conduct* (1931), foreshadowed his personal and artistic survival through the Stalinist purges of the 1930's, when a new moral direction became evident in his work, demonstrated in fragments of a novel he never finished. Although he again wrote lyric poetry during World War II, Pasternak answered Soviet postwar restrictions on creativity by mainly supporting himself with his translations, producing versions of works by Johann Wolfgang von Goethe, Friedrich von Schiller, and William Shakespeare. He also began the novel that he eventually considered his finest achievement, *Doctor Zhivago*, in which he discussed and analyzed the disintegrative reality of Russia's conversion to Communism. At the end of 1946 he met his great love, Olga Ivinskaya, the model for the heroine of the novel, and although the Soviet authorities imprisoned her in an attempt to silence Pasternak's apolitical praise of Christian values, he nevertheless completed the novel and allowed it to be published in 1957 in Italy. The Soviet regime retaliated by forcing Pasternak to refuse the Nobel Prize awarded him in 1959, the year his 1957 autobiography, *I Remember*, appeared in the West. Crushed by depression and fear for those he loved, Pasternak died of leukemia in early 1960, and two months later, as he had dreaded, Ivinskaya was rearrested and sentenced again to prison.

Analysis

All of Boris Pasternak's fiction illustrates the tragic involvement of a poet with his age. Just prior to World War I Russian literature was dominated by the figure of Vladimir Mayakovsky, who embodied a strange combination of symbolist mythmaking with the fierce futurist rejection of traditional forms. Bordering on the theatrical, Mayakovsky's self-dramatization pitted the gifted literary artist's elevated emotions and extreme sensitivity against his supposedly dull and unappreciative or even hostile audience, an artistic tendency which Pasternak recognized and from which he tried to liberate himself in his early stories.

"The Story of a Contraoctave," written in 1913 and as yet untranslated, stems from Pasternak's Marburg years and his exposure there to German Romanticism. Centered upon a German organist who, caught up in a flight of extemporaneous performance, unknowingly crushes his son to death in the instrument's works, this story exhibits the Romantic artist's "inspiration," his lack of concern for ordinary life, and the guilt which society forces upon him. Pasternak's first published story, "The Mark of Apelles," written in 1915 at the height of his admiration for Mayakovsky, explores the problem of Pasternak's simultaneous attraction to and dismay with the neoromantic posture. In this story, two writers agree to a literary competition which quickly spills over into real life when one, clearly named for Heinrich Heine, the German nineteenth century poet whose irony punctured the naïve bubble of Romantic idealism, outdoes the heavy-handed idealistic fantasy of his opponent Relinquimini by arousing and responding to genuine love in Relinquimini's mistress. A similar pair of antagonists forms the conflict in "Without Love," written and published in 1918 and originally intended as part of an unfinished longer work, although it actually furnished material for *Doctor Zhivago*. "Without Love" paradoxically shows an activist living in a peculiar never-never land, while a lyric dreamer's adherence to the truth of remembered experience illustrates Pasternak's inability to adapt his artistic inspiration to political service.

"Letters from Tula," written in 1918, again juxtaposes reality and art, but here the Russia of Pasternak's own time provides his setting. A powerful contrast develops between the reactions of a young poet and an old retired actor to a film crew working near the town of Tula. The poet, passing through on the train, is in the grasp of a violent passion for his distant lover. The mediocrity of the vulgar filmmakers appalls him, but as he tries to write to his beloved, he becomes even more disgusted with his own self-consciously arty efforts at conveying his emotion. On the other hand, the aged actor, who wholeheartedly detests the philistine cinema and the loss of tradition it caused, uses his own successful artistic representation. Made grindingly aware by them of his age and his loneliness and most of all of his need for "the human speech of tragedy," the old man returns to his silent apartment and re-creates a part of one of his performances, which in turn calls up a valid response of healing memory.

In *Safe Conduct*, his first autobiography, Pasternak wrote, "In art the man is silent, and the image speaks." The young poet's silence in "Letters from Tula" would eventually foster his creativity, but it had to be purchased at the sacrifice of his youthful arrogance and the painful achievement of humility.

The old actor attains his creative silence because he is the only one in the story who could make another speak through his own lips. Thus the humble willingness to serve as the vehicle of art, allowing experience to speak through him, becomes an important stage in Pasternak's artistic development, enabling him to move beyond romantic self-absorption toward an art that needs no audience.

Pasternak wrote one of his masterpieces, "The Childhood of Zhenya Luvers," during 1917 to 1919, intending it originally as the opening of a novel but finally publishing it by itself in 1922. This long short story shares the childlike innocence of *My Sister Life*, the height of Pasternak's lyric expression, also appearing that year. In the first section of the story, the world of childhood impressions becomes a part of Zhenya's experience. Little by little, the shapes, colors, smells—all the sensory images to which the young child responds so eagerly—impinge upon her consciousness, are assimilated, and finally arrange into an order which becomes more coherent as she grows older. Zhenya's impressions of her surroundings also gradually give place to her emotional impressions of people and situations, as the child's apprehension of "things" progressively is able to grasp more complex relations between them. Zhenya's world is at first markedly silent, as is the world of the angry young lover and the old actor in "Letters from Tula"; Pasternak's impressionistic technique allows few "realistic" details, preferring to let lovely and strange combinations of images flood the child's developing awareness of her life.

In the second part of this story, Pasternak shifts his attention from Zhenya's instinctive grasp of emotions through images given to her by the bewildering world of adulthood. As Zhenya matures, she begins to respond to the essential sadness of things by assuming, as children do, that she herself has committed some sin to cause her misery. When Zhenya's household is turned upside down by her mother's miscarriage and she is sent to the home of friends, she learns how to deal with adult condescension and cruelty. At the moment that Zhenya realizes her own participation in the body of mankind, her simultaneously Christian and singularly Russian consciousness of shared suffering, her childhood abruptly ceases.

One of the pervasive themes of Pasternak's work, the suffering of women, is thus treated in "The Childhood of Zhenya Luvers," reflecting Pasternak's anguish at being "wounded by the lot of women" that underlay his fascination with the tragic Mary, Queen of Scots. Zhenya Luvers, however, evokes the growth into recognition of adult responsibility that is basic to the human condition, extending from fragments of sense impressions into the ability to make the only sense of her world a Christian knows: the participation in its suffering. For Pasternak, Zhenya Luvers also marks the childhood of the girl whom his great love Olga Ivinskaya called "the Lara of the future," the woman at the heart of *Doctor Zhivago*. The capacity to grow and mature through the experience of suffering makes Zhenya the personification of Pasternak's betrayed Russia, trusting and defenseless in the grip of the godless aggression that followed the 1917 Communist Revolution.

All of Pasternak's works of the 1920's reveal his growing awareness of the poet's responsibility to mankind, continuing to lead him from his earlier lyric expression of romantic self-absorption toward the epic presentation of his moral impulse. "Three Chapters from a Story" and *Aerial Ways* (1924), as well as his long narrative poetry of the decade, also illustrate Pasternak's attempt to come to grips with the cannibalistic tendency of revolutions to devour the very forces that unleashed them. By 1929, in another long short story titled simply "The Story," Pasternak reached a new manifestation of his creative position. His young hero Seryosha comes to visit his sister, exhausted and dismayed by the chaos around him in the turmoil of 1916, when Russia's contribution to the struggle against Germany was faltering because of governmental ineptitude and social tensions. Pasternak's impressionistic glimpses of the disorder swirl around Seryosha like nightmarish, demonic scenes, until he lies down on a shabby cot to rest, losing himself in memories of the bittersweet prewar years when his artistic vocation had come to him.

Seryosha had been a tutor to a well-to-do family, but he saw his real mission as saving the world through art. Pasternak's "suffering women," here a sympathetic prostitute and later a widowed Danish governess trapped in poverty, awaken Seryosha's compassion and lead him to begin a story within "The Story," the tale of "Y_3," a poet and musician who intends to alleviate the suffering of some of his fellow men by selling himself at auction. As Seryosha's retrospective experiences flash through his tired mind, he suddenly becomes distressingly aware of his own failure in those earlier years. At the very time when he was self-consciously creating his gloriously idealistic artistic work, he was overlooking the genuine self-sacrifice of a young acquaintance being called into the Army, ignoring the man so completely that he could not even remember his name, and now, miserable himself, guilt overmasters Seryosha.

"The Story" employs Pasternak's early impressionistic technique of unprepared-for, disruptive shifts in plot, setting, and time, but at the same time, its portraiture and characterization are both more intimate and more realistic than those he had previously created. The element Pasternak had added to Zhenya Luver's recognition of the necessity of shared suffering was now Seryosha's guilty realization of the need for self-sacrifice, a distinct shift from a passive to an active participation in the fate of Russia. By setting "The Story" in the context of the gathering revolution, whose true meaning the oblivious "artist" cannot grasp until it has swept him up, Pasternak establishes the grounds for his subsequent opposition of creative moral man to deathly political machine. "The Story" unmistakably illustrates Pasternak's growing preference for longer and more realistic prose forms, and thematically it demonstrates his tendency, increasing steadily during the period just before the Stalinist purges of the 1930's, to integrate his own experience with that of his suffering fellows, a distinct foreshadowing of the life and poems of Yuri Zhivago that Pasternak was yet to create.

For many of Russia's artists, Mayakovsky's suicide in 1930 marked the end of faith in the ideals of the 1917 revolution. The title of Pasternak's 1932 collection of verse, *The Second Birth*, reflects his new orientation, for in one of the poems an actor speaks: "Oh, had I known when I made my debut that lines with blood in them can flood the throat and kill!" During the decade of terror, Pasternak inclined still further toward a realistic novel of the revolution, although only six fragments of it remain, the last short pieces of fiction he wrote. "A District in the Rear" and "Before Parting," both written in the late 1930's, treat autobiographical motifs from 1916, the strange prelude to the revolution, with none of Pasternak's earlier swift flashes of impression nor any penetration of the creating artist's consciousness. "A District in the Rear," however, links family love with the stirrings of the artistic impulse, since the hero senses the feelings of his wife and children as "something remote, like loneliness and the pacing of the horse, something like a book," as he approaches the decision to leave them and sacrifice his life "most worthily and to best advantage" at the front.

The four remaining story fragments, "A Beggar Who Is Proud," "Aunt Olya," "Winter Night," and "The House with Galleries," do not involve the events of 1917 but rather Pasternak's childhood reminiscences of the 1905 revolution, possibly because in the late 1930's he was as yet unable to deal fully with the poet's relation to the Communist movement and its aftermath. Only after he had lived through World War II and met Olga Ivinskaya could Pasternak express his experiences through the fictional perspective of Doctor Zhivago, binding the moral and the creative, the personal and the objective, the loving and the sacrificial elements of human life into an organic whole. While all of Pasternak's short fiction are steps toward that goal, each piece also independently reflects successively maturing phases of his recognition, as he wrote toward the end of his life, that to be a great poet, writing poetry was not enough; that it was essential to contribute in a vital way to his times by willingly sacrificing himself to a lofty and lovely destiny. Accordingly, the personae of Pasternak's short fiction—the romantic poet, the lyric dreamer, the aging actor, the maturing girl, the suffering woman, the self-sacrificing husband and father—all finally coalesced into the figure of his Christian "Hamlet":

> The noise is stilled. I come out on the stage . . .
> The darkness of the night is aimed at me
> Along the sights of a thousand opera glasses.
> Abba, Father, if it be possible,
> Let this cup pass from me. . . .

Major publications other than short fiction
NOVEL: *Doctor Zhivago*, 1957.
POETRY: *Bliznets v tuchakh*, 1914 (*Twin in the Clouds*); *Sestra moya zhizn*, 1922 (*My Sister Life*); *The Poems of Doctor Zhivago*, 1954 (in full with the novel in 1959); *Kogda razgulyayetsa*, 1959 (*When the Weather Clears*); *Poems, 1955-1959*, 1960; *Sochineniya*, 1961 (*The Collected Works of Boris Pasternak*); *Stikhotvorenia i poemy*, 1965 (*Short Lyrics and Epic Poems*).
NONFICTION: *Safe Conduct*, 1931; *I Remember: Sketch for an Autobiography*, 1959; *Letters to Georgian Friends*, 1967.

Bibliography
Conquest, Robert. *The Pasternak Affair: Courage of Genius.*
Gladkov, Alexander, ed. *Meetings with Pasternak: A Memoir.*
Ivinskaya, Olga. *A Captive of Time.*

Mitzi M. Brunsdale

CESARE PAVESE

Born: Santo Stefano Belbo, Italy; September 9, 1908
Died: Turin, Italy; August 27, 1950

Principal short fiction

Feria d'agosto, 1946 (*August Holiday*); *Il mestiere di vivere*, 1952 (*This Business of Living*); *Notte di festa*, 1953 (*Festival Night*); *I racconti*, 1960; *Selected Works of Cesare Pavese*, 1968.

Other literary forms

Cesare Pavese also published translations of English and, especially, American writers (Defoe, Dickens, Joyce, Melville, Stein, Faulkner); novels, among which the best known is *La luna e i falò* (1949, *The Moon and the Bonfires*); and poetry, *Lavorare stanca* (1936, *Hard Labor*), and *Verrà la morte e avrà i tuoi occhi* (1951).

Influence

Pavese's contemporary American writers exercised a profound influence and fascination on him and his writings; from the beginning he showed interest in those authors, and, in fact, he wrote his doctoral degree on Walt Whitman. His literary style, both in short narratives and in novels, shows traits that come directly from the American works which he had translated into Italian. His translations of such authors also eventually contributed toward a marked influence of American literature upon young Italian writers.

Story characteristics

Pavese's short stories and other short pieces are not different from his novels and even his poems; his themes deal invariably with his own lost childhood, emitting a sense of loneliness which cannot be remedied by friendship alone; indeed, he had lost true faith, both his religious faith in God and his belief in the human togetherness which he thought could be found in mankind. Thus a deep feeling of nostalgia for his native Piedmont region frequently appears in his writing. The emotions found in both his creative and noncreative works reflect a melancholy which ultimately cast Pavese into personal torment, despair, and frustration.

Biography

Pavese was born into a humble but fine family that lived in the country and worked on the soil. Educated at the University of Turin, he later took a stand against Fascism and was interned for ten months in a Calabrian town; however, he was free to continue writing. After the war he enlisted in the Communist Party but, disenchanted with this regime even more than with the previous one, he left it, complaining that such a party denied people freedom of action and personal thought. Unhappy love affairs, a dissatisfaction with himself in spite of his rising literary fame (he received the Strega Prize for his novel *La bella estate* in 1950), disillusionment with political parties, and inability to develop a normal life (true love, a wife, children, and a home) all contributed to his unhappiness. Pavese committed suicide on August 27, 1950.

Analysis

It may be stated that Cesare Pavese's prose is his forte; his translations, poems, and essays are to be taken as a testimony of his multilateral talents but not of his artistic skill and ability; these activities were secondary in his career except as avenues for expressing literary inventiveness. His short stories, such as those found in his early *Notte di festa* (*Festival Night*), represent his first artistic achievement. The protagonist of "Carogne" is Rocco, who escapes from prison with the sole purpose of killing the woman who betrayed him while he was in prison. Rocco seems resigned to the fact that he will surely be apprehended for such a murder; yet his own law has to be obeyed first, no matter what happens to him. Thus Pavese creates an atmosphere, possibly reflecting his own internal turmoil, which can be described as fast-moving yet emotionally subdued and filled with an indirect pathos. Other stories deal with priests, women, true love, and solely physical love. In one of these, "Carcere," Pavese is more autobiographical than in the preceding stories, relating personal details of his own detention in prison for his anti-Fascist activities. We also learn of his love affairs, and we find in his portrayal of the little Calabrian town the real inner spirit of Pavese, who sees in the people something with which to quiet his own soul, although his attempts were in vain to a great extent.

His *Diario*, which is in reality a collection of short stories, recollections, and comments on a variety of subjects, reveals the author ultimately as a lonely person. In this work, Pavese's life and experiences are set down. He is always forthright and at times abrupt, but never superficial or approximate, as some critics have stated; he is often brief, conveying perhaps the idea of lightness. His stories also afford insight into his outlook on life and on his imminent self-destruction, which he had been contemplating for some time. No doubt his unhappy love affairs disturbed him, yet he writes in his diary that one does not kill oneself "on account of a woman"; one commits suicide only because love, any love, exposes one to the naked, the miserable, and the vacuum or nothingness in life. In one story, "Misoginia" from *I racconti*, Pavese shows his hatred of women. It has been said that he wrote it after one of his many unhappy love affairs; but does he really hate women? "Misoginia" is the story of a man who cannot obtain the object he thought he could find in a woman; thus, he "hates" them all. The title of the story is erroneous, however, because a woman for Pavese, as revealed here and in his other works, represents life and warmth; only a woman, together with the children she bears, can take man away from solitude.

In general, Pavese did not really write of any experience which did not relate directly or indirectly to his own life experiences, his own hometown, and his belief that he was only happy as a child, although he did not then realize it. This belief recurs and haunts the author, and he finds himself returning again and again to a Piedmontese or Turin setting. It is because of such a penchant that we have his best-known novel, *The Moon and the Bonfires*, on which Pavese's fame really rests. The story can be defined as a long short story; it treats of a foundling who emigrates to America penniless but makes a fortune; he returns to his hometown and relates all that he still remembers of his childhood and is astonished that his town is now so changed. The novel is in reality a collection of episodes, or, if a story, it is a disconnected one. The only continuous thread in this book is the author's insistence on the past, the beautiful events of his boyhood, the recollection of his friends such as Muto, a friend of his youth, or even Cinto who was lame, for Pavese wished he could "see life with Cinto's eyes." His love for America as the great country of his dreams becomes truly his dream only as he is happy in the belief that the souvenirs from his past can make him happy. At one point, referring to things past in reference to Irene and Santina, he exclaims that he remembers Irene's yellow flowers, and "I remember them as if it were yesterday." The past is what occupies his thoughts.

The seemingly idle happenings which he remembers are typical of all Italy, not only of Piedmont but also of Campania, for example: nicknames, the "geloni" (cold sores) at one's feet, the "falò" or bonfires so popular during a religious holiday, the killing of a big pig in the month of November to keep the meat over the hard winter days, the sackrace, the "palo unto" or grease pole with gifts tied on top which go to whomever is able to reach the top, and even the old-fashioned urinal kept under the bed. The story itself ends with a bonfire that burns the attractive body of Santa while, we may suppose, the moon looks over everyone from above. The style of this particular work, not very different from Pavese's shorter pieces, is nervous in its staccato style; the narrative abounds in short sentences and parsimonious description; the sentences are almost skeletal at times. Finally, the story becomes poetic with much imagery, reminding us that Pavese was also a good poet. His language makes use of the dialect or popular jargon, but only to a small extent; for the most part, his language is standard Italian without any pretense to unusual stylistic devices. It is a living, everyday language, not dialectal in the sense that it is peculiar to a certain region of Italy alone. Often, but not as frequently as in his friend and contemporary Calvino, there is in Pavese's prose a flavor of the supernatural, or the *fiabesco* (a fairy tale tone), which adds a welcome touch to the narrative. It is clearly nostalgia for his own lost childhood that is significant in all of Pavese's work; thus, in a real sense he was an Italian immigrant.

Major publications other than short fiction

NOVELS: *La spiaggia*, 1942 (*The Beach*); *Il carcere*, 1942 (*The Political Prison*); *La casa in collina*, 1947 (*The House on the Hill*); *La bella estate*, 1949 (*The Beautiful Summer*); *La luna e i falò*, 1949 (*The Moon and the Bonfires*).

POETRY: *Lavorare stanca*, 1936 (*Hard Labor*); *Verrà la morte e avrà i tuoi occhi*, 1951; *Poesie edite e inedite*, 1962.

NONFICTION: *La letteratura americana e altri saggi*, 1951 (*American Literature: Essays and Opinions*); *Il mestiere di vivere*, 1952 (*This Business of Living*); *Selected Letters*, 1966.

Ferdinando D. Maurino

THE PEARL-POET

Born: Unknown; flourished in England in the latter half of the fourteenth century

Principal works

The works generally attributed to the Pearl-Poet are the four untitled poems, written in the hand of a single copyist and contained in the British Library manuscript known as Cotton Nero A. x. These poems have come to be known as *The Pearl*, *Cleanness* (sometimes titled *Purity*), *Patience*, and *Sir Gawain and the Green Knight*. Although precise dates of composition cannot be determined, most scholars believe that the poems were written in the latter half of the fourteenth century and that the order of their composition was *The Pearl*, *Cleanness*, *Patience*, and *Sir Gawain and the Green Knight*. The Early English Text Society has published a facsimile of the manuscript (*Pearl, Cleanness, Patience and Sir Gawain, reproduced in facsimile from the unique MS. Cotton Nero A. x. in the British Museum*, intro. Sir Israel Gollancz, EETS O.S. 162, London: 1923), and Malcolm Andrew and Ronald Waldron have prepared a modern edition of the poems which contains a bibliography and a glossary (*The Poems of the Pearl Manuscript*, 1978). Modern translations of the poem include Marie Borroff's *Pearl: A New Verse Translation* (1977); Borroff's *Sir Gawain and the Green Knight* (1967); and John Gardner's *The Complete Works of the Gawain-Poet* (1965).

Influence

The Pearl-Poet poems are written in the tradition of the alliterative revival which reflects the form and conventions of Old English poetry. Although the author of these poems was contemporaneous with Geoffrey Chaucer, the Pearl-Poet poems echo earlier poetic modes and are thus representative of poetry which was then being written in the provinces, whereas Chaucer's poems were written for a courtly London audience. Of the four poems, *The Pearl* and *Sir Gawain and the Green Knight* are the best known, in part because they defy reductive or simplistic interpretations. *The Pearl* draws upon the forms of dream-vision, exemplum, elegy, and allegory to consider various psychological and theological principles; and *Sir Gawain and the Green Knight* uses motifs of the romance, the quest, and the trial to explore a wide array of questions concerning human thought, behavior, and ideals. *Cleanness* and *Patience*, simpler in structure and content, are poems in the homiletic tradition which clarify and expound upon Scriptural passages.

Biography

The identity of the Pearl-Poet remains a mystery. The general time of the poems' composition is known, and many scholars believe that the poet lived in the Northwest Midlands, but no absolute evidence attesting to this fact exists. There is no proof, moreover, that the poems are the work of one poet, although most critics subscribe to this theory. Evidence contained in the poems seems to indicate that the poet was an educated person who was familiar with the Bible and the patristic writers as well as with such literary works as the *Romance of the Rose* (c. 1250), the *Aeneid* (c. 29-19 B. C.), and *The Divine Comedy* (c. 1320). The intricate structures of *The Pearl* and *Sir Gawain and the Green Knight* betoken as well a poet of considerable artistry. While the religious confidence implicit in *The Pearl*, *Patience*, and *Cleanness* reflects a mind which is theologically traditional, the sympathetic treatment of the erring Sir Gawain seems to testify to a sensitivity which is humanistic. Beyond these tentative conclusions, however, critics hardly dare go.

Analysis

The Pearl-Poet's lesser-known works, *Cleanness* and *Patience*, are poems in the homiletic tradition; that is, they take the form of sermons accompanied by illustrations which illuminate a particular Scriptural passage or doctrinal point. The poems are presented in much the same way as a medieval preacher would attempt to instruct his congregation in that they focus upon an important Christian tenet and elucidate it by exempla and discussion.

Although *Patience*, the third poem in the manuscript, begins with a recitation of the Beatitudes, the poem concentrates on the particular virtue of patience, defining it in the poem as unquestioning obedience to God's will. The poem uses the story of Jonah to illustrate the futility of impatience represented by resistance to divine governance. Jonah, like the narrator in *The Pearl*, must learn that, since human perception cannot possibly fathom God's plan and since human logic cannot possibly understand the concept and the implications of divine justice, the only sensible course of action is patient acceptance of the divine will. The poem thus examines a single virtue by means of a single biblical narrative, thereby presenting a clearly focused exemplification of an important Christian attribute.

As in *The Pearl*, the poem records the education of a misguided individual, and Jonah's three stages of education conform to his three attempts to resist God's will. In the first incident, having been directed to go to Ninevah to warn its sinful people, Jonah reveals his complete misunderstanding of the nature of God when he rationalizes his disobedience; he is convinced that there will be danger to his person, and that either God means him mischief or else sits so high that He will be unconcerned if Jonah comes to difficulty in Ninevah. Foolishly believing that he can find a place not under God's watchful eye and hide there until God has forgotten him, Jonah flees, only to experience the terrible storm at sea. His assumptions about the limitations of God's power having been proven false, at this point Jonah accomplishes his first step in understanding as he acknowledges to the crew his sinful condition and urges them to cast him overboard. Dropping directly into the whale's mouth, he remains miserably in its belly for three days and nights until he advances to a second stage in enlightenment when he acknowledges his own insufficiency and his absolute dependence on God. Although he does express faith in God's protection and vows obedience, Jonah still does not realize that obedience means having confidence in the rightness of God's actions, especially when those actions, according to earthly logic and human modes of perception, may not seem right or just.

In Ninevah, Jonah does exactly what God directs; having warned the people so convincingly that they all repent, do penance, and appeal for mercy, Jonah is then utterly outraged when, instead of destroying the people as he had predicted, God forgives them. Thoroughly angry with God for causing him to be a liar, Jonah chastises God for His act of mercy; although he himself, in the belly of the whale, sought, received, and benefited from God's forgiveness, Jonah does not yet understand that the grace God showed to him should be and is similarly available to all humankind. Unable to see that divine justice is a different concept from earthly justice and that, furthermore, justice must always be tempered by mercy, Jonah retreats to an isolated spot where he builds a hut which God uses to complete the third part of Jonah's lesson.

God transforms the hut into a wondrous leafy bower while Jonah sleeps and permits Jonah to enjoy it for one day; then, again while Jonah sleeps, God destroys the hut. When Jonah decries this as a deliberate act of malice on God's part, the anthropomorphic figure of God uses Jonah's own response to the destruction of his hut to illustrate how God feels about the destruction of His creation and why He is therefore merciful. The poem then ends abruptly with a final observation that, while patience is indeed a noble virtue, it is not always pleasing to the individual who must display it.

The poem, then, provides an extended analysis of the concept that patience entails not only passive acceptance but absolute faith and active obedience as well. In sum, through the study of Scriptural narrative the Pearl-Poet juxtaposes the divine and the human perspectives to the end of disclosing the inadequacy of human understanding and conceptual power, and the utter necessity therefore of submitting to heavenly governance. More sharply focused than *Cleanness*, and more simply structured than *The Pearl*, *Patience* provides an exemplum wherein the hero is so human that the sermon analyzing the tropological interpretation is contained within the narrative itself.

Cleanness, the second poem in the manuscript, uses the technique of exemplum and sermon to develop the idea, based on the sixth Beatitude, that God's greatest wrath is reserved for the sin of impurity. The poem focuses on three major biblical incidents—the Flood, the destruction of Sodom and Gomorrah, and the fate of Belshazzar—to illustrate God's attitude toward various manifestations of uncleanness. Although all three sins seem superficially unrelated (two are sexual in nature while the third concerns desecration of the sacred), the poem's tropological level of meaning conjoins them by emphasizing their mutual illustration that both the body and the soul, as possessions of God, should be maintained in a pure state.

The expositions of the three Old Testament stories allude as well to other biblical tales which serve as foils and thus further exemplify the divine attitude toward sin. To the three main segments of the poem are attached small sermons which further define and interpret the biblical exposition. The whole of the poem, however, has a unifying circular motion which is accomplished in large part by the linking of the poem's ending to its beginning. At the outset, the poem sets the stage for the Scriptural elucidations by defining a particular kind of impurity, that of hypocritical priests who, while wearing the garments of purity, are inwardly sinful and who therefore misuse the sacrament which is Christ's body. The poem clearly specifies that those beings dedicated to God's service should be always pure, a theme repeated at the poem's end when the temple vessels dedicated to God's service are desecrated by Belshazzar at his feast. The poem is thus unified by the deliberate pulling together of the end and the beginning as the hypocritical priests are linked with the desecrated vessels. This kind of structural circularity reflects that of *The Pearl*, and is typical of poems by the Pearl-Poet.

Having declared that God's severest anger is aroused by sins of the flesh, the poem's narrator cites the parable of the man who offends his host by wearing rags to the wedding feast; one who is clothed in the filth of evil deeds is, the narrator states, equally offensive to God. In order to provide a contrasting example to the first illustration of God's great anger, the narrator recalls Satan and Adam, wrongdoers who incurred divine wrath but whose punishments were mitigated because their particular sins were not uncleanness; although God was angry with Satan, he did not punish as severely as he could have, and although similarly angry with Adam, God eventually sent the gift of the virgin to Adam's descendants, thereby tempering the punishment he had inflicted. Those sinners of Noah's generation, however, who committed unnatural deeds of the flesh and became as fiends, even to the point of begetting giants, caused God to regret ever having created humankind. Sickened by their filthy deeds, God mercilessly punished with the flood those guilty of unclean sexual acts. Deliberately evoking pity and horror by specific details of the flood, the narrator makes all the more pointed the sermonical discussion which follows. The exemplum, of course, proves the necessity of being free from sinful spots and therefore appropriately dressed to enter God's presence.

This explanatory sermon also notes that, while indeed keeping His promise never again to flood the earth, God nevertheless continues to punish humankind for that same sin, a sin which is, in essence, contempt for the self. This discussion leads to the next instance of uncleanness punished, this time in Sodom and Gomorrah for the specific fleshly sin of homosexuality. Again, however, the narrator presents examples first of God's goodness, showing how God gently forgave Sarah for laughing, and then denying that she had laughed, at God's promise that she and Abraham should have a child. God's graciousness is further evidenced by His agreement to spare the cities if even ten good men were found. Like the flood, the destruction of the cities is vividly described, again as preparation for the following interpretive sermon which advises, among other things, that one prepare for God's grace as one would for a lady's love, advice which alludes specifically to the *Roman de la rose*.

This sermon also serves as a transition to the poem's last major segment since, after citing the nativity as the ideal of cleanness, the narrator discloses that God's anger at the two preceding sins of the flesh is equaled by His anger at the sin of profanation. The doctrine that things which are God's should always remain clean is illustrated by the fate of Belshazzar, who profaned the vessels of Solomon's temple which had been dedicated to God's service. Once again the exemplum which warns is accompanied by a positive example, this time that of Nebuchadnezzar, who was forgiven by God for his arrogance. Belshazzar, however, is not so fortunate, and the prophecy on the wall, which Daniel interprets, is fulfilled by Belshazzar's death for having befouled God's sacred vessels.

The poem thus presents three ways in which God has punished uncleanness, and, although the first two sins are sexual and the third concerned with desecration, all three involve a similar profanation of God's possessions, since the human body and the holy vessels belong equally to God. The three sins are thus linked through their allegorical and tropological levels of meaning to the necessity of preserving the soul and the body in a state of sinlessness so that one is always suitably arrayed to enter God's presence. The poem, in the homiletic tradition, is a straightforward exposition of biblical narratives.

The Pearl, one of the two most important poems in the manuscript, is the first-person narrative of a grieving father who mourns the death of his two-year-old daughter. While visiting the grave of his "lost pearl," he experiences a dream-vision in which he is transported to a location near paradise where his daughter, strangely mature and bedecked with pearls, corrects a number of his misperceptions concerning Christian doctrine. The world of the narrator, which frames this dream-vision, provides an element of circularity which, by linking the poem's beginning and end, helps to unify the poem. Additional unity occurs through the repetition of key words which connect the various stanzas; a word from the last line of each stanza is repeated in the first line of the succeeding stanza, so that the poem coheres internally as it manifests a continual circular motion.

The title given to this poem is thus exceedingly appropriate since the pearl is the symbolic heart of the poem. Embodying a multitude of meanings, the pearl seems to represent not only "the pearl of great price," but also the lost child who becomes queen of heaven, innocence, salvation, Christ himself, and God's love. Having absolute perfection of form, the pearl also symbolizes eternity, inestimable worth, and that transcendent beauty which is both physical and spiritual in nature. These symbolic values of the pearl emerge from the dialogue occurring in the dream-vision between the grieving parent and his pearl, the lost child.

The prologue to the dream-vision, establishing the dreamer's situation, uses the conventions of elegy to indicate the pearl's great worth to him and therefore the dimensions of his loss, and the conventions of courtly romance to indicate his love for her. The prologue also reveals the extent to which the dreamer's understanding and acceptance of his loss are hampered by the limitations of his narrowly mundane perspective. He grieves not simply because the physical reality of the pearl is lost to him, but because it suffers disfigurement and destruction in the earth. In spite of the dreamer's awareness that there is cyclical renewal in nature, he is emotionally paralyzed by his sense of deprivation. Similarly, although reason has tried to reconcile him to the loss, his powerful grief makes mental persuasion ineffective; and, although he has knowledge of Christian consolation, his miserable spirit steadfastly resists such comfort. Thus the dreamer, bound by a temporal and material perspective, has no real access to any Christian doctrine which might temper his grief; he is therefore doomed to exist perpetually in bitterness, bewilderment, and raw emotionality. The pearl, however, helps the dreamer to move from his state of desolation to a state approaching consolation and acceptance. In the course of describing this transformation of the dreamer, the poem illuminates a number of central Christian paradoxes.

Transported in his dream to a place across the river from paradise, the dreamer encounters his lost child, arrayed in rich garments and splendid pearls. First explaining the differing worlds in which they exist, the maiden reveals to the dreamer that his misery is caused not by his loss of her but by his willfulness and his lack of faith, which prevent him from truly understanding what her death means. His exclusive reliance on tangible reality and the dictates of reason causes him to doubt her spiritual existence and, in effect, to disobey God's plan. In response to his request that she speak of her life, the maiden reveals that she is the bride of Christ and queen of heaven. The astonished dreamer, again displaying the limitations of understanding which his mortal rationality impose, inquires if she is Mary, and how this could be so. Indicating that earthly concepts of hierarchical stratification do not apply in heaven, where God's grace rules, the maiden explains that even while Mary is unique and peerless, nevertheless all in heaven are kings or queens and equal members in Christ.

When the dreamer protests that this, according to the earthly logic which defines the parameters of his understanding, is incredible, the maiden provides the corrective by reciting the parable of the vineyard to illustrate that grace is available to all. Heavenly justice does not, like earthly justice, depend on a human perception of rationality; furthermore, no amount of human effort could ever be sufficient really to earn or "deserve" salvation. The poet seems here to show clearly a belief in grace, rather than good works, as a means for achieving salvation. When the dreamer points then to the Scriptural pronouncement that reward should be commensurate with merit, and that she, dying in childhood, could not have done sufficient penance to merit her exalted place, the maiden responds by asserting the inherent value of the innocent; since she was unstained when she died, she was actually in a better state than the person who had lived long and who therefore had more time in which to sin. Whereas grace *comes* to the sinner through the mechanism of contrition, penitence, and sorrow, the maiden can testify from her own experience that it *belongs* to the innocent because of God's right reason.

Having helped the dreamer to reshape his attitude, and having proven the legitimacy of her place in heaven, the maiden draws upon Scripture to educate the dreamer further. She alludes to the book of Revelation in disclosing that she is one of the 144,000 virgins seen by John on the hill of Sion in the New Jerusalem, and she refers both to the Old Testament book of Isaiah and to the New Testament book of John as she defines the form and nature of Christ and his sacrifice. Her discussion serves to authenticate the prophets as well as to demonstrate further the workings of heaven; since Christ, like the pearl, is pure, fair, and spotless, it is fitting that each sinless soul should be his worthy spouse.

The dreamer, now of docile spirit, is nevertheless still troubled because his earthbound mind cannot reconcile what appear to be spatial and temporal anomalies. He wishes to visit her dwelling place to confirm by his own senses the existence of such vast lodgings and the location of her New Jerusalem, since he knows well the Old Jerusalem is in Judea. Again attempting to explain the differences between the physical and the spiritual realms, the maiden observes that since her world can be experienced only spiritually, and since the dreamer's mortality prevents his entering her world, he must view it from afar.

The poem's account of the jeweled city and its golden streets is considerably indebted to the details contained in Revelation. As the dreamer gazes in rapture upon the very throne of the Trinity, the moon rises, seeming to signal a vast procession of maidens who, like his child, wear the pearl of great price upon their breasts. Suddenly, within the procession approaching the throne of Christ, the dreamer sees his "little queen," whom he had believed to be still standing near him. Observing her obvious happiness there in the presence of Christ and in the company of her peers, the dreamer feels a madness of love which compels him to attempt to swim the river which separates him from the city. As he immediately discovers, however, to do so is not in accord with Christ's pleasure, and the dreamer is abruptly roused from his sleep, torn from the vision, and returned to the herb garden where the vision began.

The epilogue to the dream-vision is in content almost a reverse of the prologue. Whereas earlier the dreamer rejected Christian consolation, refused to acknowledge the spiritual realm, and resisted God's plan, he now accepts Christian doctrine, rejoices in his pearl's spiritual existence, and demonstrates submission to the divine will. In a new state of mind and from his new perspective, the dreamer can confidently assert from his own experience God's availability, reliability, and friendship. As a result of this lesson in the herb garden, he has achieved a new state of knowledge from which he is able to commit his pearl to God.

The structure of the poem, which relies upon the device of the dream-vision, allows a transcendent spiritual experience to be presented within a physical frame. In addition to the dream-vision, the poem's reliance on the technique of personal narrative permits the reader easy access to a profound Christian experience, the movement into grace. As this movement occurs, the poem's fundamental nature shifts from elegy to *consolatio*, as the dreamer casts off his attitude of doubt, resistance, and grief and assumes one of faith, acceptance, and happiness. In this sense, the poem is related also to the tradition of the exemplum, since the poem illustrates by the dreamer's example the appropriate response to bereavement. The poem's ultimate accomplishment, then, is to enable the dreamer and the reader to achieve that theological enlightenment which precedes the greater state of Christian faith.

Sir Gawain and the Green Knight, the last of the Pearl-Poet's poems, is acknowledged by virtually all critics to be the masterpiece of the manuscript. The poem superimposes upon the chivalric background of an Arthurian romance such important topics as the initiation, the quest for perfection, and the trial of the hero. While the poem permits interpretation at many levels of meaning, it is nevertheless irreducible to a statement of particular themes. Even as it examines the heroic, the Christian, and the courtly ideals, the poem simultaneously considers a question even more profound: the degree to which civilized values can exercise control over the natural instincts. The poem records the conflict between Sir Gawain's sincere dedication to civilized behavior, as shown by his commitment to such idealized codes of conduct as chivalry, heroism, and Christianity, and his innate, primitive, and overwhelming desire to maintain the existence of his self. In illuminating this conflict, the poem addresses a fundamental issue: the ultimate effectiveness of civilizing processes.

The poem establishes Sir Gawain as the highest representative of the most civilized community, Arthur's court; Gawain is portrayed as the bravest, the noblest, the purest, and the most devout—in sum, the knightly paragon. The poem therefore tests not only Gawain's personal morality but also, through Gawain as its best representative, the collective virtue of Arthur's Round

Table. To do this, the poem examines Gawain's behavior during four times of trial: the challenge of the Green Knight to Arthur's court, the knightly quest Gawain undertakes in search of the Green Knight, the lady's attempted seduction of Gawain, and the Green Knight's return blow. These trials, drawing upon such Celtic themes as the beheading, the exchange of winnings, and the temptation, reflect as well an additional theme, game-playing. Gawain's problem throughout the poem is that he believes he is playing one game while he is, in fact, in the midst of another. For example, Gawain assumes that the purpose of the Green Knight's challenge is to test Gawain's courage in finding the Green Knight and in receiving the return blow; in fact, however, the test is of Gawain's loyalty to his pledged word as it was given to his host, Bertilak. Similarly, in encounters with Bertilak's wife, Gawain believes that his chastity and his courtesy are being tested, when what is actually being tested is his ultimate commitment to both the Christian and heroic codes. When Gawain, by accepting the green girdle which he believes will save his life, fails these tests, he behaves in a manner which is, of course, very human, but which conforms to neither the heroic nor the Christian code. In failing to maintain his ideals under pressure, Gawain demonstrates that any code of conduct is only as strong as the human limitations of those who are dedicated to it. In this sense, the external conflict between the Green Knight, a nature deity, and Sir Gawain, the model of civilized behavior, mirrors Gawain's internal conflict between his primitive, life-preserving instinct and his civilized ideals.

This conflict is set into motion when the Green Knight interrupts Arthur's New Year's celebration with an offer to exchange axe strokes with a member of Arthur's court. When Gawain volunteers and strikes the head off the Green Knight, the creature picks up his head, reminds Gawain to come to his dwelling in a year for the return blow, and rides off. When, en route to the Green Knight a year later, Gawain comes upon the castle of Bertilak de Hautdesert, he makes another pact, this time to exchange winnings: Bertilak will give whatever game he obtains from his hunting to Gawain in exchange for any winnings Gawain may obtain while he remains in the castle.

The first day finds Bertilak hunting a noble deer while Gawain, home in bed, must courteously and unoffensively resist the sexual advances of Bertilak's wife; having accepted from her one kiss, Gawain exchanges this for Bertilak's deer. The next morning Bertilak hunts a ferocious boar while Gawain, again at home in bed, must more directly use all his skill and wit to withstand the lady's more vigorous attempts at seduction; receiving two kisses, Gawain again exchanges them for Bertilak's boar. On the third day, however, Bertilak finds only a foul but crafty fox, while Gawain faces a different sort of temptation: Bertilak's wife offers him her girdle, a green and gold sash which protects the life of the wearer. On this day Gawain fails to exchange all his winnings; although he gives to Bertilak the lady's three kisses in exchange for the fox, he keeps the girdle. By this action Gawain violates the agreement with Bertilak to exchange winnings and violates his pledge to present his unguarded neck to the Green Knight's axe; more importantly, however, by relying on the girdle's magic rather than on divine care, he violates his avowal of faith in Mary's protection. At this moment all of the values to which Gawain subscribes—heroic, chivalric, and Christian—are dwarfed by his desire to remain alive.

When he faces the Green Knight, Gawain flinches at the first swing which the Green Knight then checks; the Green Knight himself holds back the second blow, even though Gawain holds steady; and at the third stroke Gawain's neck is nicked ever so slightly. At this moment, Gawain learns that the Green Knight and Bertilak de Hautdesert are one and the same, that this trial has been the result of Morgan Le Fay's machinations, and that the three blows corresponded to the degree of honesty Gawain displayed in the exchange; in other words, if Gawain had been honest in the exchange—that is, remained faithful to his ideals—he would have suffered no injury at all by the blows. Thoroughly chastened at having discovered that his honor could, indeed, be compromised, Gawain decides to wear the green sash forever as a badge of humility to remind him of his cowardice, his covetousness, and his faithlessness. Arthur's court, however, adopts the sash as a badge of honor, evidently failing to understand its true significance for both Gawain and for themselves.

Sir Gawain, then, is presented as a very credible human being in his desire to please everyone and at the same time to save his life. The poem seems clearly to treat Gawain gently, to forgive his lapse since he is, after all, only human. The larger questions of Morgan's motivation and the ultimate effect of Gawain's lapse on the court are, however, unanswered. The poem's ending is sufficiently ambiguous that the reader is unsure if Morgan has done the court a good turn by, in effect, purging it of pride, or if she has merely caused embarrassment to Arthur and to Gawain, and has actually had no lasting effect upon the court at all.

The poem thus encompasses many layers of meaning as it presents to the reader a richly informative and entertaining portrayal of medieval life. The poem's intricate structure, which enfolds bedroom scenes within hunt scenes so that the action in one setting informs the action in the other, contains as well a number of set pieces which detail such aspects of medieval life as venery and the disposal of game, the arming of the knight, the conduct of feasts, and the art of courtly conversation. The poem is perhaps most valuable, though, in its delineation of a fundamental human dilemma, the opposing impulses, on the one hand, to preserve one's life and, on the other, to preserve one's allegiances to civilized ideals. In indicating that even the best of humans may fall short in such a test, the poem displays a sympathetic attitude toward humanity which is perhaps more typical of Renaissance than of medieval thought.

Although all of the Pearl-Poet's poems are typically medieval in form and content, in their use of timeless narrative elements they transcend their particular period of generation. *The Pearl*, in attempting to explain the complex process of bereavement and consolation, exemplifies the psychological principle that loss must be acknowledged and accepted before mental and emotional healing can occur. *Sir Gawain and the Green Knight*, in examining the conflict between the forces of civilization and the primitive instinct for self-preservation, uses such narrative strands as the quest, the trial, and the initiation, thematic elements which are employed by innumerable writers. The Pearl-Poet, then, like all writers of fiction, drew his subjects from that body of material held in common by all writers of imaginative literature, material which contains universal and atemporal human experiences.

Bibliography
Benson, Larry. *Art and Tradition in* Sir Gawain and the Green Knight.
Bishop, Ian. Pearl *in Its Setting: A Critical Study of the Structure and Meaning of the Middle English Poem.*
Moorman, Charles. *The Pearl-Poet.*

Evelyn Newlyn

S. J. PERELMAN

Born: Brooklyn, New York; February 1, 1904
Died: New York, New York; October 17, 1979

Principal short fiction

Dawn Ginsberg's Revenge, 1929; *Parlor, Bedlam and Bath*, 1930 (with Quentin J. Reynolds); *Strictly from Hunger*, 1937; *Look Who's Talking*, 1940; *The Dream Department*, 1943; *Crazy Like a Fox*, 1944; *Keep It Crisp*, 1946; *Acres and Pains*, 1947; *Westward Ha! Or, Around the World in Eighty Clichés*, 1948; *Listen to the Mocking Bird*, 1949; *The Swiss Family Perelman*, 1950; *A Child's Garden of Curses*, 1951; *The Ill-Tempered Clavichord*, 1952; *Perelman's Home Companion*, 1955; *The Road to Miltown: Or, Under the Spreading Atrophy*, 1957; *The Most of S. J. Perelman*, 1958; *The Rising Gorge*, 1961; *Chicken Inspector No. 23*, 1966; *Baby, It's Cold Inside*, 1970; *Vinegar Puss*, 1975; *Eastward, Ha!*, 1977.

Other literary forms

S. J. Perelman's more than twenty-five books include essays, stories, autobiography, and plays. He has also written screenplays for film and television, and he is best known for his work with the Marx Brothers on *Monkey Business* (1931) and *Horse Feathers* (1932). For his contribution to *Around the World in Eighty Days*, he shared an Academy Award in 1956; he also received a New York Film Critics Award.

Influence

Perelman has acknowledged debts to H. L. Mencken, Stephen Leacock, Ring Lardner, George Ade, Robert Benchley, and especially James Joyce, whom he considered the greatest modern comic writer. Perelman's influence on other writers is difficult to measure because, although he was the leader of the "dementia praecox" school of humor closely associated with *The New Yorker*, he is not the inventor of the techniques of verbal humor he used so well and because his type of writing is now on the decline. There seem to be clear mutual influences between Perelman and several of his contemporaries: James Thurber, Dorothy Parker, Groucho Marx, and Nathanael West, his brother-in-law. French surrealists admired his style, and contemporary black humorists often use the techniques he mastered; but one hesitates to assert direct influence on writers such as Joseph Heller and Kurt Vonnegut, Jr. Perelman's type of writing seems to have been taken over by television, film, and perhaps the New Journalism. Woody Allen is often mentioned as an heir to Perelman and Thurber. In his critiques of American style, Perelman may be a predecessor of writers such as Tom Wolfe, Hunter Thompson, and Terry Southern.

Story characteristics

Parody, satire, and verbal wit characterize Perelman's story/essays. Most of his works are very short and tend to begin as conversational essays which develop into narrative or mock dramatic episodes and sometimes return to essay. Perelman calls them *fueilletons* (little leaves), "comic essays of a particular type." They seem formally related to the earliest American forms of short story, Benjamin Franklin's bagatelles and early American humor.

Biography

After graduating from Brown University in 1925, Sidney Joseph Perelman began his career as a writer and cartoonist for *Judge* magazine. After a brief time at *College Humor* and his marriage to Laura West, he began writing full time and in 1931 became a regular contributor to *The New Yorker* and other major magazines. He worked occasionally in Hollywood writing motion picture screenplays, but spent most of his life in New York City and on his Pennsylvania farm. He collaborated to write several successful plays; his usual collaborator on films as well as plays was Laura, although on *One Touch of Venus* (1944), he worked with Ogden Nash.

Analysis

Among *The New Yorker* humorists with whom S. J. Perelman is associated, he is probably one of the lesser lights, showing neither the versatility, the variety, nor the universality of Parker or of Thurber. Although critical estimates of his achievement vary, there is general agreement that his best work, done mostly before 1950, shows a marvelous gift for verbal wit.

Norris Yates best summarizes the world view reflected in Perelman's work: Perelman values normal family life, "integrity, sincerity, skepticism, taste, a respect for competence, a striving after the golden mean, and a longing for better communication and understanding among men." Yates sees Perelman's typical persona (the "I" of the pieces) as a Little Man resisting the forces of American cultural life which would "invade and corrupt his personality and impel him toward neuroses," the forces which seem determined to destroy the values Perelman holds. According to Yates, these forces manifest themselves for Perelman most decisively in "the mass media, which are, on the whole, the offspring of technology's unconsecrated marriage with Big Business."

Perelman's "autobiographical" work reveals his version of the Little Man. A favorite type of *The New Yorker* humorists, the Little Man is a caricature of a typical middle-class, early twentieth century American male, usually represented as helpless before the complexities of technological society, cowed by its crass commercialism, dominated by desperate, unfulfilled women, sustaining himself on heroic fantasies of a bygone or imaginary era. Thurber's Walter Mitty has become the classic presentation of this character type. Perelman's personae seem related to the type, but vary in several significant ways.

In *Acres and Pains*, the major collection of his adventures on his farm, he makes his persona into a city dweller who has naïvely tried to realize a romantic agrarian dream on his country estate, but who has come to see the errors of his ways. Perelman uses this reversal of the rube in the city to debunk a sentimental picture of country life by exaggerating his trials. Many episodes show good country people betraying the ideal with which they are associated. Contractors, antique dealers, and barn painters rob him of purse and peace. "Perelman" differs from the Little Man type in that, although he may at any time fall victim to another illusion, he knows and admits that country life is no romance. In these sketches, he also differs from the Little Man type in his relationship to wife and family. He is not dominated by a frustrated woman. He and his wife are usually mutual victims of pastoral illusion, although often she suffers more than he. This "Perelman" is most like the typical Little Man when he deals with machines. For example, when his water pump goes berserk during a dinner party, he handles the problem with successful incompetence: "By exerting a slight leverage, I succeeded in prying off the gasket or outer jacket of the pump, exactly as you would a baked potato. . . . This gave me room to poke around the innards with a sharp stick. I cleaned the pump thoroughly . . . and, as a final precaution, opened the windows to allow the water to drain down the slope." The major difference between this persona and Walter Mitty is that the former is competent; he escapes neurosis and resists with some success his crazy world. By splitting the narrator into a present sophisticate (a mask that often slips) and a former fool, he tends to shift the butt of humor away from the present narrator and toward the man who believes in romantic ideals and toward the people who so completely fail to live up to any admirable ideals. The latter are typified by the contractor who digs "Perelman's" pool in a bad place although he knows the best place for it. Asked why he offered his advice when the pool was dynamited rather than before it was begun he virtuously replies, "It don't pay to poke your nose in other people's business." Implied in these tall tales of mock pastoral life are criticisms of the values which oppose those Yates lists: dishonesty, hypocrisy, greed, naïveté, incompetence, overenthusiasm, deliberately created confusion, and lying.

Looking over the full range of Perelman's first-person sketches, one sees significant variation in the presentation of the persona. In *Acres and Pains*, the narrator is much more concrete than in many other sketches in which the "I" is virtually an empty mind waiting to take shape under the power of some absurd mass-media language. Perelman is acutely sensitive to this language as a kind of oppression. Many of his sketches explore "sub-dialects" of American English in order to expose and ridicule the values that underlie them. "Tomorrow—Fairly Cloudy" is a typical example of the author's probing of a sample of American language.

In "Tomorrow—Fairly Cloudy," Perelman notices a new advertisement for a toothpaste which promises its users rescue from humdrum ordinary life and elevation into romance and success. In his Introduction, Perelman emphasizes the absurdity of taking such ads seriously, describes the ad in detail, then introduces a dramatic scenario by observing that this ad heralds the coming demise of a desperate industry: "So all the old tactics have finally broken down—wheedling, abuse, snobbery and terror. I look forward to the last great era in advertising, a period packed with gloom, defeatism, and frustration . . . ." In the following spectacle, the children bubble excited "adese" while father despairs over his drab life:

> Bobby—Oh, Moms, I'm so glad you and Dads decided to install a Genfeedco automatic oil burner and air conditioner with the new self-ventilating screen flaps plus finger control! It is noiseless, cuts down heating bills, and makes the air we breathe richer in vita-ray particles. . . .
> Mr. Bradley (tonelessly)—Well, I suppose anything is better than a heap of slag at this end of the cellar.

Soon the Fletchers arrive to sneer at their towels and to make the Bradleys aware of all the products they do not have. The sketch ends in apocalypse as their inferior plumbing gives way and they all drown in their combination cellar and playroom. It remains unclear throughout whether this episode forecasts the forms of future advertising or its effects on the public.

Perelman exposes the absurdity of this language of conspicuous consumption by imagining its literal acceptance. In the world this language implies, happiness is possessing the right gadgets. If sales are to continue, it must be impossible for most people ever to have all the right things, ever to be happy. The Bradleys have the right oil burner, but their towels disintegrate in two days and they failed to use Sumwenco Super-Annealed Brass Pipe. This last omission costs them their lives. Not only their happiness, but also their very survival depends on their ability to possess the right new product.

Perelman's many sketches of this type culminate perhaps in "Entered as Second-class Matter," which is apparently a montage of fragments lifted (and, one hopes, sometimes fabricated) from magazine fiction and advertising. The resulting silliness may be intended as a portrait of the mass feminine mind as perceived by American magazines, 1930-1944. It ends:

> We have scoured the fiction market to set before you *Three Million Tiny Sweat Glands Functioning* in that vibrant panorama of tomorrow so that *Your Sensitive Bowel Muscles Can* react to the inevitable realization that only by enrichment and guidance *plus a soothing depilatory* can America face its problems confidently, unafraid, *well-groomed mouth-happy, breaking hair off at the roots without undue stench. Okay, Miss America!*

In such pieces, Perelman's values are clearly those Yates names. Especially important in these works is the humorous attempt to clear away the garbage of American language culture through ridicule. This aim is central to the series, "Cloudland Revisited," in which he reexamines the popular literature of his youth. Perelman varies this formula with attacks on absurd fashion and the language of fashion, one of the best of which is "Farewell, My Lovely Appetizer."

Perelman is deservedly most admired for his faculty of verbal wit. In several of his more conventional stories which seem less restrained by satiric ends, his playfulness dazzles. Among the best of these are "The Idol's Eye," "Seedlings of Desire," and "The Love Decoy." Based on the sensational plots of teen-romance, "The Love Decoy" is narrated by a coed who seeks revenge on an instructor who once failed to make a pass and who later humiliated her before her classmates by accusing her of "galvanizing around nights." Her plan is to lure him to her room after hours, then expose him as a corrupter of undergraduates. This plan backfires in a *non sequitur* when a lecherous dean arrives to assault her. The reader expects the plot to complicate, but instead it is transformed when the dean is unmasked as Jim the Penman who framed the girl's father and sent him to the pen. Other identities are revealed and the reader arrives at the end of a detective thriller. Although there is parody here of sentimental language and plot, the story seems more intent on fun than ridicule. It contains a number of Perelman's most celebrated witticisms. For example:

> He caught my arm in a vice-like grip and drew me to him, but with a blow I sent him groveling. In ten minutes he was back with a basket of appetizing fresh picked grovels. We squeezed them and drank the piquant juice thirstily.

At the center of this wit is the double entendre. Multiple meanings of words suggest the multiple contexts in which they may apply. Perelman juxtaposes these contexts, makes rapid shifts between them, and sometimes uses a suggestion to imagine a new context. The effects are sometimes surreal. The double meaning of *sent* suggests a transformation from a blow to the groin to an activity such as berrying. *Groveling* gathers an imaginary context which generates a new noun, *grovels*. While this reading seems most plausible, in another reading there are no transformations, and gathering grovels becomes a euphemistic way to describe the amorous instructor's reaction to her literal attack or to her unusually expressed affection. Perelman creates this slipperiness of meaning and encourages it to reverberate in this passage and in the language and structure of the whole work. One result is a heightened alertness in the reader to the ambiguity of language and the elusiveness of meaning, a first but important step on the way to the sort of respect for language Perelman implies in his many critiques of its abuses. This concern connects Perelman most closely with his admired Joyce and reveals his common cause with a number of his contemporaries, including Faulkner and Thurber. While Perelman has not the stature of these great writers, he shares with them a consciousness of the peculiar problems of modern life and a belief that how one uses language is important to recognizing and dealing with those problems.

Major publications other than short fiction
PLAYS: *The Night Before Christmas*, 1942 (with Laura Perelman); *One Touch of Venus*, 1944 (with Ogden Nash); *The Beauty Part*, 1961.

Bibliography
Blair, Walter and Hamlin Hill. *America's Humor: From Poor Richard to Doonesbury*.
Hasley, Louis. "The Kangaroo Mind of S. J. Perelman," in *South Atlantic Quarterly*. (Winter, 1973), pp. 115-121.
Plimpton, George, ed. *Writers at Work: The Paris Interviews, Second Series*.
Yates, Norris W. *American Humorist: Conscience of the Twentieth Century*.

Terry Heller

ISAAC LEIB PERETZ

Born: Zamosch, Poland; May 18, 1852
Died: Warsaw, Poland; April 3, 1915

Principal short fiction

Stories and Pictures, 1906; *Bontshe the Silent and Other Stories*, 1927; *Stories From Peretz*, 1947; *Three Gifts and Other Stories*, 1947; *Prince of the Ghetto*, 1948; *The Three Canopies*, 1948; *As Once We Were: Selections from the Works of Peretz*, 1951; *In This World and the Next: Selected Writings*, 1958; *The Book of Fire: Stories by I. L. Peretz*, 1960.

Other literary forms

Isaac Peretz's first publications in 1875 and 1877 were lyric and narrative Hebrew poems. In the 1890's, he edited a series of journals containing fiction, poetry, and essays. He wrote many plays: a comedy, *Once There Was a King*; a symbolic drama, *At Night in the Old Marketplace* (1907); and "The Golden Chain" (1909), which showed in four generations of a rabbinic dynasty how each link was weaker than the last. For many years he devoted himself to educating the poor, and his lectures on science and Jewish history fill several volumes. He collected and wrote about folk songs and folklore, and he was in his fifties when he began publishing the Hasidic tales for which he is most remembered. These have been translated into English, Russian, German, and Hebrew, and "Bontsha the Silent" has been performed on television.

Influence

It was reading Peretz's stories that inspired Isaac Bashevis Singer to become a writer, rather than a rabbi; his "Gimpel the Fool" is based on Peretz's "Bontsha." Bernard Malamud has, in many of his stories, reworked Peretz's themes. Peretz influenced Saul Bellow's rhetoric. Among his contemporaries, Peretz was the undisputed master. To him they submitted their literary efforts for criticism and he befriended, housed, fed, and helped to publish a large circle of disciples. Among his protégés were Joseph Opatoshu, who came to Warsaw in November of 1886 with his first short story, and was pleased with the great writer's encouragement. Sholem Asch was also helped in 1900 by Peretz to publish his first short story. David Pinski came in 1892 to show Peretz his plays and remained, as editorial assistant, for several years. Abraham-Reisen sent Peretz his poems, as did Yehoash (Solomon Bloomgarden), and he published both. In 1903, Zalman Schneor, aged sixteen, came under Peretz's personal tutelage. In 1904, Peretz Hirschbein brought his writing to "The Father of Yiddish Literature." His many protégés felt that Peretz was their literary conscience before whom they had to justify themselves; as they wrote, they continually asked themselves: "What will Peretz say?"

Story characteristics

Folktales about miracle-working rabbis or secret saints are retold in an intellectually sophisticated modern way. The folkloric material is distanced by employing a cynical narrator or by sordid historical circumstances. The magical events are made credible through believable characters speaking realistic dialogue, whose pauses, interruptions, and repetitions have the flavor of actual speech. The ironic tone, in dissonance with the enchantments it recounts; the laconic, understated style; the self-reflexivity of the narrators; and the psychological nuances of the characterizations, all make Peretz's stories seem peculiarly modern.

Biography

Isaac Leib Peretz had a strict orthodox education in Hebrew studies. One of his neighbors was so impressed with the genius of his Talmudic interpretations that he gave Isaac the key to his library. Thus, at fifteen, Peretz read his way through the secular learning and fiction of the nineteenth century, in French, German, Polish, and English, which, with the help of dictionaries he found there, he taught himself. When he was eighteen, his father arranged a marriage for him with Sarah which ended in divorce in 1876. His father-in-law, Gabriel Yehudah Lichtenfeld, was an intellectual with whom he published a book of poetry. He began the study of law and passed the bar exam in 1877. For a decade he was a practicing attorney, but his license was revoked in 1887 by Tsarist authorities for alleged radical activities. In 1878 he married Helena Ringelheim, and moved to Warsaw in 1889. He was sent by Jan Bloch to make a sociological survey of Jews in the outlying provinces of Poland to refute anti-Semitic charges that Jews controlled the economy. The poverty and starvation Peretz found are recorded in the bleak sketches called *Travel Pictures*. From 1891 to the end of his life, he was a clerk in the Jewish Community office, recording burial dates. He was deeply involved in social reform, lecturing, teaching, and founding schools and journals to educate the poor to better their lives.

Analysis

In diction, tone, and narrative perspective, Isaac Peretz valued the understated. He warned his disciples against verbosity, urging them to strip away all superfluous words. His own stories are noted for their brevity: his diction, for its precision. His tone is always restrained. His prose style is laconic, virile, and unadorned, yet capable of conveying the most subtle nuances. Before he retold a folktale, he sought out all the variant versions so that he could pare away the rhetorical flourishes and restore it to its essence. The judge at Bontsha's trial is speaking for Peretz's literary philosophy when he calls out, "No metaphors, please!" and later interrupts, "Facts! Facts! Never mind the embellishments!"

Peretz's angle of narration is always strictly controlled so that the events are viewed obliquely, or at a distance, or through a fallible narrator. By thus withholding the full resolution, he intellectually engages the reader. The enigmatic and the paradoxical are inherent in the genre in which Peretz worked: the wisdom story.

Peretz quickened the pace of the Yiddish tale. Instead of leisurely, winding sentences, he used a rush of phrases punctuated by dashes, or energy-charged fragments punctuated by ellipses—for example, the nervous staccato notes in which Bontsha's stepmother is described: "She begrudged him every bite . . . moldy bread . . . gristle of meat . . . she drank coffee with cream. . . ." The ellipsis marks are impregnated with how much has been left unsaid. The very elusiveness is suggestive.

Peretz's most popular story "Bontsha the Silent" is a paradigm for most of his fictions. Its central scene of a last judgment recurs, in some form, in all of his tales. The orthodox tradition in which he had been reared is permeated with the idea of man's being called to account after death for his behavior on earth. The details of these trials in the heavenly tribunal probably derived from his ten years' experience as a successful lawyer, a decade that certainly familiarized him with court procedure.

The trial, which is dramatized, is preceded by an account of Bontsha's death, which is summarized. The folkloric quality is preserved in the simplicity of diction, in the rhythmic repetitions, in the lack of description, in the unindividuated hero who is a type rather than a character. Without any temporal or spatial specificity, it is set in an unnamed locale which we recognize as a city because there are crowds. The reader is given no distinguishing characteristics such as physical features; he does not even know what color hair or eyes Bontsha has. Peretz has honored all the folktale conventions, in which the heroes exist only to enact the plot and any extraneous details would only distract from their function.

Bontsha's function is to enact passivity; he is, therefore, mute. His inarticulateness is stressed by implied relationships with subhuman things. His death is no more noticed than if a grain of sand had blown away; the collapse of a horse would have aroused more interest. "In his eyes there was a doglike supplication." Even nature is indifferent to his existence. His footprints have left no impression in the dust, and the wind has blown away the wooden marker over his grave. "In silence he was born, in silence he lived, in silence he died." No glasses clinked at his circumcision; no speeches were made at his bar mitzvah.

The uncomplaining porter, bowed down from a lifetime of bearing others' burdens, is welcomed into paradise by a blast from the great trumpet of the Messiah. Bontsha is terrified, convinced that they have mistaken him for someone else. Because of the ringing in his ears, he cannot hear his defending angel, but slowly he begins to recognize aspects of his life as they are recounted. Starved by a cruel stepmother, beaten by a drunken father, run over by the very man whose life he had saved, and abandoned by his wife after the birth of her illegitimate child whom he reared, only to have the child throw him out of his own house, Bontsha has never complained. The prosecutor says that because he has suffered so much in silence, he also will be silent. The great court of justice grows very still as the judge tells him to choose whatever reward he wishes:

> "Really?" he asks, doubtful, and a little embarrassed. "Really!" the judge answers. "Really! I tell you, everything is yours. Everything in paradise is yours. Choose! Take! Whatever you want!"

After a few more protestations and repeated assurances, Bontsha finally requests a hot roll with butter. In the appalling disparity between what he has been offered, and what he is able to imagine for himself, the story resists closure. He has been so conditioned to negate his own desires that none, beyond the bliss of daily bread, is available to him. In the inadequacy of this compensation for the injustice he has endured, the tale ambiguously ends:

> A silence falls upon the great hall, and it is more terrible than Bontsha's has ever been, and slowly the judge and the angels bend their heads in shame at this unending meekness they have created on earth. Then the silence is shattered. The prosecutor laughs aloud, a bitter laugh.

At whom is that dark laughter directed? Peretz leaves the enigma unresolved.

An equally famous tale, "The Three Gifts" opens with the paradigmatic scene. An ordinary soul stands before the throne watching his deeds being weighed on the scale of judgment. The accuser pours out all his sins while the advocate pours out his good deeds. Because they are in exact equilibrium, he can neither be condemned to hell, nor admitted to heaven, so he is consigned to earth to find three tokens of selfless martyrdom which will unbar the gates to paradise. Many ages pass before he finds the first tribute, a grain of sand. Robbers have murdered an elderly Jew for his bag of treasure, which turns out to be sanctified soil from the Holy Land he has saved to place under his head in the grave. The second gift is a bloody pin from the skirt of a rabbi's daughter. Her hair has been tied to the tail of a wild horse which dragged her through the streets of a medieval German town. The third is a skullcap which falls from the head of an emaciated youth being flogged to death by soldiers in a prison square.

Again, this is marked as a folktale by the minimal descriptions, by the anonymous types who perform the actions, and by the number three. Folktale heroes always have to perform three tasks. The ordinary soul, who had been neither good nor bad, "without evil intent or capacity for sacrifice," has been ennobled by vicariously participating in the communal history of persecution.

He is admitted to heaven and congratulated by "the Eternal Voice" for having brought such "truly beautiful gifts." This ironic closure is as disturbing as the prosecutor's "bitter laugh." Do the heavens require such tributes?

Peretz's most frequently anthologized Hasidic tale is "If Not Higher." He took a legend told of Rabbi Moses Leib of Sasov who disguised himself as a peasant to bring firewood to a bedridden widow and added a skeptical observer. This supplies the oblique angle of vision which Peretz so favors and turns it into a conversion story. Again the story opens just before the Days of Judgment when those who have made atonement will be inscribed in the book of life for another year. Since the rabbi always disappears at this time, his followers assume that he has ascended to heaven to intercede for them. A Litvak laughs scornfully at this and points to where it says in Scripture that even Moses could not ascend to heaven during his lifetime. Formidable rationalists who were learned in the legal codes, Litvaks were notoriously intolerant of Hasidic miracles. Thus, determined to discover where the rabbi went, the Litvak conceals himself under his bed.

The subsequent events are rendered in acoustic imagery. This mode of exposition simultaneously imposes unity and creates suspense. By focusing on what the eavesdropper can hear in the dark, his furtiveness and guilty anxiety are stressed. His fear is so great that "the roots of his earlocks pricked him like needles." He keeps himself awake by reciting an entire tractate of the Talmud. He knows that dawn has come when the sexton utters the call to prayer. He hears beds creaking, water splashing, doors opening and shutting. As he follows the rabbi into the street, lurking behind him in the shadows, he hears voices praying overhead. The thudding of his own heart seems to keep time with the rabbi's heavy footsteps in his peasant boots as they enter a wood. The rabbi takes out an ax. The Litvak hears a tree creak, then snap, then crash to the ground. He hears it being split into logs, then chopped into chips. Then he hears the rabbi tell a sick old widow that he is the peasant, Vassil, come to light her fire. As it is ignited, he hears the penitential prayers being recited. Having witnessed this simple good deed, the skeptical Litvak becomes a loyal disciple, and ever after, when another of his followers says that he ascends to heaven, he only adds, "If not higher."

Major publications other than short fiction
PLAYS: *Night in the Old Marketplace*, 1907; "The Golden Chain," 1909.
POETRY: *The Harp*, 1877; *Monish*, 1888.
NONFICTION: *Festival Journals*, 1894; *My Memoirs*, 1964.

Bibliography
Howe, Irving, ed. *Treasury of Yiddish Stories.*
Liptzin, Solomon. *The Flowering of Yiddish Literature.*
Madison, Charles A. *Yiddish Literature.*

Roback, Abraham Aaron. *I. L. Peretz: Psychologist of Literature.*
Waxman, Meyer. *History of Jewish Literature.*

Ruth Rosenberg

PETRONIUS
Gaius Petronius Arbiter

Born: c. A. D. 20
Died: Cumae, Italy; c. 66

Principal work
The Satyricon, c. 60 (earliest extant printed version, 1664).

Influence
Throughout the Middle Ages and into the Renaissance, Gaius Petronius Arbiter was known as a prose stylist and a moralist. Like the comedies of Terence, *The Satyricon* and the poems were quarried for sententious maxims. Petronius' literary influence perhaps boils down to one immortal story, "The Widow of Ephesus," the model of a candid and affirming realism, and to certain techniques of narration. Although more admired than actually imitated, Petronius is one of the few voices in which something of the *life* of antiquity can be heard.

Story characteristics
Petronius wrote Menippean satire: a potpourri of forms and styles strung on a loose picaresque thread.

Biography
The identity of the author of *The Satyricon* has only recently been agreed upon, and very little is known about his life. Gaius Petronius was governor of Bithynia and later consul. He became a member of Nero's inner circle, where he was known as *Arbiter Elegantiae* and became responsible for keeping the Emperor amused and entertained by creating new and "elegant" diversions. Denounced by the leader of Nero's Praetorian Guard, he was detained at Cumae to await the Emperor's pleasure. His tasteful suicide, the only event of his life for which an account survives, is described in the *Annals* (c. 119) of Tacitus.

Analysis
The Satyricon, Petronius' only extant work aside from a few poems, survives as a group of fragments which may represent as little as one tenth of the entire original. The nature of the work is difficult to characterize, not only because the story is impossible to reconstruct in full, but also because *The Satyricon* is unlike anything else that comes to us from antiquity. The only comparable book is *The Golden Ass* (c. 150) of Lucius Apuleius, written a century later. The book was written for Nero and his court and was probably

intended for recitation. Fragments of the text were known during the Middle Ages, but it was the rediscovery in 1650 of a codex containing the most significant and coherent section of the work, the famous *Cena Trimalchionis* (*Dinner at Trimalchio's*) that justified renewed interest in Petronius.

Sometimes considered the first realistic novel, *The Satyricon* describes the picaresque adventures of the narrator Encolpius and his sometime lover, the boy Giton, through the largely Greek cities of southern Italy. As usually reconstructed, the story begins with Encolpius engaged in a discussion of rhetoric with the teacher Agamemnon. He breaks away to pursue Ascyltos, his companion and rival for the affections of Giton. After various adventures during the day, the three spend a farcical night, interrupted by the priestess of Priapus, Quartilla, and her retinue. After a break in the surviving text, the three are brought to Trimalchio's banquet by Agamemnon. This is the *Cena Trimalchionis*, which is followed after another gap by a scene in which Encolpius meets the poet Eumolpus at a picture gallery. This provides an opportunity for poetic parodies and some roughshod art criticism. The two then dine together with Giton, and another rivalry develops over the boy. Encolpius and Giton pretend to attempt suicide, and at the height of the hubbub that follows, Ascyltos appears with an official, looking for Giton. The boy, however, hides himself by clinging to the underside of a mattress, similar to Odysseus under the ram of Polyphemos. Ascyltos leaves empty-handed, and Eumolpus and Encolpius are reconciled. After another gap, the reader finds Encolpius, Eumolpus, and Giton on shipboard, apparently fugitives. As it happens, the captain of the ship, Lichas, is an old enemy of Encolpius, while one of the passengers is Tryphaena, a woman with some claim on Giton (presumably both of these characters have appeared in parts of the story now lost). A voyage full of intrigue, suspense, and violence climaxes in shipwreck, but the three companions survive and make for Croton, a city reportedly full of legacy hunters. Beyond this point, the story becomes increasingly fragmentary, but several episodes are concerned with Encolpius' impotence and with other mishaps that befall him amid witches, priestesses, and thieves.

Fragmentary as it is, *The Satyricon* is one of the few surviving examples of several classical genres. Along with the *Apocolocyntosis* (c. 55) attributed to Lucius Annaeus Seneca, it is the only extant example of Menippean satire, a form that mixed prose, verse, and satirical observation in an episodic narrative. The result is a kind of intellectual comedy of which the closest modern relatives might be *Candide* (1759) and *Alice's Adventures in Wonderland* (1865).

Within the Menippean framework of the book there are traces of two other all but vanished genres: Roman mime and the Milesian tale. Mime, a kind of obscene farce in colloquial language, generated out of stock characters, seems to have influenced several episodes, such as those among the legacy hunters of Croton (116-117). The language of mime is explicity parodied at least once (56), and the naturalism of the book may owe something to this and other theatrical models. Milesian tales, marked by raciness and an inclination to satire, are forerunners of the novella tradition that reached maturity in Giovanni Boccaccio's *The Decameron* (1353). Two of the best-known tales in *The Satyricon* are of this type: "The Boy of Pergamum" and "The Widow of Ephesus."

In "The Boy of Pergamum" (chapters 85-87), Eumolpus tells how, while a guest in Pergamum, he schemes to seduce the son of his host by presenting himself as an ascetic philosopher. With the parents' approval, he accompanies the boy constantly to protect him from seducers. One night, noticing that the boy is awake, Eumolpus whispers a prayer to Venus: "If I can kiss this boy without his knowing it, tomorrow I will give him a pair of doves." Hearing this, the boy at once begins to snore loudly. Eumolpus takes his kisses and next morning produces two doves. The whispers become louder, the desires more extensive, the gifts more valuable, the boy's sleep more improbable, until on the third night Eumolpus promises a thoroughbred in return for consummation. He gets his wish, but since thoroughbreds are harder to come by than doves, the boy's impatience next morning breaks the spell: "Please sir, where's my horse?"

Later, Eumolpus attempts a reconciliation, but the boy, still piqued, warns him, "Go to sleep or I'll tell my father at once." Passion drives Eumolpus to force himself on his ward. No longer resisting, the boy even offers to do it again, to prove he is not so stingy as Eumolpus (the thoroughbred has not materialized). After being awakened three times by the boy, however, who asks, "Don't you want anything?," it is Eumolpus' turn to say, "Go to sleep or I'll tell your father at once."

This tale, really two linked tales, is like a primitive novella. The ribaldry of the anecdotes creates an impression of realism, but there is nothing real about the characters; they are interchangeable blanks. The boy, for example, can be, and has been, replaced by a girl without difficulty. These tales are above all formal inventions. Such familiar structures as the neat turnabout at the end, or the repetitions in threes, are formulae from which all kinds of stories can be generated. This is fiction aspiring to the efficiency of the joke.

"The Widow of Ephesus" (110-113), also told by Eumolpus, is much more impressive. A woman renowned for her virtue is widowed. Not content with ceremonial grief, she keeps vigil with the corpse in its vault, accompanied only by a devoted maid to share her grief and keep the lamp lit. Unable to dissuade her, relatives and friends leave her to her fate, praising her as a paragon of faithful love. Some robbers, however, are crucified nearby, and the soldier on guard, curious about the light he sees among the tombs, comes upon the beautiful widow. He invites her to share his supper. She refuses, but eventually the maid accepts food, and urges the widow to do the same, saying, "Your dead husband's body itself ought to persuade you to keep alive." Exhausted by hunger and grief, the woman gives in. Then, however, "the inducements the soldier had used to persuade the lady to go on living became part of his assault on her virtue." The widow consents to this too, and the couple spend three happy nights shut up together in the tomb while the parents of one of the crucified, finding no one on watch, take the body away for burial. Finding the cross empty the next day, the soldier resolves to fall on his sword rather than await punishment, but now it is the widow's turn to dissuade: "I would rather make use of the dead than kill the living." So the husband's body is taken from the tomb and fastened on the empty cross.

These are still stock characters, but not the narrative ciphers of "The Boy of Pergamum"; the story develops as it does *because* the woman is a widow, and *because* the man is a soldier. Milesian structural formulae are apparent here too in the recognition of the three nights of love and the turnabout at the end. In this tale, however, genuine human issues are raised. The nature and limits of fidelity are explored not only in the widow, once exemplary, and perhaps still so, but also in the devoted (*fidissima*) servant. The widow's love for her husband, even dead, is strikingly reflected in the parents of the robber who dare to retrieve his corpse, while the soldier's perhaps frivolous passion for her must be weighed against the honesty of her devotion to him. The story meditates too on persuasion, resistance, and acquiesence: the widow is seen, under the pressure of events, custom, and even the other characters, eventually to take command of her own story.

Eumolpus tells this as a story from his own time, but there is an earlier version in the Aesopian *Fables* of Phaedrus, and although the story is the most influential single element in *The Satyricon*, Petronius' version became authoritative only after the discovery of the *Cena Trimalchionis* revived interest in its author. "The Widow of Ephesus" was then retold by Jean de La Fontaine, and its dramatic possibilities inspired a series of stage versions, beginning with George Chapman's *The Widow's Tears* (1612) and continuing through Christopher Fry's *A Phoenix Too Frequent* (1946). The most recent dramatization is in the Fellini film *Satyricon* (1969).

Like Phaedrus, Eumolpus tells this as a fable about the fickleness of women, and so it is received by the auditors in *The Satyricon*—one even thinks the woman should be crucified for distracting the soldier from his duty. In medieval versions the treatment is the same, but modern versions, without changing the narrative appreciably, have reversed the theme, presenting the widow as sympathetic and even heroic. Fellini, for example, transforms the tale into a fable about the triumph of life and love over death; to enhance that reading, he also shifts the context, so that the story is told at the tomb of Trimalchio during his mock funeral. As the variety of versions testifies, "The Widow of Ephesus" is a triumph of economy, richer than any of the morals that can be, or have been, attached to it.

The Satyricon also bears traces of more familiar genres. Indications that Encolpius has somehow offended the god Priapus and as a result is afflicted with impotence suggest that the author may have intended a broad parody of epic, with the "wrath of Priapus" as the thread connecting many episodes that now seem unrelated, just as the "wrath of Poseidon" unifies the incidents of the *Odyssey* (c. 800 B. C.). The present state of the text, however, makes this impossible to verify. The *Cena Trimalchionis* is also to some extent imitative, a parody of Plato's *Symposium* by way of the *Satires* (35, 30 B. C.) of Horace. What strikes any reader, however, is not the sources of the episode, but its impressive originality. Although it hardly has a plot, the *Cena Trimalchionis* is a milestone in the craft of narration. In its cinematic wealth of detail, its control of shifting pace and perspective, it is Petronius' most sustained achievement as a writer.

The story is simple. When Encolpius, Giton, and Eumolpus arrive for dinner, the introduction to Trimalchio is by way of his appurtenances: a house cluttered with souvenirs, trophies, gaudy art, and the amulets of every superstition. Like Donald Barthelme, Petronius is master of his society's *dreck*; he knows how to make even the description of objects and settings eventful. The host finally appears after the first course, and the dinner begins in earnest. The sequence of outlandish *trompe l'oeil* dishes is seasoned with monologues from Trimalchio, the conversations of his guests, and the constant traffic of innumerable servants, many of them singing while they work. After several speeches full of ignorance, pretension, and platitude, Trimalchio excuses himself, and in his absence the guests gossip freely about him, one another, and their social world. Trimalchio returns with a little speech about constipation, and dinner continues, punctuated by the arrival of the drunken Habinnas (an episode obviously modeled on the entry of Alcibiades in the *Symposium*). Trimalchio, growing boozy, reads his will aloud; the former slave wants his own slaves to love him now "as much as they would if I were dead." This leads to a discussion of plans for his tomb, to a recital of his own career that begins to sound like a eulogy, and finally to a mock funeral, at the height of which the general uproar brings the fire brigade and the narrator slips away with his companions.

As even this summary can suggest, what controls the *Cena Trimalchionis* is not a plot or some authorial moral stance, but the dominant figure of Trimalchio, the *arriviste* at home among his kind. The insecurity of the exslave turned millionaire is reflected in the illusionism and impostures of his ambience, from the painted watchdog at his door to the deceptive dishes of his banquet: pea hen eggs are served nestling under a wooden hen, but the eggs are actually pastries stuffed with whole birds. A roast boar is stuffed with live thrushes that fly around the room when the carving begins. An apparent roast goose turns out to be contrived entirely of pork by a cook appropriately named Daedalus. Trimalchio's aspirations to taste are sabotaged by his native vulgarity. There is a Homeric recitation, but by way of illustrating it a slave dressed as Ajax rushes in, attacks a cooked calf dressed in a helmet, and serves up the resulting slices to the applause of the guests. Trimalchio boasts of his jewelry, and then has it weighed at the table to prove he is not lying. Above all, Trimalchio is preoccupied with death; the first thing we learn about him is that he has a clock and a trumpeter in his dining room "so he'll know how much of his life has passed." At our last glimpse, he is saying to other trumpeters, "Pretend I'm dead. Play something nice." The self-made man knows that Fortune takes as readily as she gives, so in his house, in his world, nothing is stable, nothing is what it seems. The *Cena Trimalchionis* depicts a vivid circus of ill-assorted people moving among a chaos of possessions. Its lack of a plot is purposeful, expressing the aimlessness of the world over which presides the monumentally vulgar, oddly sympathetic Trimalchio.

Although *The Satyricon* moves often toward satire, it is a special sort of satire: tolerant, generous, Horatian. Petronius' observations are penetrating but rarely condescending and in a way almost impartial. He makes way for his objects to reveal themselves. Critics who wish to see him primarily as a satirist of Imperial decadence find themselves complaining about a lack of moral focus, of "seriousness." One of the most obvious features of the book, however, its frank impartiality in sexual matters, should be a clue to the author's underlying attitude. His primary goal is realism rather than satire; his book is preoccupied with the surfaces of society, its texture, rather than its structure. Thus for example, while the narrator regularly makes judgments about what he sees, the author makes it clear that these are self-interested and unreliable. Even the judgments are part of the milieu being depicted. As objects of satire, the characters in *The Satyricon* are extremely traditional: bad poets, *nouveaux riches*, parasites, licentious women; but at the heart of Petronius' originality is a willingness to present these types on their own terms, to let them speak for themselves and about each other. The reader sees the insecurities of the loose women, the embattled pride of the self-made man. Petronius' command of several colloquial styles enables him to provide a distinguishable idiom for each of them. As a result, *The Satyricon*'s audience comes to know ostensibly stock characters from within.

This genial realism, along with the techniques of observation and language that make it possible, is Petronius' most significant contribution to the art of short fiction. If there is any statement of artistic intention in his work, it is these lines from a poem recited by Encolpius: "A kindness far from sad laughs in my pure speech;/ whatever the people do, my frank tongue reports." That candor is the hallmark of *The Satyricon*.

Bibliography

Auerbach, Erich. "Fortunata," in *Mimesis: A Representation of Reality in Western Literature*.

Corbett, Philip B. *Petronius*.
Sullivan, J. P. The Satyricon *of Petronius: A Literary Study*.

Laurence A. Breiner

LUIGI PIRANDELLO

Born: Girgenti, Italy; June 28, 1867
Died: Rome, Italy; December 10, 1936

Principal short fiction
Novelle per un anno, 1922 (*Short Stories for a Year*).

Other literary forms
Luigi Pirandello's literary interests did not stop at writing highly praised short stories; he also published novels, poetry, essays of a philological and philosophical nature, and, above all, plays, for which he is best known and for which he received the Nobel Prize for Literature in 1934. Often, however, these later works, especially the plays, have their original kernels in his short stories.

Influence
Pirandello's short stories and novels were from the very beginning semiautonomous or independent of surrounding literary influences; Italian *verismo* nevertheless exerted a temporary influence on Pirandello, especially through his acquaintance with the works of his compatriot writers Luigi Capuana and Giovanni Verga, (also from Sicily) who urged him to write stories and novels about local Sicilian lore and social conditions. Later, the Theater of the Grotesque also exerted some weight on his prose and future drama, particularly because of playwrights of the grotesque such as Luigi Chiarelli, Luigi Antonelli, and Pier Maria Rosso di San Secondo. His studies in Germany—he received a Ph.D. at the University of Bonn—must have given Pirandello a propensity toward the odd or fantastical side of life for which Romantic German literature was known; such an inclination became crystallized later into his writings and was furthered by the experience of living with his wife, who gradually became irreparably insane. He thus derived a major influence directly from life.

Pirandello must have had a natural affinity for the fantastical elements of life, since even before his wife became truly insane, many of his short stories dealt with an unexpected social behavior. In the first work, a woman who is innocent of the accusations leveled against her becomes an outcast; later, she is accepted by that same society when she is really guilty of certain deeds. Similarly, the reader finds a streak of abnormality in a person who pretends to be dead when he is living, assuming at the same time the identity of another person which he is not, as is the case with the "late" Mattia Pascal.

Story characteristics
In a sense, Pirandello's portrayal of situations and his style of writing are

monochromatic; his short stories, novels, verses, and plays depict the same atmosphere and exhibit a similar tone or sense of odd humor. Much of the author's work produces a sensation of the tragic and the hidden or mysterious, the illusion of reality, and unexpected and often confusing situations; incisive thoughts are conveyed in natural yet dramatic language. In all, his stories, style, and language are somewhat monothematic and monotonic; his work is very different from that of other short-story writers. It was not an instant success; and it took a James Joyce to recognize the importance of his writings; and it was another foreigner, Benjamin Crémieux, who introduced him to French readers.

Biography

Educated at the University of Palermo, then at the University of Rome, and finally at the University of Bonn, Luigi Pirandello settled in Rome on his return from Germany in 1894 and married Antonietta Portulano who became ill and eventually mentally deranged. To earn a living, after a financial debacle (1904), he became a professor at the Istituto Superiore Femminile de Magistero in Rome; in 1926 he established his own theater company touring Italy, most of Europe, and the Americas. His main company actress and constant friend of this period was Marta Abba, who was at times suspected of being his lover, which Pirandello denied vehemently, saying it was ridiculous since Abba was young enough to be his daughter. (In later years Abba lived in New York City devoting her time to translations and editions of his plays.) Pirandello visited the United States of America in 1935, where he was warmly received by many persons in the literary world; previously both the French and the Italian governments decorated him for his plays. The well-known actor Angelo Musco played in many of his comedies which were made into motion pictures; his play *Come tu mi vuoi* (translated by Samuel Putnam as *As You Desire Me*, 1930) was filmed in Hollywood starring Greta Garbo. In 1936, only two years after receiving the Nobel Prize for Literature, Pirandello died in Rome of a heart attack.

Analysis

Luigi Pirandello's first attempt at writing was poetry, but he soon found that prose (novels and especially short stories) suited better his natural mode of expression. Therefore, he began to write short stories, but not in a true veristic manner; he soon gave the genre a new twist, a new definition that can be termed Pirandellian. The typical Pirandellian story is eccentric, illusory, escapist, and philosophical; it deals with life's anguish, with man's isolation and torment; it probes maddening situations; it resorts to humor that leaves the reader in a paradox as if he were looking at a prism that is ever oscillating before his eyes. Pirandello never really changed; his novels follow the same trajectory as the stories, and when at the age of fifty he turned to the theater, he again returned to his past stories and novels, most of which he had written twenty or thirty years before, and converted them into plays. These plays shook the literary and theatrical world not only of Italy but also of Europe, America, and Latin America.

Among his best short stories one finds "Il Treno ha fischiato" ("The Train Whistled"), in which the protagonists must resort to an eternal illusion in order to avoid tragic results, no different from *Enrico IV* (1922, *Henry IV*); these men and women, it may be said, are from his native region, yet it can equally and irrefutably be said that they are lost souls found anywhere in the world. Mankind's problems, anguish, and the attempt to overcome them began with Adam or Abel; they belong to no nation in particular. A few other stories which posit the above-mentioned tenets that beset men everywhere are "La tragedia d'un personaggio" ("The Tragedy of Being a Character"), one of his early stories; "La carriola" ("The Wheelbarrow"); and the humorous "La marsina stretta" ("The Tight Frock Coat").

In the first mentioned short story the author is engaged in a conversation with his own characters; that is, they are living images of his inventive genius who want to live. Their author cannot disregard them any longer; they are indeed part of himself, and vice versa. He even objects to or seems to dislike the fact that "characters of my short stories go all over the world telling everyone that I am a most cruel and pitiless writer." He wishes that a kind and understanding critic could fathom his compassion and grief hidden or enclosed within "quel riso" ("that laughter"), an evident reply to Benedetto Croce and others who, Pirandello claimed to the last days of his life in a conversation with Domenico Vittorini (1935), did not understand him at all. It is evident that this short story is of paramount importance, for it contains the nucleus of one of his greatest works, *Sei personaggi in cerca d'autore* (1921, *Six Characters in Search of an Author*); and, to a lesser degree, that theme is also found in his drama *Questa sera si recita a soggetto* (1930, *Tonight We Improvise*), another play-in progress. Above all, this story marks the first time in literature that an author speaks with his creatures, which is another of Pirandello's innovations.

The story "The Wheelbarrow" is an examination of man's behavioral patterns and his yearning to give relief to life's tedium, nausea, falseness, and formality. The story concerns a man whom people assume they know, yet this man knows that he is not what others think he is; it is a Pirandellian twist that was to influence not only his later works but also the whole European theater. The man's name is on his house door on a brass plate, as is wont to be done in Italy, with Doctor, Professor, or Lawyer before the name as an identification mark of status or profession. In this case, the man seems to be all of these; he is held in high respect by all who come to see him in his study seated behind an imposing desk. After a tiring day, what this highly respected, educated man resorts to, in order to find relief from his absurd, anguished daily life, is to lift up his old female dog's hind legs and wheel her around his study for about ten feet as one does with a wheelbarrow on a patch of grass. He is not the same person people think he is. Life will certainly continue unabated in its cycles of dilemmas; he knows it, but for at least a moment in a day, he can really be crazy, filled with joy, be himself, not what the nameplate says he is. He is really a different person when alone, just as Henry IV knows he is no Emperor when he retires in his own "court." It was Pirandello himself who, being recognized at a sidewalk café by a woman who asked him if he was Signor Pirandello, answered: "No, but they say we look alike."

Relative to Pirandello's language it can be said that in no other contemporary writer can one find a greater intrinsic adhesion or corresondence between language and style and between thought and plot than in his works. The uniqueness of his wording, the freshness of his style with its incisive edge, and his ironic humor give the lie to those who say that Italian writers from southern Italy do not know Italian as well as those from the north or the center of Italy. Perhaps, relative to this linguistic assessment, one can point to only "The Tight Frock Coat," which disproves this statement. In the story, a professor has to attend the wedding of one of his women students and finds out that his frock coat is very tight only minutes before the ceremony. He puts it on anyway; almost unable to move his arms, he looks odd and ridiculous, which infuriates him. Normally, he is a patient man, nonrebellious and sedate—but under normal circumstances, not dressed and squeezed into a tight frock. Still this irritating and ridiculous coat will make him save the wedding of his student when it is about to be called off because of "a ridiculous" reason: the girl's mother had died on the same day the wedding was to take place. If the wedding had been postponed, very possibly the groom who was from another town, would not have returned months later. So, Professor Gori, wearing that frock, tight or not, becomes an imperative professor: he orders the wedding to go on; he will even be a witness for the marriage ceremony at the city hall.

Clearly, Pirandello's short stories are not traditional; their author was an innovator in the genre whose work became seminal for later writers.

Major publications other than short fiction

NOVELS: *L'esclusa*, 1901 (*The Outcast*); *Il fu Mattia Pascal*, 1904 (*The Late Mattia Pascal*); *I vecchi e i giovani*, 1908 (*The Old and the Young*); *Uno, nessuno e centomila*, 1910 (*One, No one, and a Hundred Thousand*).

PLAYS: *Così è—se vi pare*, 1917 (*Right You Are—If You Think So*); *Il piacere dell' onestà*, 1917 (*The Pleasure of Honesty*); *Sei personaggi in cerca d'autore*, 1921 (*Six Characters in Search of an Author*); *Enrico IV*, 1922 (*Henry IV*); *Come tu mi vuoi*, 1930 (*As You Desire Me*); *Quando si è qualcuno*, 1933.

POETRY: *Mal giocondo*, 1889 (*Painful Joy*).

Ferdinando D. Maurino

EDGAR ALLAN POE

Born: Boston, Massachusetts; January 19, 1809
Died: Baltimore, Maryland; October 7, 1849

Principal short fiction

Tales of the Grotesque and Arabesque, 1840; *The Prose Romances of Edgar Allan Poe*, 1843; *Tales*, 1845.

Other literary forms

Edgar Allan Poe is still regarded as a major American poet of the nineteenth century. "The Raven," a tour de force of heavy musical effects and mysterious atmosphere, is one of the most popular poems in English. Other poems feature brilliant incantatory effects, mood pictures of unreal places, and more conventional romantic lyricism. As a practical critic, Poe managed to produce (among reviews which mixed evaluation, humor, literary rage, hack work, and theory) major critical statements as well as classic judgments. He is also the author of two unique works: *Eureka* (1848), a prose poem on the universe, and *The Narrative of Arthur Gordon Pym* (1838), a fictional work of novel length.

Influence

Poe's work has had more varied strains of influence than that of any other writer of short fiction. He is often thought of as the father of the detective story and as one of the inventors of science fiction. Virtually all later writers of Gothic and supernatural fiction have been influenced directly or indirectly by Poe. By articulating the critical principles which defined its aesthetics, he made an invaluable contribution to the form of the conventional short story. More broadly, because of the response of French writers to his work and life, Poe can be seen as an early spokesman for the importance of technical and purely aesthetic approaches to literature, an emphasis which lies at the heart of modern art. Although his influence is difficult to measure, Poe's popularity from the 1840's to the present makes him a continuing presence in our culture. The numerous films adapted from his work ("The Masque of the Red Death," 1842; "The Fall of the House of Usher," 1839; and "The Pit and the Pendulum," 1843) are some of the more overt instances of the mid-twentieth century response to Poe.

Story characteristics

Poe is best known as a writer of Gothic tales, stories which depend heavily on atmosphere for their effects and which make use of supernatural and sometimes ghoulish incidents. These stories are noted for their acute rendering of the sensations and the psychological struggles of the protagonists who often feel themselves victims of powerful and mysterious forces. Although few in number, the detective stories establish firmly the interest in a chain of ratio-cination which would become typical of this intellectual handling of the terrible. Less known, Poe's humorous stories use slapstick and blunt rhetorical devices to stress what is laughable in a mechanical approach to life and art. Through his use of technology and scientific ideas, Poe is among the first of the science-fiction writers.

Biography

After being orphaned at the age of two, Edgar Allan Poe was taken into the family of John Allan of Richmond, Virginia, and reared virtually as Allan's adopted son. Tensions developed between Allan and Poe and, with the death of Allan's first wife and his remarriage, relations between the two deteriorated further, culminating in a final estrangement in 1830. Poe's short attendance at the University of Virginia in 1826 was followed by his enlistment, as Edgar A. Perry, in the United States Army. In 1827, he published his first book, a volume of poetry, *Tamerlane and Other Poems*. Following a brief matriculation at West Point, Poe turned to literature, winning first prize for a story and becoming editor of the *Southern Literary Messenger*, where his often fierce criticism brought him attention and literary notoriety. In 1836, he married his cousin, Virginia Clemm. Discharged by his publisher T. W. White in 1837, he went first to New York, then to Philadelphia, where he became an editor for *Burton's Gentleman's Magazine* and later *Graham's Magazine*. The connection with Graham was severed in 1842 and two years later Poe returned to New York. With the success of "The Gold-Bug," "The Balloon Hoax," and "The Raven," Poe's literary reputation grew, but he also became more embroiled in literary politics, personality conflicts, and social intrigue. In 1845, Poe was involved in a public dispute over his charge that Henry Wadsworth Longfellow had plagiarized. Poe's year of disaster, 1846, opened with a social scandal over some letters written to Poe by Mrs. Osgood. This was followed by the publication of his controversial New York literati series, articles which occasioned such a vicious reaction on the part of some authors that Poe sued for libel. The year was also marked by the declining health and fortunes of both Poe and his wife; Virginia died in January of 1847. In his last years, Poe was involved with several women in a confused (and confusing) struggle for emotional satisfaction and economic stability. His last major work, *Eureka*, was published in 1848. Poe died under mysterious circumstances in Baltimore in 1849.

Analysis

Both as theorist and as creative writer, Edgar Allan Poe made indispensable contributions at a crucial stage in the development of the short story. He was the first literary critic to establish aesthetic principles for regarding short fiction as high art. In his review of Nathaniel Hawthorne's *Twice-Told Tales* (1837), Poe took the position that brevity itself could be a positive aesthetic factor, contributing to the "totality" of effect upon the reader and thus to the achievement of artistic unity. He argued that short fiction had a potential for intensifying the reading experience which the novel, because of its amplitude, lacked. "During the hour of perusal [of the story], the soul of the reader is at the writer's control." According to Poe, the tale writer achieved an effect of unity in his work by being at all times conscious of his purpose and by employing with "care and skill" the technical means which would accomplish his aim. Instead of inspiration, Poe emphasized the necessity of continuous attention to rhetorical tools: "If his very initial sentence tend not to the outbringing of this effect, then he [the author] has failed in his first step." While Poe saw a number of legitimate aims for the short narrative, such as truth, an affective treatment of passion or terror, and humor, he valued control of design rather than the conveying of any particular message or moral.

Poe's ideal short-story writer was detached through his technical formulation of subject matter, but Poe also stressed the importance of the writer's identification with his materials (the result, as he saw it, of the disciplined imagination). The popularity of Poe's own stories, a continuing, worldwide phenomenon, may in fact be due to his ability (in the process of writing rather than the planning) to identify with his protagonists. The stories convey the impression that the author sympathizes with the characters' uncertainties, that he understands their fascination with their mysterious situations, and that he knows the feelings of those suddenly confronted with the unknown and the terrifying. Virtually all of Poe's well-known stories are told by first-person narrators who are able to convince readers—through sensations, details, and psychological explanation—that their involvement with the immediate surroundings and with other characters forms a drama of crucial significance. Out of these almost egotistically serious narrations emerge both the credibility for the encounter with the amazing and the growing moods of wonder that, as the stories develop, come to imply in the drama some occult relationship between inner man (soul and mind) and external situation.

Poe's best-known story, "The Fall of the House of Usher," is a good example of the conjuring of mystery, in this case with a rather neutral, prosaic narrator. Much of the first part of the story is devoted to a description of the house and surroundings and to the rather depressing atmosphere they seem to exude. Under this spell, the narrator meets again his old friend Roderick Usher and begins to discover the nature of the mysterious illnesses of Roderick and his sister Madeline. As the narrator details Roderick's symptoms and his manner of existence, it is apparent that Usher is a type of romantic, the artist of acute sensibility, but one whose sensitivity has become so refined as to prohibit any normal contact with the world. Roderick's nervous system can no longer bear strong, direct sensuous experience; he is restricted to darkened rooms, can eat only the most insipid food, and can stand only garments of a certain texture. The narrator catches just a glimpse of the apparitional Madeline. Soon he is told that she has died, and he and Roderick place the encoffined body in a vault prior to permanent entombment. Subsequently, Roderick's behavior becomes increasingly restless. On a stormy night a week later, his agitation is so intense that the narrator tries to calm him with an unimaginative tale. During the reading there is an increasing sense that the sounds in the tale are being echoed by noises in the house. Finally, as the narrator is roused to a feeling of crisis, Roderick proclaims that Madeline stands outside the door, that they have put her living in the tomb, and she has only now managed to escape. With that announcement, she enters and begins a struggle with Roderick which results in the death of both. The incredulous narrator quickly makes his escape, pausing only long enough to see behind him the house collapsing, bursting into fragments.

As in many of Poe's other works, the mood, sensations, and events of the story are so melodramatically strong that they obscure the ideas that are present. Although Poe here has made ample use of an old Gothic device— the haunted house (the setting for fantastic events)—he has also, by pointing analytically at the decadence of the overly refined, projected a critique of the romantic soul. One senses vividly the plight of that soul, but Poe's emphasis is on the implacable nature of its circumstances. In simplest terms, its impulse to seek out more refined beauty in the world of the senses has reached the stage where the world itself is threatening. Associated with that power of sensitivity, Madeline must be buried and repressed so that the encounter with the world might be more prosaic and less intense. With Madeline gone, however, Usher's essential orientation to existence is removed, and he is left directionless, objectless. Trying to help, the narrator unwittingly reengages the momentum of Usher's sensitivity; Madeline returns, and Usher is doomed.

In a series of stories concerned with bewitching female characters, Poe again used a first-person narrator to emphasize (through the psychological reactions of a male) the disturbing elements in the transcendent and earthly aspects of romantic beauty. Each story stresses the power of a beautiful lady's influence by naming her in the title: "Berenice," "Morella," "Ligeia," "Eleonora." The most successful tale of this group, "Ligeia," opens with a detailed examination of the immense learning and beauty the narrator discovers in the woman. She seems, in one respect, to represent the principle of beauty in the universe. The narrator's obsession is evident, but he is frightened as well as fascinated, for her powers are beyond the human. Her subsequent death is presented as a struggle; instead of accepting the natural course of events, she clings defiantly to life, insisting to the narrator that "Man doth not yield . . . unto death . . . save only through the weakness of his feeble will." A short time after her death, the narrator marries again, to the Lady Rowena

Trevanion. Still obsessed with his dark-haired Ligeia, he treats the fair Rowena with contempt, and even as his new wife lies dying, he is more the restless witness than the sufferer. In the death chamber the narrator begins to sense an alien presence and to imagine mysterious events as he alternates between thoughts of Ligeia and observations of Rowena. At last, just as he has convinced himself of her death, Rowena seems to rise again, but to the accompaniment of his shrieking surprise, she now appears raven-haired, not fair; she is not Rowena, but Ligeia come back, her will, or his, grotesquely triumphant.

Poe's stories often summon up the sense of another world, but in a manner that stresses its problematic relation to earthly man. The semblance of death, the return from the grave, the complicating appearance of a second woman are the somber motifs in the women stories, and the women themselves, as supernatural-seeming figures, begin to obliterate the distinction between life and death, most often in a demonic manner. Since the women are associated both with beauty and death, the male narrators' delights and unease are grounded finally in the sense of man's mortal fate (the end of all sensual pleasure) and in the vision of an abiding (though absolutely transcendent) presence in the universe.

In other stories, the absolute ground for the supernatural sense is less clear, and the characters are correspondingly more bemused, fascinated, and tortured by situations in which space and time are apparently transcended. Swept along by an unknown force powering his ship toward the South Pole, the narrator in "Ms. Found in a Bottle" feels a "new sense, a new entity is added to my soul," and is excited by some "never-to-be-imparted secret," even though he knows its attainment is destruction. The young Baron in "Metzengerstein" and Bedloe in "A Tale of the Ragged Mountains" are each involved with events they come to regard as instances of metempsychosis and reincarnation, experiences which lead eventually to their deaths. In "The Tell-Tale Heart" and "The Black Cat," the narrators are haunted and tortured by seemingly ubiquitous moral witnesses, who satanically harass them. In "The Pit and the Pendulum," the Inquisition itself offers the transcendent vision to the narrator, the idea of the soul imprisoned in the material world, constricted by space, threatened by time, and on the verge of damnation. Refusing to see these implications in his situation, this narrator persistently confines his actions to the level of practical reason and is at least partially able to cope with his predicament.

While Poe's romantic tales point toward those mysteries which must appear supernatural to earthbound man, his detective stories (which total only five) are concerned with solutions to puzzles. One of the first to work in this area, Poe created a formal perspective for later detective stories—a minor first-person narrator focusing attention on the real hero—and also invented, in Dupin, a popular detective character type, the thinking machine. Dupin is first introduced in "The Murders in the Rue Morgue" and subsequently appears in "The Mystery of Marie Rogêt" and "The Purloined Letter."

The latter story, generally regarded as Poe's finest in this vein, concerns the location of a letter being used to blackmail an unnamed but nationally prominent lady. Although the letter is known to be in the possession of the villain, a minister, known only as D__ , the Prefect of police has, as he explains to Dupin, been unable to lay hands on it. He has minutely and methodically searched both D__ 's apartment and his person, but without success. Having defined the problem, the frustrated official leaves. The story turns in the middle when, during the Prefect's second visit, the detective casually produces the letter to the dramatic amazement of the Prefect and the narrator. The latter part of the story reveals how Dupin discovered the crucial document; it has been in plain sight, but oddly obscured in a card rack where it has been disguised as a letter of little worth. In explaining this, Dupin presents a disquisition on methods of focusing the mind on the significant. He informs the narrator (and the reader) that the case's solution requires some understanding of the character of D__ (in order to allow "an identification of the reasoner's intellect with that of his opponent"), a capacity for seeing the obvious, and some flair for the theatrical. After staging a ruse, Dupin himself purloins the letter from D__ , cleverly substituting his own facsimile so that the man will unknowingly overreach himself. Like this story, the other detective narrations are all concerned with the investigation and examination of intricate details, with seeing patterns in the apparently insignificant and the puzzling. In "The Gold-Bug," Poe makes use of cryptography as a structuring device for this story of an intellectual treasure hunt.

Although they bulk comparatively large in the Poe canon (twenty-three out of fifty-seven short works that might be classed as stories), his humorous pieces are least known. Their topicality, the satire of current literary work and the references to contemporary concerns, may be one reason for this neglect. Also, several take the form of hoaxes, a brand of humor no longer popular. Their comic effect is often generated by the notion of the work as a game between writer and reader, and they feature wild, slapstick events which sometimes involve a game with the character as well. In "The Angel of the Odd," for example, after the narrator decides to place his faith in the ordinary, the Angel of the Odd appears and orchestrates the world to vex him. The narrator's insurance lapses and his house burns; his falling wig loses him one sweetheart and a speck in the eye another; he decides on suicide, is robbed of his pants by a crow, and falls over a cliff chasing it. Luckily (suicide now out of his mind), he grabs the guiderope of a passing balloon only to be confronted again by the Angel, who demands full submission. Since submission involves putting his right hand into his left back pocket and since his left arm is broken and he is hanging on with his right hand, he shakes his head. The Angel takes this for denial, cuts him loose, and he falls through his chimney into his own home. Much of Poe's humor features such an interplay of logic and illogic, expectation and event, as situations tumble wildly into one another. Thematically, Poe's satiric treatment gives rather rough mauling to a variety of ideas: didacticism in literature in "Never Bet the Devil Your Head," civilized progress in "Some Words with a Mummy," the treatment of the mentally ill in "The System of Dr. Tarr and Prof. Fether," gold fever in "Von Kempelen and His Discovery."

For Poe, immersed in the world of literary journalism, the writing of a variety of works was chiefly a means of survival; for later readers it became a testimony to his genius. Reading and editing made him familiar with some short-fiction possibilities; using what he knew of the relationship between writer and reader, he invented others. The range and general excellence of Poe's work demonstrates the wonderful fertility of his imagination, its capability for functioning in many literary directions. This imaginary brilliance, however, pushes other aspects of his art into the background. It is undoubtedly an injustice, for example, that so few readers have gone to him for his ideas, for he has much to say about the difficulties of the romantic soul in a material world and about man's relationship to his occult and transcendent visions. Poe's great gift was to have seen more clearly than any of his literary contemporaries how short fiction could work as literature, to have imagined the short story in its uniqueness, its strengths, and its possibilities.

Major publications other than short fiction
NOVEL: *The Narrative of Arthur Gordon Pym*, 1838.
PLAY: *Politian*, 1835-1836.
POETRY: *The Poems of Edgar Allan Poe*, 1965; *Collected Works of Edgar Allan Poe: Poetry, Volume I*, 1969.

Bibliography
Carlson, Eric W. *Introduction to Poe: A Thematic Reader.*
Dameron, J. Lasley and Irby B. Cauthen, Jr., eds. *Edgar Allan Poe: A Bibliography of Criticism, 1827-1967.*
Hoffman, Daniel. *Poe Poe Poe Poe Poe Poe Poe.*
Howarth, William L. *Twentieth Century Interpretations of Poe's Tales.*
Hyneman, Esther F., ed. *Edgar Allan Poe: An Annotated Bibliography of Books and Articles in English, 1827-1973.*
Jacobs, Robert D. *Poe: Journalist and Critic.*
Levine, Stuart. *Edgar Poe: Seer and Craftsman.*
Moss, Sidney P. *Poe's Literary Battles.*
_____ . *Poe's Major Crisis.*
Quinn, Arthur Hobson. *Edgar Allan Poe: A Critical Biography.*
Quinn, Patrick F. *The French Face of Edgar Poe.*
Rans, Geoffrey. *Edgar Allan Poe.*

Thompson, G. R. *Poe's Fiction: Romantic Irony in the Gothic Tales.*
Woodson, Thomas, ed. *Twentieth Century Interpretations of "The Fall of the House of Usher."*

Walter Shear

KATHERINE ANNE PORTER

Born: Indian Creek, Texas; May 15, 1890
Died: College Park, Maryland; September 18, 1980

Principal short fiction
Flowering Judas and Other Stories, 1930; *The Leaning Tower and Other Stories*, 1944; *The Old Order*, 1955; *Collected Stories*, 1965.

Other literary forms
Katherine Anne Porter, famous for her short stories, is equally famous for her collection of three short novels, published under the title *Pale Horse, Pale Rider* (1939), and for her best-selling novel, *Ship of Fools* (1962). She published two volumes of essays, and won many honors and awards for her writing, including two Guggenheim Fellowships.

Influence
Porter considered herself to be most influenced by Henry James, James Joyce, William Butler Yeats, Ezra Pound, and T. S. Eliot. While these writers influenced her technically and aesthetically, her themes and subjects certainly came directly out of her youth in turn-of-the-century rural Texas and her expatriate years in Mexico and Europe.

Story characteristics
Porter wrote in the same realistic tradition as Ernest Hemingway, whose stories hers sometimes resemble. This resemblance arises not from similar styles, but rather from similar subjects: the aimless and disillusioned youth of the World War I period; earthy, sensual peasants; nostalgic but often bitingly realistic glimpses of a past childhood in America that is now dying out (in Hemingway's case, in Upper Michigan; in Porter's, in rural Texas). Porter's characters are marked by hopelessness and failure, partly caused by the times in which they must live, but mainly growing out of their radical inability to form lasting relationships with others. She is justly famous for her style, which is marked by unobtrusive yet absolutely accurate use of adjective that gives her writing a clarity and three-dimensionality few writers can equal.

Biography
Katherine Anne Porter grew up in rural Texas. When she was two, her mother died, and from then on she was reared by her grandmother (the model for the grandmother in the Miranda stories) in a strongly matriarchal family. She ran away from school at sixteen to marry, was soon divorced, and worked for newspapars in Texas and in Colorado. In Colorado (c. 1918) she nearly died of influenza in circumstances close to those in the short novel *Pale Horse,*

Pale Rider. She went on to study in Mexico and began writing stories based on her experiences there. In 1930 she published a slim volume of stories, *Flowering Judas and Other Stories*, and her reputation was immediately established. With the help of grants she was then able to spend several years abroad in Mexico and Europe and to find visiting lectureships in universities, while she continued her sparse output of stories and short novels, and, after a gestation of nearly thirty years, produced her one novel. A perfectionist, she claimed to have thrown away trunk loads of manuscripts, only allowing what she considered her most perfect works to be published. She was married and divorced three times.

Analysis

Katherine Anne Porter wrote a number of unforgettable stories, but certainly her most famous is "Flowering Judas." As with many of her works, it was written with incredible speed, "between seven o'clock and midnight," at which time, with scarcely a word changed from the first draft, the completed manuscript was dropped into the mailbox.

The story takes place in Mexico shortly after the Obregon revolution in the early 1920's. Laura, a beautiful American girl, has been helping the revolutionaries in various small ways, mostly by carrying messages to men who are in hiding or in jail. She is a mystery to the men in the revolutionary group, for she seems to have no lover and no observable interest in men; therefore they cannot understand what her motives are in working with them. Lately, Braggioni, their leader, a fat, self-indulgent, childishly vain, but also very dangerous man, has begun courting her. Every night when she gets home he is waiting to play for her on his squealing guitar and to sing passionately to her off key. Having no choice, she endures this with an expression of "pitiless courtesy" on her face. Inwardly she feels terror, "a warning in her blood that violence, mutilation, and shocking death wait for her with lessening patience." Two other men have courted her here, but she has refused to respond to their signals.

As she sits listening to Braggioni, she is thinking about Eugenio, whom she has been visiting in his prison cell. She had brought him drugs to help him pass the time; he had saved them and taken them all today, unable to endure any further incarceration. Braggioni is increasingly restless. He tells her that May Day disturbances are coming in the city of Morelia. Catholics will have a procession marching one way, socialists the other way, until they meet. Laura cleans his revolver for him. 'Put that on, and go kill somebody in Morelia, and you will be happier,' she says softly. He leaves, and she feels she has finally got rid of him for awhile. When she goes to sleep, she at once dreams of Eugenio, who calls her "murderer," makes her eat from the bleeding flowers of the Judas tree, and takes her on a journey to death.

The story, written in a strangely echoing present tense, seems so rich and packed that the reader is astonished to look back and see it is less than ten pages long. It immediately suggests itself for symbolical interpretations, the best known of which is Ray B. West's (collected in *Katherine Anne Porter: A Critical Symposium*, 1969). West sees the story as a kind of religious allegory involving love in three guises, religious, secular, and erotic. One series of images has to do with the revolutionaries, who are socialists. Braggioni, their leader, is sarcastically called "a professional lover of man," suggesting a union of the material with the Christ-like. Erotic love is seen in Braggioni and the other two men who at some time in the story court Laura. Religious symbols accrete around Laura's childhood Catholicism and her even now sneaking off to visit a church and say a Hail Mary. It is also seen in the parade which will be marching towards the socialists in Morelia, and finally, in the overarching image of the Flowering Judas tree. Yet Laura is unable to pray meaningfully in the church and is unable to receive the advances of the men; her chief action in the revolution is to bring Eugenio the narcotics with which he kills himself. In her dream at the end he calls her "cannibal" and "murderer" and makes her eat of the Judas flowers. "This is my body and my blood," he tells her, for it has been a negative sacrament of betrayal, and Laura, the only character in the story incapable of love on any of the levels, has finally betrayed life itself.

As with all good symbolical stories, Laura's essential betrayal is grasped by the reader at the literal level; the symbols reinforce and enrich what the story's surface has already conveyed. Many of Katherine Anne Porter's other stories have been subjected to similar scrutiny, but most of them can be quite fully and accurately read and experienced at the literal level.

Mrs. Whipple, for example, in the story "He" (the characters and setting in this story are reminiscent of Porter's famous short novel, *Noon Wine*, 1937), is constantly claiming to everybody that she loves her feebleminded son more than she does the other two children put together and that she is not the least bit ashamed of him. She is always worrying that the neighbors might think she slights "Him" for the sake of Adra and Emly, the normal son and daughter. Adra, the reader learns, is weak and cowardly and Emly sickly, and the Whipple farm is going down hill. "He" is big and strong and fearless, so they take the extra blanket off his cot and give it to Emly since he does not seem to mind the cold. When they need to walk the neighbor's bull three miles over to their farm to breed their cow, they decide Adra is too nervous to handle such a dangerous animal and let Him bring it. He climbs the tallest trees after fruit, does the heaviest chores, and, when they want to kill a suckling pig for a family dinner and Adra is afraid of the savage sow, He sneaks up on it, snatches the piglet, and leaps the fence before the sow can reach him. When Mrs. Whipple slits the piglet's throat, however, He gives an anguished cry and runs off. Later He refuses to come into the room where they are eating it.

As the farm continues to lose money, Adra leaves for a job in a grocery store at the first chance he gets while Emly quits school to get a job in town. He takes over all the chores, but when He falls sick and becomes a burden, the Whipples—worrying about what the neighbors will say and hoping it will not look as if they need "charity"—allow Him to be put in a state home where He can be looked after. To their amazement, as He is carried from the farm, huge round tears begin falling from His eyes. He was the only one of the children who cared about them.

Symbolically, the reader can see that He (as the capitalized pronoun suggests) is a kind of Christ figure ("A Lord's pure mercy if He should die," a neighbor says, suggesting Christ's death for our sakes), with his innocence and love, sacrificing himself for pharisaic parents who care more for the appearance before their neighbors of loving Him than they actually care about Him. The story is clear enough, however, on its literal level: the meager and selfish parents, having the "normal" children they deserve and not recognizing the only good one, are trapped by their concern for appearances.

In "The Jilting of Granny Weatherall," a *tour de force* of stream-of-consciousness technique, the reader listens to the flowing, disorganized thoughts of the old grandmother in her final illness. As death approaches and the outer world fades from her, she keeps asking God for a sign, but she cannot help remembering the man who had run out on her on her wedding night decades before. Now, before her wedding with death, is she to be jilted again?

Some of Porter's finest stories are the so-called "Miranda" stories, collected under the title *The Old Order* (1955), stories of a young girl named Miranda, whose background and experiences clearly suggest those of Porter's own, growing up in Texas. The stories read almost like a connected autobiographical work. "I shall try to tell the truth," Porter wrote, "but the result will be fiction. I shall not be at all surprised at this result: it is what I mean to do; it is, to my way of thinking, the way fiction is made." In "The Source," the reader sees the grandmother—much like Porter's must have been— like some powerful and indomitable force, leaving her town home to go to the farm. She goes through it like a general on inspection, and everything is turned upside-down, scrubbed, whitewashed, and organized. The moment there is nothing left to do, she turns and leaves for town, where no doubt the servants are waiting in trepidation for the same thing to happen to them, in a more or less endless round.

In another of the Miranda stories, "The Fig Tree," the characters are similarly leaving town for the country. Miranda, a very little girl, is at the stage where "everything in the world was strange to her and something she had to know about." She wants especially to know "where are we going?," but she "could never find out about anything until the last minute." The adults put her off with indirect answers or euphemisms. Underlying her question about where they are going is her curiosity about death. Her mother has died, and various neighbors, farm animals, and insects have died. She knows the signs of death—it is when something does not move—and she knows what you do—the dead person or thing is ceremoniously buried, and a marker is put over the grave. Just as they are leaving for the farm, she finds a dead baby chick, buries it in a shoe box, and puts a marker over it. They shout they are leaving, so she has to run off, but at the last instant, she hears a terrifying sound coming from the grave: "Weep, weep, weep." They whisk her off, not listening to her attempts to explain, and she sobs hysterically. After a while they calm her, but what she has done stays in her mind.

At the farm they meet Great-Aunt Eliza, the grandmother's sister. The grandmother has wrapped up all life's mysteries in immutable ceremony, like the ceremony of burial, but her sister is absolutely unceremonial, dipping snuff and carting around a telescope and a microscope to search into nature's secrets. Miranda is startled to hear again the "Weep, weep, weep," but the great aunt can set her mind at ease, give her a scientific explanation: it is the calling of the tree frogs. In the last line of the story, Miranda is in a "fog of bliss," the scientific explanation freeing her from her guilt; yet "fog" carries the suggestion that when it clears, this explanation too will fall short of explaining life and death to her.

As well as "short" stories, Porter wrote "long" stories, the best of which may be "Holiday." The narrator of the story, fleeing from some unnamed trouble of her own, rents a room for a month in the vast farmhouse of the Müller family, leading members of a German colony in East Texas. She quickly falls into the routine of the house. The Low-German dialect with which they talk to one another is as incomprehensible, and yet as comforting to her as "the crying of frogs or the wind in the trees." Indeed, the large family itself—patriarchal Father Müller, matriarchal Mother Müller, and all the sons and daughters and wives and husbands and yearly children—and the endless round of chores and planting and meals are as mindless and healthy as the animal life surrounding them, and the narrator remarks on "the repose, the almost mystical inertia of their minds in the midst of this muscular life." Once she starts working with them, "I forgot to count the days, they were one like the other." In the midst of this changelessness, the great natural rhythms continue, and in the short month she stays with them, spring burgeons, a child is born, the youngest daughter is married, there is a cataclysmic storm and flood, and Mother Müller dies in the midst of the strenuous work that is all she has known, all any of them have known.

There is one member of the family, Ottilie, who is set apart, mute, dwarfish, misshapen, and palsied, the victim of a horribly crippling childhood disease. She works as hard as the rest, her job being to cook and serve the vast meals. No one talks to her or seems to realize she is present; "she moved among them as invisible to their imaginations as a ghost . . . they forgot her in pure self-defense." One day she takes the narrator into her tiny room and shows her a picture of herself as a child, when she was as beautiful as any of the other children. The narrataor thinks the others could all be parts of a single body, but Ottilie is an individual, the only one with whom, however fleetingly, she manages to have human contact. When the others go off to the funeral of the mother, the narrator is left behind, and so is Ottilie. The narrator hears her howling like a dog. She takes her out in the wagon, thinking she wants to join the funeral procession;, but she does not; once outside she laughs and is delighted with the warm spring day—she is having her holiday. The others weep easily and uncomplicatedly at the death of the mother and then forget her, as the endless round of chores continues; they will forget the very possibility of death until one day they too fall in their traces. Only the narrator with her self-consciousness and fear of death, and Ottilie, whose body is a daily reminder to her of chance and mutation and death, cannot forget. "We were both equally the fools of life, equally fellow fugitives from death." The only ones conscious of death, they are the only ones able fully to appreciate the great privilege of life. "We had escaped for one day more at least. We would celebrate our good luck, we would have a little stolen holiday, a breath of spring air and freedom on this lovely, festive afternoon."

Major publications other than short fiction
NOVELS: *Pale Horse, Pale Rider: Three Short Novels*, 1939; *Ship of Fools*, 1962.

NONFICTION: *The Days Before*, 1952; *The Collected Essays and Occasional Writings*, 1970.

Bibliography
Hartley, Lodwick and George Core, eds. *Katherine Anne Porter: A Critical Symposium.*
Hendrick, George. *Katherine Anne Porter.*

Norman Lavers

J. F. POWERS

Born: Jacksonville, Illinois; July 8, 1917

Principal short fiction
Prince of Darkness and Other Stories, 1947; *The Presence of Grace*, 1956; *Look How the Fish Live*, 1975.

Other literary forms
J. F. Powers is a slow and careful craftsman. His three short-story collections contain all of his major short fiction to date. He has also published sketches, book reviews, brief commentaries (all so far uncollected), and one novel, *Morte d'Urban*, which won the National Book Award for fiction in 1962.

Influence
Anyone familiar with *The Dubliners* (1914) will recognize in the stories of Powers his indebtedness to James Joyce. Not so obvious has been the influence of Sinclair Lewis, from whom Powers has said he learned to write satire. Evelyn Waugh and Katherine Anne Porter are also among Powers' favorite writers and have doubtlessly contributed to that combination of precise observation and ironical detachment so typical of his work. Despite these impressive influences Powers has created his own individual style which won for him in 1944 inclusion in both the O. Henry and Martha Foley Collection (for "Lions, Harts, Leaping Does") and established his reputation as a writer of carefully crafted, serious short stories.

Story characteristics
Powers' typical story deals ironically or satirically with clerical life, usually with the failure of a priest to live up to religious ideals or a devout and conscientious priest caught in the toils of a secular church.

Biography
John Farl Powers was born into a Catholic family in a town in which the "best" people were Protestant, a fact which he said "to some extent made a philosopher out of me." He attended Quincy Academy, taught by Franciscan Fathers, and many of his closest friends there later went into the priesthood. Powers himself was not attracted to clerical life, principally because of the social responsibilities, although he has said the praying would have attracted him. After graduation he worked in Marshall Field and Co., sold insurance, became a chauffeur, and clerked in Brentano's bookshop. Since his establishment as a writer he has taught briefly and reluctantly in various colleges.

In 1946 he married Elizabeth Wahl, who is also a writer, and they have five children.

Analysis

The most frequently reprinted of J. F. Powers' short stories and therefore the best known are not the title stories of his two collections—"Prince of Darkness" and "The Presence of Grace"—but rather "Lions, Harts, Leaping Does," "The Valiant Woman," and "The Forks"—stories that are firmly rooted in social observation and realistic detail but have at their center specifically moral and theological issues. Powers is a Catholic writer, not a writer who happens to be a Catholic nor one who proselytizes for the Church, but, rather (as Evelyn Waugh has said), one whose "art is everywhere infused and directed by his Faith."

For Powers the central issue is how in the midst of a fallen world to live up to the high ideals of the Church. Since that issue is most sharply seen in the lives of those who have chosen the religious life as their vocation, parish priests, curates, friars, nuns, and archbishops dominate Powers' stories. As might be expected of a religious writer who admires, as Powers does, the art of James Joyce and who learned the satiric mode from Sinclair Lewis and Evelyn Waugh, Powers' stories are frequently ironic and often satiric portraits of clerics who fail to measure up to the ideals of their priestly vocation. Many are straightforward satires. "Prince of Darkness," for example, is the fictional portrait of a priest, Father Burner, who in his gluttony, his ambition for material rewards and professional success, and his lack of charity toward sinners in the confessional, reveals himself to be a modern incarnation of the devil himself. In opposition to Father Burner is the Archbishop, an elderly cleric in worn-out slippers who in the proper spirit of moral firmness and Christian compassion reassigns Father Burner not to the pastorate he covets but to another parish assistant's role where, presumably, his power of darkness will be held in check.

"The Devil Was the Joker" from Powers' second collection resembles "Prince of Darkness" in theme and conception, except here the satanic figure is a layman who has been hired by a religious order to sell its publication in Catholic parishes. Mac, the salesman—"Fat and fifty or so, with a candy-pink face, sparse orange hair, and popeyes"—hires a young ex-seminarian to travel about with him as his companion-driver. Myles Flynn, the ex-seminarian, also becomes the drinking companion and confidant of Mac who gradually reveals himself to be totally cynical about the religious wares he is peddling, and who is, moreover, neither religious nor Catholic. Mac exploits the priests he encounters on his travels and attempts to use Myles to further his financial interests. As a way of making a sale, for example, he will frequently "take the pledge," that is, promise to refrain from alcohol. In return, he usually manages to extract from the priest to whom he made the pledge a large order for his wares. One day, after drunkenly confessing to Myles that he is not Catholic, he tries to repair the damage he imagines has been done to his position by trying to get Myles to baptize him, alleging that Myles has been responsible for his sudden conversion. It is through Myles's response that Powers provides the prospective for understanding and judging Mac. Myles perceives that Mac "was the serpent, the nice old serpent with Glen-plaid markings, who wasn't very poisonous." In conclusion, Myles not only refuses to baptize Mac, but also leaves him and attempts once more to get back into the seminary.

"Prince of Darkness" and "The Devil Was the Joker" are both loosely constructed revelations of character rather than stories of conflict and action. Powers' two best-known pieces are also the best things he has done to date, including those in *Look How the Fish Live*. Both are told from the point of view of a priest caught in a moral dilemma. In "The Forks," a young curate, Father Eudex, assistant to a Monsignor in a middle-class parish, is presented with a check from a manufacturing company that has been having labor trouble. Father Eudex, born on a farm, a reader of the *Catholic Worker* and a sympathizer with the strikers, regards the check as hush money and therefore finds it unacceptable. His superior, the Monsignor, who drives a long black car like a politician's and is friendly with bankers and businessmen, suggests that Father Eudex use the check as down payment on a good car. The Monsignor is a man of impeccable manners, concerned with the appearance of things, with laying out a walled garden, with the perfection of his salad, and disturbed by the fact that Father Eudex strips off his shirt and helps the laborer spade up the garden, and that he uses the wrong fork at dinner. Quite clearly the Monsignor represents to Powers a modern version of the secularized church; Father Eudex, the traditional and, in this story, powerless Christian virtues. At the end of the story, Father Eudex, who has considered sending the check back to the company or giving it to the strikers' fund, merely tears it up and flushes it down the toilet, aware that every other priest in town will find some "good" use for it. True goodness in Powers' stories tends to be helpless in the face of such worldliness.

In "The Valiant Woman" the same issue is raised in the conflict between a priest and his housekeeper. The occasion in this story is the priest's fifty-ninth birthday celebration, a dinner from which his one remaining friend and fellow priest is driven by the insistent and boorish presence of the housekeeper. The theological and moral issue is dramatized by the priest's dilemma: according to church law he can rid himself of the housekeeper but he can only do so by violating the spirit of Christian charity. The housekeeper, being totally unconscious of the moral implications of her acts, naturally has the advantage. Like the wily mosquito who bites the priest, her acts are of the flesh only, while his, being conscious and intellectual, are of the will. He cannot bring himself to fire her and so in a helpless rage at being bitten by a mosquito (after having been, in effect, stung by the housekeeper), he wildly swings a rolled up newspaper at the mosquito and knocks over and breaks a bust of St. Joseph.

When summarized, Powers' stories sound forbidding, when, in fact, they are—despite the underlying seriousness—delightfully humorous. About the housekeeper in "The Valiant Woman," for instance, Powers has the priest think:

> [She] was clean. And though she cooked poorly, could not play the organ, would not take up the collection in an emergency and went to card parties, and told all—even so, she was clean. She washed everything. Sometimes her underwear hung down beneath her dress like a paratrooper's pants, but it and everything she touched was clean. She washed constantly. She was clean.

And when Mrs. Stoner, the housekeeper, and the priest, Father Firman, play their nightly game of Honeymoon Bridge, Mrs. Stoner is out to "skunk" him. She handles the cards with the "abandoned virtuosity of an old river-boat gambler, standing them on end, fanning them out, whirling them through her fingers, dancing them halfway up her arms, cracking the whip over them." The priest's dilemma is amusingly symbolized in his bout with the female mosquito and in the housekeeper's cry, "Shame on you Father. She needs the blood for her eggs."

Not all of Powers' stories have been about priests. Four of those in his first collection deal with racial and religious prejudice; three are about blacks ("The Trouble," about a race riot, "He Don't Plant Cotton," in which black entertainers in a Northern nightclub are badgered by a visitor from Mississippi and quit their jobs, and "The Eye," about a lynching of an innocent black), and one about anti-Semitism ("Renner"). Two stories from *The Presence of Grace* are also not explicitly religious: "The Poor Thing" and "Blue Island." Even these apparently secular stories arise out of the same moral concern that may be seen more clearly in the overtly religious ones. In "The Poor Thing" a crippled woman, Dolly, who goes through the motions of being religious, is revealed as a pious hypocrite when she slyly exploits an elderly spinster, forcing her to serve for little pay as her constant companion. The elderly woman had been talked into accepting the position in the first place and then when she tried to leave, was falsely accused by Dolly of having stolen from her. The woman then has the choice of either returning to Dolly or having her reputation at the employment office ruined.

In "Blue Island" the oppressor is a woman who sells pots and pans by arranging "coffees" in other women's houses and then arriving to "demonstrate" her wares. Under the guise of neighborly concern for a young woman who has recently moved into the neighborhood and is unsure of herself (and ashamed of her origins), she persuades the young woman to have a coffee to which all of the important neighbor women are invited; then the saleswoman arrives with her wares and the young woman, the victim, stricken by the deception practiced on her and on the neighbors she has tried to cultivate, rushes to her bedroom and weeps, while downstairs the neighbor women file out, leaving her alone with her oppressor. In both "The Poor Thing" and "Blue Island," Powers also shows that the victims participate in their victimizing, the spinster through her pride and the young woman in "Blue Island" by denying her past and attempting to be something she is not.

Powers' best stories are undoubtedly those that bring the moral and religious issue directly into the main action. The story still most widely admired is the one written when Powers was twenty-five that established his early reputation as a master of the short story: "Lions, Harts, Leaping Does." The popularity of this story may be due not only to the high level of its art, but also because it deals so gently with the issues and creates in Father Didymus and in the simple friar Titus two appealing characters. Indeed, one of Powers' major achievements is his ability in many of his stories to create characters with the vividness and complexity one expects only from the longer novel. For this reason, if for no other, the stories of J. F. Powers will continue to engage the attention of discriminating readers.

Major publications other than short fiction
NOVEL: *Morte d'Urban*, 1962.

Bibliography
Hagopian, John V. *J. F. Powers*.

W. J. Stuckey

REYNOLDS PRICE

Born: Macon, North Carolina; February 1, 1933

Principal short fiction
The Names and Faces of Heroes, 1963; *Permanent Errors*, 1970.

Other literary forms
Reynolds Price is the author of four novels and one volume of literary essays as well as two collections of short stories, O. Henry Award winners among them. He has also published poetry and biblical translations. *A Long and Happy Life* received the award of the William Faulkner Foundation for a notable first novel, 1962; in 1970 Price's fiction received an Award in Literature from the American Academy and the National Institute of Arts and Letters.

Influence
Hailed early in his career as the legitimate heir of the great Southern writers of earlier generations, Price has since established himself as an independent master. His stories and excerpts from novels in progress appear in both little and mass-circulation magazines.

Story characteristics
Price's short-story practice has evolved and changed considerably since 1955, when he published his first story. In *The Names and Faces of Heroes*, he undertakes, often successfuly, to make the old and familiar new and his own. Stories in his second collection, *Permanent Errors*, are darker in tone, more ambitious in aim, more idiosyncratic in style and perspective, more difficult, and more challenging.

Biography
Reynolds Price received a B. A. from Duke University in 1955 and subsequently was a Rhodes Scholar at Oxford, B. Litt., 1958. In 1958 he returned to Duke where he teaches one term each year in the Department of English. He has read and lectured extensively at a number of American colleges and universities.

Analysis
Between Reynolds Price's two volumes of short stories there are several notable differences of subject, structure, style, and theme. As exemplified by "A Chain of Love" and "Uncle Grant," the earlier volume, *The Names and Faces of Heroes*, depicts in an open, rather romantic style a semipastoral

Southern world in which good country people struggle to enact the regional verities of home, family, faith, and historical continuity. There is apparent a striking fusion of observation, of detail and revelatory act, with feeling and significance.

The later volume of stories, with its chilling title, *Permanent Errors*, is less easy to read or to comprehend; the stories tend to be more elliptical and sometimes rather sketchy. Price has come to prefer the oblique slant and the quick glimpse. All the stories in this volume share a controlling effort; Price writes in his preface, "the attempt to isolate in a number of lives the central error of act, will, understanding which, once made, has been permanent, incurable, but whose diagnosis and palliation are the hopes of continuance." Two stories, "The Happiness of Others" and "Walking Lessons," illustrate such incurable errors and slender hopes.

"A Chain of Love" is a tale of the Mustian family, who also figure in two of Price's novels, *A Long and Happy Life* and *A Generous Man* (1966). The scene is a hospital to which all the Mustians accompany the family patriarch, who is being treated but who will not long survive. There is Papa, the grandfather; Mama, his widowed daughter-in-law; and her four children. Other extended-family members and friends, old and recently made, pass in and out, linked by the ties that bind. The chain of the title, however, Rosacoke, the story's protagonist, tries to extend to strangers in need as well, to the Ledwell family across the hall, whose father is dying of cancer. In her hospital vigil, Rosacoke is a credible model of compassion, love, kindness, and selflessness in the face of loneliness, pain, fear, and death surrounding her. She asserts the moral responsibility of making others happy, or at least of alleviating their unhappiness; an act is right because it does this or is undertaken to this end. It is, of course, terribly difficult work, as Rosacoke discovers, because of one's own innocence or ignorance, because one's own motives are invariably mixed, and because others do not understand or resist or cannot respond.

Although it is a tale about death and dying, "A Chain of Love" also displays Price's considerable comic powers, as Papa grimly resists the nurse with the dyed black hair who calls him "darling," as he discusses the bad things about jimson weeds with a visitor, or as Rosacoke thinks what she would like to do to Miss Willie Duke Aycock, who has designs on Rosacoke's errant boyfriend, Wesley Beavers. Price's portrayal of Rosacoke shows a genuine talent for communicating by means of style his heroine's emotional nature. Rosacoke is that rare thing in contemporary literature, a good—not a righteous—person, well understood and neither sentimentalized nor satirized.

"Uncle Grant" opens as Reynolds Price, in Oxford, England, comes upon a postcard picture of the head of the Egyptian pharaoh, Amenhotep IV, and is suddenly and powerfully reminded of Uncle Grant, Grant Terry, born around 1865, and named maybe for a general who had set free his parents.

Uncle Grant had been Price's childhood companion and for years the family's gardener, a man who could make anything grow. He lived until ninety, although in the end he grew more and more helpless. The story is both a fond history and memorial and an act of somewhat uneasy reparation on the narrator's part. Price, inevitably, naturally, had grown up and away from Uncle Grant, who had "for his own reasons loved my father and was loved by him and maybe loved me. . . ." Circling through his memories of his family and of the old man, long a fixture in the family, Price re-creates what he knows of Uncle Grant's life, speculates on what he does not, and ends up recalling his last brief visit with the old man in a rest home, when Uncle Grant had told him he would see Price in heaven—his last joke, if it was a joke: "whoever it was on," Price writes, "it was not on him."

In "The Happiness of Others," the first story in *Permanent Errors*, the scene is again Oxford, where the reader witnesses the end of a love affair. A young man, a writer, Charles Tamplin, is spending a last day with a young woman, Sara, before she takes a boat from Southampton and out of his life. They are killing time and each other. Charles Tamplin is always given his full name; he is never Charles, never Tamplin. Thus a certain measure of formality, dignity, and distance is provided him. This is in fact the kind of man he is, something of an aesthete and a prig who tends to view his experience from a self-protective, often literary attitude. He is quick, incisive, and articulate, as is Sara. The tone of the story reflects their mental state—one of heartsick anxiety, frayed nerves, and strained tempers about to snap.

Sara, by her own choice or through Tamplin's default, has become the aggressor, with Tamplin usually drawing back or in flight. Sara doubtless, and justifiably, feels that she has been badly used. Both the characters, however, possess a residual awareness of what they have had together, which intensifies their pain and the story's effect. They are united now principally in their recognition of their relation's falseness. They sit eating lunch together, "chewing each bite as long and mercilessly as though their stomachs held ravenous babies, openmouthed to suck in the streams of tepid pap." Here is an image, that of hungrily feeding babies, which becomes a refrain; it will reiterate the unfruitful quality of their relation. The child—never to be theirs—has become almost an incubus. Tamplin and Sara are eating, but they are simultaneously being eaten.

As they walk out of the inn into the sun, Tamplin notes that it gilds Sara—"it made Sara's body seem gold, warm and workable. Even the black hair transmuting quickly, through bronze to gold. They stood a moment—Charles Tamplin seeing that, she knowing he saw it, both knowing its deceit." The sun "gilds" Sara, transforms her, for a moment at least, and in the eyes of Charles Tamplin, into a precious work of art; and he is a man who sees life in terms of art, thereby often devitalizing life. Sara in the sun seems "gold, warm and workable," a distinctly sensuous figure. They "know" too much, however, know each other and their failures together too well for either to be able to respond. Walking desultorily through the town, they continue their civil war; in the church they end up trading epitaphs on the tombs, each thereby formulating his or her own view of the world and each other. Sara's memorial verses speak of relatedness; Tamplin's display his essential solitariness, a life lived almost vicariously.

Before this bleak story of parting lovers ends, Tamplin reflects on what is left, what the day now means. The prospects are ambiguous at best. One is that he will achieve a kind of altruistic abnegation, will become one of art's selfless saints. The other is that he has converted the artist's undeniable need for self-sufficiency and detachment into a cover for vanity, timidity, selfishness, and other modes of assault and withdrawal. Love and freedom appear to be irreconcilable.

Throughout *Permanent Errors*, understanding between characters is marginal and tenuous, even between those once as close as Charles Tamplin and Sara. Yet to communicate at all, Price seems to imply, we must surrender some of our own mind to participate in the ideas and attitudes of the mind we think we are addressing. Out of the attempt the most that is likely to eventuate, as it perhaps does for Charles Tamplin, is that one may at least define for oneself what one cannot impart. Such definition, in art, seems his only reward.

The last and longest story, "Walking Lessons," has the force of thematic summary. Its protagonist is a young man whose wife has recently committed suicide. To outdistance his grief, he goes to visit a friend, a lapsed medical student, Blix Cunningham, now a VISTA worker among the Navajo, who has taken up with Dora Badonie, a young Navajo woman suffering through the early stages of multiple sclerosis. Understanding among the three is marginal and discontinuous; their futures bleak; the Arizona setting beautiful, awesome, ultimately desolate and terrible. The Indians are, by the VISTA man's testimony, "weirder than snakes," and survive, barely and miserably, on Coke, Roma Tokay, Skoal Wintergreen-Flavored Chewing Tobacco, and other unknown resources. To the Indians the writer-protagonist is simply another affliction, husband of a suicide whose ghost, according to their belief, will follow him by night, He is a witch, dangerous; to Cunningham, he is an unfeeling monster, fatal.

The crisis and climax of the story evolve from the attempt of Blix, the narrator, Dora, and a few drunken hangers-on to recover Dora's grandmother's pickup truck, stuck in the mud somewhere far up the Zuni road. After failing and losing their own truck, the original three walk out, while the narrator has cause to wonder whether he will be able to make it, be deserted, or simply be killed. The long march across country through an alien and hostile environment is important not as it represents a struggle of man with nature but as it affects mental processes and psychological displacement.

Through the first hour of walking the cloud cover holds and the cold is bearable, even exhilarating, and keeps the snow frozen. The narrator begins to think he has won freedom and competence. Another hour brings more penetrating cold and a new rhythm, and the narrator realizes he may well die. Such awareness brings closer to acceptancce ties that have not previously bound the narrator to his dead wife; to Dora, knowing of her approaching death, although she ascribes her illness to touching a snake; and to Blix and Dora and their doomed union, recalling and chastising his own marriage. The end is not yet, however; during a break Cunningham asks what he must do, not about getting out, but about Dora and the rest of his life; the narrator can only say that he had made *his* way out because he wanted to.

The saving truth at last offers itself, but not as a means of escape: the narrator wanted his wife dead, but he cannot, as he is invited to do by his would-be victim, kill Dora. Finally, he asks forgiveness of his dead wife's surrogate, and—as someone begins to shoot at them from a house nearby— he steps in front of Blix. He is happy, "if being past fear and with all debts paid is a brand of happiness." There remains only the last confession: "She is dead and dumb. Hammer-dead. Her name was Beth."

The end, when it comes, is as radical as conversion and nearly as mystical: a new man emerges from the wilderness and departs for the motel. Such communication as has occurred is a triumph—framed, drawn out, diminished, and almost cut off by miles and miles of mud, snow, freezing cold, moonlight, and cliffs.

The stories in *The Names and Faces of Heroes*, Price's first collection of short fiction, are more open, more varied, more conventional, and more optimistic in tone than those of his second, *Permanent Errors*, which are, in several ways, a set of variations. One can read the earlier volume in almost any order and derive essentially the same impression—that life's rewards, whether from love or work, are present, do offer themselves, and may be grasped. A long and happy life, the title of Price's first novel, is not simply an ironic phrase. In *Permanent Errors*, the range of human options is much reduced; chaos and moral disorder insistently threaten. The characters are poised at the point where they imagine they can be understood by others— friends, lovers, family—and subsequently discover, their innocence or their egotism smashed, that they are forever opaque and incomprehensible to the world.

Major publications other than short fiction

NOVELS: *A Long and Happy Life*, 1962; *A Generous Man*, 1966; *Love and Work*, 1968; *The Surface of the Earth*, 1975.

POETRY: *Late Warnings*, 1968.

NONFICTION: *Things Themselves: Essays and Scenes*, 1972.

Bibliography
Carr, John, ed. *Kite-Flying and Other Irrational Acts: Conversations with Twelve Southern Writers.*
Hoffman, Frederick J. *The Art of Southern Fiction.*

Allen Shepherd

V. S. PRITCHETT

Born: Ipswich, Suffolk, England; December 16, 1900

Principal short fiction

The Spanish Virgin and Other Stories, 1930; *You Make Your Own Life, Short Stories*, 1938; *It May Never Happen and Other Stories*, 1945; *The Sailor, Sense of Humour, and Other Stories*, 1956; *Collected Stories*, 1956; *When My Girl Comes Home*, 1961; *Blind Love and Other Stories*, 1969; *The Camberwell Beauty and Other Stories*, 1974; *Selected Stories*, 1978; *On the Edge of the Cliff*, 1979.

Other literary forms

V. S. Pritchett's published works include a half-dozen novels, two biographies, two volumes of memoirs, five books of literary criticism, and six travel books, in addition to his ten collections of short fiction.

Influence

Pritchett is considered to be among the best English writers living today. His career spans five decades, from the late 1920's to the present. Although his more than thirty published volumes include nearly all prose forms, from fiction to essay to travel to biography to autobiography, his most influential and memorable work lies in his short fiction, of which he has published ten volumes.

Story characteristics

Although his career as a short-story writer spans five decades, during a time when the form underwent strange mutations at the hands of numerous experimenters, Pritchett seemed to have found a congenial style and manner at the beginning and varied from it very little throughout his career. His stories are marked by vivid characterization, polished style, and a lively wit that can range from gentle to caustic. Still, the reader senses that Pritchett feels affection for his characters, even as he exposes their most ridiculous foibles.

Biography

Victor Sawdon Pritchett's many travel books attest that he has often ranged beyond his native England. He has spent much time in the United States, where he has served as visiting professor or writer in residence at a number of colleges and universities. Pritchett is a foreign Honorary Member of the American Academy of Arts and Letters and the American Academy of Arts and Sciences. Knighted in 1975, Pritchett currently lives in London.

Analysis

Even if V. S. Pritchett had not stated in his Preface to *The Sailor, Sense of Humour, and Other Stories* that the short story "is the only kind of writing that has given me great pleasure," we could sense it in the sheer quantity of stories he has produced, from his first collection in 1930 to his most recent in 1979. More remarkable than the number of his stories is their unflagging quality. Rarely is a Pritchett story anything less than a delight. His work from beginning to end strikes us as so polished, so professional that we might falsely conclude that writing for Pritchett was an effortless task, that he could blithely dash off a couple of stories between lunchtime and tea. On the contrary, his memoirs and essays indicate that Pritchett sees writing as a serious craft requiring hard work, and each story is the product of careful consideration and frequent revision.

Despite the quantity and consistent high quality of his work, Pritchett is less well known, especially to Americans, than many of his contemporaries. This is perhaps due to the fact that, rather than explore new avenues of expression or deliberately strain the conventions of the short-story form, as many of his fellow writers chose to do, Pritchett early in his career found a type of story and a manner of presentation that suited him, and he varied from it rarely.

Pritchett's stories are conventional in that he does not radically manipulate or ignore the conventions of characterization, plot, setting, and syntax. Although he is not a pioneer in the genre, neither are his stories likely to become dated, as might stories employing outworn "innovations." The best of his stories are timeless in that they always focus on the one thing endlessly fascinating to readers: human beings. If his characters are often eccentric, even "fantastic," this means that they simply are "the more certain to be true," in the author's own words. Pritchett emphasizes characterization in his short stories rather than plot, but this does not mean that no interesting action is involved. Rather, action serves to elucidate character. In Pritchett's stories the reader's great fun comes from two perceptions at once: that the characters are sometimes weak, sometimes silly, sometimes ridiculous; but that it is just these foibles that make them so human, so much like ourselves.

Pritchett's best-known stories are the title stories to his collections. From early to late in his career, these stories exhibit the qualities that have endeared Pritchett to followers of short fiction: polish, careful craftmanship, vivid characterization, and a brand of wit which seems as playful as the swipes of a kitten's paw but which, like the kitten's paw, sometimes draws blood. "You Make Your Own Life," from an early collection of the same title, is a curious example: "curious" because the central events—betrayed passion, attempted suicide, permanent disfigurement—are the stuff of tragedy, or at least melodrama.

This is a familiar pattern in Pritchett's fiction. Most of his stories are comic, but most have a core of action that *could* have been serious, even tragic. The catalyst for the transformation from tragedy to comedy lies in the manner, not the matter, of the story's telling. The author of a comic piece often strives for a certain distancing effect between his reader and the events of the story, particularly if the events are painful. Pritchett achieves this distancing in one or a combination of three ways: *always* through the use of clever word choice, humorous descriptions, witty images; less often through the use of an omniscient author who is detached from the action; and frequently through the use of a first-person narrator who is once removed, emotionally, from the action.

The latter is the prime element in "You Make Your Own Life." Even though the narrator is no more than the auditor of the narrative, as in all Pritchett's stories his personality has a major, if subtle, impact on our reaction to events described. Smug, bored, and supercilious, the narrator sits irritably in a barber shop, in what he considers to be a dull little English town where nothing ever happens, and waits his turn at the chair. As in much comedy, a good deal of humor arises through incidentals, details that contribute little or nothing to the formal complication of the action. For example, a newspaper account tells of a man who identifies the body of his wife at an inquest of a drowning, only to meet her on the street three days later; and the indignation of the narrator grows when a dandy "has everything" in the chair for which the narrator waits.

When the narrator finally ascends the barber's chair, the heart of the action begins in the form of the barber's account of the life and woes of Albert, the dandy in the chair prior to the narrator. Albert, it happens, is a consumptive, a condition brought about by courting a young lady in the fog and damp. Worse, his dandyish appearance is a sad attempt to cover up the hideous scar across his throat, the emblem of a suicide attempt after the young lady rejected him. The woman, ironically, is now the barber's wife; indeed, the barber courted her during the time when the tragic events unfolded. The events are made ironic, and finally comic, by the barber's tone: flat, disinterested, objective, as if he were discussing the weather or any other bit of gossip habitual to a barber shop. When this flat tone and random order of events are combined with the narrator's initial boredom, then slight interest, then astonishment as the tale gets more violent and sordid, the resulting story resembles nothing so much as a vaudeville routine with the narrator as straight man.

The narrator of "You Make Your Own Life" has been an unwilling agent in the humor of the story; but often in Pritchett's works the narrator becomes both agent and principal in the story's ironies, as is the case with "It May Never Happen" (1945). The narrator of the story is a young man who goes to work for his pushy, pompous, lecturing, but essentially good-natured Uncle Belton. Uncle Belton forewarns the young man about his partner, Mr. Phillamore, who is a "true gentleman." (Uncle Belton, an uncle by marriage, is himself "none too certain about aitches and double negatives.") When he finally meets the formidable Mr. Phillamore, the narrator finds a shy, bumbling, painfully inoffensive little man only lately "freed" from his mother's apron strings. Humorous little incidents occur over the years as the narrator observes his uncle, Mr. Phillamore, and the secretary, Miss Croft, as they wage war with competitors in the precarious upholstery business. The climax comes when shy Mr. Phillamore corners Miss Croft, for whom both he and the narrator have had long-smoldering passions, and kisses her while professing his love. She screams. Mr. Phillamore resigns and joins a competitor.

The characters in "It May Never Happen" are perhaps a little too "pat," a little too recognizably Dickensian for us initially, yet the ending is all Pritchett's. Long after the fiasco in the office, the narrator passes Mr. Phillamore in the street, and Mr. Phillamore stares back as if the narrator were "the most ridiculous thing on earth." This puts the story in its ironic perspective. The narrator has devoted *years* of his young manhood, after all, in apathetic service to a pompous uncle and a business with obviously no future. The one infatuation of his youth has been devoted to an uninspiring secretary for whom he will not risk even one humiliating scene, as, at least, the retiring Mr. Phillamore has done. At least Mr. Phillamore has broken away, while the narrator remains, ridiculous, without a past that can so much as recall a blush.

After an examination of only two stories—stories not at all alike in characterization, action, or tone—we can already see a pattern developing that will mark a large proportion of Pritchett's stories over the years. We can expect them to have varying degrees of humor, of course; humor is a "given" with Pritchett. We can expect them to concern male-female relationships— love, or at least lust—and we can expect these relationships, generally, to end badly for one or more of the characters involved. We can expect, even amidst our laughter, to be slightly disturbed by a character—the destructively passive young man who wastes his years, the pitiful Albert who regularly bares his neck to the barber married to his former love—who is, finally, more tragic than comic.

A decade after "It May Never Happen," in 1956, we find the pattern still holding true with "Sense of Humor," from *The Sailor, Sense of Humour, and Other Stories*. Much as in "You Make Your Own Life," the narrator is a very cynical young man, a traveling salesman, in a small English town, looking for a way to pass the time. The most attractive way seems to be Muriel, the clerk in the local hotel, who wants rather desperately to escape small-town life. As the story progresses, Humphrey, the salesman, professes to feeling great affection for Muriel, although we suspect him to be incapable of very deep emotion of any sort; and Muriel responds. The romance blossoms under the nose of Colin, a mechanic, who was Muriel's chief romantic interest until Humphrey's appearance. Colin is a rather slow, doltish young man, and worse, from Muriel's point of view, he has no sense of humor. Still, she cannot help feeling some affection for him even as he harasses her and Humphrey on their rides into the countryside.

The story is mostly sardonic up to this point. None of the characters is particularly admirable, certainly not the miserly, egotistical narrator. In typical Pritchett fashion, the story becomes more interesting and more comic at the same time that it verges on the tragic. Following Humphrey and Muriel on the way to Humphrey's parents, Colin runs his motorcycle under a bus and dies. Muriel grieves heroically, but that night surrenders herself to Humphrey for the first time, moaning Colin's name under Humphrey's caresses. As it happens, Humphrey's father is a mortician, and he prepares Colin's body, which Humphrey is to drive in the hearse back to Colin's mother for burial. Muriel insists on riding in the hearse, partly because it is her duty, but primarily because she had never ridden in a hearse before. Her first ride is marvelous. People stop and lift their hats. "It's like being the king and queen," she laughs.

The last section of the story, tracing the hearse's progress, is superficially bright, cheery as a sunny English day, but the casket carrying poor ruined Colin gives us pause. Neither Muriel nor Humphrey is worth his life; despite her recent hyperbolic grief she has not a tear for Colin; and Humphrey's chief worry is that the previous night's passion may force them to get married sooner than he had hoped, cutting into his savings. The sardonicism underlying the first section of the story flares again. At the last line of the story—Muriel's comment on a passerby who refuses to raise his hat—our laughter is bitter as alum: "People ought to respect the dead," she says.

Not all of Pritchett's stories are so sardonic. Especially later in his career we see conflicts involving true passions, characters with whom we suffer and empathize. Even then, however, the characters are generally doomed to failure; either they misunderstand their own passions or they misinterpret the effect of those passions on their object. In none of the stories, whether largely serious in intent or farcical, is a cutting wit far beneath the surface; and in none of them do we fail to encounter at least one of Pritchett's dazzlingly eccentric characters. They inhabit his stories as they inhabit the world. Finally, Pritchett's stories are of and for the world. Even while they are decidedly English and decidedly middle-class, their polish, wit, and comic exposure of the common foibles of humanity allow them to transcend time and place.

Major publications other than short fiction

NOVELS: *Claire Drummer*, 1929; *Shirley Sans*, 1932; *Nothing Like Leather*, 1935; *Dead Man Leading*, 1937; *Mr. Beluncle*, 1951; *The Key to My Heart*, 1963.

NONFICTION: *Marching Spain*, 1928; *In My Good Books*, 1942; *The Living Novel and Later Appreciations*, 1946 (revised edition 1964); *Books in General*,

19ᴐ3; *The Spanish Temper*, 1954; *London Perceived*, 1964; *The Offensive Travelier*, 1964; *New York Proclaimed*, 1965; *Dublin: A Portrait*, 1967; *A Cab at the Door*, 1968; *George Meredith and English Comedy*, 1970; *Midnight Oil*, 1971; *Balzac*, 1973; *The Gentle Barbarian: The Life and Work of Turgenev*, 1977; *The Myth Makers: Literary Essays*, 1979.

Bibliography
Beachcroft, T. O. *The Modest Art: A Survey of the Short Story in English.*
Hughes, Douglas A. "V. S. Pritchett: An Interview," in *Studies in Short Fiction.* XIII (Fall, 1976), pp. 423-432.

Dennis Vannatta

JAMES PURDY

Born: Ohio; July 17, 1923

Principle short fiction

Color of Darkness, 1957 (privately printed in 1956 as *63: Dream Palace* and *Don't Call Me by My Right Name and Other Stories*); *Children Is All*, 1962.

Other literary forms

In addition to two major collections of short stories, James Purdy's published works include novels, plays, and poetry. Since the publication of his first novel, *Malcolm*, in 1959, Purdy has emerged as a novelist of diverse talents and established a significant reputation despite rather mixed critical reviews. Additional novels include *The Nephew* (1960), *Cabot Wright Begins* (1964), *Eustace Chisholm and the Works* (1967), *I Am Elijah Thrush* (1972), *In a Shallow Grave* (1976), and *Narrow Rooms* (1978). The first two volumes of a projected trilogy, *Sleepers in Moon-Crowned Valleys*, have also appeared: *Jeremy's Version*, (1970) and *The House of the Solitary Maggot* (1974). Purdy is also the author of several volumes of poetry and plays.

Influence

A succinct evaluation of Purdy's influence on American letters during the past three decades requires not only an exploration of his writings but also a consideration of the critical response to his work. There is, perhaps, no other American writer whose works so consistently encompass two major themes of contemporary fiction: the absurdity of life in the modern world and the disabling aberrations of the spirit created by such a world. Although Purdy's veritable hall of mirrors of contemporary life has met mixed reviews, he is generally acclaimed both in America and abroad as a powerful and original spokesman for his time. Dramatizations of his one-act play, *Children Is All* (1962), and several of his stories have been produced Off Broadway; his works have been translated into more than fifteen languages.

Story characteristics

Although Purdy is often linked with the so-called Southern Gothic school of writers that includes Eudora Welty, Truman Capote, Flannery O'Connor, and Carson McCullers, his works do not fit squarely within the demography of Southern Gothic. He bears an equal affinity, at times, with the naturalists, and his style is often that of a realist. In decrying the immoral atmosphere of modern America, Purdy establishes a landscape where images of human alienation, indifference, and cruelty form a tableau for living in a meaningless world.

Biography

Born in, as he claims, an unknown place in Ohio in 1923, James Purdy attended the University of Chicago and the University of Pueblo in Mexico, served as an interpreter in Latin America, France, and Spain, and taught for three years at Lawrence College in Wisconsin. After beginning a full-time writing career in 1953, his initial attempts to publish in America were thwarted by repeated rejections of his manuscripts by what he refers to as the "New York literary establishment." The private publication of his first collection of short fiction in 1956 and the subsequent support of Dame Edith Sitwell marked his introduction to the literary scene. Purdy was awarded a National Institute of Arts and Letters grant in 1958 and a Ford Foundation grant in 1961, and he was a Guggenheim Fellow in 1958 and 1962. He has continued to produce novels and collections of poetry and short fiction during regular two- to three-year intervals since his first collection of short fiction was printed by an American publisher.

Analysis

James Purdy's exegesis of the spiritual wasteland of contemporary America through his short fiction encapsulates the moral dilemma of modern man, acting out his dramas in a world where archetypal patterns are fragmented, where human values are defaced, and where language has lost its oracular power. In order to verify his own deeply felt sense of the ills in society, Purdy establishes a kind of counterpoint of the banal and the grotesque in his fiction. Characters in his stories often act in a compulsive manner, not weighing their actions but holding to patterns of inconceivable violence. Much of Purdy's short fiction evolves at the point of coalition between the grotesque and the normal; new facets of a character or new dimensions of a world suddenly confront the reader, and a cruel sense of the reality of life is established.

When Purdy's first collection of short fiction, *Color of Darkness* (initially printed privately as *63: Dream Palace* and *Don't Call Me by My Right Name, and Other Stories*) appeared in the United States in 1957, he was acclaimed as a strange and unusual writer in search of a mode of expression for modern despair. In subsequent novels such as *Malcolm* and in the first two novels of his projected trilogy, *Sleepers in Moon-Crowned Valleys*, as well as in his second major collection of short fiction, *Children Is All*, Purdy's penchant for illuminating the aberrations of life in America's towns and people marks him as *engagé* in existentialist terms. As he reflects the texture of contemporary experience, Purdy explores through the microcosm of short fiction the "soul-scape" of the American psyche and finds it wanting, salvageable only by that redeeming factor which is the wistfulness of hope expressed through lyrical language. Stating his premise that "this is an age of exhibitionists, not souls," Purdy examines the absurdity of a world indifferent to the human spirit and the aberrations of the spirit which mirror that world. Through the metaphysical and symbolist techniques of language, he reflects not only the crisis of man in an alien world but man's linguistic crisis in expressing his alienation.

In many of his short stories, Purdy places his characters on that "darkling plain" between faith and doubt which he signifies as the territory of the American spirit. Within the gravitational pull of this plain, life is absurd at best and terrifying at worst. The title story, "Color of Darkness," in his first major short-story collection indicated Purdy's concern for the world of the spirit as he discourses upon its possibilities and failures within the construct of actions versus words.

"Color of Darkness" evolves around the relationship of a father, his young son, Baxter, and a housekeeper, Mrs. Zilke. The circumstances of the father's domestic and business life are sketchy. Baxter's mother is identified as having "run off"; the only tangible evidence of her existence is Baxter, the father's wedding ring, and the father's memory of her "warm, comforting voice." For the father, only his work "had any real meaning, but its meaning to everything else was tenuous." Essentially, the story is about a man who, as he says, does "not know people," a man who has substituted being "out in the world" for the passions of human involvement. Totally absorbed by his addiction to his "success," the father deals with his son and the housekeeper in platitudes. His only relationship to the reality of his domestic existence is the nagging feeling of guilt experienced when he cannot remember the color of his wife's eyes, "a thing which *should* have been terrifying but which was not."

Serving as a surrogate parent to both the father and Baxter is the house-keeper, Mrs. Zilke, who responds in kind to the father's speech which is laden with truisms. She excuses his lack of knowledge of people because he is "out in the world," and he, in turn, views Mrs. Zilke as being fully in control of her world which was "round, firm, and perfectly illuminated." Although the father feels that his parental obligation is assured by Mrs. Zilke's presence and by his own sense of gratitude to her, he is troubled by his son's attachment to a toy crocodile as a sleeping companion and readily agrees to Mrs. Zilke's suggestion that the purchase of a dog will alleviate his son's loneliness. Prodded by his son to recall the color of the dog of his own childhood, the father focuses on nothing but colorless memories, and the boy supplies the response, "a gray dog."

The final symbolic gesture of the father's break with his human past comes with the removal of his wedding ring which he wore because "he wanted men to think he was married, he supposed." Later, Baxter puts the ring in his mouth and refuses to relinquish his "golden toy" despite the entreaties of his father and Mrs. Zilke. The climax of the story occurs when Baxter, forced by his father to expel the ring, violently kicks his father in the groin, an act both physical and symbolic, and counters his father's platitudes with direct and obscene language. Writhing with "exquisite pain," the father assumes the animalistic pose so often associated with the child; yet, in his refusal for help, he verifies his spiritual withdrawal from his son's anguish. The "Color of Darkness" is then the color of indifference.

From the spiritual torpor of the protective guise of platitudes which allow no human understanding in "Color of Darkness," Purdy explores the latent terror inherent in the archetypal figure of mother as queen of hell, castrator, and avenging fury in another of the early stories, "Why Can't They Tell You Why?" The victim in this story, as in much of Purdy's fiction—particularly in his novel *Malcolm*—is the fatherless child. Malcolm finds himself thrust from a dimly remembered Eden of grand hotels and fatherly companionship into a world of sexual infidelities and barren marital relationships where he becomes an initiate in the death throes of sexual and alcoholic excesses. The fatherless child Paul in "Why Can't They Tell You Why?" finds his own selfhood through the discovery of some old photographs of his dead father "in his different ages and stations of life." Through his eavesdropping on conversations between his mother Ethel and her friend Edith "who studied psychology at an adult center downtown" and "often advised Ethel about Paul," Paul establishes an identity inseparable from his father of the photographs. He remains out of school, ostensibly with emotional problems which merit Ethel's lengthy telephone consultations with her friend Edith.

The story achieves terrifying dimensions when Ethel finds Paul sleeping with the photographs and interrogates him about why he keeps the mementos of a father he has never known. Determined to separate the son from the tangible ghost of his father, who, through the photographs, has become for Paul a kind of generative source for his own being, Ethel forces Paul along with his pictures into the basement near the furnace. At this point in the story, she assumes the awesome aspect of an avenging fury, burning the photographs as she threatens Paul with confinement in a mental asylum. Paul, reduced to an animalistic state, clings to his only vestiges of selfhood—the photographs. The last image of Paul as a crazed and dying animal which had "spewed out the heart of his grief" is Ethel's, translated through the bile of the mother's own revulsion toward her son.

In Purdy's fictional world familiar and homely images of the American scene suddenly erupt to reveal the perverseness of spirit fostered in a technological, impersonal civilization. Accusations, desertions, and deformities of spirit mirror the frustrations of characters who, deprived of moral absolutes, insulate themselves against their own common bond of humanity. In two of Purdy's early stories, "Man and Wife" and "You Reach for Your Hat," estrangement within the bonds of marriage becomes a metaphor for the human condition. In "Man and Wife," Peaches Maud, the blowsy, middle-aged wife of Lafe Krause, a man who has lost his job because of his predilection toward other men, desires at all costs to maintain the front of being "human." Despite the painfully revealing accusations of Lafe when he says to Peaches, "You never let me show you nothing but the outside," Peaches refuses any conversation—which she calls "mental talk"—about his or her emotional states. Lafe further reveals his sense of shame and worthlessness in seeking a response from Peaches to a potentially damning question: "Have you been satisfied with me?" Twice removed from the agony that Lafe is experiencing—first by her refusal to discuss his psychological problems and then by her preoccupation with the erratic motor of the refrigerator (a machine which also fails)— Peaches annihilates Lafe with the castrating revelation that his mother had told her about his dubious sexual preferences prior to their marriage.

The spiritual desertion inherent in "Man and Wife" assumes dramatic proportions in "You Reach for Your Hat," a story about a young widow, Jennie Esmond, whose husband died in World War I. Jennie's friend, Mamie Jordan, finds it distressful that Jennie's behavior does not parallel her own romanticized view—reinforced by Hollywood films—of young love, tragic death, and beautiful, eternal grief. In an attempt to examine what she believes to be Jennie's curious state of disinterestedness in her widowhood, Mamie joins Jennie in a drinking bout; the revelations which ensue during their conversation become a kind of elementary exploration of the female psyche.

The reality of Jennie's loveless marriage and her observations about the sordid and self-serving facets of their relationship fragment Mamie's own perceptions of love, for "she had come for such a different story." Jennie reveals her own inadequacy to cope with the realities of marriage, because her mother had convinced her that her beauty would serve as a transport to "better things" than household drudgery and "this lonely period." When Mamie comes to terms with the reality of Jennie's life, "something gray and awful entered the world for her." She pleads with Jennie, "Leave me my little mental comforts." Jennie, compassionate at last, realizes that Mamie's dream of romantic love has perished and that the tangible and momentary comforts she could offer are as removed from the reality of grief as the plastic endings of Hollywood films.

Shaped by the same celluloid forces which have dictated the aesthetics of Mamie's idealized romantic code, Maud, the main character in "A Good Woman," evades the dismal dimensions of life in a small town by escaping daily to a movie and soda fountain world with a friend. Maud's friend, formerly of St. Louis, acts as a catalyst in fostering Maud's growing dissatisfaction with her life. Unable to respond to her friend's questions regarding her happiness, her marriage, or metaphysical questions about the meaning of life in general, Maud faces a bleak future by fantasizing about her past, a time of "real romance" when Obie, her husband, was a traveling jazz musician instead of a traveling salesman. Maud's bizarre encounter with the lecherous old druggist who extracts a few kisses in exchange for her overdue soda bill marks the turning point of the story. Momentarily restored to a carefree state by the sexual advances and flattery of the druggist, Maud retreats to memories of an idealized girlish state of camaraderie with her mother, a state far removed from the brutal reality of the tawdry present.

The inability to bridge those emotional constructs that separate human beings and estrange them from their own intrinsic humanity remains a major motif in Purdy's later stories. "Mrs. Benson" evokes a sense of the same chilling unconcern for another human being as does Edith Wharton's frequently anthologized "Roman Fever." Centered around the annual reunion of a mother and daughter in Paris, the story defines a pattern of lovelessness and materialism which has shaped Rose Benson's relationships, a pattern obviously to be repeated by the daughter, who views these reunions as "such a pleasure."

Purdy's only resolution of bizarre and tortured states of being within the construct of a society insensitive to human pain and grief and hope lies in his oracular use of language. Although his parables of contemporary American life stand in stark relief against a backdrop of spiritual bankruptcy, his lyrical prose forces a kind of linguistic crisis upon the reader as new and unaccustomed juxtapositions of the ordinary and the grotesque reveal a world urgent in its appeal for reform and regeneration.

In a powerful elegy to death in life and life in death, "Eventide," Purdy explores the archetypal relationships of mother to son and change to death to suggest such a regeneration. Two black sisters, Mahala and Pluny, share the loss of sons but remain locked away from each other's pain by the introversion of grief. Pluny's son George died as a child; Mahala's son Teeboy has defected by straightening his hair and forming a liaison with a white woman. Sent by Mahala to the white district to talk to Teeboy, Pluny returns with the deadly knowledge that Teeboy will no longer be a part of Mahala's world. That knowledge evokes for Pluny a vision of her infant son, dead for seventeen years, yet secure in an eternalized state of infancy. In the sharing of Pluny's vision, Mahala moves into a space inhabited by the perfection of memory associated with the dead where "the night was so black and secure." Moving like a tone poem across the sensibilities of the reader, "Eventide" asserts the poetical power of Purdy to temper human despair through the alchemy of language.

Because of Purdy's insistence that the moral fiber of American life has degenerated in proportion to the immoral influence of American affluence, his subject matter of loveless lives and corrupted sensibilities could be a depressing fare for the reader if it were not for the dark humor which illuminates his prose like foxfire. This kind of black humor becomes a defense mechanism against the imbecility of a menace-laden world and negates the violence done by humans to humans.

Purdy's world, then, becomes a world of time measured in soda fountain afternoons, a world of dreams shaped by the celluloid and tinsel of Hollywood, a world of narcissistic parents and victimized children, a world in which the polarization of faith and doubt leaves humanity exiled and unable to know refuge. The documentation of loss through the lyrical voice of despair becomes for Purdy a moral undertaking of grave importance to American letters.

Major publications other than short fiction
NOVELS: *Malcolm*, 1959; *The Nephew*, 1960; *Cabot Wright Begins*, 1964; *Eustace Chisholm and the Works*, 1967; *Jeremy's Version*, 1970 (first novel in a projected trilogy, *Sleepers in Moon-Crowned Valleys*); *I Am Elijah Thrush*, 1972; *House of the Solitary Maggot*, 1974 (second novel of the trilogy); *In a Shallow Grave*, 1976; *Narrow Rooms*, 1978.

PLAYS: *Mr. Cough Syrup and the Phantom Sex*, 1960; *Children Is All*, 1962 (two plays and stories); *The Wedding Finger*, 1974; *A Day After the Fair*, 1977 (plays and stories); *Two Plays*, 1979.

POETRY: *An Oyster Is a Wealthy Beast*, 1967; *Mr. Evening: A Story and Nine Poems*, 1968; *On the Rebound: A Story and Nine Poems*, 1970; *The Running Sun*, 1971; *Sunshine Is an Only Child Poems*, 1973.

Bibliography
Adams, Stephen D. *James Purdy*.
Chupack, Henry. *James Purdy*.
Schwarzchild, Bettina. *The Not-Right House: Essays on James Purdy*.
Sitwell, Edith. Introduction to *Color of Darkness*.

Peggy C. Gardner

THOMAS PYNCHON

Born: Glen Cove, New York; May 8, 1937

Principal short fiction

"The Small Rain," 1959; "Mortality and Mercy in Vienna," 1959; "Low-Lands," 1960; "Entropy," 1960; "Under the Rose," 1961; "The Secret Integration," 1964.

Other literary forms

In addition to his short stories, Thomas Pynchon has published one piece of reportage—"A Journey into the Mind of Watts," in *The New York Times Magazine*, June 12, 1966—however, he is best known as a novelist. His first novel, *V.* (1963), won the William Faulkner Foundation Award for best first novel; *The Crying of Lot 49* (1966) won the Rosenthal Foundation Award of the National Institute of Arts and Letters. Pynchon's masterwork and last published novel to date is *Gravity's Rainbow* (1973), which won the National Book Award (shared with I. B. Singer) and which was unanimously chosen by the literature committee for the Pulitzer Prize. The committee was over-ruled by the Pulitzer advisory board, however, which found the novel to be obscene and obscure.

Influence

Pynchon is one of the most important—and controversial—American writers of the last twenty years. His bizarre plots and characters, his audacious sense of humor, his sometimes shocking depictions of violence and sexuality, and his apocalyptic themes have won both admiration and hostility from readers and critics; he is one of those authors to whom there is rarely a moderate response. Pynchon is especially important because his own scientific and technical background and training have made him one of the few novelists outside science fiction to use facts, images, and metaphors from the physical sciences.

Story characteristics

Pynchon's stories, as well as his novels, typically deal with bizarre characters living under extreme conditions and with a personal or social order threatening either to destroy itself violently or to lapse into complete inertia and stasis. One of his major and continuing themes is that of paranoia, expressed through characters who fear the collapse of their world—either privately or cosmically—or who fear that their own lives, or life in general, are being controlled by outside forces.

Biography

Thomas Ruggles Pynchon is one of the most intensely private writers who has ever lived, even outdoing J. D. Salinger in his quest for seclusion and privacy. Only his close friends are even sure of what he looks like—the last available photograph of him is from high school. What is known of Pynchon is available only from public records. He was graduated from high school in 1953 and entered Cornell that year as a physics student, but in 1955, he left college and entered the Navy. He returned to Cornell in 1957, changing his major to English, and was graduated in 1959. He lived in New York for a short time while working on *V.*, then moved to Seattle where he worked for the Boeing Company assisting in the writing of technical documents from 1960 to 1962. Since that time, his whereabouts have been uncertain, although he seems to have spent much time in California and Mexico. In addition to the Faulkner, Rosenthal, and National Book Awards (and the Pulitzer, which he was denied), Pynchon in 1975 was awarded the Howells Medal of the National Institute of Arts and Letters and the American Academy of Arts and Letters; he refused, however, to accept the prize. He is reportedly now at work on two new novels.

Analysis

Not counting two excerpts from his second novel which were printed in popular magazines, Thomas Pynchon has published only six short stories, one of them—"The Small Rain"—in a college literary magazine. Nevertheless, the stories are important in themselves and as aids to understanding Pynchon's novels. Most of the stories were written before the publication of Pynchon's first novel, *V.*, and share the thematic concerns of that novel. The characters of these stories live in a modern wasteland devoid of meaningful life, which they seek either to escape or to redeem. Often they feel that the world itself is about to end, either in a final cataclysm or by winding down to a state lacking energy and motion, characterized by the physical state known as entropy: the eventual "heat death" of the universe when all temperature will be the same and all molecules will be chaotically arranged, without motion or potential energy. Although the responses of the characters in the first stories vary widely, they all indicate a similar degree of hopelessness.

Pynchon's first nationally published short story, "Mortality and Mercy in Vienna," illustrates many of these themes. The protagonist, a career diplomat named Cleanth Siegel, arrives at a party in Washington, D. C., only to find that the host, a look-alike named David Lupescu, is abandoning the apartment and appointing Siegel to take his place. In the course of the party, Siegel finds himself listening to the confusing details of his guests' convoluted and pointless sexual and social lives. Although he takes on the role of a father-confessor and although he wants to be a healer—"a prophet actually"—he has no cure for these people's problems. He does find a cure of sorts, however, in Irving

Loon, an Ojibwa Indian who has been brought to the party. Siegel recalls that the Ojibwa are prone to a psychic disorder in which the Indian, driven by a cosmic paranoia, comes to identify with a legendary flesh-eating monster, the Windigo, and goes on a rampage of destruction, killing and eating his friends and family. Siegel speaks the word "Windigo" to Loon and watches as the Indian takes a rifle from the wall. As Loon begins shooting the members of the party, Siegel himself escapes. Like Mister Kurtz in Conrad's *Heart of Darkness* (1902), to whom he explicitly compares himself, Siegel finds the only salvation possible to be extermination.

The presentation of the modern world as a spiritual wasteland and the theme of paranoia continue throughout these early short stories, as well as *V.*, but none of Pynchon's other characters is able to act as forcefully as Siegel, even though his action is a negative one. The later stories, however, also demonstrate Pynchon's greater ability and growth as a writer. "Mortality and Mercy in Vienna," relying as it does on references to Joseph Conrad and T. S. Eliot and on a narrative voice which generally tells rather than shows, presents itself too self-consciously as a story even as it strives for verisimilitude. Pynchon's next story, "Low-Lands," demonstrates his growth in a short period of time.

Dennis Flange, a former sailor now unhappily married, is thrown out of the house by his wife because of a surprise visit by his old Navy friend, Pig Bodine (who also later appears in *V.* and *Gravity's Rainbow*). He takes refuge with Pig in a shack in the local garbage dump which is presided over by a black caretaker. This caretaker has barricaded his shack against gypsies who are living in the dump, but that night when Flange hears someone call him he goes outside. There he meets a young woman named Nerissa who leads him to her room in a tunnel beneath the dump. At the story's end, Flange seems prepared to stay with her.

The title of "Low-Lands" comes from an old sea chantey which causes Flange to think of the sea as "a gray or glaucous desert, a wasteland which stretches away to the horizon, . . . an assurance of perfect, passionless uniformity." This "perfect, passionless uniformity" might be an apt description of Pynchon's view of modern life, his great fear of the ultimate end to surprise and adventure. Cleanth Siegel's response to this same fear is to obliterate the problem; Dennis Flange's response is to hide from it. Flange fears the uniformity suggested by his "low-lands," but he also desires it, wishing not to be exposed and lonely on that wasteland surface, "so that he would be left sticking out like a projected radius, unsheltered and reeling across the empty lunes of his tiny sphere."

In order not to be left "sticking out," Flange has taken refuge in his marriage and his house but finds that they can no longer shelter him. He finds his surrogate for a hiding place in the gypsy girl, Nerissa. Within Nerissa's underground room, he knows he can find at least a temporary sanctuary. Like the underground refuge of Ralph Ellison's Invisible Man, this room suggests a place of recuperation and preparation to reemerge into life. In Nerissa herself, the image of the sea is restored to life: "Whitecaps danced across her eyes; sea creatures, he knew, would be cruising about in the submarine green of her heart." This ending, with its gypsies and secret tunnels, suggests the possible existence of alternatives to the wasteland of modern society, a possibility to which Pynchon was to return in *The Crying of Lot 49*; at the time, this ending made "Low-Lands" one of the most positive of Pynchon's short stories.

A tone of hope, although somewhat more muted, can also be found in "Entropy," the best-known and perhaps most successful of Pynchon's short stories. Here Pynchon returns to the scene of "Mortality and Mercy in Vienna"—a party taking place in Washington, D. C.—but theme, characters, and plot are now handled with much more sophistication. The party itself is a lease-breaking party being hosted by one Meatball Mulligan, whose guests arrive and depart, engage in various kinds of strange behavior, and pass out at random. Upstairs, a man named Callisto lives in another apartment which he has converted into a hermetically sealed hot-house with the aid of a French-Annamese woman named Aubade. The story shifts back and forth between the two apartments although Meatball and Callisto are connected only by the fact of living in the same building and by the theme of entropy which concerns them both.

Although there is in "Low-Lands" a brief reference to the Heisenberg principle of nuclear physics (that an event is affected by the fact of being observed), "Entropy" is the first of Pynchon's works to make sustained use of information and metaphors drawn from science and mathematics—a use which has become one of his hallmarks as a writer. Entropy manifests itself in the story in two different forms: as *physical* entropy—the tendency towards randomness and disorder within a closed system—and as *communications* entropy—a measure of the lack of information within a message or signal. In both cases, the tendency is toward stasis and confusion—lack of motion or lack of information; in either case and in human terms, the result is death.

Physical entropy is especially frightening to Callisto, which is why he has barricaded himself within his apartment. Since he fears that the "heat death" of the universe is imminent, he has built a private enclave where he can control the environment and remain safe. The concept of physical entropy can also be applied to Meatball's party as the behavior of the individual partygoers becomes more and more random and disordered. Ironically, Meatball manages (at least temporarily) to avoid chaos and to reverse entropy, while Callisto fails. Realizing that he can either hide in a closet and add to the chaos and mad individualism of his party or work "to calm everybody down, one by one," Meatball chooses the latter. Callisto, on the other hand, fails to stop entropy within his own apartment. An ailing bird which he had been holding, trying to warm, dies in his hands after all; he wonders, "Has the transfer of heat ceased to work? Is there no more. . . ."

Part of the reason for Callisto's failure has to do with communications entropy. Order in communication is essential for the maintenance of order in Callisto's hothouse. Aubade brings "artistic harmony" to the apartment through a process by which all sensations "came to her reduced inevitably to the terms of sound: of music which emerged at intervals from a howling darkness of discordancy." Noise from Meatball's party threatens to plunge that music back into discord, and with the death of Callisto's bird, Aubade can no longer continue her effort. She smashes the window of the apartment with her fists and with Callisto awaits the triumph of physical entropy "and the final absence of all motion."

The fact that Meatball can bring order to his party suggests that order must be consciously created, not merely maintained as Callisto has sought to do. Even with Meatball's effort, his resolution of discord is not permanent and the final image of the party trembling "on the threshold of its third day" is not reassuring. Pynchon's message seems to be that of the physicists: entropy is an inevitable condition although it can be reversed for a while in some places. "Entropy" is notable for its organization and style as well as for its subject matter. The characters and the alternation of story lines are models for Pynchon's first novel, *V.*, but the story succeeds on its own as well. This "contrapuntal" structure combined with a number of references to music makes it evident that the story is structured like a musical fugue.

"Under the Rose," Pynchon's last short story before *V.*, is also especially interesting for its style and structure. Set in Cairo at the turn of the century during the Fashoda crisis—when Britain and France nearly came to war over the colonization of the Sudan—the story is Pynchon's first re-creation of a historical setting and his first successful use of a narrative limited to the point of view of a single character. With very little authorial intrusion, Pynchon skillfully describes the activities of two spies, Porpentine and Goodfellow, in seeking to prevent the assassination of the British ambassador and the international war which would inevitably follow. The story was later reworked by Pynchon, broken up into eight vignettes seen through the eyes of outside spectators, and installed as Chapter Three of *V.*

These early stories are generally characterized by a pessimism concerning the possibilities of human action and change. They are also marked by a sense of social isolation; with the exception of "Under the Rose," there is little or no suggestion of the political, economic, and social pressures that shape life, and even in that story, these pressures are subordinated to a suggested nameless, hostile, possibly nonhuman intelligence at work in history. Following the publication of *V.*, however, Pynchon has steadily moved back into the world, combining his imaginative perception of the condition of modern life with a recognition of the forces which can play a part in shaping that condition. That recognition is first manifested in Pynchon's last independent short story to date, "The Secret Integration."

"The Secret Integration" centers on a group of children living in the Berkshire town of Mingeborough, Massachusetts, who act in league to subvert adult institutions and encourage anarchistic liberty. The adults are seen as constantly seeking to make the children conform to their way of life: for example, Grover Snodd, "a boy genius with flaws," is certain that adults are planting Tom Swift books for him to read in order to foster a sense of competition and avarice as well as to promote racism.

Racism is, in fact, the key theme of the story. Carl Barrington, a central member of the children's gang, is himself black, his parents having recently moved into Northumberland Estates, a new development in Mingeborough. These newcomers are resented by the white adults of the town, and the children are aware of the presence of racism in their families, even though they do not quite understand it. There is also a flashback to the night the children—one of them a nine-year-old reformed alcoholic—go to the town hotel to sit with a black jazz musician because the adults in Alcoholics Anonymous are unwilling to help a black. After a night-long vigil, the boys see the musician hauled away by the police and never learn what really happens to him. In retaliation and as an affirmation of color, the boys stage a raid on the local train at night wearing green-colored masks and costumes to scare the passengers.

Color is a threat to Mingeborough and to a white way of life which thrives on the competition, separateness, and blandness exemplified by Tom Swift. The Barringtons are a special annoyance because they live in Northumberland Estates, which seems to have been built purposely to suppress differences and encourage uniformity. This development is like the "low-lands" of Dennis Flange, but with an important difference: rather than an abstract psychological condition, it is a real, physical place with more than enough correlatives in the nonfictional world to make it all too recognizable.

The children, however, are able to overcome this prejudice; even though Grover only understands the word "integration" as a mathematical term, they accept Carl as an equal. Yet in the end, the group capitulates. They find garbage dumped on the Barringtons' front lawn and recognize it as having come from their own houses. Unable to cut themselves off from their parents and repudiated by the Barringtons themselves, they say good-bye to Carl, who, it turns out, is imaginary, "put together out of phrases, images, possibilities that grownups had somehow turned away from, repudiated, left out at the edges of towns. . . ." The children return to the safety and love of their parents "and dreams that could never again be entirely safe."

"The Secret Integration" is concerned once again with the quest for possibilities and alternatives, which is the theme of *The Crying of Lot 49*, and with the prevalence of racism, which is one of the many concerns of *Gravity's*

Rainbow. Although the children admit defeat, one still feels the hope that life will be somewhat better once they have grown up, that they will retain some of the lessons they have learned.

It is impossible to say whether Pynchon will ever return to the short-story form for its own sake, and certainly his stories are less important than his novels. Nevertheless, these works are helpful introductions to this writer's sometimes complex and baffling ficitonal world and some of them—especially "Entropy" and perhaps "The Secret Integration"—will stand on their own as minor classics.

Major publications other than short fiction
NOVELS: *V.*, 1963; *The Crying of Lot 49*, 1966; *Gravity's Rainbow*, 1973.

Bibliography
Levine, George and David Leverenz, eds. *Mindful Pleasures: Essays on Thomas Pynchon.*
Mendelson, Edward, ed. *Pynchon: A Collection of Critical Essays.*
Plater, William M. *The Grim Phoenix: Reconstructing Thomas Pynchon.*
Slade, Joseph W. *Thomas Pynchon.*

Donald F. Larsson

MORDECAI RICHLER

Born: Montreal, Quebec, Canada; January 27, 1931

Principal short fiction
The Street, 1975.

Other literary forms
Although primarily a novelist, Mordecai Richler has written in many forms including essays, articles, film scripts, journalism, television plays, and children's literature. Two of his novels, *Cocksure* (1968) and *St. Urbain's Horseman* (1971), have won Canada's foremost literary prize, the Governor General's Award. His novel, *The Apprenticeship of Duddy Kravitz* (1959), was made into a motion picture which won the Golden Bear Award at the Berlin Film Festival in 1974. Richler's screenplay for this film was also nominated for an Academy Award and won a Screenwriters Guild of America Award.

Influence
Richler's early novels and stories reveal the author's immersion in the realism of Jean-Paul Sartre, Albert Camus, and Louis-Ferdinand Céline. Characters are presented with all their foibles and humanity, in all their absurdity and suffering. Richler relies on his memories of the Montreal ghetto where he was reared, and the stories are often almost autobiographical. In his later work, his approach is the same, using the memories of his origins, but he makes more use of black comedy. In the vein of Evelyn Waugh and George Orwell he is a writer with increasing intellectual and satirical distance. His work has been translated into French, German, Japanese, Spanish, Italian, Swedish, Dutch, and Hebrew.

Story characteristics
Richler's stories are sardonic and humorous; often they are reflections on life in a Jewish-Canadian ghetto. Although not as bitingly satirical as his later novels, the early stories are filled with ironic social criticism.

Biography
Born in Montreal, Mordecai Richler attended Sir George Williams University from 1949 to 1951. He left school to work as a writer in London, England, and later worked briefly as a news editor for the Canadian Broadcasting Company. For almost twenty years he resided in London, publishing much of his work there. In 1972, Richler returned to Montreal where he now lives with his wife and children. He has twice won Canada's Governor Gen-

eral's Award and is a member of the editorial board of the Book-of-the-Month Club.

Analysis

George Woodcock says of Mordecai Richler, "The worlds he creates are not autonomous entities re-made each time. Rather, they belong to a fictional continuum that perpetually overlaps the world in which Richler himself lives and feels, thinks and writes." The reader receives a distinct impression of the primacy of memory over imagination in Richler's work. Most of his stories and novels deal with the characters and situations of the Montreal ghetto of his early years; the stories in his collection *The Street* and the scenes of many of the novels examine with compassion and realism the lives of Canadian and immigrant Jews in this restricted and variegated environment. Most of the author's work functions within this frame of reference, with only an occasional change of focus. A peripheral character in one story comes under more thorough scrutiny in another. Often a new character will be introduced to interact with the established ones. The reader is given a continuity of the values and traditions of the old world as they evolve in the setting of their new Canadian world. There seems to be, then, no clear distinction between the fictional and the autobiographical elements of Richler's narrative.

The importance of Richler's work, consequently, is the analysis of age-old human problems found in familiar situations. He sees things with little sentimentality; life is filled with illusions, poverty, despair, and selfishness. Richler reacts positively in spite of these negative aspects, although showing how limiting they are. This view is emphasized by a keen sense of the ridiculous which sharpens our perceptions and evaluations. Absurd as his characters sometimes are, however, Richler still has a tender attitude toward them. Despite their moral and social blindness, they are human beings, desperately trying to control their own lives, and the author wants the reader to understand them rather than love them. Although their environment is a Jewish neighborhood with its own laws, legends, and language, these characters speak to all readers; in fact, they become even more authentic by belonging to a particular social setting. The external circumstances only show more clearly that their reactions are human and universal.

The story "The Summer My Grandmother Was Supposed to Die" is perhaps Richler's best. Here the author forces the reader to confront lingering death and its implications for a family. The story is graphically realistic. Since life must go on, even in tragedy, the reader is shown the absurd black comedy of ordinary existence. As are all the stories in *The Street*, this one is in the format of a recollection by old Malka's grandson, Jake Hersh. Dr. Katzman discovers that Malka has gangrene, and he says she will not last a month; he says the same thing the second, third, and fourth months. She remains bedridden for seven years; hers is a common story of the courageous person with an incredible will to live. The grotesque nature of the situation is dramatized very quickly when Jake says, "When we sat down to eat we could smell her." While Mr. and Mrs. Hersh wait for her to die, saying it will be for the best, the neighborhood children wait to peek up the nurse's dress. The grotesque and the ridiculous are simply integral parts of life—and death.

Malka, the widow of Zaddik, one of the Righteous, is described as beautiful, patient, shrewd, and resourceful. When she was married to the Zaddik, these qualities were necessary since he often gave his money away to rabbinical students, immigrants, and widows. As Jake says, this "made him as unreliable a provider as a drinker." Their sons are prominent men, a rabbi, a lawyer, and an actor, but it is left to Jake's mother to take care of Malka. No one, it seems, wants the old woman despite all that she has done for them; she becomes an inconvenience, "a condition in the house, something beyond hope or reproach, like a leaky ice-box." Jake can no longer kiss her without a feeling of revulsion, and he wonders if she knows that he covets her room. The shock of the tragic illness over a period of time gives way to resignation. Malka becomes only a presence, no longer recognizable as a human being. Instead of love being engendered by the grandmother's plight, there is resentment.

After the fourth year of her illness the strain begins to show. Mrs. Hersh is openly scornful of her husband and finds fault with her two children; she also takes to falling asleep directly after supper. Hersh seeks escape more often to Tansky's Cigar & Soda, and people tell him that he might as well be a bachelor. Malka's children finally take her, against her will, to the Jewish Old People's Home. With the reminder of death gone from the home, family relationships improve. Mrs. Hersh no longer needs the comfort of her bed, her cheeks glow with health, and she even jokes with her children. Mr. Hersh begins to come home early, no longer finding it necessary to go to Tansky's. Malka is seldom mentioned.

When Jake asks if he can move back to his room, however, his mother's caring instinct returns, and she decides to bring Malka home. The cycle of despair starts again, and the family returns to their habits of escape. Mr. Hersh says, "I knew it, I was born with all the luck." For two more years there is no change in Malka's condition; she seems to gain her strength at the expense of the family. The tension is almost unbearable for the Hershes. The fatigue and morbidity are most noticeable in Mrs. Hersh, but they are also evident in each member of the household.

Finally, in the seventh summer, Malka dies. When Jake returns home from a baseball game, he is not allowed to see her; he is only told what he and his sister will receive from their grandmother's belongings. When Jake's sister Rifka tells him that he can now have Malka's room, he changes his mind, saying "I couldn't sleep in there now." Rifka, sensing his discomfort, approaches his bed with a sheet over her head to frighten him. When all the family members gather together, cousin Jerry is skeptical of their reactions, claiming that now everyone will be sickeningly sentimental. Mr. and Mrs. Hersh, however, are openly scornful of these relatives, especially the rabbi, who did very little to comfort Malka during her illness. Ironically, Dr. Katzman tries to console this religious man. The rabbi can be pensive, but he does not feel the emotions of being involved. The comfort and simple decency of being allowed to die at home gave Malka the courage and strength to live, but the demands of caring for her has sapped the strength of the family.

Richler also examines the problem of involvement when an outsider, Mervyn Kaplansky, moves to the St. Urbain area. Within the borders of his Montreal ghetto, peopled with established families and the Jewish immigrants, there is an exaggerated emphasis on getting ahead, most forcefully presented by Richler in his novel *The Apprenticeship of Duddy Kravitz*. Any display of talent is treated with admiration, especially if that talent is recognized in the United States. Of course, there is a great deal of difference between the pressure to succeed and actual success, and expectations are often greater than achievement itself. "Some Grist for Mervyn's Mill" illustrates this point and its consequences. Mervyn, a short, fat man from Toronto about twenty-three years of age, rents a room in the Hersh household. When he says that he is a writer, Mrs. Hersh is enraptured. Mervyn even carries with him a check for $14.50 which he received from the *Family Herald & Weekly Star*. This small check has given Mervyn a great ego; he says, "I try not to read too much now that I'm a wordsmith myself. I'm afraid of being influenced, you see."

Mervyn is now writing a novel entitled *The Dirty Jews* "about the struggles of our people in a hostile society"; he spends much time discussing this book and other literary matters with Mrs. Hersh. Again, Mr. Hersh is alienated from the family and goes to Tansky's to play cards. In order to finish the novel, Mervyn rarely leaves his room. Thinking that this is bad for him, Mrs. Hersh arranges a date for him with Molly Rosen, the "best looker" on St. Urbain Street. The match is unsuccessful, but Mervyn writes to her anyway. All the letters, however, come back unopened. Mervyn's love-life seems to parallel his unattained success as a writer.

Ironically, roles begin to reverse when Mr. Hersh sees a story, "A Doll for the Deacon," supposedly published under Mervyn's pseudonym. For Mr. Hersh this is proof that Mervyn is a writer, and he overlooks his faults as well as his overdue rent, now treating the budding wordsmith as an author in full flower. He clips out material from papers for him, takes him to meet the boys at Tansky's, and talks more tenderly to him than he does to his own children. Mervyn soon becomes more important to Molly, even though she knows that a publisher has rejected his novel. Winning the praise of Mr. Hersh and the fancy of Molly puts a great deal of pressure on Mervyn. He knows that he has gained recognition on false pretenses, although he never doubts his talent as a writer.

To prove something to the locals, Mervyn concocts a lie about receiving an advance from a United States publisher. Unfortunately, Mr. Hersh proclaims a celebration including the men from Tansky's and the Rosens, and at the party Molly announces their engagement. Mervyn can only drink heavily and suffer the pain caused by his deceit. Later he tells Jake that Molly only wanted his fame; before the rumors of his success, he was an object of ridicule, but with established fame, everyone feels possessive. Mervyn is now accepted for what they think is his achievement, and to save face, Mervyn perpetuates the illusion by showing Mr. Hersh a telegram with an offer from Hollywood. He leaves immediately, saying that he must check out the offer. A few days later the Hershes receive a bill for the telegram, and no one sees Mervyn again. The boys at Tansky's are scandalized, and Molly is disgraced. After a month Mr. Hersh starts to receive money from Toronto for the unpaid rent, but Mervyn never answers any of his letters.

Richler is at his best satirizing the subtle human relationships which make up the social fabric. The consequences of almost insignificant and innocent efforts have a kind of ripple effect until a number of people are involved; the microcosm around St. Urbain Street is only a focus for broader social problems. Personal human contact creates deception, pain, family alienation, and only very rarely a sense of joy. Individuals struggle in a social context with only a hope that things will get better. Richler's characters, then, are survivors who exist not as victims of a cruel, impersonal fate, but as victims of their own actions. There is no significant harm done when Mervyn is exposed as a fraud. Life resumes at Tansky's, and Mr. Hersh has merely to take a severe ribbing from his friends. For most of Richler's people, this is what life is all about—a comedy of bearable suffering in which only minor victories, at best, are won.

Major publications other than short fiction

NOVELS: *The Acrobats*, 1954; *Son of a Smaller Hero*, 1955; *A Choice of Enemies*, 1957; *The Apprenticeship of Duddy Kravitz*, 1959; *Stick Your Neck Out*, 1963; *Cocksure: A Novel*, 1968; *St. Urbain's Horseman*, 1971; *Joshua Then and Now*, 1980.

NONFICTION: *Hunting Tigers Under Glass: Essays and Reports*, 1969; *Shovelling Trouble*, 1973; *Images of Spain*, 1977.

Bibliography
Sneps, G. David. *Mordecai Richler*.
Woodcock, George. *Mordecai Richler*.

James MacDonald

ALAIN ROBBE-GRILLET

Born: Brest, France; August 18, 1922

Principal short fiction
Instantanés, 1962 (*Snapshots*).

Other literary forms
Alain Robbe-Grillet's published works include novels, short stories, many essays on literary theory (eight collected in the influential volume *For a New Novel: Essays on Fiction*, 1963), and several motion picture scripts. The film *Last Year at Marienbad*, for which Robbe-Grillet wrote the script, received the Academy Award for best foreign film in 1961.

Influence
Robbe-Grillet is the leading figure behind the "New Novel"—sometimes called "objective" literature—which appeared in France in the mid-1950's and 1960's. Because he is "objective" literature's most skilled practitioner and most widely published theorist, he has from his earliest works endured both savage criticism and extravagant praise. Although his fiction may seem strikingly unconventional, Robbe-Grillet himself placed it in a line of fictive development beginning with Honoré de Balzac and progressing through Stendhal, Gustave Flaubert, Fyodor Dostoevski, Marcel Proust, Franz Kafka, James Joyce, William Faulkner, and Samuel Beckett. Although few in number, his short stories capture "objectivist" concerns in purest form; they have been translated into most Western languages and are frequently anthologized.

Story characteristics
Robbe-Grillet's stories are "objective" in that they are composed almost entirely of detailed descriptions of apparently meaningless objects, gestures, and scenes. Robbe-Grillet may seem to ignore conventional concerns for characterization, plot, and meaning; yet these same concerns often underlie the "objective" surfaces of the stories.

Biography
Trained as an agronomist, Alain Robbe-Grillet has lived for most of his life in France, although his job as an engineer for the *Institute des Fruits Tropicaux* took him to Guinea, Morocco, Guadeloupe, and Martinique. He also has served as *Chargé de Mission, Institute Nationale de la Statistique* and since beginning his writing career in the early 1950's has served as literary adviser for the *Editions de Minuet* in Paris.

Analysis

Readers first encountering Alain Robbe-Grillet's short stories often find them difficult or even baffling for two reasons. For one, the term often used to describe them—"objective"—is misleading. The stories are not objective in the sense of the narrator being dispassionate or uninvolved; on the contrary, narrative point of view is always totally subjective, even obsessive, by Robbe-Grillet's own admission. The stories are objective only in that they are composed of carefully arranged and minutely described scenes, and a "scene" may be no more than a seemingly insignificant object or untranslatable gesture. The fact that the narrator singles out certain objects from all those available and the fact that his descriptions of these objects are always warped to his own often unreliable perspective made the stories quite subjective indeed.

A misunderstanding of the label "objective" may lead to a more fundamental misconception about Robbe-Grillet's stories. A cursory reading of any one of the stories may reveal no more than a series of flat, dispassionate descriptions—in minute detail and photographic accuracy, generally repeated again and again—of static scenes containing no inherent interest. Yet closer analysis shows that the scenes themselves are *never* static, that the descriptions, albeit in great detail, are shifting, contradictory, and teasingly indefinite. No matter how firm his "objects" apparently are, we are always on shifting ground with Robbe-Grillet. Like the best writers, he forces the reader to engage in the process of construction and analysis. What we are often unprepared for is his refusal ever to supply answers.

The six stories in his one slender collection, *Snapshots* (first published as *Instantanés* in 1962), capture Robbe-Grillet's theories in purest fictive form. The title is as misleading as the label "objective." A snapshot is a flat, static picture that records a scene with total accuracy; it removes us from the scene through both time and distance (from the camera to its target). Certainly, Robbe-Grillet's descriptions are mostly visual: colors, shapes, and positional determiners (left, right, behind, below) dominate the descriptions. The other senses are involved sparingly, and when they do appear—the smell of hot coffee in "The Dressmaker's Dummy," for example—they are startlingly affective and effective.

Yet the static accuracy of the snapshot is undermined throughout the collection. Consider "The Dressmaker's Dummy," the first section of Robbe-Grillet's story "Three Reflected Visions" which was alternately applauded and maligned by critics. The dummy is obviously one of the three "visions" of the title. A "vision," however, can be something that we actually see or, more commonly, something that we only imagine; it is characteristic of the author to complicate our apprehension of the "visions." One complication arises from the "reflected" nature of the visions. The first section, for example, presents at least three versions (visions?) of the dressmaker's dummy: the dummy itself; its reflection in the mirror above the mantel; and its reflection in the mirror in the wardrobe. In addition, the two mirrors reflect each other and thus replicate their reflections of the dummy. A temporal complication occurs when the narrator describes the room a second time, after its furniture has been rearranged for a fitting. The dummy is not described; we learn only that it is not in its "accustomed" place. The two views of the room demonstrate the interrelatedness of time and place: a recurring theme in Robbe-Grillet's fiction. The concept of time is meaningful only through alterations in place and our recognition and memory of such alterations. In the same vein, alterations in place can occur only through time.

A final complication occurring in not only this story but also every Robbe-Grillet fiction is the language itself. The most commonly repeated words in the author's vocabulary are "perhaps," "almost," "might," "vaguely," "probably," "hidden," and so forth—words that intentionally blur the focus of Robbe-Grillet's photographic lens. Willingly or not, the reader is drawn into the process of composing the scene and making decisions by the conjectural nature of the author's diction. Even his positional determiners often complicate more than clarify. In one passage in "The Dressmaker's Dummy," for example, we find eight "lefts" and "rights" in the space of less than a hundred words; rather than exact, the passage is comically confusing.

The same types of problems that we encounter in "The Dressmaker's Dummy" are found in "The Way Back," only intensified. Here the narrative focus is not only blurred but totally disoriented as well. A scene that seems initially pellucid becomes dizzily labyrinthian as the "plot"—for want of a better term—folds back upon itself in time and place. The components of the scene are few: a narrator who always talks in first-person plural (a frequent tool of Robbe-Grillet; the "we" becomes, in effect, the reader); his two friends, Franz and Lagrand; an island, separated from the mainland by a narrow strip of water; a jetty, in the process of being (or has just been or is about to be) covered with the rising tide; two houses; and, near the end, a man with a boat.

In the first paragraph of the story, the mainland is just coming into view; "we" are clearly on the island. Within two pages, however, the narrator is contrasting the "desiccated" plants on the island to those at "our" feet. Somehow, inexplicably, we are now on the mainland. Shortly we are back at precisely the same point of focus as we were in the first paragraph, the language repeated almost verbatim. So it goes throughout the story. We are either on the island or on the mainland, worrying about getting onto the island before the water covers the jetty or worrying about getting off the island before the same thing occurs. The few bits of dialogue are repeated once, twice, thrice—always complicating, never elucidating, our task of untangling objects and events. "The Way Back" has the same fascinations and frustrations of any labyrinth with no way out, no hope of escape.

The two best-known of Robbe-Grillet's stories are "In the Corridors of the Metro" and "The Secret Room." Like "Three Reflected Visions," "In the Corridors of the Metro" is divided into three titled sections. "The Escalator" describes a group of people on an escalator, "A Corridor" describes a group of people (the same as before?) walking down a narrow underground corridor, and "Behind the Automatic Door" describes that same group crowded behind a closed door waiting for it to be opened. In all three, the author's "conjectural" vocabulary prevents definitive views of the scenes. The point of view is as pinched, claustrophobic, limited, and as frequently obstructed as that of any individual's in the crowd.

The individuals in Robbe-Grillet's metro are as expressionless, mute, and mechanical as the stone and steel tunnels down which they rush as mindlessly as lemmings. Is it Robbe-Grillet's intention for us to read the story in this way? Is it the author's "theme" that modern man has re-created himself in the image of his own mindless technology? Robbe-Grillet's very refusal to analyze, instruct, or draw conclusions invites us to do the same for him. Whatever conclusions we reach, however, are always our own; they are not to be found in the works themselves.

The last story in the collection, "The Secret Room," is probably the most frequently anthologized. Its popularity undoubtedly stems from its blending of traditional fictive concerns—action, narrative, suspense—with Robbe-Grillet's "objective" style. The story opens with a "snapshot": an object of hemispheres and curves, smeared with a red stain, in a room of shadows and diffused light. The image presented is vague, indefinite, and tentative. Succeeding "snapshots" present more information but are contradictory and confusing. The object becomes, clearly, a woman, nude, stabbed through the breast. She is first described as being entirely alone. As the focus sharpens and broadens, we see a man standing on a stairway some distance away. In the next view—with no transition, no apparent movement—the man is standing over his now chained "victim," at first dead but now alive. The shutter blinks once more, and the man is silhouetted in an open door at the top of the stairs. His victim is dying, dead.

Detractors of Robbe-Grillet might seize upon the popularity of "The Secret Room" as the proof of the failure of his "objective" style. The story is interesting, they might argue, precisely because it contains at least in rough form the elements of traditional fiction which Robbe-Grillet generally abjures: suspense, atmosphere, and an implied plot (the capture, torture, murder, flight). Some might further argue that the style of the story is more the decadent painter Gustave Moreau's (to whom the story is dedicated) than the author's. Yet Robbe-Grillet's literary interest in eroto-sadism is longstanding, and the technique is purely his own. Robbe-Grillet is *always* concerned with atmosphere: he often repeats in his criticism that a certain tone is the primary effect for which he reaches. The plot, if it exists, is certainly not sequential.

The series of pictures begins at the end, backs up to before the murder, then moves forward to a point somewhere before the first scene. The story has the same tension, then, between confused time/place relationships as does "The Way Back."

If it proves nothing else, "The Secret Room" shows that the claim that Robbe-Grillet's fictions are nothing more than flat descriptions of objects is a misleading oversimplification at best. No story is formed by only one picture; the "snapshots" are layered one on the other as in a cubist painting, each one superficially clear and static yet always altering slightly what went before, changing the focus and the angle of view, deliberately distorting what the author has gone to great lengths, seemingly, to make so understandable. The result is a type of short story that teases us into developing our own analysis, composing our own thematic statements, and supplying our own motivations for actions real or suspected. Devilishly, maddeningly, Robbe-Grillet forces us into the position of investing with meaning what is only and always ineffable.

Major publications other than short fiction

NOVELS: *Les Gommes*, 1953 (*The Erasers*); *Le Voyeur*, 1955 (*The Voyeur*); *La Jalousie*, 1957 (*Jealousy*); *Dans le labyrinthe*, 1959 (*In the Labyrinth*); *La Maison de rendezvous*, 1965; *Projet pour une Révolution à New York*, 1970 (*Project for a Revolution in New York*); *Topologie d'une cité Fantôme*, 1976 (*Topology of a Phantom City*).

NONFICTION: *Pour un Nouveau Roman*, 1963 (*For a New Novel: Essays on Fiction*).

Bibliography

Fraizer, Dale Watson. *Alain Robbe-Grillet: An Annotated Bibliography of Critical Studies 1953-72.*

Morrissette, Bruce. *Alain Robbe-Grillet.*

Stoltzfus, Ben. *Alain Robbe-Grillet and the New French Novel.*

Sturrock, John. *The French New Novel: Claude Simon, Michel Butor, Alain Robbe-Grillet.*

Szanto, George H. *Narrative Consciousness: Structure and Perception in the Fiction of Kafka, Beckett, and Robbe-Grillet.*

Dennis Vannatta

PHILIP ROTH

Born: Newark, New Jersey; March 19, 1933

Principal short fiction
Goodbye, Columbus, 1959.

Other literary forms
Philip Roth has published nine novels, many of which were excerpted as self-contained short stories in numerous magazines. He has also published essays of literary criticism and a screenplay. *Goodbye, Columbus* won the National Book Award in 1959, and the title novella was made into a motion picture in 1969.

Influence
While Roth's writings are not only of Jewish subjects and concerns, his art is often linked to other Jewish writers including Saul Bellow and Bernard Malamud. His novels have achieved a wide readership, and his short stories and episodes from his longer fiction have been published in some of the foremost magazines in America. His work has also been widely anthologized.

Story characteristics
Roth's stories exhibit a wide range of technique, from mordant satire to brooding and pensive tales. While the stories range from starkly realistic portrayals of urban and suburban society to surrealistic tales, Roth's fiction always exhibits a keen sense of place, an accurate ear for patterns of speech, and a gift for concision and pace.

Biography
Philip Roth was reared in Newark, New Jersey, where he was influenced by the rising urban Jewish culture which predominated the intellectual and cultural life of part of that city. After graduating from Weequahic High School, he took his B. A. at Bucknell University in 1954, and his M. A. at the University of Chicago in 1955. After a stint in the United States Army, he returned to the University of Chicago where he completed most of his work towards a Ph.D. and taught literature. In addition to the National Book Award, Roth won second prize in the O. Henry Prize Story Contest of 1960 for "Defender of the Faith"; he won a Guggenheim Fellowship in the same year. Roth has also been the recipient of a grant from the National Institute of Arts and Letters.

Analysis
Philip Roth's only collection of stories is the 1959 volume, *Goodbye, Co-*

lumbus, which contains the title novella and five additional short stories. Roth has produced numerous other individual stories, however, which have been printed in such magazines as *The New Yorker, Esquire, Harper's Magazine*, and *Atlantic Monthly*. Additionally, portions of several of his novels were first released as short stories. The shorter fiction serves to introduce the reader both to Roth's typical range of styles and to his complex themes. The author's Newark-Jewish background lends a prominent urban-ethnic flavor to his early fiction; but read in the context of his later work, which deals far less directly with "Jewish" matters, it becomes clear that the Jewish elements in his work are used to exemplify larger concerns endemic to American society as a whole.

Technically, Roth's fiction runs the gamut from broad satire to somber realism to Kafkaesque surrealism. Beneath the wide range of styles, however, is the strain of social realism which attempts to depict, often without overt judgment, the pressures brought to bear on the modern individual searching for (or trying to recover) moral, ethical, and cultural roots in a society which prides itself on the erasure of such differences in its attempt to achieve homogeneity. Implicit in many of the stories is the problem of the leveling down into a normalcy of behavior which, although perhaps a socially acceptable way of "getting along," nevertheless mitigates against the retention of cultural eccentricities or personal individuality. While Roth's Jewish milieu provided ample opportunity to observe this phenomenon, much of his later (and longer) fiction explores these matters in non-Jewish settings.

"Eli, the Fanatic" embodies many of Roth's themes and techniques. Taking place in suburban America, the tale concerns a young, "secularized" Jewish lawyer, Eli Peck, who is retained to convince a European Jew who operates a resident Jewish academy in the town (aptly and symbolically named Woodenton) to close his establishment. The town is embarrassed by the presence of the yeshiva, since it calls the largely gentile residents' attention to the Jewishness of some of the inhabitants who wish to blend in peacefully with the rest of the population. Significantly, it is the Jews who hire Eli, and not the gentiles, Jews who believe all too literally in the "melting pot" theory of assimilation. Of particular annoyance is one resident of the yeshiva—a Hasidic Jew who wears the traditional long black coat and wide-brimmed hat and walks about the town shopping for supplies for the school.

When Eli confronts the headmaster, he is touched by the old man's integrity and his fierce but philosophically stoical attachment to his cultural and religious roots—an attachment, however, which Eli cannot share. Eli realizes that the old man will never abandon his school and has no "respect" for the zoning laws which prohibit such establishments. Eli attempts a compromise. After soliciting reluctant approval from his clients, he tries to persuade the old man to insist that his Hasidic employee wear modern garb, in the hope that the visible manifestation of the enclave will be removed and thus mollify the community. Eli is informed by the headmaster that the clothes the man wears are the only ones he owns, and that, after escape from the holocaust, they are the "only things he has left." Eli realizes that the remark is symbolic as well as literal—that the clothes are a symbol of the identity not even the Nazis could take away from the man. Nevertheless, Eli brings to the yeshiva two of his own suits in the hope that the man will adopt the nonoffensive dress.

Although he does so, much to the temporary relief of Eli and the modern Jewish community, he also leaves his old clothes on Eli's doorstep and parades about the town in Eli's ill-fitting clothes as a kind of silent reproach to a town which would rob him of his identity. Only Eli senses the meaning of the man's act. In what can only be termed a mystical transformation, Eli feels compelled to put on the Hasidic garb, and he begins to walk through the village, achieving a "conversion" to the values and sense of belonging that the man had represented. Moreover, as he literally "walks in the man's shoes," he defies the leveling and dehumanizing impetus represented by his role in enforcing the town's desires. He finally visits the hospital where his wife has recently given birth to their first son, and is berated by her and several of the town's citizens and accused of having another of what has apparently been a series of nervous breakdowns. Eli realizes that this time he is totally sane and lucid; but at the close of the story he feels the prick of a hypodermic needle, and the reader knows that he will be tranquilized and psychoanalyzed back to "normalcy."

The story illustrates the major concerns in Roth's fiction. Eli is a normally nonaggressive hero who nevertheless is prodded to assert his individuality actively and thus assuage his own guilt. The pressures of society exert a counter force which annihilates this thrust toward individuality. The story is not really about conversion to an obscure form of Judaism so much as it is about the desire to resist the loss of cultural identity and personal individuality. In a world of diminished passions, the Rothian hero attempts to assert himself in the midst of the society which inhibits him. Unlike the "activist" heroes of much of American fiction who "light out for the territory," or who "make a separate peace," Roth's activists stand their ground and attempt to triumph over, or at least to survive within, the society—often without success.

Not all of Roth's heroes are activists: many become *passive* victims to these societal forces. "Epstein," an early story which appeared in the *Paris Review*, and, like "Eli, the Fanatic," was incorporated into *Goodbye, Columbus*, illustrates this secondary pattern. The central character, Lou Epstein, is an apparently financially and socially successful owner of a paper-bag company. An immigrant to America as a child, he has achieved success by subscribing to the essentially Protestant work ethic of his adopted country.

Epstein's life, however, has not been happy. A son died at age eleven, and he broods about his company falling into the hands of a stranger. His wife, Goldie, is aging rapidly and unattractively; and while Epstein is not young, he feels youthful sexual drives which do not tally with his wife's rejection of them or her diminished appeal. He is henpecked, and his wife is a compulsive housekeeper. His only daughter has become fat, and her fiancé is a "chinless, lazy smart aleck." Epstein is, in short, going through a mid-life crisis, surrounded by signs of unfulfilled goals and waning capacities and opportunities.

Jealous of the "zipping and unzipping" which accompany midnight teenage assignations in his living room, thus heightening the frustrations of his airless marriage, he begins an affair with the recently widowed mother of his brother's son's girlfriend. The woman represents all that his life lacks and all that his wife is not—sensuousness, lust, adventure. The "Calvinist" gods are not mocked, however, because Epstein comes down with a suspicious rash which his wife discovers to her horror, resulting in a hilarious, but apocalyptic battle waged by the naked pair over the bedsheets which Goldie seeks to burn. The next day, Epstein, seeking to confront his amour, collapses in the street with a heart attack; and at the close of the story, his wife, riding in the ambulance with Epstein, assures him that he will be all right. "All he's got to do," the doctor tells her, "is to live a normal life, normal for sixty." Goldie pleads, "Lou, you'll live normally, won't you? *Won't you?*"

Normal, of course, means a return to the external success and internal misery of his life before the liberating affair. The issue is not the morality of the situation, but the desperate attempt to control one's life consciously and seize experience. Epstein laments, "When they start taking things away from you, you reach out, you *grab*—maybe like a pig, even, but you grab. And right, wrong, who knows! With tears in your eyes, you can even see the difference!" Epstein is returned unwillingly to the world of "normalcy." He is trapped—even biologically trapped—by a society which has adopted essentially Protestant-Calvinist values which distrust appetites, roots, and eccentric behavior, and which inculcates a sense of moral guilt which is essentially the same as so-called "Jewish guilt."

In another early story (with no Jewish characters) entitled "Novotny's Pain," the title character, conscripted into the army as a willing, if frightened, recruit, suffers unspecified and clearly psychosomatic lower back pain which Novotny endures in the hope that it will eventually go away. He clearly is not a "gold-bricker." He is engaged to be married, and when out on pass, he and his girl friend enjoy a rich and acrobatic sex life despite the occasional pain from his back.

Novotny, in desperate discomfort and moral unease, seeks medical help; but tests reveal nothing pathologically wrong. The young man admits that he fears going into battle, but also sincerely asserts that if the root of the pain can be removed he would be more than willing to do his duty. The army authorities regard him, however, as a mental case, or worse; and eventually he is given a dishonorable discharge. Novotny wonders if he is being punished for all the ecstatic sex and happiness he has had with his fiancée which his back has not prevented him from experiencing; but even after he marries her, although threats that the discharge will destroy his civilian prospects turn out to be groundless, Novotny still suffers twinges of pain which correspond to his twinges of guilt. At the end, Novotny asks himself a central question: "What good was it, being good?" All of Roth's heroes try to deal with the concept of "goodness," but are impaled on the varying definitions of the term: goodness arising out of socially acceptable conformity, or goodness coming from an existential attempt to define one's self satisfactorily in terms of needs, roots, and desires.

The acerbity of Roth's vision, his honesty in portraying the deficiencies in American culture and values, and his refusal to prescribe overt solutions have led to critical charges of anti-Semitism and defeatism. His characters' valiant, if often thwarted, attempts to achieve some identity and sense of placement, however, belie the latter charge; and the honest, if not always affectionate, portrayal of both Jewish and non-Jewish characters in similar situations negate the former accusation.

Roth's later and longer works have taken stylistic risks (such as a male character who undergoes a Kafkaesque metamorphosis into a woman's breast—a transformation no less odd than Eli's); and, while his work has taken on a chameleonlike variety of forms and subjects, his themes and concerns remain largely those of his early short fiction.

Major publications other than short fiction
NOVELS: *Letting Go*, 1962; *When She Was Good*, 1967; *Portnoy's Complaint*, 1969; *Our Gang*, 1971; *The Breast*, 1972; *The Great American Novel*, 1973; *My Life as a Man*, 1974; *The Professor of Desire*, 1977; *Ghost Writer*, 1979. NONFICTION: *Reading Myself and Others*, 1975.

Bibliography
McDaniel, John N. *The Fiction of Philip Roth.*
Meeter, Glenn. *Philip Roth and Bernard Malamud.*
Pinsker, Sanford. *The Comedy That "Hoits": An Essay on the Fiction of Philip Roth.*
Rodgers, Bernard F., Jr. *Philip Roth.*
——————— . *Philip Roth: A Bibliography.*

                                                                                    David Sadkin

JOHN RUSKIN

Born: London, England; February 8, 1819
Died: Brantwood, Coniston, England; January 20, 1900

Principal short fiction

Harry and Lucy Concluded: Or, Early Lessons, 1826-1829; *Chronicles of St. Bernard,* 1836; *Leoni: A Legend of Italy,* 1837, 1868; *The King of the Golden River,* 1851.

Other literary forms

John Ruskin's first literary attempt was writing poetry when he was six years old; by 1832 he was imitating Byron and Shelley. At Oxford, he won the Newdigate Prize for poetry in 1839. His fame, however, rests on his volumes of critical prose on art, geology, metaphysics, nature, political economy, and the reformation of society. *Modern Painters,* five volumes published between 1843 and 1860, was a revolutionary critique on the pictorial arts as moral equivalents of a culture. *Unto This Last* (1860) was more revolutionary; in it, Ruskin defended the rights of labor in industrializing England. *Fors Clavigera* (1871-1884), collected letters written to English workers, probed the causes of crime and poverty. "The Nature and Authority of Miracle," written for the Metaphysical Society in 1873, dealt with the phenomenon of the universe. Numerous other essays and letters combining Ruskin's sense of morality with his aesthetic principles appeared in journals on art and architecture.

Influence

Ruskin reintroduced the medieval art treasures to Protestant England; he also advanced agriculture, industry, and education by establishing St. George's Guild in 1875 for the workingmen of England. By championing the pre-Raphaelites, as he had Turner, Ruskin helped to establish the Pre-Raphaelite movement. Internationally, he affected the fiction of Leo Tolstoy and Marcel Proust, who translated Ruskin's work into French. In America, Ruskin, Tennessee, was founded in 1896 on his principles of social justice.

Story characteristics

Fantasy and legendary stories are matched by moral tales and realistic accounts of life in an Alpine village. The fairy tale, dealing with good and evil on a simple basis, has the greatest appeal because of its dialogue and descriptive passages.

Biography

The son of first cousins, John James Ruskin and Margaret Cock, John

Ruskin was of Anglo-Scottish heritage. The father of John James, John Thomas Ruskin, strongly disapproved of his son's engagement to his sister's daughter; he slit his throat ten days after the death of his wife, following years of insanity. The marriage occurred a few months after their deaths. John Ruskin was born a year later to his thirty-seven-year-old mother, a devout Evangelical who had dedicated her son's life to the church. Her early Bible training and intensive love for her son profoundly affected his life and writing. His father's business—Ruskin, Telford, and Domecq, wine merchants—allowed the family to travel extensively throughout Europe. Educated by private tutors and at Oxford University, Ruskin, a precocious child who taught himself to read at four years of age, was both a Classical and a modern scholar. He was the first Slade Professor of Art at Oxford, lecturing there to an appreciative audience. Three unhappy love affairs were the low points in his life. Rejected by Adele Domecq, he later married Effie Gray, born in the house where his father committed suicide. After six years, the marriage was annulled because of Ruskin's impotency. He later fell in love with Rose LaTouche, a young Irish girl thirty-two years his junior. Ruskin experienced long periods of insanity during the last decade of his life. During the productive years, he was honored by Oxford and Cambridge Universities, and societies were founded in England, Scotland, Ireland, and America to study his works.

Analysis

The short fiction piece for which John Ruskin is remembered is *The King of the Golden River*, a fairy tale set in an imaginary Alpine village which mixes characters from the real world with those of the fairy world and purports to entertain rather than instruct the reader. Actually, it was written in 1841 for thirteen-year-old Effie Gray while Ruskin recovered from his rejection by the beautiful daughter of his father's Spanish partner. *Harry and Lucy Concluded* and *Chronicles of St. Bernard,* never completed, add nothing to Ruskin's fame as a storyteller. Several versions of *Leoni: A Legend of Italy* exist, but none of them are spellbinders.

Harry and Lucy Concluded: Or, Early Lessons, written when Ruskin was seven years old, follows the style of Maria Edgeworth, the Irish novelist who wrote short moral tales for children. Ruskin had intended to write four volumes; he finished three of them. His laborious method of writing certainly delayed completion: he imitated a printer, using large and small lettering to demonstrate different type sets, and included a page of errata to carry out the effect of its being a printed book.

Harry and Lucy Concluded reveals two topics of Ruskin's mature work: travel observations and geological findings. Harry (based on Ruskin himself) and Lucy, his fictitious sister, enjoy life, with Harry assuming a mentor's role in explaining natural events. Ruskin's later skill in sketching and engraving is apparent in this juvenile work. Harry's explanation of the positive and negative aspects of clouds which produce electricity and rain is complemented by sketches of a mountain and clouds. Young Harry wastes no time in pointing out the sights on journeys; much of what he describes relates to the earth and natural things. Young Ruskin also presents an early portrait of his mother and father, the parents of Harry and Lucy. Mamma is stern and moralistic while Papa is more easygoing and literary; both are in the background while Harry explores the world of animals, minerals, machinery, engines, astronomy, and boats.

This early work, remarkable for its scope and craftsmanship, is a significant accomplishment for a child. Although the record of the family's adventures lacks maturity, it justifies Ruskin's faith in himself. He wanted to learn as much as he could about the physical world, especially the geological and astronomical nature of the universe, by observing natural phenomena. Later, he would pursue the same quest for information, going to nature for his information and acquiring a copious amount of facts for his work. The methodology which he established before he was ten years old was the same method he used to document his observations on art, architecture, and sociopolitical systems.

Ruskin was on unsteady ground, however, when he wrote *Chronicles of St. Bernard* and *Leoni: A Legend of Italy*. He was hopelessly in love with Adele Domecq, Catholic and convent-educated. They were written to impress her and show his acceptance of Catholicism, absolutely rejected by his mother, unhappy with John's infatuation. The early preoccupation with Catholic customs eventually led to his fascination with the art and architecture of Catholic artisans, the source material for *Modern Painters* and *The Stones of Venice* (1851-1853). Throughout his long lifetime, Ruskin did not stray far from the beauty of Rome and the art centers of Italy. His early attempt to become part of that culture to please Adele indicates his willingness to change the opinions set in his mind by his mother.

Chronicles of St. Bernard seems to be a kind of Gothic thriller, although it is difficult to say with certainty, since Ruskin only completed the introduction and two chapters. The introduction describes the Hospice at the pass of St. Bernard in the Alps and acquaints the reader with the people staying at the inn. It satirizes an English geologist who speaks only in geological terms, missing the magnificent beauty of the mountains. To discover the quartz in the cavity out of which rare mountain flowers grow, he wantonly destroys the flowers.

Ruskin then presents a favorable picture of the monks caring for the French, German, Scotch, and English travelers and a very unfavorable picture of a Frenchwoman who is obviously a nuisance, complaining of everything about her trip. When all the travelers go off in different directions, the narrator finds himself alone with a monk who tells him of a manuscript which contains the story of Velasquez, the novice, whose body is buried in the chapel under a square slab of black marble.

The narrator in Chapters One and Eleven repeats what he read in the manuscript. It is a travelogue of an elderly English gentleman, his daughter Ada, Velasquez, a handsome young man, and their servants going to Venice by gondola. They are being rowed by a swarthy man, not very skilled, who replaces the gondolier just as the party sets off for Venice. The new gondolier's role is not defined, but it is evident he is more interested in the conversation of the party than in rowing. On reaching Venice, a spirited dialogue ensues between Peter Hayward, the English servant, and Giacomo, his Italian counterpart. Hayward is an abomination, a prig who continually criticizes Italian society while praising the superiority of the English nation. Giacomo ignores the attacks, obviously accustomed to the complaints. He tells of a local legend associated with a decaying building on a narrow canal off the main canal. It belonged to a young nobleman whose betrothed died while he was off fighting against the Turks. Coming home during her funeral, he revived her; they married and had one son, who is still living in the house and who possesses great evil powers. He received these powers from his mother, who was never the same after her return from the dead.

The manuscript ends at this point, and any number of conclusions can be drawn from the sketchy beginning. Ruskin was experimenting with fiction and was rather uncomfortable with the experience. He wanted to deal with evil forces; later in life they haunted him, and he constructed a literary framework for the battle between the demonic and the angelic powers, but he could not develop the theme. On a natural level, Ruskin does develop the fight between good and evil in *Leoni: A Legend of Italy*. Still under Adele's spell, he wrote this love story between Giulietta and the bandit Leoni. In his autobiography, Ruskin candidly admits that Leoni was he, "typical of what my own sanguinary and adventurous disposition would have been had I been brought up a bandit." Giulietta, was Adele who was amused rather than impressed by his literary accomplishment. In the romantic tale, Giulietta does not know that Leoni is a bandit, thinking that he is Francesco who cannot reveal his love to her father because of a family feud. Her brother Garcio knows nothing of the affair, but his life was spared by Leoni in a fight because he could not kill the brother of the woman he loved.

Leoni, an Italian Robin Hood, has to choose between his life and his love. Deciding he has no right to bring the noble Giulietta into his squalid existence, he sings a farewell song, revealing his identity. She cannot bear the separation, and flees with Leoni. The escaping lovers are discovered, and Garcio pursues them. He gets close enough to Leoni to kill him and aims his gun, but Giulietta, throwing herself in front of Leoni, is killed instead. Enraged, Leoni kills Garcio, and a great slaughter follows. The victorious bandits then look for their leader. They find his maniacal figure, haggard and unsteady, pacing to and fro at the locale of the battle. The tragic ending would scare away any woman, and Adele was no exception.

Both Velasquez and Leoni are embryonic Byronic heroes, dark and brooding characters. Byron was one of Ruskin's favorite authors, and it is not surprising that he should imitate his style. Although Velasquez's life is not told, there are enough signs to indicate a tragic ending. Leoni is a tragic figure, losing his beloved; instead of joining her in paradise, however, he haunts the living. Neither character is a fit companion for a beautiful woman, and the proper mix for a happy love relationship is not present in either tale.

Ruskin wrote a happy ending for *The King of the Golden River* although he was suffering from a severe depression after Adele Domecq's marriage to a French nobleman. Having a low opinion of fiction—Dickens, he thought, "taught us nothing—only painted it perfectly for us"—Ruskin nevertheless acknowledged that his fairy tale was inspired by Dickens and Grimm, along with his feeling for the Alps. The happy ending gave pleasure to children, and that was as it should be. Although Ruskin believed the tale to be "totally valueless, . . . I can no more write a story than compose a picture," it went through ten editions in his lifetime and has been frequently anthologized to the present day.

The King of the Golden River: Or, The Black Brothers, A Legend of Stiria, is set in an Alpine village. This didactic tale was not published until 1851 when he was still married to Effie Gray, for whom the preface states it was written, "solely for her amusement, without any idea of publication." The tale perfectly suited the Victorian sensibility, however, and the fine illustrations by Richard Doyle, more than ensured the success of the publication.

There are five main characters: Schwartz, Hans, and Gluck are brothers who own Treasure Valley, watered by the Golden River. Schwartz and Hans, the elder brothers, are ugly, cruel, and greedy; rich farmers, they kill everything that might threaten their crops and work their servants without wages—earning the nickname "Black Brothers." Gluck, a twelve-year-old, is handsome, kind, and generous. The other characters are fairies: South-West Wind and the King of the Golden River. South-West Wind comes to Gluck on a stormy night, wet and hungry, asking to be housed and fed. Fearing his brothers but following his own instincts, Gluck lets the fairy in and is about to feed him when his brothers return. They force him out, but not before the fairy says he will be back at midnight. He returns as a high velocity wind, destroying their home, crops, and farmland. The brothers having lost everything, are now desolate. They have some gold bars left which they melt down, but they squander the money drinking while keeping Gluck busy at the furnace.

Gluck's favorite mug is thrown into the flames, despite his protest, and out of it emerges the King of the Golden River, an eighteen-inch golden dwarf who informs Gluck that whoever throws three drops of holy water into the source of the Golden River will turn it into gold; if they throw unholy water, they shall be turned into black stones. The brothers fail and are turned into black stones. Gluck succeeds, but the river does not turn into gold; rather, another river springs up from the rocks and waters the parched land. In time, Treasure Valley becomes fertile; Gluck and all the inhabitants prosper, proving that the "inheritance, which had been lost by cruelty, was regained by love."

Major publications other than short fiction
POETRY: *Poems*, 1835, 1837; *Salsette and Elephanta*, 1839; *Poems—J. R.*, 1850; *The Poems of John Ruskin*, 1891.

NONFICTION: *On the Old Road*, 1834-1885, 1885; *The Diaries of John Ruskin*, 1835-1889; *The Seven Lamps of Architecture*, 1849; *Pre-Raphaelitism*, 1850; *The Stones of Venice*, 1851-1853; *The Construction of Sheepfolds*, 1851; *The Harbours of England*, 1856; *The Geology of Chamouni*, 1858; *The Unity of Art*, 1859; *Munera Pulveris*, 1862; *On the Forms of the Stratified Alps of Savoy*, 1863; *Sesame and Lilies*, 1865; *War*, 1866; *The Ethics of the Dust*, 1866; *The Crown of Wild Olive*, 1866; *Time and Tide*, 1867; *The Queen of the Air*, 1869; *The Future of England*, 1869; *Lectures on Art*, 1870; *Samuel Pront*, 1870; *Verona and Its Rivers*, 1870; *Fors Clavigera*, 1871-1884; *The Range of Intellectual Conceptions Proportioned to the Rank in Animated Life*, 1871; *Aratra Pentelici*, 1872; *Instructions in Elementary Drawing*, 1872; *The Eagle's Nest*, 1872; *The Relation Between Michael Angelo and Tintoret*, 1872; *The Nature and Authority of Miracle*, 1873; *Ariadne Florentina*, 1873; *Love's Meinie*, 1873-1878; *Val d'Arno*, 1874; *Deucalion*, 1875-1883; *Proserpina*, 1875-1886; *Mornings in Florence*, 1875-1877; *The Brantwood Diary of John Ruskin*, 1876-1884; *St. Mark's Rest; The History of Venice*, 1877-1884; *Guide to the Principal Pictures in the Academy of Fine Arts at Venice*, 1877; *Publications of St. George's Guild*, 1878-1885; *Notes by Mr. Ruskin on His Drawings by the Late J. M. W. Turner*, 1878; *Letters Addressed by Professor Ruskin to the Clergy on The Lord's Prayer and the Church*, 1879-1880; *The Laws of Fiesole: A Familiar Treatise on the Elementary Principles and Practice of Drawing and Painting as Determined by Tuscan Masters*, 1879; *The Bible of Amiens*, 1880-1885; *Elements of English Prosody for Use in St. George's Schools*, 1880; *Arrows of the Chace*, 1880; *The Pleasures of England*, 1884-1885; *Catalogue of a Series of Specimens in the British Museum Illustrative of the More Common Forms of Native Silica*, 1884; *The Art of England*, 1884; *The Storm Cloud of the Nineteenth Century*, 1884; *Praeterita*, 1885-1889; *Hortus Inclusus*, 1887; *Ruskiniana*, 1890-1892; *Letters from John Ruskin to William Ward*, 1893; *Lectures on Landscape*, 1897.

Bibliography
Benson, Arthur C. *Ruskin: A Study in Personality.*
Collingwood, W. G. *The Life of John Ruskin.*

James, William. *John Ruskin and Effie Gray.*
Leon, Derrick. *Ruskin: The Great Victorian.*
Quennell, Peter. *John Ruskin: The Portrait of a Prophet.*
Rosenberg, John D. *The Darkening Glass: A Portrait of John Ruskin's Genius.*
Viljoen, Helen Gill. *Ruskin's Scottish Heritage.*
Whitehouse, J. Howard. *Ruskin's Influence Today.*
Wilenski, Reginald H. *John Ruskin: An Introduction to Further Study.*

Eileen A. Sullivan

SAKI
Hector Hugh Munro

Born: Akyab, Burma; December 18, 1870
Died: Beaumont Hamel, France; November 14, 1916

Principal short fiction

Reginald, 1904; *Reginald in Russia*, 1910; *The Chronicles of Clovis*, 1911; *Beasts and Super-Beasts*, 1914; *The Toys of Peace*, 1919; *The Square Egg*, 1924.

Other literary forms

Saki's fame rests on his short stories, but he also wrote novels, plays, political satires, a history of imperial Russia, and journalistic sketches.

Influence

A comic chronicler of England's ruling class, Saki was to the Edwardians what Oscar Wilde had been to the *fin de siècle* and Evelyn Waugh, Nancy Mitford, and P. G. Wodehouse would be to the next generation. His descriptions of pre-War fashions and foibles are widely anthologized.

Story characteristics

Saki's elegant satires are brief, witty, and utterly unsentimental. Whether fanciful, bitter, or downright gruesome, they constantly rely on epigrams, ironic reversals, practical jokes, and surprise endings to pique interest without arousing feeling. Saki's perennial subjects are the members of a privileged class in pursuit of more privilege. His characters are not so much individuals as individuated parts of the social organism he dissects for his audience's amusement and education.

Biography

Born in colonial Burma to a family that had for generations helped to rule the British Empire, Hector Hugh Munro grew up in a Devonshire country house where, reared along with his brother and sister by two formidable aunts, he had the secluded and strictly supervised sort of childhood typical of the Victorian rural gentry. This upbringing decisively shaped—or perhaps warped, as some sources suggest—his character. After finishing public school at Bedford, Munro spent several years studying in Devonshire and traveling on the Continent with his father and sister. In 1893, he went to Burma to accept a police post obtained through his father's influence. Much weakened by recurrent malaria, he returned to Devonshire to convalesce and write. In the first years of the twentieth century he turned to journalism, wrote political satires, and served as a foreign correspondent in Eastern Europe and Paris. At this time he adopted the pseudonym "Saki," which may refer to the cupbearer in *The Rubáiyát of Omar Khayyám* (1859) or may contract "Sakya Muni," one of the epithets of the Buddha. After 1908, Saki lived and wrote in London. Despite being over-age and far from robust, he volunteered for active duty at the outbreak of World War I. Refusing to accept a commission, to which his social position entitled him, or a safe job in military intelligence, for which his education and experience equipped him, Munro fought as an enlisted man in the trenches of France. He died in action.

Analysis

Saki is a writer whose great strength and great weakness lie in the limits he set for himself. Firmly rooted in the British ruling class that enjoyed "dominion over palm and pine," Saki wrote about the prosperous Edwardians among whom he moved. His stories, comedies of manners, emphasize the social side of the human animal as they survey the amusements, plots, and skirmishes that staved off boredom for the overripe leisure class whose leisure ended in August, 1914, with the onset of World War I.

Just as Saki wrote about a particular class, so he aimed his stories at a comparatively small and select readership. Although he was indifferent to wealth, Saki subsisted by his pen; so he was obliged to write stories that would sell. From the first, he succeeded in producing the "well-made" story savored by literate but not necessarily literary readers of such respected journals as the liberal *Westminster Gazette* and the conservative *Morning Post*. His debonair, carefully plotted stories full of dramatic reversals, ingenious endings, and quotable phrases do not experiment with new literary techniques, but perfect existing conventions. Without seeming to strain for effect, they make of Hyde Park an enchanted forest or treat the forays of a werewolf as an ordinary country occurrence. Like the Paris gowns his fictional duchesses wear, Saki's stories are frivolous, intricate, impeccable, and, to some eyes, obsolete.

If Saki's background, subjects, and techniques were conventional, however, his values and sympathies certainly were not. As a satirist, he mocked the people he entertained. His careful portraits of a complacent ruling class are by no means flattering: they reveal all the malice, pettiness, mediocrity, and self-interest of people intent on getting to the top or staying there. His heroes—Reginald, Clovis, Bertie, and the like—are aristocratic iconoclasts who share their creator's distaste for "dreadful little everyday acts of pretended importance" and delight in tripping the fools and hypocrites who think themselves exceptional but walk the well-worn path upward. "Cousin Theresa," a variation on the theme of the Prodigal Son, chronicles the frustration of one such self-deluder.

In Saki's version of the parable, the wandering brother—as might be expected in an age of far-flung Empire—is the virtuous one. Bassett Harrow-cluff, a young and successful bearer of the "white man's burden," returns from the colonies after having cheaply and efficiently "quieted a province, kept open a trade route, enforced the tradition of respect which is worth the ransom of many kings in out of the way regions." These efforts, his proud father hopes, might earn Bassett a knighthood as well as a rest.

The elder brother Lucas, however, a ne'er-do-well London bachelor, claims to have his own scheme for certain success—a refrain that, appended to a song and embodied in a musical revue, should catch the ear of all London: "Cousin Theresa takes out Caesar,/Fido, Jock, and the big borzoi." Fate bears out Lucas' prophecy. Theresa and her canine quartet enthrall the city. Orchestras acquire the four-legged accessories necessary for proper rendition of the much-demanded melody's special effects. The double thump commemorating the borzoi rings throughout London: diners pound tables, drunks reeling home pound doors, messenger boys pound smaller messenger boys. Preachers and lecturers discourse on the song's "inner meaning." In Society, the perennial mystifications of politics and polo give way to discussions of "Cousin Theresa." When Colonel Harrowcluff's son is knighted, the honor goes to Lucas.

Saki's parable offers two lessons: an obvious one for the "eminent," a subtler one for the enlightened. If the reader takes the story as an indictment of a foolish society that venerates gimmicks and ignores achievements, that rewards notoriety rather than merit, he classes himself among the Bassett Harrowcluffs. For the same delicate irony colors Saki's accounts of both brothers' successes: whether this treatment whimsically elevates the impresario or deftly undercuts the pillar of empire is problematic. As Saki sees it, administering the colonies and entertaining the populace are equally trivial occupations. To reward Lucas, the less self-righteous of two triflers, seems just after all.

Saki, then, does not profess the creed of the society he describes; both the solid virtues and the fashionable attitudes of the adult world come off badly in his stories. In contrast to other adults, Saki's dandy-heroes and debutante-heroines live in the spirit of the nursery romp; and when children and animals appear (as they often do) he invariably sides with them. "Laura," a fantasy in which a mischievous lady dies young but returns to life first as an otter and then as a Nubian boy to continue teasing a pompous fool, is one of many stories demonstrating Saki's allegiance to *Beasts and Super-Beasts* at the expense of men and supermen.

Saki's favorites are never sweetly pretty or coyly innocent. The children, as we see in "The Lumber-Room," "The Penance," and "Morlvera," are cruel, implacable, the best of haters. The beasts, almost as fierce as the children, tend to be independent or predatory: wolves and guard dogs, cats great and small, elk, bulls, and boars figure in Saki's menagerie. Embodied forces of nature, these animals right human wrongs or counterpoise by their example the mediocrity of man throughout Saki's works, but nowhere more memorably than in the chilling tale of "Sredni Vashtar."

In "Sredni Vashtar," Conradin, a rather sickly ten-year-old, suffers under the restrictive coddling of his cousin and guardian, Mrs. De Ropp, a pious hypocrite who "would never, in her honestest moments, have confessed to herself that she disliked Conradin, though she might have been dimly aware that thwarting him 'for his good' was a duty which she did not find completely irksome." Conradin's one escape from her dull, spirit-sapping regime is the toolshed where he secretly cherishes Sredni Vashtar, the great ferret around whom he has fashioned a private religious cult. Offering gifts of red flowers, scarlet berries, and nutmeg that "had to be stolen," Conradin prays that the god Sredni Vashtar, who embodies the rude animal vitality the boy lacks, smite their common enemy the Woman. When Mrs. De Ropp, suspecting that the toolshed harbors something unsuitable for invalids, goes to investigate, Conradin fears that Sredni Vashtar will dwindle to a simple ferret and that he, deprived of his god, will grow ever weaker under the Woman's tyranny. Eventually, however, Conradin sees Sredni Vashtar the Terrible, throat and jaws wet with a dark stain, stalk out of the shed to drink at the garden brook and slip away. Mrs. De Ropp does not return from the encounter; and Conradin, freed from his guardian angel, helps himself to the forbidden fruit of his paradise—a piece of toast, "usually banned on the ground that it was bad for him; also because the making of it 'gave trouble' a deadly offense in the middle-class feminine eye."

The brutal vengeance of "Sredni Vashtar" demonstrates that Saki's preference is not founded on the moral superiority of children and animals. "The Open Window," probably Saki's most popular story, makes the point in a more plausible situation, where a "self-possessed young lady of fifteen" spins from the most ordinary circumstances a tale of terror that drives her visitor, the nervous and hypochondriacal Mr. Frampton Nuttel, to distraction. In the Saki world the charm and talent of the liar makes up for the cruelty of her lie; and the reader, cut adrift from his ordinary values, admires the unfeeling understatement of Saki's summing up: "Romance at short notice was her specialty." The reader joins in applauding at the story's end not injustice— the whimpering Nuttel gets no worse than he deserves—but justice undiluted by mercy, a drink too strong for most adults most of the time.

What Saki admires about the people and animals he portrays is their fidelity to absolutes. They follow their natures singlemindedly and unapologetically; they neither moralize nor compromise. Discussing the preferences of a character in his novel *When William Came* (1913), Saki indirectly explains his own austere code: "Animals . . . accepted the world as it was and made the best of it, and children, at least nice children, uncontaminated by grown-up influences, lived in worlds of their own making." In this judgment the satirist becomes misanthropist. Saki endorses nature and art, but rejects society.

It is this moral narrowness, this refusal to accept compromise, that makes Saki, despite the brilliance of his artistry, an unsatisfying writer to read in large doses. His dated description of a vanished world is really no flaw, for he does not endorse the dying regime but clearly shows why it ought to die. His lack of sentiment is refreshing; his lack of emotion (only in such rare stories as "The Sheep," "The Philanthropist and the Happy Cat," and "The Penance" does Saki credibly present deep or complex feelings) does not offend present-day readers long inured to black comedy. Saki's defect is sterility. He refuses to be generous or make allowances as he considers society, that creation of adults, and he sends us back empty-handed to the world of compromise where we must live.

Major publications other than short fiction

NOVELS: *The Unbearable Bassington*, 1912; *When William Came*, 1914.

PLAYS: *The Death-Trap*, 1924; *Karl-Ludwig's Window*, 1924; *The Watched Pot*, 1924.

NONFICTION: *The Rise of the Russian Empire*, 1900; *The Westminister Alice*, 1902.

Bibliography

Drake, Robert. *Saki: Some Problems and a Bibliography.*
Gillen, Charles H. *H. H. Munro (Saki).*
Lambert, J. W. "Introduction" in the *Bodley Head Saki.*
Munro, Ethel. *A Biography of Saki.*

Peter W. Graham

J. D. SALINGER

Born: New York, New York; January 1, 1919

Principal short fiction

Nine Stories, 1953; *Franny and Zooey*, 1961; *Raise High the Roof Beam, Carpenters and Seymour: An Introduction*, 1963; *The Complete Uncollected Stories of J. D. Salinger*, 1974.

Other literary forms

In addition to his short stories, J. D. Salinger has written one novel, *The Catcher in the Rye*, 1951.

Influence

The two decades following World War II may, with little exaggeration, be called the Age of Salinger. Not only is Salinger one of the best-selling authors since the war (*The Catcher in the Rye* has sold more than six million copies to date, placing it in the top fifty on the all-time list), but also he has received so much academic attention that one critic labeled this wealth of criticism the "Salinger Industry." Despite the academic overkill, however, Salinger's best work has an enduring quality that is enjoyed by a whole new generation of readers, most of whom were scarcely born when his major work was published.

Story characteristics

Rarely does anything "happen" in a Salinger short story. His structural development instead more closely resembles a dramatic scene filled with dialogue than an action-filled plot. He typically focuses on the conflict between an innocent, childlike character and the vulgar adult world. The typical Salinger hero is more preoccupied with spiritual realities than with the significance of temporal events.

Biography

Because of his reclusiveness little is known of Jerome David Salinger's life. He was born on January 1, 1919, the son of a Jewish father and an Irish mother—the same lineage as his fictional Glass children. He attended Valley Forge Military Academy (the model for Pency Prep in *The Catcher in the Rye*), where he wrote a school song still sung there. He enrolled in New York University for a semester in 1937 and in Ursinus College for a semester in 1938 and took a creative writing class at Columbia in 1939. Because his creative writing teacher was also the editor of *Story Magazine*, Salinger was first published there in March, 1940. In 1942 he was drafted into the army. He lugged his typewriter off to Europe and began publishing in such well-paying "slick" magazines as the *Saturday Evening Post, Collier's,* and *Esquire.* While in Europe, the story goes, Salinger is supposed to have met Ernest Hemingway, who expressed his delight with Salinger's work by blowing the head off a chicken with his Lugar. Discharged from the army in 1946, Salinger published his first story in *The New Yorker* and began his famous alliance with that magazine. The only personal interview Salinger ever granted was to a sixteen-year-old high school girl for the Clairmont, New Hampshire, *Daily Eagle* (November 13, 1953). He has now been silent for more than fifteen years, completely secluded on his New Hampshire farm, publishing nothing.

Analysis

Nine Stories contains, in their order of publication, all the stories written over a period of exactly five years (January 31, 1948, to January 31, 1953) which J. D. Salinger felt worth preserving. The nine stories form a thematic unit, moving from a suicide in the first one to a passive and transcendent acceptance of death in the final one. Each of the stories focuses on a moment of insight, or "epiphany," in the consciousness of the central character as he struggles between the innocent, imaginative world of the child and the crass, vulgar world of the adult.

"A Perfect Day for Bananafish" is probably the most enigmatic and frequently discussed of Salinger's short stories, and in many ways it provides the thematic key to Salinger's work. "A Perfect Day for Bananafish" is the first of the Glass family stories and introduces the fabulous Seymour Glass on the last day of his life. The story opens in a Florida hotel with Seymour's wife Muriel, whom Seymour has dubbed "Miss Spiritual Tramp of 1948," talking to her mother on the telephone. During the conversation the reader learns that Seymour has been exhibiting "funny" behavior—driving a car into a tree, insulting people, and playing the piano in the hotel lobby—and that Muriel is a rather shallow and snobbish girl who is as concerned with painting her nails and tweezing out hairs in her mole as she is with Seymour's emotional condition. The second scene shifts to the beach, where Seymour, like so many of Salinger's sensitive characters, is more comfortable with children than adults. Seymour talks with a delicate, birdlike young girl named Sybil and takes her into the water to look for "bananafish." Bananafish, explains Seymour, "swim into a hole where there's a lot of bananas. They've very ordinary fish when they swim *in.* But once they get in, they behave like pigs. Why, I've known some bananafish to swim into a banana hole and eat as many as seventy-eight bananas." Bananafish then die from "banana fever." In the final scene Seymour leaves the beach and returns to the room where Muriel is asleep. He calmly takes out a pistol and shoots himself.

Readers of Salinger's work have been strongly divided over the meaning of the bananafish parable and Seymour's consequent suicide. One view is that the bananas represent the mushy, bland temptations of a materialistic society. A bananafish then imprisons himself in a banana hole, through the surfeit of sensual pleasure, instead of remaining in the freedom of the open ocean. Banana fever is the disease of an unspiritual, overly materialistic society. Seymour, according to this view, is himself a bananafish, and his suicide is seen as despair over his own banana fever. One does not have to be a bananafish, however, in order to see a bananafish (Sybil sees them too), and another interpretation is that Seymour is the only spiritually perceptive person in a world filled with Spiritual Tramps. If one remembers that the epigraph that begins *Nine Stories* is a Zen Koan ("what is the sound of one hand clapping?"), then it is possible to view Seymour's suicide, like Teddy's death in the final story, as a positive act that comes from superior self-knowledge. For Zen teaches that in order to find the liberation of Nirvana one must learn to let go of one's life—to lose one's life is to find it.

Whether the Zen overtones of *Nine Stories* are as directly applicable to Seymour's death as they are to the later stories, "A Perfect Day for Bananafish" nevertheless illustrates the type of conflict that typifies a Salinger story: the sensitive and distraught adolescent (or child, or childlike adult) who is disturbed, nearly to the point of despair, by the vulgarity of the adult world. The typical Salinger protagonist is usually rescued from his despair through a private revelation which reveals either a transcendent reality, or a vision of childhood innocence, or both. Sometimes the realization that innocence is irrecoverable is part of the epiphany as well, as in "The Laughing Man" and "Pretty Mouth and Green My Eyes."

In "Uncle Wiggily in Connecticut" Salinger gives us his most touching rendition of how the crass adult world works to destroy innocence. The story opens in a darkening house in a Connecticut suburb (reminiscent of a banana hole) as Eloise Wengler receives a surprise visit from her former college roommate, Mary Jane. The reader learns from the dialogue that Eloise was once engaged to another member of the Glass family, Walt, who was killed in a freak accident during the war. The imaginative and spontaneous quality of Eloise's past relationship with Walt contrasts with her present loveless marriage. Walt Glass could make Eloise laugh and see the Candyland world of Uncle Wiggily, whereas her husband Lew is "unintelligent," takes the commuter train home, and fakes Jane Austen. This conflict is further personified in Eloise's myopic daughter, Ramona, whose real father, the story hints, was Walt Glass. Ramona shows traces of Walt's imaginative spontaneity in inventing an invisible playmate, "Jimmy Jimmereeno," yet Eloise seems determined to bully her into conformity. After Eloise and Mary Jane have talked over old times and drunk too much, Ramona reenters and announces that "Jimmy Jimmereeno" got "runned over" by a car. Eloise sends her to bed, but discovers later in the evening that Ramona is sleeping on the edge of her bed so as not to disturb her new imaginary playmate, "Mickey Mickeranno." Eloise angrily demands that Ramona move to the center of the bed, destroying the illusion. Suddenly filled with remorse over her loss of Walt and her treatment of Ramona, Eloise then goes downstairs to ask Mary Jane desperately, "I was a nice girl, wasn't I?" Her new awareness, as one critic has noted, is like someone in hell who has just realized where he is, but is unable to escape.

If there seems to be little hope for the Seymours and the Eloises in Salinger's fictional world, then the story of Staff Sergeant X in "For Esmé—with Love and Squalor" marks the thematic turning point in *Nine Stories*. The unidentified narrator of the story states that the story is intended "to edify, to instruct"—and the result is the triumph of successful communication between isolated human beings. The story unfolds in two scenes: the first describes the forces of love as the narrator recounts how he first came to meet Esmé in Devonshire, England, in 1944. During a rainy afternoon on his last day of a military training course, the narrator wanders into a church to observe a children's choir practice. He is especially taken by a thirteen-year-old girl with an "exquisite face," whom he later meets in a civilian tearoom across the street. With charming adolescent precocity, Esmé tells the narrator about her life: she and her brother Charles are orphans, their father having been "s-l-a-i-n" in North Africa, and Esmé continues to wear his navigator's chronometer on her slender wrist. Charles then tells the narrator a riddle ("What did one wall say to the other? Meecha at the corner!"), and the episode ends with the narrator promising to write an "extremely squalid and moving" story for Esmé.

The second scene is the squalid part and takes place in Bavaria several weeks after V-E Day. The narrator has suffered a nervous breakdown "rather like a Christmas tree whose lights, wired in series, must all go out even if one bulb is defective." His sense of identity is so shattered that he can only refer to himself in the third person, as Staff Sergeant X. Four times Sergeant X tries to reestablish successful communication with the outside world. In his first attempt he tries to respond to an anonymous inscription—"Dear God, life is Hell"—written in the flyleaf of a book he has found. His reply, however, is illegible. Next he tries to respond to an insensitive letter from his brother asking him for "a couple of bayonets or swasticas" for his kids, but Sergeant X can only tear it up and throw it away. His third confrontation is with his jeep partner, "Corporal Z," a predatory, glory-seeking soldier who has thrived on the war. Sergeant X can only turn away from him in disgust, throwing up in a trash can. Finally he opens a package that contains a letter from Esmé and the gift of her father's wristwatch, which she sends him as a "lucky talisman." The quixotic gesture of affection from Esmé lifts Sergeant X out of his despair and he is able to sleep. The selfless act of a child, whose beatific sign reaches through the horrors of war, keeps Sergeant X's 'f-a-c-u-l-t-i-e-s intact."

Although the final scene of "For Esmé—with Love and Squalor" involves spiritual regeneration, it is not overtly religious. The final two stories of *Nine Stories*, however, mark Salinger's increasing preoccupation with Zen Buddhism. Only through religion, Salinger suggests more and more strongly, can the squalor of life be overcome. "Daumier-Smith's Blue Period" is the story of a young twenty-year-old artist who fabricates an alias (Jean de Daumier-Smith—Salinger's own initials) and applies for a teaching position at a Montreal correspondence art school. The school is run by an inscrutable Japanese and is housed above an orthopedic appliance shop. Most of Daumier-Smith's students are unschooled amateurs who offer him little challenge: a Toronto housewife whose favorite artists are Rembrandt and Walt Disney, and a society photographer who submits a drawing of the "familiar, everyday tragedy of a chaste young girl, with below-shoulder-length blonde hair and udder-sized breasts, being criminally assaulted in church." His most sensitive pupil, however, is a nun, Sister Irma, who paints religious scenes alive with the teeming crowds of ordinary humanity. The selfless passion in Sister Irma's paintings leads Daumier-Smith to two epiphanies, or "Experiences," which help him regain his lost sense of identity and self-worth.

The first Experience happens one night as he stares into the window of the orthopedic appliance shop and comes to the conclusion that he will "always at best be a visitor in a garden of enamel urinals and bed pans, with a sightless, wooden dummy-deity standing by in a marked-down rupture truss." It is a bleak vision of egoless despair. The next night, however, Daumier-Smith again passes the orthopedic appliance shop window; this time a "hefty girl of about thirty" is rearranging the display. She stumbles over an enamel basin and falls; Daumier-Smith instinctively reaches out to catch her, bumping his fingers on the glass. He then sees the sun speeding toward his nose "at the rate of ninety-three million miles a second." After the blinding flash, in place of the urinals and bedpans, he sees a "shimmering field of exquisite, twice-blessed enamel flowers." In these two Zen-like experiences, Daumier-Smith first renounces his false sense of self-importance, and then achieves the wisdom of learning to see beauty in the sterile instruments of the sickroom.

In a tradition that has its roots in Huck Finn, Nick Carraway, and Nick Adams, Salinger's fiction dramatizes the isolation of the sensitive individual in a confusing and sometimes absurd world. Salinger heroes walk on the periphery of society as observers rather than participants, and they stay there—even Daumier-Smith, whose recovery seems to be complete, returns home only to watch "the American Girl in Shorts." Salinger's heroes struggle to make a private peace with the world, not to rejoin it. Withdrawal into private visions of religious mysticism, Salinger suggests, is the only intelligent response to contemporary society, and love is the only reality. Yet love for Salinger has a kind of asexual purity, and nowhere in his fiction is there a well-adjusted relationship between a man and a woman. Part of Seymour's motivation in his suicide, for example, seems to be an inability to handle his relationship with his wife; and Franny Glass, who apparently recovers from her nervous breakdown in *Franny and Zooey*, has a similar difficulty in handling a sexual relationship with her boyfriend. Adult sexuality is clearly a part of the phony and squalid world from which Salinger's characters retreat—as in "Pretty Mouth and Green My Eyes," the darkest of the nine stories. Salinger's wisest characters are children who are not bothered by libidinous concerns.

Salinger's fiction is curiously devoid of social criticism as well. As unhappy as the world makes his characters, they rarely take any overt action against it, and rarely does Salinger address larger social problems. His Glass family, for example, is half-Jewish (as is Salinger himself), yet only once, in "Down at the Dinghy," does he approach the larger ethnic concern of anti-Semitism. It is the story of four-year-old Lionel Tannenbaum, who has "run away" to the sailboat on the dock of his family's summer cottage because he has heard the maid refer to his father as a "big sloppy kike." Lionel, of course, does not understand what a kike is—he recognizes the slur as only a vague insult—and his running away is more the recurring pattern of childlike retreat than any anger against racism. Although the Salinger hero may feel rage over external conditions, he keeps his silence and makes only private gestures of protest. As Seymour Glass says in the later story, "Raise High the Roof Beam, Carpenters," the Gettysburg Address was a harmful thing for children to memorize because it celebrates a battle in which 51,112 men died. The only appropriate response for Lincoln, Seymour says, was to shake his fist at the audience and walk off the platform.

In the two decades following World War II, when most Americans were either trying to carve their own versions of the American Dream or else advocating social protest against that dream, Salinger's fiction sounded the call of retreat. The enormous popularity of his work indicates a growing undercurrent of agreement. *Franny and Zooey* was the number-two best seller in 1961, the year of the Bay of Pigs invasion, and number five in 1962, the year of the Cuban Missile Crisis. *Raise High the Roof Beam, Carpenters and Seymour: An Introduction* was the number-three best seller in 1963, the year of the Kennedy assassination. It now seems that Salinger has applied the silent retreat of his fictional characters to his own work: readers have not heard from him in more than fifteen years.

Major publications other than short fiction
NOVEL: *The Catcher in the Rye*, 1951.

Bibliography
Belcher, William F. and James W. Lee, eds. *J. D. Salinger and the Critics*.
French, Warren. *J. D. Salinger*.

Lundquist, James. *J. D. Salinger.*
Miller, James E. *J. D. Salinger.*

Robert J. McNutt

WILLIAM SANSOM

Born: London, England; January 18, 1912
Died: London, England; April 20, 1976

Principal short fiction

Fireman Flower and Other Stories, 1944; *Three*, 1946; *South: Aspects and Images from Corsica, Italy and Southern France*, 1948; *The Equilibriad*, 1948; *Something Terrible, Something Lovely*, 1948; *The Passionate North: Short Stories*, 1950; *A Touch of the Sun*, 1952; *Lord Love Us*, 1954; *A Contest of Ladies*, 1956; *Among the Dahlias and Other Stories*, 1957; *Selected Short Stories*, 1960; *The Stories of William Sansom*, 1963; *The Ulcerated Milkman*, 1966; *The Vertical Ladder and Other Stories*, 1969; *Hans Feet in Love*, 1971; *The Marmalade Bird*, 1973.

Other literary forms

In addition to his short fiction, William Sansom wrote novels, children's books, travel books, criticism, and other works; he was also an editor of stories (*Choice: Some New Stories and Prose*, 1946; Edgar Allan Poe's *The Tell-Tale Heart and Other Stories*, 1948) and translator of Astrid Bergman's *Chendru: The Boy and the Tiger* (1960). He won grants from The Society of Authors and was elected Fellow of the Royal Society of Literature (1951).

Influence

Despite Sansom's wartime histories and excellent travel books, his sensitive children's books, and even his powerful novels it is as a strikingly prolific and first-rate short-story writer that Sansom had his chief influence. Although few could equal his photographic eye and even fewer could write as successfully as he did in the style and tradition of Franz Kafka, inevitably his achievement—he was in the view of many the leading British short-story master at the time of his early death—tempted others to adopt his manner and his method. Yet imitators could not copy Sansom's jaded and alert persona, see both people and machinery as at one and the same time quite real and ominously symbolic, view the "ordinary" from an eccentric point of view, find "trivial" events and "shallow" people as worthy of analysis and yielding startling insights, copy his detailed sense of place, and try to write about the astonishing aspects of everyday events.

In fine, Sansom was not "the English Kafka," as once was said; and now there is no English (or American) Sansom. The thirty-three stories he personally collected for *The Stories of William Sansom* received the unequivocal praise of another eminent master of short fiction, Elizabeth Bowen, who termed William Sansom a "short-storyist by birth, addiction, and destiny."

Good as they are, Sansom's novels tend to be recalled in terms of brief episodes, highlighted scenes. His short stories, however, remain in the memory whole and intensely vivid. In an age in which the novel is more admired than the short story, perhaps his greatest contribution has been to show irrefutably the essential glories of the more economical form.

Story characteristics

Sansom's thirty-three representative stories in the collected edition of 1963 have no common factor except high quality, a certain emphasis upon the sense of place, and the importance of both sensation and stance. The stories range from the frightening to the farcical and from the psychological to the melodramatic. Some are dedicated to surfaces and some to deep symbols, some to satire and some to sadness. If one has to single out *the* Sansomesque essence and state it in a word, the word has to be *mood*—but the way that it is achieved, whether with a mosaic of physical facts or an insight of psychological penetration, with a seemingly lucky odd angle of vision or an obviously careful buildup of literary texture, varies from one story or sketch or tale or allegory to the next. Sansom constantly reinvents the short story to tell of anything from deeply disturbing horrors to seemingly innocuous anecdotes.

One more thing is always there: what Sansom called "a state of continual wonder at life." He added: "Even if the subject or episode is sordid, or plain humdrum, that amazement is still there. It is the sense of this which I want to convey to others."

Biography

The London where William Sansom was born, the England where he lived, the Europe where he traveled and studied, are very much part of his work, meticulously detailed and significantly depicted. The world in which he lived in all its extraordinary and ordinary aspects he reports with facility in amazing and concrete particularity. He began with nightmare tales in the style of Kafka in *Fireman Flower and Other Stories*, based upon experiences in the Fire Service in the London Blitz of World War II. He says "the Blitz taught me to write seriously" and after writing thereafter for periodicals (*Horizon, New Writing, Cornhill Magazine*) and for the screen he "risked the purely literary life" at age thirty: it was "now or never," he reported.

His novels, from *The Body* (1949) on, although *The Face of Innocence* (1951) is an important fiction, never put him in the first rank; but his short stories gave him a really significant place in literature. From 1944 until his death in 1976 he was a professional writer who never forgot what he learned in his travels as a student in Germany and elsewhere (a sense of place), advertising (grab the attention and hold it), or in The Blitz ("the suddenly more serious texture of life, and the foreshortened expectation of it.").

Analysis

Calling William Sansom's descriptive power "a steady fireworks," American short-story writer Eudora Welty wrote that he "makes you see, hear, taste, touch and smell to his order," and when places not only come alive for the reader but also take on an eerie, unforgettable significance, he is at his very best. Sansom is often said to have a sense of isolation and *Angst* (borrowed from Kafka), this sense is exemplified by the story "Episode at Gastein." In this long story Sansom has the space he requires to work his magic; the geography interpenetrates with an otherwise ordinary story of an aged aristocrat (Ludwig de Broda) whose affair with a charming and much younger woman (Laure Perfuss) is shattered by the intervention of a young ski instructor. The story ends sadly and it is the quality of the writing, "rather than the terrain of his observation" (as one critic says), that makes the story so evocative, so echoing. Not even *The Cautious Heart* (1958), with all the scope of a novel, exceeds "Episode at Gastein" in evoking a place and relating it to a story of the "sad, muted comedy of middle-aged love."

Another excellent story is "A Helping Hand," in *The Marmalade Bird*, in which a Greek peasant robs and rapes a lady tourist and then hacks off some of her hair, crams it under the hat he steals from her, and in this foolish disguise sets off for Athens, hoping to get away unnoticed. Where another writer would have made this a violent and horrible story, Sansom concentrates on the feelings of the principals, especially the arousal of the peasant and the victim's subsequent wishing him well. Although the word *eccentric* is frequently used in discussing Sansom, here he is not off center at all: he has simply chosen (as critics have noted) a sentient center that would have been "authentically after the heart of Henry James or Joseph Conrad."

A number of Sansom stories could be adduced to prove his famed brilliance, from the pervasiveness of horror created in a West Highland landscape for a couple on a holiday to the shenanigans in a seaside hotel for retired actors when hilarity results from its being mistaken for a hotel by a bunch of contestants in a silly beauty contest. In "The Vertical Ladder," terror results from the situation when Flegg, a prideful young man climbs up the ladder on the side of a frightening storage tank only to discover that the top rungs, rusted, will not let him reach the top and his acrophobia and dizziness will not permit him to descend. Terror is also the final product of an astonishing relationship suddenly developed between a young lady and a strangler who creeps in her window at night in "Various Temptations." Who but Sansom could describe what a man thinks when, fighting a fire in wartime London, a brick wall collapses on him ("The Wall"), or how a man feels when he gallantly dashes into the ocean ("To the Rescue!") to save a drowning child, has to give up, and has to face the scorn of another man who did succeed in effecting the rescue?

Harvey Breit praises Sansom for not attempting what he cannot do but it is difficult to see what is beyond his powers. He can deal with philosophical questions and farcical stock situations, but generally he is more English than continental and avoids both the speculative and the stereotypical. He has the experience to write of burning buildings in World War II ("Fireman Flower") and the audacity to create a character called World Whore One (in *Hans Feet in Love*, 1971, a novel composed of related stories or sketches). He can chart the movement from panic to despair in the gentleman who runs into a lion loose in the zoo—and is ignored by the lion ("Among the Dahlias"). He can seriously talk to the reader at length ("How Claeys Died") or in passing, with a wry smile: "It was plain that the conversation was not to become general" ("The Smile"). He can make something of the *nothing* of quotidian lives ("Down at the Hydro") or describe a "queer-eyed" girl and a young man whose eyes "bristled with sneaky contempt" and make readers ask *what are they going to do?* as if Sansom were a mere reporter rather than the creator of these fictitious characters.

In 1971 Gavin Ewart wrote in *London Magazine* that "Sansom is certainly one of the best short story writers in England now. The best, some people would say." John Lucas hailed him in *Contemporary Novelists* (1972) as "at his best one of the most gifted writers we have" and averred that "with the exception of Angus Wilson there is no other writer who has done as much . . . to keep the short story alive and well." Now Sansom himself is, unfortunately, no longer alive; his stories, however, will live for a very long time.

Sansom, who told *Who's Who* his favorite recreation was watching, did not write grandiosely despite his great gifts. In fact, his novels tended to feature individual scenes, and some critics tended to review them as short stories that had been allowed to get out of hand. The 15,000 words of his "Episode at Gastein" leave nothing more to be said, and the very much briefer "The Vertical Ladder" shocks because of its concentration as well as its subject: even the gasometer Flegg climbs is no higher than a tenement, just high enough to tempt and defeat adolescent bravado. Critic Frederick R. Karl complained that Sansom was also a miniaturist in feelings and thoughts: "The range of Sansom's fiction is great, but it is a range of location and situation rather than one of emotion and ideas. . . . His body of work is stylistic, not intellectual." Craftsman Elizabeth Bowen understood more, however, stressing that sensation was the subject and the substance of a Sansom story and the emotions "sensations of emotion." This was perfectly suited to the short story's length, for one cannot string out a crisis in a story that is "a matter of bringing sensation to a peak where it must either splinter or dissolve because it can no more." The necessity for economy plays right into the hands of Sansom's imagination, an imagination that a reviewer for *The New York Times* once called "forceful, at times all but hallucinated," one that Hillary Corke in *The New Republic* saw as forever asking the question related more to sensation than to intellect. In operating in this way Sansom got right to the heart of the short story; as Bowen says, he "is not writing *for* effect, he is dealing *in* it, and masterfully."

Major publications other than short fiction
NOVELS: *The Body*, 1949; *The Face of Innocence*, 1951; *A Bed of Roses*, 1954; *The Loving Eye*, 1956; *The Cautious Heart*, 1958; *The Last Hours of Sandra Lee*, 1961 (also published as *The Wild Affair*, 1964); *Goodbye*, 1966;. *A Young Wife's Tale*, 1974.

NONFICTION: *The Icicle and the Sun*, 1958; *The Bay of Naples*, 1960; *Blue Skies, Brown Studies*, 1961; *Away to It All*, 1964; *Grand Tour Today*, 1968.

Bibliography
Allen, Walter E. *The Modern Novel in Britain and the United States.*
Burgess, Anthony. *The Novel Now.*
Lucas, John. "William Sansom," in *Contemporary Novelists.*
Michel-Michot, Paulette. *William Sansom: A Critical Assessment.*
Nemerov, Howard. "Sansom's Fictions," in *Kenyon Review.* XVII (1955), pp. 131-134.
Val Baker, Denys, ed. *Modern British Writing.*

Leonard R. N. Ashley

WILLIAM SAROYAN

Born: Fresno, California; August 31, 1908
Died: Fresno, California; May 18, 1981

Principal short fiction

The Daring Young Man on the Flying Trapeze, 1934; *Inhale and Exhale*, 1936; *Three Times Three*, 1936; *Little Children*, 1937; *Love, Here Is My Hat and Other Short Romances*, 1938; *The Trouble with Tigers*, 1938; *Peace, It's Wonderful*, 1939; *My Name Is Aram*, 1940; *Fables*, 1941; *Dear Baby*, 1944; *The Saroyan Special*, 1948; *The Assyrian and Other Stories*, 1950; *The Whole Voyald and Other Stories*, 1956; *William Saroyan Reader*, 1958; *After Thirty Years: The Daring Young Man on the Flying Trapeze*, 1964.

Other literary forms

William Saroyan has published more than forty-five books, including novels, plays, and several volumes of memoirs and autobiography. Among his most famous plays are *My Heart's in the Highlands* (1939) and *The Time of Your Life*, which in 1939 was awarded the Pulitzer Prize, which Saroyan rejected because he "did not believe in official patronage of art." His screenplay, *The Human Comedy*, was one of the most popular wartime films and was later revised into a successful novel. Saroyan's talents also extend to songwriting, and his most famous effort was "Come On-a My House."

Influence

In America, Saroyan has been an immensely popular writer, but many critics have dismissed him as "sentimental." His European critical reception, however, has been almost universally positive. In France and Italy, for example, Saroyan is regarded as one of the major American writers, and his work has been widely translated. His short stories, well over five hundred in number, have been published in numerous magazines throughout the world and collected into widely read anthologies. His characters' cheerful attitude in the face of cultural and financial adversity has won the author many adherents; and his unique style has been emulated by other writers who lack his unique outlook and control of craft.

Story characteristics

Autobiographical in mode, Saroyan's stories draw upon the author's experiences growing up in an Armenian neighborhood in Fresno, California. His stories relate the experiences and insights of the downtrodden and struggling working classes of various ethnic backgrounds, who, despite adversity, retain a zest for life, who savor all experience, and who maintain their sensitivity, receptivity, and good humor against often overwhelming economic and social odds. The stories range from whimsical, almost plotless, rambles to nostalgic and elegiac evocations of rich texture and locale. Even when not writing in the first person, Saroyan's own consciousness pervades his work, lending all of his fiction a unified voice and vision.

Biography

William Saroyan was born in Fresno, California, in 1908. His father, who died when William was two, was a minister-turned-grape farmer; upon his death, young Saroyan spent seven years in an orphanage, after which his family was reunited. He worked at many odd jobs, including a stint as a telegraph operator, spending most of his time, as he has to this day, in Fresno and San Francisco. His first short stories began to appear in 1934 and found instant success. In his first year as a writer his work appeared in the O'Brien volume of *The Best Short Stories*, and he published what is still his best-received volume of short stories, *The Daring Young Man on the Flying Trapeze*. Since then he has produced an amazingly prolific stream of short stories, plays, novels, and memoirs. He was twice married to Carol Marcus, by whom he had two children. Saroyan lived for a time in Europe, but has since returned to America.

Analysis

While William Saroyan has cultivated his prose to evoke the effect of a "tradition of carelessness," of effortless and sometimes apparently formless ruminations and evocations, he is in reality an accomplished and conscious stylist whose influences are varied and whose total effect is far more subtle than the seemingly "breezy" surface might at first suggest. His concern for the lonely and poor—ethnic outsiders, barflies, working girls, children—and their need for love and connectedness in the face of real privation recall Sherwood Anderson. All of Saroyan's best work is drawn from his own life (although the central character must be regarded as a persona, no matter how apparently connected to the author). In this aspect, and in his powerful and economical capacity to evoke locale and mood, Saroyan is in the tradition of Thomas Wolfe. The empathetic controlling consciousness and adventurous experiments with "formless form" also place Saroyan in the tradition that includes Walt Whitman and Gertrude Stein. It might also be noted that Saroyan's work shows the influence of Anton Chekhov in his use of seemingly "plotless" situations which nevertheless reveal some essential moment in the characters' lives and philosophical insight into the human condition.

Certainly, while the tone of Saroyan's stories evolves from the richly comic to the stoical to the sadly elegiac mood of his later work, his ethos stands counter to the naturalists and the ideologically programmatic writers of the 1930's, the period during which he produced some of his best work. Often his stories portray the world from the perspective of children, whose instinctual embrace of life echoes the author's philosophy. Saroyan has written, "If you will remember that living people are as good as dead, you will be able to perceive much that is very funny in their conduct that you might never have thought of perceiving if you did not believe that they were as good as dead." Both the tone and outlook of that statement are paradigmatic.

The title story of his first and most enduring collection, "The Daring Young Man on the Flying Trapeze," is still one of the most ambitious stylistic exercises of the Saroyan canon, and an embodiment of the first phase of his career. The impressionistic style uses a welter of literary allusions in a stream-of-consciousness technique to portray the inner mind of an educated but destitute writer during the Depression who is literally starving to death as his mind remains lucid and aggressively inquiring. The poignant contrast between the failing body and the illuminated mind might evoke pity and compassion on the part of the reader, but somehow Saroyan invokes respect and acceptance as well.

The story begins with the random associated thoughts of the half-dreaming writer which reveal both the chaos of the present era—". . . hush the queen, the king, Karl Franz, black Titanic, Mr. Chaplin weeping, Stalin, Hitler, a multitude of Jews . . ."—and the young protagonist's literary erudition: ". . . Flaubert and Guy de Maupassant, a wordless rhyme of early meaning, Finlandia, mathematics highly polished and slick as green onions to the teeth, Jerusalem, the path to paradox."

Upon awakening, the writer plunges into "the trivial truth of reality." He is starving, and there is no work. He ironically contemplates starvation as he combines the food in a restaurant into a mental still life; yet without a shred of self-pity, and with great dignity in spite of a clerk's philistine and patronizing attitude, he attempts to obtain a job at an employment agency where the only skill which the writer can offer to a pragmatic world is the ability to type. He is relieved when there is no work because he can now devote his remaining energies to writing a literary last will and testament, an "Apology for Permission to Live."

He drinks copious amounts of water to fill his empty belly, steals some writing paper from the Y.M.C.A., and repairs to his empty apartment to compose his manifesto. Before beginning to write, he polishes his last remaining coin—a penny (he has sold his books for food, an act of which he feels ashamed)—and savors the "absurd act." As he contemplates the words on the coin which boast of unity, trust in God, and liberty, he becomes drowsy; and he takes final leave of the world with an inner act of grace and dignity reminiscent of the daring young man of the title. His last conscious act of thought is the notion that he ought to have given the coin to a child.

A child could buy any number of things with a penny. Then swiftly, neatly, with the grace of the young man on the trapeze he was gone from his body. . . . The city burned. The hearded crowd rioted. The earth circled away, and knowing that he did so, he turned his lost face to the empty sky and became dreamless, unalive, perfect.

The story embodies Saroyan's control of his materials and the sensitive and ironic understatement for which he is famous. While the stories written during the Depression express bitterness about the situation, Saroyan eschews political solutions of any particular stripe and emphasizes the dignity of the individual and his tenacious connection to the forces of life and survival with grace and good humor.

A second collection which gained worldwide fame is the series of interconnected stories which form the book *My Name Is Aram*. Told through the eyes of the title character, a young boy in the milieu of Armenian Fresno, the collection reveals the characteristics of the stories of the middle part of Saroyan's career and foreshadows the direction taken in his later work. The reader sees childlike adults and children imbued with the burdens of adulthood. Throughout, the collection explores the often contradictory claims of emotional, poetic, and instinctive needs and the claims of reality. The author's vision is dualistic. Some of the stories show a happy symbiosis between the poetic and the rational needs of his characters; others portray the conflicting demands unresolved. Even in the latter case, however, his characters cheerfully accept their fate, not with a stoicism so much as with a recognition that such a condition is a necessity to life and does not preclude savoring the moments of beauty which occur even in the midst of squalor or hardship.

The first aspect of the mature and late phase of Saroyan's writing is aptly illustrated by the story "The Summer of the Beautiful White Horse." Typical of Saroyan's boyhood reminiscences, this tale concerns the seven-year-old Aram Garoghlanian and his slightly older cousin Mourad, who "borrow" a horse from their neighbor's barn and keep him for months at an abandoned farm, enjoying clandestine early morning rides. The owner of the horse, John Byro, complains to the boys' uncle Khosrove, a Saroyan eccentric who responds, "It's no harm. What is the loss of a horse? Haven't we all lost the homeland? What is this crying over a horse?" When the owner complains that he must walk, the uncle reminds him that he has two legs. When Byro laments that the horse had cost him sixty dollars, the uncle retorts, "I spit on money." Byro's loss of an agent to pull his surrey brings a roar of "Pay no attention to it!"

Uncle Khosrove's attitude is typical of the charming impracticality of many of Saroyan's characters. When the boys at last secretly return the animal, the farmer is merely thankful that it has been returned and makes no attempt to find out who had stolen it. He marvels that the horse is in better condition than when it had been stolen. The story charmingly resolves the conflicting demands of the poetic and the practical (in favor of the poetic).

"Pomegranate Trees" illustrates the darker and more elegiac side of the later Saroyan canon. Uncle Melik purchases some arid desert land which he intends to farm. The land is obviously impossible to render productive; yet the uncle persists in tilling the soil, planting his crops, and beating back the encroaching cactus while holding little dialogues with Aram and the prairie dogs. He decides against all reason to produce pomegranate trees, since he associates the fruit with his Assyrian past; but the trees are stunted, and the fruit yield is merely enough to fill a few boxes. When the meager harvest fails to bring a high enough price to suit Melik, he has the fruit sent back to him at still more expense. For the uncle, the enterprise has nothing to do with agriculture. "It was all pure aesthetics. . . . My uncle just liked the idea of planting trees and watching them grow."

The real world of unpaid bills intrudes, however, and the man loses the land. Three years later Aram and his uncle revisit the land which had given Melik such quixotic pleasure. The trees have died and the desert has reclaimed the land. "[T]he place was exactly the way it had been all the years of the world." Aram and his uncle walk around the dead orchard and drive back to town. "We didn't say anything because there was such an awful lot to say, and no language to say it in."

There is nominal defeat, yet the still wistfully remembered joy in attempting the impossible for its own sake is a counterweight to the sadness of the finality of the experience. Such a resonance is at the heart of Saroyan's ethos, expressed in countless stories which have made him a popular favorite, and which are beginning to elicit a high critical acclaim as well.

Major publications other than short fiction

NOVELS: *The Human Comedy*, 1943; *The Adventures of Wesley Jackson*, 1946; *The Twin Adventures*, 1950; *Rock Wagram*, 1951; *Tracy's Tiger*, 1951; *The Laughing Matter*, 1953; *Mama, I Love You*, 1956; *Papa, You're Crazy*, 1957; *Boys and Girls Together*, 1963; *One Day in the Afternoon of the World*, 1964.

PLAYS: *My Heart's in the Highlands*, 1939; *The Time of Your Life*, 1939; *Three Plays*, 1941; *Razzle-Dazzle*, 1942; *Get Away, Old Man*, 1944; *Jim Dandy, Fat Man in a Famine*, 1947; *Don't Go Away Mad and Other Plays*, 1949; *The Cave Dwellers*, 1958.

NONFICTION: *The Bicycle Rider in Beverly Hills*, 1952; *Here Comes, There Goes, You Know Who*, 1962; *Not Dying*, 1963; *Look at Us, Let's See, Here We Are*, 1967 (with Arthur Rothstein); *Letters from 74 rue Taitbout: Or, Don't Go, But If You Must, Say Hello to Everybody*, 1969; *Places Where I've Done Time*, 1972; *Sons Come and Go, Mothers Hang in Forever*, 1976; *Chance Meetings*, 1978; *Obituaries*, 1979.

Bibliography

Floan, Howard R. *William Saroyan.*

Heiney, Donald. "William Saroyan," in *Recent American Literature*.
Kherdian, David. *A Bibliography of William Saroyan*.

David Sadkin

JEAN-PAUL SARTRE

Born: Paris, France; June 21, 1905
Died: Paris, France; April 15, 1980

Principal short fiction
Le Mur, 1939 (*The Wall*).

Other literary forms
Jean-Paul Sartre is best known as the major exponent of the Existentialist philosophy, which can be traced throughout his vast aesthetic production: novels, plays, short stories, essays, and books of literary criticism and philosophy. Some of his works have been adapted for television and the cinema.

Influence
Because one of the major tenets of existentialism is action, and the committing to action (*engagement*) of one's beliefs, Sartre's fiction can be viewed as one of the world's best examples of didactic literature, fulfilling Alexander Pope's prescription that literature should "delight and instruct." Not that every work must be interpreted along existential lines; on the contrary, Sartre was such a gifted artist that each work succeeds on its own merits. Knowledge of the existential ethic, however, permits seeing broad possibilities of interpretation along philosophical lines. His creative writing can be viewed as an artistic extension of his philosophy, and is largely responsible for the mid-century Literature of the Absurd, leading to the New Novel and the New Cinema.

Story characteristics
Sartre's one volume of short fiction, *Le Mur* (1939, *The Wall*), may be the best example of his creative talent. As was the case for Gustave Flaubert half a century before him, the limits of the short story encouraged this otherwise prolific author toward self-control and self-discipline. The result is an outstanding collection of stories, each of which presents some kind of "wall" or barrier that separates the narrator from others or from the "real" world. In Sartre's view, the bourgeois world of preestablished order and determinism had been replaced by a world out of control, disorganized, chaotic, and by extension absurd; these qualities were heightened by the accelerating events of World War II. Sartre believed that it is man's commitment to action that lends a semblance of order and rationality to life and leads to humanism. As a result, instead of presenting omniscient narrators who control their worlds like gods (Honoré de Balzac, for example, or the modern novelist François Mauriac), Sartre observed that "God isn't a novelist—and neither is François Mauriac!" To present this absurd world, Sartre used a very humanly limited

and highly subjective narrator whose mental and philosophical evolution constituted the subject of his short stories.

Biography

A cousin of the celebrated Dr. Albert Schweitzer, Jean-Paul Sartre was born in Paris, received a distinguished education at the École Normale Supérieure, won first place at the *aggrégation* examinations in philosophy (second place went to Simone de Beauvoir, the novelist and philosopher with whom Sartre has been associated ever since), and then taught philosophy at *lycées* in Le Havre and in Paris. In 1933, he went to Berlin to study phenomenology with Edmund Husserl. During the war he was taken prisoner and spent some time in a German camp. After his release, he returned to Paris, where he continued teaching, writing, and working with the Resistance. The war lent substantial validity and appeal to his expression of the existential philosophy, and Sartre acquired considerable fame and success. (It must be remembered that Sartre did not found the philosophy of existentialism, but was rather one of its chief exponents. Its origins lie with the Danish philosopher Søren Kierkegaard (1813-1855), the German Edmund Husserl with whom Sartre studied in Berlin, Martin Heidegger and Karl Jaspers, and the French Christian philosopher Gabriel Marcel. Some trace its lineage back to Blaise Pascal. Rather than being a systematic, rational philosophy, existentialism is instead an attitude, and its followers are split into two distinct groups, atheistic and Christian existentialists.

After the war, Sartre established, with friends Simone de Beauvoir and Maurice Merleau-Ponty, the literary and political review *Les Temps Modernes* to develop the applications of existentialism. After that time he published prodigiously in all genres. In 1964, he was awarded the Nobel Prize for Literature, but he refused to accept the honor on the grounds that it might compromise his philosophical and literary integrity. He continued to be active politically, philosophically and aesthetically until his death in 1980.

Analysis

In contrast to his more celebrated novels and plays, Sartre's single volume of short stories has attracted little public acclaim. This is perhaps because short fiction is less flamboyant and allows literary critics less scope for discussion. Like the reputation of Flaubert a century earlier, Sartre's reputation is based on other publications. Also like Flaubert, Sartre produced a single collection of short fiction that crystallized his aesthetic, and this aesthetic owes a great deal to the nineteenth century master who so obsessed him, and whose life bears such striking similarities to his own. The pieces that make up this slender volume contain in microcosm both the theories and the techniques that distinguish France's leading twentieth century intellectual.

Entitled *The Wall*, the collection presents characters questioning their relationship to the world, to other people, and essentially, to their own identity. The world exists, but has no meaning. In fact, existence is the only fact of which there is any certainty, and it is from man's existence that he creates essence and meaning. As a result, the meaninglessness of the world creates disgust in man, what Sartre calls nausea, and this disgust extends from him to others, to his relationships with others, and to his social institutions. Consequently, any significant act must be one that is moral, humanitarian, and fraternal. Because man is the sum total of his actions, it is easy for him to evaluate people and to know what and who they really are. This consciousness creates a new sense of responsibility and, simultaneously, a new sense of freedom.

The approach of World War II created a climate that was particularly favorable for the success both of the philosophy and of its aesthetic representation in *The Wall*. The title story is representative of all the others and will suffice as an example. Set in Spain during its Civil War, it has obvious applications to the French situation and to the universal dilemma of the captive, be he a civil prisoner or a prisoner of war, religion, or conscience. According to Sartre, the immediate reaction of cynicism and despair soon leads to an acknowledgment of the world's absurdity, and upon this fundamental notion all positive actions must be based. Pablo, captured with other Republican guerrillas, suffers not only discomfort but also great mental anguish while waiting for the inevitable moment of execution. Stalling for time, he provides false information to his captors to lead them on a wild goose chase after a guerrilla leader. To his surprise, he is not executed with the others, and later on, he learns why: the false information he had provided, by the wildest of chances, proved accurate. The guerrilla leader was killed, and Pablo was in fact responsible for this absurd death.

Recounted by Pablo in a stream-of-consciousness narrative, Sartre effectively grips his reader in this intense drama of the mind. With a colloquial vocabulary and brutal choice of detail, the verisimilitude of the experience cannot be escaped: the reader, too, is a captive in this absurd universe. When a man is up against the wall faced with the one fact of life, the inescapable certainty of death, then life acquires new meaning. This is the foundation of Sartre's existentialism.

Major publications other than short fiction

NOVELS: *La Nausée*, 1938 (*Nausea*); *Les Chemins de la Liberté* (*The Roads to Freedom*); *L'Âge de Raison*, 1945 (*The Age of Reason*); *Le Sursis*, 1945 (*The Reprieve*); *La Mort dans l'Âme*, 1949 (*Troubled Sleep*); *La dernière chance* (uncompleted).

PLAYS: *Les Mouches*, 1943 (*The Flies*); *Huis clos*, 1944 (*No Exit*); *Les Mains sales*, 1948 (*Dirty Hands*); *Le Diable et le bon Dieu*, 1951 (*The Devil and the Good Lord*); *Les Séquestrés d'Altona*, 1959 (*The Condemned of Altona*).

NONFICTION: *L'Être et le Néant*, 1943 (*Being and Nothingness*); *L'Existentialisme est un humanisme*, 1946 (*Existentialism is a Humanism*); *Qu'est-ce que la littérature*, 1947 (*What Is Literature*); *Baudelaire*, 1947; *Saint Genet, comédien et martyr*, 1952; *Critique de la raison dialectique*, 1960; *Les Mots*, 1964 (*The Words*); *L'Idiot de la famille: Gustave Flaubert*, 1972.

Bibliography

Bauer, George. *Sartre and the Artist*.
Idt, Geneviève. Le Mur *de Jean-Paul Sartre*.
McMahon, Joseph H. *Humans Being: The World of Jean-Paul Sartre*.
Peyre, Henri. *Jean-Paul Sartre*.
Thody, Philip. *Jean-Paul Sartre: A Literary and Political Study*.

Robert W. Artinian

MARK SCHORER

Born: Sauk City, Wisconsin; May 17, 1908
Died: August 11, 1977

Principal short fiction
The State of Mind, 1947; *Pieces of Life*, 1977.

Other literary forms
Mark Schorer was a prolific and successful writer in several genres, including biography, literary criticism, and the novel.

Influence
During the 1940's and 1950's Schorer was known mainly as a very skillful writer of fiction. As he turned his attention to literary scholarship and criticism, his reputation in those fields began to overwhelm his reputation for fiction. Unfortunately, his *Pieces of Life*, a fine work, was not noticed by many readers and quickly went out of print. His short stories deserve to be better known.

Story characteristics
Schorer wrote traditional rather than experimental stories, concentrating on psychological and sociological description. Some of his early stories are set in his native Wisconsin and he may well have become a regional writer like his boyhood friend August Derleth if he had not left the state.

Biography
Mark Schorer earned a B. A. at the University of Wisconsin, an M. A. at Harvard, and a Ph.D. in English from the University of Wisconsin. Later he became a professor, scholar, and one of this country's most eminent literary critics. He taught for many years at the University of California at Berkeley and briefly at other universities, including several abroad.

Analysis
Academics who write fiction are often very concerned with technique and use their critical skills to help them fill their work with symbols and image patterns and to develop characters and plot as do the literary masters. They also frequently create fiction that is dense with ideas. In short, they write the kind of stories that they enjoy teaching. At their worst, academics write mechanical stories that are much less satisfying than those created by non-academics who look into their hearts and write. At their best they are technically competent but not obtrusively so and they organically relate ideas to their plots; the result is a first-rate story such as Lionel Trilling's "Of This

Time, Of That Place." Mark Schorer's stories are not academic in these ways; the only obvious clues in them to his occupation are the professors who appear in some of them. Rather, most of his stories are autobiographical; their effectiveness is a result of his sensitive response to the events of his life and of his ability to use the knowledge he gained from those events. His literary training and his years in a sophisticated academic environment no doubt increased his sensitivity. A comment about the relation between art and life that Schorer makes in "The World We Imagine: Notes on the Creative Act and Its Function" is a useful guide to his own short stories: "the world that we create . . . depends in large part on the world that we inhabit."

In one sense the world that Schorer inhabited was the same world that all individuals inhabit, and this similarity of experience helps make his short stories significant. Schorer chronicles the universal experience encountered during the course of life: adjustment during childhood to tensions within the family and to the larger world outside the family, crises in career and marriage, and minor traumas at midlife caused in part by the persistence of memory. Schorer also describes aspects of life lying in both directions beyond the spectrum of everyday experience. In "The World We Imagine: Notes on the Creative Act and Its Function" he quotes T. S. Eliot on this expansion of experience: "the artist, I believe, is more *primitive*, as well as more *civilized*, than his contemporaries, his experience is deeper than civilization, and he only uses the phenomena of civilization in expressing it." In that essay Schorer describes the primitive or nighttime world that is invisible to the ordinary person and refers to its manifestations in the work of many other writers. A line of poetry that Schorer borrows from Wallace Stevens and uses as the epigraph of *The State of Mind*—"It was evening all afternoon"—suggests that in much of his own fiction Schorer tries to depict the nighttime world, which he probably experienced as a child.

The first story in *The State of Mind*, "In the Night," is, as its title implies, an excursion into the world of the night and a study of the dominant emotion of that world: fear. Many of this story's details indicate that the main character is about to travel into a more disturbing time. He is thirteen years old and thus on the threshold of adolescence, and it is autumn, the prelude to winter. Moreover, the story opens at dusk, and the disturbing loss of light as night approaches is exacerbated by an eerie mist. More frightening than imagining these future times is the trip backward through time that the boy takes by means of his memory. He repeatedly tries to remember one event for each year of his life, working backward from the year when the story takes place. This reverse chronicle includes only unpleasant experiences: a death, sickness, and, most disturbing of all, the events he can place in time, his mother's temporary flight from the family, although she went only a few feet from their house. This event happened when the boy was eight, and he can remember back to his fifth year but then "he always came finally to the place where there was nothing but darkness in the room under the eaves and the wind blowing and the train's whistle in the night, a sound that made him afraid in the lonely dark, as if he were all alone in the house and as if there were no people in the world, and sometimes he called his mother." These motifs— fear, train, mother, dark, loneliness—keep weaving into the story, but the boy is never quite able to understand their interrelations and to remember the cause of this emotion-laden cluster of images.

The boy later walks to the station to watch the arrival of the evening train, which fascinates him but also has a "monster engine" and is frightening. The cause of the boy's fright is, unbeknownst to him, implied by this experience at the depot. By this point he has traveled into the night world: when he walks back home "the night [is] black." Again he tries to remember his way back beyond the time when he was five years old, conjuring up a memory of his father's brutality and his mother's threat to leave later, an occurrence that he describes as having happened "once." This memory causes him to run home in panic to make sure that his mother is there. It thus becomes clear— and the boy recognizes it at least unconsciously—that his mother's threat to leave is the memory from his fifth year that he had been repressing. He had associated with it the train, the vehicle of escape from the village. Although he does not articulate his discovery, he has found the cause of his fear, the entrance into the nighttime world.

That world is revealed in a different way in "What We Don't Know Hurts Us," another story in *The State of Mind*. As it opens, the center of attention is Charles Dudley, who has recently moved to California from Boston and is being tormented by a yard that is regressing into a jungle and by a house that has been torn apart but not put back together. It soon becomes evident that the rest of his family is unhappy, too; his wife tells him that "it's no pleasure for me, either, living the way we are, nor is it for the children." His life is not the kind he wants: "he connected happiness with a certain luxury, and, probably, sexuality with elegance and freedom . . . and he knew that it was foolish to let impossibilities, as they faded, become forms of minor torture." Serious as these difficulties are, they are daytime phenomena, not the kind of nighttime horrors described in "In the Night."

The nighttime horrors in "What We Don't Know Hurts Us" are those that confront Dudley's son Gordon. He has found or, as his father and his principal suspect, has stolen a dollar and given it to another boy. Dudley sees only a problem with honesty, but his wife recognizes that Gordon gave the money to the boy, another pariah, to solidify his only friendship. To her this episode is touching proof of her son's frustration and loneliness, conditions that are exacerbated by her husband's lack of understanding and concern. After Gordon's problems are depicted, Dudley's problems can be viewed from a different perspective, and they seem trivial compared to his son's. Dudley's problems are important to him mainly because he fails to recognize the troubles that afflict others and, more important, because he fails to recognize how widespread loneliness is. That is, Dudley is trapped in his own ego so that he does not even perceive, much less try to alleviate, the loneliness suffered by others. In Schorer's terms, he sees only the daytime world: this story appropriately opens with a reference to "the mid-afternoon winter sun."

One's suspicion that many of the stories in *The State of Mind* are based on events that happened to Schorer is confirmed by *Pieces of Life*. The stories in that later book alternate with brief sketches that describe incidents in Schorer's life. In one of the sketches, for example, he describes his mother's leaving the family for a brief time, as does the mother in "In the Night." These sketches begin with his boyhood and proceed to his first meeting with his wife and then skip suddenly during his account of that meeting to a tender portrait of his relationship to her at the time he was writing *Pieces of Life*. Of these "autobiographical interstices" he writes that he

> . . . wanted the characters in the stories to act out their problems before a darker backdrop than the stories themselves provide, nothing lugubrious, nothing narcissistic certainly, nothing self-pitying, I trust, but yet something more shadowy, bleaker, than what goes on downstage.

The imagery in that statement suggests that these bits of autobiography are intended to show how Schorer became acquainted with the night and how he became interested in writing stories that reveal the nighttime world.

The central image of "A Lamp" seems to derive from a grotesque object that, according to one of the autobiographical interludes in *Pieces of Life*, stood in the home where Schorer grew up. Franklin and Flora Green, a middle-aged couple, are living temporarily in an apartment in Rome that contains the lamp, which "pretended to be a gigantic stalk of lilies." The Greens have been desultory tourists in Rome, but the lamp and a couple they see in a store window change their lives. The story ends as they tell each other about identical dreams that they had had. This strange ending is appropriate for this story, which has little physical action but subtly describes the characters' dramatic change in sensibility.

Like the two stories discussed above, "A Lamp" is about replacing superficial perception with incisive perception, but in this story, the penultimate one that Schorer wrote, the more incisive perception does not reveal horror. That is, "A Lamp" is a more optimistic story than the two earlier ones. The first sign of a change in the couple is unexpected: "suddenly he found himself looking at her. Something in her distracted tone had drawn his eyes to her, and he was *looking* at her. This was a shock because with it he knew that he had not really looked at her for years." Similarly, the significance of the couple observed in the store window is their "intense involvement, the absorption of one in the other." Soon Flora begins to ponder the lamp and she realizes that it and her name communicate a message that she cannot quite understand: that the lamp is a parody of nature and that her name, with its connotations of nature, suggests that she, too, is a parody. In other words, she is insufficiently involved with and thus insufficiently perceptive about her husband and the world in general. Both she and Franklin begin to take notes on their sightseeing, hoping thereby to sharpen their perceptions. This theme of increased perception is reinforced by the narrative voice's vivid rendering of Rome and of minute details. The meticulous observation can be seen in a description of some objects in the store window:

> a black armoire appliquéd with elaborate scrolls of mother-of-pearl, a commode with ormolu mounts, two long case clocks with intricate marquetry, a tochère in the window that held an ormolu clock in the shape of an urn, its pendulum swinging swiftly, and from the ceiling, a veritable crystal arbor of glittering lusters.

Schorer's final published story, "The Unwritten Story," seems to be auto-biographical only in the sense that while he was teaching in Italy he probably observed some details that he uses in it.. It is more subtle than the stories analyzed previously, but they provide a context in which its meaning can be grasped. It describes the efforts of Leslie and Marilyn Warden to relive a day they had spent fifteen years before. They find the town where that previous day's swimming trip began and even find the boatman who had accompanied them, but in the fifteen-year interim everything has dwindled. This story, however, is not about the melting snows of yesteryear. When it ends as Leslie asks Marilyn, "who's the best unpublished writer that you know?" one can see that it is about Leslie's realization of his own ineptness. Because of an inheritance, he had been able to stop teaching in order to write, but he has not written, which calls into question the value of his life. Nor can he respond as sensitively or graciously as does his wife to the events and people they encounter. In fact, he cannot even drive his car competently. The tone at the end of the story is calm and the meaning somewhat obscure, but Leslie is another of Schorer's characters who has finally seen the nighttime world.

Both "A Lamp" and "The Unwritten Story" are fine works, just as *Pieces of Life* is a solid book and Schorer's early novel *A House Too Old* (1935), which is a fictionalized version of his native Sauk City's history, is very interesting. It is unfortunate that his fiction is not better known.

Major publications other than short fiction

NOVELS: *A House Too Old*, 1935; *The Hermit Place*, 1941; *The Wars of Love*, 1954.

NONFICTION: *William Blake: The Politics of Vision*, 1946; *Sinclair Lewis: An American Life*, 1961; *The World We Imagine: Selected Essays*, 1968; *D. H. Lawrence*, 1969.

Bibliography
Derleth, August. *Writing Fiction*.
Stark, John. "Wisconsin Writers," in *1977 Wisconsin Blue Book*.

John Stark

DELMORE SCHWARTZ

Born: Brooklyn, New York; December 8, 1913
Died: New York, New York; July 11, 1966

Principal short fiction
In Dreams Begin Responsibilities, 1939; *The World Is a Wedding*, 1948; *Successful Love, and Other Stories*, 1961.

Other literary forms
Besides being an author of short fiction, Delmore Schwartz was a poet, critic, editor, and a prolific letter writer to all the leading literary luminaries in the world, including Ezra Pound, W. H. Auden, T. S. Eliot, and Robert Lowell, all of whom valued his opinions on their work. A book of his children's verse, *"I Am Cherry Alive," the Little Girl Sang*, has recently been published. He was also a playwright.

Influence
Although Schwartz's poems have been widely anthologized, only a few of his stories were reprinted until the recent flood of memoirs and biographies of Schwartz revived an interest in him; a book of short stories is now in preparation. To his contemporaries, he was a celebrity who embodied all their aspirations. John Berryman dedicated ten of his *Dream Songs* "to the sacred memory of Delmore Schwartz." Robert Lowell, Meyer Schapiro, and Harvey Shapiro all wrote poems about him. Saul Bellow fictionalized his life in *Humboldt's Gift* (1975). Alfred Kazin wrote about him in *New York Jew* (1978). James Atlas' *Delmore Schwartz: The Life of an American Poet* (1977) is the definitive summation of the extraordinary extent of his influence on the intellectuals of the 1930's and 1940's.

Story characteristics
Schwartz's great theme was the driving ambition instilled into Jewish sons by their immigrant parents who had deferred all their own gratifications as a sacrifice laid on the altar of their sons' success. This strenuous burden was internalized as a compulsion.

Biography
From earliest youth, Delmore Schwartz's entire identity was shaped by his expectation that he would become a great American writer. Tied in with this grandiose fantasy was the anticipation of inheriting great wealth. Although his father had been a millionaire, the crash of the stock market in 1929 eroded much of his fortune, and a dishonest executor dissipated the remaining funds. Schwartz, however, continued to hope for his legacy until as late as 1946. His

childhood was much damaged by his parents' arguments. When Delmore was nine, in 1923, his father left, but his mother resisted a divorce until 1927. Schwartz attended the University of Wisconsin and then transferred to New York University, where he received his B. A. in 1935. That same year he finally received a few thousand dollars from his father's estate and enrolled in Harvard graduate school in philosophy, having to leave school in March, 1937, however, because of debts. From 1940 to 1947 Schwartz taught at Harvard as a Briggs-Copeland Fellow. Schwartz's first marriage—to Gertrude Buckman on June 14, 1938—ended in divorce. On June 10, 1949, he married Elizabeth Pollet. Schwartz was a frequent contributor to *Partisan Review*, of which he was an editor from 1946 to 1955. Later, from 1962 to 1966, he taught at Princeton and Syracuse Universities. He died at fifty-two without having fulfilled his great early promise. A paranoid failure, he was destroyed by drugs, drink, and many shock treatments. His obituary noted that he was the poet who had won the Bollingen Prize in 1960.

Analysis

The extent to which Delmore Schwartz was venerated by his contemporaries seems, on the basis of his few surviving stories, almost incomprehensible today. He is now more known as the topic for other writers rather than for what he himself wrote. The thirty-five poems, verse play, and short-story collection, called *In Dreams Begin Responsibilities* (1939), which he published at twenty-five, made him world famous. The story which gives the volume its title is, like everything else he wrote, autobiographical.

The story is divided into six parts. It opens on a Sunday afternoon, June 12, 1909, in Brooklyn as his father is courting his mother. They take the street car to Coney Island to inhale the sea air from the boardwalk and to watch the strollers promenade in their Sunday clothes. They ride the merry-go-round and snatch at the brass ring. Later they eat dinner, while his father boasts of all the money he will make, and then proposes. His mother begins to cry because this is what she has wanted him to say ever since she met him. They have their picture taken, but the photographer corrects their pose so many times that his father becomes impatient; his smile becomes a grimace, hers "bright and false." Then they argue about having their fortune told, and in terrible anger, he strides out of the booth. The story of his parents' courtship is narrated by their child, who watches it as if it were a movie, reacts to the scenes being portrayed on the screen, and is threatened with expulsion from the theater by the rest of the audience who object to his interruptions. Finally the usher reprimands him, seizing his arm and dragging him away. He awakens on the morning of his twenty-first birthday, a bleak, snowy, wintry day.

The undisguised autobiographical elements of this story are the use of Schwartz's actual birthday, December 8, which took place four years after this mismatched couple was married; the use of his real mother's name, Rose;

the grouping of his real relatives around the dinner table; and the depiction of his father's financial ambitions. To a certain extent, the cinematic presentation could also be considered autobiographical since Schwartz was a lifelong movie addict. Saul Bellow, in his fictionalized version of Schwartz's life, shows him as an aficionado of old films and portrays him as acting out scenes from the movies he doted on, quoting from them, and even scripting one collaboratively and composing a scenario for another.

The psychological implications of this perspective are frightening. The author on his birthday night five times tries to interrupt the film which will end in his conception. Once he freezes a frame into a still shot. Three times he actually leaves his seat because he cannot endure what is coming, but he returns in horrified fascination to watch it being relentlessly played out to the end, except that he is forcibly expelled from the theater for having created such commotion with his outcries. He awakens in the cold present of his own manhood to the recognition that this has been an anxiety dream. To have wished his parents not to marry is to have wished his own extinction. To suffer such fears of dissolution, as Schwartz did nightly, is to suffer from insomnia, a condition for which Schwartz was famous. He dreaded sleep because it meant losing control. Much of his erudition resulted from the thousands of books he read at night to fend off his terrors, taking fistfuls of benzedrines to stay awake.

The Brechtian alienation effect of interrupting the narrative flow in each of the sections of the story is an authorial strategy which makes the experience of the reader conform to the experience of the author, who is also the narrator. It is a perfect narcissistic mirroring technique: the content reflects the form, which reflects the theme; the home movie being replayed on the dream screen reflects a past in which he could not have participated in any other guise because he had not yet been born. Just so, a youth must reconstruct the images of his parents' youth, as well as images of their parents, from faded images in old-fashioned clothes on family photos.

The story opens in the subjunctive mood, "I feel as if I were in a motion picture theater," then shifts into the indicative. The author's use of the present tense throughout to describe things in the distant past has a curious effect; if all the verbs were changed to their past-tense form, this story would become a simple retrospective narrative. Their obtrusive presentness makes the artificiality more conspicuous. This is not a story intended to entertain, but a series of obsessive images which relentlessly thrust themselves upon the dream screen and which can no more be stopped than the paralyzed dreamer can obliterate the visions that insist upon playing themselves out in his consciousness.

The first interruption is posed as a break in the film. Just at the point when his mother's father is indicating his doubts about the contemplated engagement, "something happens to the film." The audience protests by clapping vigorously until it is fixed. Instead of going on, however, it replays the same scene again, and once more, the grandfather critically watches the prospective husband of his eldest daughter, worried about his character. This is both effective literary technique and valid psychology. The reiterated episode foreshadows the imminent disaster. To the narrator, the recurrent scene is a way of coping with his own sense of foreboding. The father is awkward and uneasy. The narrator, totally identified with him, "stirs uneasily also, slouched in the hard chair of the theater," and at the end of this second section, he begins to weep.

The third section is based on a contrast of perceptions, and it ends like an incremental repetition with another gush of tears while the old lady sitting next to him pats him consolingly on the shoulder and says, "There, there, all of this is only a movie, young man, only a movie." Because he knows that it is not, however, he stumbles out over the feet in his row to hide his uncontrollable grief in the men's room. The double irony of the movie's being real, while the old lady seeking to assure him of its unreality is herself unreal, augments the solipsism which the story so terrifyingly expresses. The narrator's parents feel no "danger"; they are "unaware"; they stare at the ocean "absently." "Overhead the sun's lightning strikes and strikes, but neither of them are at all aware of it." The unborn son, watching their "indifference" to the ocean's force, harshness, and fierceness, is shocked. "I stare at the terrible sun which breaks up sight, and the fatal, merciless, passionate ocean . . . and finally shocked by the indifference of my father and mother, I burst out weeping once more." He is as divorced from them, in the intensity of his perceptions, as they are from each other and from the miracles of nature. Their reactions are stereotyped and superficial; they look at the bathing suits and buy peanuts. He sees the "terrifying sun and the terrifying ocean."

Part Four begins: "When I return, feeling as if I had awakened in the morning sick for lack of sleep, several hours have apparently passed and my parents are riding on the merry-go-round." Their mechanical revolution in endless cycles is an appropriate metaphor for the meaningless rounds of their lives. When his father proposes in the restaurant, the son stands up and screams: "Don't do it. It's not too late to change your minds, both of you. Nothing good will come of it, only remorse, hatred, scandal, and two children whose characters are monstrous." The entire audience glares at him, the usher approaches brandishing his flashlight, and the old lady tries to tug him back down into his seat; and because he cannot bear to see what is happening, he shuts his eyes. The irony of his behavior is that shutting his eyes cannot obliterate the pictures because he is already dreaming them with his eyes shut. No amount of protest can stop the film that is unreeling in the theater of his mind, and there is nowhere that he can go to escape it.

The fifth episode is a *tour de force*. The photographer who wants to fix a beautiful image of them and cannot find a way of posing them so that the picture will be "right" is, of course, the artistic son, who wants to "fix" them forever in his word picture as the shapers and reflectors of his identity, but he is frustrated by their inadequacies from defining them permanently. The print that emerges from the photographer's dedicated efforts is patently false.The writer that emerges from their doomed conjunction is condemned to uncertain and fluctuating ego boundaries.

In the sixth part, a terrible quarrel arises in the fortuneteller's booth. Enraged, the father stalks out yanking at her arm, but she stubbornly refuses to budge, so he strides away. The son, in terrible fear, screams "What are they doing?" The ensuing passage mirrors both the actions and the words of the preceding one. "The usher has seized my arm and is dragging me away, and as he does so, he says: 'What are *you* doing? Don't you know that you can't do whatever you want to do? Why should a young man like you, with your whole life before you, get hysterical like this?' " As the usher drags him through the lobby of the theater into the cold light, he awakens into the bleak winter morning of his twenty-first birthday. His fortune has been foretold; it is a cold and bleak one with which he enters chronological maturity, aware that he will never attain the emotional maturity which this day should mark.

The protagonist of another story, "America! America!," is Shenandoah Fish. This is one of a number of self-mocking names Schwartz invented for his personae. He felt sharply the incongruity of his Latinate first name and his Hebraic surname, so all his fictional surrogates have equally incongruous names. His alter egos are Shenandoah Fish, Marquis Fane, Richmond Rose, Berthold Cannon, Maximilian Rinehart, Cornelius Schmidt, and Hershey Green. In "America! America!" an author, unable to write, listens to his mother's monologue about the Bauman family. He is troubled by his loss of fluency, feeling it as "a loss, or a lapse of identity." Because he feels real only when he is working, he asks anxiously, "Who am I?" As he listens to the story about the insurance agent and his family whom his mother had known for thirty years, he wonders whether "its cruelty lay in his mother's tongue or in his own mind. And his own thoughts which had to do with his own life, and seemed to have nothing to do with these human beings, began to trouble him." As his mother drones on about the sons, Sydney and Dick, who were never able to make a living even in a land where everyone who is willing to work hard enough can get rich, he listens with irony and contempt. His mother interrupts her ironing to tell him that it is late afternoon and time he got dressed. As he changes from his pajamas, he stares in the mirror, thinking that no one truly sees himself as he is. "I do not see myself. I do not know myself. I cannot look at myself truly."

His mother's representation of the Baumans becomes a metaphor for the writer's handling of his subject. Her summation of the theme of the story she has just told is that the Bauman sons were spoiled by having had too pleasant a family life. They were so indulged that they became indolent and lost the will and the aggressiveness necessary for success. He feels that her judgment is external, merely gossip, and that the story would be very different if seen from the inside. As he stares at the mirror, he realizes that she has stirred up his self-contempt with her tale of waste and failure. He becomes aware that he is defending his own rationalizations; her story with its abstractions, its outlines, has exhausted him. While he had listened to it at such a distance, it remained a caricature, but as he enters into it, it becomes a self-criticism. The Baumans, who had seemed so remote from his concerns, now merge with his own ruined life, and the scorn with which he had fended them off stares back at him from the mirror. The accusation reflected there is that his own indolence and lassitude are equal to that of the Baumans', whose story has only aggravated his anxiety about lacking the volition to work, and this last scene answers the question he had asked in the first. In this story about telling a story, the cruelty is not in his mother's tongue but rather is engendered in his own mind.

Major publications other than short fiction

PLAY: *Shenandoah*, 1941.

POETRY: *In Dreams Begin Responsibilities*, 1939; *Genesis, Book One*, 1943; *Vaudeville for a Princess*, 1959; *Summer Knowledge*, 1959.

NONFICTION: *Selected Essays of Delmore Schwartz*, 1970.

Bibliography

Atlas, James. *Delmore Schwartz: The Life of an American Poet.*
McDougell, Richard. *Delmore Schwartz.*

Ruth Rosenberg

WILLIAM SHAKESPEARE

Born: Stratford-upon-Avon, England; April 23(?), 1564
Died: Stratford-upon-Avon, England; April 23, 1616

Other literary forms

William Shakespeare wrote no short prose fiction; his "short" works include the narrative poems *Venus and Adonis* (1593) and *The Rape of Lucrece* (1594). His best-known works are his thirty-seven plays and his collection of sonnets.

Influence

Shakespeare's influence, directly or as inspiration, is incalculable. Among later writers of short fiction who have acknowledged his power are Herman Melville, Charles Dickens, Henry James, D. H. Lawrence, Joseph Conrad, and James Joyce. Something of his influence can be traced in *Shakespeare: The Critical Heritage* (edited by Brian Vickers), but in a very real sense the whole history of post-Renaissance Western civilization's attempt to understand itself owes a debt to Shakespeare comparable to that it also owes to John Calvin, Karl Marx, and Sigmund Freud.

Biography

William Shakespeare was born into a respectable provincial family and moved to London in the late 1580's. There he was involved in the theater business as playwright, actor, and shareholder until about 1610. He continued his career as playwright for another two or three years but spent most of his last six years living in his childhood hometown.

Analysis

William Shakespeare did not, as far as is known, write any examples of short fiction, except perhaps for the short erotic verse narratives, *Venus and Adonis* and *The Rape of Lucrece*. His influence, however, on all subsequent fiction writers has been so immense that any analysis of the characteristics or development of short fiction in our cultural history would be incomplete without some account of his work. Shakespeare, with his extraordinary generative power and his *Nachleben*, or afterlife, constitutes the primary instance of what Harold Bloom describes as a "strong" writer, and thus provides unavoidable and seemingly inimitable ways of understanding all fiction. History and the understanding of history move through Shakespeare's works in ways that no other writer of whom we have record has ever approached. The last three centuries of literature have developed implicitly as responses to the Shakespearean understanding of fictionmaking and of art's place in daily life. Shakespeare's works are the supreme test of other individual works and of our theories of what constitutes the greatness and relevance of art.

Early in his career, Shakespeare came close to writing short fiction when he composed, as a sideline to his theatrical activities, two examples of the then-fashionable Ovidian verse romance. The first, *Venus and Adonis*, an odd mixture of classical mythology and surprisingly (and incongruously) detailed descriptions of country life, is designed to illustrate the story of the beautiful youth Adonis' seduction by a comically desperate and aging goddess Venus. It is a relatively static, decorative, yet amusing piece, and many of its faults would be transformed to advantage within the plays. The second, *The Rape of Lucrece*, a more serious work celebrating a model of chastity from Roman history, is a poetically more mature work than the earlier piece. Strongly declamatory, its rhetorical power is at times close to that of *Richard III* (1592-1593) and *King John* (1596-1597). While both *The Rape of Lucrece* and *Venus and Adonis* were clearly popular with a young, sophisticated, and courtly audience, neither allowed Shakespeare to express his most effective qualities as a writer. He turned to the public theater, which became the most important articulation of the era's dynamic forces. This blossoming of the theater was partially due to Shakespeare's genius and partially due to the complex changes in the sociocultural fabric of the age. In turning to the theater, Shakespeare contributed to a rare but crucial phenomenon in cultural history in which a literary form deeply rooted in the reality of its time also manages to be commercially viable.

Although he did not take part in the short-lived but vigorous experimentation with short prose fiction of the 1580's and 1590's, Shakespeare nevertheless was a keen reader of all the popular fiction of his age. Similar to most Elizabethan dramatists, he ruthlessly raided Giovanni Boccaccio, Cynthio, William Painter, Sir Philip Sidney, and John Lyly for plots, motifs, and ideas for his plays. Indeed, he often brooded more over the creative fictional possibilities of the stories than did the original authors. In *Measure for Measure* (1604-1605), for example, he took the story, found in Cynthio's collection of prose tales, the *Ecatommiti* (1565), of a woman giving herself to a corrupt judge to save the life of her brother, and turned a crude melodrama into a profound and moving dramatization of the moral complexity of guilt, forgiveness, and compassion. *The Merchant of Venice* (1596-1597) combines the theatrical possibilities of two traditional folktales—the lover gaining his lady by correctly answering a riddle and the vicious creditor who tries to take a pound of flesh in payment for a bad debt—which he could have found in collections such as the medieval *Gesta Romanorum* (1473) and Ser Giovanni's *Il Pecorone*. Once again Shakespeare enriches the short folktale far beyond its original, and the result is not only an entertaining piece of theater, but also a disturbing exploration of prejudice, cultural hegemony, and the brittleness of chance in human life. A great deal of what Shakespeare bequeathed to subsequent writers and readers can be discovered from the study of his extraordinarily creative adaptions of short prose fiction written or collected by his contemporaries. He seized upon the demands of form, atmosphere, and insight in ways that only the prose writers Miguel de Cervantes Saavedra in Spain or (earlier) Boccaccio in Italy approached.

Above all else, what Shakespeare bequeathed to later readers and writers was a fascination for and an exploration of the varied problems and possibilities of his medium, particularly an understanding of the ways in which art could be used to express, understand, and transcend the currents of quotidian ideas and feelings.

Writers of prose fiction in Renaissance England were, in contrast to Shakespeare, relatively uneasy before open-ended meanings in art. The traditional medieval intimacy between storyteller and audience, which rested on an implicit community of values and allegiances, continued in such courtly fiction as George Gascoigne's or Sidney's, but increasingly (and especially with the spread of printing, the growth of a printed book rather than an oral audience, and the impact of new classes of readers), writers became uneasy about their relationship with their audiences. Many writers overcompensated by the use of heavy didacticism, trying to render the audience as passive as possible, fixing and limiting meaning rather than expanding it. The prose fiction of the age tended therefore to be static, emblematic, resistant to rather than accepting of flux and unpredictability. Not until the eighteenth and the nineteenth centuries did prose fiction, in all its technical and intellectual possibilities, seem sufficiently able to articulate the crucial features of the age in the way the theater had in Shakespeare's time.

What Shakespeare seems to have been conscious of, along with other dramatists such as John Webster, Ben Jonson, and Thomas Middleton, was the distinctive character of the medium—in particular, the theater's unique focus on emotional participation and enactment. The term "theater" is used instead of drama because the medium in which he worked was not primarily the printed word but, rather, the complex interaction of word, voice, idea, and action that constitutes theater. A play, as Michael Goldman puts it in *Shakespeare and the Energies of Drama* (1972), "takes place between two sets of bodies, ours and the actors." A play emerges only in performance—even if for readers it initially is performed mentally. As his career matured, Shakespeare realized that the crucial challenge to the dramatist was, indeed, to develop the interaction of his philosophical interests with the audience's lives. This exploration of art as a meditation completed by the enactment of others constitutes a crucial part of Shakespeare's gift to posterity: readers, writers, and all human beings struggling to understand themselves and their place in history.

The dramatist's role as the writer of theatrical scripts thus becomes that of anticipating and manipulating a potential audience's responses. Shakespeare does this, first, by exploiting all the given possibilities of his medium: the stage. Shakespeare takes advantage, for example, of the physical nearness of spectator to actor, especially by using the soliloquy or the aside, or by exploiting the way sound and sight can add both distinct detail and emotional concentration to what might otherwise (as in a prose tale) have to be left unclear or else overemphasized. Second, and even more important, he knew that the crucial responsibility for the enactment of his plays lay with his director, his actors, and his audiences. Great dramatists such as Shakespeare, however, seem to see the nature of their medium not as a limiting factor but as a liberating one: theater provides a community built on the awareness that meanings in art are not given but must be made, made anew in every per-formance and by every new audience in different times and circumstances.

Shakespeare seemed to have used two basic techniques in drawing his audience into the experience and the enactment of a play. At times, as throughout *Troilus and Cressida* (1601-1602) or in the blinding of Gloucester in *King Lear* (1605), Shakespeare seems to draw from the audience an uneasy or even painful awareness of their imprisonment in the experience of the play, as they sense their uneasiness before and alienation from its actions. The audience is simultaneously appalled and fascinated. At other times, he en-courages observers to lose themselves in the immediate gratification of won-derment or wish fulfillment, in the enactment (often without, or with relatively few, words) of miracle or fantasy. The awakening of the statue in *The Winter's Tale* (1610-1611), or the dance and song signifying blessing and fruition, at the end of *As You Like It* (1599-1600), are instances in which the audience is roused and exhorted to become part of the vision.

Neither technique, the experience of the theater as alienation or as wish fulfillment, forces the acceptance of explicit and so limited meanings. The plays subtly lead—and always with the acknowledgment of the audience's freedom, such as Jacques in *As You Like It*, to refuse to participate—to the necessary fusion of performance, audience response, and action that consti-tutes the making of meaning. Either way, the audience is encouraged to see the play's meanings in its own participation in it, individually and collectively. It cannot be forced to make any particular meaning, or meaning at all, just as Jacques cannot be forced to dance with the "country copulatives," but the audience is offered a vision, and the offer includes an invitation to take a part within it.

The exaltation of the fictionmaking capacities of man which animates Shake-speare's plays (and which interestingly contrasts with the uncertainty and self-deprecation of so many writers of prose fiction in his time) is accompanied by a strain of skepticism about the nature and the power of his art. It is as if Shakespeare needed to test most severely what he took most seriously. Explicit references to poets and poetry in the plays tend to be largely satiric, voiced in skeptical or outright contemptuous speeches by such characters as Hotspur (*Henry IV, Part I*, 1596-1597) or Theseus (*A Midsummer Night's Dream*, 1595-1596). Shakespeare, indeed, established many of the conventional suspicions of fiction with which writers have had to grapple: the making of fiction is an art of deception (*Two Gentlemen of Verona*, 1594-1595); that poetry is merely pretentious and bombastic speech (*Love's Labour's Lost*, 1595); absurd and superficial (*Romeo and Juliet*, 1594-1596; *As You Like It*), akin to madness or self-deception (*Twelfth Night*, 1599-1600), essentially escapist and irrelevant to society's real concerns (*Love's Labour's Lost*), socially parasitical (*Timon of Athens*, 1605-1608), powerless in an authoritarian society (*Julius Caesar*, 1599-1600); and even (in *The Tempest*, 1611, perhaps his greatest fantasy about the poet's power) that it must be finally abandoned and renounced, as an activity that takes the poet outside the normal boundaries of humanity, within which the poet like every other ordinary man must struggle to find meaning.

This strain of skepticism about his own vocation cannot be ignored. Indeed, it provides the material of some of Shakespeare's most telling meditations on human nature. *A Midsummer Night's Dream*, for example, takes as part of its subject the pretentiousness of some of the contemporary justifications of poetry. Its story is that of a foursome of lovers, escaping parental and political pressure by fleeing from the city to the woods. While there they undergo a succession of confusions, mistakes, and eventually self-discoveries manipulated by a mildly malicious but ultimately benign world of fairies. The final scene shows the lovers, reconciled with one another and with their superiors, gathering to celebrate the marriage of the Duke, Theseus, to Hippolyta, Queen of the Amazons. All are entertained with a play by a group of well-meaning but incompetent rustics, who have also been confused by the fairies in the woods while rehearsing their play. In this final scene, the audience laughs at the naïveté and ignorance of Bottom and his friends for their confusion of fiction and reality, their pomposity and naïve intermingling of comedy and tragedy, farce and melodrama. Interestingly, much of their confusion is of matters about which the writers of prose fiction in the period clearly felt uneasy, most especially the relationships between fact and fantasy, history and imagination, and the place of the narrator in his work. Despite mocking the mechanics' crude efforts, however, there is also a sense of their warmth, fellowship, and good intentions. The audience feels uncomfortable being identified with the cynical sophistication of the watching courtiers, whose critical judgments may be accurate but whose spirit is ungenerous. Art works not merely by rationality and according to sophisticated critical theories, but by feeling—by creating a sense of felt community. When Bottom attempts to expound his apparent dream of being wooed by the Fairy Queen, he stutters into silence. His dream is, nevertheless, real; what seems problematic is any reductive explanation, any account that takes away from the immediate felt experience.

For the hard-nosed rationalist, unless art can be analyzed, partitioned, and its "themes" or "ironies" detached, it is difficult to account for within the complex fabric of so-called "real" life. Hence, there is the temptation to declare that art is somehow separate from all other human acts, its "autonomy" being its main justification. Such defensiveness and fear, Shakespeare suggests, are understandable since fiction is so highly valued, but finally destructive of that value. Reductive explanation would leave the control of life, in all its unsystematizable complexity, to the Theseuses of the world, men who confidently dismiss the accounts of the lovers' experiences as "fairy toys" and lump together "the lunatic, the lover, and the poet" as amusing diversions but finally all, like the poet's creation, "aery nothing." Shakespeare's audience, however, has indeed seen in its own "shaping fantasies" the events Theseus so firmly dismisses as being unreal; the lovers' confusion, despair, and wonderment and the plots and antics of the fairies have been as real as his wedding. It is suggested that so-called reality, the world we encounter when we leave our theater seat or close our book, is as problematic as the world in which we have participated during the performance. Both simultaneously require and yet resist interpretation; both require our willingness to participate in and allow ourselves to be vulnerable before experience, and to let that complex interaction of surprise and familiarity, thought and feeling, which constitutes our imaginative life, open itself before the experience of art.

A Midsummer Night's Dream considers fictionmaking in general, but, as was suggested earlier, Shakespeare was fascinated especially by the reality of his own medium, the theater, in ways that none of the prose fiction writers in his age were or perhaps had the opportunity or terminology to be. Shakespeare certainly inherited, like John Lyly or Thomas Nash, Thomas Deloney or John Ford, a host of commonplaces, mainly theological or philosophical platitudes, about the theater. For example, the *theatrum mundi*, the world as theater, either of God's judgments or simply of human actions, was a medieval commonplace which had been used in various ways by humanist educators, by Reformation divines, and by the Elizabethan political establishment. The description of man's life consisting of many roles, parts, or "acts," as Jacques rather cynically describes it in *As You Like It*, was an equally common metaphor. Shakespeare seems to have taken an uncommon interest in these analogies between life and the theater. We can see his interest in the interrelations of fictionmaking and other aspects of human reality in such useful technical devices as the play-within-the-play of *Hamlet* (1600-1601), for example. Moreover, he saw it as a potent means for examining the profound questions his art struggled to articulate: what, if any, realities lie beneath or within the inchoate variety and mutability of human experience? And how might the theater influence that process of self-understanding?

It is in *Hamlet* that Shakespeare draws us most disturbingly into the perplexities of the theater metaphor. *Hamlet*, perhaps the world's best-known play, concerns the task given a young prince by the ghost of his father to revenge his murder by his brother, Hamlet's uncle, who has married the former King's wife and now reigns in his place. Roles, illusions, playing, and the confusion of appearance versus reality dominate the emotional world of the play: we are confronted by a succession of figures self-consciously aware that the court of Denmark calls into question any stable or essential expression of personality and demands continually shifting roles. Such anxiety about identity centers on a man who seems, paradoxically, most aware of the destructiveness of poses and roles and yet who is most creative when he is conscious of his own. When unambiguously acting in the so-called "real" world of the court, Hamlet is preoccupied and paralyzed by "seeming," by his consciousness of "actions that a man might play"—the courtier, the mourner, the madman, the lover, the ambitious prince. Each role is a set of attitudes, seemingly unrelated to one another, which Hamlet tentatively tests within the confusing dislocations of his world. Are there any redeeming values, beliefs, or commitments, or any stability, in a world (ours and not just Hamlet's) where all men are disguised or guarded, pressured and pressuring others by the roles seemingly inevitably forced upon them? Even if we could discover them, how could we translate them into "action," (the play's most problematic word)? "The play's the thing/Wherein I'll catch the conscience of the King" is Hamlet's hope, but when Claudius does indeed rush guiltily from the performance, the consequences are not what Hamlet foresees. The ghost's word is confirmed, certainly, but what becomes more powerful is Claudius' immediate, clearsighted, and ruthless desire to protect himself. Similar to the dramatist himself, Hamlet finds that the script he has written can be cut, changed, and adapted. What we take out of the theater depends in part on what we bring in, and we translate our perceptions and imperceptions (remembering Claudius' puzzlement or recalling generations of directors' disagreement about what he sees) into actions in part determined by the world outside the play.

Not only does the power of Hamlet's dramaturgy appear problematic, but also, as the play proceeds to a tragic yet strangely arbitrary and wasteful end, we become increasingly doubtful whether there are any actions or values other than "acting" and "seeming." We become part of the mood of paralysis that haunts the play, a paralysis that extends from *Hamlet* to our world. As we sit in the theater and then leave it, do we carry any more reassurance that we are walking into a real world where our actions can be genuine, comprehensive, and integral with our real commitments?

Hamlet introduces us, in fact, to what was at once one of Shakespeare's most profound metaphors and an all-too-present social reality in his age— the court. In *Hamlet*, as in many Jacobean plays, the court seems to act as the metaphor for the inescapable, contingent, unpredictable world into which we have been thrown and in which we are trapped until we die. The court was the most powerful social institution in Shakespeare's age. Its dominance extended far beyond mere political, social, and ecclesiastical powers; its demands penetrated the lived reality of virtually every person in England. When Hamlet returns to the Court of Denmark, he finds it a "prison," unlike his ambitious friends Rosencrantz and Guildenstern, who are only too anxious to accept its demands and play the roles it requires. The question, again, which the play thrusts at us is: what values and commitments are possible and real in such a world? The court provides Shakespeare with his most telling metaphor for trying to deal with this paralyzing question.

The court's power, however, had a quite specific literary impact on Shakespeare and his contemporaries. All over Europe, even if belatedly in England, the courts of the bustling Renaissance nation-states conducted an intense campaign to use the arts—music, architecture, painting, literature—for their own self-aggrandizement. In England the most evident signs of this attempt to marshal literature into the service of the court are in the tradition of court poetry and prose fiction and, under the reign of James, in the elaborate, costly displays of state propaganda in the court masque. The court aesthetic, with its emphasis on conformity, order, obedience, display, and ornamentation as essential manifestations of the rich, even God-given, ideology which it expressed, constituted a most powerful set of pressures upon the writer in Shakespeare's time. How did Shakespeare respond? To what extent was he aware that his own medium, the theater, was also in part dependent upon court favor, and to what extent did the enormously powerful aesthetic of the court determine and limit his vision? Such questions, it will readily be seen, are unquestionably relevant for our understanding of Shakespeare. Any writer, like the rest of us, lives within complex and changing structures of belief, value, and feeling that make up the most important, even if only partly conscious, aspect of our lives. It is often the mark of the great writer that he simultaneously accepts his historical limitations while he struggles relentlessly to understand, articulate, and so help transcend them. What distinguishes a Shakespeare from a Nash, a Deloney, or an Aphra Behn is the fierce willingness to immerse himself in his age and its given and dominant modes of being, while at the same time asserting their inevitable historicity and, thus, their final powerlessness over men and women who struggle to change and direct them.

With such considerations in mind, one can see Shakespeare's fascination with the court and the court aesthetic in an interesting perspective. The dominant mode of court literature, as a survey of the prose fiction of the period will show, was that of romance. By means of idealized heroes and heroines, pastoral or exotic settings, and improbable events, romance attempted to create an atmosphere of wish fulfillment that would at once delight and charm the spectator or reader. At the same time, it desired to reinforce or test a set of usually archaic values and beliefs that were, despite the surface escapism of romance, closely related to those of the dominant sociocultural group of the society. Romance at its most profound, such as Sidney's *Arcadia* (1590), Edmund Spenser's *The Faerie Queene* (1590, 1596), Shakespeare's own *As You Like It* or his late plays, offers not only escape but also a vision of harmony, of possibility, or of hope. The vast majority of romance written by Shakespeare's contemporaries, however, is of course not profound. It is either essentially propaganda, nostalgically recalling lost golden ages of harmony and order, or it is blatant escapism, literature written (like our own best sellers) simply to cajole and lull its readers into escaping their limits and frustrations through fantasy and not action, or it is the frustrated yearnings of the excluded or underprivileged for power or autonomy, possessed only by the dominant classes and seemingly beyond their own grasp. We can see examples of all these uses of romance in the short prose fiction of the time; they appear in Lyly's subservient propaganda, in Robert Greene's or Thomas Lodge's pastorals, in Deloney's bourgeois romances, and in the many folk stories of such heroes as Robin Hood. Every society has its typical romance paradigm, and, in all cases, despite its apparent superficiality or escapism, it is demonstrably and intimately connected to the sociocultural tensions of the society at large.

Shakespeare, it is clear, was fascinated with romance and with the ethos it articulated. His early comedies use the matter and atmosphere of romance variously to celebrate, titillate, cajole, or disturb his audiences, but he always conveys an anxiety about the uses to which romance can be put. We are always reminded, even in the otherwise most blatantly wish-fulfilling atmosphere, of a "reality" beyond and yet connected with the world of "romance," such as the court at the end of *As You Like It* to which the lovers must return, or the threat of death in *Love's Labour's Lost*. When Shakespeare turns to an even fuller exploration of romance in *Pericles* (1608), *Cymbeline* (1609), *The Winter's Tale*, and *The Tempest* (that group of plays written between 1608 and 1612 and rather loosely termed his "last" or "late" romances), he was clearly aware that he was defining his art in relation to the court and its ethos. Indeed, their settings, their tone, and much at least of their ostensible concerns are explicitly those of the court.

Cymbeline presents a picture of a court that is decadent, dandified, and tyrannical, yet one that may be redeemed by human integrity and courage. *The Winter's Tale* is built on the same structural contrast as *As You Like It* and other earlier comedies; it is a story of jealousy, tragedy, and final reconciliation. Leontes, King of Sicily, falsely accuses his wife Hermione of adultery with his childhood friend Polixenes, King of Bohemia. His jealousy seemingly brings about her death and those of his two children, a daughter, newly born and abandoned on a wild seacoast, and a son. By chance, the daughter is rescued, reared by shepherds, and falls in love with Polixenes' son. Thus, by a series of chances and a final miraculous scene in which it is revealed that Hermione is in fact alive, all are reconciled. Structurally, the play is built upon an escape from an oppressive court into a pastoral world where the jars and frustrations of court life are mysteriously healed. To this basic structure it adds a scene of illusion and celebration strikingly like the culminating scene of a Jacobean court masque. Whereas the finale of the masque takes place around the monarch, whose presence is the vital ideological as well as structural center, in *The Winter's Tale* the audience is invited to celebrate something more universal than monarchy. In the masque, it is the king, as the embodiment of the highest values and aspirations of the court, upon whom the play triumphantly focuses. In *The Winter's Tale*, it is to the audience that the play turns, to embrace us in its vision of hope and possibility and to exhort us, in Paulina's words, to "awake" our "faith" in the creative unpredictability of the human. It is a vision that acknowledges the fragility and tentativeness of human achievement to an extent that the court masque could never do. Whereas the masque explicitly existed to exclude or exorcize tragedy, rebellion, and evil, Shakespeare deliberately incorporates into his romance grim reminders of the irreversible tragic possibilities of human life. Indeed, it is their presence—Mamillius' and Antigonus' deaths, Hermione's and Leonte's aging—that makes our desire for hope and fulfillment so compelling. We are *made* to want miracles to occur, to have the seemingly unmovable artistic object, the statue, step off its pedestal, just as we desire the play to step off the stage into our lives.

Paradoxically, it was in the apparently escapist mode of romance that Shakespeare opened up the most profound consideration of the power and transforming qualities of art. Unlike most writers of prose fiction who conceived romance as a means of idealizing or reifying increasingly archaic values, Shakespeare was able to use romance to explore, qualify, and transcend the ethos of the court. Part of Shakespeare's genius, it seems, was his ability to accept the demands and pressures given by his particular historical moment and yet to point beyond it, to articulate far more than what that moment seemed to afford other writers.

The Tempest expresses Shakespeare's culminating vision of the artist's fascination with and skepticism about the power of art, and about the overriding challenge of the apparent irrelevance or powerlessness of art within society. It is the story of Prospero, the exiled Duke of Milan, who by his magical powers has conquered and civilized a desert island over which he has absolute control by means of an army of spirits and fairies. His enemies, who had exiled him, are shipwrecked on the island and are brought by Prospero's power to a degree of self-knowledge and repentance; his daughter meets and falls in love with one of them, Ferdinand, Prince of Naples. At the play's end, all are reconciled; Prospero gives up his magic power and returns to Milan. The play includes an elaborate masquelike inset; and its ostensible thematic concerns with the nature of political authority, courtly behavior, and political rebellion were all matters with which the masques which entertained and supported the Jacobean court dealt.

Like the court masque, *The Tempest* entices us into a world where the complexities of our lives are magically transformed by an apparently irresistible and benign power. At the end of the play, however, Prospero, the supreme poet-magician-scientist-monarch, dissolves the masque, removes his enemies' trance, dismisses his followers, burns his magic book, breaks his staff, and deliberately leaves the magic island to return to the world—our world of unpredictability, relativism, and partial knowledge. Security and power are given up for a more problematic world. The marvelous illusion created by art, the fantasy of an all-powerful and all-wise monarch (a fantasy cherished by the Jacobean court), the human desire to triumph over evil, limitation, and death—these are all realities which Shakespeare wants his audience to face. It is (the play's epilogue states in a startling secularization of the Lord's Prayer) only by accepting our mutual human frailty that we can possibly be "set free" and can liberate into the world the marvelous vision in which we have momentarily participated. It is our frailty, and the risk that accompanies it, that constitutes an essential part of our humanity.

It is no accident that throughout *The Tempest* Shakespeare stresses the parallels between Prospero's power and the power of art. Throughout his career he seems to have been fascinated by the power and the limitations of art and, most especially, by the question of how the experience of watching a play can be translated from imaginative to discussive and enacted meaning. Did he believe, with Percy Bysshe Shelley, that poets are the unacknowledged legislators of the world? Probably not, but he seems to have seen the role of art as that of involving (either by the cajoling persuasion of wish fulfillment or by the shock of alienation) the members of his audience in becoming aware of themselves, their place in history, and the issues, the possibilities and limitations of their lives. What follows from such recognition is then left, necessarily, to the interaction of chance, historical determination, and our sensitive resoluteness before the joy, anguish, or complexity of our world, of which Shakespeare's art has sought to make us more aware.

For the student or general reader of short fiction, then, Shakespeare stands as a frustrating and inspiring figure. He frustrates us because, except as raw material for plot or incident, he ignored the art of short fiction which in his time so badly needed a genius of his stature to give it purpose, depth, and relevance. He inspires us, however, as he has inspired four hundred years of writers and readers, by his commitment to his chosen art form and by his realization of its possibilities and limitations; by his determination that men and women and their historical struggle for meaning and authenticity should not be determined by forces outside their control; and by his belief that the strange, fragile power of art could bring about a deeper, more effective awareness of themselves and their world.

Major publications other than short fiction
PLAYS: *Romeo and Juliet* (1595-1596); *Henry IV, Part I* (1596-1597); *As You Like It* (1599); *Hamlet* (1600-1601); *Measure for Measure* (1604); *Othello* (1604); *King Lear* (1605); *Macbeth* (1606); *Antony and Cleopatra* (1606-1607); *The Winter's Tale* (1610-1611); *The Tempest* (1611).

Bibliography
Barber, C. L. *Shakespeare's Festive Comedy.*
Bullough, G., ed. *Narrative and Dramatic Sources of Shakespeare.*
Coleridge, S. T. *Shakespearean Criticism.*
Evans, G. B., *et al. The Riverside Shakespeare.*
Frye, Northrop. *A Natural Perspective.*
Gesner, Carol. *Shakespeare and the Greek Romance.*
Goddard, Harold. *The Meaning of Shakespeare.*
Kernan, Alvin B. *The Playwright as Magician.*
Knight, G. W. *The Wheel of Fire.*
Kott, Jan. *Shakespeare Our Contemporary.*
Muir, K. and S. Schoenbaum, eds. *A New Companion to Shakespeare Studies.*
Righter, Anne. *Shakespeare and the Idea of the Play.*
Spencer, T. J. B., ed. *Elizabethan Love Stories.*
Wickham, Glynne. *Early English Stages, 1300-1660.*

Gary F. Waller

IRWIN SHAW

Born: New York, New York; February 27, 1913

Principal short fiction

Sailor off the Bremen and Other Stories, 1939; *Welcome to the City*, 1942; *Act of Faith*, 1946; *Mixed Company*, 1950; *Tip on a Dead Jockey*, 1957; *Love on a Dark Street*, 1965; *God Was Here, But He Left Early*, 1973.

Other literary forms

Irwin Shaw's works include novels, plays, screenplays, articles, and short stories. His novels *The Young Lions* (1948) and *Rich Man, Poor Man* (1969) and his plays *Bury the Dead* (1936) and *Sons and Soldiers* (1943) are well known. "Out of the Fog," "Act of Faith," "Tip on a Dead Jockey," and *The Young Lions* have been filmed.

Influence

A major voice of the postwar generation, Shaw is known for his antiwar themes and memorable characters from the 1920's, 1930's, and 1940's. His short story "Walking Wounded" won the O. Henry Memorial Prize in 1944, and *The Young Lions* was viewed as one of the most important novels of World War II.

Story characteristics

Shaw's stories illuminate the lives of the men and women of his own generation. Popular for their contemporary quality as well as their technical excellence, his stories typically explore complex political and social patterns affecting the people of his times. He presents a wide range of human emotions, sometimes from inside the characters, sometimes from outside, but always with restraint and subtlety.

Biography

Irwin Shaw began professional writing for the *New Republic* after graduating from Brooklyn College. He worked as a drama critic and teacher of creative writing before serving in the Army from 1942 to 1945, and during the war he spent time in Africa, England, France, and Germany. He is a member of the Author's Guild, Dramatist's Guild, and Screen Writer's Guild, and he received a National Institute of Arts and Letters grant in 1946. He is married and has one son, with whom he lives in Switzerland and France, although he makes frequent trips to the United States.

Analysis

Irwin Shaw's stories have appeared in many respected magazines and are frequently anthologized in collections of short fiction. War, crime, financial disaster, adultery, and moral sterility provide major conflicts as Shaw presents a wide range of human emotions. "Sailor off the Bremen," "The Eighty-Yard Run," "Tip on a Dead Jockey," and "The Girls in Their Summer Dresses" are well-known examples of his narrative sophistication.

In "Sailor off the Bremen," a story of naïve revenge, an American football player learns the identity of the Nazi who disfigured his brother's face. Charley, arrogant and angry in his strength, overrules his injured brother's objections to ensnaring and punishing the offender. A series of discussions between Charley, Ernest the disfigured brother, and their friends and family develops a plot suggesting various perspectives on violence.

In a scene centered around the brothers' kitchen table, Ernest, Preminger, and Stryker, new members of the Communist party, disregard violence as a means for change. Charley and Ernest's wife Sally, however, want satisfaction for their loved one's suffering. In the course of their arguments, even the strongest Communist of the three, Preminger, admits that aside from party leanings, the Nazi ought to be punished for his cruelty not merely to Ernest but to others he has sent to concentration camps. Then Stryker, although he is usually anxious and timid, agrees to help effect the revenge because he is Ernest's friend. Finally Ernest himself is resigned.

Shaw handles characterization by focusing on suggestive details that reveal much about each of the men: Ernest's face twitches almost uncontrollably; his blind eye is concealed with a dark patch. Charley's muscular hands are cleat-marked from the previous week's game. Stryker, a dentist who is attempting to replace Ernest's teeth, has a dry, raspy voice filled with doubt. Preminger, an officer aboard the *Bremen*, is cool and confident; he looks like a Midwestern college boy despite his profession of espionage. In the background, Sally, patient and hospitable, performs kitchen duties as the men discuss their plans.

Once the decision is made, the pace quickens. Preminger identifies the Nazi, Lueger, so that Sally, Charley, and Stryker will recognize him as they watch separately from another deck of the *Bremen*. Sally manages to arrange a date with Lueger, who is well known for his affairs with women. On the appointed evening, they see a movie, stop for a drink, and then continue along the street past a corner where Charley and Stryker are waiting.

Sally escapes when Stryker asks directions of Lueger, giving Charley the opportunity to land the first blow. In a brutal climactic scene, Stryker stands guard while Charley knocks Lueger unconscious and beats him until he has lost an eye and many teeth. Sobbing and cursing, Charley continues to beat Lueger until he is satisfied that Lueger will suffer serious injury permanently. Stryker and Charley then leave the Nazi lying in a pool of his own blood. Later in the hospital Preminger identifies Lueger for a questioning detective but denies any knowledge that Lueger had enemies. The eye-for-an-eye theme of the story raises questions concerning violence and morality; clearly the social and political context makes immediate answers impossible.

"The Eighty-Yard Run" presents another kind of social dilemma. Christian Darling, a former Midwestern college football player, recalls the practice run he made that changed his football career and won for him the daughter of a wealthy manufacturer. Admired by the coaches, the students, and Louise, he appeared successful through college and afterward, when he began to manage accounts for her father in New York. As Christian muses over the long run and the intervening years, he struggles to accept the fact that he could not cope with the social and intellectual changes of the 1920's and 1930's.

Louise's father, a maker of inks, had survived the initial crash and waited until 1933 to commit suicide, leaving only debts and unbought ink behind. Christian turned to alcohol, and Louise began working for a women's magazine. Their apartment became a showcase for the sophisticated intellectuals of New York. Unable to understand the new art or the philosophies of the new breed, Christian lost Louise's respect. Although he has attempted a succession of jobs, he has never done well at any of them, until he was recently hired, for his collegiate appearance, as a traveling representative for a tailoring firm. Now as Christian reflects, he realizes that while he travels, Louise dines with new, more sophisticated men and makes the social contacts that are now so important to her. Not since the eighty-yard practice run has he had any hope of his own success. Christian, visiting his old practice field, reenacts the eighty-yard run when he thinks the field is deserted. Recalling his own ease and grace at that moment, he executes the movements of fifteen years before perfectly only to discover with embarrassment that a young couple is watching him. He leaves the field with sweat beginning to break out across his face. His situation is fixed in space and time; the story presents the effects of social and economic changes in American life as they are experienced by a particular, although representative, man.

"Tip on a Dead Jockey" spotlights the lives of American expatriate flyers in Paris after the war. When Lloyd Barber, out of work and living in a shabby Parisian hotel, learns from a friend's wife that her husband, Jimmy, has disappeared for more than a month, he realizes that Jimmy must have accepted a smuggling job he himself had refused because of its risks. In this story, like "The Eighty-Yard Run," flashbacks indicate the contrast between past security and present struggle. Barber recalls, for example, the youthful beauty of Jimmy's wife, now evidencing poverty and anguish. He gives her what he can spare of his cash and reassures her that he will try to locate Jimmy.

Barber himself is depressed and lonely; he has no job but amuses himself occasionally by going to the races, where he met Bert Smith who had offered him twenty-five thousand dollars for two flights between Egypt and France, an offer which must now account for Jimmy's disappearance. Barber searches the bars and restaurants of Paris in an attempt to locate Smith, a wealthy and educated European who had entertained him for weeks before revealing his intent to use Barber to smuggle money into France.

Barber's initial contact with Smith had been most profitble. As Barber continues his search through the streets of Paris, he recalls that Smith's tips on winning horses had paid off generously for the first two weeks of their acquaintanceship. On their last afternoon together at the track, however, perhaps the afternoon he decided against the smuggling job, Smith had recommended betting on a horse which fell, killing its jockey, an event Barber accepted as a bad omen. Barber had immediately refused Smith's offer and returned flight maps Smith had given him. That evening, preparing to dine alone, Barber had stumbled onto Smith and Jimmy, talking casually about racing, and Barber had thought nothing of it, underestimating Jimmy's financial need and gullibility.

Barber's search is unsuccessful. He returns to his room to find that Jimmy's wife has left a message requesting that he meet her at a nearby bar. There he finds her with Jimmy, suntanned and thin, eagerly spending the earnings of his crime. The couple asks him to go with them to dinner at an expensive restaurant, but Barber, despite his relief that Jimmy is safely home, only feels lonelier as he witnesses their happy reunion. He returns to his hotel room where a collection of letters reminds him of the emptiness of his own life: his ex-wife wants to know what to do with an old army pistol she found in a trunk belonging to him; his mother wants him to stop being foolish and come home to a regular job; a woman he does not love wants him to come and stay with her in a villa near Eze; none of the letters makes him feel less isolated. Finally, there is a letter from a boy who had flown as his waist-gunner during the war, and this letter, more than the rest, reminds him of the emptiness of expatriate life in Europe. The lonely hotel room, the evening chill, and the memory of Jimmy's reunion with his wife converge on Barber as he concludes that Europe is not the place for him, however adventurous he may have been in the past.

"The Girls in Their Summer Dresses" is a famous example of Shaw's skill in portraying urban life with little more than an anecdote. Michael and Frances, a young married couple, walk along Fifth Avenue in New York City on a Sunday afternoon. They decide to spend the day alone, enjoying the city, instead of visiting friends in the country as they had planned; but the husband's habit of girl-watching leads to an angry confrontation in which the beautiful women of New York become a symbol of the freedom and sexual vitality his wife resents. As a Japanese waiter cheerfully serves them drinks just after breakfast in a small bar, the husband admits his fascination with the variety of women passing daily along New York streets. Their expensive clothing, their health, and their beauty draw him like a magnet, especially as he approaches middle age.

As Frances sobs into her handkerchief, Michael finds courage to celebrate the wonderful experience of observing women, richly dressed in furs in winter or in summer dresses in warm weather. Although he reassures Frances that she is a good wife, she believes that he only wants his freedom; and he cannot convince her of his loyalty because he is not convinced of it himself. They decide to spend the rest of the day with friends after all, and as Frances walks across the bar to make a phone call, Michael cannot help admiring her figure, her legs, just as he admires the features of strangers passing along the street. Their situation is a modern one, appropriately symbolized by New York women reflecting the economic vitality of the urban setting. Although Shaw frequently stops at the surface of the modern life style, his portraits of modern men and women effectively suggest the conflicts below apparent comfort and success.

Major publications other than short fiction

NOVELS: *The Young Lions*, 1948; *The Troubled Air*, 1951; *Lucy Crown*, 1956; *Two Weeks in Another Town*, 1960; *Voices of a Summer Day*, 1965; *Rich Man, Poor Man*, 1969; *Evening in Byzantium*, 1973.

PLAYS: *Bury the Dead*, 1936; *The Gentle People: A Brooklyn Fable*, 1939; *Sons and Soldiers*, 1943; *The Assassin*, 1945; *Children from Their Games*, 1965.

NONFICTION: *Report on Israel*, 1950 (with Robert Capa); *In the Company of Dolphins*, 1964.

Chapel Louise Petty

ALAN SILLITOE

Born: Nottingham, England; March 4, 1928

Principal short fiction

The Loneliness of the Long-Distance Runner, 1960; *The Ragman's Daughter and Other Short Stories*, 1963; *Guzman Go Home*, 1968; *Men, Women, and Children*, 1973.

Other literary forms

Alan Sillitoe's twenty-five published books include ten novels, five collections of poetry, three books for children, as well as travel literature, essays, and plays. Four of his books, including *The Loneliness of the Long-Distance Runner* and *The Ragman's Daughter and Other Short Stories* have been made into films. His first novel, *Saturday Night and Sunday Morning* (1959), was also produced in a stage adaptation, and his second, *The General*, carried the film title *Counterpoint*.

Influence

Sillitoe's early novels and most of his short stories fall directly within the minor yet persistent tradition of British working-class fiction established by Charles Dickens and Mrs. Gaskell in the 1840's and carried on by George Gissing, Arthur Morrison, and Walter Greenwood. He is the foremost contemporary interpreter of working-class life, and his best-known story, "The Loneliness of the Long-Distance Runner," is widely accepted as a modern classic. His more recent work has drawn on experiences outside the working-class milieu and has revealed a willingness to experiment in form and style. His stories have been frequently anthologized and have been translated into more than twenty languages.

Story characteristics

Sillitoe writes penetrating, engaged stories often concerned with the injustices of life evident in a working-class milieu. Although at times mordantly funny, the stories mirror Sillitoe's strong social conscience and frequently force the reader to question conventional wisdom and widely held "truths" about man in society.

Biography

Born into a working-class family in the English industrial city of Nottingham, Alan Sillitoe was educated to the age of fourteen at Radford Boulevard School for Boys and worked in local factories until he joined the Royal Air Force in 1946. He served in Malaya for two years, followed by sixteen months spent in an English sanitarium recuperating from tuberculosis. During this period he read voraciously and began to write himself. From 1952 to 1958 he lived in France and Spain, where he became friends with Robert Graves. On the publication of *Saturday Night and Sunday Morning* he returned to England, where he now lives. He travels frequently and widely and has made extended visits to North Africa, Israel, and the U.S.S.R. He married the poet Ruth Fainlight in 1959 and has one son, David. He has won various literary awards, including the prestigious Hawthornden Prize.

Analysis

"The Loneliness of the Long-Distance Runner," the title story of Alan Sillitoe's first collection of short fiction, quickly became one of the most widely read stories of modern times. Its basic theme, that one must be true to one's own instincts and beliefs despite intense social pressure to go against them, is echoed in many of his best-known stories, including "On Saturday Afternoon," "The Ragman's Daughter," "The Good Women," and "Pit Strike." Such an attitude strikes a responsive chord in modern readers who feel hemmed in by the dictates of "official" bureaucracies and by government interference in their personal lives. It is important for Sillitoe's characters to establish their independence in a conformist world, yet at the same time they often subscribe to a class-oriented code of values which pits the disadvantaged working class against the rest of society.

Many of Sillitoe's stories are located in urban working-class ghettos and reflect the slum environment he knew himself as a child and young adult. In story after story these ghetto-dwellers are seen as society's underdogs, as victims of a series of injustices, real or imagined, which undermine their sense of personal dignity and self-esteem. Ernest Brown, for example, the protagonist in "Uncle Ernest," is a lonely aging upholsterer who befriends Alma and Joan, two young schoolgirls he meets at a local café. In a series of encounters, always at the café and in public view, he buys them food and small gifts and takes pleasure in learning something of their lives. He asks nothing of the girls in return, and they come to think of him affectionately as "Uncle Ernest." After a few weeks, however, he is accosted by two detectives who accuse him of leading the girls "the wrong way" and forbid him to see them again. Unable to cope with this "official" harassment, Ernest Brown retreats into alcohol and despair.

In one sense "Uncle Ernest" is an anomaly in Sillitoe's short fiction, for although it illustrates the victimization his characters often face, it chronicles a too-ready acceptance of the larger society's interference and power. For the most part his characters remain defiant in the face of directives from those in positions of authority. "On Saturday Afternoon," the story of an unnamed working-class man's attempt to commit suicide, offers a sardonic example of this defiance. The man first tries to hang himself from a light fixture, but before he can succeed the police arrive and arrest him. In response to his bitter comment, "It's a fine thing if a bloke can't tek his own life," the police tell him "it ain't your life." They take him to a psychiatric hospital and unwittingly put him in a sixth floor room and fail to restrain him. That night he jumps from the window and succeeds in killing himself.

"On Saturday Afternoon" is typical of Sillitoe's stories in its assumed attitude to social authority: although "they" interfere and place controls on an individual's right to act as he pleases, they can usually be outwitted. Here and in other stories Sillitoe's workers place great stress on "cunning," the ability to preserve individual freedom of action in a restrictive or oppressive social environment. Such an attitude is well illustrated in his best-known story, "The Loneliness of the Long-Distance Runner." The protagonist in this story is simply called Smith, the modern equivalent of Everyman. He is a seventeen-year-old boy who has been put in a Borstal, a reform school, for theft from a baker's shop. He is also an accomplished long-distance runner and has been chosen by the Governor, or warden, to represent the Borstal in a competition for the All-England Championship. As we meet Smith he is running alone over the early-morning countryside, and as he runs he considers his situation. It soon becomes apparent that he has rejected the warden's platitudes ("if you play ball with us, we'll play ball with you") and has seen through the hypocrisy of his promises as well. He recognizes the difference between his own brand of honesty, which allows him to be true to his own instincts, and the warden's, which rejects the needs of the individual in favor of social expediency. Smith's only counter to the warden's attempt to use him for his own ends is cunning. As he sees it, the warden is "dead from the toenails up," living as he does in fear of social disapproval and manipulating the inmates of his Borstal to gain social prestige. Smith, on the other hand, resolves to fight against becoming swallowed up in social convention, to be true to his own concept of honesty. Adopting such a stance means recognizing "that it's war between me and them," and it also leads to his decision to lose the upcoming race.

In the second part of this three-part story the reader shares Smith's reminiscences about his boyhood in a Nottingham slum. He first engages sympathy by telling how he impulsively took part in the theft for which he was sent to Borstal, and then moves quickly to describe the confrontations with police who investigated the robbery. In this section Sillitoe manages a difficult feat by maintaining support for his protagonist even though readers know the boy is guilty of theft. He does this by turning the investigation into a series of skirmishes between Smith and the authorities which allow the reader to be caught up in admiration of the boy's ability to outwit for a time a vindictive, slow-thinking policeman. Not unexpectedly, persistence pays off for the investigators, and in a highly original and amusing climax the stolen money is found and Smith is taken into custody. The facts are less important here, however, than Sillitoe's narrative skill in sustaining our sympathetic involvement with his protagonist. Having manipulated the reader into becoming Smith's ally by allowing conventional notions of right and wrong to be suspended, he also paves the way for the acceptance of Smith's dramatic gesture in the final section of the story.

Part Three brings the reader back to time present and the day of the race. The warden, anticipating Smith's win and the reflected glory it will bring to him, has invited numbers of influential friend to witness the competition. Ironically, none of the boys' parents is present, their invitations having been worded so that they would be likely to mistrust or misunderstand them. Details such as this add to the impression of the callousness of the Borstal authorities and help to confirm Smith's conviction that they are using the boys as pawns in a selfish social game. The purity of Smith's intentions, on the other hand, is underscored during the race by his sense of communion with the natural surroundings through which he runs and his Edenic perception of himself as "the first man ever to be dropped into this world." As he runs his thoughts alternate between lyrical commentary on the physical satisfaction of running well and consideration of his decision to lose the race and the punitive consequences this will bring him. Nevertheless he remains firm in his decision, committed to showing the warden "what honesty means if it's the last thing I do." In the end he does lose the race and makes his point, but in much more dramatic manner than he had foreseen. Arriving at the finish line well in advance of the other runners, he is virtually forced to mark time in front of the grandstand until one of his competitors passes him and crosses the line. Smith has made his point: like so many other of Sillitoe's protagonists, he refuses to be manipulated.

The fierce independence espoused by Sillitoe's working-class characters, and the rejection of what they see as unwarranted interference by society's authority figures in their personal affairs, is also evident in "The Good Women." The heroine of this story is Liza Atkin, a vital and earthy woman whom one critic called "a Nottingham Mother Courage." Liza's life, like that of Bertolt Brecht's protagonist, is plagued by economic hardship and marked by injustice and the stupidity of war. Although the story has no real plot—readers are shown a series of disconnected events which take place over a period of years—they are caught up in the problems of Liza's life and come to applaud her feisty, tough-minded manner of coping with them.

Dogged by poverty, she ekes out a precarious existence supporting her out-of-work husband and two young boys by filling a decrepit baby carriage with old rags and bits of metal from local dumps and selling them to scrap dealers, and by taking in washing from troops stationed nearby. When the means-test man attempts to deny her welfare payments because of her "business," she shouts him down so the whole street can hear. She makes her gesture of protest against war by harboring a deserter; and standing up for workers' rights in the factory where she eventually finds work, she quickly becomes known to management as "the apostle of industrial unrest." Later, when her son dies because Allied planes bombed his unit by mistake, she is devastated. She recovers, however, to become a passionate advocate of violent revolution at a time in life when most women would be settling into comfortable grandmother roles.

"The Good Women," like many of Sillitoe's stories, has strong didactic overtones. Liza Atkin, along with Smith, Ernest Brown, and the unnamed protagonist in "On Saturday Afternoon," finds herself in a world in which the dictates of society at large often contradict her personal convictions. Yet she is able to resist the pressure to conform, partly because of her strong belief in what is right (harboring the deserter to protest against war, for example), partly because she shares the habitual working-class mistrust of "them" (the authority figures who come from outside and above her own social station) and their motives. From her perspective, and from Sillitoe's, society is badly flawed, and it is up to the individual to strive for a new order in which the unjust exercise of power and the suffering it can cause are eliminated. Memorable characters such as Liza Atkin are meant to show the reader how to begin.

In "Pit Strike," which was filmed for BBC Television, Sillitoe offers yet another working-class hero, a champion of fairness and integrity. Joshua, a fifty-year-old Nottingham miner, journeys to the South of England with a number of his friends to support a strike by fellow colliers. In a well-organized program of action, the men race from one coal-powered generating station to another to form picket lines and halt deliveries of coal. In a number of cases they are confronted by police whose job it is to see that deliveries are uninterrupted. Clashes between the workers, who feel they are being treated unjustly, and the police, representing the power of society as a whole, are inevitable in such circumstances. Although Joshua acts to restrain his more belligerent companions in these confrontations, he makes his own mark in a dramatic and courageous manner. When a fully loaded coal truck is seen crawling up an incline away from a picketed power station to make its delivery at another, Joshua daringly and at great personal risk runs after it and forces open the rear gate safety catches, allowing tons of coal to fall on the highway. Although he narrowly escapes death, the gesture seems worth making, and soon after this the strike is settled in the miners' favor.

Like Joshua, the characters in Sillitoe's other stories are usually agitators, passionately and defiantly reaffirming the value of the individual spirit in a world which too often encourages unthinking conformity to social norms. Sillitoe's audience may not always concur with the views his characters express, nor wish to accept the methods they use to further their aims, but their stories nevertheless touch the reader and stay tenaciously with him, disturbing, provoking, and making him more aware of the imperfect world and of himself.

Major publications other than short fiction
NOVELS: *Saturday Night and Sunday Morning*, 1959; *The General*, 1960; *Key to the Door*, 1961; *The Death of William Posters*, 1965; *A Tree on Fire*, 1967; *A Start in Life*, 1971; *Travels in Nihilon*, 1972; *Flame of Life*, 1974; *The Widower's Son*, 1977; *The Storyteller*, 1979.

PLAYS: *Three Plays*, 1978.

POETRY: *The Rats and Other Poems*, 1960; *A Falling Out of Love and Other Poems*, 1964; *Love in the Environs of Voronezh and Other Poems*, 1968; *Storm: New Poems*, 1974; *Snow on the North Side of Lucifer*, 1979.

NONFICTION: *The Road to Volgograd*, 1964; *Raw Material*, 1972; *Mountains and Caverns*, 1975.

Bibliography
Atherton, Stanley S. *Alan Sillitoe: A Critical Assessment.*
Penner, Allen R. *Alan Sillitoe.*

Stanley S. Atherton

WILLIAM GILMORE SIMMS

Born: Charleston, South Carolina; April 17, 1806
Died: Charleston, South Carolina; June 11, 1870

Principal short fiction
Carl Werner and Other Tales, 1838; *The Wigwam and the Cabin*, 1845-1846.

Other literary forms
William Gilmore Simms was one of the most versatile and prolific writers of his day; his eighty-two volumes include novels, short stories, poetry, plays, literary criticism, essays, biographies, and histories. Simms was also highly respected in his time as a magazine and newspaper editor.

Influence
Simms is generally regarded as the preeminent man of letters in the nineteenth century South. He is often compared to James Fenimore Cooper in his ability to write historical romances capturing the panorama of nature and depicting heroic characters loftily aspiring to defend high ideals in worlds corrupted by both the foibles of human existence and the advancement of mass society. As a literary critic and commentator upon the affairs of his day, Simms was the Southern equivalent of William Dean Howells in the North as a much-lauded and respected spokesman for the cultural and literary standards of the day. Edgar Allan Poe stated in 1844 that, exclusive of Charles Brockden Brown and Nathaniel Hawthorne, Simms was the best writer of fiction in America.

Story characteristics
As "the Southern Cooper," Simms portrayed in his writings a detailed, although often highly romanticized, sense of life in the South from the frontier days to the Civil War. In his stories, he makes use of stock Southern characters to protray the uniqueness of the region and its particular blend of Romanticism and realism. In technique and style, his focus is often humorous and exaggerated, with the use of the tall tale and borrowings from local legends and traditions. His writing style is often considered to be imitative of the Romantics, particularly Sir Walter Scott, but he is also generally praised for his use of adventurous escapades in his stories and for his mastery of dialect and descriptions of natural settings.

Biography
William Gilmore Simms was the son of an Irish immigrant tradesman. His mother died when he was two, and Simms was left in the care of his maternal grandmother when his father moved to Tennessee and later to Mississippi.

Simms's formal schooling amounted to less than six years, and he was largely self-educated. At the age of twelve, he was apprenticed to a druggist but later left that trade to study law. In 1827, he was admitted to the bar in Charleston. His marriage to Anna Malcolm Giles in 1826 ended with her death in 1832. Simms's literary talents became manifest very early in his life. At nineteen, he edited the literary journal, *The Album* (1825), and two years later published his first two volumes of verse. In 1828, he cofounded and edited *The Southern Literary Gazette*. He ventured into journalism as the editor of the daily newspaper, the Charleston *City Gazette*, from 1830 until its bankruptcy in 1832. Between 1833 and 1835, he published four novels, *Martin Faber*, *Guy Rivers*, *The Yemassee*, and *The Partisan*, and established his reputation as a significant voice in American fiction. In 1836, he married Chevilette Roach and moved to her father's seven-thousand-acre plantation, "Woodlands." His newly acquired wealth freed him to pursue his literary career more fully and to venture into new avenues, such as serving, from 1844 to 1846, as a representative to the South Carolina legislature. His marriage to Miss Roach lasted until her death in 1863 and produced fourteen children. During the period from 1836 to 1860, in addition to his many literary productions, Simms was active in the editing of several magazines, including *The Southern and Western Monthly Magazine* (1845), *The Southern Quarterly Review* (1849-1855), and *Russell's Magazine* (1857-1860), which he helped Paul Hamilton Hayne to edit. Simms's fortunes were ruined by the Civil War; in 1865, "Woodlands" was burned by stragglers from Sherman's Army. Reduced to poverty, Simms spent the final years of his life editing newspapers and writing desperately to support himself and his children. He died in Charleston on June 11, 1870.

Analysis

William Gilmore Simms is often viewed as the successor to Sir Walter Scott in the fostering of Romanticism. Simms was fond of asserting that his works should be viewed as romances, filled with sweeps of the imagination, bold characterization, and clearly defined moral stances. His literary works, considered as a whole, can be viewed as an epic of the South; in the epic, there are realistic elements to be sure, but Simms was interested in realism only when it served his more consuming passion for creating works of originality and vitality that portrayed the South as it was and as it aspired to be ideally. Simms's writings, too, can be associated with regionalism and the local-color movement in American letters, for he borrowed richly from the traditions and mores of his region to capture a sense of a spirit and a time.

"How Sharp Snaffles Got His Capital and His Wife," published posthumously in *Harper's New Monthly Magazine* in October, 1870, is a short story which demonstrates at a high level of quality Simms's particular and fanciful interest in local color and Southern tall-tale humor. In early winter, a group of seven hunters, four professionals and three amateurs, gather around the campfire on a Saturday night after a week of hunting in the "Balsam Range" of mountains in North Carolina. Saturday night is dedicated among the professional hunters to what is called "The Lying Camp," in which mountaineers engaged in a camp hunt, which sometimes lasts for weeks at a time, are encouraged to tell "long yarns" about their adventures and the wild experiences of their professional lives. The hunter who actually inclines to exaggeration in such a situation is allowed to deal in "all the extravagances of invention; nay, he is *required* to do so." To be literal or to confine oneself to details of fact is a finable offense. The hunter is, however, required to exhibit a certain degree of art in his invented tales, "and thus he frequently rises into a certain realm of fiction, the ingenuities of which are made to compensate for the exaggerations, as they do in the 'Arabian Nights' and other Oriental romances."

The tale for the evening is told, in dialect fashion, by Sharp Snaffles to the "Jedge," the narrator of the story. Sharp tells the tale of how fourteen years ago he was in love with Merry Ann Hopson and sought to marry her. When Sharp appears at Squire Hopson's house and announces his intentions, the squire is amazed that a man of such poor social and economic standing as a simple hunter could even think he was worthy of Merry Ann. The squire takes Sharp over to a looking glass and asks Sharp to tell him what he sees. Sharp replies that he sees a good, honest, rugged man, not the handsomest or the ugliest in the world, but man enough for Merry Ann. The squire tells Sharp to look again and "*observe*." There is one thing Sharp has not got, the squire says, and that is capital. The squire ushers Sharp quickly away, and when Sharp returns to his cabin, he sees that the squire is right. Sharp does not have the types of possessions that would attract a woman or which would enable her to live in style. He knows he must get himself some capital, but he cannot figure out how, although he spends half the night thinking and figuring.

The next morning, Sharp awakens and goes hunting, but he has no luck. At sunset, he sits down under a tree near a peaceful lake and falls asleep. He is awakened by loud and strange sounds and looks up to see a flock of wild geese landing on the lake. Sharp calculates that there must be forty thousand geese on the lake and considers that he could get fifty cents a head for them if he could get them to the markets in Spartanburg and Greenville. After a night of plotting how to catch the geese, he sets out for Spartanburg the next day and buys all the twine, cord, plow-lines, and large fishhooks in town, "all to help make the tanglement parfect." He spends a week getting the huge net in shape; his plan is to spread it across the lake and, after the geese have landed, at a key moment pull both ends of the net in quickly and catch all of the geese. The plan works perfectly, except for the fact that after reeling all the geese in, Sharp wraps the rope around his left arm and his right thigh rather than tying it to the tree in front of him. As if of one mind and body, the geese lift from the lake and carry Sharp for several miles, high above the ground, until they hit a tree and land, Sharp and all, right in its branches. Sharp does not have to decide what to do next, for suddenly the branch he is sitting on gives way and throws him backwards into the tree trunk, which is hollow and filled with honey. Sharp is literally up to his ears in honey and fears that he will drown in the syrupy goo. Suddenly, in the midst of his prayers for deliverance, a huge bear appears at the top of the hollow tree and begins to lower himself down, bottom end first, to get to the honey. Sharp sees his chance, and grabs hold of the bear's ankle; the bear is so frightened he claws his way out of the tree, taking Sharp with him. When they get to the top, Sharp pushes the bear out of the tree; the bear falls and breaks his neck.

Safely out of the tree, Sharp realizes the potential capital available to him in the bear, the geese, and the honey. When all of his dealings are done, he has sold 2,700 geese for $1,350, the bear's hide, meat, grease, and marrow for $100, and 2,000 gallons of honey for $1,400. His wealth accumulated, Sharp then sets about the business of establishing himself as a man of capital by buying a 160-acre farm with a good house on it, furniture, and a mule for working his land. The rest of his money he has converted to gold and silver coins and loads up his pockets and his saddlebags.

As he prepares to go to Squire Hopson's, Sharp tells his friend, Columbus Mills, of the squire's talk about capital. Columbus tells Sharp that the squire has no room to talk; the squire owes Columbus a 350-dollar-note on which he has not paid a cent in three years and on which Columbus is holding the mortgage to the squire's farm as security. Sharp asks Columbus if he will sell him the squire's mortgage for the face value of the note, and Columbus agrees. Dressed in his best new outfit, Sharp then goes to Squire Hopson's house; on the way, he meets Merry Ann and tells her that they are going to be married that evening. Merry Ann thinks that he has gone slightly crazy but agrees to follow along after him and see what happens.

The squire receives Sharp coldly, but he is impressed by Sharp's rich clothing and his fancy new appearance. Sharp states that he has come on business and brings up the issue of the debt to Columbus Mills. The squire tells Sharp to tell Columbus he will pay him soon, and Sharp says that the squire misunderstands Sharp's mission. The note, and consequently the mortgage, now belong to him, and, since he plans to be married this evening, he wants the squire to move out so that Sharp and his new bride can move in in the morning. The squire is outraged, but he realizes that Sharp has got him legally and can foreclose on the farm. After some fancy maneuvering taking advantage of the squire's diminished position, Sharp tells the squire he has but one option. He takes the squire over to the looking glass and tells him to "obsarve" that the squire is a man without capital. The only way the squire can acquire any capital now and save his farm is to allow Sharp to marry Merry Ann. At first the squire protests, but when Sharp shows him the gold and silver coins in his saddlebags and his pockets he finally gives in and agrees to the wedding. Sharp fetches Parson Stovall, and the wedding is performed that evening, exactly as Sharp had promised Merry Ann. Thirteen years later, Sharp tells the Judge as the conclusion of his tale that he and Merry Ann have a happy marriage, nine beautiful children, and more capital than Sharp ever imagined.

Simms's passion for the wonderful and the mysterious is exemplified by "Grayling," a story which Edgar Allan Poe admired and which begins with the lamentation that the world has become so matter-of-fact lately that "we can no longer get a ghost story, either for love or money." To break the hold which "that cold-blooded demon called Science" has upon "all that concerns the romantic," the narrator proposes to tell a story he heard as a boy from his grandmother that involves ghosts and many things wondrous.

Set in the Carolinas in the period immediately following the Revolutionary War, the tale is of the murder of Major Lionel Spencer by Sandy Macnab. Macnab has learned that Spencer is to sail from Charleston to England to claim a large inheritance. All the Major need do to secure the estate is prove that he is Lionel Spencer. With the intention of impersonating Spencer in England, Macnab follows the Major, murders him, and throws his body in the bay.

James Grayling, a close friend of Major Spencer and an army comrade with whom Spencer camped the night before he was murdered, learns that Spencer has neither reached the tavern in the next town on his journey nor has he been seen on the road. Grayling decides to search for Spencer along the road and along the margins of the bay. After four hours, he is exhausted and sits down by a tree to rest. Suddenly, he hears a voice cry out to him, and he sees the ghost of Major Spencer, in pale garments covered with blood, appear some twenty steps ahead of him near the bay. Spencer tells Grayling that Macnab has murdered him and hidden his body in the bay. The murderer, Spencer is sure, is on his way to Charleston to sail for England, and if Grayling makes haste he may be able to intercept him before the ship's departure. Spencer pleads with Grayling to have Macnab brought to justice, and Grayling hurriedly sets out to avenge his friend's murder.

In Charleston, Grayling is able to prevail upon some merchants who knew Spencer to call the sheriff and organize a search party to board the ship and look for Macnab. The search eventually uncovers Macnab, hiding under the alias of Macleod. Macleod protests his innocence, but his guilty behavior and his faltering answers to questions from Grayling lead the sheriff to arrest Macleod as the murderer.

Macleod secures a lawyer who files a writ of *habeas corpus*, and the judge states the case against Macleod would be stronger if the body were discovered and the murder actually proven. Grayling sets out to search the bay area and find Spencer's body. After several hours of searching, he spots some buzzards in a tree near the edge of the bay; the buzzards have led him to Spencer's horse, shot through the head. More searching yields Spencer's corpse and the butt of the broken pistol which had been found in Macleod's trunk. When the evidence is presented at trial, Macnab, alias Macleod, is found guilty and hanged.

Here ends the grandmother's tale; the narrator's father, however, suspicious of such irrationalities, tells his son the ghost was an invention of Grayling's mind and that all the supposed mysterious happenings of the tale can be accounted for by natural laws. Grayling was a bold, imaginative man. When he learned his friend had not made it to the tavern, he thought of Macnab traveling along the same road and became suspicious of foul play. He also was aware that Macnab knew Spencer was on his way to England to prove his identity and claim a large fortune. The spot where the "ghost" appeared was simply one which had already struck Grayling's keen intelligence as a perfect place for an ambush; these thoughts were in his mind as he sat down to rest by the tree. Falling asleep—or so the father contends—Grayling sees a "ghost"; you will note, however, the father states, that, although Spencer told Grayling he had been murdered by Macnab, he did not tell him how or by what weapons. Neither does he reveal what wounds he has suffered. To ride to Charleston and discover the murderer onboard the very ship Major Spencer would have sailed upon for England required no great or superior logical deduction from Grayling. "The whole story," the father tells the son, "is one of strong probabilities which happened to be verified." The son hears his father "with great patience to the end," noting that the father "had taken a great deal of pains to destroy one of my greatest sources of pleasure." The son, however, chooses to believe in ghosts and to reject his father's philosophy, saying that "it was more easy to believe the one than to comprehend the other."

Both "How Sharp Snaffles Got His Capital and His Wife" and "Grayling" demonstrate Simms's penchant for stories which unmask villains, reward the just and virtuous, and show the eventual triumph of good over evil. A similar pattern can be seen in the story "The Snake of the Cabin," which focuses upon the mysterious death of Ellen Ramsay, a young maiden of health and vigor who faded rapidly into sickness and death barely a year after her marriage to Edward Stanton. At her funeral, her spurned lover, Robert Anderson, appears and accuses Stanton of using slander and witchcraft to steal Ellen away from him. Stanton is enraged, and the men have to be separated before a fight ensues. Anderson keeps up a steady vigil at Ellen's grave for several months, until he himself dies, presumably of a broken heart. Upon his death, it is discovered that he has carved matching headstones for his grave and Ellen's. Stanton, however, is adamant that the headstone is not to be erected over his wife's grave.

The tale is narrated by Mr. Atkins to a stranger who has appeared upon the scene and made inquiries about Edward Stanton. Hearing the details of the story, he tells Atkins that he has proof against Stanton which will end his claim to Ellen's estate and thus save her father, John Ramsay, the pain of having to sell several of his slaves to pay Stanton his share. The stranger is taken to Mr. Ramsay's house, where Stanton is engaged in an argument with Ramsay over how he is to receive his share of his wife's estate. The stranger listens for awhile, then asks Stanton which wife he is referring to. Stanton, obviously flustered, responds that he is talking about Ellen Ramsay, of course. The stranger responds that he thinks not, since Stanton has recently married three women in different parts of the country and claimed shares of their estates. Stanton shouts that the stranger can prove none of these charges, and the stranger reveals papers he has carried with him that substantiate his claims. Stanton is confused and shaken, and those present conclude that his behavior and the legal papers at hand reveal his guilt. The stranger unmasks himself as Henry Lamar of Georgia, the cousin and once the betrothed of a girl Stanton married and later wronged. Lamar tells Stanton he has no claim against Ellen Ramsay's estate and warns him to be out of town within forty-eight hours or Lamar will have him prosecuted.

Later that evening, Abraham, one of the slaves Stanton wanted Ramsay to sell, comes up to Ellen's brother, Jack Ramsay, and shows him a twenty-dollar bill, asking him if it is genuine. Ramsay tells him it is not and asks him where he got it. Abraham responds that he got it from Mr. Stanton, who gave Abraham twenty dollars to convince the slaves to run away with him and achieve their freedom in the North. Ramsay decides that they will hatch a plot to seize Stanton at once, and he tells Abraham to round up Lamar, Atkins, and several others to disguise themselves as the Negro slaves and meet Stanton later that night at the designated spot. The men wait for Stanton in the woods, and when he appears, they move to capture him. He escapes and runs down the path, only to be tripped up by Abraham. In trying to escape once more, Stanton shoots at Abraham and wounds him in the arm. Abraham falls, however, and lands upon Stanton's knife, driving the blade deep into Stanton's side and killing him. For his virtuous conduct in revealing Stanton's plot to Jack Ramsay and in aiding in Stanton's capture, Abraham is provided for by the Ramsay family and becomes the official recounter of the tale of Stanton's efforts to attain gain by evil and devious means. The moral of the story is presented by Lamar, who states that evil is not an exclusive possession of the wealthy or the powerful; "the same snake, or one very much like it, winds his way into the wigwam and the cabin—and the poor silly country girl is as frequently the victim, as the dashing lady of the city and city fashions."

Simms's writings are often regarded as frivolous and criticized for their heavy Romanticism and simplistic conceptions of morality. Those who find Simms's works to be insubstantial often charge him with being a dated historical writer, one whose works must fade in significance and interest as quickly as the era they depicted passes into history and into memory. While there is some obvious merit to these charges against Simms, it cannot be denied that Simms never aspired to be anything more than a recorder of his era and its particular charms and peculiarities. More than any other writer of the Old South he achieved that aim, and his collected works remain the most sensitive, insightful, and imaginative record of the formative years of Southern culture.

Major publications other than short fiction
NOVELS: *Martin Faber*, 1833; *Guy Rivers*, 1834; *The Partisan*, 1835; *The Yemassee*, 1835; *Mellichampe*, 1836; *Richard Hurdis*, 1838; *The Damsel of Darien*, 1839; *Border Beagles*, 1840; *Confession*, 1841; *The Kinsmen*, 1841; *Beauchampe*, 1842; *Count Julian*, 1845; *Katharine Walton*, 1851; *The Sword and the Distaff*, 1853; *Vasconselos*, 1853, *The Forayers*, 1855; *Charlemont*, 1856; *Eutaw*, 1856; *The Cassique of Kiawah*, 1859.

POETRY: *Poems: Descriptive, Dramatic, Legendary and Contemplative*, 1853.

NONFICTION: *The History of South Carolina*, 1840; *The Geography of South Carolina*, 1843; *The Life of Francis Marion*, 1844; *Views and Reviews in American Literature, History and Fiction*, 1845; *The Life of John Smith*, 1846; *The Life of Chevalier Bayard*, 1847; *The Life of Nathaniel Greene*, 1849.

Bibliography
Leisy, Ernest E. *The American Historical Novel.*
Parks, Edd Winfield. *William Gilmore Simms as Literary Critic.*
Ridgely, J. V. *William Gilmore Simms.*
Trent, William P. *William Gilmore Simms.*

Christina Murphy

ISAAC BASHEVIS SINGER

Born: Radzymin, Poland; July 14, 1904

Principal short fiction

Gimpel the Fool and Other Stories, 1957; *The Spinoza of Market Street*, 1961; *Short Friday and Other Stories*, 1964; *The Séance and Other Stories*, 1968; *A Friend of Kafka and Other Stories*, 1970; *A Crown of Feathers and Other Stories*, 1973; *Passions and Other Stories*, 1975; *Old Love*, 1979.

Other literary forms

Isaac Bashevis Singer's thirty published books include plays, translations, autobiography, children's fiction, novels, and short stories, for which he is best known even though he won the National Book Award for children's literature in 1970. His novel *The Magician of Lublin* (1960) was filmed in Hollywood and released as *The Magician*. The Nobel Prize for Literature was awarded to Singer in 1978 for his novel *Shosha*.

Influence

Composing most of his writings in Yiddish and translating them himself or with the help of others, Singer is the foremost writer to preserve the culture and vitality of that language. He is read, however, almost exclusively in translation so that his stories possess the qualities of the oral tradition as he combines Old World myth and setting with modern Jewish lore. His stories appear in most anthologies of short fiction, he publishes in both the major and ethnic magazines, and his work has been translated into all major Western languages.

Story characteristics

Singer presents biting, sometimes bitterly humorous stories portraying stranger-than-life characters in stranger-than-this-world situations. Myth, pacing, and language are his principal means for achieving shocking dramatic action which speaks to the reader simply and directly, but which is strangely complex as if it were a nightmare enacted as a play.

Biography

Educated at Tachkemoni Rabbinical Seminary, Warsaw, 1920-1922, Isaac Bashevis Singer lived in Poland and worked as a proofreader and translator for Literarishe Bleter from 1923 to 1933. He emigrated to the United States in 1935 and became a journalist for the *Jewish Daily Forward*, where he worked until retirement. He married Alma Haimann in 1940 and has one child. He won the National Book Award in 1970 and 1974 and the Nobel

Prize in 1978; and he is a member of the National Institute of Arts and Letters (1965), American Academy of Arts and Sciences (1969), Jewish Academy of Arts and Sciences, and the Polish Institute of Arts and Sciences.

Analysis

Isaac Bashevis Singer's best-known and most anthologized stories are often the title works from his numerous collections: *Gimpel the Fool and Other Stories*, *The Spinoza of Market Street*, *A Friend of Kafka and Other Stories*. The titles of these stories, like the titles of many others—"The Unseen," "The Man Who Came Back," "Yentl the Yeshiva Boy," "The Slaughterer," "Getzel the Monkey"—reflect the mysterious and omniscient nature of Singer's work. Although characters have names, they are not quite human and their function is to fulfill roles and destinies rather than to represent individual people. In their immediate sense, Singer's characters seem contrived and literary, bearing little resemblance to ordinary people, but it is their nonhumanness and otherworldliness which help establish Singer's themes.

Singer's fiction is about man's acceptance of life's mysteries. "Acceptance" is the key. The philosophy suggests that since the conditions of life never really change, man must learn to live with the way things are rather than demand that they be different. The narrator of the stories speaks as if he were the voice of history incanting with wondrous authority. The voice is dispassionate yet caring, and seems to tell the reader to succumb to the universal conditions which trap men. Yet, undercutting this seeming determinism and capitulation to life's forces is a haunting sense that acceptance is not quite right. The reader wants desperately to speak out and warn the characters not to give in so easily, but Singer establishes plots which have inevitable directions, and for the reader to speak out would be the same as defying the gods' will. To defy the story is to blaspheme, and it is not until we realize the gods' fallibility and malevolence that we understand how evil a thing "acceptance" can be.

In the Broadway play and film *Fiddler on the Roof*, one may see two of Singer's most important themes developing: tradition and madness. Tradition provides a kind of stability and continuity which either harbors or engenders madness. Tradition can confine people so intensely that they go mad because of it, or it can protect those who reach beyond themselves and this world through creative madness. The fiddler is mad, not insane, and whatever confinement he feels from tradition is self-imposed. Singer's characters seem either to be driven by some inner demon, or strung like puppets and manipulated beyond their control.

Singer's brother, Israel Joshua Singer, who for many years was better known as a writer than Isaac, entitled a book about their lives in Poland as *Of a World that Is No More* (1946), and this haunting nostalgia suggests many levels of Isaac's stories. Singer's use of madness, his otherworldliness, his determinism all contribute to a dreamworld quality, and as with Franz Kafka one cannot tell what is real or fanciful. Singer turns dreams into bizarre comedies which force us to the brink of absurdity.

"Gimpel the Fool," for example, opens with a tone which does not permit the reader to know whether Gimpel is a simpleton or not. He is considered by the townspeople as a fool, and certainly he manages to be caught at many foolish deeds, but Gimpel is a fool who knows what foolishness is, and so we believe that he may be wise. Even when Gimpel marries Elka, the town whore already pregnant with another man's child, we are not convinced of his foolishness. Gimpel is humane and caring, and knows very well who Elka is. So what if others, who are cruel and stupid, play tricks on a poor fool? That does not make the fool foolish, only those who would trick him.

In the second part of this four-part story the illegitimate child is born to the delight and mirth of the townspeople. Gimpel questions Elka, who explains that the child is his. She speaks as if she were talking to an idiot, not a fool, and we begin to distinguish between the two categories. Slowly, Singer infuses his story with differences: life is full of deceit, pain, and stupid convention, and anyone who believes he has conquered life is more ridiculous than Gimpel, who acknowledges his own foolish ways. Gimpel, whose foolishness was once the result of mischievous pranks, is faced with genuine troubles. Arriving home unexpectedly from his job in the bakery, Gimpel finds another man in bed with Elka and declares to himself: "Gimpel isn't going to be a sucker all his life. There's a limit even to the foolishness of a fool like Gimpel."

Gimpel is speaking for all of us who ask what it means to confront the ridiculous in life. For Singer, all things in life are ridiculous. Life itself is ridiculous, though not without reward. Gimpel goes to the rabbi for advice, who tells him to divorce Elka and her brood of harlot bastards. Gimpel is never to cross her threshold again. As he thinks more about it, Gimpel is afraid of accusing Elka unjustly. Perhaps he hallucinated the vision of another man in bed with his wife. After all, the other men in town—butchers and horse traders—took Elka's defense, and so Gimpel received permission from the rabbi to send Elka bread and money until the rabbinical court could decide how to settle the infidelity.

Elka and Gimpel live separately for nine months. Elka bears another child, a girl, in his absence but Gimpel forgives her and asks permission of the rabbis to return home. They find some obscure reference in the Torah which permits his returning to an unfaithful wife, but on the night of his return, as he rushes home from the bakery full of love for his wife, he finds the baker's apprentice in bed with Elka. Startled and unaware that Gimpel has been granted permission to return home, she sends him to the animal shed to see about the goat. When he comes back to the house and asks Elka where the apprentice has gone, she shrieks abuses at him. Trapped, he capitulates and lives with her for twenty years.

On her deathbed, Elka confesses that the children, ten of them, were not his; she had lied to him, deceived him, abused him. "As she spoke she tossed her head to the side, her eyes turned glassy, and it was all up with Elka. On her whitened lips there remained a smile." Gimpel has a dream. The Spirit of Evil comes to him and tells him there is no world to come, no God, and that he should contaminate the townspeople's bread with urine in revenge for the misfortunes they have bestowed upon him. Gimpel follows the commands of the Spirit of Evil, but before the bread can be distributed Elka comes to him in another dream and confronts him with his wretched deed, and he buries the poisoned bread and returns home to Elka's children. Gimpel decides to divide his savings among the children and go into the world as a storyteller of "improbable things that could never happen." Now, Gimpel dreams frequently, and when he dreams it is always of his town, Frampol, and of Elka, who consoles him. When he awakes he can "feel her lips and taste the salt of her tears." Gimpel continues through the world knowing that while it is imaginary, it is only once removed from the true world. Gimpel concludes that his death will be joyful; that "whatever may be there, it will be real, without complication, without ridicule, without deception. There, even Gimpel cannot be deceived."

"There," of course, is loaded with dual meaning, and we realize that we have been tricked as surely as Gimpel. Gimpel has become his own fool, not the town's, but in this final, foolish affirmation of the afterlife, we regard Gimpel's faith as the only choice there is. Life may, in fact, deceive us all, but to continue in faith, and in good faith, is to achieve man's only nobility, and that is his victory. If Elka or the townsmen wish to fool us, they may, but there is no joy in tricking a fool, and those who attempt it will find the trick reversed on them.

For Singer, the world is full of tricks. Life is a magic show, and sometimes we are the magician while at other times we become the audience, or even the poor rabbit who is transformed into a dove. We control and are controlled. Yentl, in "Yentl the Yeshiva Boy," decides that she prefers the intellectual life afforded to men, and once her father dies she sells the estate, dresses as a man, and sets forth for a life where she will not be matched and married into housewifery. In a tavern on the road, she meets Avigdor, a student in the rabbi's school at Behev. Avigdor saves Yentl, now known as Anshel, from teasing by other men and boys, and he persuades her to enter the school. It is an all-male academy, of course, but Yentl manages to conceal her sexual identity so that even Avigdor does not suspect her.

Avigdor confides his marital hopes to Yentl. He wants to marry Hadass, the rabbi's daughter, but the rabbi discovers that Avigdor's brother had hanged himself many years before and the engagement is forbidden. Heartbroken, Avigdor engages himself to Peshe, a homely widow thought of as a man killer. Yentl pleads with Avigdor not to marry Peshe, partly for his own good and partly because she realizes she wants him for herself. She is crushed between wanting a marriage with Avigdor and her manly endeavors; she is certain that if she were to tell Avigdor that she is a girl, he would marry her, and so she remains silent.

Singer's tale, unlike Shakespeare's, refuses to allow us too close to the characters. We are confronted with a situation more than with sympathetic people, and it is the situation which conveys Singer's theme. Life is an entanglement of events to which we respond out of fear, or anger, or frustration. Seldom do our actions make much difference although they may change our lives dramatically.

In a fit of calculated desperation and defiance, Yentl decides to marry Hadass, the rabbi's daughter who was not permitted to marry Avigdor. The rabbi, agreeing that Anshel/Yentl is a fine young man, consents to the engagement. Avigdor is perplexed at Anshel's sudden decision to marry the girl he once loved, but he is in no position to object. They both marry—Anshel to Hadass, Avigdor to Peshe. Anshel is happy but plagued with the misfortune of deception; Avigdor is miserable. Both marriages lead inevitably to unhappiness. Finally, Yentl confesses her secret to Avigdor, who is dumbfounded by the act. He vows never to see her again, but in spite of his vows and Jewish law, he continues their friendship and they finally declare their love for each other. Anshel divorces Hadass to the amazement of the townspeople, and disappears. Avigdor divorces Peshe, and no one knows the truth. There are great rumors. Then, Avigdor marries Hadass, a confused and shamed woman, and the town is scandalized. Soon, Hadass becomes pregnant and bears a son, who is named Anshel.

Like many of Singer's stories, "Yentl the Yeshiva Boy" does not develop to a forceful ending but works to achieve an inevitable conclusion. This quality makes Singer's stories feel like moral tales, as if the reader is supposed to derive some point based on a series of circumstances presented to him by the writer. It is, perhaps, this aspect of his writing that makes Singer seem less Western than most other contemporary writers. He combines the storytelling tradition of the Cabalists, the Bible, and the Hasidic saints, establishing cultural responses to life which becomes a universal statement about brotherhood, alienation, superstition, and pain. Singer rejects almost all of the conventional responses to life, such as marriage, God, culture, while maintaining ferociously the importance of man's spirit.

Singer is often categorized as a "Jewish" writer, or an "Old World" writer, or a nineteenth century moralist, and he may be all those things, but his stories go far beyond provincial, regional, or ethnic backgrounds. His comedy is not "Jewish humor" or his metaphors religious parables, but rather his works attack the core of human fears and desires so that one cannot really tell if life is comic or tragic, or if people are erotic or sterile, compassionate or hostile, intimate or isolated. Singer's stories leave the reader with feelings rather than ideas, and with things of the earth rather than with heaven. His is the sound of a voice uttered to explore the world, and return as an echo.

Major publications other than short fiction

NOVELS: *Satan in Goray*, 1955; *The Magician of Lublin*, 1960; *The Slave*, 1962; *The Family Moskat*, 1965; *The Manor*, 1967; *The Estate*, 1969; *Enemies: A Love Story*, 1972; *Shosha*, 1978.

PLAYS: *Schlemiel the First*, 1974; *Yentl the Yeshiva Boy*, 1978.

NONFICTION: *In My Father's Court*, 1966; *A Little Boy in Search of God*, 1976; *A Young Man in Search of Love*, 1978.

Bibliography

Allentuck, Marcia, ed. *The Achievement of Isaac Bashevis Singer.*
Buchen, Irving. *Isaac Bashevis Singer and the Eternal Past.*
Malin, Irving. *Isaac Bashevis Singer.*
_____ , ed. *Critical Views of Isaac Bashevis Singer.*
Singer, Irving. *Isaac Bashevis Singer.*

Walton Beacham

ALEKSANDR SOLZHENITSYN

Born: Kislovodsk, North Caucasus, U.S.S.R.; December 11, 1918

Principal short fiction
Prose Etudes and Short Stories, 1965; *Sobranie Sochinenii*, 1969-1970 (*Collected Works*, Vols. I and V); *Stories and Prose Poems*, 1971.

Other literary forms
Although Aleksandr Solzhenitsyn is best known for his novels and his multi-volume historical-artistic investigation of the Soviet prison system, *Arkhipelag GULag 1918-1956* (1973-1976, *The Gulag Archipelago*), in which inset tales figure notably, he has also written independent short fiction, prose poems, narrative poetry, a film scenario, essays, biography and autobiography, and drama. His short novel *Odin den' Ivana Denisovicha* (1962, *One Day in the Life of Ivan Denisovich*) was adapted for American television. Solzhenitsyn was awarded the Nobel Prize for Literature in 1970, but Soviet authorities blocked a reception ceremony. His *Nobelevskara lektsira po literature* (*The Nobel Lecture*) was published in 1972.

Influence
English versions of much of Solzhenitsyn's earlier writing are often distorted by the exigencies of transmitting their originals to the West, but the moral stature of his literary message nevertheless remains the best-known example of dissent against the Communist regime of the Soviet Union. Solzhenitsyn's life work promises to unfold not only his homeland's history but also his mammoth spiritual autobiography, of which his extant short fiction, composed during the 1950's and early 1960's, forms the earliest chapters, the initial literary transmutation of Communism's harm to his countrymen and his profound faith in the redemptive power of their suffering.

Story characteristics
Solzhenitsyn's six short stories and sixteen prose poems announce the dual foundation of his mature literary faith, his traditionalist view that the pen is mightier than totalitarian terror, and his linguistic innovation, the latter, unfortunately, not apparent in English. In his otherwise conventional realistic short fiction, Solzhenitsyn begins to invigorate Russian literary language, stultified by official Soviet cliché-ridden jargon, at the same time reawakening humanistic ideals obliterated in the Stalinist aftermath of the Communist revolution.

Biography
Aleksandr Isayevich Solzhenitsyn grew up fatherless and poor in Rostov-

on-Don, where he took his university degree in mathematics in 1941, having also studied literature by correspondence from Moscow University. After four years' unbroken service as a front-line artillery officer, he was sentenced in 1945 to eight years' hard labor in GULAG, the Soviet prison system, for criticizing Stalin in a private letter. Inexplicably exiled to Kazakhstan from 1953 to 1956, Solzhenitsyn recovered from a near-fatal cancer, taught mathematics and physics in a high school, and began to set his prison experiences down as fiction. Rehabilitated in 1956, he moved to Ryazan, near Moscow, continuing to write, and the publication of his camp novel *One Day in the Life of Ivan Denisovich* marked a brief thaw in Soviet literary restrictions under Khrushchev in 1962. Upon the retightening of censorship, Solzhenitsyn's work was banned from publication in the Soviet Union. After being expelled from the Soviet Writers' Union in 1969 and barred from formal acceptance of the Nobel Prize for Literature he had won in 1970, Solzhenitsyn was ejected from the Soviet Union in 1973. He now lives in Vermont with his second wife and children.

Analysis

Aleksandr Solzhenitsyn initially responded to his prison and labor camp experiences in easy-to-memorize poetry and later in tiny self-contained prose poems, written down in the 1950's and assembled as a rough set around 1962, although not published in the Soviet Union. Shortly after his initial success in the journal *Novy Mir* with the short novel *One Day in the Life of Ivan Denisovich* (1962), Solzhenitsyn also published his short stories "Incident at Krechetovka Station," "Matryona's House," and "For the Good of the Cause" there in 1963. Like "The Easter Procession," "The Right Hand" never appeared in the Soviet Union, although "Zakhar the Pouch" was published in *Novy Mir* in 1966, the last of Solzhenitsyn's works printed publicly in the Soviet Union. Each of these short pieces contains the germ of a larger work to come, just as each of the individuals or groups named in the titles of the stories reflects one facet of Solzhenitsyn's overriding theme of his country's agony under Communism.

The essence of Solzhenitsyn's message lies in his peculiarly Russian view of shared suffering as vital, even necessary, to human spiritual survival. To this end, he announced in his Nobel Lecture that only art, only literature, can bridge the immense gulfs of time and space between human beings, bringing experiences of those faraway others close enough so that their lessons may help overcome evil. Although Solzhenitsyn has not completed large-scale treatments of all of the themes presented in his short fiction, the individualization of experience he began with Ivan Denisovich, the lowly camp inmate whose shining humanity enables him to survive, clearly emerges from the prose poems and the short stories, its successive stages mirroring Solzhenitsyn's own existence in Stalin's prison system.

"Incident at Krechetovka Station" draws heavily upon Solzhenitsyn's wartime experience. Set in the critical autumn of 1941, this story defies all the conventions of Soviet war literature, in which the cliché of patriotic self-sacrifice predominates. Its protagonist, Lieutenant Zotov, an assistant transit officer, is sympathetically portrayed in sharp contrast to the self-serving functionaries around him, who collectively form the story's antagonist, the "system" to blame for categorically condemning both the guilty and the innocent.

"Incident at Krechetovka Station" opens in cold pouring rain with one of Solzhenitsyn's typically abrupt laconic dialogues which achieve a forceful immediacy. Zotov, a youngish man isolated by the war from his family, has gentle features that toughen as he self-consciously straightens his glasses. He observes the misery of the wretched civilians who clutter the station, but he submerges his sympathy for them in his devotion to Marxism. Soon Zotov is miserable himself, however, distressed by a growing suspicion that the war is not proceeding in tune with Party propaganda.

For more than half of the story, Solzhenitsyn shuttles between the chilly "present" and events in Zotov's past, gradually hinting at the shattering perception Solzhenitsyn himself had grasped as a youth: the vast gap between Communism's promises and reality. Zotov haltingly approaches the truth through chance encounters with other actors in the drama, first in a few poems from line officers critical of their leadership, then in the hunger and cold of the old people and the children in the town. Solzhenitsyn characteristically allows Zotov to linger over the predicament of starving Russian soldiers being repatriated, like Ivan Denisovich, to Stalin's labor camps, their only crime being their surrender to the German Army. Lonely and often despairing, Zotov tries to take refuge in his cheap volume of *Das Kapital*, but somehow he cannot finish it. Distracted by the pain of the war's victims, which his heart sees, and by his revulsion at those who prey on them, which his Communist glasses cannot quite shut out, Zotov is disturbed time and again, finally by an "incident" in the bedraggled person of Tveritinov, a former actor trying to find the military detachment from which he had somehow become separated.

Tveritinov strikes up an acquaintance with Zotov, and as they reminisce about prewar times, the actor's rich voice and winning manner create a mood that for the first time warms the dreary little station with the ceaseless rain beating down on its roof. Solzhenitsyn characteristically insinuates a darker undercurrent when they speak of 1937. Zotov associates that year only with the Soviet involvement in the Spanish Civil War, but Tveritinov, older, recalls an entirely different side to it, the height of Stalin's terrifying purges; his moment of silence, eyes downcast, reveals far more than any speech.

The rapport is suddenly shattered when Tveritinov mistakenly uses the pre-Communist name for Stalingrad. Zotov, struck by the horrifying possibility that he may be harboring an enemy of the state, deceitfully leads the actor into the arms of the security police. Not long after, when Zotov inquires about Tveritinov, he is ominously warned not to look into the matter further. This "incident" at apparently insignificant Krechetovka Station is Solzhenitsyn's metaphor for his country's wartime tragedy. So caught up in Communist zeal that they are able to see the world as Zotov at first did, only through a point of view that obliterates their vital connection to the rest of humanity, Solzhenitsyn's countrymen were being forced to share a perverted brotherhood of opportunism and betrayal, brutality, and inhumanity. As a measure of Solzhenitsyn's burningly ironic message in this story, the "incident" at Krechetovka Station remains Zotov's torment forever.

In "The Right Hand," a miniature forerunner of *Rakovyi korpus* (1968, *The Cancer Ward*), Solzhenitsyn ruthlessly depicts what Zotov might have become if he had not experienced that cruel enlightenment. The story not only excoriates a state-run hospital system that dehumanizes the very patients it purports to serve, but it also unveils the devastating fate of those whose Party blinders are not removed until it is too late. Having served Communism faithfully, a new patient, clearly terminal, is hypocritically refused admittance to a cancer clinic on a technicality, and this denial of every Party ideal he has slavishly followed snaps his last thread-thin hold on life.

Like the narrator of "The Right Hand," himself a sufferer, the man who tells the story of "Matryona's House" recently emerged from the crucible of the prison system. All he wants at the outset is to lose himself in the heart of Russia, yearning for the peace of its countryside to restore his soul. Like Solzhenitsyn himself, he takes a position as a mathematics teacher in a shabby ancient village, living in a large old ramshackle house with a sick and aged peasant woman named Matryona. Matryona owns few things, and what she does have is as decrepit as her cockroach-ridden kitchen: a lame cat, a marginal garden, a dirty white goat, and some stunted house plants. Although she had worked on the collective farm for twenty-five years, bureaucratic entanglements have choked off her dead husband's pension—she herself is entitled to nothing—and she is almost destitute. Meager as her life is, however, Matryona's goodness sustains both herself and her lodger, who comes to prize her smile even more than the bit of daily bread they share.

In a strange though altogether convincing way, Matryona's very generosity is responsible for her death. She had loved one of the villagers deeply and waited three years for him to return from World War I. Thinking him dead then, she married his brother, and when the first man returned, he cursed them both. After Matryona's six children died in infancy, she reared one of the daughters of her former sweetheart as her own, and now, feeling she has not long to live, Matryona allows the girl and her friends to dismantle the top part of her house for its lumber. In struggling to help pull the heavy timber sledge over a railroad crossing, Matryona is killed by a speeding train.

For Solzhenitsyn, generosity, purity of heart, goodness, and love, the best qualities of the Russian folk, are as endangered under Communism as they had been under the czars. Now it may even be worse; Matryona's village has become wretchedly poor, with women instead of horses plowing the kitchen gardens, and the system that promised so much offers only corruption, lackadaisical confusion, and mistrust, racing carelessly over people like Matryona on its way to some future too obscure to believe. And yet (one of the hallmarks of Solzhenitsyn's fiction is the simple "and yet" that illuminates an otherwise hopeless life), he says, Matryona, poor in all but spirit, is the one righteous person without whom not a village or a city or the world can stand. Matryona is the personification of the mystical regeneration held inviolate in the Russian people that Solzhenitsyn instinctively sought upon his release and found intuitively in her. Like the old caretaker of a tatterdemalion monument to a forgotten battle in "Zakhar the Pouch," Matryona's stubborn, patient self-sacrifice restored Solzhenitsyn's faith in humanity at a time when he had learned its opposite all too well.

In his political polemic of the early 1960's, "For the Good of the Cause," Solzhenitsyn again pits genuine human affection against villainous bureaucracy. Students of a provincial technical college have helped build themselves a badly needed building, but Party officials usurp it, with the resulting disillusion wrenching the consciences of director and teachers and breaking the will of many of the students. Their helpless, bitter frustration at official hypocrisy underlies the actions of the vicious hoodlums who aimlessly harass "The Easter Procession" in Solzhenitsyn's last short story, inhuman products of a system he feels they eventually will indiscriminately trample down.

Solzhenitsyn's short fiction, written prior to his First Communion in 1971, resembles an Easter procession of his own, advancing from the Good Friday of the repatriated Soviet prisoner of war through loving recognition of the healing goodness in the peasants Matryona and Zakhar and a clear-eyed estimate of perversion of an honest teacher's responsibility to his students, finally arriving at the realization that the Soviet system and its creatures contain the seeds of universal destruction. The only hope Solzhenitsyn can see lies in the willing acknowledgment of the bond between human beings that springs from the Christian consciousness that each of us shares his fellows' suffering. In Solzhenitsyn's short fiction, his overture to a powerful literary and spiritual mission, we recognize that however separated we are in time and space, his is the voice of our brother.

Major publications other than short fiction

NOVELS: *Odin den' Ivana Denisovicha,* 1962 (*One Day in the Life of Ivan Denisovich*); *Rakovyi korpus,* 1968 (*The Cancer Ward*); *V Kruge pervom,* 1968 (*The First Circle*); *Avgust chetyrnadtsatogo,* 1971 (*August 1914*).

PLAYS: *Olen'i shalafhovka,* 1966 (*The Love-Girl and the Innocent*); *Svecha na vetru,* 1969 (*Candle in the Wind*).

NONFICTION: *A Lenten Letter to Pimen, Patriarch of All Russia*, 1972; *Nobelevskara lektsira po literature*, 1972 (*The Nobel Lecture*); *Arkhipelag GULag 1918-1956: Op'bit Khudozhestvennopo issledovanija*, 1973-1976 (*The Gulag Archipelago: One, Parts I-II*, 1973; *Two, Parts III-IV*, 1974; *Three, Parts V-VII, 1918-1956*, 1976); *Pis'mo vozhdram Sovetskogo Soruza*, 1974 (*Letter to the Soviet Leaders*); *Bodalsra telenok s dubom*, 1975 (*The Calf and the Oak*); *Lenin v Tsiurikhe*, 1976 (*Lenin in Zurich*); *Warning to the West*, 1976.

Bibliography

Dunlop, John B., Richard Haugh, Alexis Klimoff, eds. *Aleksandr Solzhenitsyn: Critical Essays and Documentary Materials*.

Feifer, George and David Burg. *Solzhenitsyn*.

Fiene, Donald M., comp. *Solzhenitsyn: An International Bibliography*.

Labedz, Leopold, ed. *Solzhenitsyn: A Documentary Record*.

Moody, Christopher. *Solzhenitsyn*.

Mitzi M. Brunsdale

MURIEL SPARK

Born: Edinburgh, Scotland; February 1, 1918

Principal short fiction
The Go-Away Bird and Other Stories, 1958; *Voices at Play*, 1961; *Collected Stories I*, 1967.

Other literary forms
Muriel Spark's more than thirty published books include novels, plays for radio and stage, verse, critical studies of English writers, and editions of poems and letters by English writers, some of the studies and editions done with the help of Derek Stanford.

Influence
Spark is generally grouped with English writers of manners and satirists such as G. K. Chesterton, Max Beerbohm, Evelyn Waugh, and Graham Greene, and she has been called a Catholic writer. Her critical and editorial work also indicates a connection with some of the English Romantic writers, and with William Wordsworth she shares an interest in the speech of common people.

Story characteristics
Spark writes highly ironic stories and novellas rendered in a deft prose characterized by the appearance of reportorial objectivity and the occasional parodying of rhetoric and various sorts of jargon. Striking repeated images, dramatic juxtapositions, and supernatural twists press forth from a generally understated surface in which, however, language often has an edge. She develops parables which demonstrate a belief in a traditional Christian view of things and, in the more naturalistic pieces, offers studies of human needs and limitations.

Biography
Muriel Sarah Spark was educated at James Gillespie's School for Girls in Edinburgh. She married S. O. Spark in 1938; now divorced, she has one son, Robin. From 1947 to 1949, she acted as General Secretary of the Poetry Society and as editor of *The Poetry Review*. In 1951, she won the *Observor* story prize for her story "The Seraph and the Zambesi." In 1954, she converted to Roman Catholicism. Between 1957 and 1961, a number of her radio plays were broadcast; and in 1962, she won the Prix Italia for a radio play. She has also won the Black Memorial Prize (1966), has been made an officer, Order of the British Empire (1967), and has been awarded an LL.D. by the Uni-

versity of Strathclyde, Glasgow (1971). In 1976, her novel *The Abbess of Crewe* (1974), satirizing Watergate, was scheduled for filming; in 1969, a successful film version of her novel *The Prime of Miss Jean Brodie* (1961) was released. She divides her time among Rome, Nemi, and Tuscany. Currently, she belongs to the commission charged with the task of modernizing the English Roman Catholic liturgy.

Analysis

Muriel Spark's sensitive but overly cerebral narrators drift about in a way that appears aimless, or perhaps directed by an unexplained and sometimes seemingly malevolent force through a world filled with violence, snobbery, self-righteousness, various mental and emotional disturbances, marriages strained by boredom and infidelity, a preponderance of solitaries who distrust the possibility of wedded bliss or sexual happiness, and a pervasive blindness to explanations which lie beyond the currently accepted clichés. The seven deadly sins are well and at work in the violent Africa she describes and in a Europe whose greater civilization is too superficial to stop its headlong rush toward a widespread war. Most frequently, the narrators of these stories speak for themselves in the first person, showing that they feel different from those they observe and have to deal with but displaying many of the same problems, certainly the pervasive cases of "nerves." Often the narrators or the main characters are intelligent and sophisticated; just as often, they are unhappy and neurotic. In all of *Collected Stories I*, there is not one complete and lasting relationship between two human beings. Beyond the isolation of these lonely pilgrims, however, there is the sense of something more, a wholeness glimpsed occasionally from the perspective of traditional religious belief. It is the absent member for which Spark's limited creatures yearn. Several of the more fanciful tales, allegorical parables, offer clear programs of her philosophical assumptions.

Nothing is coincidence, although to the narrow rationalist the opposite may appear to be true. The narrator of "The Playhouse Called Remarkable" drops into a conversation with Moon Biglow a fanciful phrase, "I'm going to read a story to illustrate the *Uprise of My Downfall*," meaning nothing much by it, saying it's "just a way of expressing" the "venture into that bourne from which no traveller returns" or "the downward progress up to the dizzy heights, as they concern the art of letters." The truth of this last statement is "extremely truthful," Moon Biglow avers, and proceeds surprisingly to explain how, before the flood, he and his brothers came from the actual moon to this earth of their "own free will on the Downfall of" their "Uprise." An artistic intuition has penetrated at least partway to heaven. The Moon brothers came, it turns out, to offer from their artistic plenitude an antidote to the limited, the boring, and the bestial that passed for art on earth in those days. Led by one of the worst offenders in Muriel Spark's gallery of rogues, a sloganizing demagogue named Johnnie Heath, the earthlings had chanted, perhaps from the beginning

of time, the only symbol of "the purity" of their "native customs," the meaningless repetitiousness of "Tum tum *ya*, tum tum *ya*." Moon and his brothers
came to save the community from "dying out from sheer lack of anything to
do in its spare time" by teaching it "the language of poetry." They established
a playhouse to offer varied fare, at the center of which, however, was the
Moon poets' one theme.

   This is made concrete in the tale of the Moon girl whose curiosity led her
to seek out the secret of a singing mountain and who, reaching her destination,
became bound in "desperate dialogue" of song. All day, stabbed by the sun,
she stood "motionless on the mountain peak" while the sun-inspired "voice
of the mountain" mocked her "with its high wordless music." Then, when
the sun withdrew, she sang her nightly song, endowing with the flesh of words
the nature of poetic inspiration, the opposites held together in artistic tension
and thus revealed, and commanded the poets below that, knowing the truth,
they take truth down to earth. This they did and flourishingly—until Johnnie
Heath, with deadening slogans and brutal sacrifice, brought the festival to a
halt, driving Moon's five brothers from the earth. Moon alone remained to
see that "the absence of the Changing Drama of the Moon" was "felt" and
that "a race of artists" appeared "in the earth to express" what was lost. These
artists remain, appearing "whenever the tum tum *ya* movement gets afoot
and the monotony and horror start taking hold of people"; their job is to
"proclaim the virtue of the remarkable things that are missing from the earth."
Art's tension exists for us, a gift from beyond, a glimpse of wholeness. The
two forces that create this tension are hardly ever absent from Muriel Spark's
stories, although in the more naturalistic pieces the reality of "those remarkable things that are missing from the earth" grows faint, implied primarily by
human confusion and dissatisfaction. However faint, it is this reality for which
Muriel Spark bears witness in the court of our limited, too cerebral selves.

   Another fanciful parable, "Miss Pinkerton's Apocalypse," amusingly asserts
the need for artistic risk when one knows the truth but sees that common
sense dictates the propagation of a lie. With a characteristic flatness of style,
the story begins, "One evening, a damp one in February, something flew in
at the window." Miss Pinkerton and George Lake both see it and agree that
it is "a small round flattish object" that flies. George bumbles about, fears
its danger ("the thing might be radio-active"), tries out some jargon, and
begins to win the attention of the newsman who has come to take down the
story, bringing with him a cameraman who wants to photograph not the thing
itself, because the thing has left by the time they get there, but "the actual
spot" where it had been. Miss Pinkerton, an antique dealer, displays none
of George's worry; she knows exactly what the flying object is: a saucer, a
piece of Spode, propelled by a little man who sits on a "tiny stool, steering
with one hand, waving with the other" and operating "something like a sewing
machine"; but she also sees the reporter's skepticism about her version. Thus,

she comes "to a rapid decision," inventing a tale that, tipsy on sherry, she and George had invented the whole affair. She sells her lie with a giggling meant to suggest that even in confessing she enjoys her naughtiness. When George persists in telling the tale to his regulars, there is some tittering at his expense. No one believes it; skepticism has triumphed—no one, that is, except the narrator, whose "little pilot," she declares, "was shy and inquisitive" and whose saucer was "Royal Worcester." A delightful parable, it makes its point with economy of action and deft strokes of characterization, showing humorously the difficulty of belief when the truth is unfashionably decked out and when those that know the truth decide to hide it. This theme recurs with darker shadings in Spark's most naturalistic tales.

A chilling one of these, worked out with an almost demonic sense of appropriateness, is "Bang-bang, You're Dead." One of the longer forms which Muriel Spark often uses, this story spans a time period running from early childhood well into maturity by shifting about among the main character's memories of various times in the past within the framework of present action. In the present, home movies filmed in Africa eighteen years before are being shown to a group including Sybil, the only survivor of the film's principals and the story's main character. The audience surrounding her is the common lot at such events. This is shown by brief snatches of type-characterizing dialogue throughout the piece: "Wonderful colours"; "and those adorable shiny natives all over the place"; "What were those large red flowers?"; "I liked the bit where those little lizards were playing among the stones"; (spoken by the host); "I rather liked that handsome blonde fellow" (spoken by the hostess); "how carefree you all look"; and so forth. Amidst the showing of the film and this brisk patter of comments, Sybil remembers the truth of things; and her re-creation of it is given force by the dramatic juxtapositioning of her memories and the real illusion created by the seeming objectivity of the pictures. From her childhood she recalls her look-alike and playmate, Désirée, who "continually shot Sybil dead, contrary to the rules, whenever she felt like it." From her time in Africa, she remembers Désirée again, by then married to Barry Weston; she also recalls that the couple pressed invitations upon her and then used her to work out their marital problems by staging embarrassing erotic shows in front of her. From the same time, she remembers David Carter, whom she had used to try to solve her own sexual problems and to whom she had lied about his ability as a poet, even persuading herself of the truth of the lie. Finally, she remembers that, having led him on to help herself and to escape the Westons, she had then declined his proposal and that, wrenched with anger, he had come to shoot her but had gotten her double, Désirée, instead—and then himself, living just long enough to realize his mistake.

Sybil, as her name suggests, knows all about these troubled human beings (herself included), but, as in the ancient Grecian analogues, is very devious about the pride and violence surrounding the play-acting on the film. The shifting of the third-person viewpoint between the external scene of the movie-watching and Sybil's memories produces a perception of continuing irony which the reader shares with Sybil. This manipulation aligns the reader with the most intelligent of the characters in order to sting him with the realization that smart people constantly need, the knowledge that a superior brain causes as many problems as it solves. As a child, Sybil had sensed in herself an intelligence that had set her off from others ("her brain was like a knife"), which made her feel "lonely"; but pins, and needles, and knives are the instruments of penetrating injuries. In Africa, she had been used by all those needy egos and had done some using in return, lying to David and Barry about their poetry and entering into an affair "as an act of virtue done against the grain" which "for a brief time . . . had absolved her from the reproach of her own sexlessness." The moral context of these actions suggests that, from the works of pride, one does not absolve oneself.

For all the darkness, however, there is still some relief in the fact that, finally, she had told the truth to Barry, when, after the death of his wife, he had looked forward to the war so that he could be its poet. "With a sense of relief, *almost* of absolution," Sybil had said, "You'll make a better soldier than a poet." It is constructive to know how adept we are at hurting others and how difficult it is "to proclaim the virtue of the remarkable things that are missing from the earth." With film *and* an honest human memory one can make a start. Amidst the apparent order and happiness of the film's lie—all the "Wonderful colours"—she makes a start with the accustomed question, "Am I a woman . . . or an intellectual monster?" There may be one young man there who has understood her reserve, another start, but she and the reader feel the need for a greater integrity than either sex or thought will bring. Spark's best fictions make us yearn beyond their limits.

The longest and possibly the richest of Spark's short fictions is *The Go-Away Bird*, the title novella of a collection from 1958, and the final piece in *Collected Stories I*. Covering many years in the life of Daphne du Toit, it moves beyond her death to a typically ironic closing, the final actions underscoring the failure of intelligent beings to communicate. Structurally, the work is reminiscent of Waugh's technique in shifting Basil Seal between England and Africa so that each society can comment satirically upon the other. At first, Daphne develops from a child into a young woman in a violent African colony which seems light years away from civilized Europe. The props around her are whiskey and guns, the leading games adultery and revenge, and hushing up unpleasant truths, which do not prepare innocence to cope with life. After civilized Europe has finished its war, Daphne goes to England, where she is used by almost everyone she meets, including relatives symbolically enfeebled in mind and body, a dying breed. Bilked out of more money than her African uncle, Chakata, can afford and mistreated by the men she has lived with, the last a novelist, she finally returns to Africa. She has hardly gotten back when she is mistaken for a buck by Old Tuys, the now senile employee Chakata had cuckolded years before. No person is in control; even Old Tuys, who had desired revenge when he had had the consciousness to do so, does not know he has gotten it; it was not his to get. Finally, the insensitive novelist, with whom Daphne had lived in England and to whom she had told many tales of her African homeland, comes to see her grave— looking for material perhaps. He vaguely remembers some of the names he sees inscribed on the tombstones, but since he had not listened well when she was talking, he will not be able to make anything out of them. Quickly irritated by the chanting of the "go-away bird" perched just behind Daphne's grave, he loses patience, fails to recognize the muse, and leaves the land with no tale to tell.

Among the story's techniques which demonstrate the theme of human limitations and make us yearn beyond them is the bird's repeated chant throughout the story. An important ritualistic symbol "like the biblical Dove, or the Zodiacal Ram," it underscores the failure of understanding bred of the characters' not hearing or of their hearing but not comprehending. In Africa, where the gray-crested lourie's voice is "part of the background to everything" (like a god's), few people hear it; but Daphne does. Indeed, taking its words to mean that she should flee from Africa to England, she yearns toward that land; and when the war delays her trip, she falls in love with anything English that Africa yields up, taking it in, however, with dangerous selectivity. Ronald, from England, talks of having captained "the village cricket team"; in response, Daphne has a romantic vision of rural English life and fails to comprehend a bigamist at work. An art instructor sneers at the success of a fashionable rival in London; Daphne hears only the magic words, " 'Queen Anne house,' 'Kensington,' 'Chelsea.' " When she travels to England, she is used by practically everyone. Mrs. Casse, the sponsor of Daphne's London season, makes Daphne a symbolic present of another bird who warns, "Go 'way, Go 'way, *go to hell!*" When Daphne refuses to pay for her own gift and leaves the house, she merely moves her hell to two one-way affairs. Finally, she returns to Africa to hear the real bird chant one last time before calling out antiphonally, "God help me. Life is unbearable." As if in answer, Old Tuys shoots her down.

Throughout these parables of religious need, intelligent creatures construct the categories that undergird false dreams and prejudices and manufacture photographs and films and guns to chase appearances, failing to grasp "the virtue of the remarkable things that are missing from the earth" as they seal themselves in the undentable silence of their illusions.

Major publications other than short fiction
NOVELS: *The Comforters*, 1957; *Robinson*, 1958; *Memento Mori*, 1959; *The*

Ballad of Peckham Rye, 1960; *The Bachelors*, 1960; *The Prime of Miss Jean Brodie*, 1961; *The Girls of Slender Means*, 1963; *The Mandelbaum Gate*, 1965; *The Public Image*, 1968; *The Driver's Seat*, 1970; *Not to Disturb*, 1971; *The Hothouse by the East River*, 1973; *The Abbess of Crewe: A Modern Morality Tale*, 1974; *The Takeover*, 1976; *Territorial Rights*, 1979.

PLAY: *Doctors of Philosophy*, produced in London, 1962.

POETRY: *The Fanfarlo and Other Verse*, 1952; *Collected Poems I*, 1967.

NONFICTION: *Child of Light: A Reassessment of Mary Shelley*, 1951; *Emily Brontë: Her Life and Work*, 1953 (with Derek Stanford).

Bibliography

Kemp, Peter. *Muriel Spark.*
Malkoff, Karl. *Muriel Spark.*
Stubbs, Patricia. *Muriel Spark.*

William P. Keen

JEAN STAFFORD

Born: Covina, California; July 1, 1915
Died: White Plains, New York; March 26, 1979

Principal short fiction

Children Are Bored on Sunday, 1953; *Bad Characters*, 1964; *Collected Stories*, 1969.

Other literary forms

Jean Stafford's first three books were novels, *Boston Adventure* (1944), *The Mountain Lion* (1947), and *The Catherine Wheel* (1952). She also published juvenile fiction and a short, book-length interview with the mother of Lee Harvey Oswald, *A Mother in History* (1966).

Influence

The most important influence on Stafford's fiction was that of Henry James, an influence she was not able to subdue completely to the exigencies of her own geography and thematic concerns. One notices it particularly in the way she structures stories and in her way of elaborating sentences; although "Jamesian," her style is nevertheless recognizably her own. With the publication of *Boston Adventure* and the award of a prize that same year by *Mademoiselle*, her reputation as a fiction writer was quickly established. Over the years, she received numerous other awards, including grants from the National Institute of Arts and Letters, the Guggenheim and Rockefeller foundations, and the National Press Club. She also received an O. Henry Memorial Award for her story "In the Zoo" in 1955, and the Pulitzer Prize for her *Collected Stories* in 1970.

Story characteristics

Stafford's short stories, like her novels, are built on the contrast of manners, and snobbery is her ultimate theme. Her protagonists are quite often young women or girls, pitted against persons who feel themselves superior but are revealed to be morally, emotionally, and even physically corrupt.

Biography

Although born in California, where she spent part of her childhood, Jean Stafford grew up in Colorado, attended the University of Colorado (A.M., 1936), and did postgraduate work at the University of Heidelberg. Her father, at one time a reporter, had written a number of Western stories. After a year teaching at Stephens College in Missouri, she worked for the *Southern Review* in Louisiana and later wrote for *The New Yorker*. She married Robert Lowell in 1940 (divorced in 1948) and in 1959, A. J. Liebling. She died in 1979.

Analysis

It is clear from a brief preface she wrote for her *Collected Stories* that Jean Stafford did not wish to be considered a regional writer. Her father and her mother's cousin had both written books about the West, but she had read neither before she began writing. Moreover, as soon as she could, she "hot-footed it across the Rocky Mountains and across the Atlantic Ocean" and came back to the West only for short periods. Her roots might therefore remain in Colorado but the rest of her abided "in the South or the Midwest or New England or New York." The short stories in this collection, which span twenty-five years of her productive life, she grouped under headings that both insisted on the national and international character of her art and echoed universally known writers with whom she clearly wished to associate herself: Henry James, Mark Twain, Thomas Mann.

It is true, as one discovers from the stories themselves, Stafford's fiction is not limited geographically but is set in such widely separated places as Colorado, Heidelberg, France, New York, and Boston; if, therefore, one thinks of these stories as the result of social observation they do indeed have the broad national and international scope their author claimed for them. Her stories, however—and this may have been as apparent to Stafford as it has to some of her critics—are not so much the result of observation and intellectual response as they are expressions of the author's own deep obsessions. To say that, however, is not to deny that her stories have their own kind of meaning; they are not expressions of random feelings, but on the contrary reflect a consistently unified vision of life.

The thirty stories in Stafford's *Collected Stories* are unified by one pervasive theme, illness—physical, mental, and emotional—and the snobbery which she finds an accompaniment, the snobbery of aberrant behavior. Fascinated, repelled, and at times outraged by the way illness can be used to purchase power over vulnerable individuals, Stafford describes the various forms of this currency, the number of places where it can be spent, and the way it can be used by those of any age or sex willing to employ it. The emotional and physical invalids in these stories clearly think themselves superior to ordinary folk, and the tensions built up in these stories are often the result of conflicts between a protagonist (who usually appears to speak for the author) and neurotic individuals who think themselves justified in exploiting others. Sometimes there is an actual physical sickness—disease, old age—but the illness or psychological aberration frequently becomes a metaphor for moral corruption.

In "Maggie Meriwether's Rich Experience" the protagonist is a naïve young American woman from Tennessee visiting in France, who has been invited to spend the weekend at a fashionable country house. There she discovers a crowd of titled Europeans, rich, overdressed, and eccentric, who look down their collective nose at the simple girl from the American South. The reader, who sees through the eyes of the young American, sees how stupid and arrogant these aristocrats are and understands Maggie's relief at escaping to Paris where she telephones the older brother of her roommate at Sweet Briar and spends the evening delighting in the wholesome provincialism of her Southern American friends, regaling them with stories about her recent experience.

In "The Echo and the Nemesis" the combination of neurosis and snobbery becomes more convincingly sinister. This story is also set in Europe, in Heidelberg, but the two main characters are Americans. The protagonist, Sue, appears to be a rather unexceptional young woman from a family of ordinary means; the "invalid," Ramona, is an enormously fat girl from a very rich family (so she says), living permanently in Italy. Sue is at first impressed by Ramona's learning and by the stories she tells of her family's wealth, and the two girls become constant companions. At first the relationship, with frequent meetings in cafés, becomes routine, like another philosophy lecture or seminar in Schiller, but then Ramona begins a series of revelations about herself and her family that embarrass, mystify, and then entrance Sue. Ramona reveals that she had a twin sister who died at an early age, a beautiful girl of whom there were many drawings and paintings, and whose room had been turned into a shrine. Ramona next reveals that she has come to Heidelberg not to study but to lose weight, and she enlists Sue's aid. Captivated by Ramona's stories about her loose-living family, Sue readily accepts an invitation to visit Ramona's brothers at a ski resort in Switzerland.

Thereafter Ramona begins to change. She misses lunches, fails to show up for appointments, and wildly indulges herself in food. When Sue makes inquiries about the coming trip and questions her about her doctor, Ramona snaps at her and, once, even slaps her face. Ramona tells Sue that she (Sue) resembles her dead sister Martha and implies that the trip to Switzerland must therefore be called off, since Ramona's family would be too upset by the resemblance. Ramona's mysterious behavior is partially explained by Sue's discovery in Ramona's room of a photograph of a younger, thinner, and beautiful Ramona. In a final scene prior to Ramona's departure from Heidelberg, the revelation about her is made complete: Sue promises to remain her friend, and Ramona replies, "'Oh, no, no, there would be nothing in it for you. Thank you just the same. I am exceptionally ill.' She spoke with pride, as if she were really saying, 'I am exceptionally talented' or 'I am exceptionally attractive.'" When Sue responds, "I'm sorry," Ramona snaps back, "I'm not sorry. It is for yourself that you should be sorry. You have such a trivial little life, poor girl. It's not your fault. Most people do."

The neurotics in Stafford's stories are not always so aggressive and unappealing. In "The Bleeding Heart" an elderly dandy who is brow-beaten by his invalid mother attempts to establish a "fatherly" relationship with a young Mexican girl who has come East and works as a secretary in a "discreet girl's boarding school." The girl is at first impressed with the old gentleman's aristocratic bearing and imagines she would like him for a stepfather, but when she visits his mother with a plant, a gift from the school, she is appalled by the odors, the repellent condition of the mother, and the disgusting behavior of a parrot. When the old man attempts to force his attentions on her, she turns on him and tells him to leave her alone. "Rose," he tells her, "All I am asking is a little pity."

A briefer summary of several other stories will show how pervasive is this theme in Stafford's stories, both in the way characters are conceived and relationships established, and in the way the main action is resolved. The point of the story "The Liberation" has to do with the way an old couple, pathetic in their loneliness, try to prevent their young niece from marrying. At her announcement of her forthcoming marriage in Boston to a teacher at Harvard (the story takes place in Colorado), the aunt (who "suffers" from chronic asthma) wrings her hands and her uncle glares at her and both are outraged at the idea of her marrying and going off to live somewhere else. The story takes a curious turn as word comes that the girl's fiancé has died of a heart attack. The girl is at first stunned and about to resign herself to remaining in Colorado, but her uncle and aunt try to "appropriate" her grief and bind her even faster to themselves. In a panic, without luggage, the girl flees for Boston and for emotional freedom from the "niggling hypochondriacs she had left behind."

"The Healthiest Girl in Town" also takes place in Colorado, where a girl, whose mother is a practical nurse in a town inhabited mainly by tuberculosis patients and their families, is forced to become friends with two sisters because her mother nurses the girls' grandmother. At first the girl is impressed with the sisters (they also have illnesses) and their Eastern pretentiousness and ashamed of her own good health, but then, after a quarrel with them, she proudly declares herself to be the healthiest girl in town.

Two other Easterners also proud of their abnormalities are a Boston spinster in "The Hope Chest" who delights in humiliating her maid and in tricking a boy who comes to her door selling Christmas wreaths into kissing her, and an elderly woman in "Life Is No Abyss" from a rich and socially prominent Boston family whom she punishes by going to the poor house and allowing them to come and observe her in her impoverishment. "A Country Love Story" also deals with an invalid, in this instance a writer who neglects his wife and then accuses her of being unfaithful to him and so drives her to the brink of insanity. Other characters include a woman (in "The End of a Career") who devotes her life to looking beautiful and dies when her hands betray her age and a woman ("Beatrice Trublood's Story") who marries three times and each time selects the same brutal kind of husband.

"Bad Characters," which is perhaps Stafford's most amusing story, treats her usual theme comically. Here the neurotic invalid is cast as a vagabond girl with an appealing swagger, a female Huck Finn but without Huck's decency. She charms the daughter of a respectable family into shoplifting and, when the two are caught, feigns deaf-and-dumbness and allows the respectable girl (the protagonist) to bear the responsibility alone.

F. Scott Fitzgerald said that a writer has but one story to tell; Stafford tells hers in many different places, about people from rather different social levels, ages, education, and backgrounds: there is almost always an innocent charmed or somehow trapped by neurotic individuals from whom she finally escapes. Sometimes Stafford gives the stage to this neurotic individual and gradually peels away the mystery that always shrouds those who think themselves superior to others. The story holds up well in the retelling, for it is a universal and timeless theme.

Major publications other than short fiction

NOVELS: *Boston Adventure*, 1944; *The Mountain Lion*, 1947; *The Catherine Wheel*, 1952.

NONFICTION: *A Mother in History*, 1966.

W. J. Stuckey

RICHARD STEELE

Born: Dublin, Ireland; March 1672
Died: Near Carmarthen, Wales; September 1, 1729

Principal short fiction
The Tatler, 1709-1710; *The Spectator*, 1711-1712; *The Guardian*, 1713.

Other literary forms
Richard Steele is well known for his four plays, his prose work, *The Christian Hero* (1701), and his later periodicals. His plays are strongly didactic in purpose and tone, and this intention carries over to his short fiction in his periodicals. Perceived as a reformer of the stage, Steele was named Governor of the Drury Lane Theatre in order to improve the moral tone of the playhouse. His last play, *The Conscious Lovers* (1722), is often identified as "sentimental" drama whose influence changed the course of the English theater.

Influence
Steele wrote *The Tatler* and *The Spectator* in conjunction with his friend and schoolfellow, Joseph Addison. Their purpose was to bring philosophy out of closets to the tea table and to temper wit with morality and morality with wit. They matched their purpose and their abilities well, for *The Tatler* and *The Spectator* became staples in many homes in eighteenth century England and America. In their essays, Addison and Steele teach a benevolent morality based on the sermons of latitudinarian Anglican divines, but they have a lightness of touch and a quickness of wit that remove any sermonizing tone. Their essays are designed to entertain as well as to teach, and indeed the essays of *The Tatler* and *The Spectator* are enjoyable reading. In his early reading, Benjamin Franklin found that *The Spectator* was a veritable education, and he credited its style with exerting a significant influence on his own writing.

Story characteristics
Scores of short stories appear in *The Tatler* and *The Spectator* from the pen of Steele, but these are in no way finished, complex stories similar to modern short stories: the story is subservient to the theme, while the characters present illustrations of an idea, theme, or moral. The short fiction in these periodicals offers a presentation of experiences easily understood by contemporary readers, and the emphasis is upon social interaction, not solitary brooding; the purpose is to guide readers to a clearer perception of their moral responsibilities toward their fellow humans.

Biography

Educated at the Charterhouse and Oxford University, Richard Steele lived in England and made his living first as a soldier and later as a writer and a politician. Although his plays and periodicals earned him some money, he always seemed to be in debt. He married Margaret Ford Stretch in 1705, but, unfortunately, she died the following year. In 1707, he married Mary Scurlock, owner of a small estate in Wales where he ultimately retired. He became the major propagandist for the Whigs from 1710 to 1714, when they were the Opposition, and after the Whigs regained power under King George I in 1714, he was knighted as a reward for his industriousness in the Whig cause. His later life was filled with financial difficulties, family problems, and political discouragement; after a stroke he retired to Wales in 1724, where he died in 1729.

Analysis

Richard Steele's short fiction appears in *The Tatler*, *The Spectator*, and *The Guardian*, as well as in some shorter periodicals. There is a double level of fiction in all three of these periodicals: the first is the fictional creation of the narrator and his family or club, with all of the telling details that make Steele's narrators interesting; the second is the storytelling of the narrator himself. The narrator of *The Tatler* is Isaac Bickerstaff, a name made popular by Jonathan Swift in his attack on the astrologer John Partridge. Bickerstaff is an elderly, benevolent astrologer who enjoys relating humorous stories about his family and friends while good-naturedly poking fun at himself. In contrast, *The Spectator* has as its narrator Mr. Spectator, the most taciturn member of The Spectator Club and the undisputed master observer of human nature and human foibles. Because of his careful observation of those around him, Mr. Spectator is an excellent storyteller as well. Finally, the narrator of *The Guardian* is Nestor Ironside, the feisty protector of the Lizard family and adviser to the British nation. To a large degree, *The Tatler* and *The Spectator* are the mutual creation of Steele and Addison, although Steele alone signed his name to the final issue of both periodicals; in contrast, *The Guardian* is largely Steele's and is generally recognized as inferior to the two earlier works. Steele's contribution to these works is a lively imagination and a facile wit; he promotes benevolence as the proper response to the sorrows and sufferings of one's fellow humans, and he satirizes slavish adherence to fashion. Plain-dealing honesty and kindly benevolence are Steele's major moral themes in both *The Tatler* and *The Spectator*; Steele's didactic purpose is always foremost, in both his fiction and his plays.

In *The Tatler*, Isaac Bickerstaff enjoys teaching the correct way to treat one's spouse by describing his sister's marital problems. Poor Jenny Distaff has more than her share of difficulties to overcome with her spouse Tranquillus; Isaac's bachelor wisdom helps them both to achieve happiness. The essential problem is Jenny's desire for domination over her husband, and Isaac teaches her to accept her husband's superior position in marriage. At first glance, it appears that Steele is preaching a very reactionary attitude toward marriage; however, this is not quite the case. Steele believes that women are people, not objects, and that they must be treated as thinking human beings by their husbands. Such an attitude was not universally held by men in the early eighteenth century, and, although Steele's attitude may seem conservative by today's standards, he deserves to be credited with some advancement of women's situations in his own century. For example, he decries the double standard of sexual morality and the marriage contract based solely on financial considerations. Women were losers in both situations, and Steele saw and spoke against what he considered serious social evils. In *The Tatler*, Steele is master of the dramatic scene, nowhere better exemplified than in the reconciliation between Jenny and Tranquillus through the efforts of Isaac Bickerstaff.

It is reasonable to assert that Steele is fascinated by all of the various pleasures and problems in domestic relationships. Primary, of course, is courtship, marriage, and married life, but the parent-child relationship is also very important to Steele. Mr. Spectator enjoys almost nothing more than a didactic story about the improvement of marital relations, parent-child relations, or a study of the potential for happiness in an impending marriage. *The Spectator* proves the ideal vehicle for these short, succinct stories, providing a different story daily and a need for constant reinforcement of central themes. One of Steele's often reinforced themes is the difficulty caused by parents who insist on choosing a spouse for their child. In *The Spectator* 533, in a letter appealing to Mr. Spectator's sense of justice, a male correspondent describes his unhappy situation as his elderly family insist that they choose their son's wife. This twenty-two-year-old is pleading for assistance: "You have often given us very excellent Discourses against that unnatural Custom of Parents, in forcing their Children to marry contrary to their Inclinations." The same theme in a different setting appears in *The Spectator* 220, in a letter from a twenty-one-year-old woman to an elderly suitor who is appealing to her father and not to her. She complains stridently of the injustice foisted upon her by a father and a suitor who believe that she must accept the suitor because her father does. Steele lets the letter communicate its message without additional comment, but it is clear that he wholly supports the unjustly treated young woman.

Steele enjoyed using the letter device as a mode of developing his short fictions; he used letters, for example, much more often than did Addison. Letters helped him to develop various perspectives, which are more effectively presented through various points of view than through Steele's voice alone. A parallel example might be the epistolary format in Samuel Richardson's *Clarissa* (1747-1748), where four perspectives are well developed through letters. Steele is interested in brevity as well as perspective, and yet his need as an author to create perspectives other than his own is similar to Richardson's. Steele presents another of his favorite themes in a letter to Mr. Spectator from an admirer in *The Spectator* 268, wherein the correspondent laments the tragedy of so many people marrying for the wrong reasons. What are these wrong reasons? They are: money, position, power. What then are proposed as the right reasons to marry? They are: virtue, wisdom, a person's good qualities, good humor, similar manners and attitudes. In this letter—and throughout Steele's writings—marriage is spoken of reverently, as the state which may "give us the compleatest Happiness this Life is capable of." For this to happen, however, Steele warns repeatedly through precept and example, men and women must be free to choose their spouses on the basis of lasting and endearing qualities.

One of the most famous stories in *The Spectator*, "Inkle and Yarico," depicts the suffering and misery of a less than circumspect love. In *The Spectator* 11, Steele describes the selfish and mean treatment by Mr. Thomas Inkle of an Indian maiden who trusted him completely. Inkle, having landed with a group of Englishmen in America, was attacked by Indians and retreated into the woods, where he was found and protected by Yarico, the Indian maid. They fell in love, he made great promises of wealth and comfort, and, when the ship came, Yarico left her people to go with Inkle. Shortly thereafter and safe once again with his own people, Inkle sold Yarico to a Barbadian merchant as a slave. The story is a warning to both sexes, but especially to women, to be circumspect in choosing a mate. Although the potential for great happiness does exist in marriage, numerous traps for the unwary, Steele warns, may make marriage a source of great unhappiness as well.

On another narrative level, two members of Mr. Spectator's club, Sir Roger de Coverley and Sir Andrew Freeport, provide a continuing story line and numerous little anecdotes. Sir Roger is an old fashioned country squire, while Sir Andrew is a vigorous, intelligent merchant. Whereas loveable Sir Roger's ideas are as out of date as his clothing, Sir Andrew's clear concepts on the role of trade in England's future are of the utmost importance. Usually these two club members get along well, but when an argument develops on the relative value of merchants to the British nation, Sir Andrew proves his superiority. Many of these little stories subtly identify the Tories with Sir Roger and the Whigs with Sir Andrew. Both Steele and Addison were wholeheartedly committed Whigs, and, despite their assurances that *The Spectator* was nonpolitical, their political beliefs inevitably surfaced. Their propaganda is delightfully subtle, as it slowly proves Sir Roger's ineffectiveness and Sir Andrew's undeniable capability.

As one might suppose, Steele remained consistent in his attitudes on marriage, parent-child relationships, and politics as he discontinued writing for *The Spectator* in order to begin *The Guardian*. Although in some places the tone does become more stern and foreboding, there are still delightful stories in *The Guardian* which promote the values of charity, benevolence, and love rather than authority and unselfishness rather than self-centeredness. For example, Nestor Ironside himself, although he would like to appear stern and crusty, exemplifies in his own story an overriding concern with the joys and sufferings of those about him. Nestor accepts the responsibility of guiding the Lizard family upon the death of his good friend, Sir Marmaduke Lizard. The lessons he inculcates in the family are based on love of neighbor rather than of self; he leads the daughters away from vanity and pride, while he admonishes the eldest son against keeping a mistress.

Steele's approach to moral issues remained essentially fixed from 1701, the date of his lengthy explication of moral values in his prose tract, *The Christian Hero*. Steele argued there that reason is incapable of guiding the passions to virtue, that only religion is capable of aiding reason sufficiently to guide the passions effectively, and that once so directed the passions may become an additional impetus to virtue. Steele posits in *The Christian Hero* a fundamentally irrational view of human nature. For this reason, perhaps, he teaches morality in his periodicals not by precept and argument but by example and story.

The influence of *The Tatler* and *The Spectator*, and to a lesser degree *The Guardian*, was extraordinary. When one realizes that each periodical lasted less than two years, the fact of such widespread influence is all the more remarkable. In both England and America, *The Spectator* was revered in many families as a repository of moral teaching as well as an entertaining book, and one may imagine that there were many, such as Benjamin Franklin, who developed a polished writing style through imitation of *The Spectator*. Although some topics contemporary to the eighteenth century may appear of little interest today, many of the stories still prove enjoyable for twentieth century readers.

Major publications other than short fiction

NOVELS: *The Christian Hero*, 1701; *The Theatre*, 1720.

PLAYS: *The Funeral: Or, Grief à la Mode*, 1701; *The Lying Lover*, 1703; *The Tender Husband*, 1705; *The Conscious Lovers*, 1722.

NONFICTION: *Apology for the Life of Richard Steele*, 1714.

Bibliography

Blanchard, Rae, ed. *Tracts and Pamphlets by Richard Steele.*

Bond, Donald F., ed. *The Spectator.*

Evans, James E. and John N. Wall, Jr. *A Guide to Prose Fiction in* The Tatler *and* The Spectator.

Kay, Donald. *Short Fiction in The Spectator.*

Winton, Calhoun. *Captain Steele: The Early Career of Richard Steele.*

——————— . *Sir Richard Steele, M. P.: The Later Career.*

Richard H. Dammers

WALLACE STEGNER

Born: Lake Mills, Iowa; February 18, 1909

Principal short fiction

The Women on the Wall, 1950; *The City of the Living and Other Stories*, 1956.

Other literary forms

Primarily a novelist and historian, Wallace Stegner is the author of many novels, from *Remembering Laughter* (1937) to *The Spectator Bird* (1976); his best-known and perhaps his best novel, *The Big Rock Candy Mountain*, was published in 1943, and *Angle of Repose*, 1971, was awarded the Pulitzer Prize. *Mormon Country*, his first book of nonfiction, was published in 1941; it was followed by approximately a dozen others, including *Beyond the Hundredth Meridian: John Wesley Powell and the Second Opening of the West* (1954), *The Sound of Mountain Water* (essays, 1969), and *The Uneasy Chair: A Biography of Bernard DeVoto* (1974). In addition, he has edited many books, including *Great American Short Stories* (with Mary Stegner, 1957), numerous annual volumes of *Stanford Short Stories* (with Richard Scowcroft), and *The Letters of Bernard DeVoto* (1975).

Influence

Stegner's best-known work, *The Big Rock Candy Mountain*, encapsulates the most important and influential elements of his writing: the American West setting, his insightful understanding of the human situation, his probing and cogent observations on and honest portrayal of life, and his masterful writing style and technique. Stegner's greatest impact, however, may well be as a professor and as a lecturer on creative writing. For many years he was the director of Stanford University's creative writing program which, with that of the University of Iowa, became the most important creative writing program in the United States.

Story characteristics

For the most part, Stegner works most effectively in the tradition of the conventional realism of the 1940's and 1950's. His short-fiction works range from relatively brief single-episode pieces to the novella; and they are characterized by meticulous craftsmanship, expert evocation of place, and perceptive characterization. These elements exist whether he writes of children or young people in an adult world that is often incomprehensible to them or of adults unable or unwilling to cope with the increasing complexities of a changing society or their own inner anxieties.

Biography

Born in Iowa and educated in his native state, in Utah, and in California (A. B., University of Utah, 1930; M. A., 1932, and Ph. D., 1935, University of Iowa), Wallace Earle Stegner has commented that his subject and themes, both in fiction and nonfiction, "are mainly out of the American West, in which I grew up." He has taught at various colleges and universities, primarily at Stanford, where he was director of its creative writing program. He has received many awards and honors including a Guggenheim Fellowship, a Rockefeller Fellowship, the Pulitzer Prize, a National Endowment for the Humanities Senior Fellowship, and an American Academy in Rome Fellowship. Currently, he lives with his wife, author Mary Stegner, in Los Altos Hills, California.

Analysis

Of the eighteen stories comprising *The Women on the Wall*, almost half are concerned with incidents in the life of Brucie, a young boy growing up in Saskatchewan in the later years of the second decade of the twentieth century. In these semi-related stories, strongly rooted in time and place, Wallace Stegner is in complete control of his material and writes with insight and understanding which never lapse into sentimentality. The Brucie stories center around relatively commonplace subjects: the trapping of a gopher, the slaughtering of a sow, a family picnic. "Two Rivers," an O. Henry second-prize winner in 1942, is characteristic. The action is simple. Following an unhappy fourth of July (the failure of the family's dilapidated Ford and the subsequent missed ball game in Chinook, the missed parade and fireworks, climaxed by the cuff on the ear from his father), the family set off for a picnic. Very little actually happens in this effective account of family relations, but at story's end the reader shares Brucie's quiet pleasure:

> The boy looked up at his father, his laughter bubbling up, everything wonderful, the day a swell day, his mother clapping hands in time to his father's fool singing (an impromptu song about "a kid and his name was Brucie").
> "Aw, for gosh sakes," he said, and ducked when his father pretended he was going to swat him one.

In his stories about adults, Stegner's vision is considerably darker. Life was essentially good for a boy in 1917, he suggests; for an adult in the 1940's, it is likely to be just the opposite. "Beyond the Glass Mountain" (like "Two Rivers," the recipient of an O. Henry Award, second-prize, 1948) is characteristic. The narrative is structurally simple, uncluttered, and admirably economical: an account of a few moments during the reunion of two men who had been close friends during their college days. The narrator, "prepared . . . for nostalgia," finds his friend to be a pathetic alcoholic, irreparably damaged by the passing of time and a destructive marriage (For the "love of God," he thinks, "Get rid of her. . . . She'll cheat on you. . . . She'll suck you dry like an old orange skin").

"Beyond the Glass Mountain," "The View from the Balcony," "The Women on the Wall," and others similarly depict the encroachment of the always present scourges of man upon lives that might or should be "ordinary" or "happy": the itch for domination, the dark shadow of emotional instability or insanity, the tyranny of sex and the insecurity of the unloved.

The seven stories and one novella of *The City of the Living and Other Stories* share in common with *The Women on the Wall* Stegner's thoroughly disciplined narrative skill and his unblinking understanding of his characters. These later stories are more varied than their predecessors, ranging as they do from a fleabag of a California pool hall during the American Depression ("The Blue-Winged Teal," the O. Henry Memorial Award first-prize winner in 1950); to Egypt ("The City of the Living"); to Salt Lake City ("Maiden in a Tower"); to the French Riviera ("Impasse"); to an unspecified snowswept rural landscape-with-figures piece ("The Traveler"); to life among the wealthy and not-so-beautiful people in Southern California ("Field Guide to the Western Birds").

Stegner is again at his best in his shorter, less complicated, pieces. "Maiden in a Tower," for example, is virtually without incident: the drama of the story is the evocation of the past. The narrator has driven from San Francisco to a funeral home in Salt Lake City where his aunt lies awaiting burial. By coincidence, the funeral home was, a quarter of a century ago, the setting of the narrator's first love, and evokes in him memories of life in the Jazz Age and his infatuation with the girl who epitomized all the glamour, the folly, the joy of youth and love and aspiration of the past, a past as dead as the narrator's aunt and the corpse of another woman whom he contemplates in her coffin in what had been the enchanted tower of his youth. Thoroughly controlled, moving and full of emotion which never degenerates into sentimentality, "Maiden in a Tower" is a masterly piece. So too is the title story "The City of the Living," a glimpse of a father and son during a few hours of almost unbearable crisis (the son is desperately ill in a hotel in Egypt); here Stegner presents a brilliant picture of father-son relations; and the setting, with its contrast of luxury and poverty, sickness and health, is unforgettable. Stegner is equally effective in his other stories of parent-child relations which furnish subject and theme for "The Blue-Winged Teak," "Impasse," and "The Volunteer."

The novella, "Field Guide to the Western Birds," on the other hand, in spite of some memorable moments, seems rather too long for what it accomplishes, too predictable in its denouement. As social history, however, Stegner's creation of well-heeled intellectuals and pseudo-intellectuals, frauds, hangers-on and circuit riders of the "good and opulent life," narrated by a self-congratulatory retired literary agent, has about it the ring of permanence. As John Galsworthy said of his Forsytes, here are characters miraculously preserved, pickled in their own juices.

Major publications other than short fiction

NOVELS: *Remembering Laughter*, 1937; *The Potter's House*, 1938; *On a Darkling Plain*, 1940; *Fire and Ice*, 1941; *The Big Rock Candy Mountain*, 1943; *Second Growth*, 1947; *The Preacher and the Slave*, 1950 (also published as *Joe Hill: A Biographical Novel*, 1969); *A Shooting Star*, 1961; *All the Little Live Things*, 1967; *Angle of Repose*, 1971; *The Spectator Bird*, 1976, *Recapitulation*, 1979.

NONFICTION: *Mormon Country*, 1942; *One Nation*, 1945 (with the editors of *Look*); *Look at America: The Central Northwest*, 1947; *The Writer in America*, 1951; *Beyond the Hundredth Meridian: John Wesley Powell and the Second Opening of the West*, 1954; *Wolf Willow: A History, A Story, and A Memory of the Last Plains Frontier*, 1962; *The Gathering of Zion: The Story of the Mormon Trail*, 1964; *The Sound of Mountain Water*, 1969; *The Uneasy Chair: A Biography of Bernard DeVoto*, 1974; *Ansel Adams: Images 1923-1974*, 1974.

Bibliography

Lewis, Merrill and Lorene Lewis. *Wallace Stegner*.

Robinson, Forrest G. and Margaret G. Robinson. *Wallace Stegner*.

Watts, Harold H. "Wallace Stegner," in *Contemporary Novelists*. Edited by James Vinson.

William Peden

JOHN STEINBECK

Born: Salinas, California; February 27, 1902
Died: New York, New York; December 20, 1968

Principal short fiction

The Pastures of Heaven, 1932; *The Red Pony*, 1937; *The Long Valley*, 1938.

Other literary forms

A prolific writer, John Steinbeck worked in many different literary forms. He is perhaps better known to the general public as a novelist than as a short-story writer, and his Pulitzer Prize-winning novel, *The Grapes of Wrath* (1939), seems to have guaranteed him a place among the major novelists of America. His early interest in marine biology led to his coauthorship (with Edward F. Ricketts) of a difficult-to-classify picture book/travel book/popular scientific study, *The Sea of Cortez* (1941), of which Steinbeck's text alone was republished (1951) as *The Log from the Sea of Cortez*. He also wrote a travel book, *Travels with Charley: In Search of America* (1962), the narrative of his journey across America accompanied by a large poodle.

Influence

Steinbeck's influence, especially as an author of short fiction, is difficult to assess. Certainly he has had practically no following among the more experimental writers within the form, and it is an open question whether those later authors whose work resembles his are directly influenced by Steinbeck's own stories or rather by extensive literary traditions of which Steinbeck is a prominent, but by no means unique, member. His influence on the American reading public, on the other hand, has been profound, and is likely to continue for some time. Not only are many of his novels still widely read, but also his short fiction is extensively taught in American public schools, where most pupils, by the time of their graduation from high school, have been exposed to at least one, and in all probability more, of his shorter fictional works.

Story characteristics

Steinbeck may be characterized primarily as a local-color writer, but this definition should be used with care. Although it is true that Steinbeck wrote almost exclusively about California life, he did not limit himself to the exploration of colorful characters, bizarre eccentricities, or remote historical periods which the typical local-color writer prefers. Steinbeck would consider himself a recorder of the multi-faceted life of the California in which he lived, and this definition accurately characterizes his work.

Biography

John Steinbeck was born in Salinas, California, and, at least artistically speaking, he never left home. His best fictional work deals almost exclusively with California subjects, more specifically with the life he knew in Monterey County. After a short time at Stanford University (he left without completing his degree in marine biology, although that subject remained of lifelong interest) he went on a freighter to New York, where he lived briefly on a succession of odd jobs. He soon returned to California, where he worked at a trout hatchery, on fruit ranches, as a surveyor, and as a painter. He spent two winters alone in a cabin in the High Sierra, teaching himself to write. His first novel, a fictionalized biography of the English pirate Henry Morgan, was relatively unsuccessful, but after its publication (1929) he turned to the California themes which he left only rarely throughout his lifetime. He was able to support himself while writing full time, and after the award of the Pulitzer Prize for *The Grapes of Wrath* he lived in relative affluence. He was awarded the Nobel Prize for Literature in 1962, the reward of a long career dedicated to letters. He died in New York City in 1968.

Analysis

Even now, more than ten years following his death, the jury has not yet returned a tentative verdict about John Steinbeck's permanent place in American literature. Critical appraisals of Steinbeck's literary merit have vacillated wildly at least since the publication of *The Grapes of Wrath*, a novel which was uniformly praised by critics of all ideological persuasions as the outstanding American novel of the 1930's, which garnered a Pulitzer Prize for its author, and which was turned into an award-winning motion picture. Critical reaction to this perhaps too extravagant praise, however, was swift. When Steinbeck failed to write another working-class novel to continue the saga of the Okies so dramatically begun in *The Grapes of Wrath*, Marxist critics, heretofore his strongest supporters, almost to a man turned against him. He was alleged to have sold his proletarian birthright for a mess of bourgeois pottage, to have betrayed the sacred cause of the class struggle for the rewards of affluence and a safe niche in the literary establishment. The irony of the self-styled Satan whose Miltonic speeches give the title to *In Dubious Battle* (1936), a bitter novel of an abortive Communist attempt to organize the migrant workers in California, accepting a Nobel Prize some quarter of a century later for *Travels with Charley*, a nostalgic attempt to find the true meaning of America on a journey across the country with a poodle, was not lost on many of his erstwhile admirers. Steinbeck himself had not helped matters by his early statements concerning the nature of his art which, he was fond of repeating, was dedicated solely to the improvement of the lot of the working class of America. At the time of his death, then, Steinbeck was generally assumed to represent nothing more significant than another example of a typically American literary failure: the young man of promise whose promise ultimately comes to nothing.

Today, and especially on the evidence of Steinbeck's shorter fiction, this easy critical dismissal of Steinbeck's work seems equally as imperceptive as did the earlier unqualified praise: it is not so much wrong as wrongheaded, weighing Steinbeck's work and finding it wanting on the basis of criteria which are not really applicable. For it seems clear now that Steinbeck's true literary subject was not the class struggle or the presumptive future triumph of the proletariat, but rather, as the title of his best collection of short stories, *The Long Valley*, indicates, California, and especially the Salinas Valley where Steinbeck was born and lived most of his life, and about which he wrote the preponderance of his work. It is also apparent that Steinbeck's attitude toward his material is, if radical at all, expressive not so much of the doctrinaire attitudes his earlier supporters discovered in it, as of a peculiarly American matrix, often called, at least in political terms, "Populist" or "Progressive." This peculiarly American radicalism, which Alexis de Tocqueville had clearly delineated a century earlier in calling his typical American "a venturesome conservative," yearns not so much toward a New Jerusalem as it hopes for a rediscovered Eden, in which the virtues of the past, purged of their dross, will be reincarnated.

For proof of the point let us briefly consider not so much the plots of Steinbeck stories as the characters in these stories of whom the author obviously approves. We should first note that in the whole context of Steinbeck's literary world a genuine proletarian is very hard to find. Steinbeck's radicals hearken not so much to Karl Marx and Max Engels as to the "Wobblies" of the turn-of-the-century Pacific Northwest, and the mark of their virtue is quite often their love for a society which is gone yet which they will give anything, if need be, to re-create. They would all like a piece of ground and a farm— the "forty acres and a mule" of the Jeffersonian yeoman—freed not only of bondage to what Theodore Roosevelt had called "the malefactors of great wealth," but also of some of the more bothersome appurtenances of the Industrial Revolution. One of the radical organizers of the strike in *In Dubious Battle* merits our particular approval because, among other virtues, he understands the fine points of hunting dogs. There is also a revealing moment in *The Grapes of Wrath* in which the true evil of "the bank" (it is worth noting that Steinbeck's villains are almost always faceless generalizations) is indicated: not only has it driven the Okies from their farms, but also it has, for purposes of plowing, replaced the lovable existential mule with the heartless and malevolent tractor.

These particular examples may well be frivolous, but the point indicated by them is not, and it is a point which is basic to Steinbeck's art; for to Steinbeck modern life itself is often the enemy, in which his characters find themselves lost in a world they never made and want nothing to do with.

When imperceptively handled, of course, this world view degenerates into sentimentalism, but when approached with care it allows a certain kind of tragic dignity to Steinbeck's fictional world. At their best, Steinbeck's stories tell of lives which have turned out far differently from expectations, and the very modesty of these initial expectations allows the author ample scope for discussing that vague malevolence he sees at the heart of life itself. Steinbeck's tragic vision is a peculiarly American one: the ironic vision of a society which, as the historian Richard Hofstadter arrestingly put it in another context, was founded in perfection and aspired to progress.

Not surprisingly, then, Steinbeck's stories often concern themselves with variations on what has been conventionally described as the typical American literary theme: that of a boy growing up. Not that all Steinbeck's stories—or even a preponderance of them—deal with children; the point is, rather, that most of them concern themselves with a character's realization that life has turned out to be a far different book from the one he ideally would have written.

A brief glance at one of Steinbeck's justly best-known stories, "The Leader of the People," will clarify the point. The plot of this story is simple; it tells of a little boy, Jody, whose grandfather comes on a visit to the family farm. The grandfather, we discover, is more tolerated than loved by Jody's parents, who find him an intolerable old bore. Jody's father, in particular, cannot stand the old man, whom he views as a tiresome relic filled only with boring stories about the pioneer life he had known when he was young. Jody, in contrast, loves the old man and likes nothing better than to listen to the stories of the "good old days" which his grandfather tells. The stage is clearly set for a sentimental explication of how only the "good" boy Jody can sympathize with the grandfather, while the insensitive, "evil" father does nothing but put down the old man, whose sterling virtues he is too blind to see.

As Steinbeck tells the story, though, he refuses to accept the easy polarities of good and evil to which its implicit structure obviously lends itself. For one thing, the old man *is* a bore; it is quite one thing to listen to an occasional pioneer reminiscence, and quite another, as Jody's father makes clear, to have to hear the same few stories repeated over and over every time the old gentleman comes to call. For another, although Jody may like to hear the stories, it is clear that he does not understand them; his interpretation of their meaning is no more than the fascination of any small boy with stories of cowboys and Indians. For, and here is the basic irony of the story, in fact the old man *had* been one of those hardy pioneers whose virtues we are all wont to extol ritually every Fourth of July while conveniently forgetting about them for the rest of the year. He had been, in his own words, "the leader of the people," that is, the man elected as captain of a wagon train of pioneers who had come to California from the East. The phrase itself is arresting, and Steinbeck is well aware of the fact: for "leader of the people" is by no means a common term for a wagon master. In the story the old man becomes emblematic of an almost mythical generalized leader of the American people themselves to the West, and his story, as the old man himself sees it, is a story not merely of some anonymous train of settlers heading West but emblematic of the whole destiny of America, of (again in his phrase) "westering," of what others have called the "manifest destiny" of the American spirit, relentlessly pushing Westward, winning and subjugating a continent. What, the story asks, had this gained him, and the answer is not reassuring: little more than an irrelevant antique, the old man must eke out his days surrounded by descendants who are either uninterested in what he has to say or incapable of understanding.

This brief explication of "The Leader of the People" may indicate some of the ways in which Steinbeck has been habitually misunderstood. Although the story contains very strong political themes, its basic thrust nevertheless is not primarily political. That political perspective which would interpret the story as a searing indictment of the deterioration of American ideals or of the unworthy compromises America has made with her promised greatness errs by imposing a grandiose political moral upon a story whose thrust is not ultimately political at all. Although it is true that in a sense the old man represents a past way of life which is now irrelevant, still the tragedy of Jody's grandfather is basically human rather than political. The former leader of the people has grown old, and the values he espoused no longer have applicability, not because they are false but because the world has changed. Thus Steinbeck finally leaves us with a question which, if not strictly speaking a political one, nevertheless goes to the heart of a basic American cultural worry. We must admit perforce that the world and American life have both changed since the days when Jody's grandfather was the leader of the people. Can one say that either has improved?

The tragedy of Steinbeck's world, then, is quite often simply the tragedy of small things. The mistake criticism has made is to attempt to impale Steinbeck's stories with pretentious ethical and existential morals. A brief glance at one other story may clarify this point. *The Red Pony* is another often and justly anthologized tale about Jody, who is here given a pony of his own. In brief, the pony sickens and dies, and that is all there is to the story. Much criticism has attempted to imbue the death of the pony with various cumbrous symbolic meanings; yet one might argue that the significance of the story is exactly the opposite. The pony may represent Jody's childhood, the end of innocence, or something equally profound, but in the story itself it is just an ordinary pony, and Steinbeck goes out of his way to emphasize the point. A less sure or more didactic artist would have been certain to tell the reader that the pony was a gift obtainable only by sacrificing the family's most valuable worldly goods; that it was the hope of Jody for winning the 4-H prize and a future college education; that the pony was the only method by which a youth of undoubted potential could possibly have been saved from a life of delinquency; and so on. Instead, this is simply a pony that dies unromantically and whose death is without much cosmic significance one way or another. Literary critics seem to find this kind of moment unworthy of serious scrutiny in itself. Perhaps they have not had to explain to a ten-year-old child why a beloved pet has to be put to sleep; perhaps they feel that a statement such as "it's just a dog" or "we can get you another one" will assuage the child's grief. These people will in all likelihood find Steinbeck's stories trivial; others may see something of worth in them.

Major publications other than short fiction

NOVELS: *Cup of Gold*, 1929; *To a God Unknown*, 1933; *Tortilla Flat*, 1935; *In Dubious Battle*, 1936; *Of Mice and Men*, 1937; *The Grapes of Wrath*, 1939; *Cannery Row*, 1945; *East of Eden*, 1952; *Sweet Thursday*, 1954.

NONFICTION: *The Sea of Cortez*, 1941; *The Log from the Sea of Cortez*, 1951; *Travels with Charley: In Search of America*, 1962.

Bibliography

Davis, Robert M., ed. *John Steinbeck: A Collection of Critical Essays.*
French, Warren. *John Steinbeck.*
Kiernan, Thomas. *The Intricate Music: A Biography of John Steinbeck.*
Lisca, Peter. *John Steinbeck: Nature & Myth.*
_____ . *The Wide World of John Steinbeck.*
Moore, Harry Thornton. *The Novels of John Steinbeck: A First Study.*

James K. Folsom

ROBERT LOUIS STEVENSON

Born: Edinburgh, Scotland; November 13, 1850
Died: Apia, Upolu, Samoa; December 3, 1894

Principal short fiction

The New Arabian Nights, 1882; *More New Arabian Nights*, 1885; *The Merry Men and Other Tales and Fables*, 1887; *Island Nights' Entertainments*, 1893.

Other literary forms

Although a lifelong invalid confined to bed for lengthy periods, Scottish novelist, essayist, and poet Robert Louis Stevenson was famous in his own lifetime for his arduous travels. Indeed, his first published book, *An Inland Voyage* (1878), recorded a canoe trip over French rivers and canals in a chatty, discursive manner reminiscent of Henry David Thoreau. Stevenson's classics of children's literature, his tales of horror and suspense, as well as some beautiful family prayers, all continue to be widely read, even today.

Influence

Praised for his style, Stevenson had played "the sedulous ape" in youth to William Hazlitt, Charles Lamb, William Wordsworth, Charles Browne, John Bunyan, Daniel Defoe, Nathaniel Hawthorne, Michel Eyquem de Montaigne, and others. As in many careers, a meeting with a local author was a possible boyhood inspiration: when he was fifteen, Stevenson spoke with Edinburgh novelist E. M. Ballantyne, then collecting information for *The Lighthouse* (1865). "A Humble Remonstrance," Stevenson's theories of prose fiction, was directly provoked by Henry James's "The Art of Fiction." Although James and he were close friends and remained correspondents for life, Stevenson placed himself in literary opposition to the former's investigations of "the statics of character," offering instead an action-fiction whose clear antecedents are allegory, fable, and romance. Many critics, however, hold James to be more influenced by Stevenson than vice versa. Finally, Stevenson's tales of adventure and intrigue, out-of-door life and old-time romance, read by children and serving to remind adults of childhood, have had a continuous and incalculable influence since the 1880's when they were first published.

Story characteristics

For clarity and suspense, Stevenson is rarely equaled. His economical presentation of incident and atmosphere signals undoubted narrative mastery. Literary critic Northrop Frye attributes Stevenson's "stylized figures which expand into psychological archetypes" to his spareness; but these same evocative skills which allow Stevenson his immediacy also permit him an easy facility: narrative development is often replaced by merely vivid detail. Events in some stories seem "directed" by a preconceived thematic intention. Many of his tales, however, are notable for dealing with complex moral ambiguities and their diagnoses.

Biography

The only child of a prosperous civil engineer and his wife, Robert Louis Stevenson was a sickly youth, causing his formal education to be haphazard. He reacted early against his parents' orthodox Presbyterianism, donning the mask of a liberated Bohemian who abhorred the hypocrisies of bourgeois respectability. As a compromise with his father, Stevenson did study law at Edinburgh University in lieu of the traditional family vocation of lighthouse engineer. In 1873, however, he suffered a severe respiratory illness, and although he completed his studies and was admitted to the Scottish bar in July, 1875, he never practiced. In May, 1880, Stevenson married Fanny Van de Grift Osbourne, a divorcée from San Francisco and ten years his senior. The new couple spent most of the next decade in health resorts for Stevenson's tuberculosis: Davos in the Swiss Alps, Hyères on the French Riviera, and Bournemouth in England. After his father's death, Stevenson felt able to go farther from Scotland and so went to Saranac Lake in the Adirondack Mountains of New York, where treatment arrested his disease. In June, 1888, Stevenson, his wife, mother, and stepson sailed for the South Seas. During the next eighteen months they saw the Marquesas, Tahiti, Australia, the Gilberts, Hawaii, and Samoa. In late 1889, Stevenson decided to settle and bought "Vailima," three miles from the town of Apia, Upolu, Samoa, and his home until his death. His vigorous crusading there against the white exploitation of native Samoans almost led to expulsion by both German and English authorities. Stevenson's tuberculosis remained quiescent, but he suddenly died of a cerebral hemorrhage on December 3, 1894, while working on the novel *Weir of Hermiston* (1896), a fragment which many now think to be his best writing. Known to the natives as "Tusitala," the Storyteller, Stevenson was buried on the summit of Mount Vaea.

Analysis

Robert Louis Stevenson has long been relegated to either the nursery or the juvenile section in most libraries, and his mixture of romance, horror, and allegory now seems jejune. In a century where narrative and well-ordered structure have become the facile tools of Harlequin paperbacks and irrelevant to high-quality "literature," Stevenson's achievement goes quietly unnoticed. To confine this technique of "Tusitala" solely to nursery and supermarket, however, is to confuse Stevenson's talents with his present audience.

Stevenson's crucial problem is the basic one of joining form to idea, made more difficult because he was not only an excellent romancer but also a persuasive essayist. In Stevenson, however, these two talents seem to be of different roots, and their combination was for him a lifelong work. The aim of his narratives becomes not only to tell a good story, constructing something of interest, but also to ensure that all the materials of that story (such as structure, atmosphere, and character motivation) contribute to a clear thematic concern. Often Stevenson's fictional talents alone cannot accomplish this for him, and this accounts—depending in each instance on whether he drops his theme or attempts to push it through—for both the "pulp" feel of some stories and the "directed" feel of others.

Appearing in the *Cornhill Magazine* for May 1874, an essay on Victor Hugo was Stevenson's very first publication. The short stories he began writing soon after demonstrate a strong tendency to lapse into the more familiar expository techniques either as a solution to fictional problems or merely in order to bolster a sagging theme. A blatant example of this stylistic ambiguity is the early story "A Lodging for the Night."

The atmosphere of the first part of the story is deftly handled. It is winter and its buffets upon the poor are reemphasized in every descriptive detail. Paris is "sheeted up" like a body ready for burial. The only light is from a tiny shack "backed up against the cemetery wall." Inside, "dark, little, and lean, with hollow cheeks and thin black locks," the medieval poet Francis Villon composes "The Ballade of Roast Fish" while Guy Tabard, one of his cronies, sputters admiringly over his shoulder. Straddling before the fire is a portly, purple-veined Picardy monk, Dom Nicolas. Also in the small room are two more villains, Montigny and Thevenin Pensete, playing "a game of chance." Villon cracks a few pleasantries, quite literally gallow's humor, and begins to read aloud his new poem. Suddenly, between the two gamesters:

> The round was complete, and Thevenin was just opening his mouth to claim another victory, when Montigny leaped up, swift as an adder, and stabbed him to the heart. The blow took effect before he had time to utter a cry, before he had time to move. A tremor or two convulsed his frame; his hands opened and shut, his heels rattled on the floor; then his head rolled backward over one shoulder with the eyes wide open; and Thevenin Pensete's spirit had returned to Him who made it.

Tabary begins praying in Latin, Villon breaks into hysterics, Montigny recovers "his composure first" and picks the dead man's pockets. Naturally, they must all leave the scene of the murder to escape implication, and Villon departs first.

Outside, in the bitter cold, two things preoccupy the poet as he walks: the gallows and "the look of the dead man with his bald head and garland of red curls," as neat a symbol as could be for the fiery pit of hell were Villon eventually expects to find himself. Theme has been handled well, Stevenson's fiction giving us the feeling of a single man thrown by existence into infernal and unfavorable circumstances, being pursued by elements beyond his control, the gallows and Death, survival itself weaving a noose for him with his own trail in the snow, irrevocably connecting him to "the house by the cemetery of St. John." The plot is clear and the situation has our interest. On this cold and windy night, after many rebuffs, Villon finally finds food and shelter with a "refined," "muscular and spare," "resonant, courteous," "honorable rather than intelligent, strong, simple, and righteous" old knight.

Here, the structure of "A Lodging for the Night" abruptly breaks down from fiction, from atmospheric detail, plot development, and character enlargement, to debate. What Stevenson implied in the first part of his story, he reasserts here in expository dialogue, apparently losing faith in his fictional abilities as he resorts back to the directness of the essay.

Villon takes the side of duty to one's own survival; he is the first modern skeptic, the prophet of expendiency. On the other hand, the knight stands for honor, *bonne noblesse*, with allegiance always to something greater than himself. The moral code of the criminal is pitted against the hypocrisy of the bourgeoisie. One's chances in life are determined by birth and social standing, says Villon. There is always the chance for change, implores the knight. In comparison to Stevenson's carefully built atmosphere and plot, this expository "solution" to his story is extremely crude.

"Markheim," a ghost story that deals with a disturbing problem of conscience, also contains a dialogue in its latter half. This dialogue, however, is a just continuation of the previous action. Different from "crawlers" such as "The Body-Snatcher," "Markheim" reinforces horror with moral investigation. Initial atmospherics contribute directly to Stevenson's pursuit of his thematic concern, and the later debate with the "visitant" becomes an entirely fitting expression for Markheim's own madness.

An allegory of the awakening conscience, "Markheim" also has the limits of allegory, one of which is meaning. In order for readers to understand, or find meaning in, an allegory, characters (or actors) must be clearly identified. In "Markheim" this presents major difficulties. Not only is an exact identity (or role) for the visitant finally in doubt, but so is one for the dealer. It can be said that he usually buys from Markheim, not sells to him, but exactly what the dealer buys or sells is a good question. Whatever, on this particular occasion (Christmas Day), Markheim will have to pay the dealer extra "for a kind of manner that I remark in you today very strongly."

Amid the "ticking of many clocks among the curious lumber" of the dealer's shop, a strange pantomime ensues. Markheim says he needs a present for a lady and the dealer shows him a hand mirror. Markheim grows angry:

> "A glass," he said hoarsely, and then paused, and repeated it more clearly. "A glass? For Christmas? Surely not!"
>
> "And why not?" cried the dealer. "Why not a glass?"
>
> Markheim was looking upon him with an indefinable expression. "You ask me why not?" he said. Why, look here—look at it—look at yourself! Do you like to see it? No! nor I—nor any man."

After damning the mirror as the "reminder of years, and sins, and follies—this hand-conscience," Markheim asks the dealer to tell something of himself, his secret life. The dealer puts Markheim off with a chuckle, but as he turns around for something more to show, Markheim lunges at him, stabbing him with a "long, skewer-like dagger." The dealer struggles "like a hen" and then dies. The murder seems completely gratuitous until Markheim remembers that he had come to rob the shop: "To have done the deed and yet not to reap the profit would be too abhorrent a failure."

Time, "which had closed for the victim," now becomes "instant and momentous for the slayer." Like Villon, Markheim feels pursued by Death, haunted by "the dock, the prison, the gallows, and the black coffin." The blood at his feet begins "to find eloquent voices." The dead dealer extracts his extra payment, becoming the enemy who would "lift up a cry that would ring over England, and fill the world with the echoes of pursuit." Talking to himself, Markheim denies that this evil murder indicates an equally evil nature, but his guilt troubles him. Not only pursued by Death, Markheim is pursued by Life as well. He sees his own face "repeated and repeated, as it were an army of spies"; his own eyes meet and detect him. Although alone, he feels the inexplicable consciousness of another presence:

> Ay, surely; to every room and corner of the house his imagination followed it; and now it was a faceless thing, and yet had eyes to see with; and again it was a shadow of himself; and yet again beheld the image of the dead dealer, reinspired with cunning and hatred.

Eventually, Markheim must project an imaginary double, a *Doppelgänger* or exteriorized voice with which to debate his troubles. Here, action passes from the stylized antique shop of the murdered to the frenzied mind of the murderer. The visitant, or double, is a product of this mind. Mad and guilty as Markheim appears to be, his double emerges as a calm sounding sanity who will reason with him to commit further evil. Thus, the mysterious personification of drives buried deep within Markheim's psyche exteriorizes evil as an alter ego and allows Markheim the chance to act against it, against the evil in his own nature. Stevenson's sane, expository technique of debate erects a perfect foil for Markheim's true madness.

In the end, although Markheim thinks himself victorious over what seems the devil, it is actually this exteriorized aspect of Markheim's unknown self that conquers, tricking him into willing surrender and then revealing itself as a kind of redemptive angel:

> The features of the visitor began to undergo a wonderful and lovely change; they brightened and softened with a tender triumph; and, even as they brightened, faded and dislimned. But Markheim did not pause to watch or understand the transformation.

Material and intention are artistically intertwined in "Markheim," but the moral ambiguities of Stevenson's theme remain complex, prompting various questions: is Markheim's martyrdom a victory over evil or merely a personal cessation from action? Set on Christmas Day, with its obvious reversal of that setting's usual significance, is "Markheim" a portrayal of Christian resignation as a purely negative force, a justification for suicide, or as the only modern solution against evil? What is the true nature and identity of the visitant? Finally, can the visitant have an identity apart from Markheim's own? Even answers to these questions, like Markheim's final surrender, offer only partial consolation to the reader of this strange and complex story of psychological sickness.

With Stevenson's improved health and his move to the South Seas, a new type of story began to emerge, a kind of exotic realism to which the author brought his mature talents. "The Bottle Imp", for example, juxtaposes the occult of an old German fairy tale (interestingly enough, acquired by Stevenson through Sir Percy Shelley, the poet's son) with factual details about San Francisco, Honolulu, Hawaii, and Papeete. These settings, however, seem used more for convenience than out of necessity.

The long story "The Beach of Falesá" fulfills Stevenson's promise and gives evidence of his whole talents as a writer of short fiction. Similar to Joseph Conrad's *Heart of Darkness* (1902), Stevenson's story deals with man's ability or inability to remain decent and law-abiding when the external restraints of civilization have been removed. Action follows simply and naturally a line laid down by atmosphere. Stevenson himself called it "the first realistic South Sea story," while Henry James wrote in a letter the year before Stevenson's death, "The art of 'The Beach of Falesá' seems to me an art brought to a perfection and I delight in the observed truth, the modesty of nature, of the narrator."

In this adventure of wills between two traders on a tiny island, Stevenson is able to unify fitting exposition with restrained description through the voice of first-person narrator John Wiltshire. Three decades later, using Stevenson as one of his models, W. Somerset Maugham would further perfect this technique using the same exotic South Sea setting.

Stevenson's "The Beach of Falesá," along with the incomplete *Weir of Hermiston* and perhaps the first part of *The Master of Ballantrae* (1888), rests as his best work, the final integration of the divergent roots of his talents. If he had lived longer than forty-four years, "Tusitala" might have become one of the great English prose writers. As history now stands, however, Stevenson's small achievement of clear narrative, his victory of joining form to idea, remains of unforgettable importance to students and practitioners of the short-story genre.

Major publications other than short fiction

NOVELS: *Treasure Island*, 1883; *The Strange Case of Dr. Jekyll and Mr.*

Hyde, 1886; *Kidnapped*, 1886; *The Black Arrow*, 1888; *The Master of Ballantrae*, 1888; *The Wrong Box*, 1889 (with Lloyd Osbourne); *The Wrecker*, 1892 (with Lloyd Osbourne); *Catriona*, 1893; *The Ebb-Tide*, 1894 (with Lloyd Osbourne); *Weir of Hermiston*, 1896 (unfinished); *St. Ives*, 1897.

PLAYS: *Deacon Brodie*, 1880; *Macaire*, 1885 (with William Ernest Henley); *The Hanging Judge*, 1914 (with Fanny Van de Grift Stevenson).

POETRY: *Moral Emblems*, 1882; *A Child's Garden of Verses*, 1885; *Underwoods*, 1887; *Ballads*, 1890; *Songs of Travel*, 1895.

NONFICTION: *An Inland Voyage*, 1878; *Travels with a Donkey in the Cevennes*, 1879; *Virginibus Puerisque*, 1881; *Familiar Studies of Men and Books*, 1882; *The Silverado Squatters, Sketches from a California Mountain*, 1883; *Across the Plains*, 1892; *A Footnote to History*, 1892; *The Amateur Emigrant*, 1895; *In the South Seas*, 1896.

Bibliography

Carre, Jean Marie. *Robert Louis Stevenson: The Frail Warrior*.

Einger, Edwin M. *Robert Louis Stevenson and the Romantic Tradition*.

Elwin, Malcolm. *The Strange Case of Robert Louis Stevenson*.

Furnas, J. C. *Voyage to Windward*.

Pope-Hennessy, James. *Robert Louis Stevenson*.

Saposnik, Irving S. *Robert Louis Stevenson*.

Smith, Janet Adams. *Henry James and Robert Louis Stevenson*.

Kenneth Funsten

FRANK R. STOCKTON

Born: Philadelphia, Pennsylvania; April 5, 1834
Died: Washington, D.C.; April 20, 1902

Principal short fiction

Ting-a-Ling, 1870; *The Lady or the Tiger and Other Stories*, 1884; *The Bee Man of Orn and Other Fanciful Tales*, 1887; *The Story Teller's Pack*, 1897; *A Vizier of the Two Horned Alexander*, 1899; *The Magic Egg*, 1902; *Fanciful Tales*, 1909; *Best Short Stories*, 1957.

Other literary forms

Frank R. Stockton wrote many articles for periodicals and was on the staffs of *Hearth and Home*, *The Century Illustrated Monthly Magazine*, and assistant editor of *St. Nicholas* from the time he was thrity-nine until he was forty-seven. He began as a juvenile writer, and many of his children's stories have remained popular, particularly "The Bee Man of Orn," newly illustrated by Maurice Sendak. Of his many adult novels, the best loved was *Rudder Grange* (1879), for which the public demanded two sequels, *The Rudder Grangers Abroad* (1891), and *Pomona's Travels* (1894).

Influence

Stockton's short stories were more successful than his novels. He entertained a large and faithful following during his lifetime; today he is remembered only as the author of "The Lady or the Tiger?"

Story characteristics

Stockton worked in every variety of romantic narrative: fairy tale, love story, adventure tale, science fiction, historical romance, and fantasy.

Biography

Frank R. (Francis Richard) Stockton was descended from American pioneers, one of whom, Richard Stockton, had been one of the signers of the Declaration of Independence. The third son of nine children, he was expected to become a doctor. Instead, upon graduating from high school he studied wood engraving, at which he was proficient enough to support himself until he was thirty-two, when he decided to become a journalist. Until 1880 he specialized in children's stories; then he began writing for adults, although the tone and the situations were not much different from his earlier works. He completed more than a dozen novels, comedies, satires, scientific speculations, and whimsies.

Analysis

In "The Magic Egg," Frank R. Stockton successfully employed a narrative device as old as *The Arabian Nights' Entertainments*: the frame story. The enclosed tale is about a magic show put on by Herbert Loring for a few carefully invited friends. The first part of the exhibition is a slide show projected on the screen of what Loring calls "fireworks," a kind of kaleidoscope arrangement of pieces of colored glass which form, by means of mirrors and lights, into fascinating patterns. After half an hour of this, the host brings out a table upon which he places a box containing an egg. When he touches the egg with a wand, it hatches into a downy chick that continues to grow until it is an enormous cock. Flapping his wings, he ascends to a chair placed upon the table for that purpose, his weight nearly tipping it over. The audience stands, cheers, and becomes extremely excited. Then the magician reverses the growth process and the bird grows smaller and smaller until it enters the egg again, is put back into the box, and the host leaves the stage.

The frame narrative tells how the audience assembled at the Unicorn Club by invitation at three o'clock on a January afternoon has to wait fifteen minutes, because Loring sees that two reserved seats in the front row have not yet been filled. Because the audience is becoming restless, Loring decides to begin even though someone important has not yet arrived. A few minutes after the fireworks part of the show, Edith Starr, who had been betrothed to Herbert Loring a month before, enters unobtrusively; not wishing to disturb the proceedings to find her front-row reserved seat, she sits in the back behind two large gentlemen who completely conceal her person. Her mother had had a headache so she stayed with her until she fell asleep and then came alone to "see what she could."

At this point the narration changes from omniscient to first-person, as the magician describes what is happening in a long monologue of six and a half pages which concludes the frame story. Elated with his success, Loring uses a metaphor in which he becomes the rooster that he produced. He feels as if he "could fly to the top of that steeple, and flap and crow until all the world heard me." Since the crowing cock who lords it over the hen yard is soon to be deflated, the emblem of masculine power is thus used as ironic foreshadowing, as well as summing up what preceded.

Herbert and Edith meet in her library. He has been in the habit of calling on her every night, so this is part of the acknowledged routine of the engaged lover. The remainder of the action is unfolded in dialogue. She says that she saw the audience wild with excitement. She, however, saw no chick, nor any full-grown fowl, no box, no wand, and no embroidered cloth. Nothing was what he said it was. "Everything was a sham and a delusion; every word you spoke was untrue. And yet everybody in the theatre, excepting you and me, saw all the things that you said were on the stage." Loring explains that he had hypnotized the audience with the revolving pieces of colored glass by which he had forced them to strain their eyes upward for half an hour in order to induce hypnotic sleep. He had been careful to invite only "impressionable subjects." When he was absolutely sure that they were under his influence, he proceeded to test his hypnotic powers with the illusion which they believed they saw.

"Did you intend that I should also be put under that spell?" she asks. She is indignant that he would have considered taking away her reason and judgment and making her "a mere tool of his will." She now understands that "nothing was real, not even the little pine table—not even the man!" She says a final good-bye to him, never to see him again, because she wants nothing further to do with a man who would cloud her perceptions, subject her intellect to his own, and force her to believe a lie. As the rejected suitor leaves, he says "And this is what came out of the magic egg!"

This is an inverted fairy tale. The normal formulaic plot would have ended in a marriage whose happy ending was achieved by the use of magical objects. Instead, the magic object here leads to the dissolution of the happy ending because the "princess" has a mind of her own; she is a strong-willed woman who refuses to submit to male domination. The second important aspect of the story is that it is a metaphor for the art of storytelling. The speaker, with his words alone, hypnotizes his audience into suspending their disbelief. His power over them is very like that of a magician, and Stockton, whose enthusiastic public followed his legerdemain through over a dozen novels, must have at times confronted the ambiguities of his position. The blank page must have seemed the white shell of a magic egg which he alone could "crack" to release wonders which lasted only as long as he was relating them, and then, when the cover was closed, went back to being only an object.

"His Wife's Deceased Sister" is a charming tale built on the interrelations between life and literature and on the paradox that failure results from too-great success. A newly married author in the elation of his honeymoon writes a moving story. He has supported himself quite adequately up to that time with his fictions, but this story is a masterpiece. The problem is that everything he writes afterwards is rejected because it would disappoint the public for not being on the same level which they have come to expect from him. The author then meets a pauper who earlier had the same paradoxical experience of having been ruined by the success of one story. Depressed by his visit to the pauper's room, where he sleeps on newspapers and lives by grinding heads on pins, the author consults his editor, saying he faces similar ruin. They hit on the device of an assumed name.

Once more the author is making a good, steady income when a son is born. In his first joy of fatherhood, he composes a story which is even superior to "His Wife's Deceased Sister." He buries it in a tin box with the edges soldered together, which he hides in the attic with instructions to throw away the key to the solid lock he has purchased for it. The underlying assumption is that great fiction is inspired by happy events in life, which contradicts the Freudian notion that art sublimates suffering. The problem with the plot is that the reader immediately thinks of a better solution to the author's problem. Why did he not publish it under his real name? Although this story was written merely for entertainment, the fact that the author did not ask such a question is what distinguishes his work from that of writers whose fiction has endured.

Major publications other than short fiction

NOVELS: *Rudder Grange*, 1879; *The Casting Away of Mrs. Lecks and Mrs. Aleshire*, 1886; *The Late Mrs. Null*, 1886; *The Dusantes*, 1888; *Ardis Claverden*, 1890; *The Squirrel Inn*, 1891; *The Adventures of Captain Horn*, 1895; *Mrs. Cliff's Yacht*, 1896; *The Great Stone of Sardis*, 1898.

NONFICTION: *New Jersey from the Discovery of Scheyochbi to Recent Times*, 1896.

Ruth Rosenberg

JESSE STUART

Born: W-Hollow, Riverton, Kentucky; August 8, 1907

Principal short fiction

Head o' W-Hollow, 1936; *Tales from the Plum Grove Hills*, 1946; *Clearing in the Sky*, 1950; *Plowshare in Heaven: Tales True and Tall from the Kentucky Hills*, 1958; *My Land Has a Voice*, 1966; *32 Votes Before Breakfast*, 1974.

Other literary forms

Although Jesse Stuart probably found the best outlet for his artistic expression in the short story, he published more than two thousand poems, a number of autobiographical works, and eight novels—the latter including the best-selling *Taps for Private Tussie* (1943).

Influence

Through the vivid pictures that he presents of life in the Kentucky hill country in his stories, Stuart has opened up significant veins of material for other writers who follow him. While not adding new dimensions to the short story, he has nevertheless produced many excellent examples in that genre.

Story characteristics

Virtually all of Stuart's stories deal with the hill country of eastern Kentucky, where generations ago people dropped off from the movement West to settle in the hills and hollows of what has come to be a part of Appalachia. The life depicted in these stories is hard, and the people who live it are fundamentally religious and close to the earth. A natural storyteller, Stuart has captured not only the idiom of his characters, but also the very essence of their relationship to one another and to the natural world around them. He does not take solely the realist's approach, but blends in a strain of romantic optimism.

Biography

A native of Kentucky, Jesse Hilton Stuart was educated at Lincoln Memorial University. Following his graduation, be began a career as a writer and teacher. Over the years he has produced more than thirty books. He spent 1937 in Scotland as a Guggenheim Fellow, and during World War II he served in the United States Navy. He and his wife Naomi Deane have made their home on a working farm in W-Hollow, the area of Kentucky that he has made famous through his writings.

Analysis

America's southern highlands have long been viewed as an area removed from the influences of the "civilized" world; and indeed, for over a century they were. Rich in folklore and tradition, these highlands have provided stimulus to a vast number of writers as far back as William Gilmore Simms. The majority produced rather second-rate novels and stories that relied on melodrama, sentimentality, and effusive description of natural setting to carry their plots. A few of the more recent writers, however, have risen above that level to present the southern highlanders and their land in a more graphic and realistic light. Jesse Stuart is one such writer.

Once commenting that as a child he "read the landscape, the streams, the air, and the skies," Stuart had "plenty of time to grow up in a world that I loved more and more as I grew older." With his abiding love and respect for the people and the land of this picturesque region, Stuart, in a fashion matched by few American regional writers, brings the southern highlands into sharp focus for his readers. His short stories—the fictional form in which he is at his best—are a journey of exploration into the many aspects of life in the region. Using his home place of W-Hollow as a vantage point and springboard, Stuart treats various themes and motifs in his stories: religion, death, politics, folklore, sense of place, nature, and the code of the hills. While these themes are treated from a realistic stance, through all of them runs the romantic idea of the ever-renewing power of the earth.

A story that clearly illustrates this blending of realism and Romanticism is "Dawn of Remembered Spring." Like so many of Stuart's stories, this one has an autobiographical ring to it. The main character is Shan, a young boy who appears in a number of Stuart's stories. In this particular instance, Shan is being cautioned by his mother not to wade the creek because of the danger of water moccasins. Just a few days prior, Roy Deer, another youngster, was bitten by a water moccasin and is now near death. To Shan's comment that all water moccasins ought to be killed, his mother agrees but adds, "They're in all these creeks around here. There's so many of them we can't kill 'em all." As idyllic as one side of life in W-Hollow may be, there is the ever-present factor of death, in this case symbolized by water moccasins.

Shan, however, is not to be deterred by his mother's warning; and, armed with a wild-plum club, he sets out wading the creek to kill as many water moccasins as he can. It is a suspenseful journey as Shan, frightened but determined, kills snake after snake. "This is what I like to do," he thinks. "I love to kill snakes." He wades up the creek all day, and when he steps out on the bank at four o'clock, he has killed fifty-three water moccasins. As he leaves the creek, he is afraid of the snakes he has killed and grips his club until his hands hurt, but he feels good that he has paid the snakes back for biting Roy Deer—"who wasn't bothering the water moccasins that bit him. He was just crossing the creek at the foot-log and it jumped from the grass and bit him."

As he goes near home, Shan sees two copperhead snakes in a patch of sunlight. "Snakes," he cries, "snakes a-fightin' and they're not water moccasins! They're copperheads!" The snakes are wrapped around each other, looking into each other's eyes and touching each other's lips. Shan's Uncle Alf comes upon the scene and tells Shan that the snakes are not fighting but making love. A group of onlookers soon gathers, including Shan's mother who asks him where he has been. "Killin' snakes," is his reply. To her statement that Roy Deer is dead, Shan says that he has paid the snakes back by killing fifty-three of them. At this point his mother, along with the rest who have gathered at the scene, is spellbound by the loving copperheads. She sends Shan to the house to get his father. As the boy goes, he notices that the snakes have done something to the people watching: "Their wrinkled faces were as bright as the spring sunlight on the bluff; their eyes were shiny as the creek was in the noonday sunlight."

In "Dawn of Remembered Spring" Stuart has juxtaposed images of death and life; Shan has killed fifty-three snakes, and Roy Deer has died from his snake bite. The two copperheads making love reminds the reader and the people watching that, cruel though nature may be at times, there is always the urge for life. The hate that demands revenge is somehow redeemed in the laughter that Shan hears from the group—a laughter "louder than the wild honeybees I had heard swarming over the shoemake, alderberry, and wild flox blossoms along the creek."

In "Sylvania Is Dead" Stuart uses the death motif to bring out the prevalent stoicism of the highlanders as well as their ability to see humor in even a sorrowful situation. While some may see the humor in this story as being overdone, actually it is the humor that contributes most to the poignancy of the theme. The story opens as Bert Pratt and Lonnie Pennix are on their way to the funeral of the story's namesake. It is September, and nature is presented through images of death: "The backbone of the mountain was gray and hard as the bleached bone of a carcass. The buzzards floated in high circles and craned their necks." When the men reach Sylvania's cabin at the top of the mountain, they see a large crowd already gathered and buzzards circling low overhead. Lonnie pulls his pistol and shoots into the buzzards, scaring them away. When Skinny, Sylvania's husband, runs from the cabin scolding them for firing guns at such a sorrowful time, they respond that they were only trying to shoo away buzzards. Skinny says it is all right, for buzzards are a "perfect nuisance in a time like this."

The humor in the story derives from Sylvania's size and her occupation. She weighs six hundred and fifty pounds; her husband, only about one hundred. Her occupation has been moonshining, and as one of the men digging her grave says, "I say we'll never miss Sylvania until she's gone. She's been a mother to all of us." Sylvania is so big that when she was caught "red handed" by the revenuers on one occasion, she simply laughed and said that even "if they could get her out of the house, they couldn't get her down the mountain."

Getting Sylvania out of the house now is the big problem. Building a coffin that takes six men to carry, they finally get Sylvania in it, but it will not go through the door. The only answer is to tear down the chimney. Before carrying the coffin out, however, the men stop for a drink from Sylvania's last barrel. "I patronized Sylvania in life and I'll patronize her in death," Bert says. The drinks from Sylvania's last barrel, combined with the sorrow at her death, make the crowd noisy. As the coffin is carried to the grave, there is laughing, talking, and crying, accompanied by another pistol shot at circling buzzards. Finally Sylvania is lowered to her rest, and, as Skinny is led back to his cabin, there are "words of condolence in the lazy wind's molesting the dry flaming leaves on the mountain."

The human drama played out at this mountaintop funeral is marked not predominantly by sorrow, but by acceptance. Sylvania was mother to them all in life, and it is only fitting that her "children" should see her to her grave. The humor in the story is not strained or out of place; on the contrary, it fits. Humor is part of the hard life lived close to nature that is common to the people of Stuart's fictional world—as much a part as are Sylvania's moonshine and the buzzards circling overhead.

In "Sunday Afternoon Hanging" Stuart again blends the comic element with grim realism, as an old man describes to his grandson what old-time hangings in Blakesburg, Kentucky, were like. Viewing the electric chair as a poor substitute for a hanging, he points out that at a hanging "everybody got to see it and laugh and faint, cuss or cry." Indeed, they would come from as far as forty miles for such an opportunity. As he relates one particular incident to his grandson, the reader is made aware of a combination of characteristics in the people Stuart writes about—violence, vengeance, fatalism, and a desire to escape the tedium of their daily lives.

The Sunday afternoon hanging that the old man describes is the result of the brutal murder of an elderly couple by five men—Tim and Jake Sixeymore, Freed Winslow, Dudley Toms, and Work Grubb. They are all sentenced to hang on the same day, and hundreds of people congregate to witness the affair. In contrast to the grizzly vengeance to be exacted, the day is bright, with a June wind blowing and roses in bloom. Providing music for the event is a seven-piece band dressed in gaudy yellow pants with red sashes and green jackets. "It was the biggest thing we'd had in many a day," recalls the old man. "Horses broke loose without riders on them and took out through the crowd among the barking dogs, running over them and the children. People didn't pay any attention to that. It was a hanging and people wanted to see every bit of it."

The procedure for the hanging is to have each man brought to the hanging on a horse-drawn wagon standing on his coffin. After a rousing number by the band and a confession from the condemned, the wagon is pulled away, leaving him "struggling for breath and glomming at the wind with his hands."

When he is pronounced dead, the procedure begins for the next man. As each man is hanged, the gruesome scene becomes even more so. The last to hang is Tim Sixeymore, and he is so large that he breaks six ropes before the execution is finally carried out. His confession, reminiscent of the ballad "Sam Hall," begins, "Gentlemen bastards and sonofabitches. Women wenches and hussies and goddam you all." As the hanging is completed and the parents of the Sixeymores carry off their dead sons, the band plays softer music. The crowd breaks up, "getting acquainted and talking about the hanging, talking about their crops and the cattle and the doings of the Lord to the wicked people for their sins"; and so life goes on. The blending of the comic and the tragic in "Sunday Afternoon Hanging" is so subtle that one is not sure whether to be horrified at the terrible vengeance exacted amid frivolity and hatred or simply to accept such an apparent contradiction as do the people of Blakesburg.

Whatever his feelings of admiration for the people about whom he writes, Stuart is not blind to that aspect of their individualism that encourages violence. A number of his stories, for example, deal with feuding and moonshining, which, although they are usually thought of now in a more or less humorous vein, were in reality serious and often deadly activities. Fiercely proud, Stuart's characters consider such activities their own business and go about them in their own way, as shown in the story "The Moonshine War."

Combining moonshining and feuding, this story is narrated by Chris Candell, whose father in earlier days was one of four moonshiners in Greenwood County, Kentucky. With the help of his three sons, Charlie, Zeke, and Chris, he moonshined for twenty years before his wife prevailed upon him to lay his sins on the mourner's bench in the Methodist Church and give up "the business." Shortly after, the federal agents close in on the other three families that are still moonshining—the Whaleys, the Fortners, and the Luttrells—sending members from each to prison for varying terms.

When Willie Fortner is released because of his youth, he returns to Greenwood County, vowing revenge on the other families because he thinks that they helped the federal agents to discover his father's still. Two weeks later Jarwin Whaley is found stabbed to death. In quick succession two more deaths by stabbing occur, of Lucretia Luttrell and Charlie Candell, Chris's brother. There is no real evidence to connect these crimes to Willie Fortner, and, although he is arrested, he is acquitted, moving Zeke Candell to say, "Damn this circumstantial evidence stuff! We've got to take the law into our own hands." Before the Candells can do anything, however, Willie Fortner is killed in an auto wreck, the only one of five in the car who is. Chris's father, obviously attributing Willie's death to the Lord, says that "we'll have peace. The knife killings are over."

Stuart does not condemn any of the actions in "The Moonshine War," but, as in all his stories, he accepts the characteristics of his highland ancestors.

Indeed, in another story, "My Father Is an Educated Man," he says of the fiercely independent men of his family now sleeping in the Virginia, West Virginia, and Kentucky mountains, "Though I belong to them, they would not claim me since I have had my chance and unlike them I have not killed one of my enemies." The code of conduct that arises from such a life view may be a combination of savagery, civility, and moral contradiction, but it attests to the belief of the highlander that he is master of his own destiny.

For those wishing to see another side of Stuart's writing, there is the volume of stories entitled *Save Every Lamb* (1964). Virtually all of the stories in this volume are autobiographical in background and have nature themes. In them Stuart hearkens back to another era—a time "when everybody in the country lived by digging his livelihood from the ground." It was a time when man was in tune with the natural world about him and was better for it. "My once wonderful world has changed into a world that gives me great unhappiness," Stuart says in the Introduction to *Save Every Lamb*. For the moment, at least, Stuart in these stories takes the reader back with him to that wonderful world of his youth.

In all of his stories Stuart writes with an easy, almost folksy, style. Avoiding experimentation and deep symbolism, he holds his readers by paying close attention to detail and by painting starkly graphic scenes as he brings to life the characters and settings of W-Hollow. As a regionalist, Stuart draws constantly on his background in his stories, with the result that his style is underlined by an autobiographical bias, which contributes strongly to the sense of immediacy that marks all his work. Just as William Faulkner has his microcosm of the universe in Yaknapatawpha County, so too does Stuart in W-Hollow, and the American literary chronicle is the richer for it.

Major publications other than short fiction

NOVELS: *Trees of Heaven*, 1940; *Taps for Private Tussie*, 1943; *Foretaste of Glory*, 1946; *Hie to the Hunters*, 1950.

POETRY: *Man with a Bull-Tongue Plow*, 1934; *Album of Destiny*, 1944; *Kentucky Is My Land*, 1952; *Hold April*, 1962.

Bibliography

Clarke, Mary Washington. *Jesse Stuart's Kentucky*.
Foster, Ruel E. *Jesse Stuart*.

Wilton Eckley

THEODORE STURGEON

Born: Staten Island, New York; February 26, 1918

Principal short fiction

Without Sorcery, 1948; *E Pluribus Unicorn*, 1953; *Caviar*, 1955; *A Way Home*, 1955; *A Touch of Strange*, 1958; *Aliens 4*, 1959; *Beyond*, 1960; . . . *And My Fear Is Great and Baby Is Three*, 1965; *The Joyous Invasions*, 1965; *Starshine*, 1968; *Sturgeon in Orbit*, 1970; *Sturgeon Is Alive and Well*, 1971; *The Worlds of Theodore Sturgeon*, 1972; *To Here and the Easel*, 1973; *Sturgeon's West*, 1973 (with Don Ward).

Other literary forms

Theodore Sturgeon wrote newspaper stories in the late 1930's and has written book reviews for a variety of publications since the 1950's. He has published a Western novel, a (pseudonymous) historical romance, a realistic vampire novel, a film novelization, and four science-fiction novels, in addition to contributing scripts for two episodes of the television series *Star Trek*. He has won the International Fantasy Award (1954, for *More than Human*), and the science fiction Hugo and Nebula (1970, for "Slow Sculpture").

Influence

Sturgeon's main influence in science fiction and fantasy writing has been in terms of style and theme. An unabashed romantic in a field that claims allegiance to futuristic hardware and "realistic" extrapolation, he has been consistently popular despite (or because of) his unorthodoxy. His style is impressionistic and heavy with imagery, but it varies with his subject matter. Ray Bradbury and Samuel R. Delany claim him as a mentor, and Kurt Vonnegut, Jr., used him as a model for his fictional science-fiction writer, wise but unacclaimed Kilgore Trout.

Story characteristics

Sturgeon's stories lie at the edge of science fiction, concerned with people first, scientific and technological innovations second. He has a tendency toward sentimentality, like the stereotype of "women's magazine" stories, as he tries to portray human reactions to love and the pain and yearning of its absence, for an audience largely resistant to such personal communication in its fiction.

Biography

Theodore (Edward Hamilton Waldo) Sturgeon has led one of those archetypal writer's lives, roaming the world and doing many different kinds of jobs. As a child, he wanted to be a circus performer, even gaining an athletic scholarship to Temple University, but his career in gymnastics was stopped by rheumatic fever. As an adult, he has sold newspapers, collected garbage, sailed the seas as an engine-room wiper, worked as a musician, a ghostwriter, and a literary agent, operated a bulldozer, a gas station, and held several door-to-door sales positions. Married five times, usually to younger women, he has fathered six children.

Analysis

In a commercial literature devoted to galaxy-spanning concepts of paper-thin consistency, mechanical characters of whatever origin (human, alien, metal, or chemical), and wooden verbal expression, Theodore Sturgeon was an anomaly as early as 1939, when his stories began appearing in science-fiction magazines. A writer more of fantasy than of science fiction, whose predilection for words over machines was immediately apparent, Sturgeon was concerned with specific fantasies less for themselves than as means to the end of writing about human beings and human problems. Unlike those of so many of his colleagues, his tales usually take place in small, circumscribed locations, where love and healing can overshadow lesser, more conventional marvels and wonders.

Although style has always been somewhat suspect in science fiction, Sturgeon (along with Alfred Bester and Ray Bradbury) has fought a rear-guard action throughout his career. His example speaks louder than theory about the importance of words, especially in terms of the planned resonance of images and the conscious manipulation of symbols to invite emotional response to his romantic, even utopian view of the relationship between man and his technologies. Viewing "science" as "wisdom," he writes of the search for wholeness, often without the aid of conventional means of attaining knowledge. He is antimachine in a way, but more opposed to man's self-enslavement to mechanical procedures, be they metal or mental. Illustration of his themes calls forth as often as not a kind of fantasy which bears a close relationship to magic, events being caused by words and gestures. His is not a "science" which tediously accumulates and interprets observations of the world as it can be measured with instruments fashioned by and limited to man's rational capacities.

There is no typical Sturgeon story, so varied is his surface subject matter, which incudes many traditional science-fiction "inventions" and "discoveries," space travel, planetary exploration, matter transmission, cloning, alien contact, and paranormal powers among them. Sturgeon's stories usually speculate on love and sex in terms often considered radical for their market. Like D. H. Lawrence, he shows concern for the roots of human behavior in publicly repressed areas of behavior and thought; like Lawrence, too, he may have exaggerated the usefulness for everyone of his own particular cures. More sentimental than Lawrence, he is also more experimental, obviously with respect to subject matter, but also in terms of literary forms, playing with chronology, point of view, and other elements of storytelling in a way highly unusual for science fiction prior to the mid-1960's.

Sturgeon sold some remarkable "horror" stories in his early years of writing, such as "It," told from the point of view of a putrescent monster as dead as it is alive, and "Bianca's Hands," about a man in love with, and eventually strangled by, the hands of a girl with the mind of an idiot. In "Killdozer," he created a masterpiece of contemporary terror in which two members of an eight-man construction crew on a deserted Pacific island barely withstand and defeat a malevolent alien consciousness which has taken possession of one of their bulldozers. The television motion picture made from this story did not do it justice. The most anthologized of Sturgeon's early pieces, however, is "Microcosmic God," whose popularity he resents, because its relatively clumsy handling and apparently ruthless attitude toward certain life forms are uncharacteristic of his best work and his own self-image.

Primarily narrative, what dialogue there is being rather stiff and self-conscious, "Microcosmic God" is somewhat of a self-parody, with its protagonist a "Mister Kidder" and his antogonist a stereotyped grasping banker named Conant who would exploit Kidder's discoveries to take over the world. Almost lost in the reader's obvious antipathy to Conant's manipulation of human beings is its direct parallel to Kidder's even more ruthless manipulation of the tiny conscious beings whose evolution he has accelerated purely to satisfy his own curiosity.

Explicitly science fictional, the story is not rooted in the practical experience with details of construction machinery which makes "Killdozer" so dramatically convincing. Kidder's literal creation of an entire race for experimental purposes is couched, rather, in more theoretical and conceptual detail. The story's headlong pace races past problems in verisimilitude, in keeping with the simplistic morality of good (Kidder) versus evil (Conant), but intrusive commentary by the narrator reminds us sporadically that this is a fable, even if it does not specifically single out Kidder for censure.

Characterizing Kidder only minimally—both men are comic-book figures—the story shows his impatience with other people, with orthodox science (he claims no academic degrees), and with practical applications for his findings. In Conant, his alter ego, the reader sees explicitly the potential for abuse in his work, which reflects back on Kidder's own amorality. A god to his creatures, Kidder is a stand-in, not for the "mad scientist" whose image Sturgeon specifically disavows, but for the shortsighted tinkerer, representing all those who endeavor by mechanical means to improve the lot of human beings. The danger within the story is that, when Kidder dies, the creatures will conquer our world; the real danger to which the story points is that the misapplication of science to means or ends in the real world will do the same.

Irresponsibility is also the theme of "Mewhu's Jet," in which an alien visitor with fabulous technological powers turns out to be a young child; of "The Sky Was Full of Ships," in which a naïve meddler unwittingly calls to Earth a menacing alien fleet; and of "Maturity," in which that quality is disavowed as the ripeness immediately preceding death. Sturgeon, however, was also concerned with the other side of the coin. In "Thunder and Roses," the beautiful Starr Anthim tries, in a nuclear-devastated America, to prevent late retaliation that might wipe out all human civilization. In "Saucer of Loneliness," another girl preserves the message given her by a miniature flying saucer, which assuages her despair with the knowledge that loneliness is shared. In "The Skills of Xanadu," an entire planet's people have overcome dependence on ugly machine technology and achieved a utopian state which is both dynamic and transferable.

Communication is central to these stories, as it is to "Bulkhead," in which the "partner" assigned to a space pilot with whom he has an intense love-hate relationship turns out to be another part of himself, part of a schizophrenic condition deliberately induced by his employers for his own good. In the classic novella, "Baby Is Three," centerpiece of the award-winning novel *More than Human* (1953), a "gestalt" being, composed of adolescent parapsychological misfits, fights to define its identity, which the last section of the novel will provide with maturity, responsibility, even community. Although this is arguably Sturgeon's best story ever, the novel to which it was converted is too well-known to require analysis here of one of its parts.

The many ways that love and sex connect fascinated Sturgeon as early as "Bianca's Hands," but several provocative variations on this theme occupied him in the 1950's. *Venus Plus X* (1960) hypothesized physiological bisexuality in a "utopian" community on Earth. *Some of Your Blood* (1961) is a psychological case study of physiological vampirism. In "Affair with a Green Monkey," a psychologist obsessed with adjustment confuses gentleness with homosexuality, completely misjudging a humanoid alien whose sexual equipment would put to shame the best-endowed pornographic film star. His best treatment of "aberrant" sexuality is probably "The World Well Lost."

Again attacking the obsession with normalcy of America in the 1950's, Sturgeon describes a future world enchanted by the love for each other and for things earthly of a couple of unexpected alien visitors, before their home world requests the return of the "loverbirds." Having once sent an ambassador to Earth and found it wanting, the planet Dirbanu has stonewalled further contact attempts until this time, when humans' intolerance at being kept out prompts them to sacrifice the fugitives in quest of anticipated interplanetary relations. The "prison ship," however, is crewed by two men whose perfect record results from a complementarity unrecognized by Rootes and unspoken by Grunty. Discovery of the aliens' telepathic powers threatens the tongue-tied Grunty, whose threat to kill them is countered by two things: the fact that Dirbanu wants them dead, and the reason why.

Dirbanu females are so different in appearance from males that all human beings look to them to be of the same sex, and just as repulsive as the two fugitive "loverbirds." Acknowledging their homosexuality, the alien prisoners recognize the same propensity in their captors. Rootes's tales of heterosexual exploits are repetitive and hollow-sounding, while Grunty suffers consciously from an involuntary attraction to his partner which he can never voice, for all the poetry that swirls within his mind. Grunty lets the prisoners escape in a lifeboat which will isolate them for years before, if ever, they reach planet-fall. Although Rootes berates him, Dirbanu is grateful for the presumed deaths; they still will have nothing to do with Earth, however, and their bigotry strikes a sympathetic chord in Rootes, as presumably it would back home. For all the "space opera" trappings, the tenuous coincidences, and the dated attitude toward homosexuality—even contextually, it seems inconsistent with an Earth that pursues, the reader is told, many other euphoric and aphrodisiac thrills—the story evokes with minimal sentimentality a love that literally "cannot speak its name" and the pathetic intolerance that will not let it.

In contrast to such a plot-laden construct, "The Man Who Lost the Sea" is as near to stream-of-consciousness style as market considerations would allow. Exploring the senses, hallucinatory experiences, and memories of the first astronaut to reach Mars alive, the story weaves past and present, childhood and adulthood, mechanical and psychological drives into a haunting impression of a time which might prove as traumatic and epoch-making as the emergence of the first air-breathers out of the sea of life's origin on Earth. As shifting point of view and chronology represent the man's dazed mental and emotional state, Sturgeon only gradually reveals the nature of the man's predicament (his ship has crashed and there is no way back), until the emotional shock of simultaneous gain and loss has prepared the way for the triumphant irony of the protagonist's dying exultation: "We made it!"

Sturgeon's rather few stories of the 1960's and 1970's continued to deal with love and responsibility, especially healing, but often in a talky mode. His greatest success in that period is "Slow Sculpture," named best of the year by science-fiction fans and readers alike. This novella is a loving exploration of how an unnamed "man" and a "girl" come tentatively to know each other, although the specific means are entwined with science-fiction and fantasy motifs as the two people are with each other and with the fifteen-foot bonsai tree that grows in his garden. Like other Sturgeon protagonists, the man is a polymath, credentialed in law and in two kinds of engineering, who in this instance practices medicine without a license.

That his cure for her cancer works the reader is asked to take on faith as she does, since establishment means and methods are deliberately eschewed, and the "technology" that he uses is more obscured than revealed by the metaphorical language with which he describes it. There are some appropriate "special effects," suggesting the interrelatedness of house and garden, house and mountain, man and tree, matter and energy, mind and body. The medium and the message, however, are primarily communication, in conversation which may be more expressive than it is true to life, but which is far from stilted. The speeches, moreover, are contextually true, since the man, whatever his healing powers for others, fends off the girl's involvement with him, her own halting attempts to connect with the anger, fear, and frustration in him at the world's resistance to all he has offered to better it.

Throughout the story, the dominant symbol is the bonsai, which resists "instruction" because it knows how it should grow, which achieves its form by compromising between its essential nature and the manipulation to which it is subjected, not by its "owner" but by its "companion." As in many of Sturgeon's works, but never more appropriately, the prose itself is "sculptured," reminding the reader that the magic of fantasy resides less in the act than in the telling of it.

Sturgeon's stories are in some ways "hopelessly romantic," conjuring impossible cures and utopian solutions, even when they are not projected long ahead and far away. Like the best science fiction, they lead the reader back to the present, not to external realities, but rather to emotional confrontations with human problems, situations, characters. Although the reader may detach himself from the ostensible subjects, removed from the here and now, the situation of the writer, often as a stand-in for the reader-as-dreamer, is frequently apparent, sometimes intensely personal. For all of their variety, Sturgeon's stories betray an almost obsessive concern for wholeness and healing, for communication and toleration of the misfit, and often for "September-June" relationships between "men" and "girls." That his work has maintained, even increased its popularity as he has written less and less suggests that he has mined a vein of ore rich in its appeal, to women as well as men, to the adolescent in everyone. Almost despite their paraphernalia of science fiction and fantasy, Sturgeon's modern-day fairy tales communicate what his characters continually try to: the truth of emotion and the magic of words.

Major publications other than short fiction

NOVELS: *The Synthetic Man*, 1950; *More than Human*, 1953; *I, Libertine*, 1956 (published by "Frederick R. Ewing"); *The Cosmic Rape*, 1958; *Venus Plus X*, 1960; *Some of Your Blood*, 1961; *Voyage to the Bottom of the Sea*, 1961.

Bibliography
Friend, Beverly. "The Sturgeon Connection," in *Voices for the Future*. Edited by Thomas D. Clareson.
Moskowitz, Sam. "Theodore Sturgeon," in *Seekers of Tomorrow: Masters of*

Modern Science Fiction.
Sackmary, Regina. "An Ideal of Three: The Art of Theodore Sturgeon," in *Critical Encounters.* Edited by Dick Riley.
Samuelson, David N. "Theodore Sturgeon: *More than Human,*" in *Visions of Tomorrow: Six Journeys from Outer to Inner Space.*

David N. Samuelson

PETER TAYLOR

Born: Trenton, Tennessee; 1917

Principal short fiction

A Long Fourth and Other Stories, 1948; *The Widows of Thornton*, 1954; *Happy Families Are All Alike*, 1959; *Miss Leonora When Last Seen and Fifteen Other Stories*, 1963; *The Collected Stories of Peter Taylor*, 1970; *In the Miro District and Other Stories*, 1977.

Other literary forms

Peter Taylor published a novel, *A Woman of Means*, in 1950. His two volumes of plays, *A Tennessee Day in St. Louis* and *Presences: Seven Dramatic Pieces*, appeared in 1956 and 1973, respectively. Other works have appeared in periodicals but have yet to be issued in book form: the play *A Stand in the Mountains* and the poem "The Furnishings of a House." Four of the stories in *In the Miro District and Other Stories* are presented in the form of narrative poems.

Influence

Taylor's association with the writers of the Southern Renaissance has long been acknowledged. At various times he studied under Allen Tate, John Crowe Ransom, Robert Penn Warren, and Cleanth Brooks; but Taylor's subordination of social themes and his rejection of idealistic mythmaking in favor of ironic domestic realism has, from the beginning of his career, indicated his independence from agrarian programs. His sensibility, techniques, and themes are often compared with those of Jane Austen, Henry James, and Anton Chekhov, evidence enough perhaps that the South is not his subject, but his metaphor.

Story characteristics

Taylor's sometimes long, always meticulously well-crafted yet leisurely narratives portray urbanized, upper-middle-class characters from the middle South. These remarkably complex and believable characters move through trying times with manners and morals born of traditional good breeding and of the need to retain their identities in the face of corrosive change. Taylor's most characteristic fiction, like that of Austen, avoids extremes, preferring, in its deft creation of genteel social comedy, irony to satire and gentle humor to burlesque. Some critics have called him "classical," a reference to his restraint and stylistic clarity.

Biography

When Peter Hillsman Taylor was seven years old, his family, leaving the small town of Trenton, began a series of moves which took them to Nashville, St. Louis, and finally Memphis. Taylor was graduated from Memphis Central High in 1935, worked his way to England on a freighter in the summer, and upon his return to the United States studied under Tate and Ransom. His first two stories were published in *River* in 1937; but when Ransom left Vanderbilt for Kenyon College in that year, Taylor dropped out of school and began selling real estate. In 1938, Taylor followed Ransom to Kenyon, graduating in 1940. He spent from 1941 to 1945 in the Army, stationed in the United States and in England, and married the poet Eleanor Ross in 1943. The Taylors have two children, a son and a daughter. Peter Taylor has taught at a number of universities; since 1967, however, he has been Commonwealth Professor of English at the University of Virginia. He has won a number of awards, among them a Guggenheim Fellowship (1950), Fulbright Award (1955), O. Henry Award (1959), Ford Foundation Fellowship (to study theater in England, 1961), Rockefeller Grant (1964), and American Institute and Academy of Arts and Letters Gold Medal for the Short Story (1978). He has been elected to membership in the National Institute of Arts and Letters (1969) and the American Academy of Arts and Sciences (1974).

Analysis

Despite the fact that his stories have appeared often in prestigious "best of the year" collections, Peter Taylor remains one of the most neglected writers of contemporary fiction. Those who know his work well, however, admire him as a craftsman of care and integrity who generally refuses to deal in the thematically or stylistically sensational, polishing instead his inch of domestic ivory in the tradition of Austen and James, writers with whom he is often compared. His rare use of such Southern fictional staples as grotesquerie, violence, and myth always shows the taming hand of a thoroughly "classical" sensibility.

Taylor has left his distinctive mark on a largely untouched body of material: the daily lives of upper-middle-class urbanized Tennesseans whose roots are in the rural or small-town South. His stories exhibit the strong sense of place and the preoccupation with history typical of the Agrarians; but, although the cultural forces which shape and plague his characters are always in evidence, it is the effect of such forces on the individual which is Taylor's real concern. Seldom does he allow the background of sociological elements in his works to overwhelm the individual in the foreground.

The story "Guests" is an excellent example of Taylor's distinctive mixture of comedy of manners and modern despair; and it reveals clearly one of the author's most characteristic attitudes toward the rural South. Lawyer Edmund Harper and his wife Henrietta, in one of the latter's schemes to "brighten the lives of people . . . whose lives [don't] seem absolutely to require her touch," have brought unwilling country relatives "bodily" to their house in Nashville for a short visit. The conflict between the country values of the elderly Kincaids and the city values of the Harpers provides the humor in the story as well as the occasion for protagonist Edmund's experience of self-discovery. "[W]anting to be no trouble," the reticent Kincaids merely tolerate their hosts' hospitality, refusing to give the Harpers any direct information about their own needs or preferences, despite the fact that Cousin Johnny is in ill health and on a strict diet.

The incompatibility of the couples' life-styles produces a complicated set of tensions, especially between the two women, as Cousin Annie tries to make minimal accommodation to her hostess' philanthropic impulses and yet preserve her and her husband's moral integrity. The Harpers' efforts to be most obliging—searching for acceptable entertainment, attempting to discover whether the cousin prefers to be addressed as "Cousin Johnny" or "Mr. Kincaid"—move the plot forward. The old lady's obviously inhibiting effect on Cousin Johnny angers Edmund, who would like to get to know the old man better and who feels, "Here is such a one as I might have been, and I am such a one as he might have been." The turning point in this struggle for communication occurs when, after accepting Edmund's invitation to lunch, Cousin Johnny goes upstairs to dress but does not come back down. Assuming that Cousin Annie has prevented the old man's going, Edmund is furious because he realizes that he and Johnny will never have a chance to talk. The next morning, the old lady informs Edmund and Henrietta that Mr. Kincaid has died, not unexpectedly, during the night.

These are memorable characters, characters whose very habits of mind are embodied in precisely rendered details of dress, speech, and behavior. Such details as Cousin Johnny's lisle socks and his tendency to wince whenever addressed stamp these characters deeply into our minds. It is Edmund's internal conflict and his feeling of emptiness and futility at the end, however, which point the reader toward the most important concerns of the story. Upon learning of Cousin Johnny's death, Edmund is seized with grief—not grief for the old farmer, but for himself. Henrietta's do-goodism has, this time, exposed the emptiness and sterility of the city couple's lives. The Harpers have no children, and it was Henrietta who had caused the reluctant Edmund to leave the small town of Ewingsburg, "where they had grown up and where he first practiced law." Standing at the foot of the bed in which the dead man is lying, Edmund finally, in internal monologue, speaks earnestly to Cousin Johnny:

> You buried yourself alive on that farm of yours, I buried myself alive here. But something in the life out there didn't satisfy you the way it should. The country wasn't itself anymore. And something was wrong for me here. By "country" we mean the old world, don't we Cousin Johnny—the old ways, the old life, where people had real grandfathers and real children, and where love was something that could endure the light of day—something real, not merely a hand one holds in the dark so that sleep will come.

Few of Taylor's characters speak so directly or so eloquently about their "country" origins; but the loss Edmund feels at the death of his alter ego is present in nearly every Taylor protagonist. It is clear from the above quotation that the "country" is, in Taylor's stories, a place to which *no* one can return— a simple, perfect place not only beyond the city limits, but also beyond the modern world.

The humor in "Guests" is certainly not broad, but it is somewhat broader than that in most Taylor stories, and its central conflict, although not titanic, is strong and clearly defined. In fact, most of Taylor's stories are of lower intensity. Taylor prefers a literal, commonplace diction and sentence structure and a correspondingly uneventful plot that is closer to that of "real life" than to that of most fiction.

"A Wife of Nashville," like "Guests" a much-admired story, is a superb example of Taylor's characteristically leisurely and indirect approach. The reader is introduced to the Lovells by reference to their servants in the first sentence: "The Lovells' old cook Sarah had to quit to get married in the spring, and they didn't have anybody else for a long time." Helen Ruth, the wife of the title, says of the black men and women who come looking for work, "When they knock on the porch floor like that, they're bound to be from the country, and they're better off at home where somebody cares something about them."

The Lovells themselves are from Thornton, the fictional town from which so many Taylor characters hail. Also like the Harpers in "Guests," they are more conspicuously people *from* somewhere than they are residents *of* somewhere. Helen Ruth's loneliness can be attributed in part to the unsatisfying role Nashville city life has forced upon her. It is not, however, suggested that she can live happily back in Thornton; her brief return there during the separation from her husband, John R., leaves her frightened and resigned to those "mysteries" which preclude any real intimacy in their marriage. Like Edmund Harper, she has in a way been "buried alive" simply by *being* from the country.

Helen Ruth's sense of loss, however, seems to stem from less obvious matters. Indeed, the reader is well into the story before he is sure hers is the significant conflict. Rather than presenting a tightly focused plot, Taylor presents what seems to be a series of anecdotes about the four black women the Lovells have employed over the years. The narrative wanders back and forth in time in the manner of a leisurely reminiscence. The reader learns of the sometimes surly Jane Blakemore, who came to Nashville with them from Thornton and who left after less than three years because, she said, the first baby made her nervous; of the secretive and morbidly curious Carrie, who left after five years to become an undertaker; of the illiterate and pious old Sarah who, after six years, left for Chicago with a man named Racecar; and finally, of the loyal and good-hearted Jess McGehee, who stayed with them the longest, but who finally left to seek the glamorous service of movie stars in California. Each of these characters is skillfully drawn, each as distinctive as good fiction can make her.

Helen Ruth, however, is the "wife of Nashville" and it is finally her story. She and John R. are fascinating, "round" characters, despite their apparently subordinate position early in the narrative. Some relationship between their marital problems and the stories about their hired help is suggested in the first few pages. For example, the major events in Helen Ruth's married life are oriented in time by such phrases as "in the era of Jane Blakemore." John R. refers to the excellent service of Jess McGehee by saying, "The honeymoon is over, but this is the real thing this time"; and he refers to the other servants as Helen Ruth's "earlier affairs." The full significance of these figures of speech gradually becomes obvious as the reader begins to realize the appropriateness of devoting most of the story to the servants: Helen Ruth's mundane experiences with these women have been the most substantial things in her life.

Like Jess McGehee (who keeps a scrapbook of the Lovells' daily lives), Helen Ruth has been living through other people. In the last section of the story, she helps Jess perpetrate a lie about a dead brother, a ploy to allow Jess to escape in search of her dreams. Both women have been disturbed by an awareness of the triviality of their lives, and in the last scene they are paralleled in many ways. Jess, who seems unaware of her mistress's knowledge of her plan, answers the phone "in a voice so like Helen Ruth's it [makes] the boys grin." When Jess tells the Lovells that the call is a telegraph message about the death of her "baby brother," John R. and the two grown boys look on in astonishment at Helen Ruth's reaction, at the depth of her sudden grief. The two women hug each other and weep. Jess apparently thinks she has fooled them all, but after Jess has left the house, Helen Ruth reveals what she has learned from the neighbors. Then she faces her three baffled men with the overwhelming need to explain her own and Jess's actions: "She felt that she would be willing to say anything at all, no matter how cruel or absurd it was, if it would make them understand that everything in life only demonstrated in some way the lonesomeness that people felt." When she speaks, however, she cannot make them understand; they sit, "their faces stamped with identical expressions, not of wonder, but of incredulity." The story ends with Helen Ruth playing Jess's role, pushing the teacart out of the bright sun parlor and into the dining room, symbolically "dark and cool as an underground cavern" and ironically "spotlessly clean"—sterilely clean—"the way Jess McGehee had left it."

"A Wife of Nashville" is Chekhovian, not only in its sharp insight into character, but also in its lack of compelling linear progression and its portrayal of slight events. The surfaces of the Lovells' lives are unruffled. The Lovells are even thought to be quite happily married—and one guesses that Taylor would say they are, relatively speaking. Theirs is a quiet desperation, one which produces John R.'s psychosomatic back pains and Helen Ruth's fruitless return to Thornton. John R.'s business partner commits suicide, it is implied; Sarah's husband has accidentally killed Sarah's son, the reader is told. Such momentous things, common enough in most Southern literature, do not happen to the Lovells—indeed, such things happen to remarkably few of Taylor's characters.

This is a quieter, more stable world than, say, that of Southerner Flannery O'Connor. There are few grotesques and mental defectives in Taylor's world. There is no lightning bolt of violence to open the eyes of laughably stupid characters, no blast of revelation to lift them from petty, earthly concerns. Most of Taylor's characters have their eyes somewhat open already, and discoveries, when they do come, are gradual, more limited, and more social in their import. In Taylor's world characters must learn to accommodate, not rise above; they must accept inevitable losses and questionable gains. Helen Ruth has a "nice family" in the conventional sense of the phrase; her husband has provided for her well. She has, by the standards of her class, a solid life; but she also has "her loneliness, the loneliness from which everybody, knowingly or unknowingly, suffer[s]."

Taylor's world is often bleaker than O'Connor's or the Agrarians', lacking as it does the former's refuge of the spiritual and the latter's refuge of the rural. Edmund Harper articulates what most of Taylor's characters will not even think directly about: "Other people seem to know some reason why it is better to be alive than dead this April morning. I will have to find it out. There must be something." When Taylor's characters do find refuge, it is in the social, a realm in which even his victors lose as much as they gain.

A common pattern in these stories is that of a character whose individuality proves so painful to maintain that capitulation to a stereotyped social role is his final, chosen defense. A number of Taylor's most attractive characters thus stereotype themselves. Aunt Muncie, the retired mammy of "What You Hear from 'Em?," when she finally realizes that the successful Tolliver boys whom she reared are never coming back to live in Thornton, adapts to a black stereotype, "laugh[ing] and holler[ing] with white folks the way they liked her to . . . talking old-nigger foolishness." The eccentric and wonderful Miss Leonora in "Miss Leonora When Last Seen," when faced with the final rejection by Thomasville, the little town she has dedicated her life to raising to her own cultural standards, cuts and colors her hair in the manner of conventional Southern ladies, dons a predictably ordinary dress, and becomes "one of those old women who come out here from Memphis looking for antiques and country hams and who tell you how delighted they are to find a Southern town that is truly unchanged." More recently there is Major Basil Manly of "In the Miro District" who, when he finally realizes he can make no meaningful connection with the future (embodied in his rebellious grandson), yields to the present "like an old general accepting total defeat with total fortitude." Manly resigns himself to playing the role Nashville society expects, the role of the garrulous old Civil War veteran reliving a colorful past. He becomes the cliché right down to the black serge suit, starched collar, and string tie. Each such defeat is a sad loss, but Taylor is never a sentimentalist. He treats even these characters with a stoic mixture of nostalgia and irony. As glorious as the fiercely idealistic Miss Leonora undeniably is, one can agree with the story's narrator that she and her family have inhibited the healthy growth of the town they created.

Like many other writers, Taylor has suffered misrepresentation at the hands of anthologists. "The Fancy Woman," perhaps his most often anthologized story, is uncharacteristically harsh. The Nashville trollop Josie Carlson is a satisfying protagonist in an effective story, and her failure to see beyond the surface vulgarity of her sample of the genteel South is definitely a Taylor touch. She is not, however, as critics point out, a standard Taylor protagonist; and neither are the grotesque and incestuous Dorsets in the prize-winning "Venus, Cupid, Folly, and Time." This latter story is haunting in its creation of mystery and decadence, and its unhurried exposition and leisurely historical epilogue spring directly from the Taylor aesthetic. Finally, however, at the story's core is a Gothic fantasy many Southerners might have written.

Early in his career Taylor established his temperate approach and narrow range, and he has worked brilliantly within his acknowledged limits. *In the Miro District and Other Stories*, dealing as it does at times with alcoholism, sex, and physical violence, extends these limits somewhat. In his modest search for variety, he has even cast four stories into the form of narrative poems. Still, with the notable exception of one character's shocking self-mutilation, Taylor's art continues to be far less galvanic than that of nearly all of his contemporaries. This later volume expresses typical Taylor concerns: the emphasis upon the alienating effects of time, the preoccupation with history, and the exploration of the paradoxes of social roles. Also, one finds a number of fully developed, complex characters, as real and strange as people met outside of books.

Major publications other than short fiction
NOVEL: *A Woman of Means*, 1950.

PLAYS: *A Tennessee Day in St. Louis*, 1957; *A Stand in the Mountains*, 1971; *Presences: Seven Dramatic Pieces*, 1973.

Bibliography
Blum, Morgan. "Peter Taylor: Self-Limitation in Fiction," in *Sewanee Review* (Autumn, 1962), pp. 559-578.

Brown, Ashley. "The Early Fiction of Peter Taylor," in *Sewanee Review* (Autumn, 1962), pp. 588-602.

Griffith, Albert J. *Peter Taylor*.
Shenandoah (Winter, 1977).
Smith, J. P. "A Peter Taylor Checklist," in *Critique* IX,3 (1967).

Ron Smith

WILLIAM MAKEPEACE THACKERAY

Born: Calcutta, India; July 18, 1811
Died: London, England; December 24, 1863

Principal short fiction
The Yellowplush Correspondence, November, 1837-July, 1838; *Comic Sketches and Tales*, 1841; *The Bedford Row Conspiracy*, 1840; *Jeames's Diary*, 1846; *A Shabby Genteel Story*, 1852; *Men's Wives*, 1853.

Other literary forms
William Makepeace Thackeray published seven novels during his lifetime, and the unfinished *Denis Duval* was printed posthumously in 1864. *Vanity Fair* (1847-1848) and *Barry Lyndon* (1844), which was recently filmed, are considered his masterpieces. Thackeray was a prolific contributor to periodicals of parodies, satires, humorous sketches, essays, reviews, and articles. He was a correspondent for many newspapers, and an editor of several magazines. He also issued popular Christmas annuals for many years.

Influence
In the last decade of his life, Thackeray was considered one of Britains' most powerful novelists. Soon after his death, however, his reputation declined, and the enormous popularity he enjoyed from his contemporaries has not yet been restored. His novels form an appraisal of English social history from 1690 to 1863 and English moral codes of that time.

Story characteristics
Thackeray experimented with every sort of first-person narration. By manipulating his various personae, he created subtle distinctions in tone. Even when Thackeray employed an omniscient narrator, he was always a mask, distinct from the author. For his Victorian audience, this mediating voice was one of the pleasures of reading Thackeray, who built on the oral nature of storytelling. To moderns, however, the tendency to tell rather than to dramatize seems an intrusive disruption of illusion, and thus, they sometimes do not appreciate the very commentary that made him so popular in his own time.

Biography
Born in India, William Makepeace Thackeray was the only son of Richmond and Ann Becher Thackeray. His grandfathers on both sides of the family had been with the Indian civil service, and after his father died in September, 1815, he was sent to school in England. He attended schools in Southampton, Chiswick, and Charterhouse; the bullying he received there was later fiction-

alized. One of his first pen names was Michael Angelo Titmarsh, adopted because his nose was broken by a classmate, as Michelangelo's had been three centuries earlier. He called his school "Slaughterhouse" for the brutality he endured there. His mother remarried, and he spent 1828 in Devon with her and Major-General Henry Carmichael-Smythe. From February, 1829, to July, 1830, he attended Trinity College, Cambridge. He traveled in Germany until May, 1831, and met Johann Wolfgang von Goethe in Weimar. He briefly studied law in England. In 1832, he spent four months in Paris, and from 1834 he began training as a professional artist since he had always had a talent for drawing. On August 20, 1836, he married Isabel Shawe, whose neurotic, domineering mother became the model for all the terrible mothers-in-law in Thackeray's fiction. Their daughter Anne was born in June, 1837; she later became a novelist and the editor of her father's letters to Edward Fitzgerald, and of his complete works. She married Sir Richmond Ritchie of the India office. Jane was born in July, 1838, and died eight months later. Harriet, born in May, 1840, was to marry Sir Leslie Stephen in 1867. In 1840, Isabel became so depressed that she attempted suicide and in 1846 she was declared incurably insane. The fortune Thackeray had inherited was dissipated by 1833, and the professional gamblers who swindled him out of his money figure in several of his stories. His stepfather invested in a paper so that Thackeray could write for it, but it failed, leaving them financially ruined. He wrote for twenty-four different periodicals between 1830 and 1844 trying to support his family, even applying to Charles Dickens for the job of illustrating the *Pickwick Papers* (1836-1837). Finally, the publication of *Vanity Fair* in 1848 made him a public figure. He began a series of public lectures which took him twice to America, from 1852 to 1853 and from 1855 to 1856. He died at the age of fifty-three on Christmas Eve, 1863.

Analysis

William Makepeace Thackeray's "Yellowplush" was first introduced in *Fraser's* in November, 1837, and was republished in America and translated into German. In 1845, the footman was revived in *Punch*, having been promoted to Charles James De La Pluche, Esq., through successful speculation in railway shares. On his first appearance in "Miss Shum's Husband," Yellowplush tells how he got his name. His mother, who always introduced him as her nephew, named him for the livery of a famous coachman, Yellowplush. Although he was illegitimate, he has gentlemanly tastes, and his cockney speech is spiced with affectations. His employer, Frederic Altamont, takes rooms in a crowded house in John Street. The footman reports that they breakfast from his master's tea leaves and dine on slices of meat cut from his joints, but Frederic endures this to be near his loved one Mary. In the next episode and with his next employer, Yellowplush has descended to petty thievery (which he calls his "perequisites") himself. During his courtship,

Altamont refuses to reveal where he works, but assures Mary that he is honest and urges her never to question him about what it would cost her misery to learn.

After their marriage, Frederic and Mary move to an elegantly furnished house in Islington, from which he mysteriously disappears each day. After their baby is born, Mrs. Shum becomes a daily visitor. This mother of twelve daughters who spent her time reading novels on the drawing room sofa, scolding, screaming, and having hysterics, is the first of the terrible mothers-in-law so prominent in Thackeray's fiction, including Mrs. Gam, Mrs. Gashleigh, Mrs. Cuff, Mrs. Crum, Lady Kicklebury, and Mrs. Baynes. They are always snobbish, interfering, and domineering. Mrs. Shum undermines the mutual affection in her daughter's household by implanting suspicions. "Where does his money come from? What if he is a murderer, or a house-breaker, or a forger?" When Mary answers that he is too kind to be any of those things, Mrs. Shum suggests that he must be a bigamist. At this moment, as Mary faints, Mrs. Shum has hysterics, the baby squalls, the servants run upstairs with hot water, and Frederic returns. He expels Mrs. Shum, double-locks the door, and tries to appease his wife without exposing his secret. His in-laws set up a spy network and finally discover that he is a crossing sweeper. Frederic sells his house and starts a new life abroad. His footman renders his snobbish judgment of the whole affair:

> Of cors, I left his servis. I met him, a few years after, at Badden-Badden, where he and Mrs. A. were much respectid, and pass for pipple of propaty.

The satire depends for its effect on the dissonance between the social pretensions and the misspellings in which they are conveyed. In Victorian England, a gentleman did not work for a living, and a footman conscious of his position could not work for a laborer. He could "pass" abroad, because foreigners were unable to tell the difference between inherited and earned money. Obviously, only income from property qualified one to enter society.

"Dimond Cut Dimond" is about Yellowplush's next master, who is penniless but titled. He is the Honorable Algernon Percy Deuceace, fifth son of the Earl of Crabs. If he had been a common man, he would have been recognized as a swindler, but since he is a gentleman, with his family tree prominently displayed in his sitting room, his gambling is considered acceptable. Dawkins, just out of Oxford, moves in with his entire fortune of six thousand pounds to establish himself as a barrister. Deuceace manipulates an introduction by tripping the servant carrying Dawkins' breakfast tray. He substitutes a pastry he has purchased for this purpose with an elaborate letter, claiming it had been sent to him by an aristocratic friend. Once they are acquainted, he suggests a game of cards, which he deliberately loses as a setup.

The scheme is complicated by a second con man, Richard Blewitt, who tells Deuceace that Dawkins is his pigeon to pluck, and that he means to strip this one alone since he already has him securely in his claws. Deuceace makes a deal to split the gains; after he wins, however, he coldly announces to Blewitt, who has come for his share, that he never had any intention of keeping his promise. Blewitt "stormed, groaned, bellowed, swore" but gets nothing, and the villain escapes to Paris, telling Yellowplush that he can come too if he likes.

Thackeray, as a student, had actually lost large sums to such gamblers. The insolent criminality with which Deuceace robs both Dawkins and Blewitt is not condemned by his footman, who is engaged in robberies of his own. "There wasn't a bottle of wine that we didn't get a glass out of . . . we'd the best pickens out of the dinners, the livvers of the fowls, the forcemit balls out of the soup, the egs from the sallit . . . you may call this robbery—nonsince—it's only our rights—a suvvant's purquizzits." In the eyes of the footman, the cold-blooded malice of his master is superior to the blustering passion of Blewitt.

The next episode, "Foring Parts," tells how Deuceace has posted a sign on his door, "Back at seven," and departed, owing the laundress. The footman learns that to gain respect in France, one must be rude. His master had abused the waiters, abused the food, and abused the wine, and the more abusive he was, the better service he got; on his example, the footman also practices insolence because people liked being insulted by a lord's footman. Deuceace writes to Lord Crabs for his allowance; but the answer comes back that since all of London knows of Deuceace's winnings, could he instead lend Lord Crabs some money. He encloses clippings from the newspapers about the transaction. Shortly afterward, a retraction appears in the paper for which Deuceace had sent a ten-pound note, with his compliments. The narrator comments that he had already sent a tenner before it came out, although he cannot think why.

"Dorothea" appeared in 1843 along with "Miss Loewe" and "Ottilia" as part of "Confessions of Fitz-Boodle." Since their narrator is a leisured gentleman, these stories differ in pace and tone from the Yellowplush series; Fitz-Boodle's aristocratic birth and classical education enable him to make social commentary of a different sort. The story turns on his failure to have learned dancing at Slaughterhouse school, where he learned little that was useful. He adds ruefully, however, that such is the force of habit that he would probably send his sons there, were he to have any. In a series of semiscenes typical of Thackeray's style, Fitz-Boodle describes the many dancing lessons he has taken from various instructors in London, in Paris, and finally in Germany, from Springbock, the leader of the Kalbsbraten ballet.

The continual shifting of temporal perspectives is also typical of Thackeray. He interrupts chronology for an amiable digression which meanders back to the starting point, and also digresses into the future consequences of an action, or presents retrospective memories of an event from years later. For example, the discursive soliloquy on dancing is suddenly interrupted by "The reader, perhaps, remembers the brief appearance of his Highness, the Duke." This is followed by an elaborate description of the Duke's pump, the whole point of which is that Speck, who designed it, is Dorothea's father. He ingratiates himself into the family by sketching the pump, and is consequently introduced to the beauty, whose charms inspire him to classical allusions. Then the narrative redoubles again:

> In thus introducing this lovely creature in her ball-costume, I have been somewhat premature, and had best go back to the beginning of the history of my acquaintance with her.

Next follows a history of the Speck family leading up to the narrator's first glimpse of her, and the narrative resumes.

The next semiscene, midway between summary and dramatization, is characteristic of Thackeray's refusal to disguise his fictions, to mount them dramatically. His narrators set the stage, but do not retire from it; they remain to pose alternatives, suggest possibilities, speculate, and muse expatiatingly. Thackeray constructs a model which the reader must then fill in; by concealing as much as he discloses, he forces the reader's participation in completing his paradigm, using a pronoun shift to the second person which asks "you" to participate. Thackeray appeals to universality (an eighteenth century device probably derived from his study of Henry Fielding, whom he had both imitated and parodied), and the interjected "I have often said" is a strategy found throughout his work. *Vanity Fair* contains countless "Captain Rawdon often said" interspersings, a technique that allows the author to interpolate commentary and to leave the rest to the reader's imagination. The story concludes with the ball at which Fitz-Boodle has managed to sign up Dorothea for a waltz, and his subsequent fall on the dance floor.

"Mr. and Mrs. Frank Berry" is part of the story sequence called *Men's Wives* which first appeared in *Fraser's* in March, 1843. In two parts, it shows Frank as a boy bravely battling the school bully and being hero-worshiped by the narrator; then, in a later encounter, he is seen as a uxorious husband who has shaved off his mustache and grown fat and pale. Part One is called "The Fight at Slaughter House." After the preliminaries, as the air resounds with cries of "To it, Berry!" there is a typical Thackerayan footnote, "As it is very probable that many fair readers may not approve of the extremely forcible language in which the combat is depicted, I beg them to skip it and pass on to the next chapter."

This chapter is entitled "The Combat at Versailles," and this time the heroic Frank is not the victor. Mrs. Berry has "a rigid and classical look" and wears a miniature of her father, Sir George Catacomb, around her thin neck. Her genteel coldness is aptly caught in her maiden name, Miss Angelica Catacomb. She spends her time making notes in the Baronetage on her pedigree, and she entertains her guest with an icy silence. After several pages about the other guests, Thackeray provides the apostrophe that if there had been anything interesting, "I should have come out with it a couple of pages since, nor have kept the public looking for so long a time at the dishcovers and ornaments of the table. But the simple fact must now be told, that there was nothing of the slightest importance at this repast."

The narrator then tells how Angelica controlled her husband's smoking, drinking, and conversation. The narrator decides to rescue Frank from his captivity and orders claret, which, after sufficient quantity has been consumed, leads to riotous singing. He feels free enough to complain, when he is inebriated, about having to spend his evenings reading poetry or missionary tracts out loud, about having to take physics whenever she insists, about never being allowed to dine out, and about not daring even to smoke a cigar. In a moment of daring, the narrator accepts an invitation for the next night, but he is not permitted to keep the appointment, and the next time he meets Frank, the latter sheepishly crosses over to the other side of the street; he is wearing galoshes. The boy who was courageous enough to beat the school bully has turned into a henpecked husband.

Major publications other than short fiction

NOVELS: *The Fatal Boots*, 1839; *Catherine*, 1839-1840; *Barry Lyndon*, 1844; *Vanity Fair*, 1847-1848; *Rebecca and Rowena*, 1850; *Pendennis*, 1848-1850; *Henry Esmond*, 1852; *The Newcomes*, 1853-1855; *The Virginians*, 1857-1859; *Lovel the Widower*, 1860; *The Adventures of Philip*, 1861-1862; *Denis Duval*, 1864.

PLAY: *The Wolves and the Lamb*, 1854.

POEM: *The Chronicle of the Drum*, 1841.

NONFICTION: *Flore et Zephyr*, 1836; *Our Street*, 1840; *Mrs. Perkins' Ball*, 1847; *Doctor Birch and His Young Friends*, 1849; *The Kickleburys on the Rhine*, 1850; *The Rose and the Ring*, 1854; *The Tremendous Adventures of Major Gahagan*, 1855; *A Legend of the Rhine*, 1879.

Bibliography

Dodds, John Wendell. *Thackeray: A Critical Portrait*.
Elwin, Malcolm. *Thackeray: A Personality*.
Loofbourow, J. *Thackeray and the Form of Fiction*.
Ray, Gordon N. *Thackeray: The Age of Wisdom, 1847-1863*.
_____ . *Thackeray: The Uses of Adversity, 1811-1846*.
Ritchie, Anne Thackeray. *Thackeray and His Daughter: The Letters and Journals of Anne Thackeray Ritchie*.
Tillotson, Geoffrey. *Thackeray the Novelist*.

Trollope, Anthony. *Thackeray.*
Welsh, Alexander, ed. *Thackeray: A Collection of Critical Essays.*
Wheatley, James H. *Patterns in Thackeray's Fiction.*
Williams, Ioan M. *Thackeray.*

Ruth Rosenberg

DYLAN THOMAS

Born: Swansea, Wales; October 27, 1914
Died: New York, New York; November 9, 1953

Principal short fiction

Portrait of the Artist as a Young Dog, 1940; *Selected Writings of Dylan Thomas*, 1946; *A Child's Christmas in Wales*, 1954; *Quite Early One Morning*, 1954; *Adventures in the Skin Trade and Other Stories*, 1955; *A Prospect of the Sea and Other Stories*, 1955; *Early Prose Writings*, 1971.

Other literary forms

The incantatory readings Dylan Thomas gave on American campuses in the 1950's inspired a new interest in lyric poetry. His verse drama, *Under Milk Wood* (1954), was made into a major motion picture starring Elizabeth Taylor and Richard Burton, and Emlyn Williams toured America with a one-man show composed of excerpts from Thomas' short stories. A satiric mystery novel, written collaboratively, was withheld from publication until recently, because of its libelous nature. Between 1940 and 1949, Thomas wrote many film scripts and gave more than fifty broadcasts for the BBC, many of which have been published. Recordings of his readings proved so popular that a company was formed to manufacture "talking records" of his readings as well as those of other poets.

Story characteristics

Thomas' stories written after 1938 are genial, lyrical, comic evocations of his childhood and are peopled with his relatives, friends, and Swansea neighbors. They are exuberant satires of provincial life, full of wit and charm. The earlier stories are allegorical representations of initiations into sex or death not distanced by an observing narrator. Interpretive strategies must be employed similar to those used in reading lyric poetry, since these are truly prose-poems with their own controlled inner coherence. The seeming spatial and temporal distortions are externalizations or objectifications of the protagonist's inner state. The apparent metamorphoses, or transformations, are simply literalized metaphors.

Biography

Dylan Marlais Thomas' father, John David, married Florence Hannah Williams in 1903. Having graduated from the University of Wales in Aberystwyth in 1899, with a first in English, he resented being a provincial schoolmaster. It was in his father's extensive library that Thomas educated himself to be a poet. The chapel-going farmers who are the aunts and uncles of the stories were his mother's family. His home, 5 Cwmdonkin Drive; his maid,

Patricia; the park he played in; Daniel Jones, with whom he wrote collaborative verse under the name of Walter Bram; the Dame's School he attended at age seven, and the Swansea Grammar School which he left on July 19, 1931, a total academic failure in everything but English—all figure in his stories. Between 1930 annd 1934, he composed 250 poems in the four notebooks, which are now in the Lockwood Library at Buffalo, New York; these constitute three-quarters of his entire work. He continually quarried these poems for his later publications. Both an amateur actor and a reporter, Thomas used his experiences on the *South Wales Daily Post* in the story, "Old Garbo." The literary meetings, hosted every Friday by Bert Trick, the socialist grocer, are described in "Where Tawe Flows." Thomas published his first book on December 18, 1934, and his important relationship with Pamela Hansford Johnson resulted from his winning a poetry contest. He moved to London and published his second book on September 10, 1936. On July 11, 1937, he married Caitlin Macnamara; the couple had three children: Llewelyn, Aeron, and Colm. In the 1940's, Thomas wrote scenarios for Strand Films and gave radio talks. He lived in a seafront home in Laugharne except for his American tours; his trip to a writer's congress in Prague on March 4, 1949; his fellowship in Italy in 1947; and his trip to Persia in January, 1951, to make a film on Iranian oil. His sudden death at the age of thirty-nine interrupted Igor Stravinsky's plan to compose an opera with him.

Analysis

Dylan Thomas' ten stories in *Portrait of the Artist as a Young Dog* are charming reminiscences of his relatives, school friends, and neighbors in the town where he grew up. Their wit and accessibility made them immediately popular, in contrast to the dark, subjective stories he had written prior to 1938, for which he had difficulty finding a publisher. In March, 1938, he wrote to Vernon Watkins that "A Visit to Grandpa's" was "the first of a series of short, straightforward stories about Swansea." Published on March 10, 1939, in the *New English Weekly*, it told of a boy's waking up on a mild summer night to the sounds of "gee-up and whoa" in the next room where his grandfather, wearing his red waistcoat with its brass buttons, is reining invisible horses. On their morning walks, the grandfather has expressed his wish not to be buried in the nearby churchyard. When he is missing a few days later, the entire village is summoned to go in search of him, and they find him on Carmarthen Bridge in his Sunday trousers and dusty tall hat on his way to Llangadock to be buried. They try to persuade him to come home to tea instead.

In "The Peaches," first published in the October, 1938, issue of *Life and Letters Today*, the naïve narrator tells of his spring holiday on a farm in Gorsehill. His uncle Jim drives him there in a green cart late one April evening, stopping for a drink at a public house. The squeal coming from the wicker basket he takes inside with him prepares the reader for the fact that cousin Gwilym will note that one of the pigs is missing the next day. The terror of being abandoned in a dark alley is assuaged by Aunt Annie's warm welcome of him later that night at the farmhouse. He enters, small, cold, and scared, as the clock strikes midnight, and is made to feel "among the shining and striking like a prince taking off his disguise." Next morning, Gwilym takes him to see the sow, who has only four pigs left. "He sold it to go on the drink," whispers Gwilym rebukingly. The boy imagines Jim transformed into a hungry fox: "I could see uncle, tall and sly and red, holding the writhing pig in his two hairy hands, sinking his teeth in its thigh, crunching its trotters up; I could see him leaning over the wall of the sty with the pig's legs sticking out of his mouth." Gwilym, who is studying to be a minister, takes him to the barn which he pretends is his chapel and preaches a thunderous sermon at him, after which he takes up a collection.

Next, the complication begins. Gwilym and Jim are told to dress up for Jack Williams, whose rich mother will bring him in an automobile from Swansea for a fortnight's visit. A tin of peaches has been saved from Christmas; "Mother's been keeping it for a day like this." Mrs. Williams, "with a jutting bosom and thick legs, her ankles swollen over her pointed shoes," sways into the parlor like a ship. Annie precedes her, anxiously tidying her hair, "clucking, fidgeting, excusing." (The string of participles is typical of Thomas' prose style; one sentence [in "Return Journey"] contains fifteen.) The rich guest declines refreshments. "I don't mind pears or chunks, but I can't bear peaches." The boys run out to frolic, climb trees, and play Indians in the bushes. After supper, in the barn, Gwilym demands confessions from them, and Jack begins to cry that he wants to go home. That night in bed, they hear Uncle Jim come in drunk, and Annie quietly relating the events of the day, at which he explodes into thunderous anger: "Aren't peaches good enough for her!" At this, Jack sobs into his pillow. The next day Mrs. Williams arrives, sends the chauffeur for Jack's luggage, and drives off with him, as the departing car scatters the hens and the narrator waves good-bye.

Two aspects of the point of view are significant. The first, its tone, is what made all the stories so immediately beloved. The genial Chaucerian stance, which perceives and accepts eccentricities, which notes and blesses all the peculiarities of humanity, is endearing without being sentimental, because the acuteness of the observations stays in significant tension with the nonjudgmental way in which they are recorded. This combination of acuity and benevolence, of sharpness and radiance, is the special quality of Thomas' humor. The second aspect of the author's style is its expansion and contraction, which indicates the view of a visionary poet. The narrator is both a homesick, cold, tired little boy, and "a royal nephew in smart town clothes, embraced and welcomed." The uncle is both a predatory fox and an impoverished farmer, as he sits in "the broken throne of a bankrupt bard." The splendid paradise where the narrator romps is simultaneously a poor, dirty "square of mud and rubbish and bad wood and falling stone, where a bucketful of old and bedraggled hens scratched and laid small eggs." The "pulpit" where Gwilym's inspired sermon is "cried to the heavens" in his deepest voice is a dusty, broken cart in an abandoned barn overrun with mice; but this decrepit building on a mucky hill becomes "a chapel shafted with sunlight," awesome with reverence as the "preacher's" voice becomes "Welsh and singing." The alternate aggrandizement and diminution of the perceptions energize the style as the lyric impulse wars with the satiric impulse in the narrator's voice.

The naïve narrator of the third of the *Portrait of the Artist as a Young Dog* stories entitled "Patricia, Edith and Arnold" is totally engrossed in his imaginary engine, whose brake is "a hammer in his pocket" and whose fuel is replenished by invisible engineers. As he drives it about the garden, however, he is aware of his maid, Patricia, plotting with the neighbor's servant, Edith, to confront Arnold with the identical letters he wrote to both of them. The girls take the child to the park as it begins to snow; Arnold has been meeting Edith there on Fridays, and Patricia on Wednesdays. As the girls wait for Arnold in the shelter, the boy, disowning them, pretends he is a baker, molding loaves of bread out of snow.

Arnold Matthews, his hands blue with cold, wearing a checked cap but no overcoat, appears and tries to bluff it out. Loudly he says, "Fancy you two knowing each other." The boy rolls a snowman "with a lop-sided dirty head" smoking a pencil, as the situation grows more tense. When Arnold claims that he loves them both, Edith shakes her purse at him, the letters fall out all over the snow, and the snowman collapses. As the boy searches for his pencil, the girls insist that Arnold choose between them. Patricia turns her back, indignantly. Arnold gestures and whispers to Edith behind Patricia's back, and then, out loud, chooses Patricia. The boy, bending over his snowman, finds his pencil driven through its head.

Later, during a discussion of lying, the boy tells Patricia that he saw Arnold lying to both of them, and the momentary truce, during which Patricia and Arnold have been walking arm in arm, is over. She smacks and pummels him as he staggers backward and falls. The boy says he has to retrieve the cap that he left near his snowman. He finds Arnold there, rereading the letters that Edith dropped, but does not tell Patricia this. Later, as his frozen hands tingle and his face feels on fire, she comforts him until "the hurting is gone." She acknowledges his pain and her own by saying, "Now we've all had a good cry today." The story achieves its effects through the child's detachment. Totally absorbed in his play, he registers the behavior of the adults, participating in their sorrows without fully comprehending them. In spite of his age-appropriate egocentricity and his critical remarks about her girth (her footprints as large as a horse's), he expresses deep affection for her and such concern as he is capable of, given the puzzling circumstances.

The narrator of "The Fight" is an exuberant adolescent. Although he is fourteen, he deliberately adds a year to his age, lying for the thrill of having to be on guard to avoid detection. The self-conscious teenager is continuallly inventing scenarios in which he assumes various heroic postures. The story tells of his finding an alter ego, as gifted as he, through whom he can confirm his existence, with whom he can share his anxieties, collaborate imaginatively, and play duets. The opening incident illustrates Dylan's testing himself against the adults about him. He is engaged in a staring contest with a cranky old man who lives beside the schoolyard when a strange boy pushes him down. They fight. Dylan gives Dan a bloody nose, and gets a black eye in return. Admiring each other's injuries as evidence of their own manliness, they become fast friends.

Dylan postures, first as a prizefighter, then as a pirate. When a boy ridicules him at school the next day, he has a revenge fantasy of breaking his leg, then of being a famous surgeon who sets it with "a rapid manipulation, the click of a bone," while the grateful mother, on her knees, tearfully thanks him. Assigned a vase to draw in art class, the boys sketch inaccurate versions of naked girls instead. "I drew a wild guess below the waist." This boyish sexual curiosity leads him mentally to undress even Mrs. Bevan, the minister's wife, whom he meets later at supper at Dan's house, but he gets frightened when he gets as far as the petticoats.

Dan shows Dylan the seven historical novels he wrote before he was twelve, plays the piano for him, and lets him make a cat's noise on his violin; Dylan reads Dan his poems out of his exercise book. They share feelings, such as their ambivalences toward their mothers, a love tinged with embarrassment. They decide to edit a paper. Back upstairs, after supper, they imitate the self-important Mr. Bevan and discuss the time Mrs. Bevan tried to fling herself out the window. When she joins them later, they try to induce her to repeat this by pointedly opening the window and inviting her to admire the view. When he has to leave at 9:30, Dan announces that he "must finish a string trio tonight," and Dylan counters that he is "working on a long poem about the princes of Wales." On these bravura promises, the story closes.

Thomas called these luminous remembrances of his youth "portions of a provincial autobiography." The stories he wrote earlier, drafts of which exist in "The Red Notebook" which he kept from December, 1933, to October, 1934, were not published until later. Considered obscure, violent, and surrealistic, their difficulties are due to the use of narrative devices borrowed from lyric poetry. In "A Prospect of the Sea," for example, the scenery seems to contract and expand. A boy lying in a cornfield on a summer day sees a country girl with berry-stained mouth, scratched legs, and dirty fingernails jump down from a tree, startling the birds. The landscape shrinks, the trees dwindle, the river is compressed into a drop, and the yellow field diminishes into a square "he could cover with his hand." As he masters his fear and sees she is only "a girl in a torn cotton frock" sitting cross-legged on the grass, things assume their proper size. As she makes erotic advances, his terror rises again, and everything becomes magnified. Each leaf becomes as large as a man, every trough in the bark of the tree seems as vast as a channel, every blade of grass looks as high as a house. This apparent contraction and expansion of the external world, is dependent upon the protagonist's internal state.

Thomas uses another device commonly employed in lyric poetry, the literalized metaphor. Because a thing seems like another, it is depicted as having been transformed into that other thing. For example, the "sunburned country girl" frightens the lonely boy as if she were a witch; thus, in his eyes, she becomes one. "The stain on her lips was blood, not berries; and her nails were not broken but sharpened sideways, ten black scissorblades ready to snip off his tongue." Finally, not only space and character are subject to transformations, but also time. As the narrator fantasizes union with this girl, he attains a mystical vision of history unrolling back to Eden. The story ends as it began; she disappears into the sea. He had imagined, at the beginning, as he dabbled his fingers in the water, that a drowned storybook princess would emerge from the waves. The apparent obscurities are resolved by seeing the plot of this story as simply the daydreams of a lonely boy on a summer's day.

"The Orchards" is another prose-poem about a man's attempt to record a vision in words. Marlais has a repetitive dream about blazing apple trees guarded by two female figures who change from scarecrows to women. He tries and fails to shape this into a story, and finally sets out on a quest. Striding through eleven valleys, he reaches the scene he has dreamed of, where he reenacts the kissing of the maiden as the orchard catches fire, the fruit falls as cinders, and she and her sister change to scarecrows. These smoldering trees may be related to the sacrificial fires of the Welsh druids on Midsummer Day. The woman figure might be connected with Olwedd, the Welsh Venus, associated with the wild apple. Marlais' adventure, however, is a mental journey undertaken by the creative writer through the landscape of his mind, and the temporal and spatial fluctuations are the projections of that mind, mythicized.

"The Tree" illustrates this same process. A gardener tells a boy the story of Jesus, reading the Bible in his shed by candlelight. While he is mending a rake with wire, he relates the twelve stages of the cross. The boy wants to know the secrets inside the locked tower to which the bearded gardener has the key. On Christmas Eve, the gardener unlocks the room through whose windows the boy can see the Jarvis Hills to the east. The gardener says of this "Christmas present" in a tone which seems prophetic: "It is enough that I have given you the key."

On Christmas morning, an idiot with ragged shoes wanders into the garden, "bearing the torture of the weather with a divine patience." Enduring the rain and the wind, he sits down under the elder tree. The boy, concluding that the gardener had not lied, and that the secret of the tower was true, runs to get the wire to reenact the crucifixion. The old man's obsessive religiosity has been transmitted to the boy, who takes it literally: "a tree" has become "The Tree," "a key" has become "The Key," and a passive beggar stumbling from the east has become Christ inviting his martyrdom.

"The Visitor" is the story of a dying poet, Peter, tended lovingly by Rhiannon, who brings him warm milk, reads to him from William Blake, and at the end pulls the sheet over his face. Death is personified as Callaghan, whose visit he anticipates as his limbs grow numb and his heart slows. Callaghan blows out the candles with his grey mouth, and lifting Peter in his arms, flies with him to the Jarvis Valley where they watch worms and death-beetles undoing "brightly and minutely" the animal tissues on the shining bones through whose sockets flowers sprout, the blood seeping through the earth to fountain forth in springs of water. "Peter, in his ghost, cried with joy." This is the same assurance found in Thomas' great elegies: death is but the reentry of the body into the processes of nature. Matter is not extinguished, but transformed into other shapes whose joyous energies flourish forever.

Major publications other than short fiction

NOVEL: *The Death of the King's Canary*, 1976 (with John Davenport).
PLAY: *Under Milk Wood*, 1954.
POETRY: *18 Poems*, 1934; *Twenty-five Poems*, 1936; *The Map of Love*, 1939; *Deaths and Entrances*, 1946; *In Country Sleep*, 1952; *Collected Poems, 1934-1952*, 1952.

Bibliography

Ackerman, John. *Dylan Thomas: His Life and Work.*
Brinnin, John Malcolm. *Dylan Thomas in America.*
Cox, C. B., ed. *Dylan Thomas: A Collection of Critical Essays.*
FitzGibbon, Constantine. *The Life of Dylan Thomas.*
Korg, Jacob. *Dylan Thomas.*
Maud, Ralph. *Dylan Thomas in Print: A Bibliographical History.*
Maud, Ralph, ed. *The Notebooks of Dylan Thomas.*
Moynihan, William T. *The Craft and Art of Dylan Thomas.*
Pratt, Annis. *Dylan Thomas' Early Prose: A Study in Creative Mythology.*
Rolph, John Alexander. *Dylan Thomas: A Bibliography.*

Ruth Rosenberg

JAMES THURBER

Born: Columbus, Ohio; December 8, 1894
Died: New York, New York; November 2, 1961

Principal short fiction

Is Sex Necessary?, 1929 (with E. B. White); *The Owl in the Attic and Other Perplexities*, 1931; *My Life and Hard Times*, 1933; *The Middle-Aged Man on the Flying Trapeze*, 1935; *Let Your Mind Alone! And Other More or Less Inspirational Pieces*, 1937; *Fables for Our Time and Famous Poems Illustrated*, 1940; *My World—And Welcome to It!*, 1942; *The Great Quillow*, 1944; *The White Deer*, 1945; *The Thurber Carnival*, 1945; *The Beast in Me and Other Animals: A New Collection of Pieces and Drawings about Human Beings and Less Alarming Creatures*, 1948; *The 13 Clocks*, 1950; *Thurber Country: A New Collection of Pieces About Males and Females, Mainly of Our Own Species*, 1953; *Further Fables for Our Time*, 1956; *The Wonderful O*, 1957; *Alarms and Diversions*, 1957; *Lanterns and Lances*, 1961; *Credos and Curios*, 1962.

Other literary forms

James Thurber's more than twenty published volumes include plays, stories, sketches, essays, verse, fables, fairy tales for adults, reminiscences, biography, drawings, and cartoons.

Influence

Thurber's writings are widely known and admired in English-speaking countries and his drawings have a world following. He has been compared with James Joyce in his command of and playfulness with English and he invites comparison with most of his contemporaries, many of whom he parodies at least once in his works. He greatly admired Henry James, referring to him often in his works and parodying him masterfully several times, for example, in "Something to Say." While Thurber is best known as a humorist (often with the connotation that he need not be taken seriously as an artist), his literary reputation has grown steadily. His short story "The Secret Life of Walter Mitty" became an instant classic after it appeared in 1939 and was subsequently reprinted in *Reader's Digest*. Since 1961 several major studies and a volume in the Twentieth Century Views series have appeared, all arguing that Thurber should rank with the best American artists in several fields including the short story. In 1980, "The Greatest Man in the World" was chosen for dramatization in the American Short Story series of the Public Broadcasting Service.

Story characteristics

Thurber is best known as the author of humorous sketches, stories, and reminiscences dealing with urban bourgeois American life. To discuss Thurber as an artist in the short-story form is difficult, however, because of the variety of things he did which might legitimately be labeled short stories. His essays frequently employ stories and are "fictional" in recognizable ways. His "memoirs" in *My Life and Hard Times* (1933) are clearly fictionalized. Many of his first-person autobiographical sketches are known to be "fact" rather than fiction only through careful biographical research. As a result, most of his writings can be treated as short fiction. Thurber seemed to prefer to work on the borderlines between conventional forms.

Biography

James Grover Thurber was born and grew up in Columbus, Ohio. There he absorbed the Midwestern regional values which remained important to him all his life: a liberal idealism, a conservative respect for the family, a belief in the agrarian virtues of industry and independence, and a healthy skepticism about the human potential for perfecting anything. He lost his left eye in a childhood accident which led to almost complete blindness forty years later. He began his writing career as a journalist, earning his living primarily as a reporter in Ohio and France before he joined *The New Yorker* in 1927. There his friendship with E. B. White provided opportunities for him to perfect and publish the stories he had been working on since college at Ohio State University. Within five years of beginning at *The New Yorker*, he was one of the best-known humorists in America. A prolific writer, he published more than twenty volumes in his lifetime and left many works uncollected at his death. He received numerous awards for his work including honorary degrees from Williams College (1957) and Yale (1953) and the Antoinette Perry Award for the revue, *A Thurber Carnival* (1962). His drawings were included in art shows worldwide. He was the first American after Mark Twain to be invited to *Punch's* Wednesday Luncheon (1958). Stricken with nearly total blindness in the early 1940's, he nevertheless continued writing until his death.

Analysis

There is disagreement among critics as to the drift of the attitudes and themes reflected in James Thurber's work. The poles are well represented by Richard C. Tobias on the one hand and the team of Walter Blair and Hamlin Hill on the other. Tobias argues that Thurber comically celebrates the life of the mind: "Thurber's victory is a freedom within law that delights and surprises." Blair and Hill see Thurber as a sort of black humorist laughing at his own destruction, "a humorist bedeviled by neuroses, cowed before the insignificant things in his world, and indifferent to the cosmic ones. He loses and loses and loses his combats with machines, women, and animals until defeat becomes permanent." While Tobias sees women as vital forces in Thurber's work, Hill and Blair see Thurber as essentially a misogynist bewailing the end of the ideal of male freedom best portrayed in the Western film and pathetically reflected in the fantasies of Walter Mitty. In fact, it seems that critics' opinions regarding Thurber's attitudes about most subjects vary from one text to the next, but certain themes seem to remain consistent. His weak male characters do hate strong women, but the males are often weak because they accept the world in which their secret fantasies are necessary and, therefore, leave their women no choice but to try to hold things together. When a woman's strength becomes arrogance as in "The Catbird Seat" and "The Unicorn in the Garden," the man often defeats her with the active power of his imagination. Characterizing Thurber as a Romantic, Robert Morseberger lists some themes he sees pervading Thurber's writing: a perception of the oppression of technocracy and of the arrogance of popular scientism especially in their hostility to imagination; an antirational but not anti-intellectual approach to modern life; a belief in the power of the imagination to preserve human value in the face of contemporary forms of alienation; and a frequent use of fear and fantasy to overcome the dullness of his characters' (and readers') lives.

Because "The Secret Life of Walter Mitty" is so well known, it will receive a little less attention here than it deserves in order to give more attention to the variety of forms Thurber practiced. Mitty lives in a reverie consisting of situations in which he is a hero: commander of a navy hydroplane, surgeon, trial witness, bomber pilot, and condemned martyr. The dream is clearly an escape from the external life which humiliatingly interrupts it: his wife's mothering, the arrogant competence of a parking attendant and policeman, the humiliating errands of removing tire chains, buying overshoes, and asking for puppy biscuits. In his dreams, he is Lord Jim, the misunderstood hero, "inscrutable to the last"; in his daily life he is a middle-aged husband enmeshed in a web of the humdrum. R. C. Tobias sees Mitty as ultimately triumphant over dreary reality. Blair and Hill see him as gradually losing grip of the real world and slipping into psychosis. Whether liberated or defeated by his imagination, Mitty is clearly incompetent and needs the mothering his wife gives him. Often described as a bitch, she is actually just the wife he needs and deserves; she seems to exist as a replacement ego to keep him from catching his death of cold as he somnambulates. The story's artfulness is readily apparent in the precise choice and arrangement of details such as sounds, objects, and images which connect fantasy and reality. The technical devices are virtually the same as those used by Faulkner and Joyce to indicate shifts in levels of awareness in their "free-association internal monologues." Mitty has become a representative figure in modern culture like Prufrock and Faulkner's Quentin Compson, although perhaps more widely known. While many of Thurber's stories are similar to this one in theme and form, they are astonishingly diverse in subject, situation, and range of technique.

Another large group of Thurber stories might be characterized as fiction-alized autobiography. One of the best of these sketches is "The Black Magic of Barney Haller" in *The Middle-Aged Man on the Flying Trapeze*. In this story, "Thurber" exorcises his hired man, a Teuton whom lightning and thunder always follow and who mutters imprecations such as "Bime by I go hunt grotches in de voods," and "We go to the garrick now and become warbs." The narrator becomes convinced that despite his stable and solid appearance, Barney is a necromancer who will transform reality with his transformed language. At any moment, Barney will reveal his true devilish form and transform "Thurber" into a warb or conjure up a grotch. It does not comfort him to learn the probable prosaic meanings of the incantations, even to see the crotches placed under the heavy peach tree branches, and at the end of the story, he feels no regret that the only man he knows who could remove the wasps from his garret has departed. The humor of these incidents is clear and a humorous meaning emerges from them. The narrator would rather hide in *Swann's Way*, reading of a man who makes himself in his book, but he feels threatened by the external supernatural power of another's language to form him. He first attempts exorcism with Robert Frost, well-known for having successfully disposed of a hired man. He quotes "The Pasture" in an attempt to make the obscure clear, but only succeeds in throwing a fear that mirrors his own into Barney. This gives "Thurber" his clue; in the next attempt he borrows from Lewis Carroll and the American braggart tradition, asserting his own superior power as a magician of words, "Did you happen to know that the mome rath never lived that could outgrabe me?" The man with the superior control of language, the man of superior imagination, really is in control; he *can* become a playing card at will to frighten off black magicians. This story is typical of Thurber in its revelation of the fantastic in the com-monplace, its flights of language play, and its concern for the relations among reality, self, imagination, and language. *My Life and Hard Times* is the best-known collection of fictional/autobiographical sketches.

Also an author of fables, Thurber published two collections of fables for our time. "The Moth and the Star" is a typical and often anthologized ex-ample. A young moth spends a long life trying to reach a star, defying his disappointed parents' wish that he aspire normally to get himself scorched on a street lamp. Having outlived his family, he gains in old age "a deep and lasting pleasure" from the illusion that he has actually reached the distant star: "Moral: Who flies afar from the sphere of our sorrow is here today and here tomorrow." The moth and the star suggest prominent images in *The Great Gatsby* (1925), one of Thurber's favorite books, but in partial contrast to that book, this story echoes the import of the great artist of the "Con-clusion" of Henry David Thoreau's *Walden* (1854). The aspiring idealist who rejects the suicidal life of material accumulation and devotes himself to some perfect work ultimately conquers time and enriches life whether or not he produces any valuable object. Because the moth, like the artist of Kouroo, succeeds and is happy, this story seems more optimistic than *The Great Gatsby*. Many of the fables are more cynical or more whimsical, but all are rich in meaning and pleasure like "The Moth and the Star."

Critics and scholars have noted ways in which Thurber's career and writings parallel Mark Twain's. For example, both, as they grew older, grew more interested in fables and fairy tales. In the latter, Thurber was perhaps the more successful, publishing four fantasy stories for adults in the last twenty years of his life. Completed after his blindness, these stories are characterized by heightened poetic language, highly original variations on the fairy formulae, sparkling humor, and a common theme: in the words of Prince Jorn, hero of *The White Deer*, "Love's miracle enough." Love is the key which frees imagination by giving it strength to do and strength of imagination makes the wasteland fertile. The fairy tales may be intentional responses to the wasteland vision of T. S. Eliot, a vision which Thurber's other writings, notably "The Secret Life of Walter Mitty" and *Further Fables for Our Time*, seem to affirm. The fairy tales suggest that the ash heap of modern culture is escapable, but it seems especially significant that the mode of escape is represented in tales of magic in remote settings.

The White Deer opens in the third period of waiting for the depleted game of King Clode's hunting grounds to replenish themselves. The story develops in triads, the central one being the three perilous tasks set for the three sons of King Clode to determine which shall claim the hand of the fair princess who materializes when the king and his sons corner the fleet white deer in the enchanted forest. The sons complete their tasks simultaneously, but in the meantime, King Clode determines that the nameless Princess is not a disenchanted woman but an enchanted deer. When the returned sons are told of this, Thag and Gallow refuse her. If denied love three times, she would be a deer forever, but Jorn accepts her: "What you have been, you are not, and what you are, you will forever be. I place this trophy in the hands of love. . . . You hold my heart." This acceptance transforms her into a new and lovelier princess, Rosanore of the Northland, and the April fragrance of lilacs fills the air: "April is the cruellest month, breeding/Lilacs out of the dead land," says the "dead" voice of "The Waste Land." As King Clode later sees the full wisdom and beauty of Rosanore, he repeats, "I blow my horn in waste land." The echoes of Eliot show up repeatedly in the fairy tales, but the greater emphasis falls on the power of love and imagination which in this fairy world inevitably blossom in beauty and happiness. The cast of secondary characters and the perilous labors provide opportunities to characterize wittily the world in need of magic. There are an incompetent palace wizard as opposed to the true wizards of the forest, an astronomer-turned-clockmaker who envisions encroaching darkness ("It's darker than you think"), and a royal recorder who descends into mad legalese when the Princess's spell proves to be without precedent. Gallow's labor is especially interesting because he must make his way through a vanity fair bureaucracy in order to conquer a sham dragon, a task that tests his purse and persistence more than his love. This task allows a satire of the commercial values of modern culture. Each of the fairy tales contains similar delights as well as bizarre and beautiful flights of language: the Sphinz asks Jorn, "What is whirly?/What is curly?/ Tell me, what is pearly early?" and in a trice, Jorn replies, "Gigs are whirly,/ Cues are curly/and the dew is pearly early."

Major publications other than short fiction

PLAYS: *The Male Animal*, 1940 (with Elliott Nugent); *Many Moons*, 1943; *A Thurber Carnival*, 1962 (revue).

NONFICTION: *The Thurber Album*, 1952; *The Years with Ross*, 1959.

Bibliography

Bernstein, Burton. *Thurber: A Biography*.

Blair, Walter and Hamlin Hill. *America's Humor*.

Bowden, James. *James Thurber: A Bibliography*.

Holmes, Charles S. *The Clocks of Columbus: The Literary Career of James Thurber*.

Holmes, Charles S., ed. *Thurber: A Collection of Critical Essays*.

Morseberger, Robert E. *James Thurber*.

Tobias, Richard Clark. *The Art of James Thurber*.

Terry Heller

COUNT LEO TOLSTOY

Born: Yásnaya Polyána, Tula Province, Russia; August 28, 1828
Died: Astapova, Russia; November 7, 1910

Principal short fiction

Tales of Army Life, 1856; *Tales for Children*, 1872; *The Death of Ivan Ilyich*, 1886.

Other literary forms

Count Leo Tolstoy's long life was extremely productive and artistically varied. He started writing at an early age, publishing first in 1851; and he turned out long and short novels, plays, and an enormous number of essays, ranging in subject from his own spiritual experiences to art and aesthetics. Although he is best known for his long novels, *War and Peace* (1865-1869) and *Anna Karenina* (1873-1877), he considered many of his shorter pieces to be of great significance; their influence in his lifetime was equal to that of the larger works.

Influence

Educated by tutors and then at the University of Kazan, Tolstoy was familiar with the best literature of his era; but his earliest influence was from nature, with which he was on close terms at the family estate and which he never long neglected in his writing. The great variety of his work, touching on topics including history, religion, education, philosophy, art, and social problems, helped him to exert much influence on nearly all thinking people of his era— there is much evidence of the lively reactions that his writings produced in the readers of his time. Since then, his worldwide fame has not diminished; in fact, in recent years a more balanced evaluation of his major works has been achieved. The general opinion still holds them very high; and translations of his writing are innumerable, with, often, several varied ones of the same item.

Story characteristics

As with the other forms in which he wrote, Tolstoy reflects a wide scope of themes and topics in his short fiction. His tone is often ironic, but it is usually eased by a note of compassion and even a stern Christian faith. Many of his early stories have the quality of folktales: simplicity, directness, candor. In some of the later pieces, however, there is more subtlety and an increased complexity of moral vision.

Biography

Count Leo Nikolayevich Tolstoy enjoyed a privileged childhood on the family estate, Yásnaya Polyána, where he chiefly remained in his adult years. After a youthful period of dissipation in Moscow and St. Petersburg, he joined the army, serving in the Caucasus (the setting of several of his tales), and then returned to the estate and a life of literary effort and social work, chiefly on behalf of the serfs. The major "event" of his life was a profound conversion to a special kind of Christian fervor which led to his opposition to all institutionalized forms in society (such as government, the army, organized religion, and private property). The irregularity of his convictions caused him to leave home on a journey which ended with his death at a lonely railroad station. His philosophy was so individual that it came to be called Tolstoyanism, and its effects were felt in Russian society for years after his death.

Analysis

Although many of Count Leo Tolstoy's best-known longer works were written when he was young (*War and Peace* was begun when he was in his early thirties), the most popular short stories date from his later years. It is notable that many of the characteristics of his early fiction persist into the tales of his middle and old age. The blunt observations of peasant life, with no romanticizing of the hard life which the serfs endured, and the uncomplicated narrative line, with few characters and often a biblical directness, can be found in the stories from any period.

It would be difficult to isolate any particular philosophical principles from a survey of his short stories. One current view is that in these pieces he subjugated ideas to art and concentrated on writing a truthful but often unexplained impression of a human situation. One can detect, however, an occasional tone of didacticism, usually pointing in the direction of an uplifting Christian revelation. Thus, in a well-known story written in 1872, not long before the years of his "conversion" to the intransigent brand of Christianity that controlled his mature thought, Tolstoy reveals a clear intention to urge the acceptance of God's will. The very title, "God Sees the Truth, but Waits," suggests the theme of the tale, which is simply that a quiescent subjugation of the self to the intentions of God is true virtue. Also, there is a note of mystery, a hint that human beings can never know the reason for God's actions.

Typically, the narrative is quite simple. Ivan Aksionov, a successful and happily married young merchant, undertakes a journey and stops at an inn on the way. He occupies a room adjoining that of another merchant; the next morning, while traveling on, he is arrested for the robbery and murder of the man in the next room. The evidence is overwhelming: the inn was locked from the inside, so that no one could have sneaked in; and a blood-stained knife is discovered in Ivan's luggage. Although he protests his innocence, his trial is swift and the punishment severe. After being flogged, he is consigned to the mines in Siberia for life. At first, before he is sentenced, Aksionov has hope of relief from the Tsar, to whom his wife has sent a petition. The request, however, is not accepted. Worse, Ivan's wife begins to doubt his innocence: ". . . tell your wife the truth; was it not you who did it?"

Aksionov is crushed by this suspicion and vows to abandon seeking help from any source but God, and he says to himself, "It seems that only God can know the truth; it is to Him alone that we must appeal, and from Him alone expect mercy." He spends twenty-six years in prison, becoming increasingly somber and religious. When, finally, the man who did commit the crime arrives at the prison and admits his guilt to Ivan, the old prisoner is first stirred by anger and later by resignation, so that when Makar, the true criminal, threatens him and then begs his forgiveness, Aksionov is unmoved. He even refuses to inform on Makar regarding an attempt to escape. Ivan's attitude seems to be one of complete acceptance of the Divine will: "God will forgive you! Maybe I am a hundred times worse than you." As he utters these words, Aksionov's heart grows light; he is content to remain in prison, hoping only for an early death, which indeed comes to him.

The tale is related with biblical simplicity, and the message is clear. This narrative is similar to those that helped to establish Tolstoy as a great writer of fiction in his youth; but, in this case, the extremely forceful and even grim vision of the ignorance of man concerning God's intentions and judgments gives the story an almost metaphysical power. It is easy to believe that, as early as 1872, Tolstoy's mind was already tending toward the mystical faith that he was to embrace not many years later.

In 1886, after the great success of *Anna Karenina* and the striking effect of his explanation of his conversion, *A Confession* (1884), Tolstoy published two stories whose differences of technique illustrate the virtuosity of his genius and the depth of his penetration into human emotions. The uncomplicated little tale, "How Much Land Does a Man Need?," deals with a perennially popular Russian topic of the era: the obsession of the peasants (all now freed by the Tsar, in 1861) with the ownership of the land. Possibly because of the renunciation of the outer world by Tolstoy, the story is told much like a parable, with the Devil tempting the chief character, Pahóm, with the possibility of possessing more and more land. Although the peasant and his family are reasonably comfortable, Pahóm sells almost all his possessions and buys more land, and he prospers. Then he learns of a district far in the West where he can purchase large tracts of land for a small price. After investigating, he sells everything and removes his family to the region of the Bashkírs, a tribe that controls the land in question. They seem ignorant but are good-natured and appear grateful for the gifts which Pahóm has provided in order to encourage negotiation. The Bashkírs are amused at the peasant's passion for land; however, they strike a congenial but somewhat unusual agreement: Pahóm may purchase, for a thousand rubles (which seems a very low price to him), as much land as he can circumscribe, while walking, in one day.

The eager peasant agrees readily. The next day he starts out to encircle as large a plot as he can, and the tragedy is that, as the reader has by now suspected, he wants too much land. He dies of overexertion just as he reaches his starting point after having extended his range to a great distance. The ending of this story, which by the close has begun to take on some features of an Aesop fable, is related in a brief and ironic fashion. The Bashkírs express regret. Their Chief notes proudly how much land Pahóm covered. Then, the peasant's servant digs up just enough land for Pahóm to lie in: "Six feet from his head to his heels was all he needed." The final authorial comment, with its element of irony, is typical of Tolstoy's short fiction, whether written near the beginning of his career or, as with this tale, in his ripest years.

The other story published in the same year, 1886, was received with acclaim upon its appearance in Russia and has become something of a classic in Western literary circles. *The Death of Ivan Ilyich* is, however, very different from most of Tolstoy's short pieces. As is often the case, the tale was inspired by a fact of real life, an account that Tolstoy read of the death of a judge in his home province of Tula in 1881. The original intention was to create a simple diary of the jurist's weeks before his demise. Tolstoy, however, saw the opportunity to create a work of art by adopting the third-person point of view and telling the pathetic story in a matter-of-fact fashion. The unemotional tone of the narrative does indeed help to create a devastating effect for the account of the death of Ivan from cancer.

As usual, there is a theme; but, in this case, it is presented in a more than usually subtle manner. Ivan Ilyich is, by the customary standards, an honest man: he does not accept bribes; he is faithful to his wife; he labors diligently in his profession, attending closely to the letter of the law. As his illness progresses, however, and his self-analysis becomes more probing, he realizes that he has lived an essentially selfish life and has become a heartless legalist. At the close, shortly before his agonized death, Ivan Ilyich realizes that it is the life of the spirit that counts. He meets death with relief and calm resignation: "Death is finished. . . . It is no more!" With these words, Ivan expresses his recognition that what he has been suffering, both mentally and physically, has truly been death and that the condition into which he is entering is the great escape from death.

The plot of *The Death of Ivan Ilyich* is deceptively simple. The reader learns of his passing, and then an uncomplicated survey of the several months of Ilyich's life leading up to his death is presented. The striking impact is achieved not so much by the events themselves, such as the slight injury to his side that causes the cancer to take root, but by the carefully observed details, such as the cynical concerns of his colleagues regarding the probable effects of Ilyich's death upon their careers. Even his wife finds him, after a short time, a great trial. She and his daughter come to visit him regularly;

but they are embarrassed, and they leave as soon as possible. The several physicians whom Ivan consults are also a severe annoyance for him. They give him a number of different and occasionally conflicting diagnoses and courses of treatment, none of which is efficacious. (In fact, the only medication that is of any use is the morphine that deadens his increasing pain, but also depresses him.)

Only one person is of any real comfort: Gerásim, the peasant boy who sits with him now and then and who lifts his legs for long periods to ease his pain. The boy's simple good will and genuine sympathy are a high tribute by Tolstoy to the finer qualities of the Russian peasantry (at this point in his life, Tolstoy was beginning to look upon the former serfs with an attitude of almost fanatic admiration). The most significant passages in the tale are those in which Ilyich examines his life, first seeking a reason for this ghastly curse to have fallen upon him, and then attempting to understand what his existence has signified. His unsatisfactory conclusions concerning the latter topic lead him to the elevated realizations that brighten his last hours.

Tolstoy had for a number of years been interested in the subject of death and the common phenomenon of the paralyzing fear of it that seizes most people. In *The Death of Ivan Ilyich* he has, in a controlled, unsentimental, simple, and yet profound manner, dealt with the subject. None of Tolstoy's middle-length writings has achieved such critical and popular success as this unforgettable account of a man's struggle with a terminal illness and his final apprehension of one of the greatest of spiritual truths.

In an often-anthologized story, "After the Ball," written when Tolstoy was seventy-five, the undiminished powers of a superb short-story writer emerge impressively. This popular tale advances two thematic points, one overtly and the other indirectly; most remarkable, however, is the familiar but still important fact that the behavior of people is controlled by their roles and surroundings, and thus may surprise us greatly. A youthful love affair of Tolstoy when attending Kazan University is probably the source of the plot, but the force of the themes and the artfulness of the technique are those of a mature writer.

The first theme, that chance plays a greater role in human affairs than environment, is set forth immediately by the narrator, a middle-aged gentleman named Ivan Vasilevitch, who proceeds to support his contention by telling of some events that changed the entire course of his life, events that developed by accident. The young Ivan is a happy-go-lucky student at a provincial university, much in love with a beautiful girl, Varyenka. This charming young lady seems to have in abundance the qualities of grace and elegance.

Happily, Ivan has been asked by a local nobleman to a ball to which Varyenka and her family have also been invited. The young student is in transports of joy at being near his beloved. When he gets an opportunity to dance with her, his happiness is almost too much to bear. Indeed, Ivan begins to feel that "I was no longer myself, but some unearthly creature unconscious of evil and capable of nothing but good." In true romantic fashion, Ivan's love begins to extend to all people. When Varyenka is asked to persuade her father to dance, the young man notices with admiration and then affection the impressive appearance and bearing of the dignified and handsome old gentleman, an officer with many decorations: "He was clearly an officer of the old school."

The sense of realism that such a romantic tale, up to this point, might lack in the hands of a lesser author is provided by well-realized details. For example, although the Colonel is well built and vigorous, Ivan notices that his aged legs are not as nimble in the dance as they doubtless once were. His affection for the old officer is confirmed, however, when the Colonel stops dancing and urges the young man to waltz with his daughter. Ivan dances the night away, completely in love and fearing only that something might happen to destroy his happiness.

Something does, in the most unexpected (yet, in harmony with Tolstoy's respect for verisimilitude, believable) manner. The colonel declines to dance further because he has to rise early the next morning. Ivan, who cannot sleep because of his rapture, leaves his room and strolls down a nearby boulevard to the parade ground. There he witnesses a horrible scene. A company of soldiers is punishing a deserter by forcing him to run the gauntlet: the helpless recruit is dragged between rows of men who mercilessly beat him with switches. In an understated passage, Tolstoy causes Ivan to recognize that the officer commanding the troops is Varyenka's father. Not only is he conducting the punishment; he is encouraging greater savagery, even punishing a soldier who does not strike vigorously enough. Ivan tries to hear what the wretch is crying out; it is always the same words: "Brothers, have pity on me." No pity, however, is shown, especially by the Colonel in command.

The now shocked and distressed young lover makes his way home. In the overtly ironic passage in the story, Ivan says that he thought then that the Colonel must know something that he did not and that if he could only learn what it was, he would not be so unhappy and could understand what he had seen: "But try as I might I couldn't understand what it was the colonel knew." The second theme of the tale emerges when Ivan explains that after this experience he was never able to enter the military, or any other kind of government service. Tolstoy's opposition to virtually all forms of organized action, commencing well before 1903, when this piece was published, is well known. No essay or treatise, however, could make his point about the cruelty and inhumanity of organized governmental actions so well as this brief and moving narrataive. The contrast between the Colonel as a loving and considerate father and as an inhuman martinet with his troops is breathtakingly accomplished and, as usual, is enhanced by Tolstoy's restraint.

Some critics have claimed that, although Tolstoy attained repeated success in his short fiction, his true genius is best expressed in the less restricted form of the long novel. There is no questioning the sweep and power of such works as *Anna Karenina* and *War and Peace*; but Tolstoy's delicate insights and concentrated moral force, combined with a sensitive perception of human motive, have provided the world with a body of short stories unsurpassed by any other writer of any nation or era.

Major publications other than short fiction
NOVELS: *Two Hussars*, 1856; *Family Happiness*, 1859; *The Cossacks*, 1863; *War and Peace*, 1856-1869; *Anna Karenina*, 1873-1877; *The Kreutzer Sonata*, 1889; *Resurrection*, 1899; *Father Sergius*, 1911; *Hadzhi Murad*, 1911.
PLAYS: *The Power of Darkness*, 1886; *The Live Corpse*, 1900; *The Cause of It All*, 1910.
NONFICTION: *Childhood*, 1852; *Boyhood*, 1854; *Youth*, 1857; *What I Believe*, 1883; *A Confession*, 1884; *What Then Must We Do?*, 1893; *The Kingdom of God Is Within You*, 1893; *What Is Art?*, 1897-1898; *Recollections*, 1908.

Bibliography
Bayley, John. *Tolstoy and the Novel.*
Berlin, Isaiah. *The Hedgehog and the Fox.*
Crankshaw, Edward. *Tolstoy: The Making of a Novelist.*
Greenwood, E. B. *Tolstoy: The Comprehensive Vision.*
Lavrin, Janko. *Tolstoy: An Approach.*
Maude, Aylmer. *The Life of Tolstoy.*
Simmons, Ernest J. *Introduction to Tolstoy's Writings.*
Troyat, Henri. *Tolstoy.*

Fred B. McEwen

JEAN TOOMER

Born: Washington, D. C.; December 26, 1894
Died: Doylestown, Pennsylvania; March 30, 1967

Principal short fiction
Cane, 1923.

Other literary forms

All of Jean Toomer's best fiction appears in *Cane*, which also includes fifteen poems. Toomer later wrote fragments of an autobiography and several essays, the most important of which are found in *Essentials: Definitions and Aphorisms*, 1931.

Influence

Toomer was directly influenced by his friend Waldo Frank and by Sherwood Anderson; although more experimental than *Winesburg, Ohio* (1919), *Cane* shares many of its techniques and themes. Less directly, Toomer has much of Walt Whitman's Romanticism, particularly in his desire to make language incantatory, but not in an open love of all men. Although *Cane* was widely recognized among a small group at the time of its publication, its idiosyncrasies of vision and language made its influence small. In the 1960's, however, the book was rediscovered, and Toomer is now represented in most anthologies of American literature.

Story characteristics

Poetic, lyrical, elliptical, and suggestive, Toomer's best stories portray dreamers trapped in a hostile or indifferent society. Although there may be violent action in the tales, it is subordinated to the imagistic sketching of mood and character.

Biography

Born in Washington, D. C., Jean Toomer stayed in the North for his education, attending the University of Wisconsin and the City College of New York. He began writing and was published in the little magazines of his time before moving South to become a schoolteacher in rural Georgia, an experience which he uses in "Kabnis," the final part of *Cane*. Married twice to whites, Toomer was often equivocal about his blackness, partially because of his involvement in Unitism, the philosophy of Gurdjieff. Toomer's later essays and stories expound his version of the philosophy and are often weakened by an excess of mystery and a deficiency of manners. In later life, he lived among the Quakers in Pennsylvania. Toomer died in 1967.

Analysis

Divided into three parts, Jean Toomer's *Cane* consists of short stories, sketches, poems, and a novella. The first section focuses on women; the second on relationships between men and women; and the third on one man. Although capable of being read discretely, these works achieve their full power when read together, coalescing to create a novel, unified by theme and symbol. Like all Toomer's work, *Cane* describes characters who have within a buried life, a dream that seeks expression and fulfillment; *Cane* is a record of the destruction of those dreams. Sometimes the dreams explode, the fire within manifesting itself violently; more often, however, the world implodes within the dreamer's mind. These failures have external causes—the inadequacy or refusal of the society to allow expression, the restrictions by what Toomer calls the herd—and internal ones—the fears and divisions within the dreamer himself, as he struggles unsuccessfully to unite will and mind, passion and intellect, what Toomer in the later story, "York Beach," calls the wish for brilliant experience and the wish for difficult experience.

The one limitation on the otherwise thoroughgoing romanticism of this vision is Toomer's rigorous separation of mankind into those who dream, who are worth bothering about, and those who do not. While the struggle of Toomer's characters is for unity, it is to unify themselves or to find union with one other dreamer, never to merge with man in general. Like Kabnis, many find their true identity in recognizing their differences, uniqueness, and superiority. At the end of "York Beach," the protagonist tells his listeners that the best government would be an empire ruled by one who recognized his own greatness.

Toomer's dreamers find themselves in the first and third sections of *Cane* in a Southern society which, although poor in compassion and understanding, is rich in supportive imagery. In the second part, set in the North, that imagery is also absent, so the return of the protagonist to the South in Part Three is logical, since the North has not provided a nurturing setting. Although the return may be a plunge back into hell, it is also a journey to an underground where Kabnis attains the vision that sets him free.

The imagery is unified by a common theme: ascent. Kabnis says, "But its the soul of me that needs th risin," and all of the imagery portrays the buried life smoldering within, fighting upward, seeking release. The dominant image of the book, the one that supplies the title, is the rising sap of the sugarcane. Cane whispers enigmatic messages to the characters, and it is to cane fields that people seeking escape and release flee. Sap rises, too, in pines, which also whisper and sing; and at the mill of Part One, wood burns, its smoke rising. The moon in "Blood-Burning Moon" is said to "sink upward," an oxymoronic yoking that implies the difficulty of the rising in this book.

A second pattern of imagery is that of flowing blood or water, although generally in the pessimistic *Cane*, water is not abundant. In "November Cotton

Flower," dead birds are found in the wells, and when water is present, the characters, threatened by the life it represents, often fear it. Rhobert, in a sketch of that name, wears a diver's helmet to protect him from water, life which is being drawn off. Dreams denied, blood flows more freely than water.

"Esther," the most successful story in *Cane*, comes early and embodies many of the book's major themes. It opens with a series of four sentences describing Esther as a girl of nine. In each, the first clause compliments her beauty, the second takes the praise away; the first clauses of each are progressively less strong. Esther represents the destruction of potential by a combination of inner and outer forces. On the outside there is her father, "the richest colored man in town," who reduces Esther to a drab and obsequious life behind a counter in his dry goods store. "Her hair thins. It looks like the dull silk on puny corn ears." Then there is King Barlo, a black giant, who has a vision in the corner of town known as the Spittoon. There, while townspeople gather to watch (and black and white preachers find momentary unity in working out ways to rid themselves of one who threatens their power), Barlo sees a strong black man arise. While the man's head is in the clouds, however, "little white-ant biddies come and tie his feet to chains." The herd in Barlo's vision, as in Toomer's, may destroy the dreamer.

Many, however, are affected by what Barlo has seen, none more so than Esther, who decides that she loves him. The fire begins to burn within. As she stands dreaming in her store, the sun on the windows across the street reflect her inner fire, and, wanting to make it real, Esther calls the fire department. For the next eighteen years, Esther, the saddest of all Toomer's women, lives only on dreams, inventing a baby, conceived, she thinks, immaculately. Sometimes, like many of his characters, sensing that life may be too much for her, knowing that "emptiness is a thing that grows by being moved," she tries not to dream, sets her mind against dreaming, but the dreams continue.

At the end of the story, Esther, then twenty-seven, decides to visit Barlo, who has returned to town. She finds the object of her dream in a room full of prostitutes; what rises is only the fumes of liquor. "Conception with a drunken man must be a mighty sin," she thinks, and when she attempts to return to reality, she, like many Toomer characters, finds that the world has overwhelmed her. Crushed from without, she has neither life nor dreams. "There is no air, no street, and the town has completely disappeared."

So, too, in "Blood-Burning Moon," Toomer's most widely anthologized short story and also from the woman-centered first section, is the main character destroyed emotionally. Here, however, the destructive force is primarily internal. Among the most conventional of Toomer's stories, "Blood-Burning Moon" has both a carefully delineated plot and a familiar one at that: a love triangle. What is inventional is the way Toomer manages the reader's feelings about the woman whom two men love. Both men are stereotypes. Bob Stone is white and repulsively so. Himself divided and content to be, he makes his mind consciously white, and approaches Louisa "as a master should." The black, Tom Burwell, is a stereotype too: having dreams, he expresses his love sincerely, but inarticulately; denied or threatened, he expresses himself violently.

The first two sections open with rhythmic sentences beginning with the word "up"; Louisa sings songs against the omen the rising moon portends, seeking charms and spells, but refusing the simple act of choosing between the two men. Because Louisa does not choose, the story comes to its inevitable violent climax and the death of both men. There is more, however: when Louisa is last seen she too has been destroyed, mentally, if not physically. She sings again to the full moon as an omen, hoping that people will join her, hoping that Tom Burwell will come; but her choice is too late. Burwell is dead, and the lateness of her decision marks the end of her dreams. Like Esther, she is separated from even appropriate mental contact with the world that is.

Barlo's vision, then, is accurate but incomplete as a description of what happens to Toomer's protagonists. While it is true that the herd will often destroy the dreamer, it is just as likely that the dreamer, from inaction, fear, and division, will destroy himself. The four stories of Section Two all focus on pairs of dreamers who can isolate themselves from the rest of society, but who cannot get their dreams to merge. In "Avey" it is the man who, focused on his own dreams, refuses to listen to and accept the value of Avey's. In "Bona and Paul," Paul, a black, takes Bona away from the dance, not, as everyone assumes, to make love to her, but to know her; but knowing a human is denied him because Bona assumes she already knows him, "a priori," as he has said. Knowing he is black, she "knows" that he will be passionate. When he is interested in knowledge before passion, she discovers that to know *a priori* is not to know at all and flees him, denying his dream of knowing her.

In "Theater" the divided main character, sitting half in light, half in shadow, watches another dreamer, the dancer on stage, Dorris. She is dreaming of him, but, although "mind pulls him upward into dream," suspicion is stronger than desire, and by the end of the story John has moved wholly into shadow. When Dorris looks at him, "She finds it a dead thing in the shadow which is his dream." Likewise, in "Box Seat" Muriel is torn between the dreamer Dan, who stands with one hand lying on the wall, feeling from below the house the deep underground rumbling of the subway, literal buried life, and Mrs. Pribby, the landlady, rattling her newspaper, its thin noise contrasting with the powerful below-ground sound. Muriel chooses respectability. At the theater, to which Dan has followed her, she is repelled by a dwarf who offers her a rose; Dan rises to his feet to proclaim that Jesus was once a leper. This last, insistent image, suggesting the maimed sources of beauty that Muriel is too timid to accept, also indicates the overexplicit inflation of claims that damages some of Toomer's fiction. Although in *Cane* most of the stories are under control, some seem rather too sketchy; "Box Seat," however, foreshadows the fault that mars all of Toomer's later fiction: the sacrifice of dramatic idea in favor of, often pallid, philosophical ones.

The last and longest story in *Cane* integrates the themes, making explicit the nature of the destructive forces. The story is "Kabnis," a novella, and the force is sin, a word contained backwards in Kabnis' name. It is the story of a black man out of place in the rural South, threatened not so much by whites as by his own people, by his environment, and by his sense of himself.

As the story opens, Kabnis is trying to sleep, but he is not allowed this source of dream; instead, chickens and rats, nature itself, keep him awake. He wants to curse it, wants it to be consistent in its ugliness, but he senses too the beauty of nature, and as that prevents him from hating it entirely, he feels that even beauty is a curse. Intimidated by nature, Kabnis is also attacked by society, by the local black church, of which the shouting acclamations of faith torture Kabnis, and by the black school superintendent who fires him for drinking. As in "Box Seat," the protagonist is thus caught between expressions of life, which are yet too strong for him, and its repression, which traps him. So positioned, Kabnis, like Rhobert, is a man drowning, trying vainly to avoid the source of life. From this low point, for the only time in the book, Toomer describes the way up, and Kabnis gains enough strength to throw off his oppression.

He has three friends: Halsey, an educated black who has been playing Uncle Tom; Layman, a preacher, whose low voice suggests a canebrake; and Lewis, a *Doppelganger* who suggests a version of what a stronger Kabnis might have become and who drops out of the story when Kabnis does indeed become stronger. Once fired, Kabnis takes up residence with Halsey, a Vulcan-like blacksmith who gives him work repairing implements, work for which Kabnis is ill-suited. In his basement, however, Halsey has his own buried life, an old man, Father John, and in the climactic scene, the three men descend into the underground for a dark night of the soul, for the *Walpurgisnacht* on which Kabnis confronts his own demons. Prefiguring the descents in such black fiction as Richard Wright's "Man Who Lived Underground" and Ralph Ellison's *Invisible Man* (1952), this is likewise a descent during which the values of the world above, met on unfamiliar terrain, are rethought. It is a night of debauchery, but also the night when the destructive illusions and fears of the men are exposed.

Father John represents those fears; when he speaks, his message is sin; but Kabnis knows, and for the first time can say, that because of sin the old man has never seen the beauty of the world. Kabnis has, and as he says. "No eyes that have seen beauty ever lose their sight." Kabnis then proclaims a new role for himself: if he is not a blacksmith, he may be, having known beauty, a wordsmith. "I've been shapin words after a design that branded here. Know whats here? M soul." If sin is what is done against the soul and if the soul of Kabnis is what needs the rising, then, as Kabnis says, the world has conspired against him. Now, however, Kabnis acknowledges and confronts that conspiracy, no longer fearing it or Father John. Exhausted by his effort, Kabnis sinks back, but Halsey's sister, Carrie K, does indeed carry K. She lifts him up, and together they ascend the stairs into the daylight, as the risen sun sings a "birth-song" down the streets of the town.

The end is not unequivocally optimistic: it is too small and too tentative a note in this large catalogue of the defeated and destroyed. *Cane* does, however, suggest finally that as destructive as dreams may be, once one has seen beauty, if he can free himself from repression, from sin, he may re-create himself. "Kabnis is me," wrote Toomer to Waldo Frank, and he had more in mind than just his use of his experiences. For what Toomer has done in *Cane* is to chart the varieties of sin that society has done to people and, more importantly, since individuals are always more interesting than society to Toomer, that people have done to themselves. Wholeness is the aim, a wholeness that breaks down barriers between mind and will, man and woman, object and subject, and that allows the potential of dreams to be fulfilled. That the wholeness is so difficult to achieve is the substance of Toomer's short fiction; that Toomer achieves it, both for a character in "Kabnis" and more permanently in his only successful work, a book uniting fiction and poetry, songs and narration, images of fire and water, of descent and ascent, is his testimony that wholeness can be achieved by those who dream of it.

Major publications other than short fiction
NONFICTION: "Winter on Earth," in *The Second American Caravan*, 1928; *Essentials: Definitions and Aphorisms*, 1931; "Chapters from *Earth-Being*: An Unpublished Autobiography," in *Black Scholar*, January, 1971.

Bibliography
Bone, Robert A. *The Negro Novel in America*.
Durham, Frank. *The Merrill Studies in* Cane.
Rosenblatt, Roger. *Black Fiction*.
Turner, Darwin T. *In a Minor Chord*.

Howard Faulkner

FRANK TUOHY

Born: Uckfield, Sussex, England; May 2, 1925

Principal short fiction
The Admiral and the Nuns and Other Stories, 1962; *Fingers in the Door and Other Stories*, 1970; *Live Bait and Other Stories*, 1978.

Other literary forms
Frank Tuohy has written three novels, a biography of William Butler Yeats, a travel book of Portugal, numerous articles for British newspapers, and television scripts for British public television.

Influence
Tuohy's stories are so distinctively his own that it is difficult to detect specific influences except in some of the early stories in which one feels the presence of Graham Greene and James Joyce. Clearly Tuohy has learned from these and other writers (possibly also Henry James) but has absorbed them completely into his own manner. The artistry of his stories has been recognized by critics and writers alike and he has received important prizes, including the James Tait Black Memorial Prize, the Geoffrey Faber Memorial Prize, the Katherine Mansfield Short Story Prize, and the E. M. Forster Award of the American Institute of Arts and Letters; he has also had a Society of Authors' Travelling Fellowship, and for his most recent collection of short fiction, *Live Bait and Other Stories*, he was awarded the Heinemann Award in 1979.

Story characteristics
Each of Tuohy's stories is like a small novel of manners, in which persons of different classes, nationalities, races, religions, political persuasions, and ages are brought into a cultural or social conflict which reveals an underlying moral conflict as well. There is a relentless truth-seeking quality about most of Tuohy's stories, a scalpellike cutting away at pretense in order to reveal the rottenness underneath: class or money, moral or racial snobbery are all revealed as means of concealing the exploitation of the weak and the corruption of those with power.

Biography
Frank Tuohy's father was Irish, his mother Scottish. Tuohy was educated in Stowe School, King's College, Cambridge. His home is in southern England, although he has traveled widely and lived for extended periods in Finland, Brazil, Poland, Japan, Portugal, and the United States. He has taught

and lectured and has written reviews and articles for newspapers and journals. His travels and his interest in journalism have had a decisive influence on his fiction, for he thinks of himself as an observer of the world, not as a writer expressing his inner self. The contrast and conflict of manners and cultures has become the chief subject of his fiction.

Analysis

An initial impression of Frank Tuohy's short stories is likely to be that they are the observations of a sharp-eyed and widely traveled reporter who is filling us in on life in such diverse places as Japan, Poland, South America, London, rural England, New England, and New York. Tuohy does have a remarkable talent for direct observation, for bringing before our eyes the look and feel, the sound and even the smell of actual places. The gestures of his characters, their speech, and their actions all ring true. He convinces the reader that, for example, this is the way it must be in the grim Communist world of Warsaw or the formal, alien world of Tokyo or the rumbling platform of a commuter train outside London. Tuohy's accuracy of observation and precision of language, although doubtless a reflection of his own interest in being literally truthful to the physical realities of the places he writes about, are all part of his strategy for supporting and making real his underlying view of life.

For despite the variety of locales, of character types, and even of subjects, Tuohy's three short-story collections are bound together by an overriding vision of the world as a place of moral confusion. Here and there one finds in unlikely places remnants of an older, more civilized way of life, but generally one finds, also in unsuspected places, moral baseness of the sort that would have made a decent man in former times put his hand firmly on his sword. These are modern times, however, and the decent men are either themselves victims or confused individuals who cannot in these confusing days sort out the proper from the improper way of acting.

The best people in Tuohy's stories are usually women. In the title story of his first collection, *The Admiral and the Nuns and Other Stories*, an English woman, the daughter of an English admiral, is living in the interior of a South American country with her Polish husband. The place is a company town; the husband is employed as an engineer at a nearby factory; the neighbors, who are nationals of the country, have developed a deep dislike for the English woman and her husband and have, in effect, instituted a community-wide boycott. The grounds of dislike are these: the English woman is a dreadful housekeeper and cannot discipline her children; her husband drinks too much and pursues women. Tuohy's point is made clear by his narrator, also English, who sees that the woman is charming and valiant, having been formed by her father (the admiral) and trained by the nuns in her convent school. She remains loyal to her husband and, throughout her ordeal (which concludes with their deciding to return to Poland), keeps her chin firmly up.

There is a dreariness, however, in this kind of life and more dreariness ahead, and the narrator's admiration is tempered by what he regards as the woman's limitations: "she was one of those people whom experience leaves untouched. But she was durable. After all, she was an Admiral's daughter." As for the nuns, the narrator "cannot decide whether they had given her the worst, or the best education in the world."

A more clearly admirable character is the young mulatto woman in "A Survivor in Salvador," the last story in the first collection. The protagonist of this story is an exiled Polish prince who has arrived in San Salvador without money but with a packet of cocaine which he is attempting to sell. Without friends, liable to deportation if caught with the drug, without food or shelter, he is befriended by the girl who herself has been a victim of various kinds of exploitation, including sexual abuse by the chief of police. The girl, Antonieta, befriends the prince, becomes his mistress, keeps him from starving, and when he is seriously ill from exposure nurses him. Christophe, the prince, in return does what he can to show his love for Antonieta.

It frequently happens in Tuohy's stories that the main character or characters are exiled Europeans living in a simpler or more integrated culture in which even the poor are bound together by some mutually shared consciousness. The prince in Salvador perceives that even the most despised are not alone as he is. The prince is not usual in Tuohy's fiction, however, for most of Tuohy's exiles are unaware of their loneliness and alienation and are likely to regard those from simpler, more integrated cultures as inferiors to be exploited.

Exploitation of the weak or innocent—one of Tuohy's themes, and related to it, the snobbery that appears to be one of its causes—is treated in the title story of his second volume of short stories, *Fingers in the Door and Other Stories*. The story takes place on a train traveling to London; the occupants of a first-class carriage are Andrew Ringsett, a successful real estate agent who has moved up in the world, his overdressed wife, their spoiled, teenage daughter, Caroline, and for a time, an elderly woman in an ancient fur whom the agent's wife Merle recognizes as someone from a higher social class who (she believes) will always snub her (although, as Tuohy remarks, the snobbery is all in Merle's head). The train stops at a station, the husband alights for a few moments, and when he reenters the carriage through an outside door the train lurches suddenly and the steel door slams shut on his fingers. The husband is in terrific pain, but his wife, embarrassed before someone whom she regards as her social better, apologizes for him to the old woman. The daughter merely stares out the window, outraged that her trip to London has been ruined by her father's accident. The old woman rises from her place in the carriage and addresses the wife, telling her to look after her husband; to the man, she offers her sympathy and the advice to seek immediate medical

assistance. It is the husband, however, who exhibits the most admirable behavior. He sees immediately that his wife is embarrassed and humiliated and
puts his arm around her and tries to make light of his injury. He has something
in common with other Tuohy characters who have not lost the power to feel
affection.

In Tuohy's third collection, *Live Bait and Other Stories*, the theme of exploitation becomes predominant and as his camera eye moves closer to home,
to New England and New York and then to England itself, the sense of moral
confusion becomes more acute, the remoteness from human feeling even
more profound.

In "Evening in Connecticut" an English visitor is attending a dinner party
in the home of a very rich old man, an important benefactor of Barford
College, and finds himself in a world which seems detached from reality, a
kind of battered Eden in which things are plentiful but life abstract. What
the visitor discovers, at last, under the banter and expensive food and drink,
is the kind of exploitation Tuohy has found in other times and places but not
in so odious a form: the elderly white-haired host informs his English guest
that he regularly makes trips to England where an English doctor who shares
his tastes has found him a suitable girl of the lower classes whose parents do
not object. The English visitor is outraged but paralyzed by the social conventions and his own timidity. Later he believes that he was on the point of
rising to his feet and attacking, but that, "surely, was self-delusion." In this
kind of society, the sexual exploitation of children appears to be indistin-
guishable from any other kind of gratification.

Two other stories, both set in England, develop the same theme. In "A
Summer Pilgrim" an elderly white-haired poet who once taught in Japan and
now is retired and living in southern England is visited by a Japanese woman
who is making a kind of literary pilgrimage, armed with camera to photograph
her dear poet and a stack of his books to be autographed. The girl, who has
been reared to behave dutifully, is timid and self-effacing and is used by her
host in a shocking way.

The assault on innocence is also the subject of the title story of *Live Bait
and Other Stories*. Here, a twelve-year-old boy, a scholarship pupil in a school
attended mainly by the rich, accompanies a school acquaintance on a fishing
expedition to a lake on the property of an elderly rich aunt and her eccentric
son, Major Peverill. The boy is asked about his father's profession and is
treated insultingly by both the old woman and by her son, who advises the
boy, Andrew, to be grateful for being invited into the society of his betters
and then, when the boy admits that he is a scholarship student, laughs in his
face. Andrew's interest, however, is in the fishing; what in particular excites
him is the gardener's account of a twenty-pound pike that inhabits the lake.
He contrives to haul off his father's fishing gear and a boat that is usually
kept locked away at the lake. His upper-class friend quarrels with him and

makes insulting remarks about Andrew's mother; Andrew then fishes for the pike by himself. He hooks the big fish but it breaks his line, and while he is rolling about on the ground in anger he is being watched by Major Peverill, who then attempts to molest him. Andrew escapes but is drawn back to the lake by the hope of catching the pike; this time he is visited by the Peverill's granddaughter, a strange girl who tries to be friendly until she discovers that Andrew is using a live frog for bait; she then runs off to denounce him to her family. Andrew lands the pike but is borne down on by Major Peverill and his laborers, and, from the other side of the lake, by his mother. Andrew is obliged to surrender.

It is impossible to indicate in so sketchy a summary the important effect of this story, for what Tuohy does is to catch, without sentimentalizing, the way a twelve-year-old boy at this particular time and place is himself "live bait" to those about him, using him to get some strange pleasure, social superiority, adventure, or sensual indulgence. One is made to feel, rather than merely to understand, the meaning of what has happened.

It is also impossible to indicate in summary the kind of pleasure afforded by Tuohy's fiction, for despite the many stories about failure of one sort or another, there is nothing depressing nor cynical nor fashionably despairing about his writing. Life should be better than this—that is the assumption behind the fiction—but Tuohy is an observer-commentator, a truth-teller. His stories say, in effect, that this is the way life is: awful, incredible, confusing, painful, but always fascinating (even, in retrospect, the boring bits) when it can be seen for what it is. The act of seeing, of feeling, of experiencing the "bite down on the rotten tooth of fact," is what gives Tuohy's stories their characteristic pleasure. That, however, is the kind of pleasure the best writers have always given.

Major publications other than short fiction
NOVELS: *The Animal Game*, 1957; *The Warm Nights of January*, 1960; *The Ice Saints*, 1964.
NONFICTION: *Portugal*, 1969; *W. B. Yeats*, 1976.

W. J. Stuckey

IVAN TURGENEV

Born: Orel, Russia; October 28, 1818
Died: Bougival (near Paris), France; September 8, 1883

Principal short fiction

A Sportsman's Sketches, 1852.

Other literary forms

Not all of Ivan Turgenev's writings have survived, especially some early pieces. Of those extant, however, virtually all have been translated into English (as well as numerous other languages). They include—aside from more than forty short stories—novels, plays, and novellas. Much of his work was censored by the Russian government, and a number of items received hostile reviews and outraged commentary by critics, political writers, and the public. Turgenev was, nonetheless, never ignored, and his writings had a great influence on Russian thought.

Influence

Well read in Greek and Roman classics, Turgenev was also familiar with the major works of such Western writers as Shakespeare, Dickens, Shelley, Keats, and Byron (the early influence from England was chiefly Romantic) and with classics from Germany and France. He was fluent in several languages, having, for example, commenced the study of English when he was eleven, and his extensive travels enhanced his familiarity with European languages and literature. He is credited with being the first Russian author to become popular in the West, and a number of prominent Western writers have acknowledged his influence on them, Gustave Flaubert, Henry James, Guy de Maupassant, and Alphonse Daudet among them. His influence in Russia was largely as a liberalizing force; but his persisting popularity in the West, where his writings are frequently republished and anthologized, is based chiefly upon the delicacy of his style and the perceptiveness of his characterization. As typically American a work as Sherwood Anderson's *Winesburg, Ohio* (1919) was created in the tradition of Turgenev's *A Sportman's Sketches*.

Story characteristics

The often lyrical, romantic nature of many of Ivan Turgenev's tales does not conceal from the perceptive reader the insightful presentation of a wide range of characters found in Russian life, from downtrodden serfs to elevated but idiosyncratic nobles. The sense of place is very strong, Turgenev being primarily a writer of the country, as Fyodor Dostoevski was chiefly an urban author. Turgenev's stories usually have little plot, the emphasis being on character and setting; nearly all of his stories are based on events and people that the author knew. He is frequently given credit for being the Russian writer who best understood and best drew Russian women characters. Although his stories deal with an era of great ferment in Russia, often the tone is autumnal and almost serene, partly a result of his interest in the past. He is noted for the endings of his tales, which frequently provide no climax but rather create a subtle irony that leaves the reader to make what he can of the suggested but not explicit meanings.

Biography

Ivan Sergeyevich Turgenev was descended from Tartar ancestry that had recently, by Russian standards, achieved enormous property and wealth. The comfort that this background afforded him was spoiled by the rigid and often capricious discipline of his family, especially his mother. Ivan, the second of three brothers, was reared on the family estate of Spasskoye; and the fierce temper of his mother, combined with his appreciaton of the beauties of nature on the estate (and the misery of the peasants who served the family on it) combined to form, in his writing, an appealing vision of the Russian countryside joined with a sensitive understanding of human nature in often unhappy circumstances. He was provided with considerable money, as a rule, permitting him to travel and to study in Moscow, St. Petersburg (now Leningrad), and Berlin. After abandoning thoughts of a career in university teaching, Turgenev devoted himself to writing. His career was generally a success, marred only by occasional brushes with the government (one resulting in imprisonment briefly and then house arrest for several months), quarrels with leading artists like Tolstoy and Dostoevski, and an infatuation for the opera singer Pauline Viardot-Garcia, an emotion undiminished by her relative indifference and the presence of her husband. This attachment helped to encourage the melancholy treatment of romantic love found in so much of Turgenev's fiction, which seems to support his claim, written in a letter to a correspondent: "You will find my whole biography in my works." At his death, he was clearly recognized as a profound influence on Russian literature and thought and on many leading Western authors.

Analysis

It may be tempting to think of Ivan Turgenev chiefly as a political writer, in view of his extraordinary influence on the Russian government (some historians believe that his writings began the movement that led to revolution); but, in truth, he was a sensitive, detached literary artist. His devotion to his art can easily be seen in his short fiction. The best-known stories of Turgenev are those found in his early collection, *A Sportsman's Sketches*, although a few later tales are occasionally reprinted. Nearly all of his work first appeared in periodicals. Perhaps the most striking conclusion to be drawn from a survey of his short fiction is that there are many similarities between later stories (such as "A Desperate Character"—also "The Desperate One"—written in 1881, two years before his death) and very early ones (such as "The Hamlet of the Shchigrov District," first published in 1849). Although the action of the stories varies considerably, there are pervasive elements of tone and style that seem unchanging. The flavor of the tales is that of a reminiscence, the form that many of them take, with subtle touches of irony and elements of quite realistic verisimilitude. There is also the directness and simplicity of the folk tale, as well as the note of universality. Three of his most frequently reproduced early stories, "Bezhin Meadow," "The District Doctor," and "The Hamlet of the Shchigrov District," reveal clearly the truth of Turgenev's assertion that he "never started from *ideas* but always from *characters*."

The "Bezhin Meadow," judged by several critics to be one of Turgenev's best stories, reveals his interest in folklore, country life, and the variety of human behavior. As in all the stories in *A Sportsman's Sketches*, the narrative is told in the first person by a hunter who has met someone interesting during his rambles. In this case, the unnamed narrator has become lost and encounters five boys who are tending some horses near a river. After a typically beautiful and detailed picture of the charms of the scene, the hunter joins the boys around their fire and listens to their discussion of ghostly events and mysterious phenomena, some of them based on stories that Turgenev had heard as a child and others common beliefs among the peasants of his region. The boys, Fedya, Pavel (or Pavlusha, a nickname), Iliusha, Kostya, and Vanya, all believe in ghosts and spirits; and their tales are accepted with considerable readiness by the others. The leader of the group is Fedya, the oldest, about fourteen, who essentially guides the talk but it is Iliusha who has had most of the supernatural experiences (and who knows the most about such matters), having been in the presence of a hobgoblin in a paper mill at night. Of course, such a spirit cannot be seen but Iliusha and his fellow workers definitely hear the intruder and observe the movement of the water wheel and various pieces of machinery worked by the goblin. The episode ends in a manner that somewhat predicts the kind of close to which Turgenev brings a number of his stories: the spirit coughs and sneezes, and the workers in their fear scramble over one another trying to hide. This reduction from the ghostly to the prosaic is enforced by the casual inquiry by Fedya: "Well, now, is them spuds cooked yet?"

Kostya then relates an experience told him by his father. The local carpenter, Gavrila, has been noticed to possess a markedly gloomy expression, and Kostya has learned how he comes to have it: Gavrila was searching for nuts in the forest and became lost. As he sought the way home, he was accosted by an evil water sprite, whom he rejected, making the sign of the cross over himself. She burst into tears, told him of her sorrow at being turned away, and in effect placed a curse on him—"kill yourself with grief also, to the end of your days"—because he refused to live with her. Gavrila immediately saw his way out of the forest, but he has remained miserable ever since. Some parallels between this incident and Nathaniel Hawthorne's "Young Goodman Brown" may strike the reader, but the differences are more interesting: Turgenev's providing few details, having the story told by a credulous boy, and leaving the reason for the protagonist's sadness unstated (the boys wonder what it was about the encounter that really caused Gavrila to be so grim).

After another brief mysterious episode, related by Iliusha, in which the spirit of a drowned man apparently has entered a small white lamb, the group is startled by the barking of the dogs. When Pavel investigates, he concludes that the animals smelled something evil, perhaps a wolf. The narrator breaks into the tale, as he occasionally does, to note his admiration for the courage of Pavel: "What a splendid boy!" There follows some discussion regarding the possibility of the presence of wolves and an exchange of opinions about when and where one might see "the departed" people one has known and might view those who are going to die in the coming year (this part of the conversation bears a clear relation to the old English legends about the eve of Saint Mark). The latter topic leads to a review of attitudes and events concerning previson in general, with a few anecdotes to illustrate these matters, one of which reveals Turgenev's humorous bent: an old woman thought that the Day of Judgment was upon her, because of a solar eclipse, and broke all the pots in the kitchen so that no one could eat upon such a day: "There was rivers of cabbage soup all over the place." Then another amusing tale is recounted, one concerning the violent behavior of a group of villagers who believed that the evil demon Trishka was threatening them, since a man was seen coming down a hill into town with his head enlarged to gigantic proportions. Everyone screamed; all ran in various directions; one old man fell into a ditch, and his wife became "stuck under a gate, screaming for all she was worth, scaring her own yard dog so that it tore loose off of its chain, and over the wattle fence it went"—the villagers were chagrined to learn that the figure was that of the local cooper who was simply carrying a large tub on his head, the easiest way to transport the ungainly vessel. The boys laugh, but then "fell silent for a moment, as is so often the case when people are talking out of doors." This authorial generalization is one of the recurrent devices by which Turgenev achieves universality for his stories and reminds the reader of the presence of the narrator. Such categorical observations also inform Turgenev's stories with an air of sympathetic concern.

After the boys hear a piercing scream from a distance, they try to guess what the source can be, and the tale moves toward its somber closing. The lads talk over "forest friends," lament the insanity of a local girl who was driven mad by being submerged in a river for a time, and are reminded of the watery death of another boy, Vassya, who drowned in the same river. This latter tragedy is given a grim significance when Pavel returns from the river, where he went to fill their kettle, and says flatly, "Well, lads,. . .it's a bad business. . . .I heard Vassya's voice." The band is chastened and fearful; they decide to try to sleep, after Pavel concludes the discussion with a comment that apparently summarizes their thoughts on the subject of the supernatural: "No man can get around his fate." "Bezhin Meadow" closes with the melancholy irony that Turgenev often provides, along with a sense of apparent inconsequence that marks his tales as very much akin to those of folklore. After sleeping for the rest of the night, the narrator wakes to a beautiful day, nods farewell to Pavel, the only lad yet awake, and departs. Then he remarks, "I must add, to my regret, that in the same year Pavel was no longer among the living. He did not drown; he was killed in a fall off a horse. A pity; he was a fine lad!" This sort of relatively unstructured story, with occasional intrusions by the narrator and composed of more than one plot, reminiscent of the old device of causing a series of stories to be told by different narrators, as found in *The Decameron* (1353) and *The Canterbury Tales* (1380-1390), suggests the early influence of Turgenev's life in the country and also his reading of national poets such as Alexander Pushkin and Mikhail Lermontov.

A more unified story is "The District Doctor," which well illustrates Turgenev's ability to tell a pointed story briefly and with a focused emphasis on character rather than plot. Although it lacks the rural charm of "Bezhin Meadow" and the sense of comradeship that warms the reader's view of the boys, "The District Doctor" demonstrates what may be seen as a more sophisticated type of narration, despite a few "old-fashioned" techniques (such as the narrator's saying, "he told me a rather curious incident; and here I will report his tale for the information of the indulgent reader"). Again, the plot of the piece is so elementary as to be clearly secondary. The narrator is returning home from a visit to a remote part of the country and falls ill in a small town. The district doctor tends him and relates to him the story of a patient he had treated years earlier, a young girl who fell in love with him, as he did with her, and then died. The power of the story lies in the sensitivity of the doctor's feelings, his sense of loss and regret (common emotions in Turgenev's heroes, as is well illustrated in his masterpiece *Fathers and Sons* (1862), and his frustration at his helplessness to cure the ailing girl. In accord with his habit of changing the tone of a story at the close, Turgenev causes the doctor to remark casually about the dullness of his wife and to propose a game of preference (a new card game in Russia at the time): "We sat down to preference for halfpenny points. Trifon Ivanich won two rubles and a half from me, and went home late, well pleased with his success." Such a prosaic ending to what has really been a story of tragic, or at least pathetic, theme can be discovered in a number of Turgenev's tales; it may be regarded as his attempt to keep his literary feet on the ground, never straying far from the everday elements of life and human behavior. The directness and carefully developed mood of this tale have, however, caused it to be regarded as something of a classic, especially in the genre of the early short story. Its tight focus helped later authors grasp the importance of brevity and concentration in short fiction.

Turgenev is particularly celebrated for his introduction into Russian fiction of an important character type, the "superfluous man," the man who, though talented and educated, feels that he has never been able to accomplish anything of note and believes that his life is wasted. Thus, he is indeed "superfluous," unneeded by society. This type is most prominently developed in *Father and Sons*, but such characters abound in his short stories as well. "The Hamlet of the Shchigrov District" tells the life story, in capsule form, of such a person. As usual, there is a narrator, and, on a visit to a country house where he is to stay overnight, he meets Vasily Vasilyich, which is all that the narrator can persuade this strange man to reveal of his identity. After the party, attended by a number of local dignitaries, of whom Turgenev makes considerable fun in his customary ironic way—one of them, in responding to a question, declares, "That remains buried in the obscurity of the unknown, as a friend of mine, an attorney, is in the habit of saying when he is asked whether he takes bribes. . ."—the narrator and Vasily share a bedroom. Since neither wishes to sleep, this "Hamlet" offers to explain how it is that such a man as he, well-traveled, well-educated, certainly not stupid, ends up being scorned or ignored by polite society, with no profession and a small income. The essential reason is that he is devoted to reflection (as Shakespeare's Hamlet is, for a time, incapacitated by his penchant for melancholy thought), after a life of fruitless endeavor and misguided efforts. His greatest disappointment is that he is not "original": "I am of the opinion that life on earth's only worth living, as a rule, for original people: it's only they who have a right to live." Vasily has arrived at this gloomy conclusion after a childhood in which he was dominated by his mother (as was Turgenev) and, later, robbed by his uncle in Moscow, "after the custom of guardians," and abandoned to the confusions and hypocrisies of life at the university. (The autobiographical implications of this tale are intensified by a passing reference to Vasily's younger brother, who died young from a crippling but unspecified disease, as Turgenev's brother perished at age eighteen of epilepsy.)

In Moscow, Vasily was unable to distinguish himself either socially or academically. His study abroad was equally unmarked by brilliance, and he returned home to live in the country, which bored him to death (and still does). He married a retired colonel's daughter, about whom he refuses to speak harshly, but he is compelled to admit that her grim dullness led him to consider hanging himself. In a typically ironic and pessimistic aside, Vasily remarks that a friend of his wife's family "had in his youth raised disproportionate expectations, but had come, like all of us, to nothing." His ambivalence toward his mate, who died in the fourth year of their marriage during pregnancy (Vasily never had a child), is best seen in his remarks concerning his feeling when viewing her at the funeral: "A sweet, sweet creature she was, and she did well for herself to die!" Following his wife's death, Vasily makes several attempts to create a place for himself in government service, as a contributor to a literary journal, and finally as a sort of country gentleman. Of course, all efforts fail; and Vasily says of himself that he "saw clearly, more clearly than I saw my face in the glass, what a shallow, insignificant, worthless, unoriginal person I was!" As is often the case, the tale has no climax. Vasily simply remarks that he muddles along uselessly with his life, and then he goes to sleep. When the narrator is awakened the next morning, his companion for the night has already left. Thus closes an early vision of the "superfluous man," a type that seems to have been prevalent among the Russian upper classes in mid century. The nineteenth century critic, N. G. Chernishevsky, commented that this sort of weak-willed person was a typical phenomenon in Russian high society. Evidently Turgenev thought so, too, since one of the last things that Vasily says is, "There are many such Hamlets in every district. . . ."

A Sportsman's Sketches was a tremendous success upon its initial publication in 1852, and it remained a landmark achievement in short fiction for decades. An impressive story, which he started writing when collecting the pieces for his book, was not completed by Turgenev until 1874, at which time it was added to a subsequent printing of the collection. This story, "A Living Relic," was dedicated to George Sand and received a glowing reaction from the already famous French author. In a letter composed three months after he finished the piece, Turgenev said "It is all a true incident." In fact, the story is much less an incident than a character sketch. The character, though, is a striking person.

She is Lukerya, an old woman whom the narrator, in this story given the name, Piotr Petrovich, encounters in an old shanty on an obscure estate to which he is driven by a rainstorm while hunting. Lukerya had been a servant at the family estate, Spasskoye (using the actual name of his family estate, Turgenev makes little attempt to advance this tale as fiction), where she was noted for her beauty and liveliness. Now she is an invalid, having suffered incurable damage to her spine as a result of a fall down a flight of stairs. Despite her suffering, thinness, and copper-colored skin, Piotr finds that her face is "positively beautiful, but strange and dreadful." In this phrase, the reader detects the persistent combination of the horrible and wonderful in life that pervades Turgenev's work. Lukerya's spirit is a marvel, as are her lack of resentment toward God, her resignation ("there are others worse off still"), even her forgiveness of the young man who abandoned her after the calamity. In essence, the theme of her discourse is a universal lesson, seldom so movingly presented: one should learn to appreciate the details of life, as has Lukerya during her seven years of immobility. She notes the bees buzzing, the occasional flight of a sparrow past the window; and the visit of a chicken to pick up crumbs or the appearance of a butterfly are wonderful events: "that's a great treat for me." She amuses herself by singing and with occasional visits from local girls. Lukerya's fortitude, strengthened, she admits by praying—although she does not do so often ("Why should I weary the Lord God? What can I ask Him for? He knows better than I what I need.")—is strained at times. For instance, when she hears a mouse scratching or a cricket chirping, "That's when it's a good thing—not to think." This suppression of thought, which has a surprisingly modern tone, is clearly something that Lukerya must practice a great deal.

She, however, refuses Piotr's offer to help. She has adjusted to her harshly circumscribed life, and she now wants no other. The only item she desires is a fresh bottle of opium, since it is a great help for the pain; but she never complains of her suffering. The narrator learns that in the village she is known as "the living relic." A few weeks later, he discovers that she has died, at the shockingly early age of twenty-eight or twenty-nine (she was not certain). As usual, the story closes with no real climax, only the narrator's comment that the bells which the pathetic creature has heard before her death could not have come from the church, which was out of earshot, but perhaps "from above. Probably she did not dare to say—from heaven." This low-keyed ending suggests an attitude of doubt regarding divine benevolence that reappears in much of Turgenev's later fiction. It may have been a result of his preoccupation with death in later life. The lesson of Lukerya's love of life and submission to it, however, seems to have influenced him, as witnessed by his statement, written four years after "A Living Relic": "Love is stronger than death and the fear of death. Only by it—only by love—does life go on and maintain itself."

Turgenev's mind returned to social and profound topics near the close of his life. In 1881, two years before his death, he composed "A Desperate Character," which is a survey of the pointless life of his cousin. The story is told in a typically episodic fashion, with the narrator, this time an older man identified only as "P.," who relates the events to a group of listeners who have been discussing current affairs. P. tells the story of his unhappy cousin Misha for the purpose of illustrating that there were desperate men in the past, and that the contemporary phenomenon of desperation is not new.

After a brief summary of the dreary, exceedingly regular household into which Misha was born, the speaker reveals his early reaction to the boy (at this time only thirteen), which was that he was quite handsome, even "pretty," but had a somewhat disconcerting smile and an almost ferocious laugh. P. recalls that an old retired police captain predicted that the boy would be a rebel; and a rebel he turns out to be, selling his family's estate for a pittance after his parents' death and adopting a dissolute life, including excessive drinking and wild parties (one in particular, with a band of gypsies, shocks P. considerably). At this point, P. remarks, "I have seen something of riotous living in my day; but in this there was a sort of violence, a sort of frenzy of self-destruction, a sort of desperation!" This trait does not diminish; and, each time that P. sees his cousin, who visits him when in need of money, at irregular, often widely spaced intervals, the young man seems more grimly desperate, even to the point of taking extremely perilous chances and doing foolish acts, such as shooting himself in the hand, plunging his horse into a deep ravine, and allowing himself to be dragged along after a fast-moving sledge. In all the turmoil that P. reveals about Misha's life, two interesting facts are displayed: Misha follows a code of honor that will not allow him to lie, and he has what he regards as a compelling reason for his behavior. When asked why he lives so wildly, he replies, "wretchedness." This misery he attributes to "the poverty,. . .the injustice, of Russia. . .one's so wretched at once—one wants to put a bullet through one's head!"

So, what P. recounts is really the story of a prolonged suicide; and the unhappy narrative is unrelieved except for a few of Turgenev's ironical asides, such as his observation about some clothes that P. gives to Misha: "clothes of mine, which, as is always the way with poor relations, at once seemed to adapt themselves to his size and figure." After several further fruitless attempts to bring meaning to his life, Misha dies of dissipation in a remote district. His remark, on an earlier occasion to his cousin P., seems to have been borne out: "There's no saving me!" Misha's revolt against society (at one point, P. tries to make a place for Misha in his own house, but the young man cannot stand such an uneventful existence) and his pessimistic vision of life mark him as a late example of Turgenev's image of the "superfluous man," one who is devastatingly aware of his uselessness. Turgenev, however, is sympathetic and even appears to beg the question of the problem with such men. He closes the tale with the assertion that, so far as the reason for "the thirst for self-destruction, the wretchedness, the dissatisfaction," is concerned, "I leave the philosophers to decide."

In this late story, one perceives a profound fact of Turgenev's short fiction: that behind the evident casualness of the tale there is great skill and enormous effort. Turgenev was a far more conscious artist than many of his contemporaries realized. Possibly, a number of these figures were blinded to his art by the political elements that they detected, or thought they did, in his work. Perhaps the wisest judgment of Turgenev's stories, however, was pronounced by a Western author whom he influenced profoundly, Henry James, who wrote that "the deep purpose pervading them all is to show us life itself."

Major publications other than short fiction

NOVELS: *Rudin*, 1856; *A House of Gentlefolk* (also *A Nest of Gentlefolk*), 1858; *On the Eve*, 1860; *Fathers and Sons*, 1862; *Smoke*, 1867; *Spring Torrents* (also *Torrents of Spring*), 1871; *Virgin Soil*, 1877.

PLAYS: *The Weakest Link*, 1847; *The Parasite*, 1848; *The Bachelor*, 1849;

The Provincial Lady, 1850; *A Month in the Country*, 1850.
POETRY: *Parasha*, 1843.
NONFICTION: *Poems in Prose*, 1882.

Bibliography
Berlin, Isaiah. *Russian Thinkers.*
Freeborn, Richard. *Turgenev, the Novelist's Novelist.*
Garnett, Edward. *Turgenev, A Study.*
Hingley, Ronald. *Russian Writers and Society, 1825-1904.*
Magarshack, David. *Turgenev: A Life.*
Pritchett, V. S. *The Gentle Barbarian: The Life and Work of Turgenev.*
Yarmolinsky, Avraham. *Turgenev: The Man, His Art and His Age.*

Fred B. McEwen

MARK TWAIN
Samuel Langhorne Clemens

Born: Florida, Missouri; November 30, 1835
Died: Redding, Connecticut; April 21, 1910

Principal short fiction

The Celebrated Jumping Frog of Calaveras County, and Other Sketches, 1867; *Mark Twain's Sketches: New and Old,* 1875; *The Stolen White Elephant,* 1882; *The £1,000,000 Bank-Note and Other New Stories,* 1893; *The Man That Corrupted Hadleyburg and Other Stories and Essays,* 1900; *The $30,000 Bequest and Other Stories,* 1906; *The Mysterious Stranger and Other Stories,* 1916; *The Complete Short Stories of Mark Twain,* 1957; *Selected Shorter Writings of Mark Twain,* 1962.

Other literary forms

As a professional writer who felt the need for a large income, Mark Twain published more than thirty books and left many uncollected pieces and manuscripts. He tried every genre, including drama, and even wrote some poetry that is seldom read. His royalties came mostly from books sold door to door, especially five travel volumes. For more than forty years, he occasionally sold material, usually humorous sketches, to magazines and newspapers. He also composed philosophical dialogues, moral fables, and maxims, as well as essays on a range of subjects which were weighted more toward the social and cultural than the belletristic but which were nevertheless often controversial. Posterity prefers his two famous novels about boyhood along the banks of the Mississippi, *The Adventures of Tom Sawyer* (1876) and *The Adventures of Huckleberry Finn* (1884), although Twain also tried historical fiction, the detective story, and quasiscientific fantasy.

Influence

Twain's Western tales quickly became a popular although almost inimitable model. More generally, his witticisms are still quoted both for passing relevance and as examples of mordant insight, tellingly phrased. Twain is universally acknowledged to have brought to American writing a style that is flowing yet idiomatic, highly figurative yet grounded in colloquial directness. Today, any narrative by a nonconforming adolescent or a picaro invites comparison, even when unjustified, with *The Adventures of Huckleberry Finn.* Twain's literary reputation is established; in addition, his worldwide fame as a personality, a creative spirit, an individualist, and an American continues to grow.

Story characteristics

At his best, Twain's distinguishing trait is an escape from type. His worst failures usually involve an attempt to fit into conventional forms; for example, he had a great fondness for O. Henry-style climaxes, but his carefully plotted stories seldom close memorably. Likewise, Twain's finest stories differ greatly from one another. Good or bad, they range from jovial comedy and even low farce to stock sentimental pieces, from vapid melodrama to thinly veiled jeremiads, from crafted jokes to rambles of free association. Insofar as Twain should be identified with any pattern of plot, it must be with the first-person anecdote.

Biography

After his education was cut short by the death of a stern father who had more ambition than success, at the age of eleven Mark Twain was apprenticed to a newspaper office, which, except for the money earned from four years of piloting on the Mississippi, supplied most of his income until 1868. Then, he quickly won eminence as a lecturer and author before his marriage to wealthy Olivia Langdon in 1870 led to a memorably comfortable and active family life which included three daughters. Although always looking to his writing for income, he increasingly devoted energy to business affairs and investments until his publishing house declared bankruptcy in 1894. After his world lecture tour of 1895-1896, he became one of the most admired figures of his time and continued to earn honors until his death in 1910.

Analysis

Many readers find Mark Twain most successful in briefer works, including his narratives, because they were not padded to fit some extraneous standard of length. His best stories are narrated by first-person speakers who are seemingly artless, often so convincingly that critics cannot agree concerning the extent to which their ingenuousness is the result of Twain's self-conscious craft. While deeply divided himself, Twain seldom created introspectively complex characters or narrators who are unreliable in the Conradian manner. Rather, just as Twain alternated between polarities of attitude, his characters tend to embody some extreme, unitary state either of villainy or (especially with young women) of unshakable virtue. Therefore, they too seldom interact effectively. Except when adapting a plot taken from oral tradition, Twain does better with patently artificial situations, which his genius for suggesting authentic speech make plausible enough. In spite of their faults, Twain's stories captivate the reader with their irresistible humor, their unique style, and their spirited characters who transfigure the humdrum with striking perceptions.

"The Celebrated Jumping Frog of Calaveras County" is generally regarded as Twain's most distinctive story, although some readers may prefer Jim Baker's bluejay yarn, which turns subtly on the psyche of its narrator, or Jim Blaine's digressions from his grandfather's old ram, which reach a more physical comedy while evolving into an absurdly tall tale. In "The Celebrated Jumping Frog of Calaveras County," Jim Smiley's eagerness to bet on anything in the mining camp may strain belief, but it is relatively plausible that another gambler could weigh down Smiley's frog, Daniel Webster, with quailshot and thus win forty dollars with an untrained frog. Most attempts to find profundity in this folk anecdote involve the few enveloping sentences attributed to an outsider, who may represent the literate Easterner being gulled by Simon Wheeler's seeming inability to stick to his point. The skill of the story can be more conclusively identified, from the deft humanizing of animals to the rising power and aptness of the imagery. Especially adroit is the deadpan manner of Wheeler, who never betrays whether he himself appreciates the humor and the symmetry of his maunderings. Twain's use of the oral style is nowhere better represented than in "The Celebrated Jumping Frog of Calaveras County," which exemplifies the principles of the author's essay "How to Tell a Story."

In 1874, Twain assured the sober *Atlantic Monthly* that his short story "A True Story" was not humorous, although in fact it has his characteristic sparkle and hearty tone. Having been encouraged by the contemporary appeal for local color, Twain quickly developed a narrator with a heavy dialect and a favorite folk-saying that allows a now-grown son to recognize his mother after a separation of thirteen years. While she, in turn, finds scars confirming their relationship on his wrist and head, this conventional plot gains resonance from Rachel's report of how her husband and seven children had once been separated at a slave auction in Richmond. Contemporaries praised "A True Story" for its naturalness, testimony that Twain was creating more lifelike blacks than any other author by allowing them greater dignity, and Rachel is quick to insist that slave families cared for one another just as deeply as any white families. Her stirringly recounted memories challenged the legend of the Old South even before that legend reached its widest vogue, and her spirit matched her "mighty" body so graphically that "A True Story" must get credit for much more craftsmanship than is admitted by its subtitle, "Repeated Word for Word as I Heard It."

In "The Facts Concerning the Recent Carnival of Crime in Connecticut," in which Twain again uses first-person narration with a flawless touch for emphasizing the right word or syllable, the main character closely resembles the author in age, experience, habits, and tastes. Of more significance is the fact that the story projects Twain's lifelong struggles with, and even against, his conscience. Here the conscience admits to being the "most pitiless enemy" of its host, whom it is supposed to "improve" but only tyrannizes with gusto while refusing to praise the host for anything. It makes the blunder, however, of materializing as a two-foot dwarf covered with "fuzzy greenish mold" who torments the narrator with intimate knowledge of and contemptuous judgments on his behavior. When beloved Aunty Mary arrives to scold him once more for his addiction to tobacco, his conscience grows so torpid that he can gleefully seize and destroy it beyond any chance of rebirth. Through vivid yet realistic detail, "The Facts Concerning the Recent Carnival of Crime in Connecticut" dramatizes common musings about shame and guilt along with the yearnings some persons feel for release from them. If it maintains too comic a tone to preach nihilism or amorality, it leaves readers inclined to view conscience less as a divine agent than as part of psychic dynamics.

The shopworn texture of "The £1,000,000 Bank-Note" reveals Twain's genius for using the vernacular at a low ebb. Narrated by the protagonist, this improbable tale is set in motion by two brothers who disagree over what would happen if some penniless individual were loaned a five-million-dollar bill for thirty days. To solve their argument, they engage in an experiment with a Yankee, Henry Adams, a stockbroker's clerk stranded in London. Coincidence thickens when, having managed by the tenth day of the experiment to get invited to dinner by an American minister, Adams unknowingly meets the stepdaughter of one of the brothers, and woos and wins her that very night. Having just as nimbly gained a celebrity that makes every merchant eager to extend unlimited credit, he endorses a sale of Nevada stocks that enables him to show his future father-in-law that he has banked a million dollars of his own. The overall effect is cheerfully melodramatic and appeals to fantasies about windfalls of money; the reader can share Adams' pleasure in the surprise and awe he arouses by pulling his banknote out of a tattered pocket. It can be argued that the story indicts a society in which the mere show of wealth can so quickly raise one's standing, but Twain probably meant Adams to deserve respect for his enterprise and shrewdness when his chance came.

"The Man That Corrupted Hadleyburg" is one of the most penetrating of Twain's stories. It achieves unusual depth of character and, perhaps by giving up the first-person narrator, a firm objectivity that lets theme develop through dialogue and incident. It proceeds with such flair that only a third or fourth reading uncovers thin links in a supposedly inescapable chain of events planned for revenge by an outsider who had been insulted in Hadleyburg, a town smugly proud of its reputation for honesty. Stealthily he leaves a sack of counterfeit gold coins which are to be handed over to the fictitious resident who once gave a needy stranger twenty dollars and can prove it by recalling his words at the time. Next, the avenger sends nineteen leading citizens a letter which tells each of them how to claim the gold, supposedly amounting to forty thousand dollars. During an uproarious town meeting studded with vignettes of local characters, both starchy and plebeian, eighteen identical claims are read aloud; the nineteenth, however, from elderly Edward Richards, is suppressed by the chairman, who overestimates how Richards once saved him from the community's unjust anger. Rewarded by the stranger and made a hero, Richards is actually tormented to death, both by pangs of conscience and by fear of exposure. Hadleyburg, however, has learned a lesson in humility and moral realism and shortens its motto from the Lord's Prayer to run: "Lead Us into Temptation."

"The Man That Corrupted Hadleyburg" exhibits Twain's narrative and stylistic strengths and also dramatizes several of his persistent themes, such as skepticism about orthodox religion, ambivalence toward the conscience but contempt for rationalizing away deserved guilt, and attraction to mechanistic ideas. The story raises profound questions which can never be settled. The most useful criticism asks whether the story's determinism is kept consistent and uppermost—or, more specifically, whether the reform of Hadleyburg can follow within the patterns already laid out. The ethical values behind the story's action and ironical tone imply that people can in fact choose to behave more admirably. In printing the story, *Harper's Monthly* may well have seen a Christian meliorism, a lesson against self-righteous piety that abandons true charity. The revised motto may warn that the young, instead of being sheltered, should be educated to cope with fallible human nature. More broadly, the story seems to show that the conscience can be trained into a constructive force by honestly confronting the drives for pleasure and self-approval that sway everyone.

Many of these same themes reappear in quasisupernatural sketches such as "Extract from Captain Stormfield's Visit to Heaven." Twain never tired of toying with biblical characters, particularly Adam and Eve, or with parodies of Sunday-school lessons. He likewise parodied most other genres, even those which he himself used seriously. In his most serious moods he preached openly against cruelty to animals in "A Dog's Tale" and "A Horse's Tale," supported social or political causes, and always came back to moral choices, as in "Was It Heaven or Hell?" or "The $30,000 Bequest." Notably weak in self-criticism, he had a tireless imagination capable of daringly unusual perspectives, a supreme gift of humor darkened by brooding over the enigmas of life, and an ethical habit of thought that expressed itself most tellingly through character and narrative.

Major publications other than short fiction
NOVELS: *The Gilded Age*, 1873 (with Charles Dudley Warner); *The Adventures of Tom Sawyer*, 1876; *The Prince and the Pauper*, 1882; *The Adventures of Huckleberry Finn*, 1884; *A Connecticut Yankee in King Arthur's Court*, 1889; *The American Claimant*, 1892; *Tom Sawyer Abroad*, 1894; *The Tragedy of Pudd'nhead Wilson*, 1894; *Personal Recollections of Joan of Arc*, 1896.

NONFICTION: *The Innocents Abroad*, 1869; *Roughing It*, 1872; *A Tramp Abroad*, 1880; *Life on the Mississippi*, 1883; *Following the Equator*, 1897; *Christian Science*, 1907; *Europe and Elsewhere*, 1923; *Mark Twain's Autobiography*, 1924; *Mark Twain's Notebook*, 1935; *Mark Twain Speaking*, 1976.

Bibliography
Ferguson, J. DeLancey. *Mark Twain: Man and Legend.*
Gibson, William M. *The Art of Mark Twain.*
Kaplan, Justin. *Mister Clemens and Mark Twain.*
Smith, Henry Nash. *Mark Twain: The Development of a Writer.*
Tenney, Thomas A. *A Reference Guide to Mark Twain.*

Louis J. Budd

JOHN UPDIKE

Born: Shillington, Pennsylvania; March 18, 1932

Principal short fiction
The Same Door, 1959; *Pigeon Feathers and Other Stories*, 1962; *Olinger Stories: A Selection*, 1964; *The Music School*, 1966; *Bech: A Book*, 1970; *Museums and Women and Other Stories*, 1972; *Too Far to Go: The Maples Stories*, 1979; *Problems and Other Stories*, 1979.

Other literary forms
Although John Updike is best known for his novels and short stories, his more than thirty-five published books include witty verse, children's fiction, essays, a play, and numerous book reviews. His novel *The Centaur* (1963) won the National Book Award. His popular novel *Rabbit, Run* (1960) was filmed in Hollywood and released on the West Coast in 1970. A film version of his short story "The Music School" appeared on public television in 1977 as part of "The American Short Story" series. A collection of his short stories, *Too Far to Go: The Maples Stories* (1979), was shaped into a television drama which was broadcast on a commercial network in March of 1979.

Influence
Despite occasional adventures into myth and experimentation, in technique Updike is primarily a realist, capturing in his fiction both the virtues and the shortcomings of American life. In general, his early stories deal with lower-middle-class life in small Pennsylvania communities; most of his later stories, somewhat in the tradition represented by John Cheever, portray the world of upper-middle-class New England suburbia. Unlike most contemporary realists, however, Updike brings to bear on an increasingly secular world an essentially affirmative and religious vision. Although always laced with irony and at times clearly satiric, his short fiction is a cautious testimony to what is good in America. His stories have reached most of his readers through *The New Yorker*, a magazine whose editorial policy suits well his close observation of the commonplace and his characteristically mild and sophisticated tone. His books frequently reach the best-seller lists, and his stories continue to be widely anthologized. Updike's work manages to appeal to critics and the public, to skeptics and believers.

Story characteristics
Updike's delicate, vividly sensory stories depict American middle-class characters in ordinary settings and situations. In language rich with imagery and frequently dazzling with rhythms, puns, and alliteration, Updike moves

his characters toward discreet changes in sensibility. A brilliant stylist, he invests mundane details with an almost miraculous importance. Some stories are so lacking in momentous events and so filled with subtle perceptions, thoughts, and emotions that they have the quality of sensuous essays.

Biography

John Hoyer Updike grew up in Shillington, Pennsylvania. When he was thirteen, his family moved to a farm ten miles outside of town, although he continued to attend the same Shillington High School where his father taught science. Upon graduation, Updike attended Harvard, marrying Mary E. Pennington in 1953 while still an undergraduate and taking his A. B. in 1954. He then studied for a year on the Knox Fellowship at The Ruskin School of Drawing and Fine Arts in Oxford, England. From 1955 to 1957 he worked on the staff of *The New Yorker* magazine. Updike has four children from his first marriage, which ended in divorce. In 1977 he remarried; his second wife is Martha F. Ruggles. Updike describes himself as a Congregationalist and a Democrat. He has won several awards: Guggenheim Fellowhsip (1959), Rosenthal Award (1960), National Book Award for Fiction (1964), O. Henry Prize (1967-1968). He has been elected to the National Institute of Arts and Letters and to the American Academy of Arts and Letters.

Analysis

In 1964 John Updike wrote, in the Foreword to his *Olinger Stories: A Selection*, "if of my stories I had to pick a few to represent me, they would be, I suppose, . . . these." Critics, anthologists, and the public had already begun to agree that the Olinger stories were his best and most representative. Nostalgic, carefully crafted, and filled with an awe of life, these are the stories which early created Updike's reputation as a brilliantly gifted short-story writer. As is his novel *The Centaur*, Updike's Olinger stories are set in and near Olinger, Pennsylvania, a small town modeled closely on the author's hometown of Shillington. In these stories Updike lingers over mundane treasures from his own past; indeed, the fictional town clearly calls to its sensitive and sometimes openly reminiscing protagonists: O, linger! it says, in its inescapable pun.

There is more to these stories, however, than simple autobiography. To critics who had suggested that the stories are merely memories dressed up as fiction, Updike replied that "the point, more or less, of all these Olinger stories" is obvious: "*We are rewarded unexpectedly.* The muddled and inconsequent surface of things now and then parts to yield us a gift." In his Foreword, Updike wrote, "In my boyhood I had the impression of being surrounded by an incoherent generosity . . . , a quiet but tireless goodness." Updike does not ignore the frustration and suffering he sees in the world, but he depicts such things more for contrast than for realism. Despite the confusion and pain in many of his stories—particularly the more recent ones—in them we can detect a continued sense of life's "generosity," its "quiet but tireless goodness."

A major aim, then, of Updike's early stories is to capture the beauty and goodness of life, characteristics which make themselves known, the author feels, in small details and sudden realizations. Thus, Updike is more concerned with awareness than event, with successive states of mind than narrative development. This concern for subtle interior states can lead, as in "The Crow in the Woods," to nearly plotless fictions of mystic revelation. Indeed, Updike's Christian vision, unlike that of Flannery O'Connor, contains a strong element of American transcendentalism, a Romantic philosophical stance which presents sensitive perception of the physical world as the way to mystic revelations of the unity and goodness of all creation. Updike's later story "Hermit" dramatizes one man's instinctive search for the kind of natural experience Henry David Thoreau celebrates in *Walden* (1854).

Updike is a storyteller, however, not a philosopher, and in his best stories he resists the temptation to philosophize at the expense of art. Most of his stories have conventional, if muted, plots and memorable, if ordinary, characters. A number of the Olinger stories reflect the Updike family's move from Shillington to a small farm some miles away, a move Updike has said may have been "the crucial detachment" of his life. In "Pigeon Feathers," probably Updike's most popular story, David Kern's family has just moved from Olinger to a farm outside of town. The story begins, "When they moved to Firetown, things were upset, displaced, rearranged. A red cane-back sofa that had been the chief piece in the living room at Olinger was here banished, too big for the narrow country parlor, to the barn, and shrouded under a tarpaulin." Thus is established at the outset the sense of dislocation, the feeling of banishment, and even, in that word *shrouded*, the theme of death. David, the protagonist, is at the disorienting age of fourteen, an age between childhood and adulthood, and it is he who feels, like the furniture, "upset, displaced." Trying to "work off some of his disorientation" by arranging his mother's books, David comes across H. G. Wells's *The Outline of History* (1920) in which he reads, to his horror, Wells's account of Jesus. The irreverent dismissal of Jesus as "an obscure political agitator, a kind of hobo," plunges David into religious doubt.

Over supper the familiar argument between his mother and father, about the relative merits of "natural" and "modern" farming, increases the tension in him; his mother swears that the land has a "soul"; his father, a chemistry major in college, says, "the earth is nothing but chemicals." In this scene and others in the story, the grandmother, blinking and waggling with senility and Parkinson's disease, is a vivid reminder of death. It is death, the loss of the promise of afterlife, that David fears most. In the outhouse that night the boy is "visited by an exact vision of death" in which he sees himself crushed and elongated deep in the earth amid shifting strata of rock. Back in the farmhouse, David endures his parents' continuing argument, the terms of which ("the human animal," "earthworms," "Dark Ages") torture him further. In bed the boy prays for reassurance, begging Christ to touch his uplifted hands, but falling asleep "uncertain if they had been touched or not." The next day, at catechetical class, David's doubt turns to anger as Reverend Dobson evades his questions about an afterlife and heaven and makes him feel ashamed. David believes that both he and Christianity have been betrayed. Back home neither his grandfather's tattered Bible nor his mother's humanistic arguments confirm for him the "promise" of afterlife, the promise he feels gives physical life meaning. He comes to believe that even his mother is part of the conspiracy of lies he sees all around.

Nevertheless, in the months which follow David does not lose all hope. He is cheered by the sight of clergymen's collars, even by "the cartoons in magazines showing angels or devils," and he keeps alive "the possibility of hope." Thinking leads to doubt; therefore, he attempts to drown his thoughts in trivial experience. He ceases reading, because even the light humor of P. G. Wodehouse seems hollow and bitter. He plays pinball. As summer approaches and school finally ends, he instinctively immerses himself in sights and sounds—in the "rapt violence" of his father's work, in the "strange mechanical humming that lay invisibly in the weeds and alfalfa and orchard grass," in the intricate "embellishments" of his dog's ears, skull, and fur. A subtle shift of tone makes itself felt in this section. There is a growing sense of wonder in David's view of the world. In his escape from painful thoughts into sensory experience, the boy has actually prepared himself for a return to faith. In his intuitive feeling that this dog is both intricately *designed* and somehow associated with the earth (which up to now has been joined in his mind with annihilation and decay), David has moved to the brink of a revelation about the meaning of life and death.

On his fifteenth birthday David is given a .22 rifle. At first, trying it out on tin cans, he uses it as he had the pinball machine, as a device for mindless fun, an escape from thinking. Then his mother suggests that he exterminate the pigeons which roost in the barn and foul the unused furniture stored there. Entering the "small night" of the barn, David enters the final stage of his growth in the story. The barn, dark and mysterious, suggests death, and it is in the barn that David, in dealing out death, confronts his fear directly. His pleasure in sharpshooting grows into a kind of joy as he drops pigeons "[o]ut of the shadowy ragged infinity of the vast barn roof." He feels "like a beautiful avenger," paradoxically feeling "the sensation of a creator."

David emerges into the daylight changed, matured. (His mother says, "Don't smirk. You look like your father.") His involvement with life, even in the taking of it, has prepared him for a final awareness. As he begins to bury the pigeons, the beauty and clear design of these worthless birds seems a sudden undeniable argument for afterlife. Symbolically taking on, like clothes, the glory of the birds, David is "robed in this certainty: that the God who had lavished such craft upon these worthless birds would not destroy His whole Creation by refusing to let David live forever."

David, a typical Olinger protagonist, is an intelligent, perceptive, sensitive boy, capable of sharp insights—and deeply troubling thoughts. "Pigeon Feathers" dramatizes his struggle with religious doubt. His dislocation from the home of his early childhood parallels the more profound dislocation that occurs with the change from boyhood to manhood. In the story the reader sees David's thoughts and feelings about religion, about life and death, gain more depth, more maturity. Despite the rapture of the ending, however, one should not be misled into thinking that "Pigeon Feathers" offers the answer to such ancient and mystifying questions. David's answer at the end is *his* answer, not necessarily Updike's. After all, David's final revelation is really only a personal version of the traditional argument from design, an argument the shortcomings of which Updike, well-read as he is in theology, doubtless knows. The irony of the last sentence seems clear: David's idea that his own death would somehow "destroy" God's "whole Creation" is almost ludicrous in its egotism. Despite his mental and emotional growth, David is not an infallible theologian at the end of the story. Surely one can affirm God, design, and the meaningfulness of life without tying all of those things so closely to one's own personal needs.

The ending, however, is not a joke on the story's protagonist either. As questionable as the final affirmation might be when the reader examines it logically, it is emotionally quite satisfying. David has won for himself a measure of assurance, the most, Updike's stories suggest, anyone can hope for; he is, indeed, "rewarded unexpectedly." His "gift" is a new state of mind which soothes his fears and makes him responsive to beauty. The ending imparts genuine religious ecstacy, and yet the irony of David's limited perspective allows Updike to avoid sermonizing.

In "Pigeon Feathers" Updike exhibits not only his ability to blend irony and affirmation within the traditional framework of the growing-up story; but he also exhibits his considerable skill as a stylist. Indeed, it is his style which most often draws critical comment. In a few stories, his prose becomes so lush and self-conscious it threatens to strangle plot, setting, theme, and characters; in "Pigeon Feathers," however, style effectively complements the other elements. The story is told for the most part in economical, essentially straightfoward language. David's joyful revelation at the end, however, provides Updike with a situation appropriate for his most poetic prose. Whatever irony there is in the logic of David's experience, there is no irony in the style. The beauty of the style seems a kind of logic in itself, urging one toward the boy's conclusions. Updike's training in the visual arts and his verbal precision are powerfully evident in these closing sentences. Sex, an element which becomes a major theme in later Updike stories, is, in "Pigeon Feathers," present only in a minor motif. As is true of most stories about growing up, David's story manifests a sexual dimension. The boy's sexual maturation is presented symbolically. His use of the rifle to "create"; the hole under the ridge of the barn roof into which he shoots; the role of his mother in suggesting the killing, and then the burial, of the birds—all of these have Freudian implications and work to reinforce the growing-up theme.

Olinger Stories: A Selection is a re-collection, drawn from Updike's first two books of short stories, *The Same Door* and *Pigeon Feathers and Other Stories*. After issuing *The Music School*, *Bech: A Book*, and *Museums and Women and Other Stories*, Updike again re-collected earlier stories in order to form a loose narrative sequence. This second re-collection, *Too Far to Go: The Maples Stories*, focuses on the disintegrating marriage of Joan and Richard Maple, characters who attempt to settle into domestic life in a Boston suburb.

Although it is true, as some critics have pointed out, that Updike's work does not fall neatly into philosophical or stylistic phases (his basic outlook and high level of craftsmanship have remained more or less constant), one can detect a shift of emphasis in his stories which corresponds roughly with the shift from Pennsylvania to New England, from youth to middle age. In his stories of adultery, separation, and divorce, of which the Maples stories are the most notable examples, Updike emphasizes another aspect of his outlook: his concern with guilt. Updike lists himself as a Congregationalist, but he is no twentieth-century Puritan. His lyrical celebrations of sex and his fundamentally affirmative response to life rest uneasily with Puritan notions of the evil of the flesh and the fearful drudgery of this world. Still, Updike's marriage stories reveal an almost Calvinistic preoccupation with guilt and pain. Joan and Richard Maple suffer a great deal; they weep openly in several of these stories.

In the story "Giving Blood" the Maples have not yet begun to talk directly of separation or divorce, but the story begins, "The Maples had been married now nine years, which is almost too long." During the drive to Boston where they are to give blood, Richard, who is bitter about Joan's forcing him to come, harangues her, finally calling her smug, stupid, and sexless. Once they are inside the hospital, however, Richard's attitude begins to change. He has never given blood before, and his irrational fear of the process makes him, the major image motif implies, feel small and helpless, like a child. His insecurity and the unfamiliar surroundings make the Maples "newly defined to themselves." Richard feels like "Hansel orphaned with Gretel" and has to fight down the urge to giggle. The Maples check off their childhood diseases, and when they lie near each other on the beds, Richard sees Joan's "feet toed in . . . childishly," and thinks, of her hair, that "[f]rom the straightness of the parting it seemed her mother had brushed it." Later Joan refers to the plastic bags full of their blood as "little doll pillows."

"Giving Blood," like many of Updike's best stories, is a vividly realistic story about ordinary people doing ordinary things. (Even the Maples' blood types are "the most common types.") When looked at more closely, however, one finds that Updike has shaped reality with art, with symbolic patterns which reveal not only the deeper workings of his characters' minds but also the significance of the story's events. Joan and Richard, symbolically in bed, are also symbolically children, innocent and clear-sighted again. Richard feels that the extraction of the blood sample from his finger is "the nastiest and most needlessly prolonged physical involvement with another human being he [has] ever experienced." This shared ritual makes it possible for the Maples, particularly Richard, to see their marriage with new eyes. Surely the most intimate "physical involvement with another human being" Richard has ever experienced has been marriage, but is it the "nastiest" and "most needlessly prolonged"? Although he might have said so at the beginning of the story, Richard's feeling toward Joan is changing as he takes on his innocent child's eyes. They are sharing a mysterious experience which, like marriage, involves private and mysterious functions of their physical bodies. Richard feels that their blood is running together and mingling literally, as it should metaphorically in sex and love.

In their return to childhood, Richard and Joan seem to have cast off the deadening hostility that nine years of marriage have given them. As they leave the hospital, Richard whispers, "Hey, I love you. Love love *love* you." In the car, they feel "illicit," as if they have "stolen something." The feeling of innocence they have gained seems exhilaratingly wrong, as if they have somehow slipped magically out of the necessary guilt and pain of adulthood. On the way home, Richard gaily proposes that they stop for pancakes, and they eat with the romantic "bashfulness" and pleasure of "two people who have little as yet in common but who are nevertheless significantly intimate to accept the fact without chatter." Like the characters of Updike's Olinger stories, the Maples have been "rewarded unexpectedly." What Richard had feared would be a painful and perhaps humiliating experience has turned out to be a thrilling return to childhood innocence and young romance.

The story is not over yet, however, and the ritual bloodletting, although it joins the couple in a new and intimate way, is not without ominous overtones. After all, these people are watching their blood run out of their bodies, a disturbing image of dying. Joan, in fact, is bled from "a tender, vulnerable place where in courting days she had liked being stroked," a clear suggestion that somehow courting has given way to, if not dying, at least alarming suffering. This is a couple "sacrificially bedded together," "[l]inked to a common loss." When the delightful breakfast is over, Richard, pretending he is "a raw dumb suitor," says, "I'll pay," and looks into his wallet. The "single, worn dollar" there infuriates him, reminding him, as it does, of the unsatisfying life he leads from day to day. To this signal that their brief return to childhood is over, Joan responds by reaching for her pocketbook. "We'll both pay," she says. No doubt the characters are as aware as the readers are of the two meanings of that closing line. The Maples will share not only the cost of the meal but also the cost of their marriage; they will pay for domesticity. As Updike has said in another story, "We pay dear in blood for our peaceful homes."

The Maples stories do not, of course, simply wallow in guilt and pain. The Maples themselves, for all the guilt they feel and engender in each other, have, as Updike has said of their name, "an arboreal innocence." One feels that their sins are forgivable, mistakes made inevitable by the Original Sin, the sin of being human. "That a marriage ends is less than ideal," Updike says in his Foreword; "but all things end under heaven, and if temporality is held to be invalidating, then nothing real succeeds." As a domestic realist, Updike feels he must be true to the pain and disappointment of life; and yet, as a romantic Christian, his basic response to the world is still one of wonder and pleasure. He says rightly that the "Maples stories . . . illumine a history in many ways happy . . . ." As in his Foreword to the *Olinger Stories: A Selection*, Updike introduces his Maples stories with a direct statement of what he feels is a major theme: "The moral of these stories is that all blessings are mixed." However mixed, blessings are what Updike continues to give his readers.

Separation and divorce are painful subjects, and yet Updike handles them with his characteristic mildness. There is no physical violence in these stories, no slapping of wives or even shrieking of obscenities. Although at times as subtly cruel as any married couple, Joan and Richard are, under the circumstances, surprisingly civilized and kind to each other. In the last story of the collection, "Here Comes the Maples," to the question, "Do you believe that your marriage has suffered an irretrievable breakdown?" they both, as if at their wedding, answer, "I do," step back from the judge's bench in unison, and kiss. There is no malicious irony here. It is not so much each other they must escape as it is the tangle of deadening social conventions that bind them. As the story "Twin Beds in Rome" makes clear, Richard and Joan seem to want each other most when their ties are most cleanly severed. Updike's implied complaint about marriage in these stories is a typical romantic one: like all institutions, marriage can rob life of its naturalness, its spontaneity, and thus its beauty. "Romance is, simply, the strange, the untried," Updike says in "Giving Blood," and the fact that the hospital where Joan and Richard Maple regain a few moments of romance also temporarily houses the exotic "King of Arabia" is certainly no accident.

Like William Wordsworth and Ralph Waldo Emerson, Updike shows the reader again and again how "strange" and "untried" even familiar things are. His piece "Wife-wooing," included among his Maples stories, is an excellent example. "Wife-wooing" exhibits many important characteristics of Updike's fiction: its tone is one of wonder; its language is rich and musical; its setting and characters are domestic and ordinary; and its vision is, despite discordant ironies, affirmative. The speaker in the story (apparently Richard Maple) celebrates, in internal monologue, the beauty and mystery of his wife. As the family sits before the fire eating hamburgers, French fries, and onion rings, Richard describes the prosaic scene before him in ecstatic and incantatory tones and in a magically immediate present tense. The reader follows his thoughts from detailed description to vivid memory. He yearns for his wife sexually, and yet she gives him no encouragement. The next day he must work, and soon, amid daily demands, he forgets about his wife. Returning home, he finds his head "enmeshed in a machine," in the details of his work. The last paragraph begins, "So I am taken by surprise at a turning when at the meaningful hour of ten you come with a kiss of toothpaste to me moist and quick . . . ." Updike ends this story, as he does so many, with a direct statement of at least one of its themes: ". . . the momentous moral of this story being, An expected gift is not worth giving." The kiss has none of the awesome ontological significance of David Kern's dead pigeons, but it is still a moment of unanticipated beauty and pleasure. Although perhaps his adult characters receive grace less often, they are still, like his Olinger children, "rewarded unexpectedly."

"Wife-wooing" also exhibits Updike's brand of modest experimentation. Updike has never been committed to an avant-garde approach to short fiction. With his romantic/religious vision, however, he has tamed a number of wilder aesthetics and brought them safely to normally conservative magazines, principally *The New Yorker*. The second-person point of view of "Wife-wooing" and its pyrotechnic alliteration ("who would have thought, wide wife, back there in the white tremble . . . .") are not the standard devices of traditional fiction. Other elements, such as the development of rich symbolic motifs (the *O*'s, the images of blood), are here woven into a density more characteristic of poetry than of fiction. Because of his great stylistic talent and his exaltation of perception, in even his most conventional stories, Updike has a tendency to allow symbolic pattern and mental event to take the place of plot. In "Wife-wooing," language and thought deliberately overwhelm the minimal plot.

In "The Music School," the title story of Updike's fourth collection, thought replaces plot entirely. The action of the story is the action of the narrator's mind. This story, another internal monologue, is rich in interlocking motifs. In this story, however, the physical events upon which Alfred Schweigen's mind acts seem so totally unconnected that the reader is startled to see a consciousness so earnestly attempting to join them. A change in the Catholic Church's communion wafer, the mysterious murder of an acquaintance, the transcendent beauty of music, the precision and "poetry" of computer mathematics—these are a few of the things Schweigen, a writer, feels he must somehow connect as he waits for his daughter in the "music school," actually the basement of a Baptist church. "The Music School" dramatizes the plight of modern man. As Schweigen struggles with images that seem to demand synthesis, the reader is presented with a vivid metaphor of the modern mind as it labors to reconcile the religious with the secular, the predictable with the random, the meaningful with the apparently meaningless—in short, to make some sense out of the world. Of course, Schweigen's struggle is suspect to begin with, dealing as it does with such apparently unrelated things. As always with Updike, one must be aware of irony: Schweigen is sure there is a connection between the murder of the computer programmer and the change in the Church's treatment of the host, but he does not understand the connection between his wife's need for a psychiatrist and his unfaithfulness to her.

Updike's meanings are always ambiguous because Updike believes that life is ambiguous, and yet, despite all of the qualifications "The Music School" forces the reader to make, the story ends in triumph. The metaphors of music and mathematics and communion fuse into a "coda," another explicit Updike message: "The world is the host; it must be chewed." Schweigen succeeds in bringing order out of chaos. His aesthetic and logical success is dazzling. The reader suspects he has not received the whole truth, but gets a wonderful truth created almost magically out of apparently random bits and intuitions. The reader has witnessed real alchemy, transubstantiation itself—gold from lead, God from bread. Updike's exquisite sensory images justify themselves: chew the world, they say. Relish its sights, sounds, and smells. Turn them into God.

Major publications other than short fiction
NOVELS: *The Poorhouse Fair*, 1959; *Rabbit, Run*, 1960; *The Centaur*, 1963; *Of the Farm*, 1965; *Couples*, 1968; *Rabbit Redux*, 1971; *A Month of Sundays*, 1975; *Marry Me*, 1976; *The Coup*, 1978.
PLAY: *Buchanan Dying*, 1974.
POETRY: *The Carpentered Hen and Other Tame Creatures*, 1958; *Telephone Poles and Other Poems*, 1963; *Midpoint and Other Poems*, 1969; *Tossing and Turning*, 1977.
NONFICTION: *Assorted Prose*, 1965; *Picked-up Pieces*, 1975.

Bibliography
Burchard, Rachael C. *John Updike: Yea Sayings.*
Detweiler, Robert. *John Updike.*
Markle, Joyce B. *Fighters and Lovers: Themes in the Novels of John Updike.*
Samuels, Charles Thomas. *John Updike.*
Sokoloff, B. A. *Comprehensive Bibliography of John Updike.*
Taylor, C. Clarke. *John Updike: A Bibliography.*
Taylor, Larry E. *Pastoral and Anti-pastoral Patterns in John Updike's Fiction.*

Vargo, Edward P. *Rainstorms and Fire: Ritual in the Novels of John Updike.*

Ron Smith

GIOVANNI VERGA

Born: Catania, Sicily; August 31, 1840
Died: Catania, Sicily; January 27, 1922

Principal short fiction

Primavera ed altri racconti, 1876 (*Springtime and Other Tales*); *Vita dei campi,* 1880 (*Life in the Fields*); *Novelle rusticane,* 1883 (*Rustic Stories*); *Per le vie,* 1883 (*Through the Streets*); *I ricordi del Capitano D'Arce,* 1891 (*Captain D'Arce's Recollections*); *Don Candeloro e C.ⁱ,* 1894 (*Don Candeloro and Co.*).

Other literary forms

The published works of Giovanni Verga are of only two kinds, fiction and drama. Since he considered his primary vocation to be that of novelist, all of his earliest publications are novels. His first play, written when he was twenty-nine, was never produced and remained unpublished until after his death. Eventually he wrote seven plays, all of them derived from his own works of fiction. He first turned to short fiction with a relatively lengthy story called *Nedda.* It was long enough, at any rate, to be accorded separate publication in a tiny volume in 1874 but was clearly not of standard novel length. This publication is generally regarded as the start of his interest in the short story as a literary form. Two years later he published his first collection of short stories, and that volume also included the previously published *Nedda.* Thereafter, he practiced this new literary form assiduously enough to make his short stories as important a part of his total achievement as were his novels. Verga is a rarity among writers of fiction in that he published no poetry—not even in his youth—and no literary criticism or travel books. Aside from his novels, short stories, and plays, only selections from his personal letters have ever appeared in print.

Influence

Verga's achievement as a writer of novels and short stories is sufficient to make him a major figure in European literature and one of the modern masters of the art of fiction. Yet his influence has not been wide outside Italy; and within his own country his influence has been felt primarily in the domain of style and, to a lesser degree, in the domains of subject matter and technique. It was Verga who found a style consonant with the ideal of his generation— for fiction to be true to life. He learned to strip away most descriptive matter and rhetorical flourishes and to produce a prose that was direct, intense, and unadorned—often close to the primitive speech patterns of the simple and uneducated characters about whom he preferred to write. This style became the standard for Italian realistic fiction, and it can fairly be said that all of the best twentieth century writers of fiction in Italy exhibit Verga's influence in

their prose style. Verga's first important successes were based on his observations of the Sicilian peasants among whom he grew up, and his work thereby
contributed to the regionalism which has been so influential in Italian literature. Verga made it respectable to take seriously the humble representatives
of the various regional cultures in Italy. Finally, one can note that Verga's
disciplined exercise of objectivity, in his techniques of presentation, was
widely imitated at the end of the nineteenth century and the beginning of the
twentieth. Eventually it was rejected by writers whose social conscience told
them that objectivity was an inappropriate posture when writing about injustice. For a generation, however, Verga's rigorously objective mode was
the dominant technique in Italian fiction.

Story characteristics

The stories which secured Verga's reputation were ones of peasant life in
Sicily, and they all feature the raw and violent emotions of those primitive
communities. Each story has only the barest of plots, involving few characters,
and the main action is occasioned by the sudden outbreak of one of man's
basic instincts, such as passion or jealousy, hunger or fear. The earliest stories
in this vein afford carefully objective glimpses of this violent existence, which
the victims undergo with a kind of fierce stoicism lending them a tragic heroism. The later stories, somewhat less rigidly objective, tend to note the suffering of this life with a tone of resigned pity which eliminated the sense of
the heroic. Still later in his career, Verga applied the same method to stories
with the urban setting of Milan, and the pessimistic vision of those stories
took on a note of bitter irony. In general, Verga's stories gaze unblinkingly
at man's painful emotional life, whatever the setting; he notes the existence
of social and economic pressures in behavior, he understands psychological
motivation, but his attention as a writer is given almost exclusively to the
more violent forms of human passion, the topic which was his greatest subject.

Biography

The city of Catania, where Giovanni Verga spent the first twenty-five years
of his life, was a cultural center for Sicily and even possessed a university;
but it was geographically so remote from the mainstream of Italy's cultural
life and so small a place, that its atmosphere was nevertheless provincial and
in some ways even primitive. Verga's family were well-to-do landowners in
a society that was agricultural at its base and still feudal in its organization.
Verga was fortunate in his schooling to have come under the influence of a
teacher who was a writer and who also encouraged his literary bent; at the
age of seventeen, Verga completed his first novel. Although he embarked on
the study of law a year later, he quickly found he had no taste for the subject
and dropped out of the university to pursue a literary career. He tried founding
a journal and published a novel at his own expense, but Catania proved an

impossible base from which to launch a literary career. In 1865 he went to Florence, where he became part of a circle of young writers, and a few years later he moved to Milan, which was even more active as a center of the arts.

During the 1870's Verga was living in Milan, publishing novels and short stories, winning a small reputation, and seeking a new literary voice for himself which would express his ideal of what fiction should be. Because of illness in his family, he made frequent trips back to Catania during that period. From these factors emerged the Verga who would be recognized as one of Europe's master storytellers. The decision to write about his native Sicily, and the development of a new, disciplined style, produced in quick succession the short-story collection *Life in the Fields* in 1880 and the novel *I Malavoglia* (translated as *The House by the Medlar Tree*) in 1881. Both volumes won quick recognition as masterpieces and inaugurated the most productive decade of Verga's career, when he was at the height of his powers and acknowledged as the leader of the new literary aesthetic called *verismo*, an Italian version of the realism and naturalism which dominated the writing of fiction everywhere in Europe during the second half of the nineteenth century.

Verga's success in the 1880's failed to make him happy. His basic view of life was pessimistic, he was always something of a loner, and while he pursued many love affairs, he always avoided marriage. He grew restless and discontent with life in a great literary center, found himself spending more and more time in his native region, and by 1894 had resettled permanently in Catania. His literary output slowed to a trickle thereafter, and he lived out his years in quiet isolation. His eightieth birthday was officially celebrated in 1920, and honors were bestowed upon him by the Italian government, but he disdained to participate in any of the public ceremonies. He died two years later of a cerebral hemorrhage.

Analysis

Giovanni Verga's first experiments with the short-story form in the 1870's were quite conventional in theme and offered no originality of form or technique. At best, critics have discerned in this work the struggles of a writer in a period of crisis seeking a new basis for his art. The publication of the group of stories about Sicily, under the title *Life in the Fields*, demonstrated that he had found that new basis. For these stories he developed a new literary language and a new style: description and rhetoric were reduced to the barest minimum possible, and characters and action were portrayed in terse, nervous prose which was more impressionistic notation than precise narrative, and which often reproduced, as direct or indirect discourse, the speech patterns of the characters themselves.

The most renowned of these stories, *Cavalleria rusticana* (*Rustic Chivalry*), exemplifies this new style fully. The opening paragraph informs the reader that the story's hero, Turiddu Macca, having completed his military service, is trying unsuccessfully to attract the attention of his former beloved, Lola, by peacocklike antics in the public square. When he learns that she has betrothed herself to another during his absence, Turiddu swears that he will destroy his rival, and Verga makes this known to the reader by switching in midsentence to implied indirect discourse, in which Turiddu's own characteristic language, including curses, is abruptly intruded into a normal third-person narrative sentence: "When Turiddu first got to hear of it, oh, the devil! he raved and swore!—he'd rip his guts out for him, he'd rip 'em out for him, that Licodia fellow!" (Although D. H. Lawrence's translation is less than accurate, it nevertheless conveys the effect of the mixed narrative mode well enough.) A few paragraphs later Verga reports a direct conversation between Turiddu and Lola, and their words include local proverbial expressions, coarse language, and rough, ungrammatical constructions—all designed to communicate impressionistically but with great economy of means the nature of the characters and of their world.

Brevity and suggestion are the keynotes of Verga's prose style. Much is left unsaid, and transitions are abrupt, unelaborated, and unexplained. Thus, after the early conversation between Turiddu and Lola, Verga quickly states that Lola married the man from Licodia, and Turiddu swore he would get even "right under her eyes, the dirty bitch" (in Giovanni Cecchetti's much more accurate translation). Without the least probing of psychological motives, Verga then recounts Turiddu's cruel courtship of a girl named Santa, who lives across the street from Lola's house, to arouse Lola's jealousy and the abrupt success of the maneuver when Lola invites Turiddu to become her lover. Swiftly and relentlessly, the action moves to its inevitable climax; there is always a minimum of explanation or analysis from the narrator and as much as possible through the vehicle of direct or reported speech by the four principal characters. The jilted Santa tells Lola's husband, Alfio, that he has been cuckolded by Turiddu. In accordance with the crude customs of local "chivalry," Alfio challenges Turiddu to a "duel" to the death, with clasp knives. The violent fight is rapidly and vividly recounted in half a page, much of it dialogue, at the end of which Alfio is seriously wounded, and Turiddu is dead, having lost the fight when Alfio suddenly threw dirt in his face, blinding him. The ironic intention in the title of the story becomes especially clear in this last circumstance: in a primitive Sicilian village, the savage, violent, animalistic resolution of an "affair of honor" provides a mocking parody of the aristocratic traditions of chivalry. The Sicilian behavior is not admirable, but it is instinctive and entirely natural, compared to the ritualistic and artificial modes of chivalry.

Verga's grasp of the essentially instinctive nature of Sicilian peasant behavior is even more starkly presented in "La Lupa" ("The She-Wolf"). The title figure in this narrative is a middle-aged peasant woman of imperious sexuality who makes a sexual slave of her own son-in-law, as though she has cast a spell over him which he is incapable of resisting, in spite of his revulsion and hatred of her. The role of primitive superstition in the relationship is emphasized by Verga's incantatory repetition of the proverbial phrase, *fra vespero e nona* ("between the hours of nones and vespers"), that time of the most intense heat in the late afternoon, when all work stops, and when Pina, the she-wolf, would come to the threshing-floor to make love with her son-in-law. The story concludes with the unforgettable vision of the son-in-law, desperate to be rid of her torment, advancing on his mother-in-law with an axe, while she unflinchingly strides toward her death, holding a bouquet of red poppies, and devouring him with her black eyes. Both are the victims of uncontrollable instinct, beyond the reach of reason, and in the story's final moment, both acquire a kind of grim, tragic heroism.

Superstition and the dark force of instinct dominate most of the stories in *Life in the Fields*. In "L'amante di Gramigna" ("Gramigna's Mistress"), for example, the story concerns a girl of good family who suddenly abandons her respectable life to follow the notorious bandit, Gramigna, because he seems to her to embody her ideal of manhood. In "Rosso Malpelo" (the title is the nickname of the hero, and means "the redheaded evil-haired one"), a young boy's character and fate are inevitably shaped by the local superstition that people born with red hair are evil and must be ostracized. Perhaps the greatest accomplishment of Verga's new style of writing in *Life in the Fields* was the immediacy with which he was able to plunge his readers into the violent emotional atmosphere of the Sicilian social system. By Verga's technique, the reader experiences this unfamiliar but fascinating world as directly as possible and with almost unnoticed mediation from the narrator.

Similar themes and similar techniques marked the new collection of short stories which Verga published three years after *Life in the Fields* under the title *Rustic Stories*. Again he dealt with the raw passions of the Sicilian peasants, although now with a diminished sense of their heroism and with a heightened sense of the bitterness of their lives. The best-known story in this collection, "La roba" ("Property"), analyzes an instance of obsessive behavior in a man who has, in an exaggerated form, the traditional and instinctive peasant attachment to the land. Mazzarò has devoted all his energy and all his means to the acquisition of land, denying himself any pleasure or indulgence in this single-minded pursuit which has dominated his whole life. The impressive opening paragraph outlines the astonishing expanse of property which had come under Mazzarò's ownership by his middle years, and the story goes on to explore, from within, the compulsions and obsessive drives which overwhelm Mazzarò's reason and his humanity, turning him into nothing more than an acquisitive machine. The story concludes, as it must, with the vision of desperation in Mazzarò when he finally realizes that his death is close and that he will have to give up his property which has been so painfully accumulated. He reels crazily about his own courtyard, killing his ducks and turkeys, and screaming: "Roba mia, vientene con me!" ("My property, come with me!").

Verga applied the same techniques to urban themes in a collection of stories about Milan, entitled *Through the Streets*. Critics generally have considered these stories somewhat less intense and therefore less effective than the Sicilian stories, but such a tale as "L'Ultima giornata" ("The Last Day") is surely in no way artistically inferior to *Rustic Chivalry* or to "The She-Wolf." It tells the story of the last hours of a vagabond who, in desperation, ends his hopeless life by throwing himself under the wheels of a train. The technical brilliance of the story lies in its indirection: it begins with an account of some well-to-do train passengers whose enjoyment is disturbed by a bump just as the train is passing through the outskirts of Milan; the next day, the newspapers report that a dead body has been found on the tracks, and soon the police investigate, following the few clues and tracking down witnesses so that a proper report can be filed on whether or not a murder for money had been involved since the victim's pockets have been found empty. The gradual unfolding of the victim's desperate plight is accomplished by the perfunctory efforts of the police, ironically operating on the wrong assumption, and in this way the final day of the suicide's life is reconstructed, clue by pathetic clue, for the reader. The story concludes with glimpses of the way various people react to "the day's suicide," demonstrating how little their lives are really touched by the event, and emphasizing the melancholy truth that life goes grimly and obliviously on.

In the decade after 1883, Verga wrote more short stories; although some of them are fine, most of them mark a decline in his creative powers. By 1894, when he returned to live in isolation in Catania, his work as a short-story writer was virtually complete. In about fifteen years of peak productivity, however, Verga had truly created the art of the modern short story in Italy and had left as his legacy nearly two dozen stories of the highest excellence, as well as another two dozen or more stories of lesser quality, as models for his successors. In doing so, Verga renewed and brought up to the artistic standards of modernity a literary tradition which had been dormant in Italy since its distinguished beginnings with Giovanni Boccaccio in the fourteenth century.

Major publications other than short fiction

NOVELS: *Una peccatrice*, 1866 (*A Sinner*); *Eva*, 1873; *Tigre reale*, 1875 (*Royal Tigress*); *I Malavoglia*, 1881 (*The House by the Medlar Tree*); *Mastro-don Gesualdo*, 1889.

PLAYS: *Cavalleria rusticana*, 1884 (*Rustic Chivalry*); *In Portineria*, 1885 (*The Porter's Lodgings*); *La Lupa*, 1896 (*The She-Wolf*); *La caccia al lupo*, 1901 (*The Wolf Hunt*).

Bibliography
Bergin, Thomas Goddard. *Giovanni Verga.*
Cecchetti, Giovanni. *Giovanni Verga.*
Ragusa, Olga. *Verga's Milanese Tales.*

Murray Sachs

VERGIL
Publius Vergilius Maro

Born: Andes, near Mantua, Italy; October 15, 70 B. C.
Died: Brundisium (now Brindisi), Italy; September 21, 19 B. C.

Principal works
Eclogae, 43-37 B. C. (*Eclogues*); *Georgics*, c. 37-29 B. C.; *Aeneid*, c. 29-19 B. C.

Other literary forms
There are several minor poems attributed with varying degrees of cogency to Vergil. Among these are the *Culex* (c. 50 B. C., *The Gnat*), *Ciris* (c. 50 B. C., the seabird), and *Aetna* (c. 50 B. C.).

Influence
Vergil is of immense and pervasive influence in Western culture. Immediately after his death, his genius was recognized by Roman educators, who made the *Aeneid* a school text. The beauty of his work survived this test as well as that provided by the Middle Ages' view of him as a magician (chiefly the result of interpretations of Vergil's fourth eclogue, the "Messianic" eclogue, which held that Vergil had been granted a prophecy of the birth of Christ). St. Augustine wept over the description of the death of Dido (Book IV of the *Aeneid*) when he was unmoved by St. Matthews' description of the Passion, and Dante made Vergil his guide to the underworld in *The Divine Comedy* (c. 1320). The Renaissance continued to value him even with the revival of Greek (and, thus Homer), although Ovid was the favorite of the little-Latined Shakespeare as well as the learned John Milton. Both Milton and his teacher, Edmund Spenser, England's Vergil, (with Geoffrey Chaucer as England's Homer) can be appreciated fully only with a knowledge of all of Vergil from the *Culex* to the *Aeneid*. The *Georgics* ("the best poem of the best poet," according to John Dryden) as well as the *Aeneid* provides much of the texture of *Paradise Lost* (1667). The eighteenth century was enraptured by the *Georgics*, and only with the growth of admiration of all things Greek in the nineteenth century, and T. S. Eliot's observation in the twentieth century that the *Aeneid* is clearly (as it is) a party poem and the consequent opposition to Vergil for his politics, together with the recurrent belief in our new Alexandrian age that a long poem is a big nuisance, has Vergil's influence been seriously lessened.

Story characteristics
The pastoral *Eclogues* are a sophisticated handling of rural simplicity. Their charm derives from the strange patina which hovers over the landscape, which

is neither an actual environment nor a mythic setting but something hauntingly more than nature provides. Like the *Georgics* and the *Aeneid* the *Eclogues* are written in hexameter meter. The contemplative life of the *Eclogues*, however, is far from the heroic life we associate with epic hexameters. However much Vergil's temperament may have been drawn to the reflective life of retirement, his intelligence told him that nature and life demand labor. Accordingly, with the tenth *Eclogue* Vergil bade farewell to Arcadian leisure and turned to the composition of the *Georgics*, a work midway between the pastoral *Eclogues* and the epic *Aeneid*, but with its insistence on the necessity of work and the worth of that work closer to the epic (as Milton perceived in *Paradise Lost* where even in Eden labor is a good). The first three books of the *Georgics* are devoted to crops (fruit trees, especially vine and olive) and animals, including horses, not usually a farm animal in the days of Vergil and a link with the heroic world of his next poem; in these Vergil surpasses his chief predecessor in nature poetry, Lucretius, not in vision and power but in harmonious involvement of poet and subject. Book IV, which deals with bee-keeping, a central farming activity in the days before sugar, has a concluding epyllion, or little epic. This is the story of Aristeus, beautiful in itself, which provides a natural link to the epic of the *Aeneid*, equally as didactic as the *Georgics* and more extensively a celebration not only of the land of Italy but also of its people, past, present, and to come.

Biography

Vergil (Publius Vergilius Maro) was born near Mantua in Northern Italy in what was then Cis-alpine Gaul on October 15, 70 B. C. His father's name is of Etruscan origin, a fact of some modest significance, perhaps, in one's understanding of the Italian wars depicted in the *Aeneid*. His boyhood was spent in relatively simple surroundings, but when he reached fifteen (putting on the *toga virilis* on the day that his greatest Latin predecessor, Lucretius, is said to have died) he went to Milan and then Rome to study rhetoric (a journey passed in reverse direction by St. Augustine four centuries later), but his public career was limited and unsuccessful, for philosophy and science were his true interests. He joined the cultural circle of the epicurean philosopher, Siro, near Naples (it is important to note that the *Aeneid* in large measure supports the Stoic, not the Epicurean, view of life). The influence of other prominent Romans not only made amends for the confiscation of his family's land following the Battle of Philippi (43 B. C.), but also introduced the poet, already in the midst of the composition of the *Eclogues*, to Octavian, the heir of Caesar, eventually to be called Caesar Augustus. Following the advice of Maecenas, the eponymous archetype of enlightened patronage, Vergil began the *Georgics*, a work which took seven years to complete, chiefly because of the care with which he composed, producing some lines in the morning and reducing them to a small number of perfected verses by the end of the day. Having celebrated first pastoral and then agricultural life, Vergil turned with the active encouragement of Octavian to the active life of the hero. The *Aeneid* slowly developed (with Books II, IV and VI the first to be completed) but it was never finished as Vergil hoped; he died with the request that the partly imperfect epic should be burned, but his executors and Augustus himself overrode his last wish and a central text of the Western imagination was thus preserved.

Analysis

The *Aeneid* of Vergil is an epic poem combining historical and mythical elements in twelve books celebrating the origin and destiny of the Roman people. It owes much to Homer, something to Apollonius Rhodius, and even something to the first Latin epic writer, Ennius. At the heart of the poem is a success story made poignant by the careful delineation of the great price of that success. Indeed, it is precisely this sense of loss which hovers over the successful plot line which makes the *Aeneid* a more richly ambiguous poem than its predecessors and all of its successors save *Paradise Lost*.

In outline the *Aeneid* tells the story of a Trojan prince Aeneas, the son of the goddess Venus and the mortal Anchises, from the time he leaves the burning city of Troy to his conquest on the site of the new Troy in Italy. In between he has many adventures, endures several temptations, displays little variety in personality, but emerges with a character experienced in Stoic fashion and representative or emblematic of the ideal Roman leader—in fact, not unlike Augustus, putatively descended from Trojan ancestors, as he seemed to some.

Book I begins as epic poems should do, *in medias res*, with the storm-tossed Trojans and their captain Aeneas driven onto the coast of North Africa not far from Carthage. The storm was prompted by Juno, ever hostile to the Trojans from the time Paris, the Trojan prince, had made his famous judgment in favor of Venus, not Juno or Minerva (to continue the Latin names); but Venus in disguise provides her son with helpful background information. He enters Carthage and sees in the newly constructed temple painted scenes of the now-famous struggles of Achilles, Priam, Hector, and even himself. He meets the Carthaginian Queen Dido, who is hospitable to the wandering Trojans, chiefly because she has known what it is to suffer as a refugee. Indeed, her statement which has moved countless readers, moved especially another sufferer and student of suffering, Sigmund Freud, who kept her lines on his desk ("My own acquaintance with misfortune has been teaching me to help others who are in distress"). Dido orders a celebratory banquet and, already smitten with love for Aeneas, asks him to tell the entire story of the fall of Troy.

Book II is Aeneas' narrative of the destruction of Troy in which ruin he lost his wife, Creusa, and with difficulty persuaded his father, Anchises, to flee along with Aeneas and his son, Ascanius (also called Iulus). This book has firmly imprinted itself in the Western imagination. Among the most vivid episodes are Sinon's treachery; the death of Laocoon and his sons; the murder of Priam by Pyrrhus (see William Shakespeare's *Hamlet* II.ii); the appeal of Creusa and the flaming sign about the head of little Ascanius; and most especially, Aeneas carrying his aged father, a necessary link with the Trojan past, and holding in his right hand little Ascanius, the necessary link with the future, struggling to keep up with his short steps to the strides of his heroic father. Meanwhile the wife, Creusa, significantly follows behind this trio of males and finally is lost in the flames of Troy. It is Creusa whose death frees Aeneas to meet the temptation of Dido and the opportunity of Lavinia, and whose ghost assures Aeneas that all is for the best as the gods have ordered it and that happiness and a kingdom await him in the West.

Book III continues Aeneas' tale of his wanderings, and along with Book X shows most the signs that Vergil would have revised or polished it if he had lived. Among the adventures are the meeting with Andromache, the widow of Hector, another of the grieving women in this masculine world; the advice of the seer Helenus to look for the huge white sow with its thirty young as a sign guaranteeing the proper place for the founding of the new Troy; the counsel to avoid Scylla and Charybdis; the description and appearance of Polyphemus; and finally, the death of Anchises in Sicily, the last landfall before the arrival in Carthage.

Book IV, the most humanly moving, the most romantic, the saddest, and the most Vergilian segment of the poem, involves the love and death of Dido. Vergil's presentation with sympathetic understanding of the defeated moved Augustine to tears, reduced Aeneas in the eyes of readers immemorial to a mere instrument of the gods rather than a feeling human being, and tempted Milton to repeat the story in the form of Adam and Eve with an antithetical resolution. Like Milton after him, Vergil had some difficulty in succeeding with the tactic of criticizing by authorial statement the all-too-moving conduct he depicts. The image of Rumor is especially memorable, but even it pales in comparison to the final lamentation and suicide of Dido, betrayed by Aeneas and destiny.

Book V is a relaxation between the two most powerful books, IV and VI; its funeral games are a more morally sophisticated version of the games in *Iliad* (c. 800 B. C.) XXIII. Although there is a relaxation in narrative tension, symbolic significance remains high, for the book is framed by two deaths. It opens with Aeneas looking backward as his fleet heads for Sicily at the walls of Troy which reflect the flames from Dido's funeral pyre, and it ends with the sacrificial death by drowning of the Trojan helmsman Palinurus. Both Dido and to a lesser degree Palinurus represent the cost in human terms of political obligation. Of the several events in the funeral games themselves the most memorable is the boxing match between the huge braggart Dares and the old champion Entellus, whose initial humiliation and ultimate regeneration reveal in small the fortunes of the Trojans in large. The psychological understanding and symbolic patterning show Vergil at his best. This book and this episode are important influences upon the imagery, structure, and theme of Milton's drama, *Samson Agonistes* (1671).

Book VI, with Aeneas' descent into the underworld guided by the Sibyl, is the greatest of the books of the poem in terms of vision and poignancy. The obstacles and dangers which Aeneas avoids in the underworld are another version of the hurdles he has had to clear throughout his career presented in the first five books. Among the memorable scenes are Palinurus with his appeal for a proper burial, and Dido, marble cold in her scorn of Aeneas' exculpatory explanation, an episode described by T. S. Eliot as the most "civilized" in Western literature. Aeneas finally reaches that part of the underworld called the Land of Joy where his father Anchises provides a vision of the destiny of his descendants, that is, a vision of the Roman future, a future already history to Vergil's contemporary audience. Of all the Roman heroes the young Marcellus, son to Octavia and nephew to Augustus, is the last, and his tragic early death foretold in the poem and experienced only recently by his readers led to his mother's swooning when Vergil read aloud the passage to her.

The sixth book brings an end to the "Odyssean" part of the *Aeneid*; Aeneas' wanderings are at an end. The last six books comprise the "Iliadic" *Aeneid*, concerned primarily with battles and the preparation for battle. As Vergil's nature was not very martial, his success in the last part of the work seems less memorable, although his profound insight into human character and into the inescapably tragic nature of existence has allowed him to create two unforgettable characters only less memorable than Dido herself. These are Turnus, the young king of the Rutulians who plays the role of the vanquished Hector to that of the avenging Achilles of Aeneas, and Mezentius, the savage tyrant, grieving at the loss of his son, indomitable in defeat. That Vergil's three most memorable characters should all suffer loss and defeat is not without significance in any analysis of the poet's sensibility and humanity.

Book VII tells of Aeneas' landing in Latium, of his dealings with King Latinus, who obeys an oracle and offers Aeneas the hand of his daughter Lavinia. By the intervention of the ever hostile Juno, however, war is created between the Trojans and the Latins. Latinus does not oppose Aeneas but Turnus does, claiming Lavinia for himself.

Book VIII has Aeneas acquire allies in the form of Evander and his son Pallas, their troops, and the Etruscan troops and their leader Tarchon. Most celebrated is the description of the shield which Vulcan forges for Aeneas. On it are depicted scenes from a Roman history, the very beginning of which Aeneas is fighting to create. At the center of the shield is depicted the Battle of Actium and the consequent triumph of Augustus.

Book IX presents the siege of the Trojan camp nearly successful in the absence of Aeneas and costing the lives of the two young men Nisus and Euryalus, who perish through the rashness of Euryalus and the profound loyalty of Nisus. Vergil stops his narrative at their deaths to expostulate on their happy fate of dying together and to argue for their immortality through his poetry. The intensity of this celebration of male bonding should not obscure the artistry with which Vergil has prepared this episode, for during the funeral games of Book V Nisus is an apparent winner in the footrace who unexpectedly slips and in that slip saves victory for Euryalus by interfering with his rival Salius. His apparent triumph in Book IX should be compared with his sacrificial return to help his less able friend.

In Book X the Trojan siege is relived, and in a great battle Pallas is killed, as are Lausus and Mezentius, son and father. The death of Mezentius is described in a particularly powerful manner, and the despoiling of Pallas by Turnus proves, like that of the Rutulians by Euryalus, to be the cause of the death of the conqueror.

Book XI provides a temporary truce and the suggestion of single combat between Aeneas and Turnus. Turnus wishes to continue the war, but in the fight loses his most valuable ally Camilla, a warrior-maiden slain by a javelin while watching another whose resplendent armor she fancies. Like Euryalus before her and Turnus after her, she dies partly through her desire for spoil.

Book XII brings Turnus and Aeneas into single combat for the hand of Lavinia and the possession of the city of Latium. Aeneas defeats Turnus, who asks for mercy. Aeneas begins to grant Turnus his request but sees the spoils of Pallas worn by Turnus and in a fit of rage kills the Rutulian king. On this note the epic ends and in its oddly un-Vergilian close provides further argument that the poet had left his work in need of some revision or addition.

The traditional Homeric devices of epic construction appear throughout the poem: the invocation to the muse, the beginning of the poem *in medias res*, the use of flashbacks, repetition by epithets and formulas, the catalogues, and the epic similes. All of these devices contribute to a written work which, while lacking the power of its Homeric, oral predecessors, surpasses them in its psychological insights and structural subtleties. We perhaps no longer share Vergil's conception of the Roman imperium, of the moral supremacy of Stoicism, or even of the nature of the hero, but the broad drama of personal desire and political obligation, of the tension between the individual and the state, remains current. Even if it were the case that a totally apolitical reader should come to the poem, he would find there the essential sadness of things expressed in language as close to perfect as language can be.

Bibliography

Camps, William Anthony. *An Introduction to Vergil's* Aeneid.
Dudley, D. R., ed. *Virgil* in *Studies in Latin Literature and Its Influence* series.

Otis, Brooks. *Virgil: A Study in Civilized Poetry.*
Poschl, Viktor. *The Art of Virgil: Image and Symbol in the* Aeneid.
Wilkinson, L. P. *The Georgics of Virgil: A Critical Survey.*

Rosemary Barton Tobin

KURT VONNEGUT, JR.

Born: Indianapolis, Indiana; November 11, 1922

Principal short fiction
Canary in a Cat House, 1961; *Welcome to the Monkey House*, 1968 (Most of the stories in the earlier collection are reprinted here).

Other literary forms
Kurt Vonnegut, Jr., has published fourteen volumes including plays, essays, short stories, and the nine novels on which his reputation is principally based.

Influence
The popular success of Vonnegut's writing has always exceeded critical recognition of his work. He has speculated on the reasons for his special popularity among young people: "Maybe it's because I deal with sophomoric questions that full adults regard as settled. I talk about what is God like, what could He want, is there a heaven, and, if there is, what could it be like?" With his work labeled as science fiction and published in paperback editions and popular magazines such as *Ladies' Home Journal* and *Saturday Evening Post*, critical attention was delayed. Since the early 1970's, however, his work has steadily received serious critical commentary.

Story characteristics
Vonnegut's stories range between the sentimental and the caustic; between satiric visions of some grotesque society of the future, which is nevertheless an extension of our own, and portrayals of life in present-day society that reassert the stability of middle-class values.

Biography
Although not specifically an autobiographical writer, Kurt Vonnegut, Jr., has frequently drawn on facts and incidents of his own life in his writing. The youngest in a family of three children, Vonnegut was born and reared in Indianapolis, Indiana. While serving in the army as an infantry scout during World War II, he was taken prisoner of war by the Germans and interned in Dresden, Germany, at the time of the 1945 Allied fire-bombing of the city that cost 135,000 lives. He himself survived only through the ironic circumstance of being quartered in an underground meat locker. Although the destruction of Dresden became a recurring motif in Vonnegut's work, not until twenty-three years later could he bring himself to write the novel of his war experiences, *Slaughterhouse-Five* (1969). After the war, Vonnegut worked in

public relations for General Electric in Schenectady, New York (called "Ilium" in his fiction), before leaving in 1950 to give full time to his writing. In 1945 he married Jane Marie Cox, settling on Cape Cod, where they reared their own three children and the three children of Vonnegut's deceased sister, Alice.

Analysis

Best-known for his novels, Kurt Vonnegut has acknowledged the ancillary interest of short stories for him. In the Preface to his collection of short stories, *Welcome to the Monkey House*, he describes the stories as "work I sold in order to finance the writing of the novels. Here one finds the fruits of Free Enterprise." Vonnegut's blunt comment, however, does not imply that the stories can be dismissed out of hand. The themes of the stories are the themes and concerns of all his work. Again in the Preface to *Welcome to the Monkey House*, Vonnegut describes those concerns in a characteristically tough style. He recalls a letter his brother sent him shortly after bringing his firstborn home from the hospital: "Here I am," that letter began, "cleaning the shit off of practically everything." Of his sister, Vonnegut tells us that she died of cancer: "her dying words were 'No pain.' Those are good dying words. . . . I realize now that the two main themes of my novels were stated by my siblings: 'Here I am cleaning the shit off of practically everything' and 'No pain.' " These terms apply equally well to the themes of Vonnegut's short stories. His muckraking is frequently social satire; his concern is with the alleviation of human suffering.

Vonnegut's short stories generally fall into two broad categories: those that are science fiction, and those that are not. The science fiction characteristically pictures a future society controlled by government and technology, whose norms have made human life grotesque. The protagonist is often an outlaw who has found such norms or conventions intolerable.

In contrast, Vonnegut's stories that are not science fiction regularly affirm social norms. Ordinary life in these stories is simply not threatened by large-scale social evil. Some of these stories indeed depict the victims of society— refugees, displaced persons, juvenile delinquents—but primarily they show such people's efforts to recover or establish conventional lives. It is within the context of conventional life that Vonnegut's protagonists can achieve those qualities that in his view give a person stability and a sense of worth. These are the qualities of modesty, considerateness (which he often calls kindness), humor, order, and pride in one's work. They are values interfered with, in the science-fiction stories, by governmental and technological controls.

Vonnegut has resented any dismissal of his work merely because it is science fiction, a kind of writing he describes as incorporating "technology in the human equation." In the novel, *God Bless You, Mr. Rosewater* (1971), Eliot Rosewater speaks for Vonnegut when he delivers an impassioned, drunken, and impromptu defense of the genre before a convention of science-fiction writers:

> I love you sons of bitches. . . . You're all I read any more. . . . You're the only ones with guts enough to *really* care about the future, who *really* notice what machines do to us, what wars do to us, what cities do to us, what big, simple ideas do to us, what tremendous misunderstandings, mistakes, accidents and catastrophes do to us.

In Eliot Rosewater's opinion, society's "greatest prophet" is an obscure writer of science fiction named Kilgore Trout, a recurring character in Vonnegut's fiction. His masterpiece, the work for which he will be revered in the far future, is a book entitled *2BRO2B* , a rephrasing of Hamlet's famous question.

The story of *2BRO2B* in Vonnegut's précis corresponds closely to his own short story, "Welcome to the Monkey House." Vonnegut writes of his fictional character, "Trout's favorite formula was to describe a perfectly hideous society, not unlike his own, and then, toward the end, to suggest ways in which it could be improved." The approach describes Vonnegut's writing as well. *2BRO2B* predicates an America crippled by automation and overpopulation. Machines have taken over most jobs, leaving people idle and feeling "silly and pointless." The government's solution has been to encourage patriotic suicide. Ethical Suicide Parlors have been widely established, each identifiable by its purple roof and each located next to a Howard Johnson's restaurant (with its orange roof), where the prospective client is entitled to a free last meal.

This is also the world of "Welcome to the Monkey House." The story takes place on Cape Cod in an unspecified future time. Fourteen Kennedys, by now, have served as Presidents of the United States or of the world. There is a world government; in fact, in this world, Vonnegut writes, "practically everything was the Government." Most people look twenty-two years old, thanks to the development of anti-aging shots. The population of the world numbers seventeen billion people. For Vonnegut, the world's dilemmma is the result of advanced technology combined with backward human attitudes. Suicide is voluntary, but everyone, under law, must use "ethical" birth control pills that, in fact, control not birth but sexuality. Their effect is to make people numb below the waist, depriving them not of the ability to reproduce "which would have been unnatural and immoral," but merely of all pleasure in sex. "Thus did science and morals go hand in hand," Vonnegut ironically concludes.

The kind of morality that could produce these pills is exemplified in J. Edgar Nation, their inventor. Walking through the Grand Rapids Zoo with his eleven children one Easter, he had been so offended by the behavior of the animals that he promptly developed a pill "that would make monkeys in the springtime fit things for a Christian family to see." In the opinion of Billy, the Poet, a renegade in this society, throughout history those people most eager "to tell everybody exactly how God Almighty wants things here on Earth" have been unaccountably terrified of human sexuality.

Billy the Poet's special campaign is to deflower Hostesses in Ethical Suicide Parlors, who are all, as part of their qualifications for the job, "plump and rosy" virgins at least six feet tall. Their uniform is a purple body stocking "with nothing underneath" and black leather boots. In this world, only death is permitted to be seductive. Billy's *modus operandi* is to single out a Hostess and send her some bawdy doggerel, calculated to offend (and to excite) narrow sensibilities. Nancy McLuhan, his present target, is more intrigued than she will admit to herself. Billy kidnaps her and takes her to his current hideout, the old Kennedy compound at Hyannis Port, now "a museum of how life had been lived in more expansive times. The museum was closed." The original lawn is now green cement; the harbor is blue cement. The whole of the compound is covered by an enormous plastic geodesic dome through which light can filter. The only "light" in which an earlier graciousness can now be seen is colored by the world's pervasive vulgarity. The current world president, named "Ma" Kennedy, but not the "real thing," keeps a sign reading "Thimk!" on the wall of her office in the Taj Mahal.

Nancy's encounter with Billy is not the licentious orgy she expects, but an approximation of an old-fashioned wedding night. Billy explains to her that most people only gradually develop a full appreciation of their sexuality. Embarrassed and confused, she tries conscientiously to resist her comprehension of his motives. As he leaves, Billy offers Nancy another poem, this time the famous sonnet by Elizabeth Barrett Browning, beginning "How do I love thee? Let me count the ways." The implication is, of course, that sexuality is one dimension of human love sorely lacking in their world. Far from being obscene, that love pursues a larger "ideal Grace," in the words of the poem, wholly unavailable either to the vulgarity of "Ma" Kennedy or to the narrow-minded purity of J. Edgar Nation. Billy also leaves with Nancy a bottle of birth-control pills that will not hamper sexual enjoyment. On the label are printed the words, "WELCOME TO THE MONKEY HOUSE." If Browning's poem risks sentimentality, the story ends in a comic readjustment of the reader's sense of proportion. Sex need not be humorless; the reader need not view himself and the human condition with the chilling seriousness and inflated self-importance of J. Edgar Nation. The reader is left with the impression that Nancy McLuhan has begun her conversion. There is a measure of hope in this world where, as Billy assures her, the "movement is growing by leaps and bounds."

Governmental domination of private life is nearly total, however, in the world of "Harrison Bergeron," whose inhabitants are tortured and shackled as a matter of course, all in the name of equality. In the United States of 2081, equality of all persons has been mandated by the 211th, 212th, and

213th Amendments to the Constitution. People are not merely equal under the law, but "equal every which way." Those people of "abnormal" capacities must wear equalizing handicaps at all times. Hazel Bergeron is a person of average intelligence, which means that "she couldn't think about anything except in short bursts." Her huband, George, however, as a man of superior intelligence, has to wear a "mental handicap radio" in his ear which broadcasts at twenty-second intervals strident noises designed to break his concentration: burglar alarms, sirens, an automobile collision, or a twenty-gun salute. A strong man as well, George wears "forty-seven pounds of birdshot in a canvas bag" padlocked around his neck.

Neither George nor his wife is able to recall that their fourteen-year-old son, Harrison, has just been arrested. They are watching on televison a performance by ballerinas also weighted down with birdshot and masked to disguise their beauty. As a law-abiding couple, George and Hazel have only fleeting suspicions that the system is a bad one. If not for such handicaps, George says, "pretty soon we'd be right back to the dark ages again, with everybody competing against everybody else." When the television announcer cannot deliver a news bulletin because he—"like all announcers"—has a serious speech impediment, Hazel's response is a well-meaning platitude, "he tried. That's the big thing." A ballerina, disguising her "unfair" voice, reads the announcement for him: Harrison Bergeron, "a genius and an athlete," has escaped from jail.

Suddenly Harrison bursts into the television studio. A "walking junkyard," he wears tremendous earphones, thick glasses, three hundred pounds of scrap metal, a rubber ball on his nose, and black caps on his teeth. In this *reductio ad absurdum* of the ideal of equality, the technology is pointedly silly. "I am the Emperor!" Harrison cries, and tears off his handicaps, revealing a man who "would have awed Thor, the god of thunder." Harrison is rival to the gods. A ballerina joins him as his empress. Freed of her restraints, she is "blindingly beautiful." Whatever the reader may perceive as ultimate human beauty, Harrison and the ballerina are that. Together the two of them dance in "an explosion of joy and grace" equally as fantastic as the shackles they have thrown off. They leap thirty feet to kiss the ceiling, and hover midair to embrace each other, "neutralizing gravity with love and pure will." They have defied the laws of the land, the law of gravity, the laws of motion. They dance out the soaring aspiration of the human spirit, for a moment made triumphantly manifest.

The United States Handicapper General, ironically named Diana Moon Glampers, then breaks into the television studio and shoots them both. Her ruthless efficiency is in marked contrast to the bumbling capabilities of everyone else. The reader is suddenly aware that the idea of equality has been made an instrument of social control. Clearly some are allowed to be more equal than others. In their home, Harrison's parents are incapable of either grief or joy. They resume their passive, acquiescent lives, having forgotten the entire scene almost as soon as they have witnessed it.

If the conventional life depicted in Vonnegut's nonscience fiction has not been made this grotesque by technology and government, it is, nevertheless, also humdrum and unaspiring. These limitations, however, are more than compensated for by the fact that ordinary people feel useful, not superfluous, and they are capable of sustaining love.

In "Go Back to Your Precious Wife and Son" the narrator's occupation is selling and installing "aluminum combination storm windows and screens" and occasionally a bathtub enclosure. He marks as "the zenith of my career" an order for a glass door for a movie star's bathtub specially fixed with a life-sized picture of the movie star's face on it. He is comically intent on installing the enclosure and on doing the job well, even as the star's household disintegrates around him. Yet if it is funny, the narrator's pride in his mundane work is also a basis for the stability in his life, a stability visibly lacking in the apparently glamorous life of Gloria Hilton, the movie star. Also installing two windows for her, he says about them, "The Fleetwood Trip-L-Trak is our first-line window, so there isn't anything quick or dirty about the way we put them up. . . . You can actually fill up a room equipped with Fleetwoods with water, fill it clear up to the ceiling, and it won't leak—not through the windows, anyway."

While the narrator is at work in the bathroom, Gloria Hilton is engaged in dismissing her fifth husband. She speaks to him, as she always speaks, in a series of fatuous clichés. She tells him now, "you don't know the meaning of love," as she had earlier seduced him away from his family with the words, "Dare to be happy, my poor darling! Oh, darling, we were *made* for each other!" She had then promptly announced to the press that the two of them were moving to New Hampshire "to find ourselves." In the narrator's (and the reader's) only glimpse of Gloria Hilton, she is without makeup ("she hadn't even bothered to draw on eyebrows") and dressed in a bathrobe. He decides, "that woman wasn't any prettier than a used studio couch." Her actual commonplaceness and utter self-absorption are patent.

Her hapless fifth husband is a writer, George Murra, of whom she had expected no less than "the most beautiful scenario anybody in the history of literature has ever written for me." In the constant publicity and tempestuousness of their lives together, however, he has been unable to work at all. He had been lured by a hollow glamour, and she by the possibility of greater self-glorification. The superficiality of their marriage is revealed in his references to her as "Miss Hilton," and her contemptuous parting words, "Go on back to your precious wife and your precious son."

In a long drinking session together after Gloria Hilton leaves, Murra explains to the narrator his earlier dreams of breaking free from the petty, marital squabbles, the financial worries, the drab responsibility and sameness of conventional life. The narrator momentarily and drunkenly succumbs to the appeal of the glamorous life; when he staggers home he immediately offends his wife. Murra is now repentant and nearly desperate for the forgiveness of his son, living at a nearby prep school. When the boy arrives to visit his father, it is apparent that the hurt and bitterness of his father's desertion have made him rigid with intolerant rectitude. The situation looks hopeless until the narrator (back to finish his job) suggests to Murra that he topple the boy from his pedestal with a kick in the pants. The gambit works, the family is reconciled, and the narrator returns home, having agreed to exchange bathtub doors with Murra. He finds his own wife gone and his own son stuffily self-righteous; but his wife returns, her equanimity restored. The new bathtub enclosure with Gloria Hilton's face on it amuses her. She is exactly Gloria Hilton's height; when she showers, the movie star's face on the door forms a "mask" for her. Gloria Hilton's glamour, of course, is all mask and pose; but his wife's good humor is genuine. The ordinary lives of the narrator and his wife have provided them with exactly what Gloria Hilton lacks and what George Murra and his son need to recover: the saving grace of humor, tolerance, and a sense of proportion.

Despite the fact that most of Vonnegut's short stories are not science fiction and similarly applaud conventional life, the happy triumph of kindness and work in this story seems contrary to the thrust of his novels. What he values remains the same, but the prospect of realizing those values becomes more desperate as the vision of normalcy recedes. The crises of the planet are too extreme and the capabilities of technology too great for Vonnegut to imagine a benign society in the future that could foster those values.

Vonnegut's novels are often described as "black humor," wholly unlike the generous good humor of "Go Back to Your Precious Wife and Son." This is another label that annoys the author ("just a convenient tag for reviewers"), but his description of black humor recalls his own lonely rebels whose cause is seriously overmatched by the monolithic enemy: "Black humorists' holy wanderers find nothing but junk and lies and idiocy wherever they go." Vonnegut has said that the writer functions like the canaries coal miners took with them into the mines "to detect gas before men got sick." He must serve society as an early-warning system so that one can work to improve the human condition while one still may.

Major publications other than short fiction

NOVELS: *Player Piano*, 1952; *The Sirens of Titan*, 1959; *Mother Night*, 1961; *Cat's Cradle*, 1963; *God Bless You, Mr. Rosewater*, 1965; *Slaughterhouse-Five*, 1969; *Breakfast of Champions*, 1973; *Slapstick*, 1976; *Jailbird*, 1979.

PLAYS: *Happy Birthday, Wanda June*, 1971; *Between Time and Timbuktu, or Prometheus-5*, 1972.

NONFICTION: *Wampeters, Foma and Granfalloons (Opinions)*, 1974.

Bibliography
Giannone, Richard. *Vonnegut: A Preface to His Novels.*
Goldsmith, David H. *Kurt Vonnegut: Fantasist of Fire and Ice.*
Klinkowitz, Jerome and David L. Lawler, eds. *Vonnegut in America: An Introduction to the Life and Work of Kurt Vonnegut.*
Klinkowitz, Jerome and John Somer, eds. *The Vonnegut Statement.*
Lundquist, James. *Kurt Vonnegut.*
Schatt, Stanley. *Kurt Vonnegut, Jr.*

Martha Meek

JOHN WAIN

Born: Stoke-on-Trent, Staffordshire, England; March 14, 1925

Principal short fiction
Nuncle and Other Stories, 1960; *Death of the Hind Legs and Other Stories*, 1966; *The Life Guard*, 1971.

Other literary forms
John Wain built his reputation as a novelist in the 1950's, his first novel being *Hurry on Down* (1953), which was published in the United States as *Born in Captivity* in 1954, and his most recent being *The Pardoner's Tale* (1979). His further efforts include several volumes of poetry, criticism, and literary biography. He has also written an autobiography and edited anthologies of essays, poetry, and fiction.

Influence
Wain has influenced contemporary letters most significantly as one of England's "Angry Young Men" of the 1950's. His reputation as a debunker of the rigidity of English society and an apologist for the alienated young man has persisted. His early achievements tend to overshadow his later work in the public eye, even though he has produced several volumes of poetry and criticism and especially astute biographies of Arnold Bennett and Samuel Johnson.

Story characteristics
Wain's stories characteristically examine the small conflicts of people in an attempt to reveal larger implications. Places such as the middle-class household, the farm, and the unfashionable resort town serve as settings; first-person narrative is the predominant voice in the stories. The style is direct and unadorned and gains its greatest energy from dialogue and from the thoughts of the characters through whose point of view the stories are told. There is usually a central and rather blatant irony stemming from the disparity between how a character regards himself and how everyone else sees him. Wain often uses children, or characters similarly limited by what is expected of them, in order to present the frustrations which people confront on a daily basis. His short fiction usually concludes with pointed irony and a statement of the theme of confinement, presenting the protagonist as a victim of a limiting world.

Biography
The son of a dentist, John Wain earned his Bachelor of Arts degree at

Oxford in 1946 and remained for the next three years as a Fereday Fellow. He also took a position as lecturer in English literature at the University of Reading, England, from 1947 to 1955, quitting the classroom to become a full-time writer in 1955. Although he objected to being classified as one of the "Angry Young Men," the label stuck. Because Wain, Kingsley Amis, and John Osborne, all near thirty years old, were writing social protest and caustic humor, they were inevitably—if artificially—grouped by critics. Despite their individual differences, they did have the collective effect of sharpening England's social sensibility and invigorating her literature.

Analysis

Typically, John Wain's stories concern the internal conflict of a viewpoint character, who is often the first-person narrator. The narrator usually is not very perceptive, whether for lack of intelligence or maturity. A frequent effect of Wain's stories is that a conflict is well developed, human narrowness is scourged with satire, and a thematic irony is made unmistakably clear. Two stories from Wain's first collection, *Nuncle and Other Stories*, provide insight into his early short fiction. Both "Master Richard" and "A Message from the Pig-Man" are dominated by the perceptions of their child-protagonists. Richard, a five-year-old prodigy, is the narrator of his story. It develops by means of the diary convention, with Richard recording his observations secretly in a notebook. The boy gauges his maturity of mind at roughly thirty-five because the conversation of adults is easily comprehensible. Such a voice puts considerable strain on the narrative credibility of the story.

Richard reads, writes, and types with the facility of an adult. Wain makes a few concessions to the age of his narrator: he faces pain and cries like any other child and throws china cups to get attention. At the other extreme, the boy has a sense of perspective that belies that of the most precocious child. He carries out a long conditioning process to prepare his parents gradually for the realization that he has learned to read on his own. The very notion of patience over a long period of time is alien to the mind of even a very bright child. Further, Richard makes jokes and uses a vocabulary of slang that cannot be accounted for, since these abilities come almost entirely from experience. The greatest breach of credibility occurs when Richard speaks of the absurd and of insanity, constructs that only time and experience—not precocity—can bring to the consciousness. The problem is that no clear frame of reference is established for the reader. The narrator's situation, environment, and comments are based on the presumption of conventional reality as the norm of the story; however, Richard's unique perception forces the reader to view the story as somewhat surrealistic. The narrative exhibits both realism and surrealism but is committed consistently to neither, and the ambivalence is disconcerting.

Richard's crisis comes with the birth of a younger brother, whom he hates jealously. As a result of his contempt for his own cruelty to his brother and for his parents, who cannot understand him, he coolly decides to commit suicide. This conclusion, which has not been prepared for in the development of the story, is more convenient than satisfying.

Unlike "Master Richard," "A Message from the Pig-Man" is thoroughly believable. Eric, the viewpoint character, is also five years old, but the narrative is third-person, giving Wain more room to maneuver in disclosing the story. The thematic function of the boy's sensibility in the story is to comment on the need to confront fear. Eric finally faces the Pig-man, whom he assumes to be a grotesque creature rather than an old man simply collecting scraps for his pigs. He goes out with some scraps at his mother's insistence and tells himself, "It was the same as getting into icy cold water. If it was the end, if the Pig-man seized him by the hand and dragged him off to his hut, well, so much the worse."

Although his fear has a comic effect, it teaches the central lesson of the story. Once he has faced the Pig-man and found him harmless, he returns home to be put off when he asks his mother and his new stepfather why his father cannot live with them. Lacking Eric's courage to face up to problems, they hedge instead of answering. The viewpoint of the child generates humor and provides insight into the deeper weaknesses of the adults; still the concluding irony is too heavy.

The stories in *The Life Guard* are more sophisticated than the earlier ones. In the title story there is overdone irony in the death of Hopper, who actually drowns when he is supposed to be acting out the part to make Jimmy look necessary as life guard. Despite the unrestrained turn of plot, the story achieves substance and interest as the narrative lets the reader see Jimmy's desperation. As a dull boy, he is in his element when he gets the job of life guard at the beach. He fears the future and lacks ambition, but he has skill and confidence in the water. Eager to prove that he is useful on the calm shore, Jimmy decides to win attention by appearing to save Hopper's life. When he sees that Hopper really is in trouble, he is faced with exactly the kind of test he had been waiting for all summer; only he fails and Hopper dies. In Jimmy's moral and physical agony as he brings Hopper to land, there is considerable dramatic energy—almost enough to make the reader overlook the predictable conclusion.

Another story from the collection, "While the Sun Shines," shows considerable control and is one of Wain's best stories by far. The conflict here between the tractor driver, the unnamed first-person narrator, and Robert, the son of the absent farm owner, is well drawn. First-person narration is particularly appropriate because the external conflict of the story is secondary to what goes on in the narrator's mind. Another man was seriously injured when the tractor overturned as he tried to mow a dangerously steep hill. When Robert orders the narrator to try the same task, he refuses more out of spite than fear. Later, however, he takes on the challenge, not for Robert's sake, but for his own, and possibly to impress Robert's roving wife Yvonne. The appeal she holds for the narrator adds a subtle dimension to the story. Although he knows she is a woman who uses men, she appeals to him more than he will admit. Thus in retrospect there is a question as to whether the narrator mastered the hill entirely for himself, as he thinks, or for Yvonne as well. Because he professes contempt for her throughout the story, his yielding to her at the end is a surprise, but a very effective one. The man who tells the story is ironically unaware of his own motives. He concludes, "What could I do? Another time, I'd have gone straight back to Mary and the kids. But today I was the king, I'd won and it was a case of winner take all." He goes from the tractor to her bed, and there is some question as to who has really won the day. The strength of the piece lies in what Wain does not say outright.

There is no doubt that Wain's concern as a writer is well placed; the problems he chooses to present are significant. The weakness in his short stories is a lack of restraint. When he makes the necessary effort to say less explicitly and more implicitly, his stories gain the light touch and resonance that mark good writing.

Major publications other than short fiction

NOVELS: *Hurry on Down*, 1953; *Living in the Present*, 1955; *The Contenders*, 1958; *A Travelling Woman*, 1959; *Strike the Father Dead*, 1962; *The Young Visitors*, 1965; *The Smaller Sky*, 1967; *A Winter in the Hills*, 1970; *The Pardoner's Tale*, 1979.

POETRY: *Mixed Feelings*, 1951; *A Word Carved on a Sill*, 1956; *Weep Before God*, 1961; *Feng: A Poem*, 1975.

NONFICTION: *Preliminary Essays*, 1957; *Gerard Manley Hopkins: An Idiom of Desperation*, 1959; *Sprightly Running: Part of an Autobiography*, 1963; *Arnold Bennett*, 1967; *Samuel Johnson*, 1975.

Bibliography
Gindin, James. *Postwar British Fiction: New Attitudes and Accents*.
O'Conner, William Van. *The New University Wits and the End of Modernism*.

                                                                          James Curry Robison

ROBERT PENN WARREN

Born: Guthrie, Kentucky; April 24, 1905

Principal short fiction
The Circus in the Attic and Other Stories, 1947.

Other literary forms

Robert Penn Warren has published ten novels, twelve volumes of poetry, a play, a biography, a collection of critical essays, two historical essays, three influential textbooks, several children's books, two studies of race relations in America, and one volume of short fiction. He has won a host of distinguished awards, including three Pulitzer Prizes, two for poetry and one for fiction. Three of his novels have been filmed, and one of them, *All the King's Men* (1946), has been presented in operatic form.

Influence

Although Warren remains best known for *All the King's Men*, it is a moot question whether he is more gifted as a novelist or as a poet. In a career extending through six decades, he has displayed the versatility of a Renaissance man in significant contributions to almost every literary genre. His work has been translated worldwide and studied in hundreds of articles and a score of books. His short stories are widely anthologized, and prepublication excerpts from his novels continue to appear regularly.

Story characteristics

Most of Warren's short fiction depicts Southern rural life in the late nineteenth and early twentieth centuries. Set down in a rich, vigorous style, the stories delineate the flow of time, the influence of the past on the present, and the difficult necessity of self-knowledge.

Biography

Robert Penn Warren was graduated from Vanderbilt University (B. A., 1925), where he was associated with the Fugitive Group of poets, and did graduate work at the University of California (M. A., 1927), Yale University, and Oxford, and as a Rhodes Scholar (B. Litt., 1930). In 1930 he contributed an essay to the Agrarian symposium, *I'll Take My Stand*. Between 1935 and 1942 he was an editor of the *Southern Review* and was influential in the articulation and practice of the New Criticism. After an active career as a professor of English at a number of American colleges and universities, he retired from Yale in 1973. He and his second wife, the writer Eleanor Clark, herself a National Book Award winner, have two children.

Warren won the Pulitzer Prize for Fiction in 1947, the Pulitzer Prize for Poetry in 1958 and 1979, and the National Book Award in 1958. In 1944 to 1945 he was the second occupant of the Chair of Poetry at the Library of Congress. In 1952 he was elected to the American Philosophical Society; in 1959 to the American Academy of Arts and Letters; and in 1972 to the American Academy of Arts and Sciences. In 1967 he received the Bollingen Prize in Poetry, and in 1970 the National Medal for Literature and the Van Wyck Brooks Award. In 1974 he was chosen to deliver the third Annual Jefferson Lecture in the Humanities. In 1975 he received the Emerson-Thoreau Award of the American Academy of Arts and Sciences; the next year the Copernicus Award from the Academy of American Poets; and in 1977 the Harriet Munroe Prize for Poetry. He is a Chancellor of the Academy of American Poets.

Analysis

Many of Robert Penn Warren's stories feature an adult protagonist's introspective, guilty recollections of imperishable childhood events, of things done or left undone or simply witnessed with childish innocence. Thus "Blackberry Winter" (the literal reference is to an unseasonable, late spring cold snap) opens with a nine-year-old boy's unbroken, secure world, a small community permeated with the presence and warmth of protective loved ones. A vaguely sinister city-clothed stranger happens by and is given a job by the boy's mother, burying drowned chicks and poults. Later the boy watches with his father and neighboring farmers as a dead cow, the yoke still around her neck, bobs down a flooding creek past fields of ruined tobacco plants. Then the boy finds a somehow shocking heap of litter washed out from under the house of his father's black help. Dellie, who lives there, is sick in bed with "woman-mizry," and after calling him to her side, gives her son little Jebb a sudden, "awful" slap. Big Jebb predicts that the cold snap will go on and on and that everything and everyone will die, because the Lord is tired of sinful people.

Later on, when the boy's father explains that he cannot afford to hire any help now but offers the stranger fifty cents for a half day's work, the stranger curses the farm and leaves, followed by the curious boy, whom he also curses. "You don't stop following me and I cut yore throat, you little son-of-a-bitch." "But I did follow him," the narrator tells us, "all the years." At the end of the story all the sureties of the boy's world have been threatened, and in the epilogue we learn that the farm was soon lost, his parents died, and little Jebb has gone to prison. The narrator, we see, has learned that the essence of time is the passing away of things and people; he has been exposed to natural and moral evil.

"When the Light Gets Green" (the reference is to a peculiar, ominous shade of greenish light just before a storm) recalls "Blackberry Winter" in its setting, characterization, and theme, as well as in its retrospective point of view. The story's first two sentences display the technique: "My grandfather had a long white beard and sat under the cedar tree. The beard, as a matter of fact, was not very long and not very white, only gray, but when I was a child. . . ." Grandfather Barden had served as a Confederate cavalry captain in the Civil War; he had been a hero, but now he is old and thin and his blue jeans hang off his shrunken hips and backside. During a bad hail storm in the summer of 1914 which threatens his son-in-law's tobacco crop, the old man has a stroke and collapses, and later upstairs in his room waits to die— unloved, as he believes. His is the necessarily uncomprehending and hopeless fight that love and pride put up against time and change. His grandson, who visits him but cannot speak, suffers the guilt of having tried and failed both to feel and to communicate the impossible love the old man needed.

Mr. Barden, as we learn in the epilogue, lived until 1918, by which time other catastrophes had intervened—the farm sold, his son-in-law fighting in France, where he would soon be killed, his daughter working in a store. "I got the letter about my grandfather, who died of the flu," the story concludes, "but I thought about four years back, and it didn't matter much." The now adult narrator is puzzled and shamed by his failure and betrayal of his grandfather. In the dual perspective of the story Warren infuses a self-condemnatory ambivalence toward the old man which gives to the narrative the quality of expiation.

"Prime Leaf," Warren's first published story, derives from the Kentucky tobacco wars of the first decade of this century, in which tobacco farmers organized in an attempt to secure higher prices from the tobacco buyers. The focus of the story is upon contention within the Hardin family, most directly between Old Man Hardin and Big Thomas, his son, but also involving Thomas' wife and young son. Old Man Hardin leaves the farmers' association rather than support the use of force against those members who object to the association's price fixing. Big Thomas, whom he had originally convinced to join the association, refuses to resign immediately. Their reconciliation occurs only after Big Thomas wounds one of a party of barn-burning night riders raiding the Hardins' property. Big Thomas decides that he will wait at home for the sheriff, but his father urges him to ride into town to justice, and on the way Big Thomas is ambushed and killed. The opposition of father and son is a contest between idea and fact, between idealism and pragmatism. Old Man Hardin is a kind and morally upright man, but is also notably detached, remote, and unyielding. To his idealism is opposed his son's stubborn practicality, born of hard experience.

In delineating the conflict of the two men, with its tragic and ironic outcome, Warren does not espouse the beliefs of either, but focuses on the incompleteness of each. Old Man Hardin, embodying the rocklike integrity of the gentleman-farmer tradition, places an unwise reliance on what he still—despite much evidence to the contrary—takes to be the due processes of law. He cannot save his son and is in a way responsible for his death. Big Thomas, firing at the night riders until his rifle jams, before yielding to his father, does not resolve in acceptable fashion the problem of ends and means.

"The Circus in the Attic" is a long and crowded tale about the meaning— or apparent meaninglessness—of history. It features, appropriately enough, a would-be local historian, Bolton Lovehart, a frail, frustrated man of aristocratic antecedents, whose deepest desire is simply to be free and himself. The only child of a weak father and an almost cannibalistically possessive mother, Bolton as a boy makes several doomed gestures of resistance. To his mother's subsequent horror, he participates in a riverbank baptismal ceremony; later he runs off with a carnival but is immediately retrieved. During his first year at college his now widowed mother has a heart attack; such at least is her story, although she will not allow a specialist to examine her and treats her son's suggestion as treason. In any event, Bolton does not return to college and life closes in on him. He begins to see a young woman, but, realizing that Bolton's mother has the stronger hold, she deliberately seduces and then abandons him.

Establishing the context of local history back to the first white settlers, Warren provides a series of vivid and ironic vignettes, one of which distinguishes between the official, heroic, United Daughters of the Confederacy version of the Civil War battle of Bardsville and the half-comic, half-sordid truth of that unremarkable little affair. One of the heroes, Cash Perkins, full of liquor, climbed on the wrong horse, a particularly mean one, and was carried, helpless and roaring, directly into Yankee rifle range. The truth of the other memorialized hero, Seth Sykes, was somewhat more involved. He cared nothing for Secession, said so publicly, and lost a stomp-and-gouge fight over it. Then he said he hoped the Yankees would come, which they soon did, to take his corn, for which they offered him a note. He would have none of it; he had offered them meat but not his corn. He resisted and was killed. Of the official, patriotic versions of these two deaths, Warren writes, ". . . people always believe what truth they have to believe to go on being the way they are."

Bolton Lovehart's major resource and consolation is the pains-taking creation of a tiny circus—complete with animals and clowns and trapeze artists and a lion tamer—which he carves in the attic office where he is supposedly composing his study of local history. Upon his mother's death (finally, she does have a heart attack), it appears that he may at last enter into a life of his own. Shortly before World War II, Bolton marries, finds a hero in his braggart stepson, a posthumous Medal of Honor winner, and becomes for a time in his reflected energy and glory a current affairs expert and historian of sorts. His wife, however, who has been unfaithful to him, is killed in an automobile crash, his stepson is taken from him, and at last he returns to the creation of those small, inanimate, innocent, wooden objects whose world alone he cherishes, controls, and understands. Bolton Lovehart's is less a fully human life than a kind of pathetic facsimile. His study of Bardsville's past—and by extension, man's study of history—seems to assert that historical causation and "truth" are unknowable, that all men are equally unimportant, and that all of us are trapped in our own dark compulsions.

Warren is commonly identified as a Southern writer and associated with such other premier representatives of that area as William Faulkner and Eudora Welty. So long as "Southern" is not equated with "regionalist" in the limiting sense of that term, the description is accurate if not very illuminating. In another sense, however, as is apparent in his short fiction, Warren is a provincial, at least insofar as he has retained an attachment to and an aware- ness of generally humanistic values—moral, social, and theological—often regarded as a vital part of the region's heritage. Thus the frequently noticeable tension between stylistic understatement (apparent in passages quoted earlier) and thematic intensity characteristic of the stories seems a reflection of a pull between the old humanistic conception of human wholeness and a naturalistic belief in the fragmented and unintegrated nature of human experience.

Warren published his last short story, "The Circus in the Attic," in 1947; since then he has published as stories fourteen prepublication excerpts from his novels. Although in his nearly twenty years as a short-story writer Warren produced some fine work, both the author and a good many of his readers have found his achievement in short fiction less satisfying than that in other genres, notably poetry and the novel.

Explanations for his limited success in and satisfaction with short fiction might start with the fact that when he wrote many of the stories collected in *The Circus in the Attic and Other Stories,* he was a beginner, at least in fiction. It is also the case, as Warren has conceded, that he wrote for the quick buck, which did not come. Most of the stories did not represent major efforts; as Arthur Miller has said of his own short stories, they were what came easier. Finally, and most importantly, the form itself seems to have inhibited Warren's natural talents and inclinations.

In writing stories in the 1930's and 1940's, Warren appears to have backed into what was for him an unhappy compromise; stories were neither long enough nor short enough, offered neither the satisfying extensive scope of the novel nor the demanding intensive concision of the poem. Short stories might occasionally serve as sketches for novels ("Prime Leaf," discussed ear- lier, is the prototype of Warren's first published novel, *Night Rider,* 1939), but Warren found that the overlap between the short story and the poem was bad for him, that stories consumed material that would otherwise have become poems. Thus, as he has said, "Short stories are out for me."

Despite such demurrers, however, Warren's achievement in the short story is that of a major talent. Warren's ear never fails him; the voices from the past and of the present always ring true. No one writing today has a better ear—one could almost say recollection, if one did not know Warren's age— for the voices of late nineteenth and early twentieth century America. His eye is open to both the panorama and to the smallest evocative detail: from the trapper looking across the mountains to the West to the cracked and broken shoe of a tramp. He is intensely alive to the natural world. This is not to say simply that the natural backgrounds of the stories are vividly realized and accurately observed, although Warren is here the equal of Ernest Hemingway or Faulkner, but that such observation and realization provide the bases for those effects characteristic of his stories, for the evocation of atmosphere, for tonal modulation, and for symbolic representation.

Major publications other than short fiction

NOVELS: *Night Rider*, 1939; *At Heaven's Gate*, 1943; *All the King's Men*, 1946; *World Enough and Time*, 1950; *Band of Angels*, 1955; *The Cave*, 1959; *Wilderness*, 1961; *Flood*, 1964; *Meet Me in the Green Glen*, 1971; *A Place to Come To*, 1977.

POETRY: *Thirty-Six Poems*, 1935; *Eleven Poems on the Same Theme*, 1942; *Selected Poems, 1923-1943*, 1944; *Brother to Dragons: A Tale in Verse and Voices*, 1953; *Promises: Poems 1954-1956*, 1957; *You, Emperors, and Others: Poems 1957-1960*, 1960; *Selected Poems: New and Old 1923-1966*, 1966; *Incarnations: Poems 1966-1968*, 1968; *Audubon: A Vision*, 1969; *Or Else—: Poem/Poems 1968-1974*, 1974; *Selected Poems: 1923-1975*, 1976; *Now and Then: Poems 1976-1978*, 1978.

NONFICTION: *John Brown: The Making of a Martyr*, 1929; *Selected Essays*, 1958.

Bibliography

Bohner, Charles J. *Robert Penn Warren*.
Casper, Leonard. *Robert Penn Warren: The Dark and Bloody Ground*.
Guttenberg, Barnett. *Web of Being: The Novels of Robert Penn Warren*.
Huff, Mary Nance, ed. *Robert Penn Warren: A Bibliography*.
Longley, John Lewis, Jr., ed. *Robert Penn Warren: A Collection of Critical Essays*.
Strandberg, Victor H. *The Poetic Vision of Robert Penn Warren*.

Allen Shepherd

JEROME WEIDMAN

Born: New York, New York; April 4, 1913

Principal short fiction
The Horse That Could Whistle 'Dixie', 1939; *The Captain's Tiger*, 1947; *My Father Sits in the Dark*, 1961; *Nine Stories*, 1963; *The Death of Dickie Draper, & Nine Other Stories*, 1965.

Other literary forms
Jerome Weidman's thirty-two published works include plays, essays, travelogue, novels, and short stories. He is best known, perhaps, for his dramatic scripts. His play *Fiorello!* won a 1960 Pulitzer Prize, he has collaborated with George Abbot to produce *Tenderloin* (1961), and he dramatized his novel, *I Can Get It for You Wholesale* (1937), in 1962.

Influence
Known best for his unpleasant, sometimes brutal, portrayal of Jewish characters, Weidman has portrayed life in the world of drama, the New York rag-trade, among others, and has published in most of the major literary and popular magazines. His work has been translated into a number of languages, including Yiddish.

Story characteristics
Often humorous, sometimes bitterly so, Weidman's stories cover the range of Jewish experience in the New York City environment and outside of it to some extent. Weidman plays heavily on Jewish traditions and uses extremely accurate Jewish dialogue to good effect. His characters are often seen to be players in a game which must be won without knowing the rules, or as parts of a puzzle which must be put together without all the pieces.

Biography
Educated in stints at City College, New York, 1931-1933; Washington Square College, 1933-1934; and New York University Law School, 1934-1937, Jerome Weidman married Elizabeth Ann Payne and has three children. He was Co-winner of the Pulitzer Prize in drama and winner of the New York Drama Critics Circle Award and the Antoinette Perry Award, all for *Fiorello!* in 1960. He is a member of the Authors Guild and Dramatists Guild of Authors League of America and the Writers Guild of America West.

Analysis
While Jerome Weidman's novels, *I Can Get It for You Wholesale* and *What's*

in It for Me? (1938), are often neglected because of his brutally realistic treatment of unsavory Jewish characters, his short stories are frequently humorous, good-natured jabs at not only the Jewish community but also the world as a whole. His early stories, particularly those in *The Horse That Could Whistle 'Dixie'*, are remarkably well constructed and display the work of a writer who has a clear conception of what he portrays. His later work, often marred by hasty writing and commercialism, retains the same sense of humor, but often lapses into the maudlin and into fits of bathos.

The people of Weidman's stories are almost universally playing the game of life, and Weidman's stories reflect the gamesmanship of their situations. The puzzles to be pieced together and the games to be played by Weidman's characters are the puzzles and games we have all played at one time or another and, as such, Weidman's stories become something of a mirror of life. The mirror is faceted and reflects many pieces of a whole, however, and it is making those pieces reflect a steady image that is the challenge for the reader and for the characters alike.

It is the task, set for himself, of the youngster in "My Father Sits in the Dark" to "figure out" why his father, night after night, sits quietly alone in his darkened house. None of the pieces the young man sorts out seems to fit. The family is poor, but his father would not worry about money. He would not worry about the family's health, either. All of the conventional answers do not fit. It is not until the young man confronts his father in the dark kitchen of the house that the pieces seem to fit. His father is an immigrant. His home in Austria did not have electricity, which made him familiar with the dark, and so dark now provides for him a comfortable, nostalgic feeling. When the son asks his father why he sits in the dark, his father replies that it helps him think. When asked what he thinks about, he replies "nothing." The implication is that the old man does not have to have a more rational reason to sit in the dark and that the son, with his rationalized, fabricated understanding of the situation, has come to an incomplete understanding, but an understanding nevertheless. The fact that Weidman is playing the conflicts of modern society off against the idyllic old world is evident, but he does not belabor the point; he only shows us the exultant son going back to bed after he finally accepts his father's explanation for sitting in the dark. The outcome makes both happy, but there is no real resolution for the reader.

The same sort of puzzle appears in "Three-Two Pitch." Harry Powell is a bright young graduate on a three-month internship to the office of the best public relations man in New York. Powell, from Cleveland, is considered a "hick," but he takes his father's advice to ingratiate himself with the secretary of the office in order to succeed. His success is such that he is prepared to marry the secretary before the action begins. D. J., Powell's employer, has a yearly commitment to have lunch with his Cleveland high school teacher, Doc Hapfel, but this year, after making the arrangements, he gets "tied up" and tells Harry to meet Hapfel and begin without him. In the course of the lunch, during which Doc becomes drunker and drunker, a series of calls from D. J.'s office (from the secretary Powell is thinking of marrying) relate that D. J. will be later and later, and after every call, Doc seems to know, intuitively, what has been said—as if he were going through a familiar ritual. When Doc finally collapses and Powell is forced to cope with the situation, he begins to put the pieces together. The lunch happens every year. D. J. always sends his intern to lunch with Doc; D. J. is always tied up; he will always come later. Doc finally admits he has not seen D. J. for years, and when Powell discovers, fortuitously, that D. J. has not been in town all day, but is in Detroit, he realizes he has been duped and used to pacify the expectations of an old man.

Weidman stresses the conflict between "hick" Cleveland and sophisticated New York, but the principal theme is the puzzle which Powell must put together. The pieces are the secretary, D. J., Doc Hapfel, and Harry Powell himself. Before Harry can solve the puzzle, he must assimilate all of the pieces and come to an understanding of the situation and of himself. When he does solve the puzzle, the solution is devastating. He understands he has no place in New York, that he has been used, and that his self-esteem has blinded him to all of these realities. Only by returning to Cleveland and entering law school, as his father counseled him to do at the first of the story, can Powell provide a definitive, if somewhat unsatisfactory, solution to the whole puzzle.

"I Knew What I Was Doing," presents life as more of a game than a puzzle, but the same unsavory undertone attaches itself to the outcome. Throughout the story, Myra, a fashion model, plays one potential escort against another until she works herself up from a mere stock clerk to a wealthy clothing buyer. By portraying her game of enticement and entrapment, Weidman shows her as a cold, calculating woman who succeeds at the game because she knows the rules so well. The irony of her role is that her chumps, the men in her life, are so predictably within the rules of the game. One of them, however, nearly upsets the game plan when he falls in love with Myra and proposes marriage almost simultaneously with her conquest of the rich clothing buyer. She retains her composure, however, and tells this, the most ensnared chump, to "paste it [a marriage license] in your hat." Weidman's characters in this story are little more than pawns being played by the queen. Weidman is not particularly interested in character here, but rather in the progress of the match. The story is, perhaps, the epitome of Weidman's depiction of game-playing.

At the other end of the spectrum is "The Horse That Could Whistle 'Dixie'." Rather than flat, featureless characters, Weidman gives us a thoroughly reprehensible father playing the age-old game of growing up with his unwilling son. After watching many children ride the ponies at the zoo pony ride and sneering fatuously at those who only ride in the horse cart and not astride the beasts, the father drags his son to the ponies and forces him to ride. Despite the child's tearful entreaties and the sensible suggestions of the attendant, who can see the child is terrified, the father forces the child to ride not once, but four times. At the end, the child was a "whipped, silent mass of tear-stained quivering fright" who had finally satisfied his father's sense of propriety. Here the game has no winner, no ending, and no understanding. The son does not understand the father's motives, the father does not understand the son's reluctance, and the crowd watching the events does not want to understand. This is the most undesirable of Weidman's games, in which a person is forced to play by someone else's rules.

From the gentle "My Father Sits in the Dark," to the savage "The Horse That Could Whistle 'Dixie'," Weidman portrays, fabricates, and manipulates the games people play and the puzzles that they are. If the reader is to understand the games and puzzles, he must abandon credulity and prepare himself for the inconsistencies that the gamesmaster builds into the game.

Major publications other than short fiction

NOVELS: *I Can Get It for You Wholesale*, 1937; *What's In It for Me?*, 1938; *I'll Never Go There Anymore*, 1941; *The Lights Around the Shore*, 1943; *Too Early to Tell*, 1946; *The Price Is Right*, 1949; *The Hand of the Hunter*, 1951; *Give Me Your Love*, 1952; *The Third Angel*, 1953; *Your Daughter Iris*, 1955; *The Enemy Camp*, 1958; *Before You Go*, 1960; *The Sound of Bow Bells*, 1962; *Word of Mouth*, 1964; *Other People's Money*, 1967; *The Center of the Action*, 1969; *Fourth Street East: A Novel of the Way It Was*, 1971; *Last Respects*, 1972; *Tiffany Street*, 1974; *The Temple*, 1975.

PLAYS: *Fiorello!*, 1960; *Tenderloin*, 1961; *I Can Get It for You Wholesale*, 1962; *Asterisk! A Comedy of Terrors*, 1969; *Ivory Tower*, 1969 (with James Yaffe).

NONFICTION: *Letter of Credit*, 1940; *Traveler's Cheque*, 1954; *Back Talk*, 1963.

Clarence O. Johnson

EUDORA WELTY

Born: Jackson, Mississippi; April 13, 1909

Principal short fiction

A Curtain of Green, 1941; *The Wide Net and Other Stories*, 1943; *The Golden Apples*, 1949; *The Bride of Innisfallen and Other Stories*, 1955.

Other literary forms

Eudora Welty's published works include novels, short stories, literary criticism, a noted volume of photographs on the South, and a children's book. *The Ponder Heart* (1954), a novel, was adapted for the stage and produced on Broadway in 1956. A musical comedy version of the novel *The Robber Bridegroom* (1942) was presented in 1974.

Influence

Recognized as one of the premier writers of the modern South, Welty embodies in her works the flavor and perceptive insight into character and place distinctive of regionalism. Her writing manifests a concern for the preservation of the distinctive Southern character, enduring amidst change, and has been praised for its ability to combine folklore, dialect, humor, and a detailed sense of locale or setting into a unified image of the South as a symbol of the human drama itself. Welty's works have received wide circulation, with two novels, *The Optimist's Daughter* (1972) and *Losing Battles* (1970), reaching the best-seller list.

Story characteristics

The majority of Welty's stories are humorous studies of the foibles of human nature. If these comic stories do rise to the level of satire, the satire is a soft one, tinged with a gentle appreciation that all of humanity can be seen from the comic or absurdist perspective. The later stories often combine elements of fantasy with realism or blend characters and themes from mythology to present the panorama of human actions against a more universal background. With Flannery O'Connor, Carson McCullers, and Harry Crews, Welty is perceived at times by critics as sustaining the tradition of the Southern grotesque or the Southern Gothic in delineating the horror and violence underlying the apparent calm surface of existence, although critics are quick to emphasize that this is a less predominant theme in her works than is the emphasis upon the comic and absurd aspects of life.

Biography

Eudora Welty attended Mississippi State College for Women in Columbus, Mississippi, from 1925 to 1927 and received her B. A. from the University of Wisconsin in 1929. From 1930 to 1931, she attended the Columbia University School of Business studying advertising, but finding this not to her liking she returned to Jackson, Mississippi, and worked for a local radio station and as a society correspondent for the Memphis, Tennessee, *Commercial Appeal* from 1931 to 1933. She worked as a publicity agent for the state office of the Works Progress Administration (WPA) from 1933 to 1936, traveling throughout the eighty-two counties of Mississippi recording information on the state's heritage and progress. Photographs Welty took during this period were published in 1971 as *One Time, One Place*, a volume widely praised for its simple and honest portrayals of Southern life. Welty's literary awards and honors have been numerous and varied. In 1942, she won the O. Henry Memorial Contest Award for the story "The Wide Net," and in 1943 she won for "Livvie Is Back." She held Guggenheim Fellowships in 1942 and 1949 and in 1944 received an award from the American Academy of Arts and Letters. She was elected to the National Institute of Arts and Letters in 1952, was awarded the William Dean Howells Medal of the Academy of Arts and Letters for *The Ponder Heart* in 1955, and in 1958 received the Lucy Donnelley Fellowship Award from Bryn Mawr College. The Ingram Memorial Foundation Award in Literature was presented to Welty in 1960; from 1958 to 1961, she served as an Honorary Consultant to the Library of Congress. In 1973, her novel *The Optimist's Daughter* was awarded the Pulitzer Prize. Welty holds honorary doctorates from the University of Wisconsin, Western College for Women, and Smith College. She was William Allan Neilson Professor of Literature at Smith College in 1962.

Analysis

Eudora Welty's fiction is a rich brocade of the finest elements of the Southern literary tradition. She is admittedly a regionalist at heart, although her writings often attain the level of universal significance in detailing the struggles of the heart for a purposeful existence. Her favorite themes, she has indicated, are separateness and the human longing for love. In delineating her artistic vision, she draws from the Southern tradition its disparate elements of folklore, tall-tale humor, dialect, romanticism, emphasis upon a personal sense of heritage and place, and an awareness of the influence of the past upon the structure and destiny of individual lives.

Welty's stories are most often appreciated for their humor and for their ability, through comic exaggeration, to show what is most fundamental about humanity. An absurdist with a light touch, Welty sees in the fabric of man's actions the essential tendencies toward self-aggrandizement which characterize the comic and absurdist aspects of his existence. The comic stories remain lightheartedly humorous and engrossing because they only suggest but do not emphasize strongly the pathos of humanity's limitations, which is the essence of all finely wrought comedy.

"Why I Live at the P.O." is a short story which embodies all of Welty's skills as a comic writer and reveals how deeply the particular character of the South is reflected in the people and settings of her stories. Also present in the story is Welty's passion for the depiction of eccentric characters who map out their destinies in accord with their rigid natures and fixed habits of mind. The story is a first-person narrative monologue recounting, in the speaker's terms, why she has left her family and is living at the post office. The narrator is identified as Sister, a common name often given to the oldest daughter in small-town Southern families by all the members of the family. Sister details for the reader all of her conflicts with her family, saving particular wrath for her younger sister, Stella-Rondo, who has been an interference and a burden in Sister's life since her appearance in the family when Sister was a year old. As the story's action begins, Stella-Rondo, who has just separated from her husband, Mr. Whitaker, returns home to China Grove, Mississippi, with her two-year-old daughter, whom she claims is adopted. Sister lets the reader know that she was going with Mr. Whitaker first, before Stella-Rondo broke them up by saying unkind things about her, and that this type of behavior has been characteristic of Stella-Rondo since her childhood. "She's always had anything in the world she wanted," Sister states, "and then she'd throw it away."

As the story builds in comic intensity, Sister's resentment and jealousy of Stella-Rondo become readily apparent. Stella-Rondo's return from Illinois on the Fourth of July upsets Sister's security in the home with her mother, uncle, and grandfather. Sister's hostility toward Stella-Rondo, who has always been the favored, spoiled child in the family, precipitates a series of quarrels with the family in which Stella-Rondo always comes out with the advantage. Sister's comment to Stella-Rondo that her daughter, Shirley-T., would look exactly like Pappa-Daddy, the grandfather, if he would shave off his beard becomes twisted into Stella-Rondo's announcement to Pappa-Daddy that Sister thinks he should cut off his beard. The comment sends Pappa-Daddy into a rage at Sister, and he spends the whole day sulking. The next provoked quarrel involves Uncle Rondo, a "certified pharmacist" with a "one-track mind" who prepares, each Fourth of July, a prescription which makes him drunk. He dresses himself in Stella-Rondo's "flesh-colored kimono" from her trousseau and wears it about, appearing in the backyard with Pappa-Daddy as Pappa-Daddy swings slowly in the hammock and loops his beard. Stella-Rondo informs him at the supper table that Sister had said he looked like a fool in that pink kimono, a statement which, in fact, Stella-Rondo had made. Uncle Rondo becomes enraged, tears the kimono off, and stomps on it, and then the next morning throws a whole string of one-inch firecrackers into Sister's bedroom. Sister is "just terribly susceptible to noise of any kind," and she makes up her mind what to do, what with "the whole entire house on Stella-Rondo's side and turned against me." She decides to move to the China

Grove Post Office, of which she is the postmistress through Pappa-Daddy's connections in the town. She systematically goes through the house gathering up whatever items belong to her and moving them to the post office.

The final section of the story serves as a coda in which the major themes of the family's eccentricities, Sister's resentment of Stella-Rondo's favored position in the family, and Sister's growing paranoia are brought together in the image of Sister living in the small post office with her possessions arranged symmetrically but "cater-cornered," the way she liked them. She has been securely isolated in the P.O. for five days and nights and finds the situation "ideal." Keeping, above all, her "pride," she works her revenge against her family by shutting them off from her and separating herself from the outside world. Some of the people in the town have taken up for her and some have turned against her, but at least she knows "which is which."

The comedy of "Why I Live at the P.O." is achieved through a variety of effects which emphasize, in particular, the eccentricities of the leading family in China Grove and which build to reveal Sister's own twisted and resentful view of the family and the world. Sister knows that Stella-Rondo has turned them all against her, but she is perfectly content to lock herself into the ideal peace of the P.O. and have nothing to do with any of them as a matter of "pride." Because Sister never sees the irony and the self-defeating effects of her actions or of her own warped perspective on reality, she remains for the reader a comic character acting out the anticipated results of her own illogical logic.

When Welty's stories probe beneath the surface of comic absurdity to reveal the violence, injustice, and inhumanity which are aspects of human existence, her works generally are perceived as belonging to the Southern grotesque or the Southern Gothic tradition exemplified by such writers as O'Connor, McCullers, and Crews. Here the comic aspects of Welty's stories blend to reveal not extravagant humor but the pathos imbedded in man's actions when his responses toward life make him either a victim or a user.

In "Keela, the Outcast Indian Maiden," the pervasive theme of man's inhumanity to man is depicted against a humorous background which serves to bring the theme into startling clarity. Were it not for Steve's anguished moral conscience and the reader's sense of the unjust manipulation of Little Lee Roy, the story would seem almost comic. Part of Welty's skill in the story is that she does not blend humorous and tragic elements into a one-dimensional whole—much like the mixing of red and blue to get purple—but allows each domain to remain separate and comment, by contrast and implication, upon the other. The effect is similar to that of two concentric circles, one inside the other, in which the tragic elements and the humorous elements touch but do not combine.

The story is perceived on three levels by characters in the story, each level indicative of developed moral or ethical consciousness. The simplest level is that of Little Lee Roy, transformed by the greed of circus owners into "Keela, the Outcast Indian Maiden." Because he is simple-minded, Little Lee Roy does not see that he has been victimized or that there is anything more than a funny, grand joke involved in his performances. Max, a local restaurant owner who comes with Steve to find Little Lee Roy, vaguely perceives that some injustice has been committed, but he does not perceive its full implications or feel personally touched by the fact that evil exists in the world. His realization is largely impersonal and clouded. Steve, the young circus barker for the show, realizes keenly and painfully his own moral culpability in the events of Little Lee Roy's life and has come seeking expiation for the pervasive sense of guilt and shame he feels.

The story's action centers upon the fact that several years ago some men from a circus captured a little club-footed black man from Cane Springs, Mississippi, put him behind bars in a side show, painted and dressed him to look like an Indian maiden, and forced him to eat live chickens for the audience's entertainment. Eventually, a man in the audience questions the performance, has the circus owners arrested and sent to jail for their crimes, and has Little Lee Roy sent home. Since he was only the barker in the show and not one of the owners or one of the men who stole Little Lee Roy away, Steve does not go to jail with the others, but he does feel he is responsible for the crime in a moral sense, even if not in a legal sense. He begins a search to find Little Lee Roy and seek forgiveness for the great sense of guilt he feels. When he finally finds Little Lee Roy with Max's help, he finds that there is little he can do to expiate his sense of responsibility. He had thought that he would give Little Lee Roy "some money or somethin'," but now he has none to give. He tries to confess to Max, seeking someone to understand, but Max is incapable of comprehending fully the image of violence and horror that Steve perceives. Finally, Steve realizes that there is nothing to be done, and that he will always be a "hitch-hiker" "feelin' bad," who cannot "stay in one place for nothin' in the world." He will travel, lonely and isolated, for the rest of his life in search of a peace he will never find.

Little Lee Roy's position is the exact opposite of Steve's. He is not troubled or haunted by what has occurred in the past. His life is peaceful and serene in that he is surrounded by his family and is neither an outcast nor a wanderer. The guilt, horror, and shame of the injustice of Little Lee Roy's forced transformation into "Keela, the Outcast Indian Maiden," have fallen not upon the victim, but upon the victimizer.

The theme of "Keela, the Outcast Indian Maiden" recalls Nathaniel Hawthorne's view of the "unpardonable sin" and of the isolation that ensues when man has cut himself off from others through sins against humanity which spring from greed, pride, or any form of unrestrained desire. The echo of Hawthorne may or may not be conscious on Welty's part, but it is clear in a number of her later stories that she strove to bring depth, texture, and universality to her writings by consciously incorporating into her works literary allusions and allusions to mythology and legend. This shift in focus in the short stories occurs concomitantly with a movement toward a greater complexity of style in Welty's endeavor to plumb and elucidate the inner life of man, the interior world of the heart and of the soul which she has described as "endlessly new, mysterious, and alluring."

The volume of short stories entitled *The Golden Apples* is an example of the movement toward greater complexity in style and meaning apparent in the later works. Each of the stories in the collection was published separately and each stands on its own, but the stories, taken together as a whole, present a cycle of experience with regard to man's elusive search for the promises of beauty, fulfillment, and meaning which "the golden apples" of William Butler Yeats's poem, "The Song of the Wandering Aengus," symbolize.

"Shower of Gold," the first story of *The Golden Apples*, is a conscious reworking in a Southern setting of the myth of Zeus and Danae. King MacLain, the center of the story's action, finds a mythological counterpart in Zeus, famed for his amorous and sportive nature with women and his numerous conquests of maidens who attracted his attention. King MacLain's wife, Snowdie Hudson, is an albino, and her mythological analogue is Danae, impregnated by Zeus in a "shower of gold" while confined in a subterranean chamber by her father. Snowdie, too, has been sequestered from the world in a house built especially for her by her father, and when she comes to tell Mrs. Rainey, the story's narrator, that she is pregnant, Mrs. Rainey's comment is that "it was like a shower of something had struck her, like she'd been caught out in something bright."

The action of the story is initiated by Mrs. Rainey's chatty and somewhat gossipy recounting of King MacLain's staged disappearance a short time after his marriage to Snowdie. King simply "walked out of the house one day and left his hat on the banks of the Big Black River." Folks in the town knew the disappearance was a staged one because King had disappeared and reappeard months and years later with no explanation many times before. They were doubly convinced when the river was dragged and no body was found. Snowdie, however, grieves for King as if he had truly drowned, prompting Mrs. Rainey's observation that no one in the town liked to think that King had treated as sweet a girl as Snowdie in such a low fashion.

Speculation about why King left Snowdie focuses upon why he married her to begin with. Mrs. Rainey feels it is because King was willful and "marrying a girl with pink eyes" was his way of telling people "this is what I think of Morgana and MacLain Courthouse and all the way between." King is, in Mrs. Rainey's opinion, a rebel and a "scoundrel." Even though King is perceived by the townspeople as an outcast and an outsider, he possesses for the people of Morgana a certain mesmeric and animal charm; he is an intriguing figure to the community because he is an element of uncontrolled primitivism, a spirit of vitality and sensuality not yet stifled by the town's demands of conformity and allegiance to respectability. Morgana is a town which is self-contained, content, and sterile, living off gossip and a passion for knowing the details of every person's life. The town goes through its predictable rounds of day-to-day existence with perfunctory calm and dullness. Mrs. Rainey describes her husband, a typical Morgana resident, as a man who "ain't got a surprise in him, and proud of it." King MacLain's free-spirited style and his adamant refusal to be tied down to society's ways stand in direct contrast to the lack of vitality in modern existence which Morgana symbolizes.

King returns to Morgana after several years to reclaim Snowdie and his family of twin sons, Eugene and Randall. He appears on Halloween, at a time when Eugene and Randall, dressed in bizarre and colorful costumes, are "playing ghosts and boogers" and scaring people. As King comes to the front door, he is scared off by the boys and runs away from the town and into the woods. After he is gone, the boys go in to tell their mother what has occurred, and Snowdie knows instinctively from their descriptions of the man that it was King they had frightened off. She rushes outside to look for him, but he is gone. Snowdie asks Old Plez, an old black man passing by, if he has seen King, and out of kindness for Snowdie's feelings Old Plez says that he has not seen anybody. Snowdie senses that Old Plez is not telling her the truth, but she lets the matter go and faces alone her bitter disappointment of having to go through King's loss a second time. For many years, devotedly and lovingly, Snowdie has pursued her dream of loving King and sharing her life with him, but her image of King and their life together proves as elusive and as illusory as "the golden apples" described in Yeats's poem. Snowdie's dream brings not fulfillment and beauty but only pain and disillusionment.

In the final images of the story's close, Snowdie is presented as living with a deep sadness about her, isolating herself from the community and having only incidental contact with the townspeople of Morgana. Not only is there disillusionment associated with her defeat, but also a certain sense of injustice, for she alone loved King with constancy and purpose and yet in the end she is betrayed by the very one she hoped most to love. The story's import is redeemed from total pessimism by the fact that Snowdie did have King to love, if only for a little while, and thus she experienced a deeper sense of the primal vitality of life than any of the other people in Morgana could ever hope to attain. The experience, for Snowdie, is a mixed one of happiness and sorrow; the story seems to suggest that Welty might confirm William Faulkner's view that life is neither total victory nor total defeat, but, instead, the cold and chilling experience of "undefeat."

Major publications other than short fiction
NOVELS: *The Robber Bridegroom*, 1942; *Delta Wedding*, 1946; *The Ponder Heart*, 1954; *Losing Battles*, 1970; *The Optimist's Daughter*, 1972.

Bibliography
Appel, Alfred, Jr. *A Season of Dreams: The Fiction of Eudora Welty.*
Bryant, J. A., Jr. *Eudora Welty.*
Howard, Zelma Turner. *The Rhetoric of Eudora Welty's Short Stories.*
Isaacs, Neil D. *Eudora Welty.*
Manz-Kunz, Marie-Antoinette. *Eudora Welty: Aspects of Reality in Her Short Fiction.*
Vande Kieft, Ruth M. *Eudora Welty.*

Christina Murphy

GLENWAY WESCOTT

Born: Near Kewaskum, Wisconsin; April 11, 1901

Principal short fiction

Good-Bye Wisconsin, 1928.

Other literary forms

Glenway Wescott has been a versatile writer, publishing novels, nonfiction prose, drama, and poetry. Like his only short-story collection, *Good-Bye Wisconsin*, his first two novels—*The Apple of the Eye* (1924) and *The Grandmothers* (1927)—are set in his native state. Both novels are solid achievements and considerably better than his other novel, *Apartment in Athens* (1945), which is set in Athens during World War II and does not rise very far above propaganda. His work in other genres is also of uneven quality. His two novellas, *The Babe's Bed* (1930) and *The Pilgrim Hawk* (1940), are first-rate, and the former deserves to be much better known. *Images of Truth* (1962), a collection of essays about fiction and fiction writers, illuminates his other work and is often interesting, even though his concept of literature as primarily a truth-telling medium is limited. The rest of his nonfiction prose, his poetry, and his short play are of lesser quality.

Influence

In substantive terms, Wescott is important mainly for his limpid prose and for *The Pilgrim Hawk*, a masterly novella that explores the symbolic meanings of the bird named in its title; *The Babe's Bed*, a similar work, is undeservedly neglected. He also is of historic interest because in the early stages of his career he was a regionalist and, more specifically, he was one of the writers who in the early decades of this century wrote works of fiction attacking rural and small-town life in the Midwest.

Story characteristics

Wescott's stories, as the title of his collection, *Good-Bye Wisconsin*, indicates, attack his home state in order to demonstrate his reasons for leaving it. They are traditional stories, technically uninteresting except when he restrains his primary motive and allows free rein to his lambent prose style. That is, he is at his best when he is unfaithful to his chosen role as a truthteller.

Biography

Glenway Wescott grew up in rural Wisconsin, the scene of *The Apple of the Eye*, *The Grandmothers*, *Good-Bye Wisconsin*, and *The Babe's Bed*. He

entered the University of Chicago at the age of sixteen and stayed for only
a year and a half. Next he spent some time with Yvor Winters, a literary
critic, who, like Wescott, believed that literature's primary function is moral
enlightenment. The next phase in his life, working at *Poetry Magazine* in
Chicago when it was publishing the best contemporary poets, was also influential, but in a negative way. Wescott reacted against those poets' experi-
mentalism and emphasis on aesthetic values and remained true to Winters'
ideas. Wescott spent much of the 1920's in France, where he knew the major
American expatriate writers. Ernest Hemingway satirizes him as Robert Pren-
tiss in *The Sun Also Rises* (1926), and Gertrude Stein, referring to his di-
minishing rate of production, said that "he has a certain syrup but it does not
pour." Later he returned to the United States and published even less
frequently.

Analysis

One of the strengths of Glenway Wescott's short stories is his evocative
description of nature. He grew up in a beautiful region of Wisconsin and was
particularly struck by its marshes, which figure prominently in *The Apple of
the Eye*. This area also lies along the line marking the farthest extent of the
glaciers, which adds to the variety of the terrain, the flora, and the fauna.
Thus, these Wisconsin regions that contain both glaciated and unglaciated
land are first-rate material for writers, and they have been effectively used
not only by Wescott but also by Aldo Leopold in *Sand County Almanac* and
by John Muir in *The Story of My Boyhood and Youth* (1913). Of his native
landscape Wescott writes in *Good-Bye Wisconsin*: "the state with the beautiful
name—glaciers once having made of it their pasture—is an anthology, a
collection of all the kinds of landscape, perfect examples side by side." In
this book he lyrically describes details from nature; for example: "the grass
is like a sponge dipped in vinegar and perfume. Persian lilacs lay wreaths on
the girls' shoulders as they pass in the lanes." His sensitive response to this
scene and to the lives of the local people make the work he published during
the 1920's, including *Good-Bye Wisconsin*, his best, except for *The Pilgrim
Hawk*.

Another characteristic of his work, his assumption in it of the role of sage,
was occasionally evident in his early work and then gradually began to dominate his writing. Regarding this subject he remarked in an interview published
in *First Person* (edited by Frank Gado):

> I would hope that everything I wrote would be helpful. . . . I'm a real believer in truth-
> telling and truth-hearing. . . . One of the things that literature does is to sharpen one's
> sense of the truth, one's ear for the truth.

In "Fiction Writing in a Time of Troubles" he asserts that instruction is the most important function of the novelist, and in his essays on individual writers—those in *Images of Truth* and his essay on F. Scott Fitzgerald that is reprinted in *The Crack-Up* (1945)—he praises writers who perform that function. Sometimes the help he offers is minimal because his point is obscure. For example, in "The Runaways" he desribes a couple who burn down their farm and run off with a carnival. Wescott's evaluations of farm life and carnival life are not precise, so it is unclear whether their choice was wise. In "Adolescence" he makes the point that that phase of life is characterized by a propensity to masquerade, but his treatment of the sexual theme is marred because one of the characters goes to a party disguised as a girl and is the object of a boy's advances. That is, Wescott's point about sexuality is unclear, as is its relation to his theme of masquerades. He is more effective when he derives his truth from analysis of images, especially when he finds multiple meanings in them, as he does in the central images of *The Pilgrim Hawk* and *The Babe's Bed*. Late in his career, however, he concluded that literature is not an effective medium for communicating truth, and this belief is one reason that he has not published a novel after 1945.

At other times Wescott's meaning is clear, perhaps too clear. In the prefatory essay of *Good-Bye Wisconsin* he recounts a train trip he took from Milwaukee to Kewaskum, the last stage of a journey home from Europe. One of his purposes is to make discursively some of the criticism of Wisconsin that he makes in fictional form in the stories that follow. The most important part of this essay is an account of his meeting with two workers. He contrasts their dislike of his beret and book to the deference shown him by a European porter who, seeing his cape, had called him "Herr Poet." Wescott does not mention his artificial English accent, one of the qualities that Hemingway satirizes in *The Sun Also Rises*. Although this account is Wescott's and he is attempting self-justification, the workers are much more sympathetic than he is. In short, his emphasis on truth-telling sometimes makes his writing too didactic—at times it also makes his prose banal—and it may not be truth that he is telling.

"In the Thicket" is one of the best stories in *Good-Bye Wisconsin*. Its plot is simple: an escaped convict comes to an isolated home, sits on the porch for a while without realizing that a young girl, who is alone, is watching him, slashes the screen on the door, and then leaves. There is considerable meaning in this story. As in most of Wescott's effective fiction, the physical setting is important. As he shows in his description of the marsh in *The Apple of the Eye*, Wescott is fascinated by wild, lonely places. In this story the thicket at first adds to the suspense, making the convict seem even more menacing. As the story unfolds, the thicket appears to be an apt metaphor for the stage of life through which the young girl is passing and perhaps for human existence. The danger posed by the man is of course general because he is an escaped convict. It is also specific because the slash he makes in the screen door has sexual connotations, which Wescott works into the story unobtrusively and effectively, demonstrating his characteristic imagistic method at its best. He also uses some heavy-handed symbolism, however, to make his point: the convict is black and the girl is an innocent white; in fact, her name is Lily. In any case, this relation between man and woman is fraught with danger, as are most such relations in Wescott's fiction. This story is in a minor key, but, except for the black-white symbolism, it is deftly composed.

"The Whistling Swan" is more complex. It tells about an aspiring composer, Hubert, who has returned from Paris to Wisconsin, to his mother and to his fiancée. Consistent with Wescott's argument in the essay in *Good-Bye Wisconsin*, this story denigrates Wisconsin. For example, Hubert once says to himself that "he did not like this country because it was merely in the process of becoming what other countries were perfectly." Here is a complaint voiced by a series of American writers stretching back at least as far as Henry James. Moreover, either nature cannot mitigate the effects of this cultural wasteland or Hubert cannot recognize nature's value: "since he had been at home, he had not seen anything extraordinary or heard anything but song-sparrows; instead there were whistles and wheels, the harsh feverish purring of the dam, the saws' incessant scream." Wescott is nevertheless more even-handed than he is elsewhere in this book because Hubert also attacks Paris. The passages in which Hubert seems to be stating Wescott's attitudes are less effective than Wescott's treatment of the central image of the story. Hubert, despairing because he is unhappy both in Wisconsin and in France and because his patron has stopped giving him money, kills a swan. The swan, because of its beauty and grace, represents Hubert's artistic aspirations; to kill it is to renounce those aspirations. Difficult as his life has become, the killing of such an innocent, beautiful creature does not seem justified. The story offers no other alternatives and is a study of a hopeless situation and of an inevitably unsatisfactory response to it.

Wescott's *Good-Bye Wisconsin* does not deserve to be as little known as it is. Fittingly, Wallace Stegner wrote about it in *Re-discoveries*, a collection of essays on works thought to be unjustifiably neglected. Stegner's essay, however, was not enough to bring Wescott back into prominence. On the other hand, Wescott has not realized his potential. He made his mark on American literature at an amazingly young age, and during the 1920's he was thought by some to be in the class of Hemingway and Fitzgerald, but except for *The Pilgrim Hawk* his career went downhill inexorably after that decade.

Major publications other than short fiction
NOVELS: *The Apple of the Eye*, 1924; *The Grandmothers*, 1927; *The Babe's Bed*, 1930; *The Pilgrim Hawk*, 1940; *Apartment in Athens*, 1945.
POETRY: *The Bitterns*, 1920; *Natives of the Rock*, 1925.
NONFICTION: *Fear and Trembling*, 1932; *A Calendar of Saints for Unbeliev-*

ers, 1932; *Twelve Fables of Aesop*, 1954; *Images of Truth: Remembrances and Criticism*, 1962.

Bibliography
Johnson, Ira D. *Glenway Wescott: The Paradox of Voice.*
Rueckert, William H. *Glenway Wescott.*

John Stark

EDITH WHARTON

Born: New York, New York; January 24, 1862
Died: St. Brice sous Foret, France; August 11, 1937

Principal short fiction

The Greater Inclination, 1899; *Crucial Instances*, 1901; *The Descent of Man*, 1904; *The Hermit and the Wild Woman*, 1908; *Tales of Men and Ghosts*, 1910; *Xingu and Other Stories*, 1916; *Here and Beyond*, 1926; *Certain People*, 1930; *Human Nature*, 1933; *The World Over*, 1936; *Ghosts*, 1937.

Other literary forms

Edith Wharton's forty-seven published books include novels, novellas, short stories, poetry, travel books, criticism, works on landscaping and interior decoration, a translation, and an autobiography. Her novel *The Age of Innocence* (1920) was awarded the Pulitzer Prize in 1921. Several of her stories have been adapted for the stage, including *The Age of Innocence, Ethan Frome* (1911), *The House of Mirth* (1905), and *The Old Maid* (1924). The dramatization of *The Old Maid* was awarded the Pulitzer Prize for drama in 1935. Films based on Edith Wharton's works include *The House of Mirth, The Glimpses of the Moon*, and *The Old Maid.*

Influence

Wharton's fiction was influenced by a number of other writers, notably George Eliot, Henry James, Honoré de Balzac, and Paul Bourget. Her fifth published book and first full-length novel, *The Valley of Decision* (1902), was a moderate success; but it was her next book, the best-selling novel *The House of Mirth*, which firmly established her reputation. By the early 1920's, Edith Wharton was one of the most respected American writers of fiction. In 1921, *The Age of Innocence* was awarded the Pulitzer Prize; in 1922 Sinclair Lewis dedicated *Babbitt* to her; in 1923 she became the first woman to be awarded the honorary degree of Doctor of Letters by Yale University. By the late 1920's, she was told that magazine advertisers would pay top prices only if their commercials appeared on the same page as a Wharton or a John Galsworthy story. She wrote prolifically until her death in 1937; and throughout her career, her work remained critically and commercially successful. Several of her books were best-sellers, and *The Children* was the Book-of-the-Month Club selection for September, 1928. She was elected to the American Academy of Arts and Letters in 1930. Although Edith Wharton's work is still the subject of a great deal of scholarly study, it is no longer widely read by the general public.

Story characteristics

Wharton's stories are elegant, polished, highly structured tales centering around upper-class New York and European society. They deal primarily with conflicts between individual freedom and a rule-oriented society, and with the related issue of the tensions which arise between an individual's private and public selves. Many of Wharton's psychological tales are told allegorically in the form of ghost stories. These stories often make use of emblematic symbols and surprise endings to convey their themes.

Biography

Edith Newbold Jones was born into the highest level of society. Like most girls of her generation and social class, she was educated at home. At the age of twenty-three she married a wealthy young man, Edward Wharton; they had no children. Wharton divided her time between writing and her duties as a society hostess. Her husband, emotionally unstable, suffered several nervous breakdowns, and in 1913, they were divorced. Wharton spent a great deal of time in Europe; after 1912 she returned to America only once, to accept the honorary degree of Doctor of Letters from Yale University in 1923. During World War I, Wharton was very active in war work in France for which she was made a Chevalier of the Legion of Honor in 1916. Realizing that after her death her friends would suppress much of her real personality in their accounts of her life, and wanting the truth to be told, Wharton willed her private papers to Yale University, with instructions that they were not to be published until 1968. These papers revealed a totally unexpected side of Wharton's character: passionate, impulsive, and vulnerable. This new view of the author has had a marked effect on more recent interpretations of her work.

Analysis

Because many of Edith Wharton's characters and themes resemble those of Henry James, her work has sometimes been regarded as a derivative of his. Each of these authors wrote a number of stories regarding such themes as the fate of an individual who challenges the standards of his society, the effect of commercial success on an artist, the impact of European civilization on an American mentality, and the confrontation of a public personality with his own private self. Further, both James and Wharton used ghost stories to present, in allegorical terms, internal experiences which would be difficult to dramatize in a purely realistic way. Wharton knew James and admired him as a friend and as a writer, and some of her early short stories—those in *The Greater Inclination* and *Crucial Instances*, for example—do resemble James's work. As she matured, however, Wharton developed an artistic viewpoint and a style which were distinctly her own. Her approach to the themes which she shared with James was much more direct than his: she took a more sweeping view of the action of a story, and omitted the myriad details, qualifications, and explanations which characterize James's work.

It is not surprising that Wharton and James developed a number of parallel interests. Both writers moved in the same rather limited social circle, and were exposed to the same values and to the same types of people. Not all their perceptions, however, were identical since Wharton's viewpoint was influenced by the limitations she experienced as a woman. She was therefore especially sensitive to such subtle forms of victimization as the narrowness of a woman's horizons in her society, which not only denied women the opportunity to develop their full potential, but also burdened men with disproportionate responsibilities. This theme, which underlies some of her best novels—*The House of Mirth* is a good example—also appears in a number of her short stories, such as "The Rembrandt."

The narrator of "The Rembrandt" is a museum curator whose cousin, Eleanor Copt, frequently undertakes acts of charity toward the unfortunate. These acts of charity, however, often take the form of persuading someone else to bear the brunt of the inconvenience and expense. As "The Rembrandt" opens, Eleanor persuades her cousin to accompany her to a rented room occupied by an elderly lady, the once-wealthy Mrs. Fontage. This widowed lady, who has suffered a number of financial misfortunes, has been reduced from living in palatial homes to now living in a dingy room. Even this small room soon will be too expensive for her unless she can sell the one art treasure she still possesses: an unsigned Rembrandt. The supposed Rembrandt, purchased under highly romantic circumstances during the Fontages' honeymoon in Europe, turns out to be valueless. The curator, however, is moved by the dignity and grace with which Mrs. Fontage faces her situation, and he cannot bring himself to tell her that the painting is worthless. He values it at a thousand dollars, reasoning that he himself cannot be expected to raise that much money. When he realizes that his cousin and Mrs. Fontage expect him to purchase the painting on behalf of the museum, he temporizes.

Meanwhile, Eleanor interests an admirer of hers, Mr. Jefferson Rose, in the painting. Although he cannot really spare the money, Rose decides to buy the painting as an act of charity and as an investment. Even after the curator confesses his lie to Rose, the young man is determined to relieve Mrs. Fontage's misery. The curator, reasoning that it is better to defraud an institution than an individual, purchases the painting for the museum. The only museum official who might question his decision is abroad, and the curator stores the painting in the museum cellar and forgets it. When the official, Crozier, returns, he asks the curator whether he really considers the painting valuable. The curator confesses what he has done, and offers to buy the painting from the museum. Crozier then informs the curator that the members of the museum committee have already purchased the painting privately, and beg leave to present it to the curator in recognition of his kindness to Mrs. Fontage.

Despite its flaws in structure and its somewhat romantic view of the business world, "The Rembrandt" shows Wharton's concern with the relationship between helpless individuals and the society which produced them. Her portrait of Mrs. Fontage is especially revealing—she is a woman of dignity and breeding, whose pride and training sustain her in very difficult circumstances. That very breeding, however, cripples Mrs. Fontage because of the narrowness which accompanies it. She is entirely ignorant of the practical side of life, and, in the absence of a husband or some other head of the family, she is seriously handicapped in dealing with business matters. Furthermore, although she is intelligent and in good health, she is absolutely incapable of contributing to her own support. In this very early story, Wharton applauds the gentlemen who live up to the responsibility of caring for such women. Later, Wharton will censure the men and the women whose unthinking conformity to social stereotypes has deprived women like Mrs. Fontage of the ability to care for themselves and has placed a double burden on the men.

As Wharton matured, her interest in victimization moved from the external world of society to the internal world of the individual mind. She recognized the fact that adjustment to life sometimes entails a compromise with one's private self which constitutes a betrayal. One of her most striking portrayals of that theme is in "The Eyes." This tale employs the framework of a ghost story to dramatize an internal experience. The story's aging protagonist, Andrew Culwin, has never become part of life, or allowed an involvement with another human being to threaten his absolute egotism. One evening, as his friends amuse themselves by telling tales of psychic events they have witnessed, Culwin offers to tell a story of his own. He explains that as a young man he once flirted with his naïve young cousin Alice, who responded with a seriousness which alarmed him. He immediately announced a trip to Europe; but, moved by the grace with which she accepted her disappointment, Culwin proposed to her and was accepted. He went to bed that evening feeling his self-centered bachelorhood giving way to a sense of righteousness and peace. Culwin awakened in the middle of the night, however, and saw in front of him a hideous pair of eyes. The eyes, which were sunken and old, had pouches of shriveled flesh beneath them and red-lined lids above them, and one of the lids drooped more than the other. These eyes remained in the room all night, and in the morning Culwin fled, without explanation, to a friend's house. There he slept undisturbed and made plans to return to Alice a few days later. Thereupon the eyes returned, and Culwin fled to Europe. He realized that he did not really want to marry Alice, and he devoted himself to a self-centered enjoyment of Europe.

After two years, a handsome young man arrived in Rome with a letter of introduction to Culwin from Alice. This young man, Gilbert Noyes, had been sent abroad by his family to test himself as a writer. Culwin knew that Noyes's writing was worthless, but he temporized in order to keep the handsome youth with him. He also pitied Noyes because of the dull clerk's job which waited for him at home. Finally, Culwin told Noyes that his work had merit, intending to support the young man himself if necessary. That night, the eyes reappeared; and Culwin felt, along with his revulsion, a disquieting sense of identity with the eyes, as if he would some day come to understand all about them. After a month, Culwin cruelly dismissed Noyes, who went home to his clerkship; Culwin took to drink and turned up years later in Hong Kong, fat and unshaven. The eyes then disappeared, and never returned.

Culwin's listeners, of course, perceive what the reader perceives: the eyes which mock Culwin's rare attempts to transform his self-centered existence into a life of involvement with someone else are in fact his own eyes, looking at him from the future and mocking him with what he would become. The eyes also represent Culwin's lesser self, which would in time take over his entire personality. Even in his youth, this lesser self overshadows Culwin's more humane impulses with second thoughts of the effect these impulses are likely to have on his comfort and security. The story ends as Culwin, surprised by his friends' reaction to his story, catches sight of himself in a mirror, and realizes the truth.

Wharton's twin themes of social and self-victimization are joined most effectively in a later story which many readers consider her best: "After Holbein." The title refers to a series of woodcuts by Hans Holbein the Younger, entitled "The Dance of Death." They show the figure of death, represented by a skeleton, insinuating himself into the lives of various un-suspecting people. One of these engravings, entitled "Noblewoman," features a richly dressed man and woman following the figure of death.

The story begins with a description of an elderly gentleman, Anson Warley, who has been one of the most popular members of New York society for more than thirty years. In the first three pages of the story, the reader learns that Warley fought, long ago, a battle between his public image and his private self; and the private self lost. Warley gradually stopped staying at home to read or meditate and found less and less time to talk quietly with intellectual friends or scholars. He became a purely public figure, a frequenter of hot, noisy, crowded rooms. His intellect gave itself entirely to the production of drawing-room witticisms, many of them barbed with sarcasm. On the evening that the story takes place, Warley finds himself reminded of one of these sallies of his. Some years earlier, Warley, who had been dodging the persistent invitations of a pompous and rather boring society hostess, finally told his circle of friends that the next time he received a card saying "Mrs. Jasper requests the pleasure," he would reply, "Mr. Warley declines the boredom." The remark was appreciated at the time by the friends who heard it; but in his old age Warley finds himself hoping that Mrs. Jasper never suffered the pain of hearing about it.

At this point in the story, Wharton shifts the scene to a mansion on Fifth Avenue, where a senile old woman prepares herself for an imaginary dinner party. She wears a grotesque purple wig, and broad-toed orthopedic shoes under an ancient purple gown. She also insists on wearing her diamonds to what she believes will be another triumph of her skill as a hostess. This woman is the same Mrs. Jasper whom Warley has been avoiding for years. She is now in the care of an unsympathetic young nurse and three elderly servants. Periodically, the four employees go through the charade of preparing the house and Mrs. Jasper for the dinner parties which she imagines still take place there.

While Mrs. Jasper is being dressed for her illusory dinner party, Anson Warley is preparing to attend a real one. Despite his valet's protests concerning his health, Warley not only refuses to stay at home but also insists on walking up Fifth Avenue in the freezing winter night. Gradually he becomes confused and forgets his destination. Then he sees before him Mrs. Jasper's mansion, lighted for a dinner party, and in his confusion, he imagines that he is to dine there. He arrives just as Mrs. Jasper's footman is reading aloud the list of guests whom Mrs. Jasper thinks she has invited.

When dinner is announced, Warley and Mrs. Jasper walk arm in arm, at a stately processional gait, to the table. The footman has set the table with heavy blue and white servants' dishes, and he has stuffed newspapers instead of orchids into the priceless Rose Dubarry porcelain dishes. He serves a plain meal and inexpensive wine in the empty dining room. Lost in the illusion, however, Warley and Mrs. Jasper imagine that they are consuming a gourmet meal at a luxuriously appointed table in the presence of a crowd of glittering guests. They go through a ritual of gestures and conversation which does indeed resemble the *danse macabre* for which the story is named. Finally, Mrs. Jasper leaves the table exhausted and makes her way upstairs to her uncomprehending and chuckling nurse. Warley, equally exhausted and equally convinced that he has attended a brilliant dinner party, steps out into the night and drops dead.

"After Holbein" is a powerful story primarily because of the contrasts it establishes. In the foreground are the wasted lives of Warley and Mrs. Jasper, each of whom has long given up all hope of originality or self-realization for the sake of being part of a nameless, gilded mass. The unsympathetic nurse, who teases Mrs. Jasper into tears, acts not from cruelty but from her inability to comprehend, in her own hopeful youth, the tragedy of Mrs. Jasper's situation. This nurse is contrasted with Mrs. Jasper's elderly maid, Lavinia, who conceals her own failing health out of loyalty to her mistress, and who is moved to tears by Mrs. Jasper's plight. Even the essential horror of the story is intensified by the contrasting formality and restraint of its language and by the tight structuring which gives the plot the same momentum of inevitability as the movements of a formal dance.

Warley and Mrs. Jasper have been betrayed from within and from without. They have traded their private selves for public masks, and have spent their lives among others who have made the same bargain. Lavinia's recollections suggest to the reader that Mrs. Jasper subordinated her role as mother to her role as hostess; and her children, reared in that same world, have left her to the care of servants. Her friends are dead or bedridden, or they have forgotten her. She exists now, in a sense, as she has always existed: as a grotesque figure in a world of illusion.

Warley, too, has come to think of himself only in terms of his social reputation—he will not accept the reality of his age and infirmity. Thus, as he drags one leg during his icy walk along Fifth Avenue, he pictures a club smoking room in which one of his acquaintances will say, "Warley? Why, I saw him sprinting up Fifth Avenue the other night like a two-year-old; that night it was four or five below." Warley has convinced himself that whatever is said in club smoking rooms by men in good society is real. None of the acquaintances, however, to whom he has given his life is with him when he takes that final step; and it would not have mattered if anyone had been there. Warley is inevitably and irrevocably alone at last.

Wharton's eleven volumes of short stories, spanning thirty-nine years, record her growth in thought and in style. They offer the entertainment of seeing inside an exclusive social circle which was in many respects unique and which no longer exists as Wharton knew it. Some of Wharton's stories are trivial and some are repetitive; but her best stories depict, in the inhabitants of that exclusive social world, experiences and sensations which are universal.

Major publications other than short fiction

NOVELS: *The Touchstone*, 1900; *The Valley of Decision*, 1902; *Sanctuary*, 1903; *The House of Mirth*, 1905; *The Fruit of the Tree*, 1907; *Madame de Treymes*, 1907; *Ethan Frome*, 1911; *The Reef*, 1912; *The Custom of the Country*, 1913; *Summer*, 1917; *The Marne*, 1918; *The Age of Innocence*, 1920; *The Glimpses of the Moon*, 1922; *A Son at the Front*, 1923; *Old New York*, 1924; *The Mother's Recompense*, 1925; *Twilight Sleep*, 1927; *The Children*, 1928; *Hudson River Bracketed*, 1929; *The Gods Arrive*, 1932; *The Buccaneers*, 1938.

POETRY: *Artemis to Actaeon*, 1909; *Twelve Poems*, 1926.

NONFICTION: *A Backward Glance*, 1934.

Bibliography

Auchincloss, Louis. *Edith Wharton: A Woman in Her Time.*
Lewis, R. W. B. *Edith Wharton: A Biography.*
Lubbock, Percy. *Portrait of Edith Wharton.*
Nevius, Blake. *Edith Wharton: A Study of Her Fiction.*
Wolff, Cynthia Griffin. *A Feast of Words: The Triumph of Edith Wharton.*

Joan DelFattore

TENNESSEE WILLIAMS

Born: Columbus, Mississippi; March 26, 1911

Principal short fiction

One Arm and Other Stories, 1948; *Hard Candy: A Book of Stories*,1954; *The Knightly Quest: A Novella and Four Short Stories*, 1966; *Eight Mortal Ladies Possessed: A Book of Stories*, 1971.

Other literary forms

In addition to his three dozen collected and uncollected stories, Tennessee Williams has written two novels, a book of memoirs, a collection of essays, two volumes of poetry, numerous short plays, a screenplay, and more than twenty full-length dramas. Among the most important of his plays are *The Glass Menagerie* (1945), *A Streetcar Named Desire* (1947), *Cat on a Hot Tin Roof* (1955), and *The Night of the Iguana* (1962).

Influence

Since Williams is known primarily as a dramatist, his stories are perhaps of greatest interest to readers of his plays, although his stories have earned him at least a long footnote among the practitioners of Southern Gothic fiction. Even when the stories are not specifically treatments of plots and characters later adpated to the stage, they share common themes and attitudes, and the shifts in outlook and style parallel those in the plays. Originally appearing in such magazines as *Story*, *The New Yorker*, *Esquire*, *Playboy*, *Vogue*, and *Mademoiselle*, Williams' short fiction has been represented as well in *Best American Short Stories*.

Story characteristics

In type, Williams' stories range from the Gothic and Poesque tale to the barely disguised autobiographical reminiscence, from the highly symbolic allegory and parable in the manner of the poet Arthur Rimbaud to the bawdy Rabelaisian fabliau. In tone, they range from the elegiac to the boisterous and slightly satiric.

Biography

Descended on his mother's side from a Southern minister and on his father's from Tennessee politicians, Thomas Lanier (Tennessee) Williams moved with his family from Mississippi to St. Louis shortly after World War I. He attended the University of Missouri and Washington University, finally graduating from the University of Iowa. After odd jobs in the warehouse of a shoe factory, ushering at a movie house, and even a stint screenwriting in Hollywood, he turned full-time writer in the early 1940's, encouraged by grants from the Group Theatre and Rockefeller Foundation. Twice winner of the Pulitzer Prize for Drama, Williams is also a four-time recipient of the Drama Critics Circle Award for the Best Play of the Year.

Analysis

Although Tennessee Williams is commonly held to be without peer among America's—many would say the world's—living playwrights, he began his career writing short fiction, with a story entitled "The Vengeance of Nitocris" in *Weird Tales* in 1928. As late as 1944, when his first theatrical success was in rehearsal, George Jean Nathan reportedly observed that Williams "didn't know how to write drama, that he was really just a short story writer who didn't understand the theatre." Today, however, in proportion to the world-wide audience familiar with Williams' dramas, only a handful know more than a story or two, usually from among the ones later transformed into stage plays. Seven of Williams' full-length dramas, in fact, have their genesis in the fiction: *The Glass Menagerie* in "Portrait of a Girl in Glass"; *Summer and Smoke* (1948) in "The Yellow Bird"; *Cat on a Hot Tin Roof* in "Three Players of a Summer Game"; *The Night of the Iguana* and *Kingdom of Earth* (1968) in stories of the same names; *The Milk Train Doesn't Stop Here Anymore* (1964) in "Man Bring This Up Road"; and *Vieux Carré* (1978) in "The Angel in the Alcove" and "Grand."

The play *The Night of the Iguana* is sufficiently different from its progenitor to indicate how Williams rethinks his material in adapting it to another medium. Both works portray a spinsterish artist, Miss Jelkes; but while Hannah in the play has fought for and achieved inner peace, Edith's harsher name in the story belies her edginess, neurosis, and lack of "interior poise." Having channeled her own "morbid energy" into painting, she discerns in the contrasting "splash of scarlet on snow . . . a flag of her own unsettled components" warring within her. When a servant at the Costa Verde hotel tethers an iguana to the veranda, Edith recoils hysterically from such brutality against "one of God's creatures," taking its suffering as proof of a grotesque "universe . . . designed by the Marquis de Sade." This picture of cosmic indifference, even malevolence, occurs in a handful of Williams stories, most notably in "The Malediction," in which the lonely Lucio exists in a meaningless universe verging on the absurd, ruled by a God "Who felt that something was wrong but could not correct it, a man Who sensed the blundering sleep-walk of time and hostilities of chance" and "had been driven to drink." Edith finds God personified in a violent storm "like a giant bird lunging up and down on its terrestrial quarry, a bird with immense white wings and beak of godlike fury."

Her fellow guests at the hotel are two homosexual writers. Squeamish and yet attracted by the forbidden nature of their relationship, Edith insinuates herself into their company only to become the object of a desperate attack on her "demon of virginity" by the older of the two. Although she has earlier hinted that she always answers, with understanding, cries for help from a fellow sufferer, she ferociously fends off his pathetic advances, metaphorically associated with the predatory "bird of blind white fury." Afterwards, however, once the younger man has mercifully cut loose the iguana, Edith feels her own "rope of loneliness had also been severed," and—instead of drawing back in "revulsion" from "the spot of dampness" left on her belly by the older writer's semen—exclaims "Ah, life," evidently having reached through this epiphanic moment a new acceptance and integration of her sexuality. Yet, unlike Hannah, whose compassionate response to Shannon in the play is for him a saving grace and who can affirm, along with Williams, that "Nothing human disgusts me unless it's unkind, violent," Edith's inability to answer unselfishly the older man's need—the cardinal sin in Williams—may have permanently maimed him by destroying his self-respect.

Williams does not capitalize fully on his gift for writing dialogue in his stories, which are almost exclusively narration. For all its interest in light of the later play, the pace of "The Night of the Iguana" is curiously desultory and enervated, which might not have been true if the story had been written from Edith's point of view. Williams does indeed prove adept at handling first-person narration in several autobiographical tales, whose content seems hardly distinguishable at times from the sections of the *Memoirs* (1975). He can, however, become annoyingly self-conscious when, in authorial intrusions analogous to the nonrepresentational techniques that deliberately destroy the illusion of reality in his dramas, he breaks the narrative line in a dozen or so stories to interject comments about himself as writer manipulating his materials, sometimes apologizing for his awkwardness in handling the short-story form, or for playing too freely with chronology or radically shifting tone. At times these stories provide some notion of Williams' aesthetic theories and practice, as when, in "Thee Players of a Summer Game," for example, he discusses the method by which the artist orders experience by a process that distorts and "yet . . . may be closer than a literal history could be to the hidden truth of it." Or these "metafictional" asides might indicate his conception of character portrayal. On that point—while without qualms at employing clinical details when necessary—Williams insists, in "Hard Candy," on the need for "indirection" and restraint rather than "a head-on violence that would disgust and destroy" if he is to remain nonjudgmental and respect the "mystery" at the heart of character.

An almost identical comment occurs in "The Resemblance Between a Violin Case and a Coffin," part of a small group of *rites de passage* stories in the Williams canon. The story centers on a love triangle of sorts as the young narrator faces the destruction of the "magical intimacy" with his pianist sister as she enters adolescence—that "dangerous passage" between the "wild country of childhood" and the "uniform world of adults"—and turns her attentions towards a fellow-musician, Richard Miles. It is as if she has deserted the narrator and "carried a lamp into another room [he] could not enter." He resents the "radiant" Richard, but also feels a frightening prepubescent physical attraction for the older boy. Like many of Williams' adult neurotics whose libidinous desires rebel against their Puritan repressions, the narrator longs to touch Richard's skin, yet recoils in shame and guilt from the boy's offer of his hand as if it were somehow "impure." Seeing Richard play the violin, however, provides an epiphany as the narrator "learns the will of life to transcend the single body" and perceives the connection between eros and Thanatos. For the narrator equates the act of playing the phallic violin with "making love," and the violin case to "a little black coffin made for a child or doll." He mourns the loss of youth and innocence and the birth of the knowledge of sin and death.

Tom, the authorial voice in *The Glass Menagerie*, confesses to "a poet's weakness for symbols," and one of Williams' own hallmarks has always been an extensive use of visual stage symbolism—"the natural speech of drama." As he remarks in one of his essays, it can "say a thing more directly and simply and beautifully than it could be said in words"; he employs symbols extensively, however, in only a handful of stories, although he does rely heavily on figurative language. In the earlier stories the imagery is ordinarily controlled and striking, as, for example, in this line (reminiscent of Karl Shapiro's "cancer, simple as a flower, blooms") describing the doctor's tumor from "Three Players of a Summer Game": "An awful flower grew in his brain like a fierce geranium that shattered its pot." In the more recent tales, however, Williams' diction frequently becomes overwrought and demonstrates some lack of control, falling into what he criticizes elsewhere in the same essay as "a parade of images for the sake of images."

If the mood of "The Resemblance Between a Violin Case and a Coffin" is tender and elegiac, the tone of a much later *rites de passage* story, "Completed," is chilling, but no less haunting and memorable. Miss Rosemary McCord, a student at Mary, Help a Christian School, is a withdrawn debutante subjected by her unsympathetic mother to a pathetic and bizarre coming-out dance. The onset of menstruation has been late in coming for Rosemary, and when it finally does arrive, she is pitifully unprepared for it. Ironically, the fullness of physical development in Rosemary coincides with a death wish; her only "purpose in life is to complete it quick." Her one understanding relative, the reclusive Aunt Ella, deliberately retreats from the external world through morphine; the drug brings her comforting apparitions of the Virgin Mary and tears of peace. Rosemary goes to live with her, aware that she has been taken captive and yet willingly submissive, ready to be calmed through drugs and her own reassuring visions of the Virgin. Her life—apparently the latest of several variations on that of Williams' own sister—is over before it began. Perhaps it is, however, only in such a sheltered, illusory life that this fragile, sensitive girl can exist.

The other "passage" that threads through Williams' stories is that from life to death, obsessed as he is with what he terms "a truly awful sense of impermanence," with the debilitating effects of time on both physical beauty and one's creative powers, and the sheer tenacity necessary if one is to endure at least spiritually undefeated. In "Sabbatha and Solitude," the aging poetess (undoubtedly semi-autobiographical) finds that the process of composition is a trial not unlike the Crucifixion that results only in "a bunch of old repeats," while in the picaresque "Two on a Party," the blond and balding queen and hack screenwriter exists at the mercy of that "worst of all enemies . . . the fork-tailed, cloven-hoofed, pitchfork-bearing devil of Time."

"Completed" is one of Williams' few recent stories—"Happy August the Tenth" is another—that can stand alongside some of his earliest as a fully successful work. Just as there is a noticeable diminution in the power of his later dramas compared with the ones from *The Glass Menagerie* through *The Night of the Iguana*, so, too, each successive volume of short fiction has been less impressive than its predecessor. As Williams' vision of the universe has darkened and become more private, the once elegiac tone has acquired a certain stridency and sharp edge; and as Williams has developed a tough, self-protective shell of laughter as a defense against his detractors, some of the dark humor—what he once called the "jokes of the condemned"—is now directed towards the pathetic grotesques who increasingly people his works, whereas once there was only compassion.

Thus, two of the most representative stories, "One Arm" and "Desire and the Black Masseur," neither of which, significantly, has ever been dramatized, appeared in his first collection. Unquestionably the most macabre of all his tales is "Desire and the Black Masseur," which details the fantastic, almost surreal sadomasochistic relationship between the insecure, sexually repressed Anthony Burns and an unnamed black masseur at a men's bath. Burns, whose name blends that of a Christian saint with the suggestion of consummation by fire—here metaphoric—suffers from an overly acute awareness of his own insignificance, as well as of his separateness and lack of completeness as a human being. Williams views the latter as an inescapable fact of the human condition and proposes three means available to compensate for it: art, violent action, or surrendering oneself to brutal treatment at the hands of others. Burns chooses the third path, submitting himself as if in a dream, finding at the punishing hands of the black first pain, then orgasmic pleasure, and ultimately death. Although the masseur thus secures a release from his pent-up hatred of his white oppressors, this tale should not be construed as a social comment reflecting Williams' attitude toward black/white relations, hardly even peripherally a concern in his work, despite his being a Southern writer. Blacks figure importantly in only two other stories. In the ribald "Miss Coynte of Greene," the title character's long-frustrated female eroticism erupts into nymphomania, her pleasure intensified by the dark skin of her sexual partners. In "Mama's Old Stucco House," Williams' gentlest foray into the black/white terrain, the failed artist Jimmy Krenning is cared for physically and emotionally after his own mother's death by the black girl Brinda and her Mama, the latter having always functioned as his surrogate mother.

That "Desire and the Black Masseur" is to be read on levels other than the literal appears clear when Williams places its climax at the end of the Lenten Season. The death and devouring of Burns becomes a ritual of expiation, a kind of black mass and perversion of the sacrifice on Calvary, even accomplished in biblical phraseology. Indeed, counterpointed with it is a church service during which a self-proclaimed fundamentalist preacher exhorts his congregation to a frenzy of repentance. What Williams has written, then, is not only a psychological study of man's subconscious desires or an allegory of the division between innocence and evil within all men, but also a parable exposing how excessive emphasis on guilt and the need for punishment at the hands of a vengeful God have destroyed the essential New Testament message of love and forgiveness. So Burns's strange rite of atonement stands as a forceful indictment of a Puritanism that creates a dark god of hate as a reflection of one's own obsession with evil, which is one of the recurrent emphases in almost all of Williams' important dramas, especially *Suddenly Last Summer* (1958) and *The Night of the Iguana.*

Something of the obverse, the possibility for transcending one's knowledge of evil and isolation, occurs in "One Arm," the quintessential—and perhaps the finest—Williams story, in which can be discerned nearly all the central motifs that adumbrate not only his fiction but also his plays. Oliver Winemiller, a former light heavyweight champion who in an accident two years earlier lost an arm, is one of Williams' "fugitive kind," a lonely misfit, cool, impassive, now tasting, like Brick in *Cat on a Hot Tin Roof* "the charm of the defeated." Since all he possessed was his "Apollo-like beauty," after his physical mutilation he undergoes a psychological and emotional change; feeling that he has lost "the center of his being," he is filled with self-loathing and disgust. He enters on a series of self-destructive sexual encounters, finally committing a murder for which he is sentenced to die.

While in confinement awaiting execution, he receives letters from all over the country from his male lovers, confessing that he had aroused deep feelings in them, that he had effected a "communion" with them that would have been, if he had only recognized it, a means of "personal integration" and "salvation." If it is not until very recently in his dramas that Williams has openly treated homosexuality with sympathy, in his stories his nonapologetic and compassionate attitude existed from the very first. Oliver's epiphany, that he had been loved, liberates him from his self-imposed insularity; ironically, however, this rebirth makes his approaching death harder to accept. On the eve of his execution, he recognizes that the Lutheran minister who visits him has used religion as an escape from facing his own sexuality, and he desperately hopes that by forcing the minister to come to terms with himself and his "feelings" he can thereby somehow repay his debt to all those who had earlier responded to him with kindness. The minister, however, recognizing a forbidden side of himself and still suffering guilt over his adolescent sexual awakening during a dream of a golden panther, which Oliver reminds him of, refuses to give Oliver a massage and rushes from his cell. Oliver goes to his execution with dignity, gripping the love letters tightly between his thighs as a protection from aloneness.

The doctors performing the autopsy see in Oliver's body the "nobility" and purity of an "antique sculpture." Yet Williams reminds his readers in the closing line that "death has never been much in the way of completion." Although the work of art is immutable, it is not alive as only the emotionally responsive person can be, for the true artist in Williams is the person who goes out unselfishly to answer the cry for help of others, and the real work of art is the bond of communion that is formed by that response. Thus "One Arm" incorporates virtually all of Williams' major attitudes, including his somewhat sentimental valuation of the lost and lonely; his romantic glorification of physical beauty and worship of sexuality as a means of transcending aloneness; his castigation of Puritan repression and guilt that render one selfish and judgmental; and his Hawthornian abhorrence of the underdeveloped heart that prevents one from breaking out of the shell of the ego to respond with infinite compassion to all God's misbegotten creatures.

Although Williams' stories, with their frequent rhetorical excesses, their sometimes awkward narrative strategies, and their abrupt shifts in tone, technically do not often approach the purity of form of Oliver's statue, they do, nevertheless—as all good fiction must—surprise the reader with their revelations of the human heart and demand that the reader abandon a simplistic perspective and see the varieties of human experience. What in the hands of other writers might seem a too specialized vision, frequently becomes in Williams' work affectingly human and humane.

Major publications other than short fiction
NOVELS: *The Roman Spring of Mrs. Stone*, 1950; *Moise and the World of Reason*, 1975.
PLAYS: *The Glass Menagerie*, 1945; *A Streetcar Named Desire*, 1947; *Summer and Smoke*, 1948; *The Rose Tattoo*, 1951; *Camino Real*, 1953; *Cat on a Hot Tin Roof*, 1955; *Orpheus Descending*, 1957; *Suddenly Last Summer*, 1958; *Sweet Bird of Youth*, 1959; *The Night of the Iguana*, 1962; *The Milk Train Doesn't Stop Here Anymore*, 1964; *Kingdom of Earth*, 1968; *Small Craft Warnings*, 1972; *Vieux Carré*, 1978.
NONFICTION: *Memoirs*, 1975.

Bibliography

Jackson, Esther Merle. *Broken World of Tennessee Williams.*
Nelson, Benjamin. *Tennessee Williams: The Man and His Work.*
Stanton, Stephen S . ed. *Tennessee Williams: A Collection of Critical Essays.*
Tharpe, Jac, ed. *Tennessee Williams: A Tribute.*
Tischler, Nancy M. *Tennessee Williams: Rebellious Puritan.*
Woods, Christine R. and Bob Woods, eds. *Where I Live: Selected Essays.*

Thomas P. Adler

WILLIAM CARLOS WILLIAMS

Born: Rutherford, New Jersey; September 17, 1883
Died: Rutherford, New Jersey; March 4, 1963

Principal short fiction

The Knife of the Times and Other Stories, 1932; *Life Along the Passaic River*, 1938; *Make Light of It: Collected Stories*, 1950; *The Farmers' Daughters: The Collected Stories of William Carlos Williams*, 1961.

Other literary forms

Best-known as a poet, William Carlos Williams nevertheless wrote in a variety of literary forms (some of them defying categorization) including poetry, novels, short stories, prose poetry, essays, autobiography, and plays. *Paterson*, his extended poem published in four separate volumes (1946-1951), with a fifth volume seving as a commentary (1958), is his most famous and enduring work.

Influence

Linda Wagner, a foremost Williams critic, says, "Williams' short stories may have had as deep an effect on contemporary fiction as his poems have had on modern poetry." Certainly, his prose shares the basic principles of his poetic theory: use of an American idiom, adherence to a locale, communication through specifics, and belief in organic form. Some of his short fiction's characteristics—apparent spontaneity, loose plot, characterization through detail, and reliance on dialogue—apply to many twentieth century short stories. Although Williams' short fiction is important to gauge the unity of his corpus, his major achievement lies in poetry.

Story characteristics

In *I Wanted to Write a Poem*, Williams says of his short stories, "I was impressed by the picture of the times, depression years, the plight of the poor." These people, with their courage and humor balanced against ugliness and deformity, form his main subjects; however, often the author as doctor-narrator is also present. He attempts to convey "The briefness of their chronicles, its brokenness and heterogeneity—isolation, color" without resorting to overt moralizing. Williams tries to present a genuine slice of life.

Biography

After attending public schools in New Jersey, spending time in Europe, and then finishing high school in New York, William Carlos Williams enrolled in the University of Pennsylvania's Medical School in 1902. While completing his M.D. there, he met Ezra Pound, Hilda Doolittle, and the painter Charles

Demuth. In 1910, he began work as a general practitioner in Rutherford, New Jersey; in addition to this practice, from 1925 on he became a pediatrician at Passaic General Hospital. Williams held these positions until several strokes forced him to retire in 1951. His medical and literary careers always coexisted. In 1909, he had his first volume, *Poems*, privately published. As his reputation grew, he traveled to Europe several times and encountered such writers as James Joyce, Gertrude Stein, and Ford Madox Ford. He married Florence Herman in 1912 and they had two sons. Williams received numerous awards, including the Dial Award in 1926, the National Book Award in 1950, the Bollingen Award in 1953, and, posthumously, the Pulitzer Prize for Poetry in 1963. He died on March 4, 1963, in his beloved Rutherford.

Analysis

M. L. Rosenthal claims that William Carlos Williams' short stories "are often vital evocations of ordinary American reality—its toughness, squalor, pathos, intensities." As such, this short fiction tends to exhibit distinctive characteristics. First, its style is the American idiom, with heavy reliance on dialogue and speech rhythm. Second, Williams inevitably writes of his own locale and stresses the Depression's dramatic effect on ordinary working people. Third, as he shows in his poem "A Sort of a Song," there should be "No ideas/But in things"; in other words, details should suggest underlying ideas, not vice versa. Fourth, Williams himself is often present, but as a doctor, never as a poet; thus biography and autobiography constitute important plot elements. Last, the author allows plot to develop organically, which affects length (the tales range from one to thirty pages) and structure (the stories may appear diffuse or highly compressed).

Williams published two main short-story anthologies: *The Knife of the Times and Other Stories* (1932) and *Life Along the Passaic River* (1938). In 1950, he collected these and other stories into a single volume called *Make Light of It*; then, in 1961, this was superseded by his complete collected stories entitled *The Farmers' Daughters*. Although these stories may indicate progressive technical sophistication or experimentation, they all treat "the plight of the poor" (as Williams says on several occasions) or the physician's frequently ambiguous role of healing the sick within an infected society.

On the choice of title for his first short-story anthology, Williams observes "The times—that was the knife that was killing them" (the poor). A typical story is "Old Doc Rivers," which provides a full background on one rural general practitioner. It also contains a strong autobiographical element because the narrator is a younger doctor (apparently Williams). An enormously complex picture emerges of Doc Rivers: efficient, conscientious, humane, yet simultaneously crude, cruel, and addicted to drugs and alcohol. The story builds this portrait by piling up specifics about the physician's personal and professional lives and interweaving case studies among the young doctor-narrator's comments. The narrator is astonished by Rivers' psychological sharpness, intuition for the correct diagnosis, and ability to inspire blind faith in his patients. As with many Williams tales, the reader's moral response is ambiguous, for when sober, Rivers is not a good doctor, yet when drunk or doped, he is at least as good as anyone else. The plot follows a roughly chronological structure which charts Rivers' gradual mental and physical decline. This story's particular strengths are its narrator voice, concrete details, re-creation of dialogue, and exploration of the doctor-patient relationship.

Williams further considers the physician-patient relationship in "Jean Beicke" and "A Face of Stone," representative of his second short fiction collection. Told by a pediatrician-narrator (but this time an established, not a beginning, doctor), "Jean Beicke" is set in a children's ward during the Depression and recounts the story of a "scrawny, misshapen, worthless piece of humanity." Although Jean is desperately ill, she wins the hearts of the physicians and nurses by her sheer resilience: "As sick as she was," the narrator marvels, "she took her grub right on time every three hours, a big eight ounce bottle of milk and digested it perfectly." Yet little Jean's symptoms puzzle the medics, and despite initial improvement, she finally dies. Up to this point, doctors and readers alike have been ignorant of her previous history, but when her mother and aunt visit the dying infant, it is learned that she is the third child of a woman whose husband deserted her. As her aunt says, "It's better off dead—never was any good anyway." After the autopsy, the doctors discover they have completely misdiagnosed Jean. The storyteller ends the tale like this:

> I called the ear man and he came down at once. A clear miss, he said. I think if we'd gone in there earlier, we'd have saved her.
> For what? said I. Vote the straight Communist ticket. Would it make us any dumber? said the ear man.

Williams thought "Jean Beicke" was "the best short story I ever wrote." One reason is its involved narrator whose sophisticated social conscience (why cure these Depression babies only to return them to a sick society?) contrasts with the nurses' instinctive (but perhaps naïve) humanitarianism. The story's careful structure takes us from external details—Jean's misshapen body, tiny face, and pale blue eyes—to internal ones—in the postmortem—and so suggests that beneath society's superficial ills lie fundamental, perhaps incurable, troubles. Once again, Williams shows his skill for catching the speech patterns of ordinary Americans, especially in the monologue of Jean's aunt. Finally, the author's main achievement is to individualize yet not sentimentalize Jean and to dramatize her life-and-death struggle so that it matters to him—and to the reader.

In "A Face of Stone," the doctor-narrator becomes the main character. A harried family doctor, he finds himself at the end of a busy morning confronted by a young Jewish couple. The husband, one of "the presuming poor," insists that he examine their baby, while the wife maintains an expressionless, stony face. As the doctor approaches the baby boy, his mother clutches him closer and is extremely reluctant to relinquish him. Frustrated and tired, the doctor is brusque and patronizing. When he eventually looks at the child, he discovers that it is quite healthy. During the winter, the people request a house call, but he refuses to go; then, in the spring, they return and still protest that the child is unwell. Conquering his annoyance at their persistence, the family doctor checks the boy and says that he simply needs to be fed regularly and weaned.

Now the physician expects the consultation to finish, but the young Jew asks him to examine his wife. The doctor is by this time exhausted and furious; however, he starts to check this passive, poverty-stricken, physically unattractive woman. Then, almost accidentally, he discovers she is a Polish Jew who has lost her whole family. Immediately, he forgets her ugliness, grasps her intense anxiety for her baby, and realizes the strong bond between wife and husband: ". . . suddenly I understood his half shameful love for the woman and at the same time the extent of her reliance on him. I was touched." The woman smiles for the first time when the doctor prescribes pain killers for her varicose veins and she senses that she can trust him.

This story effectively dramatizes the shifting reactions between patients and doctors as they try to establish a viable relationship. Often, a physician may exploit his position of power (as this one does at the beginning) and forget that his clients are human. If he does, he turns into Doc Rivers at his worst. The best relationship occurs when both parties move beyond stereotypes to view each other as individuals. Because the doctor narrates the tale, the reader follows his process of discovery, so when he stops stereotyping the couple, the reader does too. Williams once again successfully uses dialogue to convey character interaction. Also, as in "Jean Beicke," he reveals people through detail (such as the woman's ripped dress, bow legs, and high-heeled, worn-out shoes).

Williams composed few notable short stories after *Life Along the Passaic River*, mainly because he diverted his energies into longer projects (novels, plays, and *Paterson*). From the early 1940's to the mid-1950's, however, he worked on a long short story which he eventually called "The Farmers' Daughters" (and whose title he used for his collected short fiction). The title characters are Helen and Margaret, two Southern women who have been (and continue to be) betrayed by their men. Their similar background and experience form the basis of an enduring, unshakable friendship that terminates only with Margaret's death. Technically, this is one of Williams' best stories: it unfolds quickly in a "paragraph technique" as the narrator—once more a doctor—re-creates the women's conversations and letters, then links them chronologically with his own comments. The teller refers to himself in the third person, so that most of the time the story progresses through dialogue. This extract, in which Margaret and the doctor chat, illustrates the strength of using direct, idiomatic speech:

> What's your favorite flower, Margaret?
> Why?
> I just want to know.
> What's yours?
> No. Come on—don't be so quick on the trigger so early in the evening. I think I can guess.
> Petunias! (emphasizing the second syllable.) God knows I've seen enough of them. No. Red roses. Those are really what I love.

Unlike Williams' previous stories, "The Farmers' Daughters" relies on complex character depiction and development rather than on plot or theme.

Most short-story writers merely write, but Williams left behind theoretical as well as practical evidence of his interest in the genre. *A Beginning on the Short Story (Notes)* (1950) outlines his basic tenets: truthfulness, unsentimentality, and simplicity. "The finest short stories," he states, "are those that raise . . . one particular man or woman, from that Gehenna, the newspapers, where at last all men are equal, to the distinction of being an individual." From the herd of humanity, Williams succeeds in individualizing Doc Rivers, little Jean Beicke, the Jewish couple, Margaret, Helen, and all his various doctor-narrators.

Major publications other than short fiction

NOVELS: *A Voyage to Pagany*, 1928; *White Mule*, 1937; *In the Money*, 1940; *The Build-Up*, 1952.

PLAYS: *A Dream of Love*, 1948; *Many Loves and Other Plays*, 1961.

POETRY: *Al Que Quiere!*, 1917; *Kora in Hell: Improvisations*, 1920; *The Complete Collected Poems of William Carlos Williams, 1906-1938*, 1938; *Paterson*, 1946-1958; *Collected Later Poems*, 1950, 1963 (rev. ed.); *Pictures from Brueghel and Other Poems*, 1962.

NONFICTION: *In the American Grain*, 1925; *A Beginning on the Short Story (Notes)*, 1950; *The Autobiography of William Carlos Williams*, 1951; *Selected Essays of William Carlos Williams*, 1954; *I Wanted to Write a Poem: The Autobiography of the Works of a Poet*, 1958.

Bibliography

Brinnin, John Malcolm. *William Carlos Williams*.
Guimond, James. *William Carlos Williams*.
Koch, Vivienne. *William Carlos Williams*.
Miller, J. Hillis. *William Carlos Williams: A Collection of Critical Essays*.

Paul, Sherman. *The Music of Survival: The Biography of a Poem by William Carlos Williams*.
Wagner, Linda Welshimer. *The Prose of William Carlos Williams*.

Kathryn Zabelle Derounian

THOMAS WOLFE

Born: Asheville, North Carolina; October 3, 1900
Died: Baltimore, Maryland; September 15, 1938

Principal short fiction
From Death to Morning, 1935; *The Hills Beyond*, 1941.

Other literary forms
While some novelists are failed poets, a tradition that began with Cervantes in the early seventeenth century, Thomas Wolfe was a failed playwright. What makes this fact remarkable is that he seemed to know the difference between the genres and did not write transcribed and beefed-up plays, as Henry James sometimes did. What poetic talent Wolfe had he saved for the diction of his novels. One must, however, use the phrase "failed playwright" with caution. Two of his plays, neither very outstanding, were published at the close of his short life; another was produced posthumously, and two were published posthumously.

Wolfe is most famous (his fame in the 1930's was international) for his early novels. His first editor unfortunately persuaded him to stay away from the novella or short novel form, and the editor of his posthumous novels essentially pieced them together out of shorter pieces that Wolfe saw as short novels, not as parts of a rambling, protean novel. Hugh Holman's collection of Wolfe's short novels and Richard Kennedy's discovery of his last editor's defective stewardship are beginning to establish Wolfe's very real talent for the shorter forms.

The best-known of Wolfe's novels are *Look Homeward, Angel*, (1929) and *You Can't Go Home Again* (1940). Wolfe's notebooks are also very informative, not only to scholars but also to young writers interested in the processes through which a writer refines experience (and Wolfe was more able to do this than his first wave of admirers would admit). It is particularly fascinating to see how the "real" incident that inspired one of the scenes in "Death the Proud Brother" became transformed into that scene.

Influence
Wolfe's reputation, and consequently his influence, was at one time enormous both at home and abroad. Pamela Hansford Johnson's essay on him and the sales figures for the translations of his works attest to his European reputation. At home, William Faulkner said, "My admiration for Wolfe is that . . . he was willing to throw away style, coherence, all the rules of preciseness, to try to put all the experience of the human heart on the head of a pin. . . ." Wolfe has always been the writer that young writers read. It is a shattering experience for them, and for those who later become scholars of literature, to come across *Look Homeward, Angel* at the right point in

their lives (the closer to eighteen the better). Although many critics praised his work, a reaction against Wolfe set in even during his lifetime. Robert Penn Warren wrote an unfriendly review of his second novel, *Of Time and the River* (1935), praising only the section entitled "No Door." In 1936, Bernard DeVoto, in an essay called "Genius Is Not Enough," attacked Wolfe, citing his first two novels as books full of "long, whirling discharges of words, unabsorbed in the novel, unrelated to the proper business of fiction, badly if not altogether unacceptably written. . . ."

Among modern writers, Wright Morris has cited Wolfe as a man who could digest neither books nor life and whose works die of intellectual and psychic malnutrition. The controversy continues. Whether or not one likes the precise, controlled diction of what Gore Vidal has called the "National Style," or whether one believes that the meaning is also in the sound (rhetoric, diction) as well as in the meaning, is of course a matter of taste and education. It is significant, however, that two scholars have recently shown that Wolfe was trying very hard to get away from the protean novels of his first years. Louis Rubin points out, in summarizing the achievements of Richard Kennedy and Hugh Holman, that Kennedy has demonstrated "that the two novels [*The Web and the Rock* and *You Can't Go Home Again*] . . . were in fact no such thing, but a massive scissors-and-paste job" by Edward C. Aswell, Wolfe's posthumous editor. Further, even *Of Time and the River* had been flawed by editorial advice, in this case from the legendary Maxwell Perkins. Wolfe had been persuaded to change the viewpoint from first to third person, removing the novel from the accepted and at times even honored tradition of confessional fiction to the category of fiction written by an omniscience that apparently cannot remove itself from the perspective of the protagonist, so that it looks as if author and character are one, and that the writer is congenitally incapable of seeing things with the double vision so necessary to the third-person viewpoint.

Holman, in the Introduction to *The Short Novels of Thomas Wolfe* (1961), shows that much of the material Aswell rearranged to suit himself had been intended as internally coherent shorter pieces of fiction (if not yet short stories as they are known after World War II). Rubin astutely points out that readers' first encounters with Wolfe usually come when they are learning to be readers and writers and that, having learned, they proceed with the literary problems at hand rather than rereading Wolfe. Holman's book, however, will surely be followed by the publication, as it now stands, of the vast corpus of Wolfe's writing housed at Harvard. When that happens, it will surely be seen that Wolfe grew as a writer and that his later efforts are worthy of the most serious efforts in American literary scholarship.

Story characteristics
Thomas Wolfe wrote firmly within the realistic tradition. He very seldom

used sophisticated turns of viewpoint, structural techniques, or Jamesian indirection. His style was the raw, gusty "I-am-the-man-who-was-there" attitude throughout, although occasionally embellished as in "One of the Girls of Our Party" with pure, sonorous rhetoric. His short fiction as a whole—the short stories, the chapters from an uncompleted novel about the Webbers published in *The Hills Beyond*, the novellas, and the short novels—is, however, an impressive achievement, and, as Holman has demonstrated, he was concentrating more on the novella in his last years.

The short fiction depends (where this was intended by Wolfe and not by his editor) on an all-seeing, omniscient narrator, and very seldom on the interplay among characters or even the classical method of making one character desire something another one has. The narrator is all. This is sometimes the result of the editor's insistence upon Wolfe's using the third-person viewpoint; where Wolfe uses first-person, as in the *short story* "No Door," there is a wonderful integration of viewpoint, tone, and narrative strategy. The evaluation of his techniques and objectives in the short story, novella, and short novel must await further critical analysis.

Biography

Thomas Clayton Wolfe was the youngest child of Julia Elizabeth Westall and William Oliver Wolfe, a Pennsylvania mason and stonecutter who went South to find work. One of Wolfe's brothers, Benjamin Harrison Wolfe, died at age eighteen, as does the brother in *Look Homeward, Angel*. Although Wolfe's mother did run a tourist home, The Old Kentucky Home, it is important to remember that his family was very prosperous; one scholar estimates that they were financially in the upper two percent of the town's population. Although this fact does not mean that an affluent adolescent cannot suffer the torments of the damned, it nevertheless somewhat negates the concept of Thomas Wolfe as the poor, suffering, and morbidly sensitive child, which was fashioned by the early members of his literary cult. The Wolfes were German, an unusual ethnic origin in that part of Carolina, where most of the people were Scotch-Irish or English, and they lived in the western, mountain end of North Carolina, which had more in common with East Tennessee, Appalachian Ohio, and mountain Pennsylvania than with eastern North Carolina, the Tidewater of Virginia, or even northern Mississippi (the setting of Faulkner's stories). Both ethnic background and geographic environment are reflected strongly in Wolfe's works.

Wolfe was enrolled at the University of North Carolina at Chapel Hill; at that time it was the university's only campus and was restricted to males during his first two years. He majored in the classics and in English literature, and he began his writing career as a playwright with the Carolina Playmakers. By college age, Wolfe had achieved his full growth (he was six feet, six inches tall and later, as a slightly older man, weighed two hundred and fifty pounds) and in appearance was a man of epic proportions as well as epic ambitions. Wolfe went to Harvard University in 1920 to study under George Pierce Baker at the drama workshop; he left Harvard in 1923, after earning an M.A. in English and writing *Welcome to Our City*, later performed in 1947, and *Mountains*, about a family feud.

From 1924 to 1930 he led a rather unhappy existence as an English instructor at New York University, a private university on Washington Square. He was not able to find a producer for *Welcome to Our City* or *Mannerhouse*, a play about the Civil War. In 1925, he met Aline Bernstein, and their stormy relationship became the most important one in his short life. Aline Frankau Bernstein was eighteen years older than Wolfe. When she was still nineteen, she had married a broker, Theodore Bernstein, and became interested in making sets and costumes for her friends in Neighborhood Playhouse when it was founded in 1915, soon becoming the first woman member of United Scenic Artists. As her biographer says, "without intending to, she rather took the color out of those men at hand." In 1925, she met Wolfe; a relationship developed which Wolfe described as "the met halves of the broken talisman." In 1926, he went to Europe with Aline and began *Look Homeward, Angel*, with some assistance, both literary and financial, from her. In 1928, after another trip abroad with Aline and a breakup with her, he finished *Look Homeward, Angel*, and Scribner's showed interest in the manuscript. The editor who found Wolfe's gigantic manuscript and who greatly helped him during his early career was Maxwell Perkins. With Perkins' constant help, Wolfe published *Look Homeward, Angel*, which sold fifteen thousand copies and earned Wolfe about six thousand dollars. Although Wolfe, at this point in his career wanted to publish two shorter novels, one of which had already been partly set in type, Perkins gave Wolfe what modern scholars conclude was "unfortunate" advice and leadership; he advised him to work on yet another big novel. Upon Perkins' advice, he concentrated on *Of Time and the River*, dying shortly thereafter of tuberculosis of the brain, a rare condition that had not immediately been diagnosed. Although he had been working in his last years toward shorter and more controlled stories which used different viewpoint techniques, when he died, Edward C. Aswell at Harper's gave the public what they wanted: he created the "old" Wolfe by piecing together two more gigantic novels. There is no doubt that Wolfe needed editing and that he placed himself at the mercy of those who edited his works, and the massive amount of material written prior to his death became the basis from which Aswell would create *The Web and the Rock* and *You Can't Go Home Again*.

Analysis

Some of Thomas Wolfe's short stories were printed in *The Hills Beyond*, a posthumous volume compiled by Edward C. Aswell after he had published Wolfe's two "novels" of his own creation. The tough-minded old Confederate general of the story "The Dead World Relived" mourns a South ten times as full of frauds after the Civil War as before it; the story is unforgettable and furnishes a much-needed corrective to the myth that Southerners in the American literary renaissance of the 1920's and 1930's could hardly wait to start writing about the old Colonels. "A Kinsman of His Blood," is a short, concise, and moving story in its subtly achieved pathos and its nostalgia for what life and history are, rather than for what we might want them to be, and is probably the best story in the collection. The action takes place entirely in the foreground, and the story is really that of Arthur Pentland, also known from the beginning of the story as Arthur Penn. The viewpoint through which the reader sees Arthur is that of the ubiquitous Eugene Gant; the third character in the story is Eugene's uncle, Bascom Pentland, who appears in *Of Time and the River*. It could be the tale of any three men related to each other; Arthur is the son of Bascom and the only one "who ever visited his father's house; the rest were studiously absent, saw their father only at Christmas or Thanksgiving." Even so, the relation between Bascom and Arthur is "savage and hostile."

Arthur is a huge, obese, dirty, disheveled, grubby, distraught man who has trouble speaking clearly and coherently. The reader is told nothing of the history of his problems, or of Eugene's background, and knows only that the conflict is stark, ugly, and dramatic. Some of Arthur's behavior is clearly sociopathic. His table manners are not only embarrassing, but even offensive. On one occasion, he tells an anecdote about a Harvard man who climbed into a cage with a gorilla; although the man knew fourteen languages, the gorilla killed him. Arthur's summation of the incident is as frightening as anything in European fiction which tries to depict the mindless, anarchic malevolence of the crazy or the revolutionary.

Arthur decides that his grammar school teacher really loves him; even though the woman ignores his protestations of love, then tries to silence him with rudeness, he persists. He refuses to believe his mother when she tells him the woman does not really care for him, and he storms out "like a creature whipped with furies." Finally, he goes to California to see the woman. Arthur is a pitiful, subnormal, obviously seriously disturbed creature, but frightening in his obesity, his filth, his animallike inability to understand human beings. The story ends with Eugene, out walking in the rain through the South Boston slums, spotting Arthur as he shuffles along, a bundle of old newspapers under one arm. Eugene, a nice man, is glad to see him and offers to shake his hand. Arthur denies twice that he is Arthur Pentland, then says he is Arthur Penn and screams out in terror, begging Eugene to leave him alone. There is no sentimentality here; this is tragedy, however small and prosaic.

The only collection of short fiction Wolfe prepared himself and saw through publication was *From Death to Morning*; it contains the stories "No Door" and "Death the Proud Brother."

"No Door" is about a writer and his short acquaintance with "well-kept people who have never been alone in all their life," in this case a man who lives in a penthouse near the East River furnished with several sculptures by Jacob Epstein, rare books and first editions, and a view of Manhattan which displays its "terrific frontal sweep and curtain of starflung towers, now sown with the diamond pollen of a million lights." The writer is told by these people how marvelous it is to live alone with creatures of the slums. Their remarks trigger recollections of the lower depths of stinking, overcrowded, working-class Brooklyn. The writer hangs around, partly amused, partly chagrined, partly in awe of the rich man and his mistress, thinking that *they* may be the ones who will open the door to the life of glamour and ease which he, as a poor writer, yearns for. Even as he hopes, however, he knows it is useless: these creatures are foreign to him. He retails the agony and senselessness and brutality and sordidness of his existence, and the man and his mistress condescendingly and patronizingly wish his lot were theirs. Finally, at the end of the evening, he returns to Brooklyn and hears two old people discussing the death of a priest, and the story ends on a note of desperation and impotent fury.

The effect of the story depends on the consciousness of the narrator, here appearing in the first person although the reader sees him through the second person, an almost unheard-of viewpoint in English. Wolfe makes his points subtly, the length is a rather modest one for him, his satirical eye is sharp, and the rhetoric meshes with the inner turmoil lying just beneath the surface of conversation. If Wolfe had written more stories like this he might have been one of the giants of the American short story.

"Death the Proud Brother" is a very long, almost unstructured, 22,000-word novella which attempts to present as a unified narrative several unrelated incidents of death and loneliness. Wolfe said of this story, "It represents *important* work to me." The story's thematic unity arises from the narrator's successful unifying of all the incidents within his own consciousness, drawing the world to him, exercising implicit rights of selection, unlike the third-person, omniscient narrators of Wolfe's last novels. This story is a masterpiece in its conjunction of viewpoint and material. Only this viewpoint could master this material, and only disjointed, logically discrete material such as the story presents requires a first-person viewpoint.

There is no plot, but there is some structure. Wolfe describes three violent deaths. The fourth death is that of an old bum on a bench, and it occurs quietly, imperceptibly, anonymously—he is a "cipher." His death, which takes up the bulk of the novella, furnishes Wolfe with a chance to study America. If it is true that everybody talks about America but nobody can find it, then Wolfe came closest in this last movement of the novella, which was his favorite. The story is typically Wolfean in many ways; by the passion and the wise guile of his rhetoric, Wolfe becomes so thoroughly a part of the writing that he, too, becomes a cipher—the transparent narrator. It surely is no accident that the death which moves the narrator so profoundly is the death of an urban Everyman. This is the kind of story, perhaps even the story itself, that caused Faulkner to say that Wolfe had tried to put all of life on the head of a pin.

Major publications other than short fiction

NOVELS: *Look Homeward, Angel,* 1929; *A Portrait of Bascom Hawke,* 1932; *Of Time and the River,* 1935; *The Web and the Rock,* 1939; *You Can't Go Home Again,* 1940; *The Short Novels of Thomas Wolfe,* 1961.

PLAYS: *Mannerhouse,* 1948; *Welcome to Our City,* 1962 (published only in German as *Willkommen in Altamont*); *Mountains,* 1971.

NONFICTION: *The Story of a Novel,* 1936; *Thomas Wolfe's Letters to His Mother,* 1943; *The Letters of Thomas Wolfe,* 1956; *The Notebooks of Thomas Wolfe,* 1970.

Bibliography

Holman, C. Hugh. *Fifteen Modern American Authors: A Survey of Research and Criticism.*

Johnson, Pamela Hansford. *The Art of Thomas Wolfe.*

Kennedy, Richard S. *The Window of Memory: The Literary Career of Thomas Wolfe.*

Klein, Carol. *Aline.*

Nowell, Elizabeth. *Thomas Wolfe: A Biography.*

Rubin, Louis D. *Thomas Wolfe: The Weather of His Youth.*

Turnbull, Andrew. *Thomas Wolfe.*

John Carr

VIRGINIA WOOLF

Born: London, England; January 25, 1882
Died: Lewes, Sussex, England; March 28, 1941

Principal short fiction

Monday or Tuesday, 1921; *A Haunted House and Other Short Stories*, 1943; *Mrs. Dalloway's Party*, 1973 (edited by Stella McNichol).

Other literary forms

Virginia Woolf is best known for her eight novels, especially *Mrs. Dalloway* (1925), *To the Lighthouse* (1927), and *The Waves* (1931). Her literary criticism, collected in two volumes under the title *The Common Reader* (1925, 1932), expresses her aesthetic theories. Two essays, *A Room of One's Own* (1929) and *Three Guineas* (1938), concern feminist topics. Three speculative biographies are *Orlando* (1928), about a man-woman reborn through four centuries; *Flush* (1933), told through the consciousness of Elizabeth Barrett Browning's dog; and *Roger Fry* (1940), about Woolf's friend the artist and art critic. Additional essays and short stories were published posthumously.

Influence

In her own time, Woolf helped set the trend for the modern psychological novel and furthered the stream-of-consciousness technique. In the 1960's, new editions of her works spurred many critical evaluations. These continued into the 1970's when Quentin Bell's popular biography of her (1972), the establishment of a journal in her name, and editions of her diaries and letters increased scholarly effort. Her works, containing timely interests such as androgyny, became popular with the feminist movement; and Woolf became one of the leading serious British writers of the 1900 to 1945 period.

Story characteristics

Woolf sought in her writing to convey psychological states and constructed her short stories chiefly on mental processes and impressions, frequently triggered by the scene in a flashing instant, with a strong emphasis on understanding another person even without spoken communication. Because of their brevity—perhaps more conveniently than the novels—the stories may be studied as examples of her achievement of her artistic aims. In her early criticism she wrote that she wanted her writing to express "what the mind receives on an ordinary day," and that, to her, life itself is "a luminous halo, a semi transparent envelope surrounding us from the beginning of consciousness to the end." She searched for a truth beyond fact and often conveyed mystical and semimystical sensations.

Biography

A daughter in an intellectual household dominated by her father, Sir Leslie Stephen, who is best known for compiling the *Dictionary of National Biography*, Virginia Stephen suffered her first mental breakdown at the death of her mother in 1895; after her father's death in 1904 the Stephen children moved to Bloomsbury, and Virginia published her first review. A member of the informal but now famous "Bloomsbury group" following the philosophy of George E. Moore and emphasizing art and personal relationships, Virginia married Leonard Woolf in 1912 and completed her first novel in 1913. She and her husband in 1917 founded Hogarth Press in their home. Two more serious illnesses led her to dread their severity, and her feeling that another was imminent provoked her suicide by drowning.

Analysis

In the Foreword to the best-known collection, *A Haunted House and Other Short Stories*, Leonard Woolf explained that Virginia Woolf frequently wrote sketches and saved them for rewriting when an editor asked for a short story and also wrote them to rest her mind from the larger efforts of a novel. The nineteen stories in *A Haunted House and Other Short Stories* do not include two—"A Society" and "Blue and Green"—from the earlier *Monday or Tuesday* collection. *Mrs. Dalloway's Party* consists of seven stories written between 1922 and 1927 on the party theme; four of these are in *A Haunted House and Other Short Stories*; "Mrs. Dalloway in Bond Street" was previously published in *The Dial*; and two, "The Introduction" and "Ancestors," appeared here for the first time.

Many of Virginia Woolf's stories concentrate upon sensitivity to others and the importance of communication; others present a human mind fabricating or fantasizing about the background of another—unknown—person, or on a mark left by another person; or the person's effect on the environment may be analyzed at a glance. Several of the stories in *A Haunted House and Other Short Stories* demonstrate what in *Mrs. Dalloway* comes under the term "affinities," which means that an "unseen part of us" survives even after death, attached to persons and "haunting certain places." Accordingly, in the title story "A Haunted House," a drowsing person who is sensitive to the impressions left in a house by its former occupants of hundreds of years ago—a couple separated by the early death of the woman and subsequent travel of the man—feels that the couple are reunited as ghosts in this house. The house therefore still holds a "buried treasure" of their love.

"The String Quartet" consists of impressions and fantasies and snatches of conversation overheard during a concert. "Kew Gardens" records the impressions of a person sitting on a park bench, watching a snail amid the flowers, and hearing fleeting conversations of several types of people. "The Mark on the Wall," a series of reflections and speculations about relationships to objects, deplores the possibility of positively identifying the mysterious mark, left by an unknown person, and expresses a truth that transcends fact: "the mystery of life; the inaccuracy of thought! . . . how very little control of our possessions we have—what an accidental affair this living is after all our civilization." Yet the solidity of an object reassures us who worship "the impersonal world which is a proof of some existence other than ours."

The mystical relationships to objects—and the effect of an object on a person—continues in two widely varying stories, "Solid Objects" and "The New Dress." In the first a political candidate becomes so obsessed with the collection of fragments of glass and other castoffs, speculating about their origins and history, that he forgets his political ambitions. In the second an object—the dress—which is not quite right for the occasion, confirms a woman's sense of inferiority.

Somewhat similarly, in "The Shooting Party," a suitcase with pheasants placed on top of it during a moment on a train provides for a fellow traveler a meditation complete with fanciful plot about the owner of the suitcase. Also, in "The Lady in the Looking Glass," a mirror in a hallway reflects enough of sensation that it seems that "the room had its passions and rages and envies and sorrows coming over it and clouding it, like a human being," and the viewer imagines a series of thoughts for a woman reflected distantly in it. Then the woman walks closer, and obvious facts shatter the images, which nevertheless had a truth of their own.

Close to the philosophy of Mrs. Dalloway that life is lived in "secret deposits of exquisite moments," Virginia Woolf created another type of story and gave to one of the type the title "Moments of Being." In itself a retitling of "Slater's Pins Have No Points," the story catches a person suspended in a moment of being. The moment of searching for a fallen straight pin provides for a music pupil an opportunity to feel sorry for her spinsterish teacher; but the teacher in making the comment "Slater's pins have no points" turns and kindles like a "dead white star" and triumphantly possesses the moment and the pin's recovery in an embrace of the pupil—for her witticism, she thinks, unites them, and she has no knowledge of the pupil's pity.

So also an Air Force light searching for enemy aircraft in "The Searchlight" brings a moment into being; seeing the light briefly strike a balcony reminds Mrs. Ivimey of a story her grandfather told about focusing—again momentarily—a telescope on a distant girl just as she was kissed, then running miles to meet her. The girl—in another rare moment, obviously—became Mrs. Ivimey's grandmother; and the young man the grandfather had seen kissing the girl simply vanished. "The light," Mrs. Ivimey explains, "only falls here and there."

Although these stories demonstrate Woolf's aesthetic theories, so that an object or a part of the environment, or one's sense of time, makes a metaphysical statement, three other stories—"The Legacy," "The Duchess and the Jeweller," and "Lappin and Lapinova"—have more traditional character and conflict.

"The Legacy," with the compression of a one-act tragedy, presents in only eight pages a man who, with pronounced hubris, experiences recognition and reversal. As Gilbert Clandon prepares to distribute the mementos his recently deceased wife Angela has left marked for her various friends, he remembers the childishness of her delight in those objects. Even her stepping off a curb in front of a car seems to him the impetuous gesture of a child. Secure in his masculine pride and superiority, he condescends, also, to the drab little woman who served his wife as secretary, mainly, he thinks, because of his wife's foolish sympathy, although he admits she had a talent for discovering admirable qualities in others. Despising the secretary's cheap costume, he barely remembers that she, too, is in mourning for her brother. He barely perceives, also, the sympathetic and searching look she gives him as she departs with the absurd intimation that she may be able to help him. With all his male vanity, he can explain the look only with the thought that this poor lonely creature must entertain a passion for him.

Certain of his worthiness and of his wife's diary as testimony to it, he begins reading the diary—the only secret she had kept from him. It recalls to him their early married life when his wife, so ignorant, she said, was eager to learn from him, the worldy-wise and traveled member of parliament. All the tributes from his wife for the greatness of himself seem to be exactly his due, including her pride in the possibility that he might become Prime Minister. As he reads he remembers that he gradually became more "absorbed in his work" and that she had more time to herself. Her diary confirms still her selflessness in the wish that Gilbert—not herself—had a son.

With a patronizing air he continues reading and recalls the reason—if it would amuse her—that he consented to her daring request for permission to do something outside the home. After this he finds his own name occurring less frequently and the initials "B. M." occurring more frequently. Regarding the activities of "B. M.," who ignorantly shook hands with the maid, Gilbert Clandon continues to be patronizing. He knows the type, no doubt a socialist "who had never done an honest day's work in his life." Clandon's first suspicions begin to dawn when he finds a name obliterated—possibly his own—the name of someone B. M. had abused verbally. Then come his wife's regret for her own luxurious way of living, the books—*Karl Marx, The Coming Revolution*—that B. M. gave her to read, B. M.'s unexpected visit at night when "luckily" Angela was alone. The date of this visit recalls nothing to Clandon's mind except his own speech at the Mansion House dinner. The diary reveals more sessions with his wife alone with B. M. and her refusal to go away. Hotly Clandon interprets this as B. M.'s request that his wife become this man's mistress. The pages chronologically reveal Angela's increasing agitation when some appear blank, as if in the face of some urgent question nothing else could occupy her writing time. He notes, also, that the initials are dropped; the other man in her life is simply "he," with no possible confusion with himself. Gradually Clandon understands that B. M., answering the question, committed suicide for Angela; but the recognition is double— Angela also committed suicide for her lover.

Telephoning the drab secretary, Clandon learns that B. M. was the secretary's brother. Shocking as this is, there is still another stage in the recognition, a new meaning for the word "legacy," which is not merely the diary his wife left him but also this devastating truth: "She had stepped off the kerb to rejoin her lover." The reversal follows in a swift, concluding sentence: "She had stepped off the kerb to escape from him."

That a man of dignity, wealth, and position should be escaped from because his wife, to him, is something like a pet dog, or because he is concerned only with himself and regards his wife as a possession—all of these possibilities, and the attack on the male ego, make "The Legacy" superb feminist literature. That a woman could have undiscovered talents, unrevealed concerns, an informed intellect, a social purpose, a secret love—all of these confirm the feminist position. Further, there is just the slightest suspicion that, since Clandon has lost his seat in parliament and now occupies an unidentified government position, he has neither the courage nor intellect nor ability that he thinks he has. Angela's superb devotion to another man and her courage in taking her own life remain for Clandon the supreme blow, and these two factors extend the meaning of her legacy to him.

A man's pride also plays a role in "The Duchess and the Jeweller"; but in this story Oliver Bacon, unlike Gilbert Clandon, has very precise self-knowledge. He remains, nevertheless, in the grip of two feminine necessities—his deceased mother, who haunts him with her eyes staring out at him from her portrait and with her remembered counsel; and his own need for female company, although rigidly controlled. Confronted with these two conflicting factors, he succumbs to fraud by a real woman of mountainous proportions of flesh and blood; and yet he clearly understands his position and calmly acquiesces to the fraud.

His ambivalent position appears at the beginning of the story in his private apartment, a setting which marks the dichotomy between the animal and the intellect in details such as "chairs covered in hide" and "sofas covered in tapestry." Also the invitations he receives from countesses and other Honourable Ladies of wealth and standing contrast with his memories of himself as a "little boy in a dark alley." Proud of his rising from poverty and ignominy, he likes to remember his past, likes especially to luxuriate in contrasting his present wealth and influence to his beginning his career by "selling stolen dogs to fashionable women in Whitechapel." The animal side of his nature, persisting under his gilt refinement and officious manner, evidences itself in a series of animal analogies: his nose, long and flexible, like an elephant's trunk; his lifetime career of snuffling like a giant hog trying to unearth a bigger truffle, somewhere farther off; his walk, swaying like a camel at the zoo; his delight expressed with head back in a horse's neigh. He meets his match in the Duchess of Lambourne, however, who preens and flounces like a peacock, whose purse resembles a ferret's belly with its slit spilling out ten pearls like eggs. To both of these people who value wealth, these eggs are those of "some heavenly bird."

In his role as the world's most important jeweller, Oliver Bacon commands obeisance from his attendants and associates—the duchess, likewise, commands respect because of her social position. Her tendency to gamble, for which she needs to sell off various possessions without her husband's knowledge, parallels Oliver's weakness of gloating over his gains. Both therefore become susceptible to outside forces and understand each other. Attempting to sell her pearls, the duchess plays her cards with the sure instinct of a bird of prey. She mentions her three daughters at just the moment to prevent his sending the pearls to his assistant for testing. She lures him to submit to the purchase with an invitation to her estate where, amid other attractions, she promises a long weekend which he interprets as an opportunity to be alone with Diana. His mother's eyes on him momentarily cause him to hesitate while he writes a check for twenty thousand; but all his natural desires pulsate in the name Diana—goddess of the wood and of the hunt—and in the image of "riding alone in the woods with Diana!"

Immediately upon the departure of the duchess, when Oliver discovers that the pearls are "rotten at the core!" (a comment on the Duchess herself and possibly on himself), he recognizes that all the conflicting elements in his nature—his alley boy background, his pleasure in association with the aristocracy, his submission to his mother, his desire for Diana—have been epitomized in this fraud. Without regret for his victimization, he says, "Forgive me, oh, my mother! . . . For it is to be a long week-end."

The hunt figures, also, in "Lappin and Lapinova," although only in fantasy. This most conventional of Woolf's stories remains—perhaps for its conventions—the one most frequently anthologized and is another excellent example of feminist literature. The story may have been suggested when Woolf visited the future in-laws of her sister and thought they looked like rabbits, but the story ranges much further than this mere suggestion.

The story begins with the marriage of Rosalind to Ernest Thorburn, as stuffy a man as one could find in British society. Amid trite British conventions of setting and manners, Rosalind decides that Ernest looks like a rabbit, especially with his twitching nose. Immediately bored with her married life, having nothing to do but act like a proper wife, she fantasizes a Lapin tribe and makes her husband King Lappin. He aids her with a suggestion, on his return from work, that he has been chased by a hare, and Rosalind herself becomes Queen Lapinova. The fantasy, contrasting his work in the city and her lonely life at home by day with romance at night, provides a needed metaphor for her married state: "he was bold and determined; she wary and undependable. He ruled over the busy world of rabbits; her world was a desolate, mysterious place, which she ranged mostly by moonlight."

Added to his twitching nose gradually comes an accumulation of analogies: her popping eyes, her habit of holding her sewing as if her hands were paws, the rabbitlike reproduction of the Thorburns with Ernest's nine brothers and sisters. With the two of them enlarging upon any details about gamekeepers, skins, prices, and poachers, in conversations extended through a long winter they make rabbits their only means of sharing their divided worlds.

The breaking point comes at the golden anniversary celebration of Ernest's parents, when everything is done in gold and all gifts are gold except Rosalind's, an eighteenth century sand caster used to sprinkle sand over wet ink and indicative of her unconscious need for communication. For the first time Ernest's nose seems to resemble the family portraits and does not twitch at all. Literally suffocating at dinner, she revives only when she catches a phrase about the Thorburns: "But they breed so!" Her imagination quickly endows the dining room with meadows and rabbits; she would have been trapped if Ernest's nose had not twitched at the precarious moment.

Two years later Ernest's separate life of business removes him so effectively that he has difficulty remembering the game they have been playing, and Rosalind awake at night imagines her king rabbit dead. "Don't talk such rubbish," says the awakened Ernest, and effectively ends the moonlight excursions. Out of doors in daylight the London setting seems to Rosalind identical with the Thorburns' dining room, a symbol of her own trapped life. A visit to the National History Museum shows her at its very entrance a stuffed hare, a symbol of the state of her marriage. On Ernest's return from the office for this day, with much indifference and lack of sympathy, he agrees that Lapinova has been "Caught in a trap . . . killed." Woolf concludes the story, "So that was the end of that marriage."

Major publications other than short fiction

NOVELS: *The Voyage Out*, 1915; *Night and Day*, 1919; *Jacob's Room*, 1922; *Mrs. Dalloway*, 1925; *To the Lighthouse*, 1927; *The Waves*, 1931; *The Years*, 1937; *Between the Acts*, 1941.

NONFICTION: *The Common Reader: First Series*, 1925; *Orlando: A Biography*, 1928; *A Room of One's Own*, 1929; *The Common Reader: Second Series*, 1932; *Flush: A Biography*, 1933; *Three Guineas*, 1938; *Roger Fry: A Biography*, 1940; *The Death of the Moth and Other Essays*, 1942; *The Moment and Other Essays*, 1947; *The Captain's Death Bed and Other Essays*, 1950; *A Writer's Diary*, 1953; *Granite and Rainbow*, 1958.

Bibliography

Bell, Quentin. *Virginia Woolf: A Biography.*
Bennett, Joan. *Virginia Woolf: Her Art as a Novelist.*
Brewster, Dorothy. *Virginia Woolf.*
Daiches, David. *Virginia Woolf.*
Gorsky, Susan Rubinow. *Virginia Woolf.*

Grace Eckley

RICHARD WRIGHT

Born: Natchez, Mississippi; September 4, 1908
Died: Paris, France; November 28, 1960

Principal short fiction

Uncle Tom's Children: Four Novellas, 1938; *Uncle Tom's Children: Five Long Stories*, 1940; *Eight Men: A Book of Stories*, 1961.

Other literary forms

Richard Wright's best-known works are the novel *Native Son*, 1940, and the autobiographical *Black Boy: A Record of Childhood and Youth*, 1945. Like other black writers who were ignored initially by white-dominated presses, Wright was a regular contributor of articles to the Communist *Daily Worker*. Early fiction such as *Uncle Tom's Children* and *Native Son* illustrate his Marxist ideology. Like Ralph Ellison, however, he became disillusioned with the Communists, and in 1944 expressed his views in "I Tried to Be a Communist," first published in *Atlantic Monthly*. His later social protest novels develop existential themes; black experience, with its alienation and suffering, becomes a parable for the human condition.

Influence

Bigger Thomas, the protagonist of Wright's *Native Son*, is perhaps the most striking character in black literature, providing a prototype for subsequent portrayals of the rebel-victim of racial oppression. James Baldwin wrote that "no American Negro exists who does not have his private Bigger Thomas living in the skull." Wright lectured widely in Europe on the psychological problems of oppressed peoples and on Afro-American literature. All contemporary black writers are indebted to him for commanding the attention of the white world and winning respect for black writers here and abroad. Wright was instrumental in organizing the first Congress of Negro Writers and Artists.

Story characteristics

Because of Wright's early contact with Marxism and his own bitter experience of social deprivation, he belongs to the proletarian school of writing which, in turn, borrows from literary naturalism. He also uses symbolism and archetypal patterns to support his existential themes of alienation and despair. His plots usually deal with the harrowing experience of racial bigotry, which converts an innocent victim into a violent rebel. Such rebels do not live long, and the brutality which they suffer or which they perpetrate on others is relentlessly described. Yet the more subtle achievement is the psychological insight illuminating the subjective experience of oppression and rebellion.

Although there is some philosophical contradiction in the social determinism implied in Marxism and the individualism of the metaphysical rebel in existentialism, they coexist in Wright's best stories.

Biography

The poverty, racial hatred, and violence that Richard Nathaniel Wright dramatizes in fiction comes directly from his own experience as the child of an illiterate Mississippi sharecropper. Richard was six years old when his father was driven off the land and the family moved to a two-room slum tenement in Memphis, Tennessee. The father deserted the family there. Richard's mother, Ella Wright, got a job as a cook, leaving Richard and his younger brother Alan alone in the apartment. When his mother became ill, the brothers were put in an orphanage. An invitation for Ella and the boys to stay with a more prosperous relative in Arkansas ended in panic and flight when white men shot Uncle Hoskins, who had offered the Wrights a home. The family lived for some time with Richard's grandparents, stern Seventh-Day Adventists. In this grim, repressive atmosphere, Richard became increasingly violent and rebellious.

Although he completed his formal education in the ninth grade, the young Richard read widely, especially Stephen Crane, Fyodor Dostoevski, Marcel Proust, T. S. Eliot, and Gertrude Stein. The family eventually migrated to Chicago. Wright joined the Communist party in 1933 and, in 1937 in New York City, became editor of the *Daily Worker*. The publications of *Uncle Tom's Children*, *Native Son*, and *Black Boy* brought Wright fame both here and in Europe. In 1945, at the invitation of the French government, Wright went to France and became friends with Jean-Paul Sartre, Simone de Beauvoir, and other existentialists. His next novel, *The Outsider* (1953), has been called the first existential novel by an American writer. Wright traveled widely, lectured in several countries, and wrote journalistic accounts of his experience in Africa and Spain. He died unexpectedly in Paris of amoebic dysentery, probably contracted in Africa or Indonesia.

Analysis

"Fire and Cloud" in *Uncle Tom's Children* is perhaps the best representative of Richard Wright's early short fiction. It won first prize in the 1938 *Story* magazine contest which had more than four hundred entries, marking Wright's first triumph with American publishers. Charles K. O'Neill made a radio adaptation of the story that appeared in *American Scenes*.

Unlike the later works concerning black ghetto experience, "Fire and Cloud" has a pastoral quality, recognizing the strong bond of the Southern black to the soil and the support he has drawn from religion. Wright reproduces faithfully the Southern black dialect in both conversation and internal meditations. This use of dialect emphasizes the relative lack of sophistication of rural blacks. His protagonist, Reverend Taylor, is representative of the "old Negro," who has withstood centuries of oppression, sustained by hard work on the land and humble faith in a merciful God.

Wright's attitude toward religion, however, is ambivalent. Although he recognizes it as contributing to the quiet nobility of the hero, it also prevents Taylor from taking effective social action when his people are literally starving. The final triumph of Reverend Taylor is that he puts aside the conciliatory attitude which was part of his religious training and becomes a social activist. Instead of turning the other cheek after being humiliated and beaten by white men, he embraces the methods of his Marxist supporters, meeting oppression with mass demonstration. Strength of numbers proves more effective and appropriate for getting relief from the bigoted white establishment than all his piety and loving-kindness. Early in the story Taylor exclaims "The good Lawds gonna clean up this ol worl some day! Hes gonna make a new Heaven n a new Earth!" His last words, however, are "Freedom belongs t the strong!"

The situation of the story no doubt reflects Wright's early experience when his sharecropper father was driven off the plantation. Taylor's people are starving because the white men, who own all the land, have prohibited the blacks from raising food on it. No matter how Taylor pleads for relief, the local white officials tell him to wait and see if federal aid may be forthcoming. When two Communist agitators begin pushing Taylor to lead a mass demonstration against the local government, white officials have Taylor kidnapped and beaten, as well as several deacons of his church. Instead of intimidating them, this suffering persuades them to open confrontation. As the Communists promised, the poor whites join the blacks in the march which forces the white authorities to release food to those facing starvation.

The story's strength lies in revealing through three dialogues the psychological dilemma of the protagonist as opposing groups demand his support. He resists the Communists initially because their methods employ threat of open war on the whites—"N tha ain Gawds way!" The agitators say he will be responsible if their demonstration fails through lack of numbers and participants are slaughtered. On the other hand, the mayor and chief of police threaten Taylor that they will hold him personally responsible if any of his church members join the march. After a humiliating and futile exchange with these men, Taylor faces his own church deacons who are themselves divided and look to him for leadership. He knows that one of their number, who is just waiting for a chance to oust him from his church, will run to the mayor and police with any evidence of Taylor's insubordination. In a pathetic attempt to shift the burden of responsibility that threatens to destroy him no matter what he does, he reiterates the stubborn stand he has maintained with all three groups: he will not order the demonstration, but he will march with his people if they choose to demonstrate. The brutal horse-whipping that Taylor endures as a result of this moderate stand convinces him of the futility of trying to placate everybody. The Uncle Tom becomes a rebel.

Critics sometimes deplore the episodes of raw brutality described in graphic detail in Wright's fiction, but violence is the clue here to his message. Behind the white man's paternalistic talk is the persuasion of whip and gun. Only superior force can cope with such an antagonist.

Wright's most perfect short fiction is "The Man Who Lived Underground." Although undoubtedly influenced by Dostoevski's underground man and by Franz Kafka's "K," the situation was based on a prisoner's story from *True Detective* magazine. The first version appeared in 1942 in *Accent* magazine under the subtitle "Two Excerpts from a Novel." This version began with a description of the life of a black servant, but Wright later discarded this opening in favor of the dramatic scene in which an unnamed fugitive hides from the police by descending into a sewer. This approach allowed the story to assume a more universal, symbolic quality. Although racist issues are still significant, the protagonist represents that larger class of all those alienated from their society. Eventually the fugitive's name is revealed as Fred Daniels, but so completely is he absorbed into his Everyman role that he cannot remember his name when he returns to the upper world. His progress through sewers and basements becomes a quest for the meaning of life, parodying classic descents into the underworld and ironically reversing Plato's allegory of the cave.

Although Plato's philosopher attains wisdom by climbing out of the cave where men respond to shadows on the cave wall, Wright's protagonist gains enlightenment because of his underground perspective. What he sees there speaks not to his rational understanding, however, but to his emotions. He moves among symbolic visions which arouse terror and pity—a dead baby floating on the slimy water whose "mouth gaped black in a soundless cry." In a black church service spied on through a crevice in the wall, the devout are singing "Jesus, take me to your home above." He is overwhelmed by a sense of guilt and intuits that there is something obscene about their "singing with the air of the sewer blowing in on them." In a meat locker with carcasses hanging from the ceiling, a butcher is hacking off a piece of meat with a bloody cleaver. When the store proprietor goes home, Fred emerges from the locker and gorges on fresh fruit, but he takes back with him into the sewer the bloody cleaver—why he does not know.

When Fred breaks through a wall into the basement of a movie house, the analogy to Plato's myth of the cave becomes explicit. He comes up a back stair and sees jerking shadows of a silver screen. The Platonic urge to enlighten the people in the theater, who are bound to a shadow world, merges with messianic images. In a dream he walks on water and saves a baby held up by a drowning woman, but the dream ends in terror and doubt as he loses the baby and his ability to emulate Christ. All is lost and he himself begins to drown.

Terror and pity are not the only emotions that enlarge his sensibilities in this underground odyssey. As he learns the peculiar advantages of his invisibility, he realizes that he can help himself to all kinds of gadgets valued by that shadow world above ground. He collects them like toys or symbols of an absurd world. He acquires a radio, a light bulb with an extension cord, a typewriter, a gun, and finally, through a chance observation of a safe being opened by combination, rolls of hundred dollar bills, containers of diamonds, watches, and rings. His motivation for stealing these articles is not greed, but sheer hilarious fun at acquiring objects so long denied to persons of his class.

In one of the most striking, surrealist scenes in modern literature, Fred delightedly decorates his cave walls and floor with these tokens of a society which has rejected him. "They were the serious toys of the men who lived in the dead world of sunshine and rain he had left, the world that had condemned him, branded him guilty." He glues hundred dollar bills on his walls. He winds up all the watches but disdains to set them (for he is beyond time, freed from its tyranny). The watches hang on nails along with the diamond rings. He hangs up the bloody cleaver, too, and the gun. The unset diamonds he dumps in a glittering pile on the muddy floor. Then as he gaily tramps around, he accidentally/on purpose, stomps on the pile, scattering the pretty baubles over the floor. Here, indeed, is society's cave of shadows, and only he realizes how absurd it all is.

When the euphoria of these games begins to pall, Fred becomes more philosophical, perceiving the nihilistic implications of his experience. "Maybe *any*thing's right, he mumbled. Yes, if the world as men had made it was right, then anything else was right, any act a man took to satisfy himself, murder, theft, torture." In his unlettered, blundering way, he is groping toward Ivan Karamazov's dark meditation: "If there is no God, then all things are permissible." Fred becomes convinced of the reality of human guilt, however, when he witnesses the suicide of the jewelry store's night watchman, who has been blamed for the theft he himself committed. At first, the scene in which police torture the bewildered man to force a confession strikes Fred as hilariously funny, duplicating his own experience. When the wretched man shoots himself before Fred can offer him a means to escape, however, Fred is shocked into a realization of his own guilt.

The protagonist ultimately transcends his nihilism, and like Plato's philosopher who returns to the cave out of compassion for those trapped there, Fred returns to the "dead world of sunshine and rain" to bear witness to the Truth. Like the philosopher who is blinded coming out of the light into cave darkness, Fred seems confused and stupid in the social world above ground. When he is thrown out of the black church, he tries inarticulately to explain his revelation at the police station where he had been tortured and condemned. The police think he is crazy, but because they now know they accused him unjustly, they find his return embarrassing. Fred euphorically insists that they accompany him into the sewer so that they too can experience the visions that enlightened him. When he shows them his entrance to the world underground, one of the policemen calmly shoots him and the murky waters of the sewer sweep him away.

This ironic story of symbolic death and resurrection is unparalleled in its unique treatment of existential themes. Guilt and alienation lead paradoxically to a tragic sense of human brotherhood, which seems unintelligible to "normal" people. The man who kills Fred Daniels is perhaps the only person who perceives even dimly what Daniels wants to do. "You've got to shoot this kind," he says. "They'd wreck things."

Major publications other than short fiction

NOVELS: *Native Son*, 1940; *The Outsider*, 1953; *Savage Holiday*, 1954; *The Long Dream*, 1958; *Lawd Today*, 1963.

NONFICTION: *12 Million Black Voices: A Folk History of the Negro in the United States*, 1941; *Black Boy: A Record of Childhood and Youth*, 1945; *Black Power: A Record of Reaction in a Land of Pathos*, 1954; *Pagan Spain*, 1957; *White Man, Listen!*, 1957; *Richard Wright Reader*, 1978 (Ellen Wright and Michel Fabre, eds.).

Bibliography

Bakish, David. *Richard Wright*.
Brignano, Russell Carl. *Richard Wright: An Introduction to the Man and His Works*.
Borgum, Edwin Berry. "The Art of Richard Wright's Short Stories," in *Quarterly Review of Literature*. I (Spring, 1944), pp. 198-211.
Kinnamon, Keneth. *The Emergence of Richard Wright: A Study in Literature and Society*.
McCall, Dan. *The Example of Richard Wright*.
Margolies, Edward. *The Art of Richard Wright*.
Webb, Constance. *Richard Wright: A Biography*.

Katherine Snipes

WILLIAM BUTLER YEATS

Born: Sandymount, near Dublin, Ireland; June 13, 1865
Died: Roquebrune, France; January 28, 1939

Principal short fiction

John Sherman and Dhoya, 1891; *The Celtic Twilight,* 1893; *The Secret Rose,* 1897; *The Tables of the Law; The Adoration of the Magi,* 1897; *Stories of Red Hanrahan,* 1904.

Other literary forms

William Butler Yeats, a prolific writer, composed hundreds of lyrical, narrative, and dramatic poems. It was not unusual to find characters from his short stories appearing in his poems; *Michael Robartes and the Dancer,* a collection of poems in 1920, is one example. In addition to his poetry, he contributed to the Irish dramatic movement which culminated in the establishment of the Abbey Theatre in Dublin. His *Cathleen ni Houlihan* (1902) and *Deirdre* (1907) are typical plays of that early period. An accomplished essayist, Yeats wrote *The Bounty of Sweden* (1925) following his acceptance of the Nobel Prize for Literature in 1923.

Influence

By using Irish myth, folklore, and ancient Irish literature, new motifs to the artists writing in English, Yeats had an enormous influence upon the literature of Ireland and eventually of the English-speaking world. In searching for a theme to unify his work, he revitalized Irish myths and legends, particularly of the heroic pre-Christian age. He used symbols in his verse and dramatic verse plays to understand history and human personality in terms of natural events: the moon, for example, symbolized twenty-eight phases of mankind and its cyclic history. He was much more direct, however, in his short stories, which were written at the outset of his career. At that time, his tales reveal that Yeats was influenced by Irish literature, London and Sligo, and alchemy—the sort envisioned by the Theosophists of the Dublin circle of Madame Blavatsky and George (Æ) Russell. These influences were to last a lifetime, forming the subject matter of his great poems. William Carleton, William Blake, and the French symbolists influenced both Yeats's work and his selection of themes. His reputation was worldwide before his death, and many critics consider Yeats the greatest poet of our century.

Story characteristics

Love is the dominant emotion, but one subject matter dominates the stories: the war of the spiritual with the natural order of things. Consequently, an air of mysticism in which characters live in this world while obviously communicating with the spirit world pervades the dramatic episodes. "John Sherman," the exception, is realistic and commonplace without a defined conflict or credible resolution.

Biography

Born in Dublin to the painter John Butler Yeats and Susan Pollexfen of Sligo, William Butler Yeats was of Irish Protestant background. His childhood was spent in London, Dublin, and Sligo. He was educated at the Godolphin School, Hammersmith, Dublin High School, and the Metropolitan School of Art, where he fell under the spell of George (Æ) Russell and other Dublin mystics. John O'Leary, the Fenian leader, and Maude Gonne, the passionate actress and patriot, were two Irish friends, while Arthur Symons and Lionel Johnson of the Rhymers' Club were London friends. When Maude Gonne and later her daughter Iseult rejected his marriage proposal, Yeats married Georgie Hyde-Lees, an Englishwoman, in 1917. They had one son and one daughter. After the Irish Civil War, he served as Senator for the Irish Free State, 1923-1928. Yeats traveled extensively, including lecture tours to the United States. In 1899, Yeats with Lady Gregory, Edward Martyn, and George Moore established an Irish theater which led to the Abbey Theatre. With George Bernard Shaw and George (Æ) Russell, Yeats founded the Irish Academy of Letters in 1932.

Yeats received honorary degrees from the Universities of Dublin, 1922; Oxford, 1931; and Cambridge, 1933. His complex life experiences were literary source material for his works. Acutely aware of the religious and philosophical conflict facing the world, he believed that a viable literature was an alternative resolution until religion and philosophy offered another solution.

Analysis

With the exception of "John Sherman," William Butler Yeats's short stories mirror his attraction to the spirit world and reflect his fascination with good and evil. Since they were written during the *fin de siècle* period when literary and graphic artists, epitomized by the French symbolists, were expressing a world weariness and pessimism that celebrated the triumph of evil, it is understandable that Yeats's tales articulate that prevailing mood. These early fictional works also identify the themes which were to occupy Yeats's poetic genius for the remainder of his life.

An integral part of the Irish literary movement, the tales have a dual purpose: to revitalize ancient Irish myths for modern Ireland and to serve as a model for artists attempting to write in Irish about Irish subjects. In the stories Yeats celebrates the exploits of fairies and pagan Irish heroes which he discovered in the oral and written literary traditions; his tales thus become source material for other storytellers. Yeats's *The Celtic Twilight*, a collection of folklore gathered from local storytellers, became important source material for Yeats's later work. In recording the fantastic behavior of the various spirits and their relationship to the country people, Yeats stored information which he used later to dramatize his belief in communication between the material and the immaterial worlds. "Dhoya" is an excellent example of a revitalized myth, and "The Twisting of the Rope" illustrates Yeats's role as a mentor for others.

In "Dhoya," Yeats writes about a local Sligo legend. He had recently edited *Fairy and Folk Tales of the Irish Peasantry* (1888), and his imagination was stimulated by the living nature of these expressions of the conflict between the natural and preternatural worlds. "Dhoya" honors an ancient Celt who lived before the time of the Pharaohs, Buddha, and Thor. In predating the time of known heroes, Dhoya, the Celt, exists before recorded history. It follows then that Yeats's native Sligo has indeed an ancient history, for Dhoya is deserted at the Bay of Ballah, the fictional name of Sligo Bay. The Formorians, an ancient Irish tribe, abandon Dhoya, a giant of tremendous strength, because he cannot control the violent rages which come over him. While enraged, he kills those around him and destroys whatever he can touch. He is believed to be possessed by demons, and a plan is concocted to exile him to the Bay of Ballah.

Dhoya, living alone in the forests and along the beaches, experiences more frequent attacks, but they are directed against his shadow or the halcyon, the beautiful and peaceful legendary bird. Years pass, and a quality of timelessness adds to the mystical nature of the tale, for Dhoya is hundreds of years old. One day he kills a great bull, and the herd chases him until he eludes it by running into the deepest part of the bay, a spot called Pool Dhoya. To this day, and in Yeats's day, the deepest part of Sligo Bay is known as Pool Dhoya, a fact which Yeats incorporates into the story to create a living legend.

Yeats also introduces legendary characters. Dhoya ranges over the mountains where Diarmuid and Grania, pagan lovers of the written Irish literature of pre-Christian Ireland, traveled. In time, Dhoya also experiences a love like Diarmuid. It comes to Dhoya as a gentle breeze upon his forehead, nothing more; but he longs for that touch, which remains only a touch for an untold number of years. Eventually, he develops a depression which he plans to shake off by building a huge bonfire at the rising of the moon. The unhappy lover prays to the moon and makes all kinds of sacrifices—strawberries, an owl, a badger, deer, swine, birds, and whatever else he can find to appease the moon. Soon thereafter, a voice calls "Dhoya, my beloved." Trembling, Dhoya looks into the forest, sees a white form which becomes a flowering plant as he touches it. Dazed, the giant returns to his cave where he finds a beautiful woman cleaning and rearranging the spears and skins.

She throws her arms about his neck, telling him that she yearns for his love. Having left her happy people from under the lake where age, sorrow, and pain are unknown, she desires love in the changing world, a mortal love which her people cannot experience. Dhoya loves her with a mad passion which is not matched by the beautiful fairy, unnamed by Yeats. Then a man from under the sea appears to reclaim the lady. Holding a spear tipped with metal, he challenges Dhoya, whose rage returns as he fights to keep his love. He wins that battle only to lose to the fairy who reappears and challenges him to a game of chess. Before she leaves Dhoya, the fairy sings a strange love song which was part of "The Wandering of Oisin" (1889):

> My love hath many evil mood
> Ill words for all things soft and fair
> I hold him dearer than the good
> My fingers feel his amber hair.

This stanza is central to "Dhoya" and to the great poems which follow. The happy spirit is unhappy and seeks human love which is neither perfect nor perpetual—a paradox which haunts Yeats.

"John Sherman," a realistic story which Yeats called a short romance and wanted to be judged as an Irish novel, is a variation of the Dhoya theme. Although the story lacks the cultural unity of the Irish novels of William Carleton, John Banim, and Gerald Griffin, it does demonstrate the great influence upon Yeats of William Blake, whose poetical works Yeats had recently edited.

The story takes place in Ballah and London, two contrary locations representing the virtuous countryside and the villainous city. There is also a set of contrary characters who, even if they were merged, would not represent the ideal character. John Sherman of Ballah and William Howard of London have different views on almost everything, yet they become engaged to the same woman. Mary Carton of Ballah and Margaret Leland of London are different, but both are very confused about their love for John Sherman. Sherman's mother and Margaret's mother really represent the country mother and the city mother; neither has a life beyond motherhood. Such artificial characterizations doom the plot of "John Sherman," which—although intended as a love story—with a little revision could have become a comedy or farce. Certainly, it is the lightest piece of work that Yeats produced; but unlike other Irish writers, Yeats lacked a comic sense.

"Proud Costello, MacDermot's Daughter, and the Bitter Tongue," from *The Secret Rose* is a love story which exhibits the intensity of Dhoya's love for the fairy, but the lovers are mortals of the sixteenth century. Costello loves Una, daughter of MacDermot, who is promised by her father to MacNamara. Una loves Costello and sends a message to him by Duallach, the wandering piper. Costello must appear at her nuptial feast, at which she will drink to the man she loves. At the bethrothal drink, to the amazement of all, she drinks to Costello; he is then attacked by the members of the wedding party and barely escapes with his life. Una dies without seeing Costello again, but at her funeral procession he sees the coffin and is considered her murderer. Loving her still, Costello swims to the island where Una is buried, mourning over her grave for three days and nights. Confused, he tries to swim back to the mainland but drowns in the attempt. His body is brought to the island and buried beside his beloved; two ash trees are planted over their grave site. They grow tall and the branches, like lover's arms, entwine themselves, symbolic of the undying love between Costello and Una. This motif, common in folklore, appealed to Yeats's sensibility because of the implied relationship between the natural world and the affairs of mortals.

From another perspective, Yeats writes again about that relationship in "The Twisting of the Rope." This story is one of the six connected stories grouped as the *Stories of Red Hanrahan* which tell of the plight of Hanrahan, a hedge schoolmaster enchanted by a spirit on Samhain Eve, the night (the equivalent of our Halloween) on which the Celts believed spirits roamed the earth searching for mortals. Since his enchantment, Hanrahan becomes a traveling poet of the Gael who sings of the past heroic age when the ancient Irish kings and queens ruled Ireland. The people, although they welcome Hanrahan into their cottages, fear him because he is of the other world and is able to charm others, especially young and impressionable women.

One night Hanrahan is observed casting his spell over Oona, an attentive listener of his tales; but her mother and a neighbor woman, watching Oona drift into the spirit world, plan to thwart Hanrahan's influence. They cannot order the poet out of the house because he might cast a spell over their animals and fields, destroying cattle and corn, so they devise a scheme whereby Hanrahan is asked to twist a rope from the bundles of hay which the women bring to him. Feeding him more and more rope and praising him for the fine job of rope-making, they eventually get Hanrahan to the door and out of the cottage. Realizing that he had been tricked, he composes a song, "The Twisting of the Rope." Douglas Hyde, who wrote the first Irish play for the new Irish dramatic movement (*Casad-an-Sugan*, 1901), selected Yeats's short tale for production. His success in revitalizing Irish myth and encouraging the continuation of the written Irish literary tradition assures Yeats a prominent place in Irish letters.

Another aspect of Yeats's personality was his fascination with the occult, an attraction which led him to explore Christian, Jewish, and Oriental mysticism in his writings. As John O'Leary made Yeats conscious of the past political Irish culture, George (Æ) Russell, to whom *The Secret Rose* was dedicated, indoctrinated Yeats into the Dublin Theosophist Circle, which was occupied with the study of Rosicrucianism. It was a subject about which Yeats could never learn enough, and in "Rosa Alchemica" he approaches the topic through the story of the life of Michael Robartes. Yeats says in an explanatory note to the collection of poems known as *Michael Robartes and the Dancer*

(1920) that Robartes had returned to Dublin from Mesopotamia where he "partly found and partly thought out much philosophy."

This knowledge, which Robartes wants to share with his old friend, is revolutionary. It consists of an understanding that modern alchemy is not concerned with simply converting base metal to gold. On the contrary, the new science seeks to transform all things to the divine form; in other words, experiential life is transmuted to art. The process involves rituals through which novices are initiated gradually into the sect. Robartes brings his friend into a temple, but in order to proceed, he must first learn a series of intricate dance steps; then he is dressed in a costume of Greek and Egyptian orgin for the mad dance. At this point the friend, fearing for his sanity, flees from the phantasmagoria.

"The Tables of the Law" and "The Adoration of the Magi" are two other short stories that deal with religious mysteries. In "The Tables of the Law," Owen Aherne, like Michael Robartes, returns to Dublin after studying mysticism and alchemy. He hates life and cherishes a medieval book with its secrets of the spirit. Swift, Aherne thinks, created a soul for Dublin gentlemen by hating his neighbor as himself. A decade later, the narrator sees Aherne again at a Dublin bookstore; his face is a lifeless mask, drained of the energy to sin and repent as God planned for mortal man. God's law tablets make mankind commit sin, which is abhorrent to Aherne.

Michael Robartes, appearing again in "The Adoration of the Magi," promises the return of the Celtic heroes. Three men in the tale, perhaps demons, watch the death of the Wise Woman. Civilization has not progressed; Christianity has not fulfilled its mission. The hope of nations lies in the reestablishment of the aristocratic order of the Celtic civilization. To a greater degree, Yeats develops this theme in later verse, essays, and plays with a blurring of the character of Cuchulain, the pagan Irish hero, with Christ and Saint Patrick.

Yeats's reputation as a poet and a dramatist overshadows his renown as a storyteller. His tales have intrinsic worth nevertheless, and can be read as a prelude to his later great works.

Major publications other than short fiction

PLAYS: *The Countess Kathleen*, 1892; *The Land of Heart's Desire*, 1894; *The Shadowy Waters*, 1900; *Cathleen ni Houlihan*, 1902; *Where There Is Nothing*, 1902; *The Hour Glass*, 1903; *The Pot of Broth*, 1904; *The King's Threshold*, 1904; *On Baile's Strand*, 1905; *Deirdre*, 1907; *The Unicorn from the Stars*, 1908; *Plays for an Irish Theatre*, 1911; *Four Plays for Dancers*, 1921; *Wheels and Butterflies*, 1934; *Collected Plays*, 1934; *The Herne's Egg*, 1938; *Collected Plays*, 1952.

POETRY: *Mosada: A Dramatic Poem*, 1886; *The Wanderings of Oisin*, 1889; *The Wind Among the Reeds*, 1899; *In the Seven Woods*, 1903; *The Green Helmet and Other Poems*, 1910; *Responsibilities*, 1914; *The Wild Swans at*

Coole, 1917; *Michael Robartes and the Dancer*, 1920; *The Tower*, 1928; *The Winding Stair and Other Poems*, 1933; *A Full Moon in March*, 1935; *Last Poems and Plays*, 1940.

NONFICTION: *Ideas of Good and Evil*, 1903; *Discoveries*, 1907; *Poetry and Ireland*, 1908 (with Lionel Johnson); *Synge and Ireland of His Times*, 1911; *The Cutting of an Agate*, 1912; *Reveries Over Childhood and Youth*, 1915; *The Trembling of the Veil*, 1922; *Essays*, 1924; *The Bounty of Sweden*, 1925; *A Vision*, 1925; *Estrangement: Being Fifty Thoughts of 1909*, 1926; *The Death of Synge and Other Passages from an Old Diary*, 1928; *Dramatis Personae*, 1936.

Bibliography

Cross, K. G. W. and R. T. Dunlop. *A Bibliography of Yeats Criticsm, 1887-1965*.

Donoghue, Denis and J. R. Mulryne, eds. *An Honoured Guest.*

Ellmann, Richard. *Yeats: The Man and the Masks.*

Finneran, Richard, ed. *William Butler Yeats: John Sherman and Dhoya.*

Jeffares, A. Norman. *Yeats: Man and Poet.*

Jochum, K. P. S. *W. B. Yeats: A Classified Bibliography of Criticism.*

Ronsley, Joseph. *Yeats's Autobiography.*

Ure, Peter. *Yeats and Anglo-Irish Literature.*

Eileen A. Sullivan

FRANK YERBY

Born: Augusta, Georgia; September 5, 1916

Principal short fiction

"Love Story," 1937; "Young Man Afraid," 1937; "A Date With Vera," 1937; "Thunder of God," 1939; "Health Card," 1944; "White Magnolias," 1944; "Roads Going Down," 1945; "My Brother Went to College," 1946; "The Homecoming," 1946.

Other literary forms

Frank Yerby's literary works include twenty-eight novels and nine short stories. Three best-selling novels—*The Foxes of Harrow* (1946), *The Golden Hawk* (1948), and *The Saracen Blade* (1952)—have been made into motion pictures. *Pride's Castle* (1949) has been adapted and produced for a television audience.

Influence

Generally considered the "king" of the costume novel, Yerby published his first novel, *The Foxes of Harrow*, in February, 1946. By the end of the year, more than two million copies had been sold, and Yerby was well on his way to becoming one of the most popular American writers of all time. During the nine-year period of 1946-1954, Yerby published eight novels, each of which sold one million copies or more: *The Foxes of Harrow* (1946), *The Vixens* (1947), *The Golden Hawk* (1948), *Pride's Castle* (1949), *Floodtide* (1950), *A Woman Called Fancy* (1951), *The Saracen Blade* (1952), and *Benton's Row* (1954). Between 1940 and 1970, Yerby had more novels on the best-seller list than any other American writer. Among these, *The Foxes of Harrow*, *The Vixens*, and *Pride's Castle*—Yerby's most popular novels—account for total sales in excess of eight million copies. In 1948 *The Golden Hawk* was the best-selling novel of the year in sales to the public through all media, and in 1950 *Floodtide* was the only historical novel to make the best-seller list. Of the two historical novels which reached the million mark in sales in 1951, *A Woman Called Fancy* was the best seller. Yerby's twenty-eight published novels have sold more than fifty million copies, an achievement which ranks him with Grace Metalious, Mickey Spillane, Erskine Caldwell, and Erle Stanley Gardner as one of the five most popular American writers during the period from 1925 to 1960. His books have been translated into fourteen languages, including Hebrew and Japanese.

Story characteristics

Published during the 1940's, the best of Yerby's short stories focus on a segregated Southern society which is characterized by prejudice and racism. Unlike his novels, the stories are bitter, satirical protests of the mistreatment of blacks as they strive for recognition in a hostile environment. Created in a "Wrightian vein," his main characters are black antiheroes; they are outcasts, aliens in their native land, who are engaged in a futile struggle for control of their destinies.

Biography

Educated at Paine College, Augusta, Georgia (B. A., 1937), and Fisk University, Nashville, Tennessee (M. A., 1938), Frank Garvin Yerby worked in the Federal Writers Project of the WPA and studied at the University of Chicago. He taught English at Florida A. and M. College (now Florida A. and M. University), Tallahassee, Florida (1939-1940), and at Southern University, Baton Rouge, Louisiana (1940-1941). Yerby spent the war years (1941-1945) as a lab technician at Ford Motor Company and as a chief inspector for Ranger Aircraft Corporation. Although he published verse in several "little magazines" during his high school and college years, Yerby's first major success as a writer came when his short story "Health Card" appeared in *Harper's Magazine* and won the O. Henry Memorial Award for 1944. Yerby has four children by his first wife, Flora Helen Claire Williams, whom he married in 1941. Subsequently, he was divorced and married Blanquita Calle-Perez in 1956. Yerby now lives in Madrid, Spain.

Analysis

Frank Yerby's most popular and frequently anthologized short stories belong to the protest tradition in American literature. Lacking the restraint and subtlety of the novels, these stories reflect an angry condemnation of the brutal exploitation of blacks at the hands of the whites who control the power structure. Consequently, the plot often involves a black-white tension which results from the protagonist's struggle to achieve self-affirmation and human dignity, on the one hand, and the antagonist's fight to maintain the social-moral order and the arbitrary power which it represents, on the other. Through this structure, Yerby introduces the modern hero, the "rebel-victim," the antihero who attempts to impose his idealistic concepts of freedom and self-definition upon a society which demands the surrender of personal ethics in the face of conflict with the sociopolitical forces which maintain the status quo. Deprived of social sanctions, the antihero is an outsider who is unable to identify a pattern or logical reason for the "place" which has been assigned to him. He is a lonely, alienated individual whose love of liberty and intensity of feeling challenge the authority of American society and its concept of humanity.

Yerby's antihero finds himself in search of a life which denies the frustrations, compulsions, limitations, and mores dictated by convention and authority. He must push beyond the frontiers of the universe and discover that which is best, both in himself and in his world. Because he has the courage to examine his life and make those changes which seem necessary for the realization of self, he is driven to a pursuit which is destined to end in rebellion. His is a confrontation between the self and the society which, according to Ihab Hassan, has led the self "through the dark undersides of experience from which it emerged still human only to find itself outlawed by the collective authority of men who had relinquished their full humanity."

This is the encounter which Yerby describes in "Health Card," the story of Johnny Green, a black soldier stationed in the South, who has been repeatedly denied a furlough. When he receives word that his wife is coming from Detroit to visit him, Johnny persuades a black preacher's wife to rent them a room for a week. Having secured special permission from his commanding officer, he meets Lily's train and the couple walk toward the minister's house. Two military policemen stop them, however, assuming that Lily is a prostitute, and demand to see her health card. Johnny is angered by this humiliating encounter, but his efforts to retaliate are frustrated by Lily, who fears for her husband's life. Demoralized and embittered by his inability to protect his wife from such insults, Johnny can only bemoan the fact that his manhood has been compromised by the prejudice and racism of whites.

The white characters in the novel are typical racists: the military policemen, the sentry, and the soldiers in the white section of the camp all display a condescending and sometimes hostile attitude toward blacks. Only the sergeant who allows Johnny access to the Colonel, the Colonel himself, and the young M. P. corporal show a semblance of human emotion and compassion. The story is structured around two parallel episodes: the confrontation between the soldiers and their dates and the military policemen, and the conflict between Johnny and the military policemen. In the first incident, one of the white M. P.'s molests one of the black women. In turn, she rebels, the soldiers come to her rescue, and they are subdued by the back-up squads of M. P.'s, who use their billy clubs and guns. On a symbolic level, the skirmish represents a clash between the idealism of the blacks and the harsh, brutal, unrelenting reality of the power structure. The resulting violence comes as a natural result of the confrontation of these ideologies, particularly since there is no buffer, no mediator to intervene.

The second episode between Johnny and the two M. P.'s reveals Johnny as a black antihero whose self-affirmation and human dignity are destroyed because he is unable to protect his wife from the insults of the white policemen. Again, the clash is between idealism and realism, but Lily acts as a mediator to bridge the gap between what is and what should be. She understands Johnny's need to maintain his self-esteem, but she also realizes that violence and bloodshed are inevitable unless she can offset these opposing forces. The inequitable realities of life have conspired to frustrate Johnny in the pursuit of his manhood, and this manipulation leaves him forlorn and dejected.

The quest for manhood is also a dominant motif in "The Homecoming," which describes Sergeant Willie Jackson as he returns to the provincial white Southern town of his boyhood. Having fought in the war, earned a Purple Heart, and lost a leg, Jackson staunchly rejects the "place" in society which he once accepted unquestioningly. He has "grown" from boyhood to manhood, and in the process, his mood of accommodation and acceptance has changed to an attitude of protest and defiance. After refusing to address two white men as "sir" and antagonizing a white salesgirl who has overlooked him to wait on a white customer, Willie is confronted by a mob of townspeople determined to teach him a lesson. Jackson is saved, however, by an old, sympathetic Colonel who convinces the mob that Willie is a "combat fatigue" case and that he is not responsible for his actions.

The plot of "The Homecoming" unfolds through four brief episodes which involve two confrontations, a revelation, and a resolution. In each episode, the tension is created between Willie's idealism and the realism of the whites in the town. Throughout the entire story, Yerby uses descriptive images of overwhelming heat to intensify the attitudes and feelings of Willie and the white townspeople. During his initial confrontation with the two white men, Willie declares his willingness to die, if necessary, to achieve the freedom for which he has fought in the war. Sheer determination compels him to stand up to the men and refuse to accept the constraints which they seek to impose on his life. In the second encounter, Willie establishes himself as a "loner" when he enters the Five-and-Ten-Cent Store and decides that he has no one to buy anything for. Because of his idealism, however, he deliberately chooses postcards which, instead of reflecting the "real" town, give the impression which he wants his friends to have. Finally, he "insults" the white salesgirl and comes into a second conflict with reality.

Having reached the Colonel's house, Willie reveals in the third episode that he has "grown up" psychologically as well as physically. Much to the dismay of the Colonel and his black servants, Willie soberly explains his new vision both of himself and his world. He is quick to realize that Southern circumscriptions impose an insurmountable obstacle to such a vision and that he must move North if that dream is ever to become a reality. Although the Colonel never admits in Willie's presence that he is right, he recognizes Willie's claim to manhood and begins to feel compassion for and empathy with him.

Bolstered by his newfound pride and dignity, Willie sets out to catch his train in the final episode. As he approaches the station, the white men with eyes of "blue ice" close in on him as the heat becomes a "visible thing," and the final encounter between black freedom and Southern tradition seems inevitable. At this point, however, the Colonel enters as a mediator between the two opposing forces and successfully averts what would have been certain tragedy. Like Johnny Green, Willie is saved, but he loses his claim to manhood and self-respect in the process. These idealists would have preferred to fight to the death for their liberty, but in each instance, there is a counterbalancing force which prevents their action.

The clash of values and quest for freedom take a subtle turn in "My Brother Went to College." Twenty-year-old Mark Johnson, the narrator, has spent the last ten years of his life wandering from town to town in search of an elusive freedom. Finally, he experiences a nostalgic yearning for familiar faces and surroundings, and he returns to his home town to find that his father has died and that his brother has become a successful, reputable doctor in the community. The two brothers are happily reunited, and immediately, Matthew unfolds his plan for sending Mark to college and making him "respectable." Having been thoroughly impressed with the luxuries of middle-class black life, Mark assumes that these status symbols are keys to the freedom which he has never been able to find. Although he comes to realize the severe limitations placed upon Matt's life, Mark makes the decision to abandon his itinerant life-style and follow his brother's plan for success.

The tension in this story is created through a comparison of the carefree vitality experienced by Mark, as opposed to the materialistic quest in which Matt is involved. Essentially, this is the conflict between the forces of freedom and the forces of restraint which Yerby describes in the other stories. Unlike "Health Card" and "The Homecoming," however, the racial element is subtle and indirect. Mark Johnson, antihero, wanderer, and rebel, views the restraints and authority of civilized society from his unique perch on the margins of that society. He is an alien, a "lost ball in high grass," without the benefit of the trappings of stability: land, job, status, money, and material comforts. He has not acquired the wherewithal for validating his claim within the social hierarchy.

During the course of the narrative, however, Matt's efforts propel Mark into a significant encounter with the customs and traditions of society. He is immersed in scalding hot water and given new clothes (the old ones are burned) and a haircut to symbolize his new station in life. As the freedom of "the juke boxes in the river [die] away out of mind into silence," he exchanges his dream of freedom for the comforts which his brother enjoys. He realizes that as he continues the search for his identity, according to Kingsley Widmer, he must "ultimately . . . renounce rebellion and commit himself to simple love-and-misery."

Thus, Mark has redefined his concept of freedom. Although he has freed himself from the misapprehension that Matt's life-style incorporates the freedom which he has been seeking, he decides to abandon the licentiousness of his earlier life, become a conformist, and reap the benefits of an approving society. Like Matt, he begins to build the inevitable box which insures the final measure of isolation from his former self. As Mark himself comes to realize, this is "one of the saddest things . . . that I ever heard of." For he has chosen to live in a society in which light-complexioned women are "angels out of Glory," where one must watch one's grammar and avoid the vernacular—even in private conversation—and where white policemen humiliate little black boys, who are compelled to grin and shuffle. It is a society in which every single action, no matter how trivial, must be weighed in terms of the consequences and repercussions which that act might evoke from a white society.

Although Yerby's short stories frequently feature a black protagonist in a Southern setting, their appeal surpasses these physical limitations and approaches the universal. For these are stories of human yearnings, strivings, and aspirations; they are stories of the struggle for human freedom against those forces of convention and oppression which seek to limit, restrain, and control. The meaning of Yerby's short fiction, then, lies not in what it tells us about black freedom or white oppression; rather, its ultimate significance concerns a question of the boundaries and limits of human freedom within a civilized society.

Major publications other than short fiction

NOVELS: *The Foxes of Harrow*, 1946; *The Vixens*, 1947; *The Golden Hawk*, 1948; *Pride's Castle*, 1949; *Floodtide*, 1950; *A Woman Called Fancy*, 1951; *The Saracen Blade*, 1952; *Benton's Row*, 1954.

L. H. Pratt

ÉMILE ZOLA

Born: Paris, France; April 2, 1840
Died: Paris, France; September 29, 1902

Principal short fiction

Contes à Ninon, 1864 (*Stories for Ninon*); *Nouveaux contes à Ninon*, 1874; *Les Soirées de Médan*, 1880 (a contributor); *Le Capitaine Burle*, 1882 (*A Soldier's Honor*); *Naïs Micoulin*, 1884; *Contes et nouvelles*, 1928.

Other literary forms

Émile Zola is principally remembered as a novelist, and also as the flamboyant journalist who took up the defense of Captain Dreyfus during the celebrated trial of the young Jewish officer which transfixed French society at the end of the nineteenth century. In addition to novels and journalistic essays, he is the author of numerous plays, essays, literary and artistic criticism, and an early youthful attempt at poetry.

Influence

Zola will always be associated with the school of naturalism in France. He became the most widely read author of the turn of the century, in part because of the sensationalism of his subjects, in part because of his early training as a public relations clerk for the prestigious Hachette publishing firm. Because of his immense success, his aesthetic ideas were widely circulated, and a group of disciples was formed at Zola's country home outside Paris at Médan. Five regular disciples including Guy de Maupassant collaborated with Zola on a volume of short stories dealing with the war of 1870 entitled *Les Soirées de Médan*, a landmark publication that helped establish the new aesthetic. Zola had provided the theoretical background for this aesthetic in his book of criticism *Le Roman expérimental* (1880, *The Experimental Novel*), whose title suggests the main feature; a scientific approach to literature. Inspired by the medical advances made possible by scrupulous observation combined with precise analytical techniques, in particular the theories of Doctor Claude Bernard, philosopher Hippolyte Taine, and the English naturalist Charles Darwin whose *On the Origin of Species* (1859) was translated into French in 1862, Zola proposed literature as a means of experimenting on man. He specifically was interested in determining what happens when his environment is changed or his heredity tampered with; what would be the result of man's gradual addiction to certain chemical compounds? One of his best-known novels, *L'Assommoir* (1877, *Drink*), for example, attempts to examine the effects of alcohol on the working class. Other works examine prostitution, political power, industrial power (the locomotive), and capitalism.

The simplest definition of the new aesthetic—naturalism, whose name implies scientific observation of nature—would be to say that literary naturalism is realism with scientific claims. The naturalist author attempts to be objective, detached, and precise in his representation of reality, in the tradition of Gustave Flaubert, but goes further in that he attempts to demonstrate a scientific principle. Conclusions are clearly stated and justified by concrete facts, and they have moral consequences. When the newly discovered literary subject matter—the ordinary, if not outright lower-class, existence—is added to these characteristics, one understands the inevitable excess of the naturalists: envisioned is a sordid environment in which the unhealthy and the immoral exist side by side. Using Honoré de Balzac's *La Comédie Humaine* (*The Human Comedy*) as a model, Zola attempted to balance his production, but the careful reader will not fail to note his predilection for the base and ugly. In this sense naturalism came full circle in the evolution of French letters during the nineteenth century: Romanticism, exemplified by Victor Hugo was followed by realism, in the tradition of Gustave Flaubert, which finally gave way to the naturalism of Zola—a new form of Romanticism, with all its exuberance and excesses. The aesthetic in prose is largely associated with the Goncourt brothers, Maupassant, and Joris-Karl Huysmans in France; with Thomas Hardy and George Moore in England; and with Theodore Dreiser, Frank Norris, Stephen Crane, and James T. Farrell in the United States. Naturalism also affected another genre, the theater, by stressing concrete reality in opposition to any artificiality or false theatricality, and this led to movements in three important countries: the *Théâtre Libre* in France, the *Feie Buhne* in Germany, and the Moscow Art Theatre in the Soviet Union.

Story characteristics

The discussion above might suggest that Zola was a writer of "programmed" literature. Certainly his claims to scientific writing, suggesting that each work is a case study under carefully determined conditions, would reinforce this impression. Happily, the reality of his creations was quite different. On the one hand, it would be impossible to assume that an author's imaginings would have any claim to scientific objectivity; and on the other, Zola was far too creative a writer to be limited by a single theory, even his own. As a result, it is always possible to trace in his work two mutually contradictory traits: scientific determinism and lyrical counterpoint. Consequently, each story has its requisite basis in fact—a precisely defined environment, carefully constructed situations, precisely described characters, and often a scientific term or two. Then the artist takes over and adds the necessary aesthetic dimension. Zola's novels and stories are genuine works of art, eminently readable and immensely satisfying, and many of his works are full of moral and lyrical idealism. It is no accident that his first collection of short stories was designed as a series of fairy tales for children.

Zola excelled in establishing settings, conveying mood or atmosphere, and breathing life into representations of crowds acting together. Critics have emphasized his lyrical qualities and have drawn attention to the epic proportions of his creations. Although these are valid remarks regarding Zola's short stories, his best work will be found in his novels, where his vast epics find a canvas large enough to contain them. Zola's short fiction contains all his talent in microcosm, but the genre does not allow Zola to develop his talent fully.

Biography

The son of an Italian engineer, Émile Zola grew up in Aix-en-Provence with a friend who was to become equally famous in the world of art, Paul Cézanne. Both came from modest families, and Zola learned early to resent the ordered and comfortable life of the bourgeoisie around him. The early death of his father prompted the family move to Paris, where his mother could find work, and where Zola attended the *lycée*. Failing to pass his *baccalauréat*, Zola gave up his studies and took a position in the civil service, then another with the distinguished Hachette publishing house, where he rose through the ranks to become head of public relations. During this time he made various attempts to write poetry and to penetrate the world of journalism, and he succeeded in establishing himself as an author with his collection of short stories *Contes à Ninon*. The following year, his novel *La Confession de Claude* (1865, *Claude's Confession*), attracted so much attention because of its sordid details that it aroused police interest. The unhappy management of Hachette ordered Zola to choose between publishing and writing, and the young author, already in the public eye, set out to earn his livelihood by his pen.

With his flair for publicity Zola was able to exploit both his public and his art with great success. Even his ideas of naturalism were tempered by what he realized the public wanted to hear. Inspired by Balzac, he determined to develop a *comédie humaine* on his own terms; and this time he determined not only to make the cycle of novels a coherent whole, but also to ensure that the cycle would be complete and accurate in every detail, with no contradictions. His early exposure to his father's scientific career prepared him for a lifelong fascination with science and its theoreticians, and his humble origins made him especially sympathetic to the lofty position accorded the *savant*. As a result, the organizing principle for his series of novels became the aesthetic of naturalism, which he carefully defined in a series of essays inspired by scientific and particularly medical treatises. Adopting the realists' idea of a "slice of life," Zola sketched out a family tree, and then proceeded to write a novel about the major members of that family, whose name would form the title of the twenty-volume series: *Les Rougon-Macquart* (1871-1893, *The Rougon-Macquart Family*). The first volume, *The Fortune of the Rougon*, appeared in 1871; it was a good novel, but did not spark popular imagination.

Five other volumes appeared in the next five years, but it was the appearance of *Drink*, an epic about alcohol's effect on the worker, in 1877, that notoriety—and hence financial success—came to Zola. From that point on he became the most talked-about and widely read author in France. It was not that he could do no wrong: ten years later, the appearance of *La Terre* (1887, *Earth*) so outraged the critics that Zola's then-disciples publicly repudiated him, declaring that his penchant for the sordid and the gruesome had betrayed the aesthetic of naturalism. The newspapers, however, eagerly printed the work, and the public eagerly bought it.

Zola attempted to soften this criticism of his work by writing novels and stories that erred in the other extreme: they were highly idealistic. Not only were some of *The Rougon-Macquart Family* novels written in this more positive vein, but also, at the conclusion of the series, Zola embarked on two new series of novels, the romance *Les Trois villes* (1894, 1896, 1898; *The Three Cities*) and what he called *Les Quatre Évangiles* (1899, 1901, 1903; *The Four Gospels*), the gospels of population, work, truth, and justice (which at his death was incomplete and published posthumously). This idealistic bent heightened Zola's outrage when he became increasingly convinced that the Dreyfus affair was, in fact, a vast conspiracy by the established government and military to denigrate a talented young Jewish officer. With his usual lack of tact, Zola published his findings on the front page of the newspaper *L'Aurore* in a public letter whose first words were "j'accuse." Promptly prosecuted for libel, Zola fled to England and worked there until he learned that public opinion favored his position and that a retrial was imminent. His vindication helped to establish Zola as the leading author of France at the turn of the century; nevertheless, his reputation as a pornographer in fact prevented him from achieving his cherished goal: election to the Académie Française. He died of asphyxiation from a defective fireplace flue (some seriously consider that there may have been an assassination plot involved), on September 29, 1902, and was accorded a hero's public funeral, at which Captain Dreyfus was present.

Analysis

Émile Zola's talent as a short-story writer is evident from the first sentence of "La Mort d'Olivier Bécaille" (1879, "The Death of Olivier Bécaille,") included in the volume *Naïs Micoulin* of 1884. In this work the reader's curiosity is immediately piqued over the question of how a first-person narrator can deal with his own death. At first, the reader feels that Zola is perhaps presenting us with an example of a fleeting moment of consciousness after the physical body has died, as though he were presenting a distinction between body and soul, which, for a naturalist, would be an intriguing concept. As the narrative unfolds, however, the reader understands that Zola is instead exploring one of the most traditional of literary themes: the return from the dead. At age thirty-nine Zola is developing a theme that Maupassant would exploit in his story "En Famille" (1881, "A Family Affair"). In contrast to Maupassant's objective narrative used for comic effect, Zola's first-person narrative not only captures interest, but also develops it to a different effect: the reader understands, and comes to sympathize with the narrator, and shares with him his experience of death.

At the moment of death which begins the story, the narrator thinks back over his life and over the lifelong obsession that death has held for him. The story gives a rapid flashback of his youth, marriage, and move to Paris, then returns to the present moment in a seedy hotel, where the narrator is taken ill and dies. The reader shares the narrator's outburst of affection for his young wife and the aroused interest of the neighbors and especially their children. As he did so successfully in *Drink*, Zola excels in capturing the atmosphere of the crowd. His pictures of unhealthy children are particularly moving; as aware as adults, their observations are all the more startling because they are true. Thus, when the first child cries out, "Il est mort, oh! maman, il est mort," her unsophisticated breach of social etiquette adds a moment of poignancy and accentuates the verisimilitude of the plot.

At first the reader wonders if the narrator is not simply dreaming, and Zola has the narrator ask himself the same question to heighten the tension. When a neighbor refers to the imminent arrival of the coroner, however, the question is answered. The cursory examination revolts the narrator, for he is conscious of being alive, in spite of the coroner's judgment; yet, like the condemned poets in Dante's *Inferno* (c. 1320), there is no outlet by which these frustrations can be expressed. Agonizing at his inability to summon help or attention, the narrator witnesses his own body being prepared for the funeral, observes the mourning of his wife, sees himself being enclosed in his own coffin, and hears the lid being nailed down. He experiences the funeral ceremony, the horror of being buried alive, and the climactic silence of an abandoned cemetery.

In spite of a perhaps unnecessary touch of scientific determinism, the story accelerates to its dramatic conclusion. Through superhuman effort the narrator manages to pry open his coffin, claw his way out of the ground, and stumble about on the street at night, before being overcome by exhaustion and emotion and injuring his head as he falls unconscious. When he regains his senses weeks later, he quickly realizes what has happened, that he has still not been able to make contact with his young wife in order to let her know that he is in fact alive. He escapes from his benefactors to rejoin his wife, only to find that she already has settled into a new life with a new man. Zola presents this absorbing tale with the control and economy required of an effective short story. The ordinary details of one's mundane existence take on a new proportion when viewed from beyond the tomb, and Zola does not hesitate to use imagery and symbolism to enhance the primitive and religious qualities of his story.

Perhaps the best known of Zola's short stories is "L'Attaque du Moulin" (1880, "The Attack on the Mill"). It is the lead story in the collection *Les Soirées de Médan*, and along with Maupassant's "Boule de Suif," is largely responsible for the success of the collection that satirizes the Franco-Prussian war of 1870. Zola's contribution is a powerful account of man's inhumanity to man, as war interrupts a pastoral romance and prompts its protagonists to actions of heroism and patriotism, only to leave them bloodied, nature devastated, and the windmill—a symbol rich in associations—laid waste. Man's hubris ravishes both nature and humanity in this pacifist tale in which Zola demonstrates his characteristic poetic quality, which he retained despite his obsession with science. Like the Parnassian poets, his inability to follow rigorously his own aesthetic saved Zola and made possible his greatest writing. A visionary Romantic in the tradition of Victor Hugo, Zola's ability to evoke vast tableaux, both of men and of nature, along with his lyrical vision of man, lend epic proportions to his work.

Major publications other than short fiction

NOVELS: *La Confession de Claude*, 1865 (*Claude's Confession*); *Thérèse Raquin*, 1867; *Les Mystères de Marseille*, 1867 (*The Mysteries of Marseille*); *Madeleine Férat*, 1868; *Les Rougon-Macquart*, 1871-1893 (*The Rougon-Macquart Family*); *Les Trois Villes* (*The Three Cities*): *Lourdes*, 1894; *Rome*, 1896; *Paris*, 1898; *Les Quatre Évangiles* (*The Four Gospels*): *Fécondité*, 1899 (*Fruitfulness*); *Travail*, 1901 (*Labor*); *Verité*, 1903 (*Truth*).

PLAYS: *La Laide*, 1865; *Madeleine*, 1865; *Les Héritiers Rabourdin*, 1874 (*The Rabourdin Heirs*); *Le Bouton de rose*, 1878 (*The Rosebud*); *Renée*, 1887.

NONFICTION: *Mes Haines*, 1866; *Le Roman expérimental*, 1880 (*The Experimental Novel*); *Les Romanciers naturalistes*, 1881; *Le Naturalisme au théâtre*, 1881 (*Naturalism in the Theater*); *Nos auteurs dramatiques*, 1881 (*Our Dramatic Authors*); *Documents littéraires*, 1881; *Une campagne*, 1882; *Nouvelle campagne*, 1896.

Bibliography

Bernard, Marc. *Zola par lui-même*.
Hemmings, F. W. J. *Émile Zola*.
Josephson, Matthew. *Zola and His Time*.
Lattre, Alain de. *Le Réalisme Selon Zola*.
Levin, Harry. *The Gates of Horn: A Study of Five French Realists*.
Robert, Guy. *Émile Zola: principes et caractères généraux de son oeuvre*.

Robert W. Artinian